# The Manager's Bookshelf

## A Mosaic of Contemporary Views

SEVENTH EDITION

**Jon L. Pierce**
*University of Minnesota Duluth*

**John W. Newstrom**
*University of Minnesota Duluth*

Upper Saddle River, New Jersey 07458

**Library of Congress Cataloging-in-Publication Data**
The manager's bookshelf : a mosaic of contemporary views / [collected by] Jon L. Pierce, John W. Newstrom.—7th ed.
p. cm.
Includes bibliographical references and index.
ISBN 0-13-149034-6
1. Management literature—United States. I. Pierce, Jon L. (Jon Lepley) II. Newstrom, John W.
HD70.U5M32 2005
658—dc22

2004015196

**VP/Editorial Director:** Jeff Shelstad
**Project Manager:** Ashley Keim
**AVP/Executive Marketing Manager:** Shannon Moore
**Marketing Assistant:** Patrick Danzuso
**Media Project Manager:** Jessica Sabloff
**Managing Editor:** John Roberts
**Production Editor:** Suzanne Grappi
**Production Manager, Manufacturing:** Arnold Vila
**Manufacturing Buyer:** Michelle Klein
**Design Manager:** Maria Lange
**Cover Design:** Bruce Kenselaar
**Manager, Print Production:** Christy Mahon
**Composition/Full-Service Project Management:** Pine Tree Composition, Inc.
**Printer/Binder:** Phoenix Companies

Credits and acknowledgments borrowed from other sources and reproduced, with permission, in this textbook appear on appropriate page within text.



Pearson Education LTD.
Pearson Education Australia PTY, Limited
Pearson Education Singapore, Pte. Ltd
Pearson Education North Asia Ltd
Pearson Education, Canada, Ltd
Pearson Educación de Mexico, S.A. de C.V.
Pearson Education—Japan
Pearson Education Malaysia, Pte. Ltd
Pearson Education Upper Saddle River, New Jersey

10 9 8 7 6 5 4 3 2 1
ISBN 0-13-149034-6

*We dedicate this book*
*to Janet Pierce and Diane Newstrom*

# Brief Contents

# Contents

# Preface

The last twenty-five years have been marked by a proliferation of books published on topics in management, leadership, and various organizational issues. This explosion of products apparently reflects an intense and continuing fascination by managers, future managers, and the general public with the inner workings of business organizations. Bookstores around the country and sources on the Internet continue to offer a large number of management books, and many of these books have appeared on various best-seller lists—some remaining there for months and years at a time. Clearly, managers and others (including business school students at both graduate and undergraduate levels) remain intrigued by, and are searching for insights and answers in, the popular business literature.

We prepared *The Manager's Bookshelf: A Mosaic of Contemporary Views* to serve the needs of both managers and management students. A significant number of individuals in both of these groups do not have sufficient time to read widely, yet many people find themselves involved in conversations where someone else refers to ideas like vision, self-directed work teams, ethics, flow, or emotional intelligence. We believe that a laudable goal for managers as well as all students of management is to remain current in their understanding of the views being expressed about organizational and management practices. To help you become a better informed organizational citizen, we prepared *The Manager's Bookshelf,* which introduces you to more than 40 popular management books—both recent and classic.

*The Manager's Bookshelf,* as a book of concise *summaries,* does not express the views of just a single individual on the management of organizations, nor does it attempt to integrate the views of several dozen authors. Instead, *this book is a collage*—a composite portrait constructed from a variety of sources. It provides you with insights into many aspects of organizational management from the perspectives of a diverse and sometimes provocative group of management writers, including some highly regarded authors such as James Collins, Edward Lawler III, Chris Argyris, Stephen Covey, Clayton Christensen, Spencer Johnson, Michael Maccoby, Thomas Peters, Michael Porter, and Peter Senge. Through this collection we will introduce you to the thoughts, philosophies, views, and experiences of a number of authors whose works have captured the attention of today's management community—and often captivated them in the process.

This book contains a rich array of pieces. From a topical perspective, its inclusions focus on motivation, ethics, global perspectives, environmental trends, managing diversity, corporate strategy, leadership styles, and other key concerns of managers. This collection includes the views from a variety of individuals—some practitioners, some philosophers, some management consultants, and some researchers. The selections reflect a wide variety in terms of their tone and tenor, as well as the diverse bases for their conclusions. Indeed, critics have praised some of the authors' works as passionate, invaluable, stimulating, and insightful, whereas other business books have been attacked as being overly academic, superficial, redundant, glib, or unrealistic.

The nature and source of the ideas expressed in this collection are diverse. Some inclusions are prescriptive in nature, whereas others are more dispassionately descriptive; some are thoughtful and philosophical, whereas others limit themselves to reporting directly on their personal or organizational experiences; some of these works represent armchair speculation, whereas others are based on empirical study. Finally, the selections take a variety of forms. Some of the readings are excerpts extracted from the original book, some are articles written by the book's authors in which part of their overall perspective on management is revealed, and some are objective summaries of popular books that have been specially prepared for inclusion in *The Manager's Bookshelf.*

This mosaic of readings can provide you with useful insights, stimulate your thinking, and spark stimulating dialogue with your colleagues about the management of today's organizations. We hope these readings will prompt you to raise questions of yourself and your peers about the viability of many of the ideas expressed by these authors regarding the practice of organizational management. We hope—and predict—these readings will prompt you to read the full text of many of the authors' works; these books often contain rich anecdotes, compelling stories, provocative assertions, and detailed data that are not possible to include in our summaries. If these goals are met, our purpose for assembling this collection will be realized.

# Acknowledgments

We would like to express our sincere and warm appreciation to several colleagues who played key roles in the preparation of this edition of *The Manager's Bookshelf.* Their commitment and dedication to students of organizations and management, coupled with their efforts, made this edition possible.

We would also like to single out our late friend and colleague, Larry L. Cummings (Carlson School of Management at the University of Minnesota and "The Institute") for his "reflections on the best-sellers" contained in the introduction to our book. We thank Larry for taking the time to reflect on this part of the organization and management literature and to offer his insightful observations on this genre of books. He will always be remembered and valued for his intellectual contributions and for his friendship. Also (new to this edition), we value the reflective comments provided on best-sellers offered by Brad Jackson and Anne Cummings, which greatly enriched the discussion in that section.

## ◆ CONTRIBUTORS TO THIS EDITION

We would like to express our appreciation to a number of individuals who provided us with a great deal of assistance and support for the preparation of this book. Many of our management colleagues took the time and effort—always under tight time pressures—to contribute to this book by carefully reading and preparing a summary of one of the selected books. Many of these individuals wanted to offer their personal opinion, offer their endorsements or criticisms, and surface elements of their own management philosophies, but they stuck to their task at our urging. To them we express our thanks for their time, energy, and commitment to furthering management education.

The following individuals prepared book summaries for this edition of *The Manager's Bookshelf:*

### INTRODUCTION

**Kelly Nelson,** AK Steel—Argyris's *Flawed Advice and the Management Trap*

### BEST-SELLER CLASSICS

**William B. Gartner,** Georgetown University, and **M. James Naughton,** Expert Knowledge Systems, Inc.—Deming's *Out of the Crisis*
**Charles C. Manz,** University of Massachusetts, Amherst—Blanchard and Johnson's *The One Minute Manager*
**Gayle Porter,** Rutgers University—McGregor's *The Human Side of Enterprise*
**Dorothy Marcic,** Vanderbilt University—Senge's *The Fifth Discipline*
**Sara A. Morris,** Old Dominion University—Porter's *Competitive Advantage*

## HIGH-PERFORMING ORGANIZATIONS

**Penny Dieryck,** 148th Fighter Wing—Katzenbach's *Peak Performance*
**Chris Steele,** Best Buy Co.—Weick and Sutcliffe's *Managing the Unexpected*
**Stephen A. Rubenfeld,** University of Minnesota Duluth—Cascio's *Responsible Restructuring*

## ORGANIZATIONAL STRATEGY, EXECUTION, AND GOVERNANCE

**Sanjay Goel,** University of Minnesota Duluth—Kaplan and Porter's *The Strategy-Focused Organization*
**Christian F. Edwardson** —Bossidy, Charan, and Burck's *Execution*
**Allen Harmon,** University of Minnesota Duluth—Joyce, Nohria, and Roberson's *What (Really) Works*
**William Palmer,** Generations Health Care Initiatives—Conger, Lawler, and Finegold's *Corporate Boards*

## FOCUSING ON THE HUMAN DIMENSION

**Danielle DuBois Kerr,** RSM McGladrey—Lawler's *Treat People Right!*
**Jannifer David,** University of Minnesota Duluth—Ventrice's *Make Their Day*
**Kelly Nelson,** AK Steel—Csikszentmihalyi's *Good Business*
**Gary Stark,** Washburn University—Lawrence and Nohria's *Driven*

## MOTIVATION

**Stephen A. Rubenfeld,** University of Minnesota Duluth—Lawler's *Rewarding Excellence*
**Shannon Studden,** University of Minnesota Duluth—Thomas' *Intrinsic Motivation at Work*
**Anne-Marie Kaul,** American Red Cross—Katzenbach's *Why Pride Matters More than Money*

## TEAMS AND TEAMWORK

**Shannon Studden,** University of Minnesota Duluth—LaFasto and Carlson's *When Teams Work Best*
**Katherine Karl,** Marshall University—Hackman's *Leading Teams*
**David Beal,** Consolidated Papers, Inc.—Beyerlein, Freedman, McGee, and Moran's *Beyond Teams*

## LEADERSHIP

**John Kratz,** University of Minnesota Duluth—Goleman, Boyatzis, and McKee's *Primal Leadership*
**Kjell R. Knudsen,** University of Minnesota Duluth—Maccoby's *The Productive Narcissist*

## MANAGING DIVERSITY

**Kristina A. Bourne,** University of Massachusetts at Amherst—Miller and Katz' *The Inclusion Breakthrough*

## ORGANIZATIONAL CHANGE IN DYNAMIC ENVIRONMENTS

**Warren L. Candy,** Minnesota Power—Dannemiller Tyson's *Whole-Scale Change*
**Warren L. Candy,** Minnesota Power—Christensen, Raynor, and Scott's *The Innovator's Solution*

## MANAGERIAL DECISION-MAKING

**Paul C. Nutt,** The Ohio State University—Nutt's *Why Decisions Fail*
**Linda Rochford,** University of Minnesota Duluth—Murnighan and Mowen's *The Art of High-Stakes Decision-Making*
**Allen Harmon,** University of Minnesota Duluth—*Managing Crises Before They Happen*

## ETHICS AND VALUES

**Gregory R. Fox,** University of Minnesota Duluth—Kouzes and Posner's *Credibility*
**Gary P. Olson,** Center for Alcohol and Drug Treatment—Batstone's *Saving the Corporate Soul & (Who Knows?) Maybe Your Own*
**Steven B. Castleberry,** University of Minnesota Duluth—Bennis and Thomas' *Geeks and Geezers*
**Randy Skalberg,** University of Minnesota Duluth—George's *Authentic Leadership*

## MANAGING EMOTIONS AT WORK

**Gary Stark,** Washburn University—Johnson's *Who Moved My Cheese?*
**Gary J. Colpaert,** Milwaukee's Eye Institute—Frost's *Toxic Emotions at Work*
**Cathy A. Hanson,** City of Azusa—Seligman's *Authentic Happiness*

## EMERGING DIMENSIONS OF ORGANIZATIONAL ENVIRONMENTS

**Sanjay Goel,** University of Minnesota Duluth—Stiglitz' *Globalization and Its Discontents*
**Robert Stine,** University of Minnesota College of Natural Resources—Robbins' *Greening the Corporation*
**Rajiv Vaidyanathan,** University of Minnesota Duluth—Kanter's *Evolve!*

In addition to those who provided constructive feedback on previous editions, we appreciate the recommendations for inclusions in this seventh edition made by several persons. To Connie Johnson and Mandie Krueger, who patiently helped us prepare the manuscript, we want to say thank you for helping us complete this project in a timely fashion. We appreciate the supportive environment provided by Dean Kjell Knudsen and our colleagues in the Department of Management Studies here at the University of Minnesota Duluth. We especially appreciate the continued project commitment from Jeff Shelstad and the editorial support and assistance that we have received from Jennifer Simon and Ashley Keim, at Prentice Hall.

*Jon L. Pierce*
*John W. Newstrom*

# About the Editors

**Jon L. Pierce** is Professor of Management and Organization in the Labovitz School of Business and Economics at the University of Minnesota Duluth. He received his Ph.D. in management and organizational studies at the University of Wisconsin-Madison. He is the author of more than 60 papers that have been published or presented at various professional conferences. His publications have appeared in the *Academy of Management Journal, Academy of Management Review, Journal of Management, Journal of Occupational Behavior, Journal of Applied Behavioral Science, Organizational Dynamics, Organizational Behavior and Human Decision Processes*, and *Personnel Psychology*. His research interests include sources of psychological ownership, employee ownership systems, and organization-based self-esteem. He has served on the editorial review board for the *Academy of Management Journal, Personnel Psychology*, and *Journal of Management*. He is the co-author of six other books—*Management, Managing, Management and Organizational Behavior: An Integrated Perspective*, and along with John W. Newstrom, *Alternative Work Schedules, Windows into Management*, and *Leaders and the Leadership Process*. In 2000, he was inducted into the Academy of Management Journals' Hall of Fame.

**John W. Newstrom** is a Morse-Alumni Distinguished Teaching Professor Emeritus of Management in the Labovitz School of Business and Economics at the University of Minnesota Duluth. He completed his doctoral degree in management and industrial relations at the University of Minnesota and then taught at Arizona State University for several years. His work has appeared in publications such as *Academy of Management Executive, Personnel Psychology, California Management Review, Journal of Management, Academy of Management Journal, Business Horizons*, and the *Journal of Management Development*. He has served as an editorial reviewer for the *Academy of Management Review, Academy of Management Journal, Academy of Management Executive, Human Resource Development Quarterly, Advanced Management Journal,* and the *Journal of Management Development*. He is the coauthor of 19 books, including *Organizational Behavior: Human Behavior at Work* (eleventh edition, with Keith Davis), *Supervision* (eighth edition, with Lester Bittel), *Transfer of Training* (with Mary Broad), and *The Complete Games Trainers Play* (with Ed Scannell). He is a member of the University of Minnesota's Academy of Distinguished Teachers.

# About the Editors

**Jon L. Pierce** is Professor of Management and Organization in the Labovitz School of Business and Economics at the University of Minnesota Duluth. He received his Ph.D. in management and organizational studies at the University of Wisconsin–Madison. He is the author of more than 65 papers that have been published or presented at various professional conferences. His publications have appeared in the Academy of Management Journal, Academy of Management Review, Journal of Management, [illegible] [illegible]

**John W. Newstrom** is [illegible]

[illegible]

PART

# I

# Introduction

Part I contains three pieces. The first, "Understanding and Using the Best-Sellers," prepared by the editors of *The Manager's Bookshelf,* provides insight into why such a large number of management-oriented books have found themselves in the downtown bookstores, on coffee tables in homes, and on the bookshelves of those who manage today's organizations. Pierce and Newstrom discuss the rationale for this mosaic of contemporary views on organizations and management, and they provide you with insight into the nature and character of *The Manager's Bookshelf.* They challenge you to read and reflect upon this collection of thoughts and experiences. They invite you to debate the ideas and philosophies that are presented here. They encourage you to let these contemporary management books stimulate your thinking, to motivate you to look more systematically into the science of organizations and management, and to provide you with the fun of learning something new.

As a result of their concern that these contemporary books will be seen as "quick and dirty" cures for organizational woes, Pierce and Newstrom encourage you to read books such as Ralph H. Kilmann's *Beyond the Quick Fix: Managing Five Tracks to Organizational Success.* In it, he provided a valuable message, one that should serve as the backdrop to your consumption and assessment of the myriad of purported "one minute" cures for organizational problems and for the management of today's complex organizations. Kilmann encourages managers to stop perpetuating the myth of organizational and management simplicity and to develop a more complete and integrated approach to the management of today's complex organizations.

Many other writers have echoed these thoughts and cautions. For example:

- Michael Harvey (*SAM Advanced Management Journal,* Autumn 2001, p. 37) concludes that "there is an immense wrong-headedness or slipperiness in most normative approaches" to management as portrayed in various management best-sellers.
- Eric Abrahamson (*Academy of Management Review,* January 1998, p. 263) concluded that management fashions are "cultural commodities deliberately produced by fashion setters in order to be marketed to fashion followers."
- Shari Caudron (*TD,* June 2002, p. 40) notes that the fads presented in management best-sellers are taken up with great enthusiasm for a short while and then quickly discarded. This, she suggests, is done because "the tools were sold into

companies by charlatans who didn't understand the concepts but knew the right buzzwords."

- Kristine Ellis (*Training,* April 2001, p. 41) concludes that the worst of the best-sellers are promoted as "magic bullets" to solve organizational problems but often become little more than the prevailing "flavor of the month."
- Business columnist Dale Dauten (*The Arizona Republic,* February 19, 2004, p. D3) suggests that there are three types of business books on the market to avoid: the *Obvious* (compilations of clichéd truths), the *Envious* (stories of successful businesspeople), and the *Obnoxious* (books that insult your intelligence).
- Eileen Shapiro, author of *Fad Surfing in the Boardroom* (*Across the Board,* January 2000, p. 23), hints that most leadership books "ought to be stocked among the romance novels" of bookstores.
- Paula Phillips Carson et al. (*Academy of Management Journal,* 2000, p. 1154) conclude that the life spans of current management fashions have decreased. A rising wave of genuine concern over the quality of the content in popular business books has clearly emerged.
- Danny Miller and Jon Hartwick (*Harvard Business Review,* October 2002, p. 26) note that management fads usually have short life cycles and are quickly replaced by new ones. Typical fads, according to Miller and Hartwick, are simple, prescriptive, falsely encouraging, broadly generic, overly simplistic, closely matched to contemporary business problems, novel and fresh-appearing, and achieve their legitimacy through the status and prestige of gurus (as opposed to the merits of empirical evidence).
- Another cautionary perspective is provided in *The Witch Doctors.* After systematically and objectively reviewing a wide array of popular management books, authors John Micklethwait and Adrian Wooldridge conclude that managers must become critical consumers of these products. Being critical means being suspicious of the faddish contentions, remaining unconvinced by simplistic argumentation by the authors, being selective about which theory might work for you, and becoming broadly informed about the merits and deficiencies of each proposal.

Readers interested in more comprehensive and critical portraits of the management best-seller literature are encouraged to read "Management Fads; Emergence, Evolution, and Implications for Managers" by Jane Whitney Gibson and Dana V. Tesone (*Academy of Management Executive,* 2001, 15:4, pp. 122–133) and the reviews of four books on management fads in "Resource Reviews" (*Academy of Management Learning and Education,* 2003, 2:3, pp. 313–321).

In an explicit *attempt* to provoke your critical thinking about management fads, we have included (as Reading 2) a summary of *Flawed Advice and the Management Trap.* Harvard professor Chris Argyris presents two models of behavior. He voices a cautionary note when it comes to the managerial advice that is presented through the "popular management" press. Much of these prescriptions, such as those presented in Stephen Covey's *The Seven Habits of Highly Effective People* (see Reading 6 in Part II) are presented as though they are sound and valid principles of management, when in fact these prescriptions cannot be tested and therefore proven correct (workable). In order to avoid the management trap that stems from the adoption of "flawed advice," Argyris offers an alternative through Model II behavior.

Argyris has received numerous awards and is the recipient of 11 honorary degrees from universities around the world. He is the James Bryant Conant Professor Emeritus of Education and Organizational Behavior at Harvard's Graduate School of Business. He has written more than 400 articles and 30 books across a 45-year career, including *The Next Challenge for Leadership: Learning, Change, and Commitment* and (with Donald Schon) *Organizational Learning: A Theory of Action Perspective.* Interested readers may wish to read the "retrospective" comments on his career by Argyris and others in the *Academy of Management Executive* (2003, 17:2), pp. 37–55.

Currently two types of voices create "messages" relevant to management education. One is the organizational scholar (e.g., Karl Weick, Edward E. Lawler III, Lyman Porter, J. Richard Hackman), who offers us rich theories of management and organization and rigorous empirical observations of organizations in action. The other source includes management consultants and management practitioners (e.g., Bill George, Daniel Goleman, Jack Welch, Tom Peters, Stephen Covey, Bill Gates) who offer us perspectives from their lives on or near the "organizational firing line."

Traditional academics—students of tight theory and rigorous empirical study of organizational behavior—often find a large disparity between these two perspectives on management and organization. Confronted with the increasing popularity of the "best-sellers," the editors of *The Manager's Bookshelf* began to ask a number of questions about this nontraditional management literature. For example:

- Is this material "intellectual pornography," as some have claimed?
- Do we want college and university students to read this material?
- Should managers of today's organizations be encouraged to read this material and to take it seriously?
- What contributions to management education and development come from this array of management books?
- What are the major deficiencies or limitations of these books?

For answers to these questions we turned to three colleagues—Professors Larry L. Cummings, Brad Jackson, and Anne Cummings. We asked each of them to reflect upon the current and continued popularity of this literature. The questions we asked them (and their responses) are intended to help you frame, and therefore critically and cautiously consume, this literature. Their reflections on the role of the popular books in management education are presented as Reading 3 in Part I.

# Understanding and Using the Best-Sellers

*JON L. PIERCE and JOHN W. NEWSTROM*

For several decades now, a large number of books have focused on various aspects of management. These books have been in high demand at local bookstores. Several individuals have authored books that have sold millions of copies, among them Tom Peters and Bob Waterman *(In Search of Excellence)*, Spencer Johnson *(Who Moved My Cheese?)*, Jim Collins *(Good to Great)*, Bill Byham *(Zapp! The Lightning of Empowerment)*, Stephen Covey *(Seven Habits of Highly Effective People)*, Lee Iacocca *(Iacocca: An Autobiography)*, and Kenneth Blanchard and Spencer Johnson *(The One Minute Manager)*.

Some of these books have stayed on "best-seller" lists for many weeks, months, and even years. What are the reasons for their popularity? Why have business books continued to catch the public's attention through both good economic times and bad?

We have all heard newspaper stories about (and many have felt the shock waves and personal impact of) downsizing, pension fund losses, restructuring, corporate ethical scandals, and seemingly excessive executive compensation and benefits. We have all read stories about the success of foreign organizations—especially in the automotive and electronics industries. We have continued to watch bigger and bigger portions of our markets being dominated by foreign-owned and -controlled organizations. We have witnessed foreign interests purchase certain segments of America, while more and more jobs have been moved offshore. Perhaps in response to these trends, a tremendous thirst for *American* success stories and a desire to learn what would prevent some of these negative phenomena has arisen. In essence, the public is receptive and the timing is right for the writing, publication, and sale of popular management books at bookstores everywhere.

A second reason for the upsurge in management books stems from another form of competition. Many management consultants, fighting for visibility and a way to differentiate their services, have written books they hope will become best-sellers. Through the printed word they hope to provide a unique take-home product for their clients, communicate their management philosophies, gain wide exposure for themselves or their firms, and profit handsomely.

Third, the best-sellers also provide an optimistic message to a receptive market. In difficult economic times or under conditions of extreme pressures to produce short-term results, managers may be as eager to swallow easy formulas for business success as sick patients are to consume their prescribed medicines. Sensing this propensity, the authors of the best-sellers (and of many other books with lesser records) often claim, at least implicitly, to present managers with an easy cure for their organizational woes, or with an easy path to personal success. In a world characterized by chaos, environmental turbulence, and intense global competition, managers are driven to search for the ideas provided by others that might be turned into a competitive advantage.

Fourth, we are witnessing an increased belief in and commitment to proactive organizational change and a search for differentiating one's approach. An increasing number of managers are rejecting the notion that "if it ain't broke, don't fix it," and instead are adopting what Peters and Waterman portrayed as a *bias toward action.* These managers are seriously looking for and experimenting with different approaches toward organizational management. Many of the popular books provide managers with insights into new and different ways of managing. At a minimum, they are engaging in the process of benchmarking their competition and adopting "best practices" that have worked for others; hopefully, they are using the established practices of others as a springboard to new ideas themselves.

In their search for the "quick fix," generations of risk-taking American managers have adopted a series of organizational management concepts, such as management by objectives, job enlargement, job enrichment, sensitivity training, flextime, and a variety of labor-management participative schemes, such as quality circles, total-quality management, and quality of work-life programs. Each has experienced its own life cycle, often going through the stages of market discovery, wild acceptance by passionate believers, careful questioning of it by serious critics, broad disillusionment with its shortcomings, and sometimes later being abandoned and replaced by another emerging management technique (while a few advocates remain staunchly supportive of the fad).[1]

As a consequence of this managerial tendency to embrace ideas and then soon discard them, many viable managerial techniques have received a tarnished image. For example, many of the Japanese participative management systems that were copied by American managers found their way into the garbage cans of an earlier generation of American managers. The continuing demand for quick fixes stimulates a ready market for new, reborn, and revitalized management ideas. We encourage you to read and seriously reflect on the questionable probability of finding a legitimate quick fix. The search for solutions to major organizational problems in terms of "one minute" answers reflects a Band-Aid® approach to management—one that is destined to ultimately fail, and one that we condemn as a poor way to enrich the body of management knowledge and practice.

We alert you to this managerial tendency to look for "new" solutions to current organizational problems. The rush to resolve problems and take advantage of opportunities frequently leads to the search for simple remedies for complex organizational problems. Yet very few of today's organizational problems can be solved with any single approach. The high-involvement management, the learning organization, and the compassionate corporate culture advocated in today's generation of popular management books may also join the list of tried-and-abandoned solutions to organizational woes if implemented without a broader context and deeper understanding. We especially hope that the quick fix approach to organizational problem-solving that characterizes the management style of many will not be promoted as a result of this mosaic (i.e., *The Manager's Bookshelf*) of today's popular business books.

## ◆ RATIONALE FOR THIS BOOK

The business world has been buzzing with terms like *vision, alignment, flow, pride, authenticity, innovation, credibility, narcissism, paradigms, stewardship,* the *learning organization,* the *spirit of work* and the *soul of business, transformational and charismatic leaders, knowledge management, high-involvement management and organizations,* and *corporate cultures.* On the negative side, these terms feed the management world's preoccupation with quick fixes and the perpetuation of management fads. On the positive side, many of these concepts serve as catalysts to the further development of sound management philosophies and practices.

In earlier decades a few books occasionally entered the limelight (e.g., *Parkinson's Law, The Peter Principle, The Effective Executive, My Years with General Motors, The Money Game*), but for the most part they did not generate the widespread and prolonged popularity of the current generation of the business books. Then, too, many were not written in the readable style that makes most contemporary books so easy to consume.

Managers find the current wave of books not only interesting but enjoyable and entertaining to read. A small survey conducted by the Center for Creative Leadership found that a significant number of managers who participated in a study of their all-around reading selections chose one or more *management* books as their favorite.[2] In essence, many of the popular management books *are* being read by managers—probably because the books are often supportive of their present management philosophies! Many managers report that these books are insightful, easily readable, interestingly presented, and seemingly practical. Whether the prescriptions in these books have had (or ever will have) a real and lasting impact on the effective management of organizations remains to be determined.

Despite the overall popularity of many business best-sellers, some managers do not ready *any* current management books, and many other managers have read only a limited number or small parts of a few.* Similarly, many university students studying management have heard about some of these books but have not read them. *The Manager's Bookshelf: A Mosaic of Contemporary Views* presents perspectives from (but not a criticism of) a number of those popular management books. The book is designed for managers who are interested in the books but do not have time to read all of them in their entirety, and for students of management who want to be well informed as they prepare to enter the work world. Reading about the views expressed in many of the best-sellers will expand the knowledge and business vocabulary of both groups and enable them to engage in more meaningful conversations with their managerial colleagues.

Although reading the 48 summaries provided here can serve as a useful introduction to this literature, they should *not* be viewed as a substitute for immersion in the

*For a discussion on incorporating these types of management books into management training programs, see J. W. Newstrom and J. L. Pierce, "The Potential Role of Popular Business Books in Management Development Programs," *Journal of Management Development,* 8 (2, 1989), 13–24.

original material, nor do they remove the need for further reading of the more substantive management books and professional journals. The good news is that the popularity of these books suggests that millions of managers are reading them and they are exhibiting an interest in learning about what has worked for other managers and firms. This step is important toward the development of an open system paradigm for themselves and for their organizations.

*We strongly advocate that both managers and students be informed organizational citizens.* Therefore, we believe it is important for you to know and understand what is being written about organizations and management. We also believe that it is important for you to know what is being read by the managers who surround you, some of which is contained in best-sellers, much of which is contained in more traditional management books, as well as in professional and scientific journals.[3]

## CONTENTS OF THE BEST-SELLERS

What topics do these best-selling books cover, what is their form, and what is their merit? Although many authors cover a wide range of topics and others do not have a clear focus, most of these books fall into one of several categories. Some attempt to describe the more effective and ineffective companies and identify what made them successes or failures. Others focus on "micro" issues in leadership, motivation, or ethics. One group of authors focuses their attention on broad questions of corporate strategy and competitive tactics for implementing strategy. Some focus on pressing issues facing the contemporary organization such as social responsibility, globalism, the natural environment, workforce diversity, and the "virtual workplace."

In terms of form, many contain apparently simple answers and trite prescriptions. Others are built around literally hundreds of spellbinding anecdotes and stories. Some have used interviews of executives as their source of information, and others have adopted the parable format for getting their point across. As a group their presentation style is rich in diversity. As editors of this mosaic, we have necessarily had to exclude thousands of books while attempting to provide you with a rich exposure to an array of perspectives. For the most part, we have *not* included books that focus on a single executive's career success (e.g, Jack Welch or Steve Jobs), a single successful or failed organization (e.g., Wal-Mart or Southwest Airlines or Enron), or a historical reinterpretation of a key person's practices (e.g., "Leadership Secrets of Sitting Bull" [or Sir Ernest Shackleton, or Sun Tzu, or General George Patton, or William Shakespeare, or the Sopranos!])

Judging the merits of best-sellers is a difficult task (and one that we will leave for readers and management critics to engage in). Some critics have taken the extreme position of calling these books "intellectual wallpaper" and "business pornography." Certainly labels like these, justified or not, should caution readers. A better perspective is provided by an assessment of the sources, often anecdotal, of many of the books. In other words, much of the information in business best-sellers stems from the experiences and observations of a single individual and is often infused with the subjective opinions of that writer. Unlike the more traditional academic literature, these books do not all share a sound scientific foundation. Requirements pertaining to objectivity, reproducibility of observations, and tests for reliability and validity have not guided the creation of much of the material. As a consequence, the authors are at liberty to say whatever they want (and often with as much passion as they desire).

Unlike authors who publish research-based knowledge, authors of management best-sellers do not need to submit their work to a panel of reviewers who then critically evaluate the ideas, logic, and data. The authors of these popular management books are able to proclaim as sound management principles virtually anything that is intuitively acceptable to their publisher and readers. Therefore, *readers need to be cautious consumers.* The ideas presented in these books need to be critically compared with the well established thoughts from more traditional sources of managerial wisdom.

## ◆ CRITIQUING THESE POPULAR BOOKS

Although the notion of one minute management is seductive, we may safely conclude that *there are no fast-acting cures to deep and complex business problems.* Recognizing that simple solutions are not likely to be found in two hundred pages of anecdotal stories and that the best-sellers frequently present (or appear to present) quick fixes and simple solutions, we strongly encourage readers to read these popular books, looking less for simple solutions and more toward using them to stimulate their thinking and challenge the way they go about doing their business. We encourage you not only to achieve comprehension and understanding, but ultimately to arrive at the level of critique and synthesis—far more useful long-term skills.

To help you approach these works more critically, we encourage you to use the following questions to guide your evaluation:[4]

- **Author credentials:** How do the authors' background and personal characteristics uniquely qualify them to write this book? What *relevant* experience do they have? What unique access or perspective do they have? What prior writing experience do they have, and how was it accepted in the marketplace? What is their research background (capacity to design, conduct, and interpret the results of their observations)?
- **Rationale:** Why did the authors write the book? Is their self-proclaimed reason legitimate?
- **Face validity:** On initial examination of the book's major characteristics and themes (but before reading the entire book and actually examining the evidence provided), do you react positively or negatively? Are you inclined to accept or reject the author's conclusions? Are they believable? Does it fit with your prior experience and expectations, or does it rock them to the core?
- **Target audience:** For whom is this book uniquely written? What level of manager in the organizational hierarchy would most benefit from reading the book and why? Is it for you?
- **Integration of existing knowledge:** A field of inquiry can best move forward only if it draws upon and then extends existing knowledge. Was this book written in isolation of existing knowledge? Do the authors demonstrate an awareness of and build upon existing knowledge, while giving appropriate credit to other sources of ideas?

- **Readability/interest:** Do the authors engage your mind? Are relevant, practical illustrations provided that indicate how the ideas have been or could be applied? Is the language and format used appealing to you?
- **Internal validity:** To what degree do the authors provide substantive evidence that the phenomenon, practice, or ideas presented actually and directly produced a valued result? Does an internally consistent presentation of ideas demonstrate the processes through which the causes for their observations are understood?
- **Reliability/consistency:** To what degree do the author's conclusions converge with other sources of information available to you, or with the product of other methods of data collection? Do the authors stay consistent in their "pitch" from beginning to end of the book?
- **Distinctiveness:** Is the material presented new, creative, and distinctive (providing you with "value added"), or is it merely a presentation of "old wine in new bottles"?
- **Objectivity:** To what extent do the authors have a self-serving or political agenda, or have the authors presented information that was systematically gathered and evaluated? Have the authors offered both the pros *and* cons of their views?
- **External validity:** Are the ideas likely to work in your unique situation, or are they bound to the context within which the authors operated? What are the similarities that give you confidence that the recommendations made can be safely and effectively applied to your context?
- **Practicality:** Are the ideas adaptable? Do the authors provide concrete suggestions for application? Are the ideas readily transferable to the workplace in such a way that the typical reader could be expected to know what to do with them a few days later at work? Is it possible to produce an action plan directly from the material read?

These are only some of the questions that should be asked as you read and evaluate any popular management book.

## NATURE OF THIS BOOK

This is the seventh edition of *The Manager's Bookshelf.* The first edition was published in 1988. Recent language editions have also appeared in Italian, Spanish, and Chinese, pointing to the international popularity of these books. The current edition includes many books that were not previously summarized, representing a very substantial revision. *The Manager's Bookshelf* provides a comprehensive introduction to many of the major best-sellers in the management field during recent years.

Some authors have achieved such a level of market success with their first book that they have been driven to follow up their earlier success with one or more additional books. In response to this trend, this edition of *The Manager's Bookshelf* includes summaries of subsequent books written by authors whose work appeared in an earlier edition of *The Manager's Bookshelf.* Examples of "repeat" authors in this edition include Warren Bennis, Jay Conger, Edward E. Lawler III, Spencer Johnson, Jon Katzenbach, and Rosabeth Moss Kanter.

The selections contained in this book are of two types: excerpts of original material and summaries prepared by a panel of reviewers. In some cases, we provide the reader with not only the main ideas presented by the author of a best-seller, but also the flavor (style or nature) of the author's literary approach. For some selections, we obtained permission to excerpt directly a chapter from the original book—particularly chapters that are the keystone presentation of the author's major theme. In other cases, the author's original thoughts and words were captured by selecting an article (representing part of the book) that the author had written for publication in a professional journal. Here again, the reader will see the author's ideas directly, though only sampled or much condensed from the original source.

The major format chosen for inclusion is a comprehensive but brief and readable summary of the best-seller prepared by persons selected for their relevant expertise, interest, and familiarity. These summaries are primarily descriptive, designed to provide readers with an overall understanding of the book. These summaries are not judgmental in nature, nor are they necessarily a complete or precise reflection of the author's management philosophy.

Determining what constituted a management best-seller worthy of inclusion was easy in some cases and more difficult in others. From the thousands of books available for selection, the ones included here rated highly on one or more of these criteria:

1. *Market acceptance:* Several books have achieved national notoriety by selling hundreds of thousands, and occasionally millions, of copies.
2. *Provocativeness:* Some books present thought-provoking viewpoints that run counter to "traditional" management thought.
3. *Distinctiveness:* A wide variety of topical themes of interest to organizational managers and students of management are presented.
4. *Representativeness:* In an attempt to avoid duplication from books with similar content within a topical area, many popular books were necessarily excluded.
5. *Author reputation:* Some authors (e.g., Warren Bennis, Edward E. Lawler III) have a strong reputation for the quality of their thinking and the insights they have generated, and therefore, some of their newer products were included.

## ◆ AUTHORS OF THE BEST-SELLERS

It is appropriate for a reader to examine a management best-seller and inquire, "Who is the author of this book?" Certainly the authors come from varied backgrounds and that can be both a strength and weakness for the best-sellers as a whole. Their diversity of experience and perspective is rich, and yet it is possible that some authors are ill qualified to speak and portray themselves as experts.

Some of the authors have been critically described as self-serving egotists who have little to say constructively about management, but who say it with a flair and passion such that reading their books may appear to be very exciting. Some books are seemingly the product of armchair humorists who set out to entertain their readers with tongue in cheek. Other books on the best-seller lists have been written with the aid of a ghost writer (i.e., by someone who takes information that has been provided by another and then converts it into the lead author's story) or with the assistance of a professional writer who helps a busy executive organize and present his/her thoughts. Other books are the product of a CEO's reflection on his/her career or heart-felt positions on contemporary issues in organizations (e.g., authors Bill George and Larry Bossidy). A rather new and refreshing change has been the emergence in the best-seller literature of books prepared by respected academic professionals who have capably applied the best of their substantive research to pressing management problems and subsequently integrated their thoughts into book form. (Examples in this edition of such academics include Edward E. Lawler, J. Richard Hackman, Karl Weick, and Paul Lawrence.) In summary, it may be fascinating to read the "inside story" or delve into a series of exciting anecdotes and "war stories," but the reader still has the opportunity and obligation to challenge the author's credentials for making broad generalizations from that experience base.

## Conclusions

We encourage you to read and reflect on this collection of thoughts from the authors of today's generation of management books. We invite you to expand and enrich your insights into management as a result of learning from this set of popular books. We challenge you to question and debate the pros and cons of the ideas and philosophies that are presented by these authors. We hope you will ask when, where, how, and why these ideas are applicable. Examine the set of readings provided here, let them stimulate your thinking, and, in the process, learn something new. You'll find that learning—and especially critical thinking—can be both fun and addictive!

## Notes

1. See, for example, B. Ettore, "What's the Next Business Buzzword?," *Management Review,* 1997, 86:8, 33–35; "Business Fads: What's In—and Out," *Business Week* (January 20, 1986); W. W. Armstrong, "The Boss Has Read Another New Book!" *Management Review* (June 1994), 61–64.
2. Frank Freeman, "Books That Mean Business: The Management Best Sellers," *Academy of Management Review,* 1985, 345–350.
3. See, for example, a report on executive reading preferences by Marilyn Wellemeyer in "Books Bosses Read," *Fortune* (April 27, 1987).
4. See John W. Newstrom and Jon L. Pierce, "An Analytic Framework for Assessing Popular Business Books," *Journal of Management Development,* 12 (4, 1993), 20–28.

# Flawed Advice and the Management Trap

*CHRIS ARGYRIS*

*Summary prepared by Kelly Nelson*

***Kelly Nelson** is a 1991 graduate of the University of Minnesota Duluth. Since graduation, she has served in various operating management and human resource positions in the steel industry. She is currently working as a General Manager, Labor Relations at AK Steel in Ohio. She is committed to dispensing "unflawed" advice as often as possible, particularly when dispensing parenting knowledge to her son John.*

Many individuals receive and accept advice that is fundamentally flawed, which leads to counterproductive consequences. The acceptance of flawed advice stems from Model I behaviors that strive to protect oneself, while unilaterally treating all others the same (i.e., not dealing specifically and directly with behaviors in order to effect change). Model II behaviors, on the other hand, provide organizations the opportunity to share information, act cooperatively, and deal directly and firmly with behaviors in order to effect change. Organizations that adopt Model II behaviors also provide themselves the opportunity to analyze advice to ensure it is not flawed, thereby avoiding the "management trap."

## ◆ INCONSISTENT AND UNACTIONABLE ADVICE

Stephen Covey's *The Seven Habits of Highly Effective People* (1989) is based upon a set of principles that direct individuals to effectiveness through *inside-out management,* one that begins with a focus on one's self. The goal is to develop a positive atti-

Chris Argyris. *Flawed Advice and the Management Trap: How Managers Can Know When They're Getting Good Advice and When They're Not.* New York: Oxford University Press (2000).

tude through developing trust, generating positive energy, and sidestepping negative energy. Covey's strategy suggests suppressing negative feelings and putting on a "false face" of positive feedback. However, the premise of this suppression flies in the face of Covey's basic principles (i.e., to develop trust). Furthermore, the "theory" espoused by Covey cannot be tested; therefore, it cannot be proven.

This inconsistent and unactionable advice is also demonstrated by Doyle and Strauss (*How to Make Meetings Work,* 1982), management consultants who advise groups on actions to produce effective meetings. According to Doyle and Strauss, if a group is having difficulty where to begin and how, it is best to wait until the group is convinced it needs the consultant (or leader). The group will then ask for assistance and the consultant can take control and give direction to the group. In any group, this tactic may become a self-fulfilling prophecy. Further, Doyle and Strauss do not give specific guidelines on the point at which the consultant should intervene. Also, the actual behaviors of the consultant are not detailed. Similar to Covey's theory, Doyle and Strauss' theory cannot be tested; therefore, it cannot be proven.

As demonstrated by the examples of Covey and Doyle and Strauss, popular management advice is published as valid and actionable and is widely adopted. However, the advice reveals a pattern of gaps and inconsistencies, leading to unintended consequences and an inability to systematically correct the deficiencies.

## ORGANIZATIONAL CONSEQUENCES OF USING INCONSISTENT ADVICE

The most common advice for designing and implementing programs for organizational change and improvement involves the following four elements:

1. Define a vision.
2. Define a competitive strategy that is consistent with the vision.
3. Define organizational work processes that, when carried out, will implement the strategy.
4. Define individual job requirements so that employees can produce the processes effectively.

The elements are sound and understandable. However, they lead to inconsistencies when the vision, strategy, work processes, and job requirements are developed to support contradictory goals. For example, a 1996 study concluded that a vast majority of companies held only a superficial commitment to internal participative decision making. Eighty-three percent of the middle managers responding favored more involvement; yet, their supervisors did not know it. Top managers were not committed to the strategy, nor were they aware of the lack of credibility they were demonstrating.

For the four elements to succeed and to lead to consistent improvement, *internal commitment* of every employee (gained through intrinsic motivation) is needed. However, most organizations attempt to develop the elements' *external commitment* (top-down policies). This inherent inconsistency lays the groundwork for failure. The failure is demonstrated through the organization's failure to improve performance, increase profits, and develop cooperative behaviors.

## WHY FLAWED ADVICE EXISTS

If so much professional advice, even if implemented correctly, leads to counterproductive consequences, why have so many users found that advice to be helpful? Because people hold two different "theories of action" about effective behavior—one they *espouse* and one they actually *use* (i.e., *Model I*). While using Model I, people strive to satisfy their actions when they:

- Define goals and try to achieve them. (They don't try to develop, with others, a mutual definition of shared purpose.)
- Maximize winning and minimize losing. (They treat any change in goals, once they are decided on, as a sign of weakness.)
- Minimize the generation or expression of negative feelings. (They fear this would be interpreted as showing ineptness, incompetence, or lack of diplomacy.)
- Be rational. (They want to remain objective and intellectual, and suppress their feelings.)

To accomplish these ends, under Model I, people will seek to:

- Design and manage the environment unilaterally, that is, plan actions secretly and persuade or cajole others to agree with one's definition of the situation.
- Own and control the task.
- Unilaterally protect themselves, that is, keep from being vulnerable by speaking in abstractions, avoiding reference to directly observed events, and withholding underlying thoughts and feelings.
- Unilaterally protect others from being hurt, in particular, by withholding important information, telling white lies, suppressing feelings, and offering false sympathy. Moreover, they do not test the assumption that the other person needs to be protected or that the strategy of protection should be kept secret.

Following Model I behavior leads to a self-sealing loop in which the individual treats others unilaterally while protecting him/herself. As individuals follow Model I behavior, they become skilled and their actions will appear to have "worked" in that they achieve their intended objectives while appearing spontaneous and effortless. Model I behaviors are not only performed by individuals but also by groups. This provides an organization-wide network of Model I behavior in which all members are protecting themselves (whether individually or as a group). Furthermore, the Model I behaviors are enforced and perpetuated by Human Resource Department individuals who also practice Model I behaviors.

On the other hand, *Model II* behaviors involve sharing power with anyone who has competence and is relevant to deciding about implementing the action in question. Defining and assigning tasks are shared by all decision makers. In the Model II method, decision-making networks are developed with the goal of maximizing the contribution of each member.

Model I behaviors allow individuals to remain within their comfort zones and encourage all to place responsibility on problems "out there" instead of on the systematic faults of the advice being used. Hence, it is attractive and still widely used. Model II behavior forces individual behavioral change and accepts all participants as equals in the process. While pulling individuals out of their comfort zones, it requires individuals to face up to their own commitments and reflect upon their own assumptions, biases, and reasoning.

## VALIDITY AND ACTIONABILITY LIMITS TO MODEL I

The four main reasons Model I behavior produces unskilled awareness and incompetence are:

1. The advice represents *espoused* theories of effectiveness.
2. The advice, as crafted, contains evaluations and attributions that are neither tested nor testable.
3. The advice is based on self-referential logic that produces limited knowledge about what is going on.
4. The advice does not specify causal processes.

### CRITIQUING ADVICE

How can managers determine if the advice they are receiving is Model I-based advice? It is important that individuals focus on reducing inconsistencies, closing knowledge gaps, and addressing personal fear. Instead of judging others as defensive, wrong, and/or unjust, the individual must request illustrations of evaluations and attributions, and craft tests of their validity. Instead of judging others as naïve, complainers, or crybabies, one should request illustrations and tests, then inquire about how others responded to test attempts. One must also illustrate how the gaps and inconsistencies in the reasoning process are likely to backfire. Finally, evaluations and attributions about counterproductive actions must be illustrated and testing encouraged.

If most of the advice is abstract and does not specify the theory required to implement it, Model I behaviors will result. Some may espouse Model II behavior, but they will be unaware of and unable to explain the gaps. Finally, Model II behavior is more direct and is much tougher on holding people responsible for true changed behaviors.

Model I is often integrated in performance review systems. Often performance appraisals are "eased into" by the appraiser in order to save the recipient's feelings. Also, negative feedback is given in general terms, and quickly followed by positive reinforcement (often given only to get away from the negative portion of the review). Performance evaluations such as these are classic Model I examples, with inconsistencies, information gaps, and behavior not changed as a result.

On the other hand, performance evaluations based in Model II are specific, direct, and produce discussion about tough, productive reasoning that results in compelling decisions. It also facilitates change of the organization to generating internal commitment to organization values.

### GENERATING INTERNAL COMMITMENT TO VALUES TO PRODUCE DESIRED OUTCOMES

In order for an organization's values to become internal commitments on an individual level, Model II behavior needs to be practiced at all levels of the organization. Nondefensive information sharing and decision making, along with individual awareness of their own gaps and inconsistencies, provide the culture in which value commitment becomes internal to the individual.

The organization's values lead to strategic choices. High-quality choices possess four key attributes:

1. They are genuine.
2. They are sound.
3. They are actionable.
4. They are compelling.

Obstacles to high-quality strategic choices include politics, bad analyses, turbulent markets and, most commonly, flawed processes. In flawed processes, choices either do not get framed, do not get made, appear to get made but fall apart, are made but are not sound, or choices get made but the subsequent action is not timely.

To ensure strategic choices are high-quality and meet the internal commitment to values adopted by individuals, a *choice-structuring process* is necessary. The goal of a choice-structuring process is to produce sound strategic choices that lead to successful action.

The strategic choice-structuring process has five steps:

1. Frame the choice.
2. Brainstorm possible options.
3. Specify conditions necessary to validate each option.
4. Prioritize the conditions that create the greatest barrier to choice.
5. Design valid tests for the key barrier conditions.

## Summary

Model I behaviors prohibit strategic choice-structuring because protectionism and defensiveness are the bases for the behavior. In Model II environments, successful strategic choice structuring is possible because the advice adopted is not flawed. The advice adopted stipulates that (1) the theories in use should specify the sequence of behavior required to produce the intended consequences or goals; (2) the theories in use should be crafted in ways that make the causality transparent; (3) the causalities embedded in the theories in use are testable robustly in the context of everyday life; and (4) actionable knowledge must specify the values that underlie and govern the designs in use.

Model II behaviors provide organizations with the opportunity to analyze advice directly to ensure advice adopted by the organization is not flawed.

# Reflections on the Best-Sellers: A Cautionary Note

**JON L. PIERCE and JOHN W. NEWSTROM,**

**with Larry L. Cummings, Brad Jackson, and Anne Cummings**

*Dr.* ***Larry L. Cummings*** *was the Carlson Professor of Management in the Carlson School of Management at the University of Minnesota. He previously taught at Columbia University, Indiana University, the University of British Columbia, the University of Wisconsin in Madison, and Northwestern University. Professor Cummings published more than 80 journal articles and 16 books. He served as the editor of the* Academy of Management Journal, *as a member of the Academy's Board of Governors, and President of the same association. Dr. Cummings was a consultant for many corporations, including Dow Chemical, Cummins Engine, Eli Lilly, Prudential, Samsonite, Touche-Ross, and Moore Business Forms.*

***Dr. Brad Jackson*** *is Head of School at the Victoria Management School at Victoria University of Wellington in New Zealand. Brad taught previously at Denmark's Copenhagen Business School in Denmark and at the University of Calgary in Canada. Jackson's research interests include: the changing role of the CEO, the global management fashion industry, and organizational political processes associated with managing change. He has taught courses in Organizational Behavior, Change Management, Intercultural Management, Organizational Communication, and Management Learning. Jackson has published three books—Management Gurus and Management Fashions, The Hero Manager, and Organisational Behaviour in New Zealand.*

***Dr. Anne Cummings*** *taught General Management, Organizational Behavior, Teams, Negotiations, and Leadership for Undergraduate, MBA, Ph.D., and Executive Education audiences at the University of Pennsylvania's Wharton School, and recently joined the Management Studies faculty at the University of Minnesota Duluth. Dr. Cummings won the David W. Hauck teaching award at*

*Wharton in recognition of her outstanding ability to lead, stimulate, and challenge students. She holds a Ph.D. in Organizational Behavior from the University of Illinois at Urbana-Champaign, and her research has appeared in the* Academy of Management Journal, Journal of Applied Psychology, California Management Review, *and* Leadership Quarterly

This opening section provides our reflections upon management (both the body of knowledge and its practice), as well as upon the wave of management books that have almost become an institutionalized part of the popular press. We hope it will provide some helpful perspectives and point you in some new directions.

One of the world's premier management gurus, Peter F. Drucker, suggests that managing is a "liberal art." It is "liberal" because it deals not only with fundamental knowledge, but self-knowledge, wisdom, and leadership; it is an "art" because it is also concerned with practice and application. According to Drucker, "managers draw on all the knowledge and insights of the humanities and the social sciences—on psychology and philosophy, on economics and history, on ethics—as well as on the physical sciences".* Building on this, we note that *management can be defined as the skillful application of a body of knowledge to a particular organizational situation.* This definition suggests that management is an art form as well as a science. That is, there is a body of knowledge that has to be applied with the fine touch and instinctive sense of the master artist. Peter Drucker reminds us that the fundamental task of management is to "make people capable of joint performance through common goals, common values, the right structure, and the training and development they need to perform and to respond to change" (p. 4). Consequently, execution of the management role and performance of the managerial functions are more complex than the simple application of a few management concepts. The development of effective management, therefore, requires the development of an in-depth understanding of organizational and management concepts, careful sensitivity to individuals and groups, and the capacity to grasp when and how to apply this knowledge.

The organizational arena presents today's manager with a number of challenges. The past few decades have been marked by a rapid growth of knowledge about organizations and management systems. As a consequence of this growth in management information, we strongly believe that it is important for today's manager to engage in *lifelong learning,* by continually remaining a student of management. It is also clear to us that our understanding of organizations and management systems is still in the early stages of development. That is, there remain many unanswered questions that pertain to the effective management of organizations.

Many observers of the perils facing today's organizations have charged that the crises facing American organizations today are largely a function of "bad management"—the failure, in large part, to recognize that management is about human beings. It is the ability, according to Drucker, "to make people capable of joint performance, (and) to make their strengths effective and their weaknesses irrelevant. This is what organization is all about, and it is the reason that management is the critical, determining force" (p. 10). Similarly, Tom Peters and Bob Waterman have observed that the growth

*Page references are to Peter F. Drucker, "Management as a social function and liberal art," *The Essential Drucker: The Best of Sixty Years of Peter Drucker's Essential Writings on Management.* Harper Business, 2003.

of our society during the twentieth century was so rapid that almost any management approach appeared to work and work well. The real test of effective management systems did not appear until the recent decades, when competitive, economic, political, and social pressures created a form of environmental turbulence that pushed existing managerial tactics beyond their limits. Not only are students of management challenged to learn about effective management principles, but they are also confronted with the need to develop the skills and intuitive sense to apply that management knowledge.

Fortunately, there are many organizations in our society from which they can learn, and there is a wealth of knowledge that has been created that focuses on effective organizational management. There are at least two literatures that provide rich opportunities for regular reading. First, there is the traditional management literature found in management and organization textbooks and academic journals (e.g., *Academy of Management Journal, Administrative Science Quarterly, Harvard Business Review, Managerial Psychology, Research in Organizational Behavior,* and *California Management Review*). Second, the past few decades have seen the emergence of a nontraditional management literature written by management gurus, management practitioners, and management consultants who describe their organizational experiences and provide a number of other management themes. Knowledge about effective and ineffective management systems can be gleaned by listening to the management scholar, philosopher, and practitioner.

Since not all that is published in the academic journals or in the popular press meets combined tests of scientific rigor and practicality, it is important that motivated readers immerse themselves in *both* of these literatures. Yet, neither source should be approached and subsequently consumed without engaging in critical thinking.

## ◆ CRITICAL THINKING AND CAUTIOUS CONSUMPTION

We believe that the ideas promoted in these best-sellers should not be integrated blindly into any organization. Each should be subjected to careful scrutiny in order to identify its inherent strengths and weaknesses; each should be examined within the context of the unique organizational setting in which it may be implemented; and modifications and fine-tuning of the technique may be required in order to tailor it to a specific organizational setting and management philosophy. Finally, the process that is used to implement the management technique may be as important to its success as the technique itself.

This is an era of an information-knowledge explosion. We would like to remind consumers of that information of the relevance of the saying *caveat emptor* (let the buyer beware) from the product domain, because there are both good and questionable informational products on the best-seller market. Fortunately, advisory services like *Consumer Reports* exist to advise us on the consumption of consumer goods. There is, however, no similar guide for our consumption of information in the popular management press. Just because a book has been a best-seller does not mean that the information contained therein is worthy of direct consumption. It may be a best-seller because it presents an optimistic message, it is enjoyable reading, it contains simple solutions that appeal to those searching for easy answers, or because it has been successfully marketed to the public.

The information in all management literature should be approached with caution; it should be examined and questioned. The pop-management literature should not be substituted for more scientific-based knowledge about effective management. In addition, this knowledge should be compared and contrasted with what we know about organizations and management systems from other sources—the opinions of other experts, the academic management literature, and our own prior organizational experiences.

We invite you to question this best-seller literature. In the process there are myriad questions that should be asked. For example: What are the author's credentials, and are they relevant to the book? Has the author remained an objective observer of the reported events? Why did the author write this book? What kind of information is being presented (e.g., opinion, values, facts)? Does this information make sense when it is placed into previously developed theories (e.g., from a historical context)? Could I take this information and apply it to another situation at a different point in time and in a different place, or was it unique to the author's experience? These and similar questions should be part of the information screening process.

## ◆ INTERVIEWS WITH THREE ORGANIZATIONAL SCHOLARS

As we became increasingly familiar with the best-sellers through our roles as editors, we began asking a number of questions about this type of literature. We then sought and talked with three distinguished management scholars—Professors L. L. Cummings, Brad Jackson, and Anne Cummings. Following are excerpts from those interviews.

### EXPLORING THE CONTRIBUTIONS OF BEST-SELLERS

We have witnessed an explosion in the number and type of books that have been written on management and organizations for the trade market. Many of these books have found themselves on various "best-seller" lists. What, in your opinion, has been the impact of these publications? What is the nature of their contribution?

#### Larry Cummings' Perspective

Quite frankly, I think these books have made a number of subtle contributions, most of which have not been labeled or identified by either the business press or the academic press. In addition, many of their contributions have been inappropriately or inaccurately labeled.

Permit me to elaborate. I think it is generally true that a number of these very popular "best-seller list" books, as you put it, have been thought to be reasonably accurate translations or interpretations of successful organizational practice. Although this is not the way that these books have been reviewed in the academic press, my interactions with managers, business practitioners, and MBA students reveal that many of these books are viewed as describing organizational structure, practices, and cultures that are thought to contribute to excellence.

On the other hand, when I evaluate the books myself and when I pay careful attention to the reviews by respected, well trained, balanced academicians, it is my opinion that these books offer very little, if anything, in the way of *generalizable* knowledge about successful organizational practice. As organizational case studies, they are the most dangerous of the lot, in that the data (information) presented has not been systematically, carefully, and cautiously collected and interpreted. Of course, that criticism is common for case studies. Cases were never meant to be contributions to scientific knowledge. Even the best ones are primarily pedagogical aids.

The reason I describe the cases presented in books like *In Search of Excellence* as frequently among the most dangerous is because they are so well done (i.e., in a marketing and journalistic sense), and therefore, they are easily read and so believable. They are likely to influence the naive, those who consume them without critically evaluating their content. They epitomize the glamour and the action orientation, and even the machoism of American management practice; that is, they represent the epitome of competition, control, and order as dominant interpersonal and organizational values.

Rather, I think the contributions of these books, in general, have been to provide an apology, a rationale, or a positioning, if you like, of American management as something that is not *just* on the defensive with regard to other world competitors. Instead, they have highlighted American management as having many good things to offer: a sense of spirit, a sense of identification, and a sense of clear caricature. This has served to fill a very important need. In American management thought there has emerged a lack of self-confidence and a lack of belief that what we are doing is proactive, effective, and correct. From this perspective these books have served a useful role in trying to present an upbeat, optimistic characterization.

### Brad Jackson's Perspective

It is very difficult to assess the true nature of the impact that the best-sellers have on management practice. We might infer from the huge number of books that are sold each year that their impact might be quite substantial. Corporations and consulting firms purchase many business best sellers on a bulk basis. It is difficult to ascertain how many of these are actually distributed and received. The next question to consider, of course, is the extent to which these books are actually read. Anecdotal evidence (as well as personal experience!) suggests that, even with the best intentions, most readers manage to peruse the book jacket, the testimonials, the preface, and, at best, the introductory chapter. Few find the time to read the book's entire contents.

Most crucially, however, we should try to understand the nature of the impact that the reading of a best-seller, even if it is very partial, has on how the individual manager perceives the world and how she or he acts on that world as a result of being exposed to the ideas expressed in this genre of books. This is a task that is fraught with difficulty, as managers are exposed to so many different influences and are shaped and constrained by a wide range of organizational environments. In my book, *Management Gurus and Management Fashions* (Jackson, 2001), I suggest that business best sellers not only make an intellectual contribution, they also provide quite important psychological and emotional support to managers. It is no accident that we can observe the swelling of the personal growth section of the business book section during times of widespread turbulence.

During the 1990s, organizations across all sectors embraced new management ideas (management fashions) that were promoted by management gurus in business best-sellers. Organizational improvement programs such as Total Quality Management, Business Process Reengineering, The Balanced Scorecard, and Knowledge Management were seized upon as the panacea for organizations desperate to retain their competitive edge or merely survive. Vestiges of these and older programs can still be traced in the language, systems, and structures of these organizations, but their influence and attention are well past their peak. We have very little to go on in terms of understanding how these management fashions are adapted and institutionalized, but a few studies have shown that these ideas tend to be only selectively adopted or they are reworked or even actively resisted by managers and employees. The bottom line is that *it is very difficult to accurately trace the impact of best-sellers.* However, we should be prepared to accept that the final impact is likely to be quite different than what the best selling author originally intended!

### Anne Cummings' Perspective

These best-selling business books have offered my teaching a variety of important contributions:

- They offer powerful corporate examples that I use for illustrating conceptual points in class. I often find the examples of what didn't work (and the ensuing discussion about why) as useful (if not more useful!), than the examples of what did work.
- They update me on the newest terminology and techniques that managers are reading about, which helps me to communicate efficiently and effectively with them, using their vocabulary.
- They stimulate interesting conversations with Executive Education participants, who often question the value of the latest fads, and want to explore how these new ideas compare to their managerial experience and to the conceptual foundations about management that they learned a decade earlier.
- Some of the books offer basic frameworks for viewing problems and issues, and this encourages students to begin thinking conceptually. I can then nudge students towards thinking further about cause-effect relationships, contingencies, and the utility of academic research.
- Some of the books offer important insights into environmental trends, shifting managerial pressures, and even new ways of thinking about things—sometimes long before academics explore these areas.

## POSSIBLE CONCERNS ABOUT BEST-SELLERS

In addition to a large volume of sales, surveys reveal that many of these books have been purchased and presumably read by those who are managing today's organizations. Does this trouble you? More specifically, are there any concerns that you have, given the extreme popularity of these types of books?

### Larry Cummings' Perspective

I am of two minds with regard to this question. First, I think that the sales of these books are not an accurate reflection of the degree, the extent, or the carefulness with which they have been read. Nor do I believe that the sales volumes tell us anything about the pervasiveness of their impact. Like many popular items (fads), many of these books have been purchased for desktop dressing. In many cases, the preface, the introduction, and the conclusion (maybe the summary on the dust jacket) have been read such that the essence of the book is picked up and it can become a part of managerial and social conversation.

Obviously, this characterization does not accurately describe everyone in significant positions of management who has purchased these books. There are many managers who make sincere attempts to follow the management literature thoroughly and to evaluate it critically. I think that most of the people with whom I come in contact in management circles, both in training for management and in actual management positions, who have carefully read the books are not deceived by them. They are able to put them in the perspective of representations or characterizations of a fairly dramatic sort. As a consequence, I am not too concerned about the books being overly persuasive in some dangerous, Machiavellian, or subterranean sense.

On the other hand, I do have a concern of a different nature regarding these books. That concern focuses upon the possibility that the experiences they describe will be taken as legitimate bases or legitimate directions for the study of management processes. These books represent discourse by the method of emphasizing the extremes, in particular the extremes of success. I think a much more fruitful approach to studying and developing prescriptions for management thought and management action is to use the *method of differences* rather than the *method of extremes.*

The method of differences would require us to study the conditions that gave rise to success at Chrysler, or McDonald's, or which currently gives rise to success at Merck, or any of the other best-managed companies. However, through this method we would also contrast these companies with firms in the same industries that are not as successful. The method of contrast (differences) is likely to lead to empirical results that are much less dramatic, much less exciting, much less subject to journalistic account (i.e., they're likely to be more boring to read), but it is much more likely to lead to observations that are more generalizable across managerial situations, as well as being generative in terms of ideas for further management research.

Thus, the issue is based on the fundamental method that underlies these characterizations. My concern is not only from a methodological perspective. It also centers on our ethical and professional obligations to make sure that the knowledge we transmit does not lead people to overgeneralize. Rather, it should provide them with information that is diagnostic rather than purely prescriptive.

The method of extremes does not lead to a diagnostic frame of mind. It does not lead to a frame of mind that questions why something happened, under what conditions it happened, or under what conditions it would not happen. The method of differences is much more likely to lead to the discovery of the conditional nature of knowledge and the conditional nature of prescriptions.

### Brad Jackson's Perspective

I tend to be less concerned about the large volume of business best-sellers than a lot of my academic colleagues. While I wish that there were bigger public appetites for more academically oriented management books, I am generally encouraged by the widespread interest in business and management. It's important for managers to take an interest in what is going on beyond their immediate work environment and to ask questions about why things are being done in a certain way and what could be done differently. Best-sellers typically challenge the *status quo* in provocative and dramatic ways that readily engage managers' attentions. Subsequently, many managers wish to learn more and sign up for some form of formal management education. It is in this forum that they can become exposed to alternative and more rigorously researched accounts of management theory and practice that challenge some of the assumptions made in the best-sellers. I have found that encouraging managers to take a more critical reading of the business best-sellers can be highly instructive for both them and me, especially when they are presented alongside academically oriented texts which they find to be slightly less accessible, but ultimately more rewarding.

### Anne Cummings' Perspective

My greatest concern with these books is that many readers do not have the time, motivation, or managerial experience to appropriately apply the contents. Unfortunately, a few students seem to be mostly interested in "speaking the language" with bravado just to demonstrate how up-to-date they are. Others seem to want to simply imitate the successful examples that they have read about, as though these reports of alleged best practices represent a "cookbook" approach that can be easily applied elsewhere. Most managers consider their time an extremely valuable resource, and consider this reading a "luxury"; they tell me they therefore approach these readings looking for "take-aways" from each one—short lists of guiding principles, practical procedures they can implement immediately, or a simple diagram or model to organize a project or change they are leading. All students of management can benefit from remembering that the process of building solid theories and best practices from isolated case examples (i.e., inductive learning) is a complex one; some discipline and patience is required to avoid premature generalizing before valid evidence is available and well understood. The challenge is for readers to expend some real effort and apply critical thinking to these products—to analyze when and why the practices might be successful. Demanding conversations with colleagues, mentors and competitors; comparisons of apparent discrepancies; and asking tough "why" and "how" questions are all useful techniques to achieve this discipline.

## RECENT CHANGES IN BEST-SELLERS

The modern era of business best-seller popularity now spans roughly a quarter-century. Have you witnessed any changes or evolution in the nature of these best-seller books over the past decade or so?

### Brad Jackson's Perspective

Looking back, I characterize the 1990s as the "guru decade." This was the era in which a few highly influential management gurus such as Michael Hammer, Tom Peters, Michael Porter, Peter Senge, and Stephen Covey reigned supreme among the best-sellers. Their larger than life presences helped to spawn a few very powerful management ideas that drove a lot of conventional management thinking in North America and beyond. I do not see the same concentration of interest in either management gurus or management fashions in the current business book market. Instead I see a lot of niche-based ideas that are being promoted by specific consulting firms. None of these seem to have had the same pervasive influence that the gurus previously held.

On the other hand, I see a lot of interest in biographical accounts of what I call "hero managers" such as Jack Welch, Richard Branson, and Lou Gerstner. Most of these are inspirational self-celebratory accounts but, of course, there has also been a lot more interest in exposing some of the darker sides of corporate life in the wake of the Enron and other corporate scandals.

### WORDS OF ADVICE

Do you have any insights or reflections or words of advice to offer readers of business best-sellers?

#### Brad Jackson's Perspective

I like to share the advice that Micklethwait and Wooldridge (*The Witch Doctors,* 1996) give at the end of their excellent exposé on the management theory industry. They argue that because management theory is comparatively immature and underdeveloped, it is vital that managers become selective and critical consumers of the products and services offered by the management theory industry. In particular, they suggest that managers should bear in mind the following advice when making book purchase decisions:

1. Anything that you suspect is bunk almost certainly is.
2. Beware of authors who aggrandize themselves more than their work.
3. Beware of authors who argue almost exclusively by analogy.
4. Be selective. No one management theory will cure all ills.
5. Bear in mind that the cure can sometimes be worse than the disease.
6. Supplement these books with reactions from academic reviewers to get an informed and critical perspective on the value of new management theories and their proponents.

All I would add to this succinct list is to encourage managers to read more widely and to look to other disciplines such as philosophy, history, psychology, and art for supplemental insights into management practice and organizational life. I'm always surprised by how much I learn when I browse through books in the other sections of the library or bookstore.

## Conclusion

We hope that you have enjoyed reading the views of these management scholars (Professors Larry Cummings, Brad Jackson, and Anne Cummings) on the role of popular management books. In addition, we hope that the readings contained in the seventh edition of *The Manager's Bookshelf* will stimulate your thinking about effective and ineffective practices of management. We reiterate that there is no single universally applicable practice of management, for management is the skillful application of a body of knowledge to a particular situation. We invite you to continue expanding your understanding of new and developing management concepts. In a friendly sort of way, we challenge you to develop the skills to know when and how to apply this knowledge in the practice of management.

PART

# II

# Best-Seller "Classics"

Many of those books that found their way into earlier editions of *The Manager's Bookshelf* as a part of our *mosaic of contemporary views* continue to have a message that many managers reference and still want to hear. As a result, for the seventh edition of *The Manager's Bookshelf* we have included summaries of selected books published in earlier years that continue to be popular among managers today.

While working as partners for McKinsey & Company (a management consulting firm), Thomas J. Peters and Robert H. Waterman Jr. conducted research that led to their book *In Search of Excellence.* The results of their study of management practices in several dozen companies in six industries led to the identification of eight attributes that were practiced consistently and appeared to be related to organizational success. Peters and Waterman's work also sparked an interest in looking at management through a different set of lenses and defined a manager's role as coach, cheerleader, and facilitator. Subsequently, Peters co-authored *A Passion for Excellence, Thriving on Chaos, Liberation Management,* and *The Tom Peters Seminar.* Waterman wrote *The Renewal Factor* and *What America Does Right.*

Quality, customer service, total quality management, and continuous improvement have become organizational buzzwords in the past several years. One of the leaders in developing strategies for building quality into manufacturing processes was the late W. Edwards Deming. During the 1950s, Deming went to Japan to teach statistical control, where his ideas received a very warm reception. The Japanese built on Deming's ideas and moved the responsibility for quality from the ranks of middle management down to the shop floor level. Deming's ideas on quality control soon became an integral feature in Japanese management. Deming has been called by his admirers both the "prophet of quality" and the "man of the century." He certainly demonstrated a powerful force of personality and singular focus.

Total quality control (TQC) means that responsibility for quality is a part of every employee's job. Deming's *Out of the Crisis* calls for long-term organizational transformation through the implementation of a 14-step plan of action focusing on leadership, constant innovation, and removal of barriers to performance. Interested readers may also wish to examine other books about Deming and his influence in *The World of W. Edwards Deming, The Deming Dimension, Thinking About Quality,* and *Deming's Road to Continual Improvement.*

Kenneth Blanchard and Spencer Johnson, in the widely read book *The One Minute Manager,* build their prescriptions for effective human resource management on two basic principles. First, they suggest that *quality time* with the subordinate is of utmost importance. Second, they adopt Douglas McGregor's notion that employees are basically capable of *self-management.* These two principles provide the basis for their prescriptions on goal setting, praising, and reprimanding as the cornerstones of effective management.

Kenneth Blanchard was a professor of management at the University of Massachusetts, and remains active as a writer and management consultant. Blanchard has also published *The Power of Ethical Management, Gung Ho, The One-Minute Apology, Servant Leader, Whale Done, The Heart of a Leader, The Leadership Pill,* and *Raving Fans.* Spencer Johnson, the holder of a medical doctorate, is interested in stress and has written the popular book *Who Moved My Cheese?* and *The Precious Present.*

A true classic in the management literature is Douglas McGregor's *The Human Side of Enterprise,* first published in 1960. Because of the book's popularity, its timeless theme, and genuine relevance for organizations in the twenty-first century, McGregor's seminal work continues to be valuable reading.

McGregor explores alternative assumptions that managers might hold and that drive different approaches to the management of organizations and their employees. Through the presentation of two sets of assumptions—labeled *Theory X* and *Theory Y*—McGregor urges managers to see employees as capable of innovation, creativity, commitment, high levels of sustained effort, and the exercise of self-direction and self-control.

Douglas McGregor received his doctorate at Harvard University. Before his death in 1964, he served on the faculties of Harvard University and the Massachusetts Institute of Technology and was president of Antioch College. McGregor is also the author of *The Professional Manager.*

A contemporary of McGregor's, Abraham Maslow, has sometimes been called the "greatest psychologist since Freud," and a "significant contributor to the humanistic psychology movement." He is well known to psychology students for his books *Toward a Psychology of Being* and *The Psychology of Science.* However, he is equally well known to most business students for his highly popularized and defining work on postulating a hierarchy of human needs beginning at the physiological level and proceeding up through safety, social, esteem, and self-actualizing levels, and suggesting that any need level, when fully satisfied, can no longer be a powerful motivator. Maslow also published *Eupsychian Management* (which received little acclaim in the 1960s), which has been republished (with additional material from a variety of admirers) as *Maslow on Management.* In this book, Maslow lays out the underlying assumptions for a eupsychian organization. Maslow taught at Brooklyn College and Brandeis University, and while writing his final book, he was an in-depth observer of worker behaviors at the Non-Linear Systems plant in Del Mar, California.

Stephen R. Covey is a well known speaker, author of several books, and chief executive officer of the Franklin Covey Co. His first book, *The Seven Habits of Highly Effective People,* remains on best-seller lists and has sold millions of copies. In it, he offers a series of prescriptions to guide managers as they chart their courses in turbulent times. Drawn from his extensive review of the "success literature," Covey urges people to develop a character ethic based on people being proactive, identifying their values, disciplining themselves to work on high-priority items, seeking win-win solutions, listening with empathy, synergizing with others, and engaging in extensive reading and studying.

Covey has also published a "Seven Habits" book that adapts the basic principles for families. *First Things First* urges people to manage their time and life well so as to achieve goals consistent with their values. His *Principle-Centered Leadership* identifies seven human attributes—self-awareness, imagination, willpower, an abundance mentality, courage, creativity, and self-renewal—that, when combined with eight key behaviors (e.g., priority on service, radiating positive energy), help produce effective and principled leaders. His other books include *Living the Seven Habits* and *Reflections for Highly Effective People.*

Peter M. Senge is the Director of the Systems Thinking and Organizational Learning Program at MIT's Sloan School of Management. His book *The Fifth Discipline: The Art and Practice of the Learning Organization* emphasizes the importance of organizations developing the capacity to engage in effective learning. Senge identifies and discusses a set of disabilities that are fatal to organizations, especially those operating in rapidly changing environments. The fifth discipline—systems thinking—is presented as the cornerstone for the learning organization. Personal mastery, mental models, shared vision, and team learning are presented as the core disciplines and the focus for building the learning organization. Senge has also published *The Fifth Discipline Fieldbook* and *The Dance of Change.*

Michael E. Porter, a Harvard University Business School professor, continues to make contributions to our understanding of organizations and their competitive strategies. He received the 1986 George R. Terry book award for his book *Competitive Advantage: Creating and Sustaining Superior Performance,* which was published in 1985. *Competitive Advantage* was a follow-up to his earlier book *Competitive Strategy.* Porter is also the author of *Competitive Advantage of Nations.* He has argued that firms can receive above-average profits by synthesizing and applying their unique strengths effectively within their industry. They can do this either through creating a cost advantage, or by differentiating a product or service from that of their competitors. The key, which some firms seemingly ignore, is to link strategy formulation successfully with strategy implementation. Porter encouraged managers to study their industry in depth, to select a course of competitive advantage, to develop a set of strategies that adapt the firm to its external environment, and to draw on their executive leadership talents.

In *Competitive Advantage: Creating and Sustaining Superior Performance,* Porter provides insight into the complexity of industry competition by identifying five underlying forces. Low cost, differentiation, and focus are presented as generic strategies for the strategic positioning of a firm within its industry. The popularity of this book is revealed by its widespread adoption by managers and academics, as it has undergone its sixtieth printing in English and translation into many different languages. Interested readers might wish to explore "An Interview with Michael Porter" by Nicholas Argyres and Anita M. McGahan in the *Academy of Management Executive,* 2002, 16:2, pp. 43–52.

# In Search of Excellence

*THOMAS J. PETERS*
*and ROBERT H. WATERMAN, JR.*

What makes for excellence in the management of a company? Is it the use of sophisticated management techniques such as zero-based budgeting, management by objectives, matrix organization, and sector, group, or portfolio management? Is it greater use of computers to control companies that continue to grow even larger in size and more diverse in activities? Is it a battalion of specialized MBAs, well-versed in the techniques of strategic planning?

Probably not. Although most well-run companies use a fair sampling of all these tools, they do not use them as substitutes for the basics of good management. Indeed, McKinsey & Co., a management consultant concern, has studied management practices at thirty-seven companies that are often used as examples of well-run organizations and has found that they have eight common attributes. None of those attributes depends on "modern" management tools or gimmicks. In fact, none of them requires high technology, and none of them costs a cent to implement. All that is needed is time, energy, and a willingness on the part of management to think rather than to make use of management formulas.

The outstanding performers work hard to keep things simple. They rely on simple organizational structures, simple strategies, simple goals, and simple communications. The eight attributes that characterize their management are:

- A bias toward action.
- Simple form and lean staff.
- Continued contact with customers.
- Productivity improvement via people.
- Operational autonomy to encourage entrepreneurship.
- Stress on one key business value.
- Emphasis on doing what they know best.
- Simultaneous loose-tight controls.

Although none of these sounds startling or new, most are conspicuously absent in many companies today. Far too many managers have lost sight of the basics—service to customers, low-cost manufacturing, productivity improvement, innovation, and risk-

Reprinted from Thomas J. Peters, "Putting Excellence into Management," *Business Week,* July 21, 1980, © 1980 by McGraw-Hill, Inc.

taking. In many cases, they have been seduced by the availability of MBAs, armed with the "latest" in strategic planning techniques. MBAs who specialize in strategy are bright, but they often cannot implement their ideas, and their companies wind up losing the capacity to act. At Standard Brands Inc., for example, Chairman F. Ross Johnson discovered this the hard way when he brought a handful of planning specialists into his consumer products company. "The guys who were bright [the strategic planners] were not the kinds of people who could implement programs," he lamented to *Business Week*. Two years later, he removed the planners.

Another consumer products company followed a similar route, hiring a large band of young MBAs for the staffs of senior vice-presidents. The new people were assigned to build computer models for designing new products. Yet none of the products could be manufactured or brought to market. Complained one line executive: "The models incorporated eighty-three variables in product planning, but we were being killed by just one—cost."

Companies are being stymied not only by their own staffs but often by their structure. McKinsey studied one company where the new product process required 223 separate committees to approve an idea before it could be put into production. Another company was restructured recently into 200 strategic business units—only to discover that it was impossible to implement 200 strategies. And even at General Electric Co., which is usually cited for its ability to structure itself according to its management needs, an executive recently complained: "Things become bureaucratic with astonishing speed. Inevitably when we wire things up, we lose vitality." Emerson Electric Co., with a much simpler structure than GE, consistently beats its huge competitor on costs—manufacturing its products in plants with fewer than 600 employees.

McKinsey's study focused on ten well-managed companies (see Table 1): International Business Machines, Texas Instruments, Hewlett-Packard, 3M, Digital Equipment, Procter & Gamble, Johnson & Johnson, McDonald's, Dana, and Emerson Electric. On the surface, they have nothing in common. There is no universality of product line: Five are in high technology, one is in packaged goods, one makes medical products, one operates fast-food restaurants, and two are relatively mundane manufacturers of mechanical and electrical products. But each is a hands-on operator, not a holding company or a conglomerate. And while not every plan succeeds, in the day-to-day pursuit of their businesses these companies succeed far more often than they fail. And they succeed because of their management's almost instinctive adherence to the eight attributes.

## ◆ BIAS TOWARD ACTION

In each of these companies, the key instructions are *do it, fix it, try it.* They avoid analyzing and questioning products to death, and they avoid complicated procedures for developing new ideas. Controlled experiments abound in these companies. The attitude of management is to "get some data, do it, then adjust it," rather than to wait for a perfect overall plan. The companies tend to be tinkerers rather than inventors, making small steps of progress rather than conceiving sweeping new concepts. At McDonald's Corp., for example, the objective is to do the little things regularly and well.

Ideas are solicited regularly and tested quickly. Those that work are pushed fast; those that don't are discarded just as quickly. At 3M Co., the management never kills an idea without trying it out; it just goes on the back burner.

**TABLE 1** How 10 Well-Run Companies Performed in 1979

| | *Million of Dollars* | | *Percent* | |
|---|---|---|---|---|
| | ***Sales*** | ***Profits*** | ***Return on Sales*** | ***Return on Equity*** |
| IBM | $22,862.8 | $3,011.3 | 14.8% | 21.6% |
| Procter & Gamble | 10,080.6 | 617.5 | 5.6 | 19.3 |
| 3M | 5,440.3 | 655.2 | 12.2 | 24.4 |
| Johnson & Johnson | 4,211.6 | 352.1 | 6.5 | 19.6 |
| Texas Instruments | 3,224.1 | 172.9 | 5.1 | 19.2 |
| Dana | 2,789.0 | 165.8 | 6.1 | 19.3 |
| Emerson Electric | 2,749.9 | 208.8 | 7.5 | 21.5 |
| Hewlett-Packard | 2,361.0 | 203.0 | 8.2 | 18.1 |
| Digital Equipment | 2,031.6 | 207.5 | 9.7 | 19.7 |
| McDonald's | 1,937.9 | 188.6 | 8.7 | 22.5 |
| BW composite of 1,200 companies | | | 5.1 | 16.6 |

These managements avoid long, complicated business plans for new projects. At 3M, for example, new product ideas must be proposed in less than five pages. At Procter & Gamble Co., one-page memos are the rule, but every figure in a P&G memo can be relied on unfailingly.

To ensure that they achieve results, these companies set a few well-defined goals for their managers. At Texas Instruments Inc., for one, a typical goal would be a set date for having a new plant operating or for having a designated percent of a sales force call on customers in a new market. A TI executive explained: "We've experimented a lot, but the bottom line for any senior manager is the maxim that more than two objectives is no objective."

These companies have learned to focus quickly on problems. One method is to appoint a "czar" who has responsibility for one problem across the company. At Digital Equipment Corp. and Hewlett-Packard Co., for example, there are software czars, because customer demand for programming has become the key issue for the future growth of those companies. Du Pont Co., when it discovered it was spending $800 million a year on transportation, set up a logistics czar. Other companies have productivity czars or energy czars with the power to override a manufacturing division's autonomy.

Another tool is the task force. But these companies tend to use the task force in an unusual way. Task forces are authorized to fix things, not to generate reports and paper. At Digital Equipment, IT, HP, and 3M, task forces have a short duration, seldom more than ninety days. Says a Digital Equipment executive: "When we've got a big problem here, we grab ten senior guys and stick them in a room for a week. They come up with an answer and implement it." All members are volunteers, and they tend to be senior managers rather than junior people ordered to serve. Management espouses the busy-member theory: "We don't want people on task forces who want to become permanent task force members. We only put people on them who are so busy that their major objective is to get the problem solved and to get back to their main jobs." Every task force at TI is disbanded after its work is done, but within three months the senior operations committee formally reviews and assesses the results. TI demands that the managers who requested and ran the task force justify the time spent on it. If the task force turns out to have been useless, the manager is chided publicly, a painful penalty in TI's peer-conscious culture.

## ◆ SIMPLE FORM AND LEAN STAFF

Although all ten of these companies are big—the smallest, McDonald's has sales in excess of $1.9 billion—they are structured along "small is beautiful" lines. Emerson Electric, 3M, J&J, and HP are divided into small entrepreneurial units that—although smaller than economies of scale might suggest—manage to get things done. No HP division, for example, ever employs more than 1,200 people. TI, with ninety product customer centers, keeps each notably autonomous.

Within the units themselves, activities are kept to small, manageable groups. At Dana Corp., small teams work on productivity improvement. At the high-technology companies, small autonomous teams, headed by a product "champion," shepherd ideas through the corporate bureaucracy to ensure that they quickly receive attention from the top.

Staffs are also kept small to avoid bureaucracies. Fewer than 100 people help run Dana, a $3 billion corporation. Digital Equipment and Emerson are also noted for small staffs.

## ◆ CLOSENESS TO THE CUSTOMER

The well-managed companies are customer driven—not technology driven, not product driven, not strategy driven. Constant contact with the customer provides insights that direct the company. Says one executive: "Where do you start? Not by poring over abstract market research. You start by getting out there with the customer." In a study of two fast-paced industries (scientific instruments and component manufacturing), Eric Von Hippel, associate professor at Massachusetts Institute of Technology, found that 100 percent of the major new product ideas—and eighty percent of the minor new product variations—came directly from customers.

At both IBM and Digital Equipment, top management spends at least 30 days a year conferring with top customers. No manager at IBM holds a staff job for more than three years, except in the legal, finance, and personnel departments. The reason: IBM believes that staff people are out of the mainstream because they do not meet with customers regularly.

Both companies use customer-satisfaction surveys to help determine management's compensation. Another company spends twelve percent of its research and development budget on sending engineers and scientists out to visit customers. One R&D chief spends two months each year with customers. At Lanier Business Products Inc., another fast-growing company, the twenty most senior executives make sales calls every month.

Staying close to the customer means sales and service overkill. "Assistants to" at IBM are assigned to senior executives with the sole function of processing customer complaints within 24 hours. At Digital Equipment, J&J, IBM, and 3M, immense effort is expended to field an extraordinarily well-trained sales force. Caterpillar Tractor Co., another company considered to have excellent management, spends much of its managerial talent on efforts to make a reality of its motto, "24-hour parts delivery anywhere in the world."

These companies view the customer as an integral element of their businesses. A bank officer who started his career as a J&J accountant recalls that he was required to make customer calls even though he was in a financial department. The reason: to ensure that he understood the customer's perspective and could handle a proposal with empathy.

## ◆ PRODUCTIVITY IMPROVEMENT VIA CONSENSUS

One way to get productivity increases is to install new capital equipment. But another method is often overlooked. Productivity can be improved by motivating and stimulating employees. One way to do that is to give them autonomy. At TI, shop floor teams set their own targets for production. In the years since the company has used this approach, executives say, workers have set goals that require them to stretch but that are reasonable and attainable.

The key is to motivate all of the people involved in each process. At 3M, for example, a team that includes technologists, marketers, production people, and financial types is formed early in a new product venture. It is self-sufficient and stays together from the inception to the national introduction. Although 3M is aware that this approach can lead to redundancy, it feels that the team spirit and motivation make it worthwhile.

Almost all of these companies use "corny" but effective methods to reward their workers. Badges, pins, and medals are all part of such recognition programs. Outstanding production teams at TI are invited to describe their successes to the board, as a form of recognition. Significantly, the emphasis is never only on monetary awards.

## ◆ AUTONOMY TO ENCOURAGE ENTREPRENEURSHIP

A company cannot encourage entrepreneurship if it holds its managers on so tight a leash that they cannot make decisions. Well-managed companies authorize their managers to act like entrepreneurs. Dana, for one, calls this method the "store manager" concept. Plant managers are free to make purchasing decisions and to start productivity programs on their own. As a result, these managers develop unusual programs with results that far exceed those of a division or corporate staff. And the company has a grievance rate that is a fraction of the average reported by the United Auto Workers for all the plants it represents.

The successful companies rarely will force their managers to go against their own judgment. At 3M, TI, IBM, and J&J, decisions on product promotion are not based solely on market potential. An important factor in the decision is the zeal and drive of the volunteer who champions a product. Explains one executive at TI: "In every instance of a new product failure, we had forced someone into championing it involuntarily."

The divisional management is generally responsible for replenishing its new product array. In these well-managed companies, headquarters staff may not cut off funds for divisional products arbitrarily. What is more, the divisions are allowed to reinvest most of their earnings in their own operations. Although this flies in the face of the product-portfolio concept, which dictates that a corporate chief milk mature divisions to feed those with apparently greater growth potential, these companies recognize that entrepreneurs will not be developed in corporations that give the fruits of managers' labor to someone else.

Almost all these companies strive to place new products into separate startup divisions. A manager is more likely to be recognized—and promoted—for pushing a hot new product out of his division to enable it to stand on its own than he is for simply letting his own division get overgrown.

Possibly most important at these companies, entrepreneurs are both encouraged and honored at all staff levels. TI, for one, has created a special group of "listeners"—138 senior technical people called "individual contributors"—to assess new ideas. Junior staff members are particularly encouraged to bring their ideas to one of these individuals for a one-on-one evaluation. Each "contributor" has the authority to approve substantial startup funds ($20,000 to $30,000) for product experimentation. TI's successful Speak'n'Spell device was developed this way.

IBM's Fellows Program serves a similar purpose, although it is intended to permit proven senior performers to explore their ideas rather than to open communications lines for bright comers. Such scientists have at their beck and call thousands of IBM's technical people. The Fellows tend to be highly skilled gadflies, people who can shake things up—almost invariably for the good of the company.

The operating principle at well-managed companies is to do one thing well. At IBM, the all-pervasive value is customer service. At Dana it is productivity improvement. At 3M and HP, it is new product development. At P&G it is product quality. At McDonald's it is customer service—quality, cleanliness, and value.

## ◆ STRESS ON A KEY BUSINESS VALUE

At all these companies, the values are pursued with an almost religious zeal by the chief executive officers. Rene McPherson, new dean of Stanford University's Graduate School of Business but until recently Dana's CEO, incessantly preached cost reduction and productivity improvement—and the company doubled its productivity in seven years. Almost to the day when Thomas Watson Jr. retired from IBM he wrote memos to the staff on the subject of calling on customers—even stressing the proper dress for the call. TI's ex-chairman Patrick Haggerty made it a point to drop in at a development laboratory on his way home each night when he was in Dallas. And in another company, where competitive position was the prime focus, one division manager wrote 700 memos to his subordinates one year, analyzing competitors.

Such single-minded focus on a value becomes a culture for the company. Nearly every IBM employee has stories about how he or she took great pains to solve a customer's problem. New product themes even dominate 3M and HP lunchroom conversations. Every operational review at HP focuses on new products, with a minimum amount of time devoted to financial results or projections—because President John Young has made it clear that he believes that proper implementation of new-product plans automatically creates the right numbers. In fact, Young makes it a point to start new employees in the new-product process and keep them there for a few years as part of a "socialization" pattern: "I don't care if they do come from the Stanford Business School," he says. "For a few years they get their hands dirty, or we are not interested." At McDonald's the company's values are drummed into employees at Hamburger U., a training program every employee goes through.

As the employees who are steeped in the corporate culture move up the ladder, they become role models for newcomers, and the process continues. It is possibly best exemplified by contrast. American Telephone & Telegraph Co., which recently began to develop a marketing orientation, has been hamstrung in its efforts because of a lack of career telephone executives with marketing successes. When Archie J. McGill was hired from IBM to head AT&T's marketing, some long-term employees balked at his leadership because he "wasn't one of them," and so was not regarded as a model.

Another common pitfall for companies is the sending of mixed signals to line managers. One company has had real problems introducing new products despite top management's constant public stress on innovation—simply because line managers perceived the real emphasis to be on cost-cutting. They viewed top management as accountants who refused to invest or to take risks, and they consistently proposed imitative products. At another company, where the CEO insisted that his major thrust was new products, an analysis of how he spent his time over a three-month period showed that no more than 5 percent of his efforts were directed to new products. His stated emphasis therefore was not credible. Not surprisingly, his employees never picked up the espoused standard.

Too many messages, even when sincerely meant, can cause the same problem. One CEO complained that no matter how hard he tried to raise what he regarded as an unsatisfactory quality level, he was unsuccessful. But when McKinsey questioned his subordinates, they said, "Of course he's for quality, but he's for everything else, too. We have a theme a month here." The outstanding companies, in contrast, have one theme and stick to it.

## ◆ STICKING TO WHAT THEY KNOW BEST

Robert W. Johnson, the former chairman of J&J, put it this way: "Never acquire any business you don't know how to run." Edward G. Harness, CEO at P&G, says, "This company has never left its base." All of the successful companies have been able to define their strengths—marketing, customer contact, new product innovation, low-cost manufacturing—and then build on them. They have resisted the temptation to move into new businesses that look attractive but require corporate skills they do not have.

## ◆ SIMULTANEOUS LOOSE-TIGHT CONTROLS

While this may sound like a contradiction, it is not. The successful companies control a few variables tightly, but allow flexibility and looseness in others. 3M uses return on sales and number of employees as yardsticks for control. Yet it gives management lots of leeway in day-to-day operations. When McPherson became president of Dana, he threw out all of the company's policy manuals and substituted a one-page philosophy statement and a control system that required divisions to report costs and revenues on a daily basis.

IBM probably has the classic story about flexible controls. After the company suffered well-publicized and costly problems with its System 360 computer several years ago—problems that cost hundreds of millions of dollars to fix—Watson ordered Frank T. Cary, then a vice-president, to incorporate a system of checks and balances in new-product testing. The system made IBM people so cautious that they stopped taking risks. When Cary became president of IBM, one of the first things he did to reverse that attitude was to loosen some of the controls. He recognized that the new system would indeed prevent such an expensive problem from ever happening again, but its rigidity would also keep IBM from ever developing another major system.

By sticking to these eight basics, the successful companies have achieved better-than-average growth. Their managements are able not only to change but also to change quickly. They keep their sights aimed externally at their customers and competitors, and not on their own financial reports.

Excellence in management takes brute perseverance—time, repetition, and simplicity. The tools include plant visits, internal memos, and focused systems. Ignoring these rules may mean that the company slowly loses its vitality, its growth patterns, and its competitiveness.

# Out of the Crisis

***W. EDWARDS DEMING***

***Summary prepared by William B. Gartner and M. James Naughton***

***William B. Gartner*** *is a Professor at Georgetown University.*
***M. James Naughton*** *is the owner of Expert-Knowledge Systems, Inc.*

Deming provides an ambitious objective for his book when he begins by saying:

> The aim of this book is transformation of the style of American management. Transformation of American style of management is not a job of reconstruction, nor is it revision. It requires a whole new structure, from foundation upward. *Mutation* might be the word, except that *mutation* implies unordered spontaneity. Transformation must take place with directed effort.

Few individuals have had as much positive impact on the world economy as Dr. W. Edwards Deming. With the broadcast of the NBC white paper, "If Japan Can, Why Can't We?" on June 24, 1980, Dr. Deming gained national exposure as the man responsible for the managerial theory that has governed Japan's transformation into a nation of world leaders in the production of high quality goods. This transformation did not happen overnight. Since 1950, when Dr. Deming first spoke to Japan's top managers on the improvement of quality, Japanese organizations have pioneered in the adaptation of Dr. Deming's ideas.

As a result of his seminars, Japan has had an annual national competition for quality improvement (the Deming Prize) since 1951. Japan has numerous journals and books devoted to exploring and furthering the implications of Deming's theory. However, it has only been within the last few years that a number of books have been published in the United States on "the Deming Theory of Management." An overview of the ideas that underlie Deming's theory, which cut across all major topical areas in management, will be provided here.

---

W. Edwards Deming, *Out of the Crisis.* Cambridge, MA: MIT Press, 1986.

## ◆ DISEASES AND OBSTACLES

Deming's book is not merely about productivity and quality control; it is a broad vision of the nature of organizations and how organizations should be changed. Deming identifies a set of chronic ailments that can plague any organization and limit its success. These, which he calls "deadly diseases," include an overemphasis on short-term profits, human resource practices that encourage both managers and employees to be mobile and not organizationally loyal, merit ratings and review systems that are based on fear of one's supervisor, an absence of a single driving purpose, and management that is based on visible figures alone.

The reason that managers are not as effective as they could be is that they are the prisoners of some structural characteristics and personal assumptions that prevent their success. Among the obstacles that Deming discusses are the insulation of top management from the other employees in the organization, lack of adequate technical knowledge, a long history of total reliance on final inspection as a way of assuring a quality product, the managerial belief that all problems originate within the work force, a reliance on meeting specifications, and the failure to synthesize human operators with computer systems for control.

## ◆ THE CONCEPT OF VARIABILITY

The basis for Deming's theory is the observation that variability exists everywhere in everything. Only through the study and analysis of variability, using statistics, can a phenomenon be understood well enough to manipulate and change it. In many respects, using statistics is not very radical. Statistics are fundamental to nearly all academic research. But Deming asks that the right kind of statistics (analytical) be applied to our everyday lives as well. And that is the rub. To recognize the pervasiveness of variability and to function so that the sources of this variability can be defined and measured is radical. In Deming's world, the use of statistical thinking is not an academic game; it is a way of life.

The concept of variability is to management theory and practice what the concept of the germ theory of disease was to the development of modern medicine. Medicine had been "successfully" practiced without the knowledge of germs. In a pre-germ theory paradigm, some patients got better, some got worse, and some stayed the same; in each case, some rationale could be used to explain the outcome. With the emergence of germ theory, all medical phenomena took on new meanings. Medical procedures thought to be good practice, such as physicians attending women in birth, turned out to be causes of disease because of the septic condition of the physicians' hands. Instead of rendering improved health care, the physicians' germ-laden hands achieved the opposite result. One can imagine the first proponents of the germ theory telling their colleagues who were still ignorant of the theory to wash their hands between patients. The pioneers must have sounded crazy. In the same vein, managers and academics who do not have a thorough understanding of variability will fail to grasp the radical change in thought that Deming envisions. Deming's propositions may seem as simplistic as "wash your hands!" rather than an entirely new paradigm of profound challenges to present-day managerial thinking and behaviors.

An illustration of variability that is widely cited in the books on Deming's theory is the "red bead experiment." Dr. Deming, at his four-day seminar, asks for 10 volunteers from the attendees. Six of the students become workers, two become inspectors of the workers' production, one becomes the inspector of the inspectors' work, and one becomes the recorder. Dr. Deming mixes together 3000 white beads and 750 red beads in a large box. He instructs the workers to scoop out beads from the box with a beveled paddle that scoops out 50 beads at a time. Each scoop of the paddle is treated as a day's production. Only white beads are acceptable. Red beads are defects. After each worker scoops a paddle of beads from the box, the two inspectors count the defects, the inspector of the inspectors inspects the inspectors' count, and the recorder writes down the inspectors' agreed-upon number of defects. Invariably, each worker's scoop contains some red beads. Deming plays the role of the manager by exhorting the workers to produce no defects. When a worker scoops few red beads he may be praised. Scooping many red beads brings criticism and an exhortation to do better, otherwise "we will go out of business." The manager reacts to each scoop of beads as if it had meaning in itself rather than as part of a pattern. Figure 2–1 shows the number of defective beads each worker produced for four days of work.

**FIGURE 2–1** Number of Defective Items by Operator, by Day

| | Day | | | | |
|---|---|---|---|---|---|
| Name | 1 | 2 | 3 | 4 | All 4 |
| Neil | 3 | 13 | 8 | 9 | 33 |
| Tace | 6 | 9 | 8 | 10 | 33 |
| Tim | 13 | 12 | 7 | 10 | 42 |
| Mike | 11 | 8 | 10 | 15 | 44 |
| Tony | 9 | 13 | 8 | 11 | 41 |
| Richard | 12 | 11 | 7 | 15 | 45 |
| All 6 | 54 | 66 | 48 | 70 | 238 |
| Cum $\bar{x}$ | 9.0 | 10.0 | 9.3 | 9.92 | 9.92 |

$$\bar{x} = \frac{238}{6 \quad 4} = 9.92$$

$$\bar{p} = \frac{238}{6 \quad 4 \quad 50} = .198$$

$$\left.\begin{matrix} \text{UCL} \\ \text{LCL} \end{matrix}\right\} \begin{matrix} = x \pm 3\sqrt{\bar{x}(1 \quad \bar{p})} \\ = 9.9 \pm 3\sqrt{9.9 \quad .802} \end{matrix}$$

$$= \begin{cases} 18 \\ 1 \end{cases}$$

*Source:* Adapted from Deming, p. 347.

Dr. Deming's statistical analysis of the workers' production indicates that the process of producing white beads is in statistical control; that is, the variability of this production system is stable. The near-term prediction about the *pattern,* but not the individual draws, of the system's performance can be made. Near-future draws will yield about an average, over many experiments, of 9.4 red beads. Any one draw may range between 1 and 18 red beads. In other words, the actual number of red beads scooped by each worker is out of that worker's control. The worker, as Dr. Deming says, "is only delivering the defects." Management, which controls the system, has caused the defects through design of the system. There are a number of insights people draw from this experiment. Walton lists the following:

- Variation is part of any process.
- Planning requires prediction of how things and people will perform. Tests and experiments of past performance can be useful, but not definitive.
- Workers work within a system that—try as they might—is beyond their control. It is the system, not their individual skills, that determines how they perform.
- Only management can change the system.
- Some workers will always be above average, some below.[1]

The red bead experiment illustrates the behavior of systems of stable variability. In Deming's theory, a system is all of the aspects of the organization and environment—employees, managers, equipment, facilities, government, customers, suppliers, shareholders, and so forth—fitted together, with the aim of producing some type of output. Stability implies that the output has regularity to it, so that predictions regarding the output of the system can be made. But many of these systems are inherently unstable. Bringing a system into stability is one of the fundamental managerial activities in the Deming theory.

In Deming's theory, a stable system, that is, a system that shows signs of being in statistical control, behaves in a manner similar to the red bead experiment. In systems, a single datum point is of little use in understanding the causes that influenced the production of that point. It is necessary to withhold judgment about changes in the output of the system until sufficient evidence (additional data points) becomes available to suggest whether or not the system being examined is stable. Statistical theory provides tools to help evaluate the stability of systems. Once a system is stable, its productive capability can be determined; that is, the average output of the system and the spread of variability around that average can be described. This can be used to predict the near-term future behavior of the system.

The inefficiencies inherent in "not knowing what we are doing," that is, in working with systems not in statistical control, might not seem to be that great a competitive penalty if all organizations are similarly out of control. Yet we are beginning to realize that the quality of outputs from organizations that are managed using Deming's theory are many magnitudes beyond what non-Deming organizations have been producing. The differences in quality and productivity can be mind-boggling.

For example, both Scherkenbach[2] and Walton[3] reported that when the Ford Motor Company began using transmissions produced by the Japanese automobile manufacturer, Mazda, Ford found that customers overwhelmingly preferred cars with Mazda transmissions to cars with Ford-manufactured transmissions—because the warranty repairs were ten times lower, and the cars were quieter and shifted more smoothly. When Ford engineers compared their transmissions to the Mazda transmissions, they found that the piece-to-piece variation in the Mazda transmissions was nearly three times less than in the Ford pieces. Both Ford and Mazda conformed to the engineering standards specified by Ford, but Mazda transmissions were far more uniform. More uniform products also cost less to manufacture. With less variability there is less rework and less need for inspection. Only systems in statistical control can begin to reduce variability and thereby improve the quality and quantity of their output. Both authors reported that after Ford began to implement Deming's theory over the last five years, warranty repair frequencies dropped by forty-five percent and "things gone wrong" reports from customers dropped by fifty percent.

## FOURTEEN STEPS MANAGEMENT MUST TAKE

The task of transformation of an entire organization to use the Deming theory becomes an enormous burden for management, and Deming frequently suggests that this process is likely to take a minimum of ten years. The framework for transforming an organization is outlined in the fourteen points (pp. 23–24):

1. Create constancy of purpose toward improvement of product and service, aiming to become competitive, to stay in business, and to provide jobs.
2. Adopt the new philosophy. We are in a new economic age. Western management must awaken to the challenge, must learn their responsibilities, and must take on leadership in order to bring about change.
3. Cease dependence on inspection to achieve quality. Eliminate the need for inspection on a mass basis by building quality into the product in the first place.
4. End the practice of awarding business on the basis of the price tag. Instead, minimize total cost. Move toward a single supplier for any one time and develop long-term relationships of loyalty and trust with that supplier.
5. Improve constantly and forever the systems of production and service in order to improve quality and productivity. Thus, one constantly decreases costs.
6. Institute training on the job.
7. Institute leadership. Supervisors should be able to help people to do a better job, and they should use machines and gadgets wisely. Supervision of management and supervision of production workers need to be overhauled.
8. Drive out fear, so that everyone may work effectively for the company.
9. Break down barriers between departments. People in research, design, sales, and production must work as a team. They should foresee production problems and problems that could be encountered when using the product or service.
10. Eliminate slogans, exhortations, and targets that demand zero defects and new levels of productivity. These only create adversarial relationships because the many causes of low quality and low productivity are due to the system, and not the work force.
11. **a.** Eliminate work standards (quotas) on the factory floor. Substitute leadership.
    **b.** Eliminate management by objectives. Eliminate management by numbers or numerical goals. Substitute leadership.

**12. a.** Remove barriers that rob the hourly worker of his right to pride of workmanship. The responsibility of supervisors must be changed from sheer numbers to quality.

**b.** Remove barriers that rob people in management and in engineering of their right to pride of workmanship. This means, *inter alia,* abolishing the annual merit rating and management by objectives.

**13.** Institute a vigorous program of education and self-improvement.

**14.** Put everybody in the company to work to accomplish the transformation. The transformation is everybody's job.

As mentioned earlier, the fourteen points should not be treated as a list of aphorisms, nor can each of the fourteen points be treated separately without recognizing the interrelationships among them.

## Conclusions

*Out of the Crisis* is full of examples and ideas, and Deming calls for a radical revision of American management practice. To his credit, Deming constantly recognizes ideas and examples from individuals practicing various aspects of his theory. This constant recognition of other individuals provides a subtle indication that a body of practitioners exists who have had successful experiences applying his fourteen steps and other ideas.

A transformation in American management needs to occur; it can take place, and it has begun already in those firms applying Deming's theory. Deming offers a new paradigm for the practice of management that requires a dramatic rethinking and replacement of old methods by those trained in traditional management techniques. In conclusion, Deming recognizes that "it takes courage to admit that you have been doing something wrong, to admit that you have something to learn, that there is a better way" (Walton, 1986, p. 223).

## Notes

1. William B. Gartner and M. James Naughton. "The Deming Theory of Management." *Academy of Management Review,* January 1988, pp. 138–142.
2. William W. Scherkenbach. *The Deming Route to Quality and Productivity: Roadmaps and Roadblocks.* Milwaukee, WI: ASQC, 1986.
3. Mary Walton. *The Deming Management Method.* New York: Dodd, Mead, & Company, 1986.

# The One Minute Manager

***KENNETH BLANCHARD and SPENCER JOHNSON***

***Summary prepared by Charles C. Manz***

***Charles C. Manz** is a Professor of Management at the University of Massachusetts at Amherst. He holds a doctorate in Organizational Behavior from Pennsylvania State University. His professional publications and presentations concern topics such as self-leadership, vicarious learning, self-managed work groups, leadership, power and control, and group processes. He is the author of the book* The Art of Self-Leadership *and co-author of* The Leadership Wisdom of Jesus.

The most distinguishing characteristic of *The One Minute Manager* by Kenneth Blanchard and Spencer Johnson is its major philosophical theme: Good management does not take a lot of time. This dominant theme seems to be based on two underlying premises: (1) *Quality* of time spent with subordinates (as with one's children) is more important than quantity; and, (2) in the end, people (subordinates) should really be managing themselves.

The book is built around a story that provides an occasion for learning about effective management. The story centers on the quest of "a young man" to find an effective manager. In his search he finds all kinds of managers, but very few that he considers effective. According to the story, the young man finds primarily two kinds of managers. One type is a hard-nosed manager who is concerned with the bottom line (profit) and tends to be directive in style. With this type of manager, the young man believes, the organization tends to win at the expense of the subordinates. The other type of manager is one who is concerned more about the employees than about performance. This "nice" kind of manager seems to allow the employees to win at the expense of the organization. In contrast to these two types of managers, the book suggests, an effective manager (as seen through the eyes of the young man) is one who manages so that both the organization and the people involved benefit (win).

The dilemma that the young man faces is that the few managers who do seem to be effective will not share their secrets. That is only true until he meets the "One Minute Manager." It turns out that this almost legendary manager is not only willing

---

Kenneth Blanchard and Spencer Johnson, *The One Minute Manager.* La Jolla, CA: Blanchard-Johnson Publishers, 1981.

to share the secrets of his effectiveness, but is so available that he is able to meet almost any time the young man wants to meet, except at the time of his weekly two-hour meeting with his subordinates. After an initial meeting with the One Minute Manager, the young man is sent off to talk to his subordinates to learn, directly from those affected, the secrets of One Minute Management. Thus the story begins, and in the remaining pages, the wisdom, experience, and management strategies of the One Minute Manager are revealed as the authors communicate, through him and his subordinates, their view on effective management practice.

In addition to general philosophical management advice (e.g., managers can reap good results from their subordinates without expending much time), the book suggests that effective management means that both the organization and its employees win, and that people will do better work when they feel good about themselves; it also offers some specific prescriptions. These prescriptions center around three primary management techniques that have been addressed in the management literature for years: goal setting, positive reinforcement in the form of praise, and verbal reprimand. The authors suggest that applications of each of the techniques can be accomplished in very little time, in fact in as little as one minute (hence the strategies are labeled "one minute goals," "one minute praisings," and "one minute reprimands"). The suggestions made in the book for effective use of each of these strategies will be summarized in the following sections.

## ◆ ONE MINUTE GOALS

"One minute goals" are said to clarify responsibilities and the nature of performance standards. Without them, the authors suggest, employees will not know what is expected of them, being left instead to grope in the dark for what they ought to be doing. A great deal of research and writing has been done on the importance of goals in reaching a level of performance (c.f., Locke, Shaw, Saari, and Latham, 1981). The advice offered in *The One Minute Manager* regarding effective use of performance goals is quite consistent with the findings of this previous work. Specifically, the authors point out through one of the One Minute Manager's subordinates that effective use of One Minute Goals includes:

- agreement between the manager and subordinate regarding what needs to be done;
- recording of each goal on a single page in no more than 250 words that can be read by almost anyone in less than a minute;
- communication of clear performance standards regarding what is expected of subordinates regarding each goal;
- continuous review of each goal, current performance, and the difference between the two.

These components are presented with a heavy emphasis on having employees use them to manage themselves. This point is driven home as the employee who shares this part of One Minute Management recalls how the One Minute Manager taught him about One Minute Goals. In the recounted story, the One Minute Manager refuses to take credit for having solved a problem of the subordinate, and is in fact irritated by the very idea of getting credit for it. He insists that the subordinate solved his own problem and orders him to go out and start solving his own future problems without taking up the One Minute Manager's time.

## ◆ ONE MINUTE PRAISING

The next employee encountered by the young man shares with him the secrets of "one minute praising." Again, the ideas presented regarding this technique pretty well parallel research findings on the use of positive reinforcement (c.f., Luthans and Kreitner, 1986). One basic suggestion for this technique is that managers should spend their time trying to catch subordinates doing something *right* rather than doing something wrong. In order to facilitate this, the One Minute Manager monitors new employees closely at first and has them keep detailed records of their progress (which he reviews). When the manager is able to discover something that the employee is doing right, the occasion is set for One Minute Praising (positive reinforcement). The specific components suggested for applying this technique include:

- letting others know that you are going to let them know how they are doing;
- praising positive performance as soon as possible after it has occurred, letting employees know specifically what they did right and how good you feel about it;
- allowing the message that you really feel good about their performance to sink in for a moment, and encouraging them to do the same;
- using a handshake or other form of touch when it is appropriate (more on this later).

Again, these steps are described with a significant self-management flavor. The employee points out that after working for a manager like this for a while you start catching yourself doing things right and using self-praise.

## ◆ ONE MINUTE REPRIMANDS

The final employee that the young man visits tells him about "One Minute Reprimands." This potentially more somber subject is presented in a quite positive tone. In fact, the employee begins by pointing out that she often praises herself and sometimes asks the One Minute Manager for a praising when she has done something well. But she goes on to explain that when she has done something wrong, the One Minute Manager is quick to respond, letting her know exactly what she has done wrong and how he feels about it. After the reprimand is over, he proceeds to tell her how competent he thinks she really is, essentially praising her as a *person* despite rejecting the undesired *behavior.* Specifically, the book points out that One Minute Reprimands should include:

- letting people know that you will, in a frank manner, communicate to them how they are doing;

- reprimand poor performance as soon as possible, telling people exactly what they did wrong and how you feel about it (followed by a pause allowing the message to sink in);
- reaffirm how valuable you feel the employees are, using touch if appropriate, while making it clear that it is their *performance* that is unacceptable in this situation;
- make sure that when the reprimand episode is over it is over.

## OTHER ISSUES AND RELATED MANAGEMENT TECHNIQUES

These three One Minute Management techniques form the primary applied content of the book. Good management does not take a lot of time; it just takes wise application of proven management strategies—One Minute Goals, Praisings, and Reprimands. Beyond this, the book deals with some other issues relevant to these strategies, such as "under what conditions is physical touch appropriate?" The book suggests that the use of appropriate touch can be helpful when you know the person well and wish to help that person succeed. It should be done so that you are giving something to the person such as encouragement or support, not taking something away.

The authors also address the issue of manipulation, suggesting that employees should be informed about, and agree to, the manager's use of One Minute Management. They indicate that the key is to be honest and open in the use of this approach. They also deal briefly with several other issues. For example, the book suggests that it is important to move a subordinate gradually to perform a new desired behavior by reinforcing approximations to the behavior until it is finally successfully performed. The technical term for this is "shaping." A person's behavior is shaped by continuously praising improvements rather than waiting until a person completely performs correctly. If a manager waits until a new employee completely performs correctly, the authors suggest, the employee may well give up long before successful performance is achieved because of the absence of reinforcement along the way.

The authors also suggest substituting the strategies for one another when appropriate. With new employees, for instance, they suggest that dealing with low performance should focus on goal setting and then trying to catch them doing something right rather than using reprimand. Since a new employee's lack of experience likely produces an insufficient confidence level, this makes reprimand inappropriate, while goal setting and praise can be quite effective (so the logic goes). The authors also suggest that if a manager is going to be tough on a person, the manager is better off being tough first and then being supportive, rather than the other way around. Issues such as these are briefly addressed through the primary story and the examples described by its primary characters, as supplemental material to the management philosophy and specific management techniques that have been summarized here.

Eventually, at the end of the story, the young man is hired by the One Minute Manager and over time becomes a seasoned One Minute Manager himself. As he looks back over his experiences, the authors are provided with the occasion to summarize some of the benefits of the management approach they advocate—more results in less time, time to think and plan, less stress and better health, similar benefits experienced by subordinates, and reduced absenteeism and turnover.

## Conclusions

Perhaps one bottom-line message of the book is that effective management requires that you care sincerely about people but have definite expectations that are expressed openly about their behavior. Also, one thing that is even more valuable than learning to be a One Minute Manager is having one for a boss, which in the end means you really work for yourself. And finally, as the authors illustrate through the giving attitude of the young man who has now become a One Minute Manager, these management techniques are not a competitive advantage to be hoarded but a gift to be shared with others. This is true because, in the end, the one who shares the gift will be at least as richly rewarded as the one who receives it.

## Notes

1. Locke, E., K. Shaw, L. Saari, and G. Latham. "Goal Setting and Task Performance 1969–1980." *Psychological Bulletin,* 90 (1981) 125–152.
2. Luthans, F., and T. Davis. "Behavioral Self-management (BSM): The Missing Link in Managerial Effectiveness." *Organizational Dynamics* 8 (1979), 42–60.
3. Luthans, F., and R. Kreitner. *Organizational Behavior Modification and Beyond.* Glenview, IL: Scott, Foresman and Co., 1986.
4. Manz, C. C. *The Art of Self-Leadership: Strategies for Personal Effectiveness in Your Life and Work.* Upper Saddle River, NJ: Prentice Hall, 1983.
5. Manz, C. C. "Self-Leadership: Toward an Expanded Theory of Self-influence Processes in Organizations." *Academy of Management Review,* 11 (1986), 585–600.
6. Manz, C. C., and H. P. Sims, Jr. "Self-Management as a Substitute for Leadership: A Social Learning Theory Perspective." *Academy of Management Review,* 5 (1980), 361–367.

# The Human Side of Enterprise


**DOUGLAS MCGREGOR**

**Summary prepared by Gayle Porter**


*__Gayle Porter__ obtained her doctorate from The Ohio State University in Organizational Behavior and Human Resource Management and is now at Rutgers University—Camden. Articles and ongoing research interests include the effects of dispositional differences in the workplace, group perceptions of efficacy and esteem, and the comparison of influence on employees through reward systems, leadership, and employee development efforts. Her prior experience includes positions as Director of Curriculum Development for a human resource management degree program; consultant on training programs, financial operations, and computer applications; financial manager for an oil and gas production company; and financial specialist for NCR Corporation.*

*The Human Side of Enterprise* was written during an ongoing comparative study of management development programs in several large companies. In McGregor's view, the making of managers has less to do with formal efforts in development than with how the task of management is understood within that organization. This fundamental understanding determines the policies and procedures within which the managers operate, and guides the selection of people identified as having the potential for management positions. During the late 1950s McGregor believed that major industrial advances of the next half century would occur on the human side of enterprise and he was intrigued by the inconsistent assumptions about what makes managers behave as they do. His criticism of the conventional assumptions, which he labels Theory X, is that they limit options. Theory Y provides an alternative set of assumptions that are much needed due to the extent of unrealized human potential in most organizations.

## ◆ THE THEORETICAL ASSUMPTIONS OF MANAGEMENT

Regardless of the economic success of a firm, few managers are satisfied with their ability to predict and control the behavior of members of the organization. Effective prediction and control are central to the task of management, and there can be no

Douglas McGregor, *The Human Side of Enterprise.* New York: McGraw-Hill, 1960.

prediction without some underlying theory. Therefore, all managerial decisions and actions rest on a personally held theory, a set of assumptions about behavior. The assumptions management holds about controlling its human resources determine the whole character of the enterprise.

In application, problems occur related to these assumptions. First, managers may not realize that they hold and apply conflicting ideas and that one may cancel out the other. For example, a manager may delegate based on the assumption that employees should have responsibility, but then nullify that action by close monitoring, which indicates the belief that employees can't handle the responsibility. Another problem is failure to view control as selective adaptation, when dealing with human behavior. People adjust to certain natural laws in other fields; e.g., engineers don't dig channels and expect water to run uphill! With humans, however, there is a tendency to try to control in direct violation of human nature. Then, when they fail to achieve the desired results, they look for every other possible cause rather than examine the inappropriate choice of a method to control behavior.

Any influence is based on dependence, so the nature and degree of dependence are critical factors in determining what methods of control will be effective. Conventional organization theory is based on authority as a key premise. It is the central and indispensable means of managerial control and recognizes only upward dependence. In recent decades, workers have become less dependent on a single employer, and society has provided certain safeguards related to unemployment. This limits the upward dependence and, correspondingly, the ability to control by authority alone. In addition, employees have the ability to engage in countermeasures such as slowdowns, lowered standards of performance, or even sabotage to defeat authority they resent.

Organizations are more accurately represented as systems of *inter*dependence. Subordinates depend on managers to help them meet their needs, but the managers also depend on subordinates to achieve their own and the organization's goals. While there is nothing inherently bad or wrong in the use of authority to control, in certain circumstances it fails to bring the desired results. Circumstances change even from hour to hour, and the role of the manager is to select the appropriate means of influence based on the situation at a given point in time. If employees exhibit lazy, indifferent behavior, the causes lie in management methods of organization and control.

*Theory X* is a term used to represent a set of assumptions. Principles found in traditional management literature could only have derived from assumptions such as the following, which have had a major impact on managerial strategy in organizations:

1. The average human being has an inherent dislike of work and will avoid it if possible.
2. Because of this human characteristic of dislike of work, most people must be coerced, controlled, directed, and threatened with punishment to get them to put forth adequate effort toward the achievement of organizational objectives.
3. The average human being prefers to be directed, wishes to avoid responsibility, has relatively little ambition, and wants security above all.

These assumptions are not without basis, or they would never have persisted as they have. They do explain some observed human behavior, but other observations are not consistent with this view. Theory X assumptions also encourage us to categorize certain behaviors as human nature, when they may actually be symptoms of a condition in which workers have been deprived of an opportunity to satisfy higher-order needs (social and egoistic needs).

A strong tradition exists of viewing employment as an employee's agreement to accept control by others in exchange for rewards that are only of value outside the workplace. For example, wages (except for status differences), vacation, medical benefits, stock purchase plans, and profit sharing are of little value during the actual time on the job. Work is the necessary evil to endure for rewards away from the job. In this conception of human resources we can never discover, let alone utilize, the potentialities of the average human being.

Many efforts to provide more equitable and generous treatment to employees and to provide a safe and pleasant work environment have been designed without any real change in strategy. Very often what is proposed as a new management strategy is nothing more than a different tactic within the old Theory X assumptions. Organizations have progressively made available the means to satisfy lower-order needs for subsistence and safety. As the nature of the dependency relationship changes, management has gradually deprived itself of the opportunity to use control based solely on assumptions of Theory X. A new strategy is needed.

*Theory Y* assumptions are dynamic, indicate the possibility of human growth and development, and stress the necessity for selective adaptation:

1. The expenditure of physical and mental effort in work is as natural as play or rest.
2. External control and the threat of punishment are not the only means for bringing about effort toward organizational objectives. People will exercise self-direction and self-control in the service of objectives to which they are committed.
3. Commitment to objectives is a function of the rewards associated with their achievement (*satisfaction of ego and self-actualization needs can be products of effort directed toward organizational objectives*).
4. The average human being learns, under proper conditions, not only to accept but to seek responsibility.
5. The capacity to exercise a relatively high degree of imagination, ingenuity, and creativity in the solution of organizational problems is widely, not narrowly, distributed in the population.
6. Under the conditions of modern industrial life, the intellectual potentialities of the average human being are only partially utilized.

The Theory Y assumptions challenge a number of deeply ingrained managerial habits of thought and action; they lead to a management philosophy of integration and self-control. Theory X assumes that the organization's requirements take precedence over the needs of the individual members, and that the worker must always adjust to needs of the organization as management perceives them. In contrast, the principle of *integration* proposes that conditions can be created such that individuals can best achieve their own goals by directing their efforts toward the success of the enterprise. Based on the premise that the assumptions of Theory Y are valid, the next logical question is whether, and to what extent, such conditions can be created. How will employees be convinced that applying their skills, knowledge, and ingenuity in support of the organization is a more attractive alternative than other ways to utilize their capacities?

## ◆ THEORY IN PRACTICE

The essence of applying Theory Y assumptions is guiding the subordinates to develop themselves rather than developing the subordinates by telling them what they need to do. An important consideration is that the subordinates' acceptance of responsibility for self-developing (i.e., self-direction and self-control) has been shown to relate to their commitment to objectives. But the overall aim is to further the growth of the individual, and it must be approached as a managerial strategy rather than simply as a personnel technique. Forms and procedures are of little value. Once the concept is provided, managers who welcome the assumptions of Theory Y will create their own processes for implementation; managers with underlying Theory X assumptions cannot create the conditions for integration and self-control no matter what tools are provided.

The development process becomes one of role clarification and mutual agreement regarding the subordinate's job responsibilities. This requires the manager's willingness to accept some risk and allow mistakes as part of the growth process. It also is time-consuming in terms of discussions and allowing opportunity for self-discovery. However, it is not a new set of duties on top of the manager's existing load. It is a different way of fulfilling the existing responsibilities.

One procedure that violates Theory Y assumptions is the typical utilization of performance appraisals. Theory X leads quite naturally into this means of directing individual efforts toward organizational objectives. Through the performance appraisal process, management tells people what to do, monitors their activities, judges how well they have done, and rewards or punishes them accordingly. Since the appraisals are used for administrative purposes (e.g., pay, promotion, retention decisions), this is a demonstration of management's overall control strategy. Any consideration of personal goals is covered by the expectation that rewards of salary and position are enough. If the advancement available through this system is not a desired reward, the individuals are placed in a position of acting against their own objectives and advancing for the benefit of the organization only. The alternative (for example, turning down a promotion) may bring negative outcomes such as lack of future options or being identified as employees with no potential.

The principle of integration requires active and responsible participation of employees in decisions affecting them. One plan that demonstrates Theory Y assumptions is *The Scanlon Plan.* A central feature in this plan is the cost-reduction sharing that provides a meaningful cause-and-effect connection between employee behavior and the reward received. The reward is directly related to the success of the organization and it is distributed frequently. This provides a more effective learning reinforcement than the traditional performance appraisal methods. The second central feature of the Scanlon Plan is effective participation, a formal method through which members contribute brains and ingenuity as well as their physical efforts on the job. This provides a means for social and ego satisfaction, so employees have a stake in the success of the firm beyond the economic rewards. Implementation of the Scanlon Plan is not a program or set of procedures; it must be accepted as a way of life and can vary depending on the circumstances of the particular company. It is entirely consistent with Theory Y assumptions.

Theory X leads to emphasis on tactics of control, whereas Theory Y is more concerned with the nature of the relationship. Eliciting the desired response in a Theory Y context is a matter of creating an environment or set of conditions to enable self-direction. The day-to-day behavior of an immediate supervisor or manager is perhaps the most critical factor in such an environment. Through sometimes subtle behaviors superiors demonstrate their attitudes and create what is referred to as the psychological "climate" of the relationship.

Management style does not seem to be important. Within many different styles, subordinates may or may not develop confidence in the manager's deeper integrity, based on other behavioral cues. Lack of confidence in the relationship causes anxiety and undesirable reactions from the employees. No ready formula is available to relay integrity. Insincere attempts to apply a technique or style—such as using participation only to manipulate subordinates into believing they have some input to decisions—are usually recognized as a gimmick and soon destroy confidence.

In addition to manager-subordinate relationships, problems connected to Theory X assumptions can be observed in other organizational associations such as staff-line relationships. Upper management may create working roles for staff groups to "police" line managers' activities, giving them an influence that equates psychologically to direct line authority. Top management with Theory X assumptions can delegate and still retain control. The staff function provides an opportunity to monitor indirectly, to set policy for limiting decisions and actions, and to obtain information on everything happening before a problem can occur.

Staff personnel often come from a very specialized education with little preparation for what their role should be in an organization. Will full confidence in their objective methods and training to find "the best answer," they often are unprepared for the resistance of line managers who don't share this confidence and don't trust the derived solutions. The staff may conclude that line managers are stupid, are unconcerned with the general welfare of the organization, and care only about their own authority and independence. They essentially adopt the Theory X assumptions and readily accept the opportunity to create a system of measurements for control of the line operations.

To utilize staff groups within the context of Theory Y, managers must emphasize the principle of self-control. As a resource to all parts and levels of the organization, staff reports and data should be supplied to all members who can use such information to control their own job—not subordinates' jobs. If summary data indicate something wrong within the manager's unit of responsibility, the manager would turn to subordinates, not to the staff, for more information. If the subordinates are practicing similar self-control using staff-provided information, they have most likely discovered the same problem and taken action before this inquiry occurs. There is no solution to the problem of staff-line relationships in authoritative terms that can address organizational objectives adequately. However, a manager operating by Theory Y assumptions will apply them similarly to all relationships—upward, downward, and peer level—including the staff-line associations.

## THE DEVELOPMENT OF MANAGERIAL TALENT

Leadership is a relationship with four major variables: the characteristics of the leader; the attitudes, needs, and other personal characteristics of the followers; the characteristics of the organization, such as its purpose, structure, and the nature of its task; and the social, economic, and political environment in which the organization operates. Specifying which leader characteristics will result in effective performance depends on the other factors, so it is a complex relationship. Even if researchers were able to determine the universal characteristics of a good relationship between the leader and the other situational factors, there are still many ways to achieve the same thing. For example, mutual confidence seems important in the relationship, but there are a number of ways that confidence can be developed and maintained. Different personal characteristics could achieve the same desired relationship.

Also, because it is so difficult to predict the situational conditions an organization will face, future management needs are unpredictable. The major task, then, is to provide a heterogeneous supply of human resources from which individuals can be selected as appropriate at a future time. This requires attracting recruits from a variety of sources and with a variety of backgrounds, which complicates setting criteria for selection. Also, the management development programs in an organization should involve many people rather than a few with similar qualities and abilities. Finally, management's goal must be to develop the unique capacities of each individual, rather than common objectives for all participants. We must place high value on people in general—seek to enable them to develop to their fullest potential in whatever role they best can fill. Not everyone must pursue the top jobs; outstanding leadership is needed at every level.

Individuals must develop themselves and will do so optimally only in terms of what each of them sees as meaningful and valuable. What might be called a "manufacturing approach" to management development involves designing programs to build managers; this end product becomes a supply of managerial talent to be used as needed. A preferred alternative approach is to "grow talent" under the assumption that people will grow into what they are capable of becoming, if they are provided the right conditions for that growth. There is little relationship (possibly even a negative one) between the formal structure for management development and actual achievement of the organization, because programs and procedures do not *cause* management development.

Learning is fairly straightforward when the individual desires new knowledge or skill. Unfortunately, many development offerings soon become a scheduled assignment for entire categories of people. Learning is limited in these conditions, because the motivation is low. Further, negative attitudes develop toward training in general, which interferes with creating an overall climate conducive to growth. In many cases, managers may have a purpose in sending subordinates to training that is not shared with or understood by that individual. This creates anxiety or confusion, which also interferes with learning. It is best if attendance in training and development programs is the result of joint target-setting, wherein the individual expresses a need and it can be determined that a particular program will benefit both the individual and the organization.

Classroom learning can be valuable to satisfying needs of both parties. However, it can only be effective when there is an organizational climate conducive to growth. Learning is always an active process, whether related to motor skills or acquisition of knowledge; it cannot be injected into the learner, so motivation is critical. Practice and feedback are essential when behavior changes are involved. Classroom methods such as case analysis and role playing provide an opportunity to experiment with decisions and behaviors in a safe environment, to receive immediate feedback, and to go back and try other alternatives. Some applications of classroom learning may be observed directly on the job. In other cases, the application may be more subtle, in the form of increased understanding or challenging one's own preconceptions. Care must be taken so that pressures to evaluate the benefits of classroom learning don't result in application of inappropriate criteria for success while the true value of the experience is overlooked.

Separate attention is given to management groups or teams at various levels. Within Theory X assumptions, direction and control are jeopardized by effective group functioning. On the other hand, a manager who recognizes interdependencies in the organization—one who is less interested in personal power than in creating conditions so human resources will voluntarily achieve organization objectives—will seek to build strong management groups. Creating a managerial team requires unity of purpose among those individuals. If the group is nothing more than several individuals competing for power and recognition, it is not a team. Again, the climate of the relationships and the fundamental understanding of the role of managers in the organization will be critical. One day the hierarchical structure of reporting relationships will disappear from organizational charts and give way to a series of linked groups. This shift in patterns of relationships will be a slow transition, but will signify recognition of employee capacity to collaborate in joint efforts. Then we may begin to discover how seriously management has underestimated the true potential of the organization's human resources.

## Conclusion

Theory X is not an evil set of assumptions, but rather a limiting one. Use of authority to influence has its place, even within the Theory Y assumptions, but it does not work in all circumstances. A number of societal changes suggest why Theory X increasingly may cause problems for organizations needing more innovation and flexibility in their operating philosophy. It is critically important for managers honestly to examine the assumptions that underlie their own behavior toward subordinates. To do so requires first accepting the two possibilities, Theory X and Theory Y, and then examining one's own actions in the context of that comparison. Fully understanding the implications on each side will help identify whether the observed choices of how to influence people are likely to bring about the desired results.

# Maslow on Management

*ABRAHAM H. MASLOW*

It should be possible to implement an enlightened management policy into an organization, where employees can *self-actualize* (institute their own ideas, make decisions, learn from their mistakes, and grow in their capabilities) while creating *synergy* (attaining beneficial results simultaneously for the individual and the organization). Such a policy (and associated practices) would not necessarily apply to all people, because everyone is at a different level on the motivational hierarchy (from physiological to safety to love to esteem to self-actualization). Nevertheless, the assumptions that would need to be true in order to create an ideal (eupsychian) society can be identified and then explored. They include the following dimensions. People are:

- psychologically healthy;
- not fixated at the safety-need level;
- capable of growth, which occurs through delight and through boredom;
- able to grow to a high level of personal maturity;
- courageous, with the ability to conquer their fears and endure anxiety.

They have:

- the impulse to achieve;
- the capacity to be objective about themselves and about others;
- the capacity to be trusted to some degree;
- a strong will to grow, experiment, select their own friends, carry out their own ideas, and self-actualize;
- the ability to enjoy good teamwork, friendships, group spirit, group harmony, belongingness, and group love;
- the capacity to be improved to some degree;
- the ability to identify with a common objective and contribute to it;
- a conscience and feelings.

Everyone prefers:

- to love and to respect his or her boss;
- to be a prime mover rather than a passive helper;
- to use all their capacities;

---

Abraham H. Maslow, *Maslow on Management.* New York: Wiley & Sons, Inc, 1998.

- to work rather than being idle;
- to have meaningful work;
- to be justly and fairly appreciated, preferably in public;
- to feel important, needed, useful, successful, proud, and respected;
- to have responsibility;
- to have personhood, identity, and uniqueness as a person;
- to create rather than destroy;
- to be interested rather than bored;
- to improve things, make things right, and do things better.

Given this portrait of a certain type of individual described by these assumptions, we can conclude the following:

- Authoritarian managers are dysfunctional for them;
- People can benefit by being stretched, strained, and challenged once in a while;
- Everyone should be informed as completely as possible;
- These types of persons will do best at what they have chosen, based on what they like most;
- Everybody needs to be absolutely clear about the organization's goals, directions, and purposes.

In conclusion, *enlightened management is the wave of the future.* It will be seen more and more for a very simple reason that can be stated as a fundamental principle of human behavior: "Treating people well spoils them for being treated badly." In other words, once employees have experienced any aspect of enlightened management, they will never wish to return to an authoritarian environment. Further, as other workers hear about enlightened work organizations, they will either seek to work there or demand that their own workplaces become more enlightened.

# The Seven Habits of Highly Effective People

*Stephen R. Covey*

There are two types of literature on how to succeed. The first type focuses on a *personality ethic.* It claims that you are what you appear to be; appearance is everything. It accents public image, social consciousness, and the ability to interact superficially with others. However, exclusive attention to these factors will eventually provide evidence of a lack of integrity, an absence of depth, a short-term personal success orientation, and basic deficiency in one's own humanness.

The second type of success literature revolves around a *character ethic.* It provides proven pathways to move from dependent relationships to independence, and ultimately to interdependent success with other people. It requires a willingness to subordinate one's short-term needs to more important long-term goals. It requires effort, perseverance, and patience with oneself. One's character is, after all, a composite of habits, which are unconscious patterns of actions.

Habits can be developed through rigorous practice until they become second nature. There are seven key habits that form the basis for character development and build a strong foundation for interpersonal success in life and at work:

1. *Be proactive;* make things happen. Take the initiative and be responsible for your life. Work on areas where you can have an impact and pay less attention to areas outside your area of concern. When you do respond to others, do so on the basis of your principles.
2. *Begin with the end in mind.* Know where you're going; develop a personal mission statement; develop a sense of who you are and what you value. Maintain a long-term focus.
3. *Put first things first.* Distinguish between tasks that are urgent and not so urgent, between activities that are important and not so important; then organize and execute around those priorities. Avoid being in a reactive mode, and pursue opportunities instead. Ask yourself, "What one thing could I do (today) that would make a tremendous difference in my work or personal life?"

---

Stephen R. Covey, *The Seven Habits of Highly Effective People: Restoring the Character Ethic.* New York: Simon & Schuster, 1989.

4. *Think "win-win."* Try to avoid competing, and search for ways to develop mutually beneficial relationships instead. Build an "emotional bank account" with others through frequent acts of courtesy, kindness, honesty, and commitment keeping. Develop the traits of integrity, maturity, and an abundance mentality (acting as if there is plenty of everything out there for everybody).
5. *Seek to understand, and then to be understood.* Practice empathetic communications, in which you recognize feelings and emotions in others. Listen carefully to people. Try giving them "psychological air."
6. *Synergize.* Value and exploit the mental, emotional, and psychological differences among people to produce results that demonstrate creative energy superior to what a single person could have accomplished alone.
7. *Sharpen the saw.* Do not allow yourself to get stale in any domain of your life, and don't waste time on activities that do not contribute to one of your goals and values. Seek ways to renew yourself periodically in all four elements of your nature—physical (via exercise, good nutrition, and stress control), mental (through reading, thought, and writing), social (through service to others), and spiritual (through study and meditation). In short, practice continuous learning and self-improvement, and your character will lead you to increased success.

# The Fifth Discipline


**PETER M. SENGE**

**Summary prepared by Dorothy Marcic**


***Dorothy Marcic*** *is an adjunct professor at Vanderbilt University's Owen Graduate School of Management. Previously, she served as Director of Graduate Programs in Human Resource Development at Peabody College and Fulbright Scholar at the University of Economics-Prague, and held academic appointments at Arizona State University and the University of Wisconsin-La Crosse. Dorothy's research and consulting interests include how to develop the kinds of structures, values, and systems that help create learning organizations that are uplifting to employees. Addressing that issue is one of the ten books she has authored*—Managing With the Wisdom of Love: Uncovering Virtue in Organizations.

Learning disabilities can be fatal to organizations, causing them to have an average life span of only 40 years—half a human being's life. *Organizations need to be learners, and often they are not.* Somehow some survive, but never live up to their potential. What happens if what we term "excellence" is really no more than mediocrity? Only those firms that become learners will succeed in the increasingly turbulent, competitive global market.

## ◆ LEARNING DISABILITIES

There are seven learning disabilities common to organizations.

### Identification with One's Position

American workers are trained to see themselves as what they do, not who they are. Therefore, if laid off, they find it difficult, if not impossible, to find work doing something else. Worse for the organization, though, is the limited thinking this attitude creates. By claiming an identity related to the job, workers are cut off from seeing how

Peter M. Senge, *The Fifth Discipline: The Art and Practice of the Learning Organization,* New York: Doubleday, 1990.

their responsibility connects to other jobs. For example, one American car had three assembly bolts on one component. The similar Japanese make had only one bolt. Why? Because the Detroit manufacturer had three engineers for that component, while a similar Japanese manufacturer had only one.

### External Enemies

This belief is a result of the previously stated disability. *External enemies* refers to people focusing blame on anything but themselves or their unit. Fault is regularly blamed on factors like the economy, the weather, or the government. Marketing blames manufacturing, and manufacturing blames engineering. Such external fault-finding keeps the organization from seeing what the real problems are and prevents them from tackling the real issues head-on.

### The Illusion of Taking Charge

Being proactive is seen as good management—doing something about "those problems." All too often, though, being proactive is a disguise for reactiveness against that awful enemy out there.

### The Fixation on Events

Much attention in organizations is paid to events—last month's sales, the new product, who just got hired, and so on. Our society, too, is geared toward short-term thinking, which in turn stifles the type of generative learning that permits a look at the real threats—the slowly declining processes of quality, service, or design.

### The Parable of the Boiled Frog

An experiment was once conducted by placing a frog in boiling water. Immediately the frog, sensing danger in the extreme heat, jumped out to safety. However, placing the frog in cool water and slowly turning up the heat resulted in the frog getting groggier and groggier and finally boiling to death. Why? Because the frog's survival mechanisms are programmed to look for sudden changes in the environment, not to gradual changes. Similarly, during the 1960s, the U.S. auto industry saw no threat by Japan, which had only 4 percent of the market. Not until the 1980s when Japan had over 21 percent of the market did the Big Three begin to look at their core assumptions. Now with Japan holding about 30 percent share of the market, it is not certain if this frog (U.S. automakers) is capable of jumping out of the boiling water. Looking at gradual processes requires slowing down our frenetic pace and watching for the subtle cues.

### The Delusion of Learning from Experience

Learning from experience is powerful. This is how we learn to walk and talk. However, we now live in a time when direct consequences of actions may take months or years to appear. Decisions in R&D may take up to a decade to bear fruit, and their actual consequences may be influenced by manufacturing and marketing along the way. Organizations often choose to deal with these complexities by breaking themselves up into smaller and smaller components, further reducing their ability to see problems in their entirety.

### The Myth of the Management Team

Most large organizations have a group of bright, experienced leaders who are supposed to know all the answers. They were trained to believe there are answers to all problems and they should find them. People are rarely rewarded for bringing up difficult issues or for looking at parts of a problem that make them harder to grasp. Most teams end up operating below the lowest IQ of any member. What results are "skilled incompetents"—people who know all too well how to keep *from* learning.

## ◆ SYSTEMS THINKING

There are five disciplines required for a learning organization: personal mastery, mental models, shared vision, team learning, and systems thinking. The fifth one, systems thinking, is the most important. Without systems thinking, the other disciplines do not have the same effect.

### THE LAWS OF THE FIFTH DISCIPLINE

#### Today's Problems Result from Yesterday's Solutions

A carpet merchant kept pushing down a bump in the rug, only to have it reappear elsewhere, until he lifted a corner and out slithered a snake. Sometimes fixing one part of the system only brings difficulties to other parts of the system. For example, solving an internal inventory problem may lead to angry customers who now get late shipments.

#### Push Hard and the System Pushes Back Even Harder

Systems theory calls this compensating feedback, which is a common way of reducing the effects of an intervention. Some cities, for example, build low-cost housing and set up jobs programs, only to have more poor people than ever. Why? Because many moved to the cities from neighboring areas so that they, too, could take advantage of the low-cost housing and job opportunities.

#### Behavior Gets Better Before It Gets Worse

Some decisions actually look good in the short term, but produce *compensating feedback* and crisis in the end. The really effective decisions often produce difficulties in the short run but create more health in the long term. This is why behaviors such as building a power base or working hard just to please the boss come back to haunt you.

#### The Best Way Out Is to Go Back In

We often choose familiar solutions, ones that feel comfortable and not scary. But the effective ways often mean going straight into what we are afraid of facing. What does *not* work is pushing harder on the same old solutions (also called the "what we need here is a bigger hammer" syndrome).

#### The Cure Can Be Worse than the Disease

The result of applying nonsystematic solutions to problems is the need for more and more of the same. It can become addictive. Someone begins mild drinking to alleviate work tension. The individual feels better and then takes on more work, creating more tension and a need for more alcohol, and the person finally becomes an alcoholic. Sometimes these types of solutions only result in shifting the burden. The government enters the scene by providing more welfare and leaves the host system weaker and less able to solve its own problems. This ultimately necessitates still more aid from the government. Companies can try to shift their burdens to consultants, but then become more and more dependent on them to solve their problems.

### Faster Is Slower

Every system, whether ecological or organizational, has an optimal rate of growth. Faster and faster is not always better. (After all, the tortoise finally did win the race.) Complex human systems require new ways of thinking. Quickly jumping in and fixing what *looks* bad usually provides solutions for a problem's symptoms and not for the problem itself.

### Cause and Effect Are Not Always Related Closely in Time and Space

*Effects* here mean the symptoms we see, such as drug abuse and unemployment, whereas *causes* mean the interactions of the underlying system which bring about these conditions. We often assume cause is near to effect. If there is a sales problem, then incentives for the sales force should fix it, or if there is inadequate housing, then build more houses. Unfortunately, this does not often work, for the real causes lie elsewhere.

### Tiny Changes May Produce Big Results; Areas of Greatest Leverage Are Frequently the Least Obvious

System science teaches that the most obvious solutions usually do not work. While simple solutions frequently make short-run improvements, they commonly contribute to long-term deteriorations. The *non*obvious and *well-focused* solutions are more likely to provide leverage and bring positive change. For example, ships have a tiny trim tab on one edge of the rudder that has great influence on the movement of that ship, so small changes in the trim tab bring big shifts in the ship's course. However, there are no simple rules for applying leverage to organizations. It requires looking for the structure of what is going on rather than merely seeing the events.

### You Can Have Your Cake and Eat It Too—But Not at the Same Time

Sometimes the most difficult problems come from "snapshot" rather than "process" thinking. For example, it was previously believed by American manufacturers that quality and low cost could not be achieve simultaneously. One had to be chosen over the other. What was missed, however, was the notion that improving quality may also mean eliminating waste and unnecessary time (both adding costs), which in the end would mean lower costs. Real leverage comes when it can be seen that seemingly opposing needs can be met over time.

### Cutting the Elephant in Half Does Not Create Two Elephants

Some problems can be solved by looking at parts of the organization, whereas others require holistic thinking. What is needed is an understanding of the boundaries for each problem. Unfortunately, most organizations are designed to prevent people from seeing systemic problems, either by creating rigid structures or by leaving problems behind for others to clean up.

### There Is No Blame

Systems thinking teaches that there are not outside causes to problems; instead, you and your "enemy" are part of the same system. Any cure requires understanding how that is seen.

## THE OTHER DISCIPLINES

### PERSONAL MASTERY

Organizations can learn only when the individuals involved learn. This requires personal mastery, which is the discipline of personal learning and growth, where people are continually expanding their ability to create the kind of life they want. From their quest comes the spirit of the learning organization.

Personal mastery involves seeing one's life as a creative work, being able to clarify what is really important, and learning to see current reality more clearly. The difference between what's important, what we want, and where we are now produces a "creative tension." Personal mastery means being able to generate and maintain creative tension.

Those who have high personal mastery have a vision, which is more like a calling, and they are in a continual learning mode. They never really "arrive." Filled with more commitment, they take initiative and greater responsibility in their work.

Previously, organizations supported an employee's development only if it would help the organization, which fits in with the traditional "contract" between employee and organization ("an honest day's pay in exchange for an honest day's work"). The new, and coming, way is to see it rather as a "covenant," which comes from a shared vision of goals, ideas, and management processes.

Working toward personal mastery requires living with emotional tension, not letting our goals get eroded. As Somerset Maugham said, "Only mediocre people are always at their best." One of the worst blocks to achieving personal mastery is the common belief that we cannot have what we want. Being committed to the truth is a powerful weapon against this, for it does not allow us to deceive ourselves. Another means of seeking personal mastery is to integrate our reason and intuition. We live in a society that values reason and devalues intuition. However, using both together is very powerful and may be one of the fundamental contributions to systems thinking.

### MENTAL MODELS

Mental models are internal images of how the world works, and they can range from simple generalizations (people are lazy) to complex theories (assumptions about why my co-workers interact the way they do). For example, for decades the Detroit automakers believed people bought cars mainly for styling, not for quality or reliability. These beliefs, which were really unconscious assumptions, worked well for many years, but ran into trouble when competition from Japan began. It took a long time for Detroit even to begin to see the mistakes in their beliefs. One company that managed to change its mental model through incubating a business worldview was Shell.

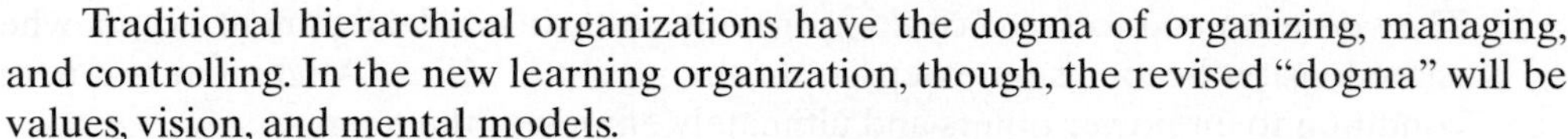

Traditional hierarchical organizations have the dogma of organizing, managing, and controlling. In the new learning organization, though, the revised "dogma" will be values, vision, and mental models.

Hanover Insurance began changes in 1969 designed to overcome the "basic disease of the hierarchy." Three values espoused were

1. *Openness* —seen as an antidote to the dysfunctional interactions in face-to-face meetings.
2. *Merit,* or making decisions based on the good of the organization—seen as the antidote to decision making by organizational politics.
3. *Localness* —the antidote to doing the dirty stuff the boss does not want to do.

Chris Argyris and colleagues developed "action science" as a means for reflecting on the reasoning underlying our actions. This helps people change the defensive routines that lead them to skilled incompetence. Similarly, John Beckett created a course on the historical survey of main philosophies of thought, East and West, as a sort of "sandpaper on the brain." These ideas exposed managers to their own assumptions and mental models, and provided other ways to view the world.

## SHARED VISION

A shared vision is not an idea. Rather it is a force in people's hearts, a sense of purpose that provides energy and focus for learning. Visions are often exhilarating. Shared vision is important because it may be the beginning step to get people who mistrusted each other to start working together. Abraham Maslow studied high-performing teams and found that they had a shared vision. Shared visions can mobilize courage so naturally that people don't even know the extent of their strength. When John Kennedy created the shared vision in 1961 of putting a man on the moon by the end of the decade, only 15 percent of the technology had been created. Yet it led to numerous acts of daring and courage.

Learning organizations are not achievable without shared vision. Without that incredible pull toward the deeply felt goal, the forces of *status quo* will overwhelm the pursuit. As Robert Fritz once said, "In the presence of greatness, pettiness disappears." Conversely, in the absence of a great vision, pettiness is supreme.

Strategic planning often does not involve building a shared vision, but rather announcing the vision of top management, asking people, at best, to enroll, and, at worst, to comply. The critical step is gaining commitment from people. This is done by taking a personal vision and building it into a shared vision. In the traditional hierarchical organization, compliance is one of the desired outcomes. For learning organizations, commitment must be the key goal. Shared vision, though, is not possible without personal mastery, which is needed to foster continued commitment to a lofty goal.

## TEAM LEARNING

Bill Russell of the Boston Celtics wrote about being on a team of specialists whose performance depended on one another's individual excellence and how well they worked together. Sometimes that created a feeling of magic. He is talking about *alignment,* where a group functions as a whole unit, rather than as individuals working at cross purposes. When a team is aligned, its energies are focused and harmonized.

They do not need to sacrifice their own interests. Instead, alignment occurs when the shared vision becomes an extension of the personal vision, Alignment is a necessary condition to empower others and ultimately empower the team.

Never before today has there been greater need for mastering team learning, which requires mastering both dialogue and discussion. *Dialogue* involves a creative and free search of complex and even subtle issues, whereas *discussion* implies different views being presented and defended. Both skills are useful, but most teams cannot tell the difference between the two. The purpose of dialogue is to increase individual understanding. Here, assumptions are suspended and participants regard one another as on the same level. Discussion, on the other hand, comes from the same root word as *percussion* and *concussion* and involves a sort of verbal ping-pong game whose object is winning. Although this is a useful technique, it must be balanced with dialogue. A continued emphasis on winning is not compatible with the search for truth and coherence.

One of the major blocks to healthy dialogue and discussion is what Chris Argyris calls *defensive routines.* These are habitual styles of interacting that protect us from threat or embarrassment. These include the avoidance of conflict (smoothing over) and the feeling that one has to appear competent and to know the answers at all times.

Team learning, like any other skill, requires practice. Musicians and athletes understand this principle. Work teams need to learn that lesson as well.

## ◆ OTHER ISSUES

Organizational politics is a perversion of truth, yet most people are so accustomed to it, they do not even notice it anymore. A learning organization is not possible in such an environment. In order to move past the politics, one thing needed is openness—both speaking openly and honestly about the real and important issues and being willing to challenge one's own way of thinking.

Localness, too, is essential to the learning organization, for decisions need to be pushed down the organizational hierarchy in order to unleash people's commitment. This gives them the freedom to act.

One thing lacking in many organizations is time to reflect and think. If someone is sitting quietly, we assume they are not busy and we feel free to interrupt. Many managers, however, are too busy to "just think." This should not be blamed on the tumultuous environment of many crises. Research suggests that, even when given ample time, managers still do not devote any of it to adequate reflection. Therefore, habits need to be changed, as well as how we structure our days.

# Competitive Advantage: Creating and Sustaining Superior Performance

*MICHAEL E. PORTER*

*Summary prepared by Sara A. Morris*

***Sara A. Morris*** *received her Ph.D. in business policy and strategy from the University of Texas at Austin. Now on the faculty at Old Dominion University, she teaches capstone courses in strategic management and graduate seminars in competitive strategy. Her current research is in business ethics and social responsibility and concerns CEO misconduct and the use of unethical techniques for obtaining competitor information.*

How can a firm obtain and maintain an advantage over its competitors? The answer lies in an understanding of industries, the five forces that drive competition in an industry, and three generic strategies that a firm can use to protect itself against these forces. An industry is a group of firms producing essentially the same products and/or services for the same customers. The profit potential of an industry is determined by the cumulative strength of five forces that affect competition in an industry.

1. Jockeying for position on the part of current competitors in the industry,
2. Potential for new competitors to enter the industry,
3. The threat of substitutes for the industry's products or services,
4. The economic power of suppliers of raw materials to the industry,
5. The bargaining power of the industry's customers.

---

Michael E. Porter, *Competitive Advantage: Creating and Sustaining Superior Performance.* New York: Free Press, 1985.

Three strategies that a firm can use to neutralize the power of these five forces are low costs, differentiation, and focus. Several specific action steps are required to execute each of these three generic strategies.

## PRINCIPLES OF COMPETITIVE ADVANTAGE

A firm creates a competitive advantage for itself by providing more value for customers than competitors provide. Customers value either (1) equivalent benefits at a lower price than competitors charge, or (2) greater benefits which more than compensate for a higher price than competitors charge. Thus, there are two possible competitive advantages, one based on costs and one based on differentiation (benefits). Each of these tactics will be discussed in detail, following an examination of the value chain.

## THE VALUE CHAIN

The *value chain,* consisting of value-producing activities and margin, is a basic tool for analyzing the large number of discrete activities within a firm that are potential sources of competitive advantage. The inclusion of margin in the value chain is a reminder that, in order for a firm to profit from its competitive advantage, the value to customers must exceed the costs of generating it. Value-producing activities fall into nine categories—five categories of primary activities and four categories of support activities. Primary activities include inbound logistics, operations, outbound logistics, marketing/sales, and service. Support activities include procurement (of all of the inputs used everywhere in the value chain), technology development (for all of the myriad of technologies that are used in every primary and support activity), human resource management (of all types of personnel throughout the organization), and the firm infrastructure (general management, planning, finance, accounting, legal and government affairs, quality management, etc.).

Firms perform hundreds or thousands of discrete steps in transforming raw materials into finished products. The value chain decomposes the nine value-producing activities into numerous subactivities because each separate subactivity can contribute to the firm's relative cost position and create a basis for differentiation. In most subactivities, the firm is not significantly different from its rivals. The strategically relevant subactivities are those that currently or potentially distinguish the firm from competitors.

Value chain activities are not independent from one another, but interrelated. The cost or performance of one activity is linked to many other activities. For example, the amount of after-sale service needed depends on the quality of the raw materials procured, the degree of quality control in operations, the amount of training given to the sales force regarding matching customer sophistication and model attributes, and other factors. Competitive advantage can be created by linkages among activities as well as by individual activities. Two ways that firms can derive competitive advantage from linkages are through optimization of linkages and coordination of linkages.

The configuration and economics of the value chain are determined by the firm's *competitive scope.* By affecting the value chain, scope also affects competitive advantage. Four dimensions of scope are:

1. *Segment scope*—varieties of products made and buyers served
2. *Vertical scope*—the extent of activities performed internally rather than purchased from outside
3. *Geographic scope*—the range of locations served
4. *Industry scope*—the number of industries in which the firm competes.

Broad-scope firms operate multiple value chains and attempt to exploit interrelationships among activities across the chains to gain competitive advantages. Narrow-scope firms use focus strategies to pursue competitive advantages; by concentrating on single value chains, they attempt to perfect the linkages within the value chain.

## COMPETITIVE ADVANTAGE THROUGH LOW COST

The starting point for achieving a cost advantage is a thorough analysis of costs in the value chain. The analyst must be able to assign operating costs and assets (fixed and working capital) to each separate value chain activity. There are ten major factors which are generally under the firm's control and which drive costs:

1. Economies (or diseconomies) of scale
2. Learning, which the firm can control by managing with the learning curve and keeping learning proprietary
3. Capacity utilization, which the firm can control by levelling throughput and/or reducing the penalty for throughput fluctuations
4. Linkages within the value chain, which the firm can control by recognizing and exploiting
5. Interrelationships between business units (in multi-industry firms), which the firm can control by sharing appropriate activities and/or transferring management know-how
6. The extent of vertical integration
7. Timing, which the firm can control by exploiting first-mover or late-mover advantages, and/or timing purchases over the business cycle
8. Discretionary policies (regarding products made, buyers served, human resources used, etc.)
9. Location
10. Institutional factors imposed by government and unions, which the firm can influence if not control outright.

Moreover, costs are dynamic; they will change over time due to changes in industry growth rate, differential scale sensitivity, differential learning rates, changes in technology, aging, and the like. Each individual value chain activity must be analyzed separately for its cost drivers and cost dynamics.

By definition, the firm has a cost-based competitive advantage if the total costs of all its value chain activities are lower than any competitor's. A firm's cost position relative to competitors depends on the composition of its value chain compared to competitors' chains, and the firm's position relative to its competitors vis-à-vis the cost drivers of each value chain activity. Two ways that a firm can achieve a cost advantage, therefore, are: (1) by controlling cost drivers, and (2) by reconfiguring the value chain through means such as changing the production process, the distribution channel, or the raw materials. A cost-based competitive advantage will be sustainable only if competitors cannot imitate it. The cost drivers which tend to be harder to imitate are economies of scale, interrelationships, linkages, proprietary learning, and new technologies that are brought about through discretionary policies.

## COMPETITIVE ADVANTAGE THROUGH DIFFERENTIATION

Successful *differentiation* occurs when a firm creates something unique that is valuable to buyers and for which buyers are willing to pay a price premium in excess of the extra costs incurred by the producer. This statement begs two questions: (1) What makes something valuable to buyers, and (2) Why does the producer incur extra costs? With regard to the first question, a firm can create value for buyers by raising buyer performance, or by lowering buyer costs (in ways besides selling the product at a lower price). With regard to the second question, differentiation is usually inherently costly because uniqueness requires the producer to perform value chain activities better than competitors.

In order to achieve a differentiation advantage, strategists must be thoroughly familiar with the many discrete activities in their own value chain(s) and in the buyer's value chain, and must have a passing knowledge of the value chains of competitors. Each discrete activity in the firm's value chain represents an opportunity for differentiating. The firm's impact on the buyer's value chain determines the value the firm can create through raising buyer performance or lowering buyer costs. Since competitive advantages are by definition relative, a firm's value chain must be compared to those of its competitors.

For each separate activity in the firm's value chain, there are *uniqueness drivers* analogous to the cost drivers described previously. The most important uniqueness driver is probably the set of policy choices managers make (regarding product features, services provided, technologies employed, quality of the raw materials, and so forth). Other uniqueness drivers, in approximate order of importance, are linkages within the value chain and with suppliers and distribution channels, timing, location, interrelationships, learning, vertical integration, scale, and institutional factors.

Buyers use two types of purchasing criteria: (1) *use criteria,* which reflect real value, and (2) *signaling criteria,* which reflect perceived value in advance of purchase and verification. Use criteria include product characteristics, delivery time, ready availability, and other factors which affect buyer value through raising buyer performance or lowering buyer costs. Signaling criteria include the producing firm's reputation and advertising, the product's packaging and advertising, and other factors through which the buyer can infer the probable value of the product before the real value can be known. Differentiators must identify buyer purchasing criteria; the buyer's value chain is the place to start.

Armed with an understanding of multiple value chains, uniqueness drivers, and buyer purchasing criteria, managers can pursue differentiation. There are four basic routes to a differentiation-based competitive advantage. One route is to enhance the sources of uniqueness, by proliferating the sources of differentiation in the value chain, for example. A second route is to make the cost of differentiation an advantage by exploiting sources of differentiation that are not costly, minimizing differentiation costs by controlling cost drivers, and/or reducing costs in activities that do not affect buyer value. Another route is to change the rules to create uniqueness, such as discovering unrecognized purchase criteria. The fourth route is to reconfigure the value chain to be unique in entirely new ways.

A differentiation-based competitive advantage will be sustainable only if buyers' needs and perceptions remain stable and competitors cannot imitate the uniqueness. The firm can strongly influence the buyer's perceptions by continuing to improve on use criteria and by reinforcing them with appropriate signals. The firm is, nevertheless, at risk that buyers' needs will shift, eliminating the value of a particular form of differentiation. The sustainability of differentiation against imitation by competitors depends on its sources, the drivers of uniqueness. The competitive advantage will be more sustainable if the uniqueness drivers involve barriers such as proprietary learning, linkages, interrelationships, and first-mover advantages; if the firm has low costs in differentiating; if there are multiple sources of differentiation; and/or if the firm can create switching costs for customers.

## ◆ TECHNOLOGY AND COMPETITIVE ADVANTAGE

One of the most significant drivers of competition is technological change. Because technologies are embedded in every activity in the value chain as well as in the linkages among value chain activities, a firm can achieve and/or maintain low costs or differentiation through technology. The first step in using technology wisely is to identify the multitude of technologies in the value chain. Then, the astute manager must become aware of relevant technological improvements coming from competitors, other industries, and scientific breakthroughs.

A firm's technology strategy involves choices among new technologies, and choices about timing and licensing. Rather than pursuing technological improvements involving all value chain activities and linkages indiscriminately, managers should restrict their attention to technological changes that make a difference. New technologies are important if they can affect (1) the firm's particular competitive advantage, either directly or through its drivers, or (2) any of the five forces that drive competition in the industry. A firm's timing matters in technological changes because the technology leader will experience first-mover advantages (e.g., reputation as a pioneer, opportunity to define industry standards) as well as disadvantages (e.g., costs of educating buyers, demand uncertainty). Thus, the choice of whether to be a technology leader or follower should be made according to the sustainability of the technological lead. When a firm's competitive advantage rests on technology, licensing the technology to other firms is risky. Although there are conditions under which licensing may be warranted (to tap an otherwise inaccessible market, for example), often the firm inadvertently creates strong rivals and/or gives away a competitive advantage for a small royalty fee.

## ◆ COMPETITOR SELECTION

A firm must be ever vigilant in pursuing and protecting its competitive advantage; however, there are dangers in relentlessly attacking all rivals. It is prudent to distinguish desirable competitors from undesirable ones. Desirable competitors may enable a firm to increase its competitive advantage (e.g., by absorbing demand fluctuations, or by providing a standard against which buyers compare costs or differentiation), or may improve industry structure (i.e., may weaken one or more of the five forces that collectively determine the intensity of competition in an industry). Characteristics of desirable competitors include realistic assumptions; clear, self-perceived weaknesses; enough credibility to be acceptable to customers; enough viability to deter new entrants; and enough strength to motivate the firm to continue to improve its competitive advantage. A smart industry leader will encourage some competitors and discourage others through tactics such as technology licensing and selective retaliation.

## ◆ SCOPE AND COMPETITIVE ADVANTAGE

An industry consists of heterogeneous parts, or segments, due to differences in buyer behavior and differences in the economics of producing different products or services for these buyers. Therefore, the intensity of competition (i.e., the collective strength of the five competitive forces) varies among segments of the same industry. Moreover, because segments of the same industry have different value chains, the requirements for competitive advantage differ widely among industry segments. The existence of multiple industry segments forces a firm to decide on competitive scope, or where in the industry to compete. The attractiveness of any particular industry segment depends on the collective strength of the five competitive forces, the segment's size and growth rate, and the fit between a firm's abilities and the segment's needs. The firm may broadly target many segments or may use the generic strategy of focus to serve one or a few segments.

The competitive scope decision requires the manager to analyze all the current and potential industry segments. To identify product segments, all the product varieties in an industry must be examined for differences they can create in the five competitive forces and the value chain. The industry's products may differ in terms of features, technology or design, packaging, performance, services, and in many other ways. To identify buyer segments, all the different types of buyers in an industry must be examined for differences they can create in the five competitive forces and the value chain. Buyers can differ by type (e.g., several types of industrial buyers, several types of consumer buyers), by distribution channel, and by geographic location (according to weather zone, country stage of development, etc.).

When the value chains of different segments in the same industry are related at multiple points, a firm can share value-producing activities among segments. Such segment interrelationships encourage firms to use a broad-target strategy, unless the costs of coordination, compromise, and inflexibility in jointly accomplishing value-producing activities outweigh the benefits of sharing. Broad-target strategies often involve too many segments, thereby pushing coordination, compromise, and inflexibility costs too high and making the broadly-targeted firm vulnerable to firms with good focus strategies.

Whereas broad-target strategies are based on similarities in the value chains among segments, focus strategies are based on differences between segments' value chains. A focuser can optimize the value chain for one or a few segments and achieve lower costs or better differentiation than broad-target firms because the focuser can avoid the costs of coordination, compromise, and inflexibility required for serving multiple segments. The sustainability of a focus strategy is determined by its sustainability against (1) broad-target competitors, (2) imitators, and (3) substitutes, the next topic of interest.

Both the industry's product or service and its substitutes perform the same generic function for the buyer (i.e., fill the same role in the buyer's value chain). The threat of substitution depends on (1) the relative value/price of the substitute compared to the industry's product, (2) the cost of switching to the substitute, and (3) the buyer's propensity to switch. The relative value/price compares the substitute to the industry's product in terms of usage rate, delivery and installation, direct and indirect costs of use, buyer performance, complementary products, uncertainty, etc. Switching costs include redesign costs, retraining costs, and risk of failure. Buyer propensity to substitute depends on resources available, risk profile, technological orientation, and the like. The threat of substitution often changes over time because of changes in relative price, relative value, switching costs, or propensity to substitute. To defend against substitutes, the focuser can reduce costs, improve the product, raise switching costs, improve complementary goods, etc.

## CORPORATE STRATEGY AND COMPETITIVE ADVANTAGE

Whereas business-level strategy is concerned with the firm's course of actions within an individual industry, corporate-level strategy is generally concerned with the multi-industry firm's course of actions across industries. By exploiting interrelationships among its business units in distinct but related industries, the multi-industry corporation can increase its competitive advantage within one or more of those industries. Porter uses the term *horizontal strategy* to refer to a corporation's coordinated set of goals and policies that apply across its business units, and argues that horizontal strategy may be the most critical issue facing diversified firms today. It is through its horizontal strategy that a corporation achieves synergy.

There are three types of interrelationships among a multi-industry corporation's business units: tangible, intangible, and competitor-induced. *Tangible interrelationships* occur when different business units have common elements in their value chains, such as the same buyers, technologies, or purchased inputs. These common elements create opportunities to share value chain activities among related business units. Sharing activities may lower costs or increase differentiation, thereby adding to competitive advantage. However, the benefits of sharing do not always exceed the costs of sharing. One cost of sharing is the need for more coordination in the shared value chain activities. Another cost is the need for compromise in the way shared value chain activities are performed; the compromise must be acceptable to both business units, but may be optimal for neither. A third cost of sharing is greater inflexibility in responding to changing environmental conditions.

A second type of interrelationship, *intangible interrelationships,* occurs when different business units can transfer general management know-how even though they have no common elements in their value chains. It is possible, though less likely, for intangible interrelationships to lead to competitive advantage. A third type of interrelationship, *competitor-induced interrelationships,* occurs when two diversified corporations compete against each other in more than one business unit. Such multipoint competition between two corporations means that any action in one line of business can affect the entire range of jointly contested industries. Therefore, for multipoint competitors, a competitive advantage in one line of business will have implications for all the linked industries.

Any diversified corporation will face impediments to exploiting interrelationships: The managers of business units that receive fewer benefits than they contribute will resist sharing; managers of all business units will tend to protect their turf; incentive systems may not appropriately measure and reward a business unit's contributions to other units; and so forth. Therefore, corporate-level executives must articulate an explicit horizontal strategy and organize to facilitate horizontal relations. Examples of organizational practices and mechanisms that are particularly helpful are horizontal structures (e.g., groupings of business units, inter-unit task forces), horizontal systems (e.g., inter-unit strategic planning systems and capital budgeting systems), horizontal human resource practices (e.g., cross-business job rotation and management forums), and horizontal conflict resolution processes.

A special case of interrelationships occurs when the industry's product is used or purchased with complementary products. Because the sale of one promotes the sale of the other, complementary products have the opposite effect of substitutes. Three types of decisions that a corporation must make regarding complementary products concern whether to control these products internally (as opposed to letting other firms supply them), whether to bundle them (i.e., sell complementary products together as a package), and whether to cross-subsidize them (i.e., price complementary products based on their interrelationships instead of their individual costs). All three types of decisions have repercussions for competitive advantage.

## IMPLICATIONS FOR OFFENSIVE AND DEFENSIVE COMPETITIVE STRATEGY

The *industry scenario* is a planning tool which may be used to guide the formulation of competitive strategy in the face of major uncertainties about the future. Constructing industry scenarios involves identifying uncertainties that may affect the industry, determining the causal factors, making a range of plausible assumptions about each important causal factor, combining assumptions into internally consistent scenarios, analyzing the industry structure that would prevail under each scenario, identifying competitive advantages under each scenario, and predicting the behavior of competitors under each scenario. Managers may then design competitive strategies based on the most probable scenario, the most attractive scenario, hedging (protecting the firm against the worst-case scenario), or preserving flexibility.

Defensive strategy is intended to lower the probability of attack from a new entrant into the industry or an existing competitor seeking to reposition itself. The preferred defensive strategy is deterrence. The old saying about "the best offense is a good defense" holds here; a firm with a competitive advantage that continues to lower its costs or improve its differentiation is very difficult to beat. Nevertheless, when deterrence fails, the firm must respond to an attack underway. When a firm's position is being challenged, defensive tactics include raising structural barriers (e.g., blocking distribution channels, raising buyer switching costs) and increasing expected retaliation.

Sometimes attacking an industry leader makes sense. The most important rule in offensive strategy is never to attack a leader head-on with an imitation strategy. In order to attack an industry leader successfully, the challenger must have a sustainable competitive advantage, must be close to the leader in costs and differentiation, and must have some means to thwart leader retaliation. There are three primary avenues to attack a leader: (1) change the way individual value-producing activities are performed, or reconfigure the entire value chain; (2) redefine the competitive scope compared to the leader; (3) pure spending on the part of the challenger. The leader is particularly vulnerable when the industry is undergoing significant changes, such as technological improvements, changes in the buyer's value chain, or the emergence of new distribution channels.

PART

# III

# High-Performing Organizations

Most organizations don't want merely to survive; they want to be effective, or even excellent, at what they do. To do so requires a prior definition of success, and defining success often encourages the managers of an organization to examine the actions of their best competitors for comparative models (benchmarks). The assumption is that if they can identify the organizational characteristics that allow others to succeed, perhaps these attributes can be transplanted (or adapted) to facilitate their own success. Consequently, a wide variety of organizations and management groups have shown considerable interest in what "high-performing organizations" actually do and what the guiding principles are.

The four readings in this section concern themselves with issues pertaining to organizational effectiveness. In *Peak Performance,* Jon R. Katzenbach reports on his in-depth study of twenty-five organizations, operating in diverse industries, including fast foods, military, air transportation, and retail. Katzenbach focuses on the way the "best" organizations harness and maximize the emotional energy of their workforces. He reports that sustained high performance is achieved through five tactics: (1) mission, values, and pride, (2) process and metrics, (3) entrepreneurial spirit, (4) individual achievement, and (5) recognition and celebration. Essential to each of these five routes to peak performance is management (leadership) commitment to achieving a balance between enterprise performance and individual worker fulfillment. As a consultant and writer, Katzenbach provides practical insights to assist others in achieving peak performance within their organizations.

Jon R. Katzenbach, as the senior partner in Katzenbach Partners LLC, a New York-based consulting firm, specializes in leadership, team, and workforce performance. He is the author (co-author) of *Teams at the Top, Real Change Leaders, The Wisdom of Teams,* and *Why Pride Matters More than Money*.

In *The Tipping Point: How Little Things Can Make a Big Difference,* Malcolm Gladwell, a staff writer for *The New Yorker,* asks several probing questions: Why did crime in New York drop so suddenly in the mid-nineties? Why is teenage smoking out of control, when everyone knows smoking kills? What makes TV shows like *Sesame*

*Street* so good at teaching kids how to read? Gladwell explores why major changes so often occur suddenly and unexpectedly.

In *The Tipping Point,* Gladwell notes that ideas, behaviors, messages, and products often spread like an infectious disease. Three factors shared by all "fads" are examined, each containing an implicit change message. The reader is encouraged to think about change and ways to make what appears to be immovable a candidate for change from the slightest push.

*Managing the Unexpected* uses the example of high-reliability organizations (e.g., aircraft carriers or nuclear power plants) to provide a model for twenty-first century organizations. The authors suggest that all organizations can and must learn to anticipate and respond to ambiguity, uncertainty, and unexpected challenges in their environments, and to do so with flexibility, consistency, and effectiveness. The primary key to this is through mindfulness, which encompasses a preoccupation with failure, a reluctance to simplify interpretations, a sensitivity to operations, a commitment to resilience, and a deference to expertise wherever it may reside.

Co-authors Karl E. Weick and Kathleen M. Sutcliffe are faculty members at the University of Michigan Business School. Weick is the Rensis Likert Distinguished University Professor of Organizational Behavior and Psychology, and he is well known for exploring unique concepts such as enactment, naive thinking, bricolage, sensemaking, organizational learning, and loose coupling. His other books include *Sensemaking in Organizations* and *The Social Psychology of Organizing;* the latter book was designated by *Inc.* magazine as one of the nine best business books ever written. He is the recipient of the Academy of Management's lifetime achievement award for Distinguished Scholarly Contributions. Sutcliffe received her Ph.D. from the University of Texas at Austin and has researched and published extensively on organizational performance, functionally diverse teams, and cognitive and experiential diversity.

Corporate downsizing, sometimes euphemistically referred to as "right-sizing" has cost tens of thousands of employees their jobs in the past decade while organizations sought to reduce their costs, redirect their resources, and improve their stock price. Wayne Cascio, in *Responsible Restructuring,* reports on the results of an eighteen-year study of major firms that destroys many common myths about downsizing's presumably positive effects. By contrast, Cascio found that downsizing has a negative impact on not only the morale and commitment of the survivors, but also on key indicators of productivity, profits, and quality. He presents an alternative to layoffs—a step-by-step blueprint that revolves around treating employees as assets to be developed, and demonstrates how responsible restructuring has worked effectively at Compaq, Cisco, Motorola, and Southwest Airlines.

Wayne Cascio is a professor of management at the University of Colorado–Denver, and also instructs in the Rotterdam School of Management. Cascio is a past chair of the Human Resources division of the Academy of Management and past president of the Society for Industrial and Organizational Psychology. A consultant and writer, he is the author of numerous other books, including *Applied Psychology in Human Resource Management, The Cost Factor, Costing Human Resources,* and *Managing Human Resources.*

# Peak Performance: Aligning the Hearts and Minds of Your Employees


***JON R. KATZENBACH***

***Summary prepared by Penny Dieryck***



***Lt. Col. Penny Dieryck*** *is Logistics Squadron Commander, 148th Fighter Wing, Duluth, Minnesota. She is responsible for the transportation, supply, fuels management, and contracting divisions for the base. She is an adjunct faculty member at the University of Minnesota Duluth, College of St. Scholastica, and Concordia University-St. Paul. Lieutenant Colonel Dieryck obtained her Masters of Business Administration and Bachelor of Science degrees from the University of Minnesota Duluth. She also attended the U.S. Air Force Air Command and Staff College, where she completed studies in Air Force tactics, national policy and strategy, and Armed Forces functions and capabilities.*


*Peak Performance* is a new way of looking into an organization and finding the key methods and ideas surrounding their exceptional success in an ever-changing, chaotic world. The main thrust of this research was to identify why various thriving corporations continued to hold a sustained superior advantage over their competitors. Through this process, it was found that these successful organizations had workforces comprised of outstanding systems that give these people the incentive to "go the extra mile" for their customers and companies. Thus the central conclusion of the research was that energized workforces deliver higher performance, where emotions take over

---

Jon R. Katzenbach, *Peak Performance: Aligning the Hearts and Minds of Your Employees.* Boston: Harvard Business School, 2000.

and the employees "get fired up." This energy, in turn, creates sustained competitive advantage for their employers.

Not surprisingly, the key to the additional emotional commitment at the front lines was found in maintaining a balance between enterprise performance and employee fulfillment. The organizations that have been successful in sustaining emotional commitment within critical segments of their workforce did so in various ways. There are also important commonalities among these enterprises: All believe strongly in the value of the individual worker, all strike the balance between fulfillment and performance, and all make clear choices and cultivate sets of disciplined behaviors. However, beyond those broad levels of abstraction, the options are many.

In order to find the keys surrounding these highly successful organizations, three major steps were followed. First, the performances of the workforces in the selected corporations were tracked over time to ensure that the performance of the employees was not a brief glimmer, but an integral part of the equation. Second, a series of in-depth interviews with executives and managers in each of the companies explored in this study was utilized to ascertain if and why they believed that their workforce was at the core of the enterprise's performance. Third, as much evidence as possible was obtained to confirm management's judgment about their workforces, and the workforces' value to the continued success of their corporations. Ultimately, the most noticeable and compelling uniqueness of these workers was their enthusiasm, energy, and emotional commitment to perform—a factor that could not be quantified.

Not surprisingly, when each institution was assessed, it was determined that its success lay within its own set of distinctive approaches, mechanisms, and tools—some exclusive and some common amongst all the high-performing organizations. The most compelling common traits, however, were in the philosophical beliefs and practices shared by leaders at all levels within these enterprises. These were:

- Strong belief in each employee, mainly the frontline employee.
- Attempts to engage their employees on an emotional as well as rational level. This emotional energy carries across the organization and has a multiplier effect on the collective performance of the entire organization.
- Tracking organizational performance and worker fulfillment with equal rigor; one is not traded off for the other.

Energizing people for performance elevates the game significantly, to the point that many employees go well beyond leaders' expectations, individual accountabilities, financial results, and short-term market objectives. The key is in finding how to unleash the full individual and collective potential of people to achieve and sustain higher levels of performance than the workers themselves thought possible, management or customers expected, and competitors can realistically achieve.

Five paths explain all the higher-performing workforce situations that were explored in depth. They are called "balanced paths" to demonstrate the importance of sustaining a dynamic balance between enterprise accomplishments and worker fulfillment. There may be redundancies in the paths, but the primary focus and value proposition of each is quite distinct. Five classifications convey the combination of energy sources and alignment approaches for highly successful organizations studied.

- Mission, Values, and Pride
- Process and Metrics
- Entrepreneurial Spirit
- Individual Achievement
- Recognition and Celebration

As the exploration into these paths was continued, the patterns of behavior for sourcing the emotional energy and channeling it into peak performance kept floating to the top. Thus, these five balanced paths became the frameworks to provide guidance to leaders to assist them with options of how to shape their own configuration or path. Whatever path a company or leader with a peak-performance workforce takes, they enjoy the common feature of a dynamic balance between worker fulfillment and company performance over time.

## THE BALANCED PATH CONCEPT

The decision to find a balance between an organization's performance and worker fulfillment is fundamental to each of the five identified paths. Every company may use different managerial methods to find this balance, but these paths or cultures lead the employees to become emotionally charged. These methods, in turn, produce higher performance than their competitors. The five defined courses emphasize the vital essence of finding the point where worker fulfillment and enterprise performance are equal.

### MISSION, VALUES, AND PRIDE PATH

Employees of the specified workforce take great pride in the aspirations, accomplishments, and reputation of the enterprise. They also take pride in the achievements of their immediate work groups and in the specific contribution they make to those groups. Often the history and heritage of the company have become powerful sources of pride and emotional energy.

### PROCESS AND METRICS PATH

The enterprise has a clearly defined set of performance measures that translate readily into individual goals. These goals emphasize specific outcomes, rather than activities that may or may not lead to outcomes. These routes provide for worker fulfillment as well as performance effectiveness. Finally, the workers play a key role in the processes and metrics that affect them.

### ENTREPRENEURIAL SPIRIT PATH

This type of organization blazes a trail characterized by high-risk, high-reward situations plus the opportunity to share significantly in the ownership of whatever the enterprise is becoming. Employees typically are energized by a dynamic, growing marketplace, high individual earnings potential, and a unique opportunity to "build something with their own minds and hands."

### INDIVIDUAL ACHIEVEMENT PATH

Members in the workforce perceive great opportunity to excel and develop as individuals. The primary force of the organization is that of tracking and rewarding individual performance, and ensuring that high achievers have ample advancement or job enrichment opportunities.

### RECOGNITION AND CELEBRATION PATH

Members of this path are constantly being recognized for all their achievements in meaningful and conspicuous ways. The nonmonetary aspects of this effort are much more important than the formal compensation program. Foremost to this path is a unique leadership philosophy, which starts at the very top of the organization and cascades to the front-line employees. Critical to this process is the fact that the celebrations must become an integral part of the management process.

## ◆ EXAMPLES OF THE BALANCED PATHWAYS

While developing the research and striving to find examples of these balanced pathways, numerous organizations, corporations, and enterprises were studied. At the heart of the institutions were the several methods utilized to get the additional emotional commitment and mileage out of their employees. Examples include:

- **Mission, Vision and Pride Path:** U.S. Marine Corps; 3M Corporation
- **Process and Metrics Path:** Avon; Hill's Pet Nutrition
- **Entrepreneurial Spirit Path:** Hambrecht & Quist; BMC Software
- **Individual Achievement Path:** The Home Depot; McKinsey & Company
- **Recognition and Celebration Path:** KFC (Kentucky Fried Chicken); Marriott Corporation

## ◆ IMPLEMENTING THE LESSONS LEARNED

Not every company or enterprise would choose to utilize one, parts, or all of these paths to sustain a competitive advantage in their marketplace. They can continue to build their profit margins through consequence management and old-fashioned bureaucratic methods. The true test is to look deeply at the core of an organization. Look at its leadership, culture, and surrounding business conditions and determine if the use of one of the balanced paths will work for the enterprise. Before implementing parts or combinations of these paths, the leadership of the organization should remember that the key to these paths is finding the pivotal balance between organization performance and worker fulfillment, and then having the discipline to stay the course and channel the energy into performance consistently over time.

To strive toward this balance of high efficiency and performance between company and employee commitment, one dynamic is noted: the energy these highly charged organizations exude. The work environment is positive, activity levels are intense, interpersonal relations are not constrained, and authority lines or formal positions are less evident. The employees play hard and work hard; they have fun while getting the job done.

Most of this energy comes from three sources: (1) charismatic leaders with impossible ideas, (2) unpredictable, vibrant marketplaces, or (3) remarkable legacies. In order to align this energy within a workplace, leaders must strategically figure out how to tap or build this energy into their organization. This may be done by:

- Building personal self-image and self-confidence of the employees.
- Sustaining consistency and focus on performance across the organization.
- Personally challenging the employees by offering more opportunities and developing their capabilities.

Finally, in striving to make organizations peak-performers, successful enterprises have found that in the equation between worker fulfillment and company performance the balance is held through enforcing disciplined behavior. This behavior is a combination of self-, peer-, and institution-enforced controls, which entail a clear set of rules.

## APPLYING THE *PEAK PERFORMANCE* LESSONS LEARNED

As the balanced paths were developed, successful organizations were studied, and factors surrounding peak-performing enterprises were identified. The question posed to all companies is, "Will this approach work for us?" To ponder and answer these questions, the corporation's leaders must determine:

- Is the *Peak Performance* workforce needed for our company?
- What are the costs and benefit factors identified for our future, and are they strong enough for us to build this type of workforce?
- Will these costs be worth the benefit to other stakeholders?

If the organization wishes to build a highly motivated, highly effective workforce, then its next move is to make the critical choices to make this vision a reality. These changes will demand more from the organization's leaders, higher standards for all employees to follow, and commitment by the company to climb the emotional peak of performance.

READING 2

# The Tipping Point

## MALCOLM GLADWELL

What do the spread of syphilis, the sudden resurgence of Hush Puppies, and the surprise popularity of the book *Divine Secrets of the Ya-Ya Sisterhood* have in common? Quite a lot, says Malcolm Gladwell, author of the lively best seller *The Tipping Point: How Little Things Can Make a Big Difference* (Little, Brown and Company, 2000).

Gladwell, a writer for *The New Yorker,* has combined a broad knowledge of social phenomena with modern theories of epidemiology to posit a theory of how social change really works. The result is a book that could alter how we think about fads—be they unexplained run-ups in dot-com stock prices or sudden fashion quirks. Why, for instance, did adolescents—and some adults who should know better—begin wearing baseball caps backward a few years ago?

Past explanations of faddish behavior have tended to focus on human irrationality (the tulip bulb mania in the 17th century; the craze over Harry Potter books today). But Gladwell argues that many so-called fads are not really fads at all; rather they are manifestations of "the tipping point," a phrase he borrows from the rational language of medical science to describe the dramatic moment in an epidemic when something changes and a disease suddenly begins to spread like wildfire through a population. According to Gladwell, ideas, products, messages and behaviors spread just as viruses do.

Case in point: Hush Puppies was a dying brand in 1994. Parent company Wolverine was about to pull the plug on the crepe-soled, brushed-suede shoe. But by autumn of 1995, Hush Puppies had become a national craze; sales had skyrocketed from fewer than 30,000 pairs the previous year to 430,000 pairs. The difference? A few young, hip, downtown New Yorkers thought the shoes were cute and funky, which, in turn, prompted a half a dozen hip and funky fashion designers to use them in shows. Suddenly Hush Puppies were the must-have footwear for the twenty-something crowd.

A freak phenomenon? Yes, but according to Gladwell, a comprehensible, predictable event—provided you understand what to look for. Hush Puppies' unexpected reprieve from the trash heap, along with the dozen or so other cases Gladwell examines in the book, exemplify three key characteristics shared by all fads: First, all are most accurately understood as the product of "contagious behavior." Ideas spread one to one, person to person—just as a disease spreads in a human population. Second,

---

From the October 2000 *Training* magazine article by Ron Zemke, "How Change Really Works," pp. 122–126. 

relatively small changes (the decision by a few well-positioned fashion designers) can have extraordinarily large effects. Finally, real change occurs in a hurry—not slowly and steadily.

"Of the three," Gladwell writes, "the third trait—the idea that epidemics can rise or fall in one dramatic moment—is the most important, because it is the principle that makes sense of the first two and permits the greatest insight into why modern change happens the way it does."

A world that follows the rules of epidemics is a very different world than the one we think we live in. We think of diseases such as influenza or the West Nile virus in contagion terms; we do not think of social change—crime waves, passing fancies, the preference of one software program over another—as the result of a contagious behavior. And yet, this is Gladwell's very point. "If there can be epidemics of crime or epidemics of fashion, there must be all kinds of things just as contagious as viruses."

By Gladwell's reckoning, the spread of an idea can be explained, if not predicted, according to the Three Rules of the Tipping Point: The Law of the Few, The Stickiness Factor, and The Power of Context. The Law of the Few says that a few people—the right people who are well-connected and influential in shaping others' opinions—can bring great focus to the previously obscure. Just as a 4-year-old with an incubating flu virus can shut down a day care center, the right person promoting the right idea at the right time can cause great change. "There are 'Typhoid Marys' for ideas just as there are for diseases."

The Stickiness Factor—the idea that there are specific ways of making a contagious message memorable—should be familiar to any trainer who has wrestled with the problem of putting enough Velcro on an idea that it sticks with the people who hear it. To illustrate stickiness, Gladwell uses one of the most successful learning efforts of the last 50 years—*Sesame Street.* Joan Gantz Cooney, *Sesame Street's* creator, borrowed from advertising, marketing and child psychology to find ways to make televised educational messages not only watchable and digestible, but memorable as well. The key to her success, says Gladwell, is that if you pay careful attention to the structure and format of your material (and if you are willing to test, revise and experiment with it), you can dramatically enhance its stickiness.

The final factor, The Power of Context, says that human beings are more sensitive to their environment than they appear to be. Though the least clear of Gladwell's arguments, it may be the most powerful for those in the organizational change business. When the New York Transit Authority wanted to decrease crime, one of its key strategies was to change the context. The agency worked not just on catching criminals but also on cleaning up subway cars and stations. The idea was to make the subway look and feel safe, to show criminals and law-abiding riders alike that someone cared and was watching. The net result: Between 1990 and 1994, the New York subway went from a place people shunned to an acceptable and convenient rapid transit system.

Gladwell makes no claim to having mastered the art of change or discovered all the rules. What he does hold, and what merits our consideration, is this summation: "Tipping Points are a reaffirmation of the potential for change and the power of intelligent action. Look at the world around you. It may seem like an immovable, implacable place. It is not. With the slightest push—in just the right place—it can be tipped."

READING 3

# Managing the Unexpected: Assuring High Performance in an Age of Complexity

***KARL E. WEICK***
***and KATHLEEN M. SUTCLIFFE***

***Summary prepared***
***by Christopher R. Steele***

***Christopher R. Steele*** *is a certified public accountant, certified internal auditor, and a 1980 graduate of the University of Minnesota Duluth. Steele's career has included roles on nuclear submarines, at Wells Fargo, Target Corporation, The Limited, and Best Buy. He retired from Best Buy, Inc., a $20 billion specialty retailer, in 2001 as Vice President—Financial Shared Services and Accounting Operations.*

A fundamental skill of high performance companies is their ability to deal effectively with unexpected challenges. In some organizations the unexpected is managed in ways that produce tragic outcomes, while in other organizations the unexpected is routinely managed successfully. There are several organizations that consistently operate under very dynamic conditions, commonly experience significant unexpected events, and yet reliably achieve their objectives. Examples of these *Highly Reliable Organizations* (HROs) include emergency rooms, hostage negotiation teams, nuclear power plants, aircraft carriers, and wilderness firefighting crews. Organizations such as these provide a template for those organizations that want to improve reliability.

---

Karl E. Weick and Kathleen M. Sutcliffe, *Managing the Unexpected: Assuring High Performance in an Age of Complexity.* San Francisco: Jossey-Bass, 2001.

## THE OBJECTIVE

Surprises are events or outcomes different from the expected that arise from an action or inaction by someone inside or outside the organization. Those skilled in dealing with the unexpected manage surprises mindfully. *Mindful management* of the unexpected requires rapid recognition of the warning signs, containment, resolve, resilience, and swift restoration of system functioning. Identifying and applying the processes used by HROs to improve the skills needed to mindfully manage the unexpected is a useful objective for organizations.

## FIVE KEY ATTRIBUTES

Highly reliable organizations have a culture and operating style that allow them to consistently and successfully manage the unexpected. This operating style provides a roadmap useful for all organizations and levels within organizations.

While the flight deck of an aircraft carrier (or hostage negotiating team) is an organization different from all others, like all businesses there are input processes, outputs, resource constraints, teams, *and* surprises. What differentiates the flight deck from many businesses is the cultural commitment to the five attributes of mindful management:

1. *Preoccupation with failure.* HROs treat lapses, small or large, as symptoms of a system failure, a failure with potentially significant consequences. HROs recognize that a number of small lapses could occur simultaneously with grave results. Consequently, HROs create a culture that encourages the reporting of errors and near misses, and they extract the lessons that can be learned from these events. They are also aware of the complacency and compromises that can accompany success and are wary of the arrogance that success may bring.
2. *Reluctance to simplify interpretations.* HROs manage their complex worlds through developing a deep and detailed view of an operation that allows for a nuanced understanding. They avoid simplifications and position themselves to see and understand as much as possible. Mindful managers create an open environment where diverse points of view are shared and reconciled.
3. *Sensitivity to operations.* Surprises frequently originate where system vulnerabilities have been present for some time without any apparent business disruption. Unexpected events are prevented when these vulnerabilities or deficiencies are identified and addressed prior to a disruption. HROs have high situational awareness and relational understandings that allow for continuous adjustments that stop small errors from cascading into big events. Sensitivity to operations requires a common language and shared goals across the organization.
4. *Commitment to resilience.* HROs are not "zero defects" organizations. While they may strive to be perfect, they are not. When mistakes occur, HROs are not disabled by those errors. Their resilience is the result of addressing problems when they are small, and developing "work-arounds" (alternative scenarios of actions)

to keep the system functioning. These two elements of resilience require deep knowledge of the system—people, process, technology and raw materials, experience, expertise, and training.

5. *Deference to expertise.* In an HRO, those with the most expertise make decisions at the front line. Top-down and decision-making authority, based on rank instead of expertise, result in high level errors that predictably exacerbate errors made at lower levels.

## UNMINDFUL MANAGEMENT OF THE UNEXPECTED

A few years ago the Union Pacific Railway merged with Southern Pacific, and optimism for improved operations at the new Southern Pacific ran high. The expertise of UP was expected to turn around the deteriorating SP. Instead, surprises, followed by disappointment, were just ahead.

Following the merger, the railroad proved to be a more dangerous place than an aircraft carrier. Soon thereafter the UP experienced six major collisions and the deaths of five employees and two trespassers. In addition to this carnage, the accidents resulted in regulatory attention. Federal regulators began riding trains and found untrained employees, poor maintenance, and crews on duty working more hours than allowed by law.

Problems were not confined to compliance issues. Railroad customers found service levels deteriorating in the form of delayed deliveries, lost shipments, and untraceable shipments. The average speed of trains dropped from 19 to 12 MPH, equivalent to a loss of 1,800 locomotives or one-fourth of the fleet capacity. Gridlock from the Gulf Coast to Chicago existed and 550 trains could not move because of a lack of locomotives or crews.

### THE UNION PACIFIC CULTURE

Union Pacific was a company focused on success, with management isolated from bad news. Slowdowns were underreported until problems were nearly irreversible. Management ranks were filled with like-minded railroaders. The homogeneity of management allowed executives to misinterpret or be blind to the early warning signs. Management defined sensitivity to operations as balance sheet improvement and cost controls. The bottom of the organization was sensitive to a railroad system grinding to a halt. The by-the-books culture at UP viewed workarounds and improvisation as insubordination. Consequently, when trains began backing up, no new actions were taken and the problems worsened. With top-down decisions made far from the yard that was at the center of the system meltdown, a deep, nuanced understanding of the problem was not possible.

Hubris and the disconnect between the Union Pacific growth strategy and its operational capabilities prevented the company from recognizing warning signs and taking early preventative measures. As problems cascaded, the rhetoric of competence and arrogance of isolated leaders proved unhelpful.

## ◆ MINDFUL MANAGEMENT ON AN AIRCRAFT CARRIER'S FLIGHT DECK

An aircraft carrier's numbers are staggering:

- Six thousand people jammed into a ninety-thousand-ton ship that is filled with nuclear weapons and jet fuel and powered by a nuclear reactor. The 1,100 foot long ship operates in an unforgiving environment of fog, heavy seas and hostile "competitors."
- Sixty-five thousand-pound planes land in "controlled crashes" on a pitching, heaving deck that is blanketed in salt water and jet fuel. Landings at night are accomplished without the benefit of lights.
- Two-million horsepower steam-powered catapults allow jets to reach 150 miles per hour in three seconds. These catapults simultaneously launch jets from the bow as other approaching planes hook arresting wires and land on the stern.

The carrier's output is a plane in the air and the subsequent safe return of the plane and its crew. Jets become airborne (and land) through people, process and technology. Businesses have the same types of inputs to transform the materials that arrive at the dock door into sales and earnings.

The attributes in short supply at Union Pacific are deeply embedded in a carrier's culture. The crew understands that success cannot be banked. From this understanding comes a *preoccupation with failure.* Landings are graded, near misses are debriefed, incidences are reported, and small problems are viewed in the context of underlying issues such as communications breakdowns.

Flight crews assume nothing and are *reluctant to simplify.* Responsibilities are clear. Communication, confirmation and verification are via voice, hand and visual cues. The *sensitivity to operations* is evidenced by the continuous communications loops and the exchange of information about flight deck operations. The constant flow of communications exists to ensure that the unexpected is noticed and addressed before it becomes an incident. The opening credits sequence in the movie *Top Gun* provides a visual example of teamwork and the continuous flow of information in an HRO.

Deep, hands-on knowledge of the carrier's equipment, technologies, crew and its capabilities enables the ship to react and improvise as necessary. The ability to creatively solve problems brings *resilience.* Finally, despite a clear chain of command and the hierarchical nature of military operations, lower level staff can override superiors when conditions and circumstances dictate. This *deference to expertise* is necessary because systems operating in a dynamic environment must be refined as conditions warrant and expectations evolve.

## ◆ BARRIERS TO MINDFULNESS

Mindful organizations are adept at both recognizing and containing the unexpected. Preoccupation with failure, reluctance to simplify, and sensitivity to operations lead to recognition while resilience and deference to expertise allow for containment.

The liabilities of success are understood by HROs. To counter the pull of pride and resulting astigmatism that accompanies success, HROs are obsessed with failure and incident reviews. Incident reviews in HROs are both frequent and timely to prevent the rewriting of history to save face and protect images.

Non-HRO organizations see close calls as evidence of skill and success. In contrast, HROs see close calls as failures from which learnings can be extracted. Post mortems are most successful when diverse perspectives and information not held in common are allowed to surface.

When the unexpected arises, containment in its early stages is required. Coping skills, capacity, capabilities, flexibility, and an ability to act while thinking are enablers to rapid containment. A non-hierarchical leadership style that shifts decision-making to the area or individual who currently has the expertise and answer is essential.

The planning process creates a barrier to both recognition and containment. Plans are developed in an environmental context and they expect the future to unfold in a predictable, systematic manner. While operating within the plan, there is no place for events not contemplated by the plan. The plan and its assumptions cause people to limit what they see and how they interpret the things occurring in their midst. The tendency is to interpret anomalies in the context of the plan and not as something requiring attention and containment.

Furthermore, plans focus capabilities in a particular direction and are unaware of how capabilities can be reconfigured to address the unexpected. Finally, plans assume that repeatable processes will yield predictable results. Dealing with a surprise requires the ability to sense something novel and then act contrary to the plan. Sizable investments in plans reduce both sensing and innovation capabilities of individuals and organizations.

## ◆ THE PATH FORWARD

A widely administered audit to assess organization mindfulness and mindfulness tendencies should be conducted across organizational boundaries, hierarchies, and specialties. If material improvement is needed, a culture and management style change is necessary.

Culture—what people think, feel and do—is a byproduct of management's beliefs, values and actions. It reflects their communications, perceived values and philosophy, the reward system, and employee beliefs and attitudes.[1] HROs have a culture of mindfulness coupled with institutional practices. Cultural properties that influence mindfulness include safe practices, being informed, reporting systems, just practices, flexibility, and the valuation of continued learning.

[1]Edgar Schein said that culture has six properties: "(1) shared basic assumptions that are (2) invented, discovered or developed by a given group as it (3) learns to cope with its problem of external adaptation and internal integration in ways that (4) have worked well enough to be considered valid, and, therefore, (5) can be taught to new members of the group as the (6) correct way to perceive, think and feel in relation to those problems."

Inattention to safe practices can lead to errors with unexpected consequences. Safety requires learning from small errors to prevent larger ones from occurring. If errors cannot be reported without fear of adverse consequences, mistakes will not see the light of day. Mistakes must be dealt with in a consistently just manner. Disciplinary action is appropriate for a few "across the line" errors, while most mistakes fall on the other side of the line. If disciplinary action is inconsistent or unjust, self-reporting of errors is unlikely. Flexible authority structures and non-hierarchical decision-making permits information to flow freely to where the expertise resides. Openness, truth, and the reconciliation of divergent interpretations shared freely across boundaries increases the collective knowledge of the enterprise, and this knowledge can be leveraged with effective management to deal mindfully with the unexpected.

Effective managers in a mindful organization:

- Allocate resources to both production and protection,
- State not only goals to be accomplished but also errors that cannot occur,
- Create an error-friendly learning atmosphere,
- Are humble, and aware of their vulnerabilities,
- Promote healthy debates by those with diverse views,
- Break down hierarchies and divisional barriers,
- Push decision-making to where the expertise resides. The deep knowledge of experts is a byproduct of a commitment to training, job rotation, feedback loops, and debriefing that accompanies the routine reporting of errors and organizational capacity.

## Conclusion

Plans, mental models, management styles, and company culture create blind spots that allow rich opportunities for learning to pass by undetected. When these opportunities go unnoticed, the chance to make small corrections to prevent a subsequent large surprise also passes. *The skills and culture of non-traditional organizations (HROs) that routinely manage the unexpected successfully are transportable to more traditional entities.* If these organizations wish to improve reliability and join the ranks of high performance companies, they have an exciting opportunity to do so through mindful management.

READING 4

# Responsible Restructuring: Creative and Profitable Alternatives to Layoffs

***WAYNE F. CASCIO***

***Summary prepared by Stephen A. Rubenfeld***

***Stephen A. Rubenfeld** is Professor of Human Resource Management at the Labovitz School of Business and Economics at the University of Minnesota Duluth. He received his doctorate from the University of Wisconsin–Madison, and was previously on the faculty of Texas Tech University. His professional publications and presentations have covered a wide range of human resource and labor relations topics, including job search behaviors, human resource policies and practices, job security, and staffing challenges. He has served as a consultant to private and public organizations, and is a member of the Society for Human Resource Management, the Academy of Management, and the Industrial Relations Research Association.*

A highly competitive business context carries with it both boundless opportunities and daunting challenges. On one hand, organizations are stimulated to become better at what they do by economizing, innovating, and honing their competitive advantage. But at the same time, the very existence of a business can be threatened by pricing pressures, declining profit margins, and burgeoning capital investment needs. This is not a situation that calls for "just getting by," mediocrity, or hoping that things will work themselves out. Intense competition is a call to action which tests the mettle

---

Wayne F. Cascio, *Responsible Restructuring: Creative and Profitable Alternatives to Layoffs.* San Francisco: Berrett-Koehler, 2003.

of organizations and their leaders. It is a situation that demands thoughtful and aggressive actions. The pressures attributable to the global marketplace, pervasive technology, and more assertive consumers are not going to abate. Decisive steps are necessary to assure that the critical elements of competitive success—price, quality, and customer service—are in place and fine tuned to support continued organizational vitality.

The active pursuit of efficiencies, effective operations, and customer responsiveness are all subjects of much organizational rhetoric, but in practice it is the cost containment part of the equation that gets most of the attention. In fact, it is easier, faster, and more predictable to cut costs than it is to increase revenues or to fundamentally improve the organization's product or service. Whether driven by a current financial crisis or the desire to avoid future problems, actions directed at cutting or controlling costs, rooting out inefficiencies, and keeping prices in check have become almost universal. Unlike earlier times, this self-imposed pressure to focus on cost containment is not limited to organizations swimming in red ink; it has become a benchmark of good business practice.

Because employment costs are the most visible and frequently an organization's largest variable cost, downsizing along with wage and benefit containment are at the heart of most efforts to enhance competitiveness. Often characterized euphemistically as organizational restructuring, the logic of these efforts to control expenses by having fewer employees is compelling: Reducing costs will increase profit margins which will produce immediate bottom-line results and help assure future success. But the promised benefits of cost containment through reducing headcount often are elusive. Whether couched in the verbiage of *downsizing, rightsizing,* or other emotionless synonyms for reducing the number of employees, the benefits tend to be fleeting. By themselves these methods rarely offer a sustainable solution to the barriers to competitiveness. Likewise, wage freezes and benefits cuts may have an immediate and visible bottom line impact, but the true savings are often reduced by diminished productivity along with undesired turnover or other employee withdrawal behaviors.

The net effect is that *restructuring that is built primarily on downsizing or containment of compensation costs will not have a positive effect on the areas where real competitiveness is built: innovation, quality, and customer service.* In the end, this approach to restructuring does not achieve the forecasted cost savings and does not help to improve long-term competitive vitality of the organization. If downsizing is not the solution, how can an organization succeed in a competitive marketplace?

## ◆ IS RESTRUCTURING BAD?

Restructuring can be constructive and even essential when a company is struggling to regain or achieve economic success. Similarly, evolving technologies, non-performing assets, or even aggressive moves by competitors can be a powerful impetus to restructure. It is obvious that job losses, layoffs, and sometimes radical changes to the jobs that remain are integral to most restructurings, but as is often the case, the devil is in the details. The issue is *how* these employment changes are made. Experience carries with it the lesson that across-the-board layoffs and hiring freezes, or similar *slash and burn* downsizing strategies, rarely achieve the promised benefits. The hidden costs and secondary impacts may even worsen the competitive crisis.

Many of the costs of downsizing are obvious and calculable. The decision to restructure typically carries with it a recognition that costs associated with severance pay, accrued vacations, benefit costs, outplacement, and additional administrative expense will be incurred. In contrast, there are many indirect costs that may be ignored or not even recognized. Even where acknowledged as potential problem areas, their severity is often underestimated. Although it may be difficult to accurately estimate their future costs and impacts, these costs are real and can have a dramatic negative impact on competitiveness. Examples of such hidden costs include:

- Reduced morale
- Risk-averse behaviors by surviving employees
- Loss of trust
- Costs of retraining continuing employees
- Legal challenges
- Reduced productivity
- Loss of institutional competencies and memory
- Survivor burnout

While these problems and costs may impede competitiveness efforts, restructuring is not inherently bad. Many businesses have successfully downsized and restructured to improve their productivity and financial success, but downsizing is not a panacea. Research conducted over the past 25 years indicates that *downsizing strategies for most organizations do not result in long-term payoffs that are significantly greater than those where there are stable employment patterns.*

## ◆ MYTHS ABOUT DOWNSIZING

When confronted by the need to reduce costs, many employers (who self-righteously proclaim that "employees are our greatest asset") turn to layoffs first when responding to a competitive dilemma. This may be fueled by a number of myths and misunderstandings about downsizing. For example, the following six myths are refuted by research and experience (facts):

*Myth 1:* Downsizing increases profits.
*Fact 1:* Profitability does not necessarily improve.

*Myth 2:* Downsizing boosts productivity.
*Fact 2:* Productivity results are mixed.

*Myth 3:* Downsizing doesn't negatively affect quality.
*Fact 3:* Quality does not improve and may go down.

*Myth 4:* Downsizing is a one-time event.
*Fact 4:* The best predictor of future downsizing is past downsizing.

*Myth 5:* Downsizing has few effects on remaining employees.
*Fact 5:* Negative impacts on morale, stress, and commitment are common.

*Myth 6:* Downsizing is unlikely to lead to sabotage or other vengeful acts.
*Fact 6:* Such behaviors are not rare and their consequences can be severe.

These findings should offer decision-makers a note of caution about the potential consequences of restructuring efforts painted with a broad brush. An obvious conclusion is that restructuring should not be done blindly, and when restructuring does appear to be necessary, it should be approached strategically and responsibly.

## ◆ RESPONSIBLE RESTRUCTURING

The approaches that employers take toward restructuring reflect significant differences in how they view their employees. Organizational decision-makers can be thought of as falling into two camps concerning their view of employees—those that see employees as *costs to be cut,* and those that see employees as *assets to be developed.* The *cost cutters* consider employees to be the source of the problem. They think of employees as commodities. Through the lens of the balance sheet, they strive to achieve the minimum number of employees and the lowest possible labor expenditures needed to run the business successfully. In contrast, the *responsible restructurers* view employee expertise and contributions as central to any solution. They consider their employees as essential in fashioning and carrying forward sustainable answers to competitiveness challenges. The initial focus of the responsible restructurers is not on reducing headcount or shrinking the budget, but rather on enhancing effectiveness and empowering employees to overcome competitive challenges.

Responsible restructurers turn to broad-based layoffs and compensation cuts only as a last resort. Their initial and primary approach is to use a variety of developmental and effectiveness-oriented practices to achieve and maintain competitive viability. These organizations are likely to:

- Flatten their hierarchical structures.
- Create an empowered, team-oriented work environment.
- Seek labor-management partnerships.
- Share information.
- Make extensive use of training.
- Demonstrate a culture of continuous learning.
- Link compensation to performance and skills.

These employers do not advocate and use these responsible restructuring strategies primarily as acts of compassion or for other altruistic reasons. They truly believe that there are benefits that come from employment stability and that the best and most sustainable outcomes are achieved when employees are part of the solution.

These companies, which include in their ranks Southwest Airlines, SAS Institute, Cisco, Charles Schwab, Procter & Gamble, and 3M, share the following critical characteristics:

1. A clear vision of what they want to achieve and how to communicate this vision to stakeholders,
2. The ability to execute and develop employee-centered initiatives, and
3. Highly empowered employees who are committed to help the organization succeed.

These companies don't start with the premise that the minimal number of employees is the best number of employees. Rather, they ask how their employees can help them fashion a solution and meet the market challenge. They know that short-term downsizing does not solve long-term problems.

## HOW DO WE MOVE FORWARD?

In addition to the basic elements of responsible restructuring already described, it is useful to keep these recommendations in mind as issues of competitiveness are confronted:

- Deal with the underlying competitive problem, not just the bottom line.
- Integrate staffing decisions with the strategic business plan and the drivers of success.
- Involve employees in shaping broad solutions as well as specific organizational responses.
- Consider the payoffs from employment stability.
- Communicate regularly, openly, effectively, and honestly.
- If layoffs are necessary, be logical, targeted, fair, and consistent.
- Give survivors a reason to stay and prospective employees a reason to join the organization.
- Empower survivors to succeed and encourage them to beware of burnout.

## Conclusion

The ultimate payoff from successfully pursuing *responsible restructuring* rather than budget slashing in responding to competitive challenges is better and longer lasting solutions. The organization also is more likely to reap the rewards of higher customer satisfaction, have the ability to respond more quickly and more successfully to future challenges, maintain a recruiting and retention advantage over its labor market competitors, and have committed employees who are not unduly risk averse. Remove the barriers to effective competition and financial success will follow.

PART

# IV Organizational Strategy, Execution, and Governance

Many of the authors in this book suggest that organizations can benefit by defining their own standard of effectiveness, especially after examining other successful firms. An organization's external environment has a powerful influence on organizational success and needs to be monitored for significant trends and influential forces. In addition, effective executives need to recognize when internal changes are necessary to adapt to the external environment.

The four readings in this section are designed to stimulate thinking about management through a focus on the management and leadership of the organization from its very top. Taken collectively, these readings suggest that organizations can (and should) proactively *take control of their destinies.* One way of doing this is by articulating an engaging vision that can systematically guide them into the future. In effect, managers are urged to have a master plan that defines their mission, identifies their unique environmental niche, builds on their strengths, and adapts to changing needs. This overall vision is then converted into operational goals by applying several very specific management practices.

In their book *The Strategy-Focused Organization: How Balanced Scorecard Companies Thrive in the New Business Environment,* Robert S. Kaplan and David P. Norton focus their attention on performance measurement. Based upon their observations, many of today's organizations continue to function with management systems and tactics that were designed for yesterday's organization. They contend that too many organizations fail to execute strategy successfully. Addressing this issue, the authors identify five key factors that are required for building a "strategy-focused organization."

Robert S. Kaplan is the Marvin Bower Professor of Leadership at the Harvard Business School. His co-author, David P. Norton, is president of Balanced Scorecard Collaborative, Inc.

*Execution: The Discipline of Getting Things Done* by Larry Bossidy and Ram Charan, with Charles Burck, is the second reading in this section of *The Manager's*

*Bookshelf.* Through numerous examples of success and failures the authors provide two themes. The first deals with "execution"—the process of moving from vision formulation to implementation. Secondly, the authors go to great length to provide insight into the mechanisms associated with making execution an organizational building block. In too many instances top management fails either because it tends to micro-manage new organizational initiatives or because they remain aloof and too far removed. Bossidy, Charan with Burck argue that it is important to find the right balance between over- and under-involvement. To this end they highlight several essential leadership characteristics.

Larry Bossidy is the chairman and former CEO of Honeywell International. He had a long managerial career serving as vice chairman and COO at General Electric Capital, which was followed by several years as CEO of Allied Signal assisting with their merger with Honeywell International. Ram Charan has taught at the Harvard School of Business and the Kellogg School at Northwestern University. He has also served as an advisor to CEOs and executive managers for over three decades.

William Joyce (professor of strategy and organization theory at Dartmouth's Amos Tuck School of Business), Nitin Nohria (business administration professor at the Harvard Business School), and Bruce Roberson (a partner with McKinsey & Company) combined to write *What (Really) Works: The 4 + 2 Formula for Sustained Business Success.* A question driving this book asks—Why do some organizations consistently outperform their competitors? What do their managers know and do?

To answer these two questions the authors analyzed data from the Evergreen Project, a major field study analyzing more than ten years of data from 160 companies and more than 200 different management practices. In *What (Really) Works* the authors report their discovery of six (4 + 2) specific management practices engaged in by all of the successful companies.

The final reading in this section on "Organizational Strategy, Execution, and Governance" is a summary of Jay A. Conger, Edward E. Lawler, III, and David L. Finegold's book *Corporate Boards: Strategies for Adding Value at the Top.* Building from their work at the University of Southern California's Center for Effective Organizations, the authors provide a review of corporate boards and their governance structures past and present. Conger, Lawler, and Finegold provide insight into areas where board performance has fallen victim to the inherent conflict that lies between the role of working with top management to form a strategic direction for the firm, while attempting to exercise independent insight over the same top management team. As the authors look to the future and more successful board performance, they highlight the advantages of a stakeholder as opposed to a stockholder model of governance.

Jay Conger is a world expert in the area of leadership development and organizational change. He is also Professor of Organizational Behavior in the London Business School and a senior researcher at the Center for Effective of Organizations at the University of Southern California, where he works with Edward E. Lawler, III and David L. Finegold. A couple of years ago, *Business Week* magazine identified Dr. Lawler as one of the most distinguished management gurus of the past century as a result of his work to advance both the understanding and management of organizations.

# The Strategy-Focused Organization

**_ROBERT S. KAPLAN and DAVID P. NORTON_**
**_Summary prepared by Sanjay Goel_**

***Sanjay Goel** (Ph.D., Arizona State University) is an Assistant Professor of Management at the University of Minnesota Duluth. His research and teaching interests are primarily in the areas of strategic management, management of innovation and technology, and corporate governance. As a management consultant in the agribusiness sector, he was involved in new project appraisals and project monitoring.*

No matter how thoughtful, creative, and detailed an organization's strategy is, it is worth nothing if it is not executed. Strategy execution has proven to be the Achilles' heel of most organizations. In fact, a 1999 *Fortune* story based on prominent CEO failures concluded that it is poor strategy execution, not strategy itself, that is the real problem behind corporate failure. The task of creating an organization that is focused on strategy execution is indeed critical to unleashing the real value trapped in an organization's strategy. Unfortunately, organizations seem to be slipping farther behind in linking strategy formulation and strategy execution. This has been due to a shift in real value within organizations from tangible to intangible assets, a shift in strategies from efficiency to knowledge-based, and a shift in decision focus from centralized to decentralized. Due to these developments, the metrics, controls, and structures used to measure strategy execution have become outdated and out of sync with the actual needs of organizations to monitor strategy execution. Five principles define a strategy-focused organization, which tighten the link between an organization's strategy and its execution.

## ◆ THE PRINCIPLES

**Principle 1.** *Translate the strategy to operational terms.* This is the first step to enabling strategy execution, the premise being that unless a strategy can be elaborated in operational metrics, it does not communicate actionable steps to the rest of the organiza-

---

Robert S. Kaplan and David P. Norton. *The Strategy-Focused Organization: How Balanced Scorecard Companies Thrive in the New Business Environment.* Cambridge, MA: Harvard Business School Press, 2001.

tion. Strategy-focused organizations translate the strategy to operational terms by developing a *strategy map,* which then serves as a framework for building *balanced scorecards* for the organization.

*Strategy maps:* A strategy map is a logical relationship diagram that defines a strategy by specifying the relationship among shareholders, customers, business processes, and an organization's competencies. The relationships establish cause-and-effect links between activities. These explicit linkages can then be communicated and incorporated in developing a balanced scorecard for the organization.

*Balanced scorecard:* A balanced scorecard provides measurement and control metrics for an organization's strategy map along four key dimensions: financial, customer, internal business process, and learning and growth perspective. Thus it highlights not just the financial and nonfinancial outcomes of an organization's strategy, but also the lead indicators and processes that would need to be monitored to achieve the desired outcomes. In this manner, it provides a framework to describe and communicate strategy in a consistent way throughout the organization. Most importantly, it establishes accountability throughout the organization for strategy execution.

**Principle 2.** *Align the organization to the strategy.* Strategy cannot be implemented if organizations do not change to accommodate the needs of the planned strategy. Balanced scorecards in a strategy-focused organization are used to align the organization with its strategy in two ways: by creating business unit synergy, and by creating synergy across shared services.

*Creating business unit synergy:* This involves clarifying the value created by common ownership of multiple businesses under a single corporation. Value could be created by any one of the four perspectives of the balanced scorecard. For instance, optimizing capital allocation could create financial synergies by increasing shareholder value. In addition, promoting cross selling could create customer synergies by increasing the share of the customer's total account.

*Creating synergies through shared services:* Synergies can be created by aligning an organization's internal units that provide shared services. These support services frequently become bureaucratic and unresponsive to the demands of strategy execution of operating divisions. These shared services can be aligned to the strategic needs of operating divisions by adopting either of the following two models:

- **The strategic partner model—**In this approach the shared service unit is a partner in the development of, and adherence to, the balanced scorecard of the operating business unit.
- **The business-in-a-business model—**In this approach, the shared service unit must view itself as a business, and the operating business units as its customers. A shared service scorecard serves as a written, explicit definition of this relationship.

**Principle 3.** *Make strategy everyone's day job.* This principle has roots in the simple fact that strategy cannot be implemented by the CEO and senior leadership of an organization. Everyone in the organization must be involved in strategy execution by developing specific activities within their own sphere of influence. Strategy-focused organizations use the balanced scorecard in three ways to align their employees to the strategy:

- **Communicating and educating.** Strategy needs to be communicated to the entire organization in a holistic manner, so that everybody understands it and is able to implement it.
- **Developing personal and team objectives.** Managers must help employees set individual and team goals that are consistent with strategic outcomes. This helps establish personal accountability, and provides metrics to self-evaluate progress.
- **Establishing an incentive and reward system.** This develops a stake among the employees in the organization's success and failure, closing the loop on accountability and organizational performance.

**Principle 4.** *Making strategy a continual process.* Strategy-focused organizations use a "double-loop" process that integrates the management of budgets and operations with the management of strategy. The balanced scorecard is used as a link between the two "loops." Three specific remedies are used to link the operations review cycle with the strategy review cycle.

- **Linking strategy and budgeting.** Stretch targets and strategic initiatives on the balanced scorecard link the conceptual part of strategy with the rigor and precision of budgets. Rolling forecasts are substituted for fixed budgets.
- **Closing the strategy loop.** Strategic feedback systems linked to the balanced scorecard provide a new framework for reporting and a new metric for monitoring strategy execution, one focused on strategy instead of operations.
- **Testing, learning, and adapting.** Using the balanced scorecard, managers can test the cause-and-effect relationships underlying an organization's strategy. These relationships can be modified to incorporate learning from experience and changed environmental conditions.

The emphasis on strategy as a continuous process, as opposed to a static and periodic statement of intent, keeps strategy current and relevant to an organization's environment. It also makes strategy easier to implement and change, when needed.

**Principle 5.** *Mobilizing change through executive leadership.* The buy-in of executive leadership is the underlying premise of a strategy-focused organization. Top management must understand that creating a strategy-focused organization is an organization change project. A successful change to a strategy-focused organization rests on performance of three critical activities by top management:

- **Mobilization.** An organization needs to understand why change is needed. In the mobilization phase, the organization is shaken up, or "unfrozen." A sense of urgency is established, a guiding coalition is formed, and a new vision and strategy is articulated for the entire organization to gather around.
- **Establishing a governance process.** The next phase defines, demonstrates, and reinforces the new cultural values in the organization. This is a democratic process, breaking existing silos and creating strategy teams, town hall meetings, and open communications.

- **Recognizing a new strategic management system.** This phase evolves as the organization begins to understand the process of being a strategy-focused organization. This phase essentially institutionalizes the new cultural values and new structures into a new system for managing. In other words, it "refreezes" the organization, albeit an organization that is more adaptable, flexible, and strategy-focused.

## COMMON PITFALLS

Pitfalls that impede the implementation of balanced scorecards to make firms strategy-focused usually fall in three categories:

1. *Transitional issues:* abandoning the project due to merger or acquisition, and/or change in leadership.
2. *Design flaws:* failing to integrate strategy into the scorecards, and not making scorecards detailed and multidimensional enough to be really balanced.
3. *Process failures:* these are exhibited in the following ways:
   - Lack of senior management commitment
   - Too few individuals involved
   - Keeping the scorecard at the top
   - A development process that is too lengthy
   - Treating the scorecard as a systems project
   - Hiring inexperienced consultants
   - Introducing the balanced scorecard only for compensation.

The message from the application of principles of the strategy-focused organization in several entities—across the public, private, and not-for-profit sectors—is that these principles work, and organizations achieve a tighter integration between their strategy and its implementation.

# Execution: The Discipline of Getting Things Done

*LARRY BOSSIDY and RAM CHARAN*

*Summary prepared by Christian F. Edwardson*

***Christian F. Edwardson*** *is in the home remodeling business and a part-time consultant after spending more than 25 years in wood products research and development. His areas of research interest are related to the home building industry, especially green building technology. He is also interested in incorporating lean manufacturing principles in home remodeling and new construction. He received a B.S. and an M.S. in Wood Science and Technology from the University of Maine and an MBA from the University of Minnesota Duluth.*

*The absence of execution is the biggest obstacle to business success today.* Execution is a discipline that nobody has previously explained satisfactorily. Successful execution requires a specific set of behaviors and techniques that companies must master if they want a competitive advantage. Leading for execution is not difficult, but a leader has to be deeply and passionately engaged in the organization, and honest about its realities. Leaders at any company or level need to master the discipline of execution to establish credibility.

## ◆ UNDERSTANDING EXECUTION

Three key points are useful to help understand what execution is:

1. *Execution is a discipline, and integral to strategy.* It is a mistake to think of execution as the tactical side of the business. Execution is a systematic process of exposing reality and acting on it. Three core processes—the people process, the strategy

Larry Bossidy, and Ram Charan, with Charles Burck, *Execution: The Discipline of Getting Things Done.* New York: Crown Business, 2002.

process, and the operations process—must be tightly linked for a company to execute effectively.

2. *Execution is the major job of the business leader.* The leader is in charge of getting things done by managing the three core processes with intensity and rigor. Picking other leaders, setting strategy, and running operations are the substance of execution that cannot be delegated. The leader sets the tone of the dialogue (the core of culture and the basic unit of work) in an organization.
3. *Execution has to be in the culture.* Execution is not a program; it is a discipline that must be understood by everyone in the organization. Execution requires education, practice, dedication, and reflection. Execution should drive the behavior of all leaders at all levels, beginning with senior leaders.

## ◆ THE THREE BUILDING BLOCKS OF EXECUTION

The first building block of execution requires a leader to practice seven essential behaviors:

1. *Know your people and your business.* In companies that don't execute, leaders are usually out of touch with the day-to-day realities of the business. It's not that they lack information—they just aren't engaged with the business or where the action is. A leader (CEO) must go to operations and conduct business reviews. Managers may not like what you tell them, but they will respect that you care enough about the business to take time for the review. The review is useful for fostering honest dialogue and helping establish the personal connection critical to launching future initiatives.
2. *Insist on realism.* The heart of execution is realism. In order to execute, leaders must establish realistic, attainable goals with those who will carry them out. Avoiding realism because it is uncomfortable is a major mistake. By confronting reality, changes can be made so that execution is successful.
3. *Set clear goals and priorities.* Leaders who execute well focus on only a few priorities that everyone understands. The matrix organization requires a small number of carefully crafted, clear priorities to avoid conflicts over who gets what, and why. Along with clear goals, strive for simplicity in general; leaders who execute speak simply and directly.
4. *Follow through.* A major cause of poor execution is the failure of business leaders to follow through. If no one is held accountable for meeting goals, no one will take the goals seriously. A leader will set up a mechanism to monitor the progress of goal achievements assigned to others.
5. *Reward the doers.* People need to be rewarded if you want them to produce specific results. This seems obvious, but many companies do a poor job of linking rewards to performance. It is important to distinguish between those who achieve and those who don't, through base pay or in the administration of bonuses and stock options.
6. *Expand people's capabilities through coaching.* One of the most important jobs of leaders is to pass on their acquired knowledge and experience to the next generation of leaders. Coaching is a vital way of expanding the capabilities of everyone in the organization. Coaching is teaching people how to get things done, and a good leader will regard every contact as a coaching opportunity.

7. *Know yourself.* Strength of character is critical to execution. *Emotional fortitude* is necessary to be honest with yourself, to deal honestly with business realities, and to assess people fairly. Emotional fortitude gives you the strength to hear the truth, to deliver the truth, and it enables you to deal with your own weaknesses. Emotional fortitude is the foundation of people skills, and is made up of four core qualities: *authenticity* means who you are is what you do and say; *self-awareness* means you know your strengths and weaknesses; *self-mastery* allows you to keep your ego in check, take responsibility for your behavior, adapt to change, and be honest in all situations; and *humility* allows you to acknowledge your mistakes.

The second building block requires creating the framework for cultural change. It is important to recognize that people's beliefs and behaviors are equally or even more important than a company strategy or organizational structure. Changing culture is difficult and often fails because it is not linked to improving the business' outcomes. A set of processes (social operating mechanisms) are needed to change the beliefs and behaviors of people in ways that are linked directly to bottom-line results.

## OPERATIONALIZING CULTURE

Clearly linking rewards to performance is the foundation of changing behavior. A company's culture will change if it rewards and promotes people for execution.

People should be rewarded both for strong achievements on numbers and adopting desirable behaviors. Linking rewards to performance is necessary to create an execution culture, but it must be implemented with the "social software of execution." The social software includes the values, beliefs, and norms of behavior (i.e., culture).

Social operating mechanisms are a key component of social software. *Social operating mechanisms are formal or informal interactions where dialogue occurs.* One difference between a meeting and an operating mechanism is that the latter are integrative. New information flows and working relationships are created because the interaction breaks down barriers among units, functions, disciplines, work processes, and hierarchies. A second difference is that social operating mechanisms are where beliefs and behaviors of the social software are practiced.

In the ever-changing business environment, the social operating mechanism is the constant, providing the consistent framework needed to create a common corporate culture. The social operating mechanism teaches people how to work together in constructive debate.

*Robust dialogue* is necessary in an execution culture. With robust dialogue, an organization will be effective in gathering and understanding information, and using it to make decisions. For robust dialogue to occur, people must go in with an open mind and a desire to hear new information and choose the best alternatives. People should be encouraged to speak candidly. Informality encourages candor and invites questions and critical thinking. It gets the truth out. *Robust dialogue ends with closure,* that is, people agree about what each person has to do and when. Because robust dialogue has purpose and meaning, it brings out reality.

The culture of a company is defined by the behavior of its leaders. In the social operating mechanism, the leader has to be present to create and reinforce desired behaviors and robust dialogue. However, success in executing the desired cultural change depends on having the right people.

The third building block is having the right people in the right place. This is a job that should be handled by the leader and not delegated to someone else in the organization. If you claim that people are your most important asset, then it is critical that you understand what each job requires and what kind of people are needed to fill the job. The best competitive differentiator a company has is its people.

Many mismatches between people and their jobs result because the leaders do not know enough about the people they are appointing. A leader who is personally committed and deeply engaged in the people process will avoid this mistake.

It is the leader's responsibility to ask what specific qualities make a person right for the job. This means understanding the requirements of the job—the three or four non-negotiable criteria that a person must be able to do to be successful. A leader must have the emotional fortitude to confront a non-performer and take decisive action. Finally, a leader must spend as much time and energy developing people as on budgeting, strategic planning, and other tasks. The payoff will be a sustainable competitive advantage.

Look for people who are good at getting things done. To build a company that has excellent discipline of execution, choose people who are *doers* (not just talkers). Search for leaders who have a drive for winning and who get satisfaction from getting things done. Good leaders will energize people, not through rhetoric, but by focusing on short-term accomplishments that lead to winning the game. Good leaders have the emotional fortitude to be decisive and able to make difficult decisions on tough issues. The best leaders get things done through others. They do not micromanage the people they lead, nor do they abandon them. Finally, every leader who is good at executing will follow through. They ensure that people are doing the things they said they would, when they said they would.

It is not easy to get the right people in the right jobs. Traditional interviews don't work for finding the qualities of leaders who execute. It requires probing people to learn about how they think and what drives them. Developing leaders requires hands-on hiring. It is important to look for energy and enthusiasm for execution. Getting the right people in the right job is a matter of being systematic and consistent in interviewing and appraising people, and then developing them through candid appraisals and feedback to encourage improvement.

With the three building blocks in place, the foundation is established for operating and managing the core processes effectively.

## THE PEOPLE PROCESS: MAKING THE LINK WITH STRATEGY AND OPERATIONS

Getting the people process right is necessary to fulfill the potential of the organization. This makes it more important than either the strategy or operations processes. A robust people process has three elements: It evaluates people accurately and in-depth; it has a mechanism to identify and develop the leadership talent needed to execute its strategies; and it fills the leadership pipeline.

Evaluating people accurately and in depth will yield information about leadership qualities and business acumen. It may be necessary to replace an excellent performer with a person better equipped to take the business to the next level. It is important to have early feedback on behavior so that an unsuited person does not rise to a critical job in the future.

Four building blocks can be used to determine the organization's talent needs over time and for planning actions to meet the need:

1. *Linking people to strategy and operations.* The business leader must make sure that the right kinds and numbers of people are available to execute the near, medium, long-term, and operating strategy of the organization. A new strategy may require new people. A high performer in the current organization may not be able to handle the challenges of a new strategic future. It is tough, but necessary, to tell some people that they aren't capable of moving to the next level. The people process will force leaders to do what has to be done.
2. *Developing the leadership pipeline.* A leadership assessment summary tool is useful to develop a picture of the pipeline. The summary compares performance and behavior for a group of individuals and identifies those who have high potential and those who are promotable. A *continuous improvement summary* is similar to a traditional performance appraisal, but it captures information on development needs and helps the individual become a better performer. The essence of talent planning and developing a leadership pipeline requires analyzing succession depth and retention risk. *Succession depth analysis* shows if the company has enough high-potential people to fill key positions. *Retention risk analysis* may be used to learn if people are in the wrong job or at risk for leaving the company. Identifying the talent avoids the danger of organizational inertia; that is, keeping people in the same job too long and conversely, promoting people too quickly.
3. *Dealing with non-performers.* People who aren't meeting their established goals are *non-performers.* Failure to meet goals means they aren't performing at a level essential for the company's success and they need to be dealt with quickly and fairly. This may mean moving someone to a job they are more suited for, but if you have to let someone go it should be done as constructively as possible. An important part of reinforcing the positive nature of the performance (execution) culture is preserving the dignity of people who leave jobs.
4. *Linking HR to business results.* The role of HR changes radically in an execution culture. HR is more important than ever in a recruitment-oriented mode and it can be a force for advancing the organization. The HR person must have the same characteristics as any effective manager; these include business acumen, understanding how a company makes money, critical thinking, a passion for getting things done, and the ability to link strategy and execution.

There is not one best system for having a robust people process, but certain rules are needed. The process must have integrity, honesty, a common approach and language, frequency, and candid dialogue. Candid dialogue is critical, as it is the social software of the people process.

## ◆ THE STRATEGY PROCESS: LINKING PEOPLE AND OPERATIONS

*The basic goal of any strategy is to be preferred by customers and achieve a sustainable competitive advantage, while making sufficient money to satisfy stockholders.* The strategic plan must be an action plan used by business leaders to reach their business objectives. The strategy must be linked to the people process. If you don't have the right people in place to execute the strategy, you need a plan to get them.

The substance of any strategy can be summed up by a few key concepts and actions that define it. By pinpointing the key concepts or building blocks, leaders are forced to be clear as they discuss and debate the strategy.

A strategy will be effective only if it is constructed and owned by those who will execute it. Through the process of developing the plan using robust dialogue, the line people will learn execution. Discussing the business and environment creates excitement and alignment and in turn strengthens the process.

A strong strategic plan addresses nine key questions:

1. *What is the assessment of the external environment?* Businesses operate within a shifting political, social, and economic environment, and the strategic plan must define the external assumptions management has made.
2. *How well do you understand the existing customers and markets?* It is important to understand who makes the purchasing decision and their buying behavior. The sales approach used with an engineer, purchasing agent, or CEO (of a small company) will be significantly different.
3. *What is the best way to grow the business profitably, and what are the obstacles to growth?* Growth can be a result of new products, new channels, new customers, or acquisitions. Whatever direction your company takes requires understanding of the obstacles and taking action to overcome them.
4. *Who is the competition?* It is important to think critically about your competitors, neither underestimating nor overestimating them.
5. *Can the business execute the strategy?* The leader must make a realistic assessment of the ability of the organization to execute the plan. It is possible to increase your capability when you know the capabilities and understand what needs to be done.
6. *What are the important milestones in executing the plan?* Milestones help leaders decide if they have the right strategy. If the milestones are missed, the direction can be changed if the strategic plan is adaptable (as it should be).
7. *Are the short term and long term balanced?* Strategy planning needs to be done in the current environment. The plan must deal with what a company has to do between the present (short term) and the future time when the plan will give peak results.
8. *What are the critical issues facing the business?* It is important to identify the issues and impediments that can keep the company from reaching its objectives.
9. *How will the business make money on a sustainable basis?* An understanding of the drivers of cash, margin, velocity, revenue growth, market share, and competitive advantage is required.

The strategic plan developed according to these guidelines and questions will provide the basis for a robust dialogue linking the strategy to the people and operating processes. The plan is less about numbers and more about ideas that are specific and clear.

A critical part of developing and adopting the plan is the strategy review. The review is a good place for the leader to learn about the people involved and assess their potential for promotion. Five key questions should be critically addressed in the review:

1. Does each business unit team know the competition?
2. Does the organization have the capability to execute the strategy?
3. Is the plan scattered or focused?
4. Have the right ideas been selected?
5. Are the linkages with people and operations clear?

## ◆ THE OPERATIONS PROCESS: MAKING THE LINK WITH STRATEGY AND PEOPLE

An operating plan provides the path for people to fulfill the strategy and achieve the end point where a business wants to go. The plan looks forward to how targets will be met. It addresses the critical issues in execution by building the budget on realities. The assumptions used in developing the plan are debated rigorously and trade-offs are made openly. Robust dialogue and debate are part of the social software that helps build the business leadership of the people involved.

The plan is built after the assumptions are agreed on. The process is done in three parts: setting targets, developing the action plan, and establishing follow-through measures after participants agree to the plan. The follow-through has three parts. The first is a memo (or other device) sent by the leader outlining what others agreed to accomplish. The second part of follow-through is a contingency plan. Companies that execute well have a contingency plan that deals with alternative scenarios, and this allows them to act quickly when faced with new situations. Finally, quarterly reviews help keep the plans up to date and synchronized and they show leaders who may need coaching to get things done.

If the operations process is run on the social software of execution, the people who must meet the targets have also set the targets. This avoids the traditional budget problem of disconnect from reality. Robust dialogue, debate, and review of the plan allows leaders to set meaningful stretch goals to maximize individual effort.

## Conclusion

The discipline of execution is based on linking the core processes of people, strategy, and operations. It starts with the leader knowing what skills a job requires and having the right people in the job. Leaders need to be where the action is—learning the realities of the business from those in the trenches. Being honest both with yourself and others is critical to getting things done. Using robust dialogue to get at the heart of an issue brings reality to each of the core processes.

The people process has to be a top priority. Success in execution depends on having doers, and doers should be rewarded because the promise of meaningful compensation ultimately drives future performance. The long-term success of the business depends on having the right strategy process. The individuals who must execute the strategy should be driving the process. The critical issues facing the business need to be identified, debated, and resolved. The final strategic plan should be clear, concise, and understood by everyone involved. An operations plan for the year sets the stage for achievement.

In an execution culture, the leader must be personally involved in the three core processes. To run the business with reality knowledge requires the leader to be involved from the start through the follow-up. This involvement and follow through allows leaders to know the capabilities of the people who work for them and the potential of the organization.

READING 3

# What (Really) Works: The 4 + 2 Formula for Sustained Business Success

*WILLIAM JOYCE, NITIN NOHRIA, and BRUCE ROBERSON*

*Summary prepared by Allen Harmon*

***Allen Harmon** is President and General Manager of WDSE-TV, the community-licensed PBS member station serving Northeastern Minnesota and Northwestern Wisconsin. He also currently serves as an adjunct instructor in the Labovitz School of Business and Economics at the University of Minnesota Duluth. Before joining WDSE, Mr. Harmon held a series of senior management positions in a regional investor-owned electric utility. He earned an MBA from Indiana University and has completed the University of Minnesota Carlson School of Management Executive Development Program.*

## ◆ INTRODUCTION

The list of companies currently at the top of their game churns constantly. Management thinkers offer a seemingly endless supply of silver-bullet cures that are half-heartedly adopted, quickly fail, and are soon abandoned. Managers await the latest autobiographies of business legends only to find that the experiences described and suggestions offered by these luminaries fail to translate easily into their own situations. By contrast, the Evergreen Project—a search for the "evergreen" source of

---

William Joyce, Nitin Nohria, Bruce Roberson, *What (Really) Works: The 4 + 2 Formula for Sustained Business Success,* New York: Harper Collins, 2003.

business success—was conceived to replace blind faith, luck, and guessing with statistically rigorous analysis of the results of previously effective organizations. The results of that study produced the 4 + 2 formula for corporate success.

## ◆ THE STUDY

An initial study of several hundred companies confirmed that, despite the caprices of the market, total return to shareholders (TRS) is useful as a primary metric of organizational performance. Successful companies, as measured by TRS, were found to be winners by almost every other measure.

From the initial group, 160 companies—four companies in each of 40 industry groups—were selected for extensive study. The companies in each group were, at the start of the study in 1986, of comparable size, had achieved similar financial performance and had similar prospects for the future. Failing companies and those conglomerates that defied classification were left out. Performance of the 160 companies was measured over two consecutive five-year periods, 1986–1990, and 1991–1995. Based on TRS performance, each company was labeled as a winner, climber, tumbler, or loser and assigned to one of four groups:

- **Winners:** Companies that outperformed their peers in both time periods
- **Climbers:** Companies that lagged their peers in the first period, but achieved performance better than their peers in the second
- **Tumblers:** Companies with better-than-peer performance in the first period, followed by under-performance in the second
- **Losers:** Companies that lagged behind their peers in both time periods. This grouping of the companies would provide insight into cause-effect relationships. Accounting for the differences in performance was the next step.

Three distinct methodologies were used to unlock the answer to what really works from the 10-year performance of the companies studied. First, all publicly available information on the 160 companies was scanned for references to 200 established management practices, and the companies were scored on each practice using a scale from 1 (poor relative to peers) to 5 (excellent relative to peers). Scores were independently verified through alternate sources, such as former executives. A second set of studies by academic experts identified connections among management practices. Analysis of hundreds of documents concerning each of the companies—analysts' reports, newspaper and magazine articles, business school case studies—confirmed the results of the first two studies.

## ◆ WHAT DOESN'T WORK

Of the 200 management practices surveyed, four popular approaches stand out for having *no* demonstrated cause-effect relationship to sustained superior performance. Over the period of the study, no correlation was found between total return to shareholders and a company's investment in technology. Despite their popularity, neither corporate change programs nor purchase and supply chain management practices contributed to superior TRS. There was no evidence that attracting better outside directors, an effort promoted as a means of improving corporate governance, improved TRS. If anything, it is better performance that attracts more astute outside directors!

## ◆ WHAT DOES WORK—THE 4 + 2 FORMULA

In fact, most of the 200 practices studied turned out to be largely irrelevant to corporate performance. That is not to say that the vast majority of these practices are counterproductive, just that they are not essential to achieving superior performance. A compelling connection was found between sustainable high performance and just eight of the practices. *Four "primary" areas of management practice—designated in shorthand as strategy, execution. culture and structure—proved essential to success.* Four "secondary" areas—talent, leadership, innovation, and mergers and partnerships—complete the set. Companies with high scores on each of the four primary areas and any two of the secondary areas had a better than 90 percent chance of being a Winner. This unique finding produced the *4 + 2 formula* in which four primary plus any two of the four secondary management practices are required for success.

## ◆ THE FOUR PRIMARY MANAGEMENT PRACTICES

### STRATEGY

Winning companies keep their attention and resources focused on growth of their core business through a *clear and focused strategy.* Positioning decisions, such as to be a product innovator, a quality leader, or a low-cost competitor do not have a significant impact on whether the company will succeed or fail. Whether the planning process invited input from all levels of the organization, or was the inspiration of the chief executive; whether long-range budgeting and planning were a part of the process; whether change was initiated in response to a takeover attempt or a change in management similarly had little effect.

What works well in the domain of strategy is:

1. Offering the customer a clear value proposition, rooted in an understanding of both the customer's needs and the company's capabilities.
2. Developing strategy from the outside in; what customers, partners, and investors say and do are more important considerations than relying on internal instincts.
3. Monitoring the marketplace and adapting the strategy to emerging trends; winners have the ability to detect trends in their own and related businesses and to act on those that count.
4. Clearly communicating the strategy with both internal and external stakeholders, including customers; internal stakeholders give the strategy life, while communicating with customers encourages them to move from being "just" customers to true business partners.

5. Growing the core business; winners achieve growth by focusing on their core business. When they do venture into other businesses, they do so before the growth potential of their core is exhausted.

### Flawless Execution

Operational excellence—flawless execution in meeting the expectations of ever more demanding and sophisticated customers—can only be achieved through effort, study, and ingenuity. It will not, the Evergreen Project showed, be achieved through outsourcing operations, buying the latest enterprise resource planning (ERP), supply chain management, or customer relations management (CRM) software, or adopting a total quality management (TQM) program.

What *does* work in the pursuit of flawless execution?

1. Consistently meeting customer expectations, Winners need not deliver extraordinary products or services, but must *consistently meet their customers' expectations* in order to build trust.
2. Empowering employees on the front line of customer contact to respond to customer needs. This also requires keeping the organization's best employees in those front line positions.
3. Eliminating waste and inefficiency, and then focusing the effort on the processes most important to meeting customer expectations.

## CULTURE

Winning requires that virtually everyone in the organization perform to the maximum of their capabilities. Evergreen Project Winners created a culture dedicated to performance and then serving the customer by:

1. *Inspiring high performance by creating and supporting a culture that holds all employees, not just managers, responsible for corporate success.* The ideal culture empowers employees to make independent decisions to improve company operations, while building loyalty to the employee's team and the company.
2. *Rewarding achievement through praise and pay, while constantly raising expectations.* Once a winning organization achieves "best in class" performance, it ratchets the goal up to "best in show."
3. *Creating an environment that is challenging, satisfying, and fun.* Winners stay on the right side of the fine line between a high-performance environment and a high-anxiety environment.
4. *Establishing clear company values, presenting them to employees, living them, and making them a part of every communication with employees.* Good ethical behavior promotes good business.

## STRUCTURE

Bureaucracy may have its place, but the Evergreen Project found that Winners focus full-time efforts on eliminating unnecessary bureaucracy. How the elements of the organization are arranged—functionally, geographically, or by product—matters not. Neither does the extent to which profit and loss responsibility is delegated to subordinate units, nor does the level of autonomy granted subordinate units to select their own unique structure. The structural attributes that *do* matter are:

1. *Simplicity.* Winners work to eliminate redundant layers, bureaucracy, and the behaviors that create and sustain them.
2. *Cooperation and information sharing across the entire organization.* Winners devote resources to break down walls between organizational fiefdoms.
3. *Putting the frontline first.* Winners place the best employees in positions where their decisions can make a difference, and keep them there.

## ◆ THE FOUR SECONDARY MANAGEMENT PRACTICES

### TALENT

About half of the Winners in the Evergreen Project dedicated significant human and financial resources to building an effective workforce and management team. It was not the resources dedicated to building the highest quality human resources staff, maintaining a fast-track management development program, or implementing a 360-degree performance review system that made a difference. Instead, it was the effort devoted to the following that worked:

1. Promoting from within; filling mid- and upper level positions with internal talent.
2. Offering top quality training and education programs; committing resources to the programs that will develop candidates for internal promotion.
3. Designing jobs that challenge the best performers; decentralization and empowerment are tools for keeping people engaged.
4. Getting senior executives engaged in the competition for the best talent; recruiting isn't just for HR any more.

### LEADERSHIP

The choice of a chief executive is crucial to the company's success. The Evergreen Project provides insight (contrary to many commonly held beliefs) into what leadership traits are consistent with becoming a Winner. The leader's decision-making style, be it independent or collaborative is irrelevant. Personal characteristics—patient or impatient, visionary or detail oriented, secure or insecure—are irrelevant as well. Success is independent of whether senior managers make major decisions on the basis of qualitative or quantitative analysis. Instead, what does work in the domain of leadership is:

1. Strengthening management's relationships with people at all levels of the organization; Winners see these relationships as the foundation of positive attitudes toward the company and its goals.
2. Focusing management on spotting opportunities and problems early; encouraging managers to anticipate change rather than dealing only with immediate difficulties.
3. Motivating the board to take an active role in governing the company by requiring a significant financial stake; when board members have their own money at risk, they tend to seek and retain stronger chief executives.

4. Pay for performance; stock price need not be the only factor considered, but executive compensation should reflect performance against pre-established goals.

### INNOVATION

The Evergreen Project provides the evidence. Barely half of the Winners were able to excel in this challenging area of management practice. Yet the potential payoffs for success—greater efficiency, new products, the opportunity to transform an industry—are difficult to ignore. Where new ideas come from makes no difference. For the companies that were successful, what worked was:

1. Introducing disruptive technologies and business models; success in innovation requires leading the industry and developing the innovative blockbusters that change the competitive landscape.
2. Using technological innovation both externally to produce new products and internally to improve efficiency.
3. Being willing to cannibalize existing products; Winners do eat their young in the battle to maintain their technological lead.

### MERGERS AND PARTNERSHIPS

In mergers and acquisitions analyzed by the Evergreen Project, 93 percent of the deals involving Winners created value, while only 9 percent of the Losers' deals did so. Why? Losers sought mergers and acquisitions to achieve diversification, or to fix a weakness in their primary practices. What worked for the Winners was:

1. Acquisition of new businesses to take advantage of existing customer relationships; making the most of both their own relationships with customers and the relationships that came with the acquired company.
2. Entering businesses that are complementary to existing strengths; picking companies with compatible cultures and strengths that extend or complete the value they offer the marketplace.
3. In creating partnerships, entering businesses that draw on both partners' strengths; successful partnerships provide benefits neither partner could have achieved alone.
4. Developing the capacity to successfully identify, screen and close deals; successful merger management is a significant business activity in itself.

## ◆ KEEPING SIX BALLS IN THE AIR

The seemingly simple 4 + 2 model challenges managers to attend to no fewer than six key elements of their business at once. The task is certainly more daunting than simply applying the panacea of the day, but the results provide significant motivation to do so. Over the ten years of the Evergreen Project study, investors in the average Winner saw their investment grow nearly ten-fold; the average loser eked out only a 62 percent gain for the entire decade. Follow-up evaluation of over forty of the original study companies for 1997–2002 affirmed the earlier study's conclusions.

READING 4

# Corporate Boards: Strategies for Adding Value at the Top

*JAY A. CONGER, EDWARD E. LAWLER III, and DAVID L. FINEGOLD*

*Summary prepared by William H. Palmer*

*William H. Palmer, a Duluth, Minnesota resident, retired from Miller-Dwan Medical Center in 2001 after serving as President and CEO for twenty-six years. He was born in Rockford, Illinois, received a BS degree in Economics and Business Administration from Rockford College and attended the University of Minnesota Graduate Program in Hospital Administration where he received a Master's Degree in Hospital Administration. He was employed as an Assistant Administrator at The Fairview Hospitals for nine years prior to his service at Miller-Dwan. He currently works with Generations Health Care Initiatives, a not-for-profit organization concerned with creating access to health care services for the uninsured in the Duluth area.*

## ◆ INTRODUCTION TO BOARDS

Until recently, corporate boards have labored in relative obscurity. That is changing rapidly as corporations grow both in size and in number and attract increasing scrutiny because of their pervasive influence on almost everyone's lives. Much of this attention has been directed toward CEOs. Given the steady stream of negative news about high profile CEOs and their lavish compensation, mega-mergers and takeovers, globalization, and (sadly) corporate scandals, it comes as little surprise that increasing attention is being directed toward boards of directors, whose job it is to hire the CEO.

---

Jay A. Conger, Edward E. Lawler III, and David L. Finegold, *Corporate Boards: Strategies for Adding Value at the Top.* San Francisco: Jossey-Bass, 2001.

Corporations are also feeling pressure from large pension funds and institutional investors who believe a strong board and sound governance practices can have a positive influence on corporate performance. State attorneys general and regulators have become increasingly active in pressing for governance reform, and the level of shareholder activism has grown significantly. The good news is that many boards have recognized these concerns and have taken steps to improve their performance. Naturally, some boards have been better at this than others, a fact which is clearly discernible in their performance and that of their corporations.

There are widely different views on what boards are expected or required to do. There are legal mandates citing fiduciary responsibilities, oversight of management, approval of corporate actions, providing counsel to management, and giving voice to the company's stakeholders. Certainly boards must concern themselves with company performance, but board members, most of whom are employed full time elsewhere, do not have the time or the knowledge to immerse themselves fully in the operations of the company. State laws generally hold that board members must act responsibly, within the law, and free from conflict of interest.

## ACCENTING KEY RESPONSIBILITIES

Board members can generally expect to spend one day a month at board meetings and perhaps another 5–6 days a year on board activities. Although this seems a substantial commitment of time for individual members, realistically it can suffice only if the board focuses on those areas and responsibilities where it can have the most impact. Among the most important are:

- **Developing mission and strategy**—Outside directors can bring expertise and a different perspective to the planning and mission process, and can provide valuable counsel to the CEO and senior management.
- **Monitoring implementation of strategic plans**—The board can stay in touch with the company's performance and keep the CEO on task by following through on the progress of strategic initiatives.
- **Appraisals**—The CEO is accountable for the performance of the firm and it is the board's job to hire, develop, guide, appraise, and (if necessary) replace him or her.
- **Developing human capital**—The board must see that systems are in place and adequate investment is made in employee development at all levels of the organization.
- **Assuring compliance**—The board must see that ethical policies and standards are in place, monitor how well management conducts business, assure adherence to relevant laws, and maintain open channels of communication, both internally and externally.
- **Preventing and managing crises**—While it is not possible to anticipate the exact form a future crisis may take, the board should develop and approve generalized response procedures, both preventative and corrective. They should be prepared to step into a management role in those situations where the CEO is either absent or is the focus of the crisis.

- **Procuring resources**—Depending on the type and size of the company, board members may have expertise or network connections which can be helpful in arranging financing, or forming strategic alliances.

  Evidence suggests that by focusing on specific activities and practices a board can enhance the quality of governance and improve organizational performance. These activities and practices largely define the job of the board and to a large degree, differentiate the roles of the CEO and the board. The board and senior management must strive to develop a mutually supportive relationship, but a balance of power between them is the surest route to high performance.
- **Key board attributes**—A board is essentially a team and it must have structure to carry out its key responsibilities. Several important elements of that structure have been identified, and they include knowledge, information, power, rewards, opportunity, time, and resources. Collectively the board must embody a high level of *knowledge* about the operations of the firm and its industry, and a more diverse knowledge about strategic planning, finance, and organizational development. The *information* needs of the board include financial and statistical information about the performance of the firm, its strategies, and the behavior of its competitors. *Power* refers to the board's standing and authority to deal with critical issues of governance and the assurance that those decisions and actions they undertake will be fulfilled. A high performance board can place significant time demands on its members. It is, therefore, critically important to attract capable members and keep them interested. It is important to *reward* them adequately. Boards must also have the *opportunity* to participate in the firm's critical decision-making and to have adequate *time* and resources to support their work.
- **Board membership**—One of the board's most important roles is to balance the power of the CEO, and therefore it is important that its membership include independent, outside members. Ideally, they should constitute a substantial majority, two-thirds to three-quarters of the membership. The best way to achieve such balance is to assign this responsibility to a nominating committee comprised entirely of outsider board members who then present their nominations to the full board for approval. The CEO should participate in the process, but the decision is the board's to make.

  There doesn't appear to be any ideal size for a board, but most seem to have between five and fifteen members. Larger, more complex corporations may require more members. More important is the right mix of technical background, managerial knowledge, and strategy expertise. A board can be viewed as an organism made up of interdependent parts, and it is therefore critical that those doing the recruiting search for evidence that a prospective member will be a team player. Membership on an effective board can be very time consuming and a board may wish to limit the number of boards on which their directors may serve. The nominating process must also consider representing the interest of *stakeholders* as well as shareholders.
- **Board leadership**—In the majority of corporations, the CEO also holds the position of board chair. Some corporations have, in the interest of balancing the power of the CEO, appointed a non-executive, independent chair or *lead director* to run the board. The difficulty with these alternate models is that they require a great deal of time and commitment to perform the work of the chair; they expose

that director to considerable liability; and they may foster ambiguity about who really is accountable for the organization's performance. Nonetheless, some firms have been successful in appointing a lead outside director who works with the CEO and whose job it is to run the board meetings and prepare the board's agenda. Other methods of balancing the CEO's power include appointing outside directors to chair the nominating and governance committees, and for the board to hold frequent executive sessions without management or inside directors present.

## ◆ INFORMATION FOR HIGH PERFORMANCE BOARDS

Typically boards receive a great deal of financial and statistical information that portrays how the firm has performed in the latest reporting period. It is important for the board to receive this information; however, too much operational detail can lead to micro-management. The board itself needs to decide the level of detail needed and ask that the information be presented in a *balanced scorecard* format sent to the board at least a week in advance of the meeting.

*The focus of the board should be strategic* and the board members should receive information that allows them to assess how well the firm is achieving its strategic objectives. Management should be providing information on markets, new product development, and competitor strategies, as well as internal information regarding human resource development, employee satisfaction, and succession planning for top levels of management. Most of the data that the board members receive will be presented by the CEO and senior managers, and this provides an important opportunity for board members to assess the capabilities of the management team. Beyond the information presented by management, boards need to develop their own internal and external channels of communication. A corporation has many *stakeholders,* including suppliers, customers, employees and investors, all of who have important perspectives on the corporation and need to be heard. In times of crisis these channels of communication can become extremely important.

## ◆ EVALUATING THE CEO

Most corporations have developed elaborate and effective systems to evaluate the performance of their employees. Only in the past 20 years, however, have CEOs been similarly evaluated by the board. The CEO has become the central figure in the popular notion of the corporation and the spectacular rise in compensation has brought a demand for greater accountability. Regular performance evaluations can do much to placate critics if the CEO's compensation is tied closely to key measures of organizational performance. A good evaluation process can keep the CEO on task and strengthen the CEO-board relationship. It also sends a very important message to employees that the CEO is subject to the same performance evaluation process as they are.

The evaluation, which should be done on an annual basis, is the proper role of the compensation committee. Prior to the beginning of the evaluation cycle, the board and the CEO should develop a workable number (5–10) of performance objectives, which should also be communicated to the senior management team who will be instrumental in attainment of the objectives. These objectives should include strategic planning, personal development, and financial targets.

These objectives should be visited at mid-year as well as year-end, and the appraisal should be delivered in person by a member or members of the board. In determining compensation, both individual and firm performance should be factored in and the level of compensation should compare closely to industry norms for comparable performance. The board should also insist that the compensation system for the CEO and senior managers be consistent with that used on all other employees in the organization.

## ◆ BOARD SELF-EVALUATION

Board self evaluations are much less common than CEO evaluations, but they are a powerful tool for improving an organization's performance. The process should occur annually and should be spearheaded by the committee responsible for nominating directors. The process should be similar in form to that used for the CEO evaluation, including objectives related to improving the board's performance and practices. Much of the input for this process can be gathered with a questionnaire asking individual directors their opinion on overall board performance and how they feel about their own participation in board activity. It is important that the board make time to thoroughly discuss the findings and develop an improvement plan and objectives.

## ◆ EFFECTS OF THE INTERNET ON BOARD GOVERNANCE

One of the biggest challenges facing corporations and their boards is the use of the Internet. It has enhanced communications allowing companies to communicate instantly with their markets, and by the same token has empowered consumers who can price shop with ease. This in turn has greatly accelerated the pace of decision-making while simultaneously creating a high level of uncertainty. The Internet has facilitated globalization and indeed spawned entirely new business models.

All of this has had a significant impact in the boardroom, affecting those attributes of high performance boards—*knowledge, information, power, rewards, opportunity,* and *time.* Certainly all boards, whether or not they are involved in e-commerce, need to have some members who have a clear understanding of the threats and opportunities posed by the Internet. Furthermore, there should be expertise on the board to deal with issues of organizational development and transformation in the e-commerce environment.

With respect to *information,* the Internet can greatly facilitate linkages with employees and external stakeholders such as customers, suppliers, and investors. The use of communication sources outside the boardroom can augment the power of board members by giving voice to a broader group of stakeholders, although there is some risk that too much focus on outside stakeholders may divert the board's attention away from the development of human resources within the corporation. Finally, the Internet and electronic communications can help the board become more efficient by allowing them to communicate and even conduct a significant portion of their business between meetings.

## ◆ TO WHOM ARE BOARDS ACCOUNTABLE?

Historically, boards have owed their primary allegiance and accountability to the owners of the corporation, the shareholders. This *property conception* of the corporation was born in the days when the company was owned and operated by a small group of investors who in effect were also the board. Through the years this concept was reinforced by the courts and regulators, and it made sense when corporations were capital intensive and return on investment was the primary driver.

When corporations began to hire professional managers, formalize a board structure and, most important, raise capital through the issuance of common stock, things began to change. In today's environment, a firm may have many diverse investors or stakeholders and the *social entity conception* has come to the forefront. The social entity model recognizes that the employee who makes a long-term commitment to an organization or the supplier who enters into a long-term contract are as much investors as the equity holder.

Board members, on the one hand, may feel pressure from shareholders, particularly large institutional shareholders and pension funds, seeking an economic return on investment, while other stakeholders such as employees or suppliers may be seeking a different end. Most boards will, therefore, be well served to adopt a stakeholder model. Access to capital is as important as ever to a firm's long-term growth and survival, but in today's economy the definition of capital increasingly means human capital, particularly knowledge workers. Many firms have used stock grants and options as a way of bringing better representation to employees, but the practice is not as widespread as it might be. In most cases it has not led to direct involvement by employees in electing directors.

## ◆ NEW FORMS OF BOARD GOVERNANCE

The practices described to this point have proven effective in building strong boards that collaborate productively with management. However, new forms of enterprise may call for a quite different membership mix. Whereas the board of a traditional manufacturing firm might require a majority of independent outsiders to best serve its stakeholders, a new high-tech start-up company might need a board heavily weighted with technically knowledgeable insiders, plus one or two venture capital representatives. Indeed, some established firms have created independent boards internally to govern the development and start-up of new ventures rather than spinning off these enterprises. This approach allows the new firm to operate free of the parent company's overhead and bureaucracy.

Partnerships and joint ventures have become attractive enterprise models because more and more firms are outsourcing ancillary functions and developing long-term relationships with suppliers. New board models with cross memberships may be needed to cement these relationships and increase the participants' security. These newer models may by definition result in a higher level of stakeholder representation than traditional models.

## Conclusion

In the twenty-first century, more will be demanded of corporate boards. It is to be expected that new forms of governance will emerge to accommodate these challenges. CEOs struggling with the challenges and opportunities of new technologies and corporate models, instantaneous communications, globalization, and lightning-quick competitive forces will be more dependent than ever on their governing boards to provide wise counsel and support in developing and implementing the right strategies.

Boards must be prepared to meet this challenge and to understand the needs of the firm's broader stakeholders. To position themselves to do this, they must first set in place the practices and develop the structure by which they will govern. They, their corporation, and its stakeholders will be well served if, in this process, they pay attention to those five attributes of high performance boards mentioned earlier: knowledge, information, power, rewards, and time and opportunity.

PART

V

# Focusing on the Human Dimension

Traditionally, many employees were promoted to supervisory and managerial positions based on their prior success in technical fields of expertise, such as engineering, accounting/finance, or sales. Often, they were ill prepared for the tremendous challenges of understanding the complexities of human behavior at work, and there was little information available to assist them. Approximately a half-century ago, the field of organizational behavior (OB) began to emerge, and its goal since then has been to establish an integrated field of knowledge based on a solid foundation of conceptual, theoretical, and research material. Borrowing initially from the fields of psychology, sociology, social psychology, and other domains, OB sought to identify the primary outcomes that organizations seek to obtain and the key causal factors that contribute to those outcomes. Although at one time focused on the academic preparation of future managers in college and university courses, several professors have become popular-press authors. Some of these have recently begun to share their insights and suggestions via practitioner-oriented "best-sellers."

Edward E. Lawler III is widely acknowledged as one of the country's premier experts on management. He is a distinguished professor of management and organization in the Marshall School of Business and director of the Center for Effective Organizations at the University of Southern California. Lawler received his Ph.D. from the University of California-Berkeley, was the recipient of a Lifetime Achievement Award from ASTD, and has been named a Fellow of the Academy of Management. He has prepared over thirty books, including *Pay and Organizational Performance, Managerial Attitudes and Performance, The Ultimate Advantage,* and *High-Involvement Management.*

Lawler suggests that treating people right is a challenging task, with payoffs for both organizations and their members. He portrays a "virtuous spiral of success" that moves beyond simply providing adequate working conditions and fair pay to induce new levels of sustained peak performance. Specific practices include "branding" the firm as a place for high achievers, recruiting and selecting high performers, and institutionalizing a leadership style that supports and rewards desired levels of individual and organizational performance. This is achieved through the integration of job design, reward systems, training programs, and a host of other recommendations.

Cindy Ventrice is the author of *Make Their Day!* Ventrice is a management consultant and workshop leader for Potential Unlimited in Santa Cruz, California, and a member of the National Speakers' Association of Northern California. As the basis for her book, she asked employees around the country to answer the question, "What kind of recognition makes your day?" She discovered that employees are often critical of existing programs and overblown special events. Ventrice suggests that there are four elements of effective recognition—praise, thanks, opportunity, and respect. These can be administered meaningfully, easily, and inexpensively to produce desired effects on morale, motivation, and profits.

Mihaly Csikszentmihalyi, the author of *Good Business,* is the C.S. and D.J. Davidson Professor of Psychology at the Peter F. Drucker School of Management at Claremont Graduate University and the director of The Quality of Life Research Center. His research interests include positive psychology, creativity, socialization, and the study of intrinsically rewarding behavior in work and play settings. Csikszentmihalyi is the author of *Flow: The Psychology of Optimal Experience, The Evolving Self: A Psychology for the Third Millennium,* and *Finding Flow: The Psychology of Engagement with Everyday Life.* He is a recipient of BrainChannels' "Thinker of the Year" award.

Csikszentmihalyi argues that workplaces can be dismal places when they have destroyed employee trust, given workers no clear goals, failed to provide adequate feedback, and taken away any sense of control. He suggests that CEOs need to recognize that the total fulfillment of a person's potential is what usually generates true happiness, and this begins with a philosophy and belief that the company will be operating successfully one hundred years from now. He articulates the eight central features underlying flow, and suggests that managers can create the conditions for flow by making the workplace attractive, finding ways to imbue the job with meaning and value, and selecting and rewarding individuals who find satisfaction in their work.

Paul Lawrence and Nitin Nohria, in *Driven,* assert that employees act as they do because of a set of conscious choices made. These choices are affected by human nature and four innate drives: 1. to acquire objects of status, 2. to bond with others in long-term relationships, 3. to learn, grow, and make sense of the world, and 4. to defend themselves and others from harm. The key to attaining well-being is to balance the four drives, while never expecting that total balance and agreement are likely outcomes.

Paul Lawrence is the Wallace Brett Donham Professor of Organizational Behavior Emeritus at Harvard Business School. Many of his twenty-four books, including *Organization and Environment,* have focused on organizational design, organizational change, and the human aspects of management. Nitin Nohria is Richard P. Chapman Professor of Business Administration and chairman of the Organizational Behavior Unit at Harvard Business School. He has co-authored or edited seven books, including *The Differentiated Network.*

READING 1

# Treat People Right!


*EDWARD E. LAWLER III*

*Summary prepared by Danielle DuBois Kerr*



***Danielle DuBois Kerr*** *is a consultant with R.S.M. McGladrey's human resources consulting practice. Danielle assists clients in their compensation and benefits needs and has experience in compensation market pricing, salary surveys, job analysis and job descriptions, salary structure design, benefits administration, and compliance. Danielle attained her Professional in Human Resources certification from the Society of Human Resources Management. She received a Bachelor of Business Administration degree from the University of Minnesota Duluth, with a major in both Human Resource and Organizational Management. She is a member of the Twin Cities Human Resource Association.*


*In today's tough business environment, organizations and people can't succeed without the other.* Organizations need to be successful so they can provide meaningful work and reward their people, but in order to be successful, organizations need high-performing people. Finding a mutually beneficial path that leads both parties to this joint definition of success seems difficult to find. *However, there is a path that can lead both individuals and organizations to their goals. It is to "treat people right."*

The challenge is to create organizational structures that provide employees with meaningful work and appropriate rewards, while motivating and satisfying them to behave in ways that help their organizations become effective and high-performing. Both parties need to understand how the other operates in order to make informed decisions about the relationship. For example, an organization may treat its people right by investing in new training and development programs. However, for the training program to be successful, the individual must decide to take on additional responsibility for learning new skills and embrace the opportunity to manage his or her own career. Without a mutual commitment to the program, neither will succeed.

---

Edward E. Lawler III, *Treat People Right! How Organizations and Individuals Can Propel Each Other into a Virtuous Spiral of Success.* San Francisco: Jossey-Bass, 2003.

## VIRTUOUS SPIRALS

Organizations that value and reward their people will motivate them to perform well, which in turn propels organizations to attain higher levels of accomplishment. When individuals and organizations achieve more and more of their goals, a *virtuous spiral* evolves. These spirals are the ultimate competitive advantage. They are win-win relationships that are hard-to-duplicate sources of positive momentum. The virtuous spiral begins with strategy, follows with organization design, and then proceeds through an iterative process of staffing–performance–rewards that continues onward.

Organizations that mishandle their human capital are susceptible to inverting this process, in turn creating a *death spiral.* During a death spiral, an organization will see both individual and organizational performance decline. These unwanted spirals can last for decades, or can be relatively fast and only last a few days.

How can a virtuous spiral be launched and a death spiral avoided? *Simply being nice to people and treating them well is not enough.* Organizations need to develop a wide array of human capital management practices that motivate people to excel and then follow through by rewarding them for high levels of performance. In turn, individuals need to make greater commitments to their own careers and organizations, at the same time becoming responsible for their own behaviors.

## THE COMPONENTS OF AN EFFECTIVE ORGANIZATION

Before organizations can effectively establish human capital management practices, they need to lay the appropriate foundation for treating people right. The organization itself must be effective. This means that the organization must have alignment among four determinants of effectiveness:

1. *Strategy:* The master plan for the organization, which include its goals, purpose, products/services, etc.
2. *Organizational capabilities:* The factors that allow an organization to coordinate and focus its behavior to produce levels of performance required by its strategy. One example is the ability to manage and develop new knowledge.
3. *Core competencies:* A combination of technology and production skills that help define and create an organization's products/services, such as an organization's ability to miniaturize its products.
4. *Environment:* The context in which the organization operates. Examples include the business climate, the state of the economy, and the political and physical environment.

The organization must have a clear understanding of these factors before it can cultivate its human capital, organizational structure, reward systems and processes. Once the organization lays its foundation for effectiveness, it can take steps to treat people right. Implementing the seven principles to treating people right will give the organization the capability of launching a virtuous spiral.

## SEVEN KEY PRINCIPLES FOR TREATING PEOPLE RIGHT

### 1. ATTRACTION AND RETENTION

*"Organizations must create a value proposition that defines the type of workplace they want to be so that they can attract and retain the right people."* Creating a value proposition communicates who the organization is, what it wants and what is has to offer. This allows an organization to attract and employ individuals who are aligned with its values and goals. Each organization should consider having multiple value propositions to attract and retain a diverse workforce. For example, rewards that are designed to retain core employees probably focus on encouraging individual commitment to the organization. Rewards for this group of employees usually include a stake in the organization through some type of stock ownership. On the other hand, some employees may not be interested in ownership, so it would be wise to develop a separate value proposition for this group. Overall, the propositions should be well thought out and focus on what the organization has to offer in order to attract and retain the right people needed to achieve a high-performing organization. In turn, a virtuous spiral could evolve.

### 2. HIRING PRACTICES

*"Organizations must hire people who fit with their values, core competencies, and strategic goals."* This requires a clear and disciplined process that allows the organization to properly assess the competencies, skills, knowledge, personality, and needs of applicants. Objective data should be collected through assessment tools such as personality tests or knowledge exams. Another valuable tool for collecting data is background checks, as past behavior has been demonstrated to be the best predictor of future behavior. An organization that does not have effective hiring practices will have a very hard time reaching a virtuous spiral.

### 3. TRAINING AND DEVELOPMENT

*"Organizations must continuously train employees to do their jobs and offer them opportunities to grow and develop."* Commitment to an organization's training and development program reinforces the value an organization places on creating a virtuous spiral. By doing so, employees' skills are essentially increased and a virtuous spiral is reinforced. Overall, supporting a training and development program is not only valuable to the organization, but also adds value to each employee as it helps ignite one's personal career spiral by providing the opportunity to learn, develop and experience new things.

### 4. WORK DESIGN

*"Organizations must design work so that it is meaningful for people and provides them with feedback, responsibility, and autonomy."* Employee motivation, satisfaction, and performance are greatly influenced by this principle, and can have a significant influence on the overall effectiveness of an organization. In order to influence these factors, organizations must make work involving, challenging, and rewarding for people. To do so organizations must:

- Avoid simplified jobs.
- Design *enriched jobs* that allow one to experience meaningfulness, have responsibility for outcomes of his or her behavior, and receive feedback about his or her results.

Not all work can be enriched to the fullest extent nor can all of the repetitive work in the world be eliminated. To combat this problem, an organization should consider making the work intrinsically satisfying, offer higher extrinsic rewards or possibly outsource simplified, repetitive work to subcontractors. That said, paying attention to the way in which work is designed could have a significant impact on employees' motivation and satisfaction, which may in turn hinder or propel a virtuous spiral.

## 5. MISSION, STRATEGIES AND GOALS

*"Organizations must develop and adhere to a specific organizational mission, with strategies, goals, and values that employees can understand, support and believe in."* Goals are a powerful motivator of behavior that can lead and direct an organization down a certain path. Accomplishment of goals gives people feelings of intrinsic satisfaction that cause them to reach for higher performance and to form a stronger commitment to the overall organizational mission and strategy. In turn, accomplishment sparks and carries the momentum of the virtuous spiral.

For the spiral to continue moving ahead, the established goals must be meaningful. Some may be noble and have a higher order mission, while others may be purely financial and performance driven. Both types have the ability to effectively influence individual and organizational results as long as there is a line of sight between the individual's behavior and the end result. For example, goals cannot be accomplished or even supported if they are hidden from the public eye. Employees must be committed to reaching goals and when they can see a direct connection between their behavior and the goal, attainment of the goal becomes more likely. In sum, when employees can understand, support, and believe in the developed mission and strategies, the potential for a virtuous spiral is greatly increased.

## 6. REWARD SYSTEMS

*"Organizations must devise and implement reward systems that reinforce their design, core values, and strategy."* Reward systems are influential in obtaining a virtuous spiral. To be effective, the systems must reward performance, be properly aligned with the organization's design, core values and strategy, and must motivate people to perform effectively. Several criteria should be considered when designing a reward system. First, the systems must have a clear line of sight between the desired outcomes and the individual behaviors needed to obtain those outcomes. Second, the size of the reward must be large enough to capture the attention of the employees and make a difference in their motivation. For example, average merit increases have been three to four percent over the past few years. If the reward were smaller than this, it might not capture their attention. However, a raise or a bonus of 10 percent is more likely to spark people's interest, in turn motivating certain behaviors. Third, if an organization has a pay-for-performance system in place, employees must possess the power, information, and knowledge they need to influence their performance. Finally, leadership must create credibility for their reward programs. This means being trustworthy and

carrying out promises. If all criteria are designed properly, reward systems can be a powerful tool in becoming a high-performing organization.

### 7. LEADERSHIP

*"Organizations must hire and develop leaders who can create commitment, trust, success, and a motivating work environment."* Individual and organizational effectiveness can be greatly affected by leadership at all levels. So how can managers be most effective? The answer is simple: Set up win-win situations (in essence, virtuous spirals). Findings from The Ohio State University in the 1950s showed that the most effective managers focused on both organizational and individual results. Satisfying the wants and needs of both groups (managers and employees) can be a challenge; however, the responsibility should not reside on the shoulders of one person. The organization's leadership must be shared, including the responsibility for motivating employees and creating a vision.

## ◆ CREATING A VIRTUOUS SPIRAL

Getting organizations to a point where they are ready to develop a virtuous spiral can be very challenging. It requires well planned strategic actions to gain momentum. To start a virtuous spiral, a strategy must be developed by effective change leaders. Next, employees must be motivated to change and a vision should be created. Finally, all seven principles of treating people right need to be implemented. All steps must be set in place; one step simply cannot be omitted. Failure to do so leads to the risk of making all adopted principles dysfunctional. Once the spiral has begun, it needs regular check-ups to make sure the organization is heading in the right direction. Depending upon changes within or outside the organization, changes may be needed to one or all of the steps used to initiate the spiral.

## ◆ FALSE AND FRAUDULENT SPIRALS

As organizations develop their own spirals, false or fraudulent spirals can wreak havoc on the ability or potential to create a virtuous spiral of success. A *false spiral* occurs when an organization thinks a virtuous spiral has been initiated, when in fact the thought is simply an illusion. A good example of this was observed in the dot-com industry during the 1990s. In general, the market value of many dot-com organizations was greatly inflated. These companies believed they were in the midst of a virtuous spiral, when in fact their market values were too high. Eventually their stock prices collapsed and the majority of these dot-coms fell into a death spiral. *Fraudulent spirals* are another type of spiral that can cause destruction. These spirals can be easily mistaken as virtuous although they are created by deceitful activities. These practices were recently uncovered at several large corporations such as Enron, WorldCom, and Adelphia. Once fraudulent behavior surfaces, the organization almost always falls into a *death spiral.* Organizations must steer clear of these two types of spirals and focus their efforts on successfully implementing the seven principles mentioned earlier.

## ◆ THREATS TO A VIRTUOUS SPIRAL

Once a virtuous spiral has been initiated, there is no guarantee that it will stay intact. Many internal and external threats can quickly turn the spiral in the wrong direction. One important and increasingly prevalent threat is environmental changes, including new competitors or industry regulations. Environmental changes are serious threats, which may call for new organizational strategies. This threat is so critical that the virtuous spiral model presented earlier was revised to take this threat into consideration. The new model again starts with an initial sequence of strategy–organizational design–staffing–performance–rewards, but then includes strategy *change,* organizational design *change,* and performance *change,* all of which are based on the fact that organizations need to pay attention to the environment and may need to react to changes by altering their initial foundation. The model then proceeds onward to iterative cycles of rewards–staffing–performance.

Environmental changes occur in many different forms and in many different frequencies. Depending upon these factors, each organization needs individually to assess when to react to the environment. When the timing is right, an organization will have the capability to change by tweaking the seven principles of "treating people right."

Environmental changes are just one type of threat to an organization's virtuous spiral. Others include:

- Economic downturn within a country
- Industry-specific economic downturn
- Mistakes or self-inflicted threats
- Fads or fashions

Any one of these threats can devastate an organization's financial performance. However, threats do not and cannot automatically cause a death spiral. A well thought out response to any threat can actually save an organization and launch it into a new virtuous spiral by causing it to rethink its strategy and re-lay its foundation.

## Conclusion

Virtuous spirals can flourish in organizations that perform well and treat people right. Despite the numerous threats to an organization, virtuous spirals can be rekindled and launched into new directions. It is important to consider and recognize that organizations serve multiple stakeholders. Meeting financial performance goals is important, but so is satisfying customers, employees, stockholders, and community members. It must be remembered that organizations are made of people, they are created by people, and they exist to serve people. *If organizations do not treat people right they should not (and often will not) exist.*

# Make Their Day: Employee Recognition That Works

*CINDY VENTRICE*

*Summary prepared by Jannifer David*

***Jannifer David** teaches Human Resource Management at the Labovitz School of Business and Economics at the University of Minnesota Duluth. Her courses include employee recruiting and selection, training and development, and introductory human resource management. Her research interests follow two tracks: international human resource management, and the use of contingent workers and how they affect the work relationships of others within organizations. She received her Ph.D. in Labor and Industrial Relations from Michigan State University. Prior to her graduate studies she worked as a Human Resources Consultant for Mercer Human Resource Consulting.*

## ◆ INTRODUCTION

*Recognition* is any form of personalized acknowledgement of an employee's accomplishments toward organizational goals. Well designed employee recognition can lead to positive employee and organizational outcomes such as high employee morale, low turnover, and even higher productivity and profits. Employee recognition, however, involves more than the presentation of a plaque or certificate. *Effective recognition must meet the personal needs of each employee.* To ensure that employees receive this level of appreciation, managers should make an effort to create work environments that incorporate meaningful recognition as often as possible from a variety of sources.

---

Cindy Ventrice, *Make Their Day: Employee Recognition That Works.* San Francisco: Berrett-Koehler, 2003.

## WHAT IS EFFECTIVE RECOGNITION?

To deliver effective recognition, managers should consider its four key elements: praise, thanks, opportunity, and respect.

- *Praise* and compliments affirm that managers understand the accomplishments of their employees and how these accomplishments positively affect the organization's mission.
- Sincere *thanks* from managers make employees feel valued. Written thank you notes or other methods of showing appreciation and delivering thanks for employees that clearly state their accomplishments are excellent reminders of their manager's appreciation.
- Employees who have performed well should be provided *opportunities* to expand their knowledge and/or control over their work. These opportunities will make employees feel trusted by their managers and will likely lead to higher organizational loyalty, commitment, and increased efforts to perform well.
- *Respect* is critical to any integrated recognition effort. Managers should minimally strive for a work environment that is safe and pleasant. Beyond this they should make an effort to get to know each of their employees and show confidence in their capabilities to show that they respect them as people as well as workers.

Recognition can motivate people through either intrinsic or extrinsic sources. Both sources are valuable tools for managers to use. *Extrinsic recognition* encompasses any items that can be bestowed upon employees from others, such as bonuses, certificates, new offices, etc. Extrinsic rewards, if used properly, can work well but they are limited because they do not provide long-lasting effects. Intrinsic motivation, however, comes from within employees. Because employees are the source of this motivation and recognition, it is tailored to their needs and is therefore more powerful than extrinsic motivation. Sources of *intrinsic motivation* (feelings that come from within) include: appropriate job design, valued purpose, and trust. Well designed jobs provide opportunities for intrinsic motivation through the satisfaction that comes from performing the job tasks. Employees with a clear purpose for their jobs will have greater intrinsic motivation, as these employees will be able to see the value of their efforts. Trusting employees to do their work without micro-managing every detail imparts employees with respect as people worthy of trust, and gives them an opportunity to decide for themselves how work should be done.

Managers must know who their employees are and what their individual needs are. Recognition must be tailored to individuals, and this can be facilitated by developing close relationships with each of them. For example, public recognition of achievement may work well for some employees, but may embarrass other employees who are extremely shy or introverted. Employees should be able to trust that managers are offering recognition because of sincere appreciation for their efforts and receive recognition that is personalized enough for them to see that management truly understands who they are as people. If this happens, then this recognition will retain its intended meaning and not become a negative interaction between employees and their managers.

## WHO IS RESPONSIBLE FOR PROVIDING RECOGNITION?

*Managers are the primary deliverers of extrinsic forms of recognition.* Most employees see their managers as the main representatives of their organization. If their managers provide good recognition, then they are likely to think their organizations provide good recognition. Unfortunately, many managers are reluctant to give recognition because they feel that it is unnecessary, have had negative reactions to recognition provided in the past, are busy doing their daily work and don't feel they have time to give recognition, or fear backlashes for perceived favoritism in their recognition efforts. Employees, however, want recognition so as to obtain feedback on their efforts. Even negative feedback can be seen as recognition if it is offered as a developmental tool and imparts to employees a sense that management trusts they are capable of making the suggested improvements. To meet this employee need, managers ought to overcome their doubts about recognition.

Managers, however, are not the only important component of successful recognition programs. Organizations that are truly successful with recognition tend to have executive leadership that embraces and promotes recognition. Company executives should set examples of good recognition habits by getting to know their employees and regularly bestowing recognition on them. Recognition from top executives in organizations can be a particularly powerful motivator for rank and file employees, who may frequently feel they go unknown and unnoticed by high-level executives. When executives place high priority on recognition, they indicate to other managers and supervisors that recognition is an important part of the work environment. These managers and supervisors will strive to include recognition in their management styles and in the work environments of their employees. Finally, to solidify their public commitment to recognition, executives should recognize their mid-level managers' efforts to provide recognition for lower level employees, thus creating a waterfall effect. Through these efforts executives can ensure that their organizations have a culture of recognition that will improve employee loyalty and organizational performance.

Human Resource departments can contribute significantly to the success of recognition programs, but their roles are typically behind the scenes. HR departments have the professional knowledge to design high-quality recognition programs. They can also provide management with information regarding the success of recognition efforts through the design and administration of employee surveys. HR professionals, however, should not be the primary *deliverers* of recognition. HR professionals are not close enough to employees to provide the personalized recognition that is necessary for these interactions to be most effective. In addition to line managers and executives, co-workers and employees themselves are generally the organizational members closest to employees' efforts and they are best suited to provide this in-depth level of feedback.

Co-workers, while not a replacement for managerial recognition, are a powerful source. *Peer recognition*—formal or informal efforts by co-workers to praise employees for their positive contributions at work—can go a long way toward creating a pleasant work environment. Peer recognition efforts can be very informal, utilizing everyday items as signs of appreciation, such as giving tools as "fix it" awards to co-workers. Organizations can also implement formal peer recognition programs whereby co-workers can either directly reward employees with company-supplied awards or they can nominate their co-workers for company-wide awards. Either approach can help employees feel that they are appreciated and improve their everyday work environment.

Self-recognition provides another method of helping employees feel appreciated and rewarded. Organizations that promote self-recognition may develop programs for employees to highlight their accomplishments during the previous business cycle and share these accomplishments with other employees throughout the organization. By giving employees control over their own recognition it ensures that employees will be recognized for those achievements that mean the most to them. This approach also helps management understand what aspects of work their employees value the most, which should assist management in developing other meaningful recognition opportunities for these employees.

## HOW SHOULD MANAGERS DELIVER EFFECTIVE RECOGNITION?

Managers can develop, perhaps in conjunction with HR departments, recognition programs that consistently see behaviors and performance worthy of recognition and reward employees accordingly. Delivering effective recognition requires managers to develop tools that address the need for recognition specific to each employee's contributions to the organization's mission, that give recognition consistently and fairly, and that make recognition an ongoing process. Recognition that specifically relates each employee's achievement(s) and/or behaviors to the organization's mission and values is most effective for improving employee morale. Therefore, organizations and managers should develop criteria for recognition that are directly related to the organization's mission and values. These criteria should be used consistently in determining who receives recognition as well as the magnitude of such recognition. Announcing these criteria will let employees know in advance what is going to be rewarded and help allay any fears of favoritism. Further, recognizing an employee for achievements and behaviors that foster the organization's mission and values helps impress upon the employee the importance of this mission.

To ensure consistency and accuracy of the recognition program, the criteria used in determining employee recognition should be based upon solid measurement techniques. Measuring organizational variables related to missions and values will help managers determine who should be recognized and reinforce within organizations that these goals are important. Measuring organizational outcomes will ensure that employees pay attention to these outcomes and strive to improve them. Measuring should be done carefully, however, as only measuring one dimension of an outcome may result in undesired employee behaviors. Measurements should be taken from multiple sources and using multiple methods to be certain that unintended and undesirable outcomes do not result from the measurement system. *Good measurements should be quantifiable, consistent over time, and provide an accurate picture of current conditions.* For more indepth analyses qualitative data may be acquired through the use of interviews, focus groups or observation, but these methods shouldn't be relied upon solely as a basis for a recognition program.

To set these ideas into action managers and supervisors should begin by trying to understand two aspects of their employees: 1. their unique contributions to the mission and values of the organization; and 2. how they prefer to be recognized. In addition to observing employees to learn how they are contributing, it is wise to sit down with them to discuss their contributions. During this conversation, managers should ask their employees how they think they are contributing to the organization's mission, what else they think they could be doing to foster the mission, and which of their tasks could be modified or eliminated because they do not currently contribute to the mission. Through this conversation, employees may come to learn more about how their jobs relate to the organization's mission and managers should learn which tasks their employees are most committed to, and therefore would be the best tasks for recognition.

To determine the best methods of recognizing each employee, managers should develop relationships with each of their employees to understand who they are. Learning what employees do in their non-work time, identifying their career aspirations, and exploring other personal traits may provide valuable information about how they would prefer to be recognized. Beyond information gathered in this fashion, managers may be more straightforward and ask their employees through surveys about how they would prefer to receive recognition for various levels of exemplary performance.

Once managers have ascertained how their employees contribute and how they would prefer to be recognized, the final stage is the actual recognition. Managers need to take what they have learned and make a concerted effort to recognize their employees whenever these opportunities present themselves. When giving this recognition managers should follow some simple guidelines:

- **Recognition efforts should be commensurate with their employees' achievements.** Large achievements should be recognized with substantial rewards, while smaller achievements should also receive recognition, but on a lesser scale.
- **Past failures with recognition shouldn't be a reason to avoid giving recognition in the future.** Those employees who are not accustomed to receiving recognition may be wary at first, but continued efforts to provide them with personalized recognition will eventually lead to successful outcomes.
- **Recognition should be offered continually.** Grandiose recognition given at irregular intervals will not be as effective for employees as frequent, smaller recognition efforts.
- **Managers should constantly look for ways to allow recognition to come intrinsically from the job** and not make it always be dependent upon external sources.

To assist managers with these guidelines, it is often a good idea to develop a plan for offering recognition. Without such a plan, recognition may be sporadic and inconsistent with huge awards for relatively small deeds and fewer awards toward the end of the year because budgets have disappeared. If recognition is new to an organization or manager, then the best approach is to start small. A pilot program of recognition efforts can be a way to begin offering recognition before committing to a large program that could be unsuccessful. Pilot programs are typically offered in one area/unit of the company and studied to ensure that the results would be beneficial to the whole organization. First, managers should assess the levels of recognition and job satisfaction that currently exist. Employee surveys may be a useful tool for this. The results of these surveys will point out areas where successful efforts already exist and places where help is needed. Both of these pieces of information are worth noting, as successful efforts may be transplanted to areas of need.

The next steps in developing a plan are to determine the funding available and to set up a timeline for deployment of the plan. Funds may come from multiple sources such as bonus pools, training programs, employee events, and a manager's discretionary funds. Managers should make use of all possible resources. Realistic timelines for delivering recognition should be set that allocate recognition events throughout the budget year. By planning ahead, managers can ensure that recognition efforts don't begin with a bang and then dwindle out toward the end of the year, causing a demoralizing effect in employees. Finally, a good recognition program should have built-in opportunities to improve. Managers should observe how their recognition is received and modify it as needed.

## Conclusion

A well designed employee recognition program can help organizations improve many employee and organizational outcomes. Employees who receive quality recognition will be motivated to perform better and will, in the long run, have higher job satisfaction. Positive employee attitudes make their managers' jobs easier and make their organizations more successful. To achieve these outcomes managers should develop recognition programs that are personalized to the employee's unique needs and take into consideration his or her contributions to organizational goals. These employee recognitions will have the positive outcomes predicted for employees, managers, and their organizations.

# Good Business: Leadership, Flow, and the Making of Meaning


***MIHALY CSIKSZENTMIHALYI***

***Summary prepared by Kelly Nelson***



***Kelly Nelson** is a General Manager, Labor Relations with AK Steel Corporation, headquartered in Middletown, OH. She is responsible for the labor negotiations of the organization's seven carbon, stainless, and specialty steel–producing facilities located in Pennsylvania, Kentucky, Ohio, and Indiana. In her position, she has daily opportunity to explore the "right" course of action and what framework provides the appropriate structure for the greater good not only of the organization, but for all stakeholders. A believer in enhancing human well-being, she receives the greatest intrinsic rewards as a parent to her son John, as a daughter, as a sister, as an auntie, as well as an enthusiastic student of human behavior.*


## ◆ INTRODUCTION

Business leaders who manage their businesses to enhance the happiness of human beings provide an environment in which individual workers flourish and reasonable profits are made. Leaders who manage their organizations with a moral obligation toward the greater good share characteristics that, if more widely adopted, will lead to businesses truly making life happier for all.

Business leaders today have become the leaders of society—much like the nobility of the past. As leaders of society, it is incumbent upon business leaders to enrich the lives of individuals in society. This obligation goes beyond the focus of the quarterly

---

Mihaly Csikszentmihalyi, *Good Business: Leadership, Flow, and the Making of Meaning.* New York: Penguin Putnam, 2003.

financial review. It reaches all aspects of life because the careers that everyone follows, and how they feel about those careers, affects how they feel about themselves as individuals, family members, community participants, and contributors to society.

## ◆ THE DUAL GOALS OF BUSINESS

As difficult as the balance is, today there are a number of CEOs who demonstrate that financially successful business enterprises can also contribute to human happiness. These individuals share common principles of good business, and firmly believe that they have an obligation to society that is broader and has longer term significance than success based solely on financial strength. These CEOs embrace the *hundred-year manager philosophy,* which dictates leading the business enterprise and making decisions based upon the belief that the company will be operating successfully one hundred years from now.

The basis of human happiness is not universal, and this makes it more difficult to conduct a business in such a way that it ensures human happiness. It is generally agreed that happiness is, as Aristotle expressed it, the *summum bonum,* or the chief good. This philosophy holds that, while people desire other goods (such as money or power) because they believe those things will make them happy, they want happiness for its own sake. In fact, businesses are built on the premise that the goods and/or services produced will make people happy, so there will be a market for the products produced.

However, *the total fulfillment of a person's potential is what usually generates true happiness.* Total fulfillment depends upon the presence of two forces—differentiation and integration. The process of *differentiation* suggests that we are all unique individuals, responsible for ourselves, with the self-confidence to develop our uniqueness. *Integration* implies that, although we are unique individuals, we all are completely immersed in networks of relationships with other human beings, our environment, our culture, and our material possessions. A person who is fully differentiated and integrated becomes a *complex individual* and one most probable to develop true happiness.

The evolution of individual complexity changes throughout the stages of one's life. It culminates at the point where an individual has an appreciation for uniqueness and is in control of thoughts, actions, and feelings, while relishing dependence and interrelatedness to others, the environment, and the culture. Although the maturation of complexity is desired and is necessary for ultimate happiness, businesses who work to support complexity not only work for financial success, but the ideal that the business exists for a greater good.

## ◆ THE BASES OF FLOW

Individuals who have developed complexity have the capacity truly to enjoy the work that they do. The total immersion one feels when completing tasks with no distinction between thought and action, or self and environment, is an element of flow, and *flow is an individual's full involvement with life.* Although individuals may feel flow from different life activities, eight conditions determine flow.

1. *Goals are clear.* The clarity of the goal allows individuals to focus their attention and to appreciate the completion of each step along the way to the goal.
2. *Feedback is immediate.* The individual knows internally whether each step is completed with the level of excellence acceptable to the individual. This can be provided by external sources; however, an individual who has achieved flow is able through knowledge and past experience to trust his or her internal standards.
3. *A balance between opportunity and capacity.* When the challenges faced by the individual are high and equal to the individual's skills, flow is possible.
4. *Concentration deepens.* As an individual focuses on the task at hand, his or her concentration deepens to the point that "thinking" is no longer necessary. Instead, the individual is focused and the process feels effortless.
5. *The present is what matters.* Concentration on the events at hand allows other worries and thoughts to be eliminated. The individual escapes in a positive manner by using his or her skill to accomplish the task.
6. *Control is no problem.* Because flow allows the individual to control his or her own performance and disregard environmental elements, the individual is in control and feels the power of his or her own control.
7. *The sense of time is altered.* The speed at which time passes depends upon two elements—how focused the mind is on the task and whether the individual's "clock" speeds up or slows down. Occasions of flow can either cause time to fly by or to appear to be passing in slow motion.
8. *The loss of ego.* The final condition of flow is the individual's loss of ego. As workers completely focus on the task at hand and their skills and activities to complete their tasks, there is no concentration left over to focus on themselves. The consumption of oneself allows one to be self-less.

The ability to enter flow, of course, does not guarantee that the individual is happy or contented. However, it provides the opportunity to grow. Individual growth, in turn, adds more happiness and accomplishment to the individual's life.

The ability to enter flow fluctuates during the day. Each individual's internal clock provides opportunities at different times. The activities faced in the individual's day also determine the propensity to enter flow, as a function of challenges (high or low) and personal skill level (high or low). If a person's challenges are high and the person's skills are high, flow is possible. This is most often achieved when the individual is involved in favorite activities. On the other hand, when challenges and skills are both low, the individual is more apt to feel apathy, such as when one is lonely or passively watching television.

As the individual's challenge level increases, but his/her skills do not increase, the individual first feels worried and then reaches anxiety. If, when at a high challenge period, the individual's skill level increases, the individual moves from anxiety to arousal. In the state of arousal, such as when learning a new skill, the individual is alert and focused. As the individual's skill level increases, it is possible to move from arousal to the state of flow.

When employees' challenges and skills are low, they feel apathetic. If their challenges do not increase but their skill level does, it leads to boredom. As skill increase, boredom turns to relaxation, which leads to control as challenges increase to meet the skill level. From the point of control, it is possible to increase both the challenges and skill level to enter flow.

Prospective leaders challenge themselves and develop their skill levels to increase the times in which they experience relaxation, control, arousal, and flow. As the proportion of time spent in these areas increases, the individual experiences more opportunities to grow in his or her complexity, leading to still more happiness and contentment in life.

Although flow is important for personal development, flow may or may not be a part of an individual's workday. Most jobs were created to get the most productivity out of individuals, but not necessarily to bring out the best in them. Managers should seek to provide career opportunities and motivational conditions that bring out the best in people. Motivation toward work is determined by three conditions: 1. the type of job available, 2. the value the culture assigns to the job, and 3. the attitude the individual has toward his or her job.

Managers who build an organization that brings out the best in workers have three options:

1. Make the objective conditions of the workplace as attractive as possible;
2. Find ways to imbue the job with meaning and value; and
3. Select and reward individuals who find satisfaction in their work.

Although there have been general improvements in the workplace over the years, there are several reasons that workers still lack the opportunity for flow in their jobs. First, the goals of individual jobs have become more obscure. Many times the individual worker does not understand either the short- or long-term goals so although they may understand *what* they are doing, they do not understand *why.* It is difficult for workers to derive true satisfaction and accomplishment if they do not understand why they are doing what they are doing.

Secondly, workers are rarely provided with clear, timely feedback. The lack of feedback prevents employees from understanding that what they are doing is important and does matter to the organization. The skills of the worker are also not necessarily matched to the skills needed in the job, and this prevents the experience of flow. Also, workers feel a lack of control in setting not only the goals of the process, but also determining the rhythm of the process. Managers who want to allow workers to achieve their best must redesign the workplace to eliminate barriers to flow.

## ◆ BUILDING FLOW INTO ORGANIZATIONS

It is possible for managers to redesign the workplace to encourage the growth of individuals to allow more flow. It takes a complete commitment from top management to create an environment that will foster flow. Because the profitability of flow does not appear neatly on a spreadsheet, it requires strong leaders who have achieved complexity and who understand business's duty to increase human well-being to redesign the workplace to achieve it.

It takes a leap of faith by top management to believe that redesigning the workplace will eventually result in improved financial results. It is especially important that top management commits to and believes in the fact that greater good results from improving the well-being of the individual.

To create an environment conducive to well-being, it is imperative that the organization's mission is understood by all participants and that individuals are provided the flexibility to adjust their individual goals to match the organization's goals. Managers must also allow individuals to fail without responding too harshly. Calculated risk-taking is important in challenging the individual and some risk-taking initiatives will result in either failure or lack of success. Individuals who are harshly criticized for risk-taking will learn to avoid risks (and the challenges they offer), and will fail to achieve flow.

Managers can best ensure that their workers understand the organization's true commitment to redesigning the workplace by communicating at every opportunity and to ensuring that feedback is provided. After managers ensure individuals are placed in appropriate jobs, given clearly understand goals, and provided with appropriate feedback, the work conditions must also include the eight properties conducive to achieving flow. The details of each person's properties may be different, so these should be handled in the work area of the individuals, with input and creation of the properties left to the individual and supported by the direct manager.

## ◆ THE SOUL OF BUSINESS

Creating a nurturing environment in which individuals are encouraged to achieve flow lays the groundwork to be an organization that improves human well-being; however, it does not ensure it. It is imperative that the organization has soul. *Soul is demonstrated by the organization when it devotes energy to purposes beyond itself.* The goals adopted by the organization for the greater good or to benefit others (without financial reward to itself) show the organization's base values. Often the concept of soul of the organization is similar to beliefs supported by religions—giving donations, assisting the poor, supporting community events, supporting volunteerism, and fighting for what is right.

Managers who believe their obligation is to improve human well-being share five common traits:

1. They are *optimistic* in both their feelings about people as well as their thoughts about the future.
2. They have *integrity,* or an unwavering adherence to principles on which mutual trust can be based.
3. They have a high level of *ambition* coupled with the perseverance necessary to overcome obstacles.
4. They also have *curiosity and a desire to learn.*
5. They possess *empathy* and have a basic respect for others.

Managers who possess these traits also possess the *self-confidence* to pursue their dreams and to support the dreams of others. These are the managers who supply the soul of business.

## ◆ CREATING FLOW IN LIFE

Business leaders can only provide the environment that is conducive to achieving flow. Everyone possesses the ability to achieve that state of challenge and accomplishment. It is important for people to build on their strengths by creating challenges to hone their own skills. It is also important to identify weaknesses and to strengthen them. In order to build on strengths and minimize weaknesses, it is important that employees pay attention. By paying attention, people will learn not only what their strengths and weaknesses are, but will see what is necessary to optimize them. Focusing attention to detail provides the greatest opportunity for learning and growth. Paying attention requires an investment of time. Individuals who lead others to greatness hone their use of time, develop healthy and challenging habits, and invest energy in their consciousness.

## ◆ THE FUTURE OF BUSINESS

In order for an organization to contribute to human well-being while also achieving reasonable profitability, the leaders of the organization must have a vision beyond the organization itself. They must envision the organization within the framework of its environment and the human environment. The leaders must also have the intrinsic need to do what is right in relation to human well-being that is based on trust and respect for others. This will allow the leaders to encourage the personal growth of the workers and to provide opportunities for flow in the workplace. Finally, it is imperative that organizations provide goods or services that truly enhance the well-being of people, and that they operate in an ethical, responsible manner.

The principles of good business have historically been gleaned from our religious beliefs and from the principles of our parents. The leaders of today's business who manage their business for improved human well-being will provide examples to be followed by future generations of business leaders.

# Driven: How Human Nature Shapes Our Choices

**_PAUL R. LAWRENCE and NITIN NOHRIA_**

**_Summary prepared by Gary Stark_**

***Gary Stark*** *is an assistant professor of management at Washburn University in Topeka, Kansas. He earned his Ph.D. in Management from the University of Nebraska. Gary's research interests include feedback seeking behavior and self-evaluation. Prior to his academic life, Gary earned his B.S. and M.B.A. degrees at Kansas State University and worked in Chicago as a tax accountant.*

## ◆ THE CALL FOR A UNIFIED THEORY OF HUMAN BEHAVIOR

The nature of mankind has been debated since the time of the ancient philosophers. The work of Charles Darwin revolutionized the approach, but has been largely ignored by social scientists, who feared such an approach to social issues implied racism. The present state of the social sciences is too fragmented for any single discipline to address the challenge of a more complete understanding of human behavior. However, since Darwin's time there have been great advances in our knowledge of the social sciences and biology. It is time to synthesize this wealth of knowledge to create a unified theory of human behavior—one that must meet several very challenging criteria:

- It must work at several levels of analysis—individual to organizational to societal.
- It should not contradict the present knowledge of the social sciences and biology.

---

Paul R. Lawrence and Nitin Nohria, *Driven: How Human Nature Shapes our Choices.* San Francisco: Jossey-Bass, 2002.

- It must be able to be tested empirically.
- It should be easy to teach, usable, and parsimonious.
- It should work in any cultural setting.

The present work is an attempt at developing this theory—one believed to meet these criteria. While the theory presented will require further testing, at the least it should stimulate new ways of thinking about human nature.

## EVOLUTION OF THE BRAIN

Hominids split off from other primates around six million years ago, but there was very little development in human technology from that time until about 80,000 years ago. According to archeological records there was, at that point, a very dramatic shift in human technology—from crude stone axes to needles, awls, scrapers, and the like. This revolutionary shift is known as the Great Leap. There is no consensus as to what caused the Great Leap, but contemporary understanding of innate skills, plus the limbic center and the frontal cortex of the brain, may shed light on the mystery.

Scientists now believe that evolution has selected in several innate skills for humans, including habitat selection, food selection, danger awareness, intuitive psychology, orientation, justice, and an ability to remember important people. None of these skills alone would account for the Great Leap, but at that critical point in time these skills became connected in the human brain in such a way that humans could use all these skills simultaneously to deal with complex problems. Modern methods of electronically scanning the brain allow us to see that this work of sorting through complex concepts occurs in the frontal cortex.

To fully comprehend the role of the human brain in the Great Leap we must also understand the limbic center, which is the seat of emotions or the ability to experience feelings. The limbic center had previously been regarded as the most primitive area of the brain, but research by Antonio Damasio indicates that individuals who have all their rational faculties (most notably a fully functioning frontal cortex), but have sustained damaged to the limbic center, experience a marked decrease in decision-making ability. They are able to solve complex problems and have fine memory and attention, but the inability to experience feelings renders them unable to make socially appropriate or personally beneficial decisions.

The limbic center plays a sophisticated role in "marking" incoming sensory messages for their relevance to human needs. Thus, when sensory information reaches the prefrontal cortex, where decisions are made, the limbic center has already done the job of eliminating several options from the decision.

Key in this "marking" theory is the idea that *the limbic center sorts sensory information based on human needs or drives.* The neuroscientists who have advocated this "marking theory" have not specified what those drives are, preferring to leave that work to social scientists.

Based on the accumulated work of biologists, anthropologists, psychologists, economists, and others, *the bases for many of the decisions in every fully functioning human are the needs to acquire, bond, learn, and defend.* These drives are the result of the natural selection process as they have allowed humanity to thrive and to propagate the species.

These drives were not fixed millions of years ago as many biologists believe, but instead were the product of Darwinian evolution. Indeed this configuration of drives, specifically the emergence of the drive to learn and the drive to bond as primary rather than secondary drives, was the critical development responsible for the Great Leap. This configuration allowed humans to form complex social contracts that allowed humans as a collective to attain the adaptive ability that has made them the most dominant species on earth.

## THE DRIVE TO ACQUIRE (D1)

*One of the innate drives of all humans is the drive to acquire.* Natural selection has favored those driven to acquire food, shelter, sexual consummation, and water. From an evolutionary standpoint, the drive to acquire seems the most obvious. This has led to the dominance of economic models of thought (and their corollary assumption that humans are driven only to acquire) in the social sciences. The economic model extends to say that human choice is based on the rational pursuit of self-interest.

There are instances where we can see some discord between the drive to acquire and rational self-interest and it is here we can see the role of emotion, or the limbic center. One example is food. Evolution has bestowed on humans a general attraction to foods with a high fat content. This is a derivative of our drive to acquire, as a diet high in fat helped our ancestors survive in times of food scarcity. Today, however, the unfettered drive to consume such food is at odds with rational self-interest—we know that such a diet increases our odds of a host of diseases, including heart disease and cancer. The eventual choice—to eat a certain food or not—reflects not only a rational choice, but a competition between emotions. The limbic center has been informed that eating has long-term negative consequences, but the limbic center also has been wired to drive us to eat.

The negative results of the drive to acquire (D1) are that one can never acquire enough, and that this drive may lead us to sacrifice absolute well-being for relative well-being. The constant drive to acquire ever more things leads us to increase our status to help ensure our ability to acquire. This drive is at the heart of conspicuous consumption. Evolutionarily, even in times of scarcity there was always some sustenance, but it went to those of highest status. While the futile battle to constantly increase status may lead to unhappiness, the job of our evolutionary needs is not to make us happy, but help us propagate. To propagate we must succeed against the competition.

On the positive side, the drive to acquire can also lead to cooperation. The drive to acquire can lead people to calculate comparative advantage, and specialize labor in such a way as to increase the well-being of all parties.

It is tempting to explain all human behavior in terms of the drive to acquire. But we should note that even Adam Smith, the father of modern economics, did not believe this. He stated that moral sentiments are just as important to understanding human behavior as is the drive to acquire. This helps explain anonymous acts of charity, not cheating when cheating cannot be detected, and other behaviors at odds with rational self-interest.

## ◆ THE DRIVE TO BOND (D2)

*Human beings have an innate desire to bond with others.* Early humans with this drive were more likely to pass these genes onto succeeding generations. Males were more likely to be selected as mates, females were more likely to nurture their children to adulthood, and children were more likely to avail themselves to such nurturing. Groups of individuals with this drive were more likely to form the cooperative bonds that helped the group face large challenges. The drive to bond accounts for the universal similarity of moral codes. Moral codes enhance adaptive cooperation.

The bonding drive is known by such terms as loyalty, friendship, love, fairness, empathy, and caring. There appears to be wide support suggesting that:

- People form social relationships very easily without evidence of material advantage.
- The breakup of social bonds is strongly resisted, even beyond any loss of material advantage.
- People spend a large amount of mental energy thinking about their social relationships.
- Many of the strongest human emotions, both positive and negative (such as elation, happiness, jealousy, and loneliness) are associated with bonding.
- People relatively deprived of social bonds are much more likely to suffer a wide variety of physical and mental pathologies.

The drive to bond can be shown to be separate from the drive to acquire. The strength of human bonds is determined *not* by the benefits *minus* costs of particular relationships, but of the benefits *plus* costs. That is, *sacrifices for the sake of a relationship seem to enhance that relationship.* Philosophically, we can all think of situations where the drive to acquire conflicted with the drive to bond. This universal conflict forms the appeal of art forms such as movies, literature, and plays that portray characters torn between such motives as love and money.

The drive to bond carries over to human interaction with social institutions. The growth of the human brain allowed humans the capacity to use symbols as abstractions of real events. When combined with the drive to bond, this allowed humanity to reinforce and extend social bonds with creeds, flags, songs, and ritual. Social institutions did not always exist. They were made possible by symbolization. These extended social bonds were key to developing the complex cultures and civilizations that allowed humanity to prosper.

With regard to work, Nobel laureate Herbert Simon points out that humans consistently exert more effort than is minimally required. Economists focus negatively on the shirking that occurs on jobs, but Simon points out that since shirking is the exception (and exceeding requirements is the norm), this demonstrates the human desire to see the success of organization they are bonded to.

The dark side of the drive to bond is the common occurrence of a "we versus they" mindset in many groups. This may only result in friendly rivalry but it can also take severe forms such as sabotage and even genocide.

## ◆ THE DRIVE TO LEARN (D3)

*Humans have an innate drive to learn about themselves and their surroundings.* This drive is represented by such terms as wonder, curiosity, and inquisitiveness. The drive to learn is evidenced through the universality of religion as a means to explain gaps in such unobservable mysteries as the purpose of life and the nature of an afterlife. Further, humans have always been fascinated by games, puzzles, and humor even in the absence of material reward. Gaps between what humans think they know and what they observe cause a dissonance that they are driven to reduce.

The drive to learn forms the basis of such needs as mastery, achievement, efficacy, and growth. All of these topics relate to the importance of learning in job design. Jobs that are too simplified and specialized frustrate the drive to learn and may lead to unintended consequences as workers look to relieve boredom. On the other hand, since people are intelligent and have a drive to learn, if management simply empowers workers to make improvements, it is possible to harness these attributes to the organization's betterment.

Unfortunately the drive to learn can lead people to believe plausible, but inaccurate, stories and ideologies. This may be dangerous when it enables cult leaders to take advantage of followers. Once it is lodged in the human brain a belief is difficult to dislodge. Another down side to the drive to learn is that we sometimes pursue new knowledge so aggressively we ignore its destructive potential. The most dramatic example is the pursuit of nuclear technology.

## ◆ THE DRIVE TO DEFEND (D4)

*Humans have an innate drive to protect themselves, their knowledge, their accomplishments, and their valued possessions.* This need manifests itself in the emotions of anger, fear, and alarm. This drive may have preceded the drive to acquire in evolution as evidenced by defense reactions in the simplest of creatures.

The drive to defend ties to other drives as we see evidence that humans defend the possessions they have acquired (D1), defend against threats to their loved ones or against threats to the relationships themselves (D2), and defend threats to their ideologies (D3). These threats and changes cause such reactions as resistance, caution, anxiety, denial, rationalization, and (if chronic) withdrawal, passivity, and helplessness.

More is known about the neurology of the defense drive than the other three drives. Evidence from other species and from electronic brain scanning of humans reveals that alarm-inducing messages can travel straight to the organs without passing through the cortex. Thus an individual can experience alarm without knowing why. This is why a defense reaction, such as fear or anger, can cause seemingly irrational behavior. In evolutionary terms this probably served as a valuable defense to physical dangers, but serves little purpose in today's world.

## FREE WILL AND DIVERSITY

The independence of the four drives often forces them into conflict. When there is no conflict the body can go about much of its business with minimal consciousness. However, conflict forces these drives into the consciousness. These conscious decisions are what is known as free will. In this way human genes do not determine our behavior, but actually require the exercise of free will.

An important question becomes, *Why is there diversity among cultures?* The short answer is environmental contingencies. Recent research reveals that 99.9 percent of human genes are the same and there is little evidence that genetic differences account for differences in the way and rate at which civilizations emerged. Technological levels have differed based on differences in the resources on which civilizations depend—namely, easily domesticated plants and animals, but also mineral resources. The availability of resources eased the transition from hunter-gatherer societies to agrarian societies and set the trajectory for cultures to move on to more complex societies.

## HUMAN NATURE IN ORGANIZATIONS

The four-drive model implies that an organization would do well to respect the needs to acquire, bond, learn, and defend in dealing with all organizational stakeholders. The beginning of the decline of GM and the rise of Japanese autos can be traced to management that paid factory workers well (met their acquisition needs), but generally ignored their learning needs by giving them mindless work. This thwarted any bonding with the organization through the stimulation of hostile or superior attitudes. Further, GM formed adversarial relationships (antithetical to the bonding drive) with suppliers—forcing short-term lowball bids (ignoring the security implicit in the drive to defend) without respecting supplier innovation (learning). The success of the Japanese auto industry in the 1980's and 1990's can be attributed to those auto firms' respect for innate needs in its dealings with employees, suppliers, customers, and regulators.

An overemphasis on any of the four needs leads to a less successful organization, and an incomplete individual. *Respect for all four needs should lead to social contracts that leave all individuals and all parties fulfilled.*

PART

# VI

# Motivation

A number of readings contained in this edition of *The Manager's Bookshelf* attempt to focus the manager's attention on the social-psychological side of the organization. Authors, concepts, and suggestions for proactive management call our attention to the importance of recognizing that all organizations have a natural (human) resource that, when appropriately managed, can lead to dramatic performance effects.

Part VI has three readings. First, Edward E. Lawler, III in *Rewarding Excellence* stresses the fact that traditional compensation systems (e.g., time, job, and seniority-based) are no longer adequate for the challenges facing organizations today and the opportunities that lie on tomorrow's doorstep. Dr. Lawler calls for a new way of thinking about the contributions that pay systems can make to organizational success.

Lawler argues that organizations must compensate people in a way that recognizes the value of their human capital, and how effectively they use their knowledge and skills in ways that help to achieve business objectives. Competitive advantage is increasingly being defined in terms of an organization's ability to capitalize on its people. Therefore an organization's reward system must encourage excellence in employee contributions, and motivate and satisfy employees to move the organization forward.

Dr. Lawler is on the faculty at the University of Southern California and director of the Center for Effective Organizations. He has his Ph.D. from the University of California, Berkeley, and has held faculty appointments at Yale and the University of Michigan. Dr. Lawler has a long and distinguished scholarly career contributing extensively to the organizational sciences.

Most managers find themselves interested in the question, "What motivates people to do their best?" In *Intrinsic Motivation at Work,* Kenneth W. Thomas addresses this question. Dr. Thomas highlights the fact that a large number of managers continue to rely upon extrinsic motivators—pay, benefits, status, bonuses, commissions, pension plans, and expense budgets—as a way to achieve high and sustained levels of employee motivation. The author suggests that a committed and self-managing workforce can be realized through intrinsic motivation. Specifically, Thomas identifies the intrinsic rewards that are needed to energize a workforce, realize organizational commitment, and achieve self-management. The solution, he argues, lies in creating intrinsically motivating jobs.

Kenneth W. Thomas, Ph.D., is a professor of management at the Naval Postgraduate School in Monterey, California. He has been on the management faculty at UCLA, Temple University, and the University of Pittsburgh. He has done extensive work on conflict management, and is the co-author of the Thomas-Kilmann Conflict Mode Instrument, which has sold over 3 million copies.

Based upon his observations of a large number of organizations (e.g., Southwest Airlines, the U.S. Marines, General Motors), Jon R. Katzenbach in his book *Why Pride Matters More than Money: The Power of the World's Greatest Motivational Force,* tackles the question "How do I motivate my employees?"—the question most frequently asked by supervisors, managers and leaders. While conventional wisdom, as practiced in most organizations, suggests that money and intimidation are the keys to sustained performance, Katzenbach asserts that the real answer is to be found in the word *pride.* He asserts that neither money nor intimidation contribute to the long-term sustainability of an organization. With regard to money he states that money is not a motivator, and that pay-for-performance programs lead to self-serving behavior and ephemeral commitment to the organization. Instead, Katzenbach notes that most employees are motivated by meaningful work, feelings of accomplishment, recognition/approval, and a sense of belonging and being a part of others in the work environment.

The author, Jon R. Katzenbach, was a senior partner and director of McKinsey and Company, a large U.S.-based consulting organization. He now directs his own firm, Katzenbach Partners, assisting organizations in such areas as workforce performance, team building, and leadership. Mr. Katzenbach is the author of several other books, including *Peak Performance, Teams at the Top, The Wisdom of Teams,* and *Real Change Leaders.*

# Rewarding Excellence

**EDWARD E. LAWLER III**

**Summary prepared by Stephen A. Rubenfeld**

***Stephen A. Rubenfeld** is a professor of Human Resource Management in the Labovitz School of Business and Economics at the University of Minnesota Duluth. He received his Ph.D. from the University of Wisconsin–Madison, and was previously on the faculty of Texas Tech University. His professional publications and presentations have covered a wide range of human resource and labor relations topics, including job search behaviors, human resource policies and practices, job security, and staffing challenges. He has served as a consultant for a number of private and public sector organizations, and is a member of the Society for Human Resource Management, the Academy of Management, and the Industrial Relations Research Association.*

Traditional approaches to employee compensation are showing their age. It is becoming increasingly evident that these pay systems, little changed over the generations, are not adequate to meet the challenges of today and the opportunities of tomorrow. The time is right for a different approach to compensation, a new way of thinking about the contributions that pay systems can make to organizational success. Compensation systems can do more than attract and retain employees; they must be accepted as critical pathways guiding the behaviors and the evolving competencies of these employees. At the same time, it is essential that compensation be used more astutely to support the firm's strategic pursuits.

Change is ongoing, but there is literally a revolution in the way that organizations are managed. Driven by intensified competition and dramatic societal changes, the pace of change has exceeded the ability of traditional business systems to respond. The standard of success is elevated and even the traditional measures of success are no longer sufficient. Firms continuously are being buffeted by demands to raise the bar of performance. Spurred on by the global marketplace and an ever more competitive business environment, firms have found the hurdles to be higher and the runners in the field to be faster. The bottom line is that success today means more than not failing. Managers have to continuously stretch and look for ways to meet the challenges of tomorrow. In this setting, organizations have to be better than most, not just

Edward E. Lawler III, *Rewarding Excellence: Pay Strategies for the New Economy.* San Francisco: Jossey-Bass Publishers, 2000.

better than some. They can tinker with systems and policies to seek incremental gains, but they must keep an open mind to new and creative ways of doing things.

Technological innovation is at the heart of these business challenges. The escalating growth of information technologies has not only made obsolete the traditional ways of running an organization, but has made the management and development of knowledge an integral element of success. It has changed what people do and how they do it. It has elevated the importance of individual work roles, and has challenged the efficacy of traditional hierarchical and bureaucratic models of organizational management. The structured and task-driven job of yesterday is gone, replaced with a much more fluid set of work expectations in which workers are knowledgeable decision makers and sensitive to the implications of their work. Beyond the competencies needed in the immediate work focus, employees also need to be constructive partners in the organization's strategic pursuits and alert to the needs of customers and other key constituencies.

These challenges have not only altered the nature of work, but have dramatically changed the relationship between employers and employees. There is no question that employment is more transitory, but at the same time there has been a widespread and dramatic shift in the amount of power employees have in their work relationship. This increased level of worker control may be attributable to a combination of favorable labor market conditions, knowledge and competencies that have value beyond the walls of the firm, and changing societal norms. But regardless of its antecedents, the growing importance of human capital to success and the increased marketplace mobility of workers challenge firms to question their long-standing assumptions about compensation. It is growing more and more clear that organizations must compensate people in a way that recognizes the value of their human capital, and how effectively they use their knowledge and skills in ways that help to achieve business objectives.

## REWARDS AND ORGANIZATIONAL PERFORMANCE

In today's business environment, competitive advantage is defined by an organization's ability to capitalize on its people—its human resources. Management systems are the key to unlocking the potential of employee contribution and can be the source of a sustainable competitive advantage. But total success cannot come from honing existing systems; a new logic must also be embraced.

While implementation details will need to be tailored to individual settings, this new logic of organization is built on several critical assumptions. The first is that there must be an effective way to influence and coordinate the contributions of employees. This must go beyond traditional hierarchical rules; it must embrace the integration of the work and the worker. Business involvement assumes that if the customer and the external market rather than a set of rules and procedures guide an employee's performance, the outcomes will be better and we will have better utilized the employees' expertise. This requires that involvement be central to our management systems and organizational culture. More specifically, employees must have extensive access to information, knowledge of the total work system, power to make decisions, and access to rewards tied to individual capabilities and contributions, as well as business outcomes.

A second hallmark of the new logic is in the definition of work and the ways in which employees can add value. With the imperative to better take advantage of our human capital, we must move beyond hierarchically based job structures and encourage individuals and work groups to develop their human capital by:

- Doing more involved tasks
- Managing and controlling themselves
- Coordinating their work
- Suggesting ideas for improvements
- Promoting better ways to serve the customer.

Beyond the work itself, organizations cannot lose sight of the importance of having integrated and comprehensive policies that attract, retain, and develop people who have the capacity to add to the firm's competitive advantage.

The reduced emphasis on hierarchical reporting relationships in favor of lateral relationships is another critical element of the new logic. This objective may be carried forward with:

- Group and team performance-based rewards
- Individual rewards for lateral learning
- Team-based work and rewards.

Other concepts important to this new logic include greater product- and customer-focused organizational designs.

How can an organization implement the elements of the new logic? First and foremost, it must realize that a holistic perspective is required—piecemeal changes will not have the desired effects. There must be an alignment and fit among the strategies, structures, processes, people, and reward systems that define the organization. Meaningful gains can only be accomplished if the change effort is pervasive and well integrated.

## DESIGN CHOICES

There is a broad array of conceptual and structural factors to consider in choosing the design for an organization's compensation system. The list of options is long and provides the latitude to fashion a compensation model that fits current needs and creates a future-oriented system for organization success. Among the dimensions or alternatives to be considered are the approach to internal and external equity, the degree to which the pay will be job- or person-based, in what ways and to what extent performance will influence pay decisions, and whether individual or group performance will be predominant. Among many other issues that can influence the design of the pay system are the reward mix, market factors, and the locus of decision making.

While the choices are many, those entrusted with spearheading the design effort must keep in mind that organizational success, both today and tomorrow, is dependent on choosing a reward structure that is responsive both to the firm's strategies for achieving success and the realities of the business environment. Likewise, while pay systems can guide and lead the change process, they also must be sensitive to the organization's internal context and capabilities.

## REWARDING PERFORMANCE

With the growing need for organizations to excel at what they do, it is logical that pay systems must encourage excellence in employee contributions, and must motivate and satisfy the employees who do the most to move the organization forward. Although there is growing acceptance that individuals who contribute more deserve greater rewards, there is less agreement on how this can best be accomplished. Nevertheless, there are some "truths" that may guide the design process:

- Rewards are not valued equally.
- Organizations are viewed in a more favorable light by job seekers where the rewards offered are seen as valuable.
- Satisfied employees are less likely to leave.
- Motivation to perform is higher when there is a connection between performance and valued rewards.

Even where there is agreement and commitment to reward performance, we are still faced with important design choices. Merit-based systems traditionally have emphasized individual performance. While there are circumstances where this still makes sense, with work becoming more dynamic and interdependent, a move toward team-based rewards and rewards based on organizational excellence becomes compelling. But here again, there are different types of teams and care must be taken to adopt the most appropriate reward structure for the specific nature and purpose of the team. Whatever plan is chosen, it is essential that the reward emphasizes collective rather than individual performance.

There also is a place for well-conceived and operationalized organizationally based reward plans as part of the overall compensation system. This is particularly true where organizational success is dependent on broad-based contributions and complex interdependencies. Here again, there are many specific options from which to choose (including gainsharing, goalsharing, profit sharing, and a variety of stock plans), and care must be taken to carefully consider strategic objectives as well as the structure of the work process in deciding whether to adopt a specific plan and how it should be configured.

## ATTRACTION AND RETENTION

Attracting, hiring, and ultimately retaining productive employees are obvious needs if firms are to achieve organizational excellence. While the level of rewards may have a direct impact on the number of individuals wanting to work in an organization, it is of utmost importance that the *right* people apply. The market viability of salaries and benefits is important, but other factors, such as the way in which pay decisions are made and the factors that determine the distribution of future rewards, are critical both to attracting the types of employees who will move the organization forward and to retaining employees who have demonstrated excellence.

Overall, systems that are job-based or seniority-based are not a particularly good way to attract and retain excellent employees. They do little to motivate desirable work behaviors or personal growth, and may even discourage work contributions at the margin. The challenge is not to focus solely on numbers when assessing attraction and retention, but rather to assess the quality dimension—has the firm hired and kept the best people? While job-based or seniority-based pay plans can still serve a purpose in some situations, organizations should be placing their emphasis on performance-sensitive plans that emphasize team contributions and organizational successes.

## ◆ DESIGN—A STRATEGIC VIEW

As organizations consider the imperative to adopt compensation philosophies and systems supportive of strategic goals, it is important that decision makers not lose sight of the importance of (1) the capabilities and competencies needed to execute the compensation plan, and (2) the motivation to use these capabilities and competencies in a way that simultaneously advances the intent of the compensation changes and the attainment of strategic objectives. While these capabilities and competencies need not be fully developed at the onset, a plan to hone them must parallel the implementation of the new or revised compensation system. These attributes must evolve to be part of the organization's culture and must be embraced by employees throughout the organization. Likewise, the basic tenet of accountability in a performance-based culture must be accepted and applied to employees at all levels.

The ultimate challenge for managers is to create and sustain a high-performance culture. Without doubt, the skills and abilities of organizational leaders will be tested as they spearhead the diagnostic, decision, and change processes. But however daunting the challenge, the reality is that reward systems must be reinvented to support a sustainable competitive advantage. The consequences of failure speak for themselves.

# Intrinsic Motivation at Work


***KENNETH W. THOMAS***

***Summary prepared by Shannon Studden***



***Shannon Studden** is a native of Milwaukee, currently living in Duluth, Minnesota. She received her Master of Science degree in Industrial/Organizational Psychology from the University of Tennessee at Chattanooga in 1994. She has worked as an internal research consultant at Duracell, USA, in Cleveland, Tennessee, and has been a member of the faculty at Tennessee Wesleyan College and the University of Tennessee at Chattanooga. She is currently an adjunct instructor of Organizational Behavior at the University of Minnesota Duluth.*


Traditionally, organizations have relied on extrinsic rewards such as salaries and bonuses to motivate employees. Rewards focused on employee behavior and depended on close supervision to determine who qualified for them and who did not. In a hierarchically structured organization, this was relatively easy to do, as multiple levels of managers with narrow spans of control were available to keep close watch over subordinates. Employees were fairly accepting of this watchdog approach because it meant they had a secure job with solid benefits.

The problem is that this type of reward system doesn't fit well with the changing face of organizations. The trend of eliminating layers of management has resulted not only in decreased employment security, but also in wider spans of control and less direct supervision of employees. This leaves supervisors with little time to micromanage employees' tasks.

The feeling of decreased employment security means that employees feel less loyal to their employers and are more likely than workers of previous generations to leave an unsatisfying job for a more attractive one, often several times in their lifetime. Therefore, to remain competitive, today's organizations need a better way to attract and retain the best employees.

---


Kenneth W. Thomas, *Intrinsic Motivation at Work: Building Energy & Commitment.* San Francisco: Berrett-Koehler Publishers, Inc., 2000.

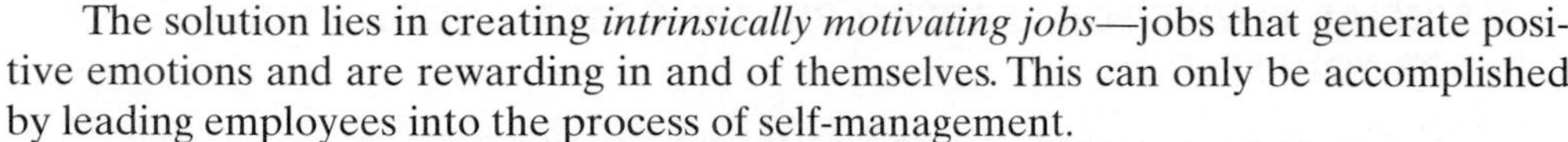

The solution lies in creating *intrinsically motivating jobs*—jobs that generate positive emotions and are rewarding in and of themselves. This can only be accomplished by leading employees into the process of self-management.

## ◆ THE PROCESS OF SELF-MANAGEMENT

Successful self-management is dependent upon four processes in progression: meaningfulness, choice, competence, and progress. First, employees commit to a *meaningful* purpose. Second, they are allowed to *choose* activities to accomplish the purpose. Third, after performing these activities, employees assess their own *competence.* Last, employees monitor their *progress* toward the purpose. These processes come together to create a continuous cycle. Ideally, an increased sense of progress leads back into an increased sense of meaningfulness and choice, and the process starts all over again.

## ◆ BUILDING A SENSE OF MEANINGFULNESS

A meaningful job elicits a passion for its ultimate purpose. When we have a job that is meaningful, we spend more time thinking about it, feeling excited about it, and increasing our commitment to it. It means we try to get around obstacles in our way of reaching the purpose and keep focused on the outcome. Because what is meaningful to one person may not be meaningful to another, a leader's job is to match individuals with tasks that have meaning for them. To build meaningfulness, leaders should:

- **Provide a noncynical climate.** Cynicism punishes excitement and passion by trivializing positive emotions. If a cynical climate has existed in the organization in the past, leaders need to openly acknowledge past mistakes, admit to the reasons behind the cynicism, and emphasize that a new choice has been made to strive toward a more positive environment.
- **Clearly identify passions.** Employees need to identify what they care most about in their jobs. Leaders can talk with each employee individually about passions and dreams, then bring the group together to discuss the passions that they have in common. Identifying common passions leads to a shared vision and unifies the team through its values. Once these passions are openly expressed, the leader must allow the group to evolve in the direction of its passions, or cynicism will be even more firmly embedded in the climate than before.
- **Provide an exciting vision.** As the vision develops more fully, it should become more concrete to make it more real. A well-formed vision will also help later in assessing progress toward goals.
- **Ensure relevant task purposes.** All day-to-day tasks must contribute to the vision. Any tasks that do not contribute to the vision should be outsourced. This reinforces the fact that the organization is dedicated to the interests and passions of the group.
- **Provide whole tasks.** Whenever possible, employees should be able to see projects through from beginning to end. This allows for a greater source of pride in accomplishment, and a better feeling for the team's overall purpose.

### SPECIAL ADVICE FOR LEADERS: BUILDING MEANINGFULNESS FOR YOURSELF

- **Create a noncynical climate for yourself.** Stop focusing on deficiencies.
- **Clarify your own passions.** Identify what really matters to you.
- **Craft your own vision.** This needs to be done before the team's vision is created, so that you can fit the vision not only to the passions of the team members, but also to your own.
- **Make your tasks more relevant.** Ask yourself what you could do at work that is meaningful to you.
- **Negotiate for whole tasks.** Make an attempt to take on the responsibility of an entire task when possible.

## BUILDING A SENSE OF CHOICE

We experience a true sense of choice when our opinions matter, when we feel that we have flexibility in our behavior, and when we feel ownership of the outcome. When we are able to make choices, we accomplish the overall goal by deciding what works best for us. A sense of choice leads to initiative, creativity, and experimentation.

Leaders have more control over their employees' sense of choice than over the other three intrinsic rewards, because choice, and not meaningfulness, competence, or progress is given to employees. To maximize a sense of choice, leaders need to provide them with basic guidelines, and allow employees to make their own decisions within established limits. Additionally, leaders should:

- **Delegate authority.** Leaders must resist the trap of waiting to delegate until employees are more skilled. Waiting for ideal conditions only causes employees to become increasingly dependent, which makes them less capable of making decisions and creates a downward spiral of dependence. The only way for employees to become more competent decision makers is to have experience making decisions.
- **Demonstrate trust.** There are three keys to demonstrate trust. First, important decisions, rather than trivial ones, should be delegated. Second, employees must be left alone to carry out decisions. Monitoring the decision-making process diminishes the sense of choice. Third, trust can be demonstrated by encouraging employees to take on new responsibilities.
- **Provide security.** Employees need to feel that experimentation is acceptable, and that mistakes will be seen as learning opportunities rather than failures. The "zero-defects" mentality so prevalent in organizations today unfortunately leaves no opportunity for mistakes. As a result, employees keep mistakes to themselves, rather than presenting them to the team as opportunities for constructive learning. This secrecy increases the probability of falsifying records and blaming others, all of which act in direct opposition to the ultimate goal of intrinsic motivation. To minimize mistakes, leaders can try to match individuals to tasks within their abilities and provide help when asked. Once this is done, it is necessary to allow employees to make their own choices about the best way to reach their goals.

- **Provide a clear purpose.** To have meaningful work and make good decisions, workers need understanding of the bigger purpose, not just knowledge of tasks.
- **Provide information.** Leaders must provide employees with access to all relevant information so that they can make well-informed decisions.

### SPECIAL ADVICE FOR LEADERS: BUILDING CHOICE FOR YOURSELF

- **Negotiate for the authority you need.** Tell your boss how giving you authority will help you or your team reach the purpose.
- **Earn trust.** Show that you are capable of self-management by your actions.
- **Don't yield to fear.** Unrealistic fears can keep you from thinking logically and intelligently.
- **Clarify your purpose.** Make sure that you understand why you are doing what you are doing.
- **Get the information you need.** Do you need more than you currently have? Personal contacts? A better information system? Access to information previously unavailable to you?

## BUILDING A SENSE OF COMPETENCE

We feel a sense of competence when our performance meets or exceeds the standards we have set for ourselves. Performing well is, in itself, intrinsically rewarding. When creating a product, competence produces a sense of craftsmanship. When performing a service, competence produces a sense of responsiveness. Competence means that we are serving our purpose.

When people feel a sense of incompetence, it results in apathy, low effort, embarrassment, low job satisfaction, and anxiety. However, too much competence can also be a problem, as it results in a feeling of little challenge, boredom, and low job satisfaction. A leader's responsibility is to find the right balance for each employee's sense of competence. To achieve the balance, leaders can:

- **Provide knowledge.** Leaders need to provide specific job-related knowledge through discussions or training.
- **Provide positive feedback.** When a task is difficult, positive feedback allows employees to make necessary adjustments in their performance. Positive feedback increases the sense of competence, while negative feedback undermines it. Negative feedback is sometimes necessary; however, because people are more sensitive to negative feedback, leaders should concentrate on positives as much as possible.
- **Recognize skill.** Recognition increases a sense of competence.
- **Manage challenge.** Leaders need to find a fit between employee ability and task difficulty. The ideal task is one that the employee is capable of accomplishing with full concentration. High satisfaction results when this type of task is done well.
- **Foster high, noncomparative standards.** High standards build competence. Just as delegating trivial decisions diminishes a sense of choice, low standards diminish a sense of competence. A sense of competence comes after having achieved a sufficiently difficult goal.

Standards must be noncomparative. Comparing employees against each other sets average competence at "mediocre." Because the goal is for all employees to aim high, comparing them relative to each other is counterproductive.

### SPECIAL ADVICE FOR LEADERS: BUILDING COMPETENCE FOR YOURSELF

- **Get the knowledge you need.** As a leader, it is your responsibility to engage in continuous learning.
- **Get the feedback you need.** Feedback lets you improve your own performance.
- **Recognize your own skill.** Acknowledge your own competence.
- **Manage challenge in your own work.** Say no when necessary. Take on more or increasingly complex responsibilities when things get too easy.
- **Set high standards for yourself.** A sense of competence comes when you feel that you have accomplished something worth accomplishing.

## BUILDING A SENSE OF PROGRESS

When we feel a sense of progress, we feel that the task purpose is steadily being achieved, that things are on track. We feel part of something successful, resulting in excitement and enthusiasm for the task. When little progress is being made, however, a sense of frustration results. We feel a loss of control, resulting in a loss of commitment.

In some ways, progress is more important than the actual attainment of the goal. Reaching the goal is significant, but there must be progress along the way to serve as reinforcement. To help build a sense of progress, leaders must:

- **Build a collaborative climate.** Conflict can halt progress in its tracks. When conflict arises, collaboration allows all of the parties involved to get what they need. For collaboration to be successful, all parties must listen to each other, take each other's point of view seriously, and direct a great deal of energy into problem solving.
- **Track milestones.** Employees need reference points to measure progress. Breaking tasks into significant advances is especially important on long tasks, where progress is sometimes difficult to see.
- **Celebrate progress.** Employees need a special time to recognize that a milestone has been reached. Celebrations intensify the positive emotions that arise from a sense of progress. This can be as simple as pausing to acknowledge that a milestone has been reached, or as complex as an all-out party.
- **Provide access to customers.** One of the best ways to gauge progress toward a purpose or goal is to have contact with the people affected by it—the customers. Seeing customer satisfaction first-hand gives employees a sense of accomplishment. When customer contact is built into the job, it serves as an ongoing reinforcement of progress.
- **Measure improvements (and reduce cycle time).** Improvements are essential to a sense of progress. It is especially important that the right things are being measured—specifically, things that the leader and team care about. Measuring cycle time is particularly useful. Cycle time improvements result in teams having to

cover fewer steps to reach their goals and encountering fewer obstacles along the way. These improvements create a sense of speed, which adds to the sense of progress.

## SPECIAL ADVICE FOR LEADERS: BUILDING PROGRESS FOR YOURSELF

- **Build collaborative relationships.** If you are experiencing noncollaborative relationships at work, share your desire to make the relationships more collaborative with the other persons, and ask them to join you.
- **Develop your own milestones** to increase your own sense of progress.
- **Take time to celebrate.** Think of celebrations as time for renewal. You need to pace yourself to avoid burnout, and to keep your energy and passion.
- **Make contact with customers**—internal and external—as often as possible.
- **Measure improvements (and track intrinsic motivation).** Try to measure improvements in team progress, quality, and intrinsic motivation. Are employees still energized by their work tasks?

These four processes propel the change from an external, managerial-driven reward system to an internal, employee-driven reward system. The subsequent increase in intrinsic motivation is critical for organizations to succeed in the work environment of the twenty-first century.

# Why Pride Matters More than Money

*JON KATZENBACH*

***Summary prepared by Anne-Marie Kaul***

***Anne-Marie Kaul*** *is the Donor Recruitment Manager for the North Central Blood Region of the American Red Cross in St. Paul, Minnesota. She and her recruitment reps are responsible for recruiting sponsors and volunteers to ensure the acquisition of over 243,000 pints of blood each year. She also has several years of experience managing financial services operational departments. Her business expertise has been in the areas of leadership and customer service. She has a B.A. from the University of Minnesota Duluth and an M.B.A. from the University of St. Thomas in St. Paul, Minnesota.*

Pride can be the key to unlocking the motivational spirit of any employee at any level and within virtually any enterprise. At the base of this building of pride is emotion. More specifically, it is critical to obtain the emotional commitment of associates, which in turn can lead to both positive and negative forms of motivation. The positive form of motivation is called institutional-building pride and the negative form is self-serving pride.

Companies that rely solely on monetary incentives to motivate employees will only realize short-term successes, because they are not taking advantage of the easily accessible building of pride that is a powerful motivating force. *Enterprises today must move beyond egos and monetary incentives to sustain not only employee satisfaction, but also economic performance and long-term growth.*

---

Jon R. Katzenbach, *Why Pride Matters More than Money: The Power of the World's Greatest Motivational Force.* New York: Crown Business, 2003.

## ◆ WHY INSTITUTIONAL-BUILDING PRIDE WORKS

In the long run, a person who is allowed to pursue worthwhile goals and endeavors will be more motivated to work harder than a person only receiving monetary incentives. When associates take pride in their work, their job satisfaction increases, their productivity is higher, and the enterprise ultimately is more likely to succeed. One of the best reasons for using pride as a motivator is that it can be quickly learned and easily applied. Before leaders use pride to motivate, it is important that they understand the other reasons why instilling pride works so well to motivate others.

- The skills and knowledge for instilling pride are mostly teachable and can be readily learned.
- Pride begets pride; there is a closed loop of energy linking pride to work performance. The anticipation of higher performance feels good and generates the emotional commitment to obtain better results.
- The fundamental correlation between pride and performance can be found in any company that depends on humans.
- Leaders don't have to wait for real success before instilling pride in others. They can tap into past accomplishments as well as future expectations to trigger emotions.

## ◆ DIFFERENCES BETWEEN SELF-SERVING PRIDE AND INSTITUTIONAL PRIDE

In companies that consistently perform better than their competition, pride is a primary driver of their higher performance. There is clear evidence indicating that in traditional larger companies, managers who instill pride also have better economic and market performance than their competitors.

Both categories of pride—self-serving and institutional-building—can be a factor in the production of good and bad results, but typically self-serving pride only produces short-term success.

### SELF-SERVING PRIDE

Self-serving pride is all about power and moncy. The individual's thought process goes something like this: "The more you can earn, the more visible you are, the more powerful and well-off you become." Power and control are believed to be all-important, so typically a person who is motivated by this type influence will switch allegiances such that there is no loyalty or commitment to the company. However, there *are* some advantages of self-serving pride, especially in situations such as in individual sports. Monetary awards not only serve as indicators of talent and achievement; they are a simple way to distinguish between performers and non-performers.

### INSTITUTIONAL-BUILDING PRIDE

*This type of pride is based on the character and emotional commitment of associates.* With institutional-building pride, people are motivated to help others and work for the good of the enterprise. They place their efforts on more basic performance factors such as customer satisfaction, peer and mentor approval, developmental opportunities, and quality of work. These in turn build self-worth, group cohesion, and personal developmental happiness—factors that lead to success.

When further comparing the two types of pride, it is important to note that institutional pride has real strength because it can work across different types of organizations, even in companies where money is not a realistic source of motivation. For example, organizations such as the U.S. Marine Corps and Kentucky Fried Chicken (KFC) have been very successful, because they have integrated institutional-building pride into the workplace. It has been demonstrated over and over again that money may attract and keep people, but it does not continue to motivate them to excel. At the end of the day, it is the feeling of pride (self-serving or institutional-building) that prompts employees to do well.

## ◆ SOURCES OF INSTITUTIONAL PRIDE

Institutional pride can come from many sources. The primary origins fall into three main categories—work results, work processes, and co-workers/supervisors.

- **Pride in the results of one's work.** This is often exhibited when employees feel good about what they have accomplished. This can arise from the product or service delivered or the kind of work done.
- **Pride in how work is done.** Employees can take pride in "doing something right." This refers to the set of values, standards, work ethic, and commitment that is applied to one's job.
- **Pride in co-workers and supervisors.** The people that an employee works with—supervisors, subordinates, or peers—can all provide job satisfaction.

Given the fact that these sources of "good" pride can be easily directed and controlled by leaders within corporations (as opposed to money), institutional-building pride should be the primary source of pride for the broader base of employees. *It is important to remember that what motivates upper level executives is very different than what motivates frontline employees, especially during difficult times.*

Why is this true? Top executives not only possess the business savvy in terms of schooling in business fundamentals, typically their individual goals are stated in terms of economic results and market share. As a result, their motivation is a function of performance logic and many rational factors. On the other hand, at lower levels, simple emotional factors from everyday occurrences are more important as a motivating source because on the front line, the performance statistics of the company are often less meaningful. The six most important non-financial elements of enterprise success that influence *all* associates are:

- Local company reputation
- Product/service attributes
- Customer satisfaction
- Work group composition
- Peer approval
- Competitive position

The good news is that these sources of pride result in the emotional commitment that motivates employees, leading to enterprise-wide success. Understanding the motivational differences between the top and the other levels of an organization is a critical challenge, but it can be learned. The enterprises that excel at engaging emotions employ leaders who are masters at cultivating institutional-building pride.

## THE FIVE PATHS TO HIGHER PERFORMANCE

There are five distinct applications or paths that motivate higher performing groups in companies that have successfully developed emotional commitment.

- **Mission, Values and Collective Pride (MVP)**—This is where companies use their rich histories of past accomplishments to instill pride.
- **Process and Metrics (P&M)**—Delivering value by measuring the right things and maintaining effective processes is a powerful source of pride.
- **Entrepreneurial Spirit (ES)**—High risk/high reward opportunities typically provide motivational direction on this path.
- **Individual Achievement (IA)**—Individual performance and personal advancement, rather than team performance, are the primary motivational sources.
- **Recognition and Celebration (R&C)**—Giving recognition and holding celebrations and special events are used to motivate others.

All of these paths lead to an emotionally committed workforce, which leads to a higher level of performance. Companies that desire to sustain an emotionally committed environment will be more successful if they integrate two of these paths, rather than concentrating on one. But what if you work for a company that does not appear to comprehend these concepts? What can a leader do as an individual to motivate the workforce?

## IDEAS FOR INDIVIDUALS NOT IN AN INSTITUTIONAL-BUILDING COMPANY ENVIRONMENT

What if the company you work for is not a well-established enterprise—one whose size, market position, and growth prospects are not highly attractive? A manager in this situation can use the case study results of General Motors to identify successful key motivating features. The following three methods are not only useful, but also easy to apply.

1. *Keep it simple.* Use one or two concentrated themes and place great significance on local sources of pride that employees can easily understand.
2. *Develop one's own unique pride-building formula.* Strong pride-influenced managers should connect to their employees in any way they can (e.g., by tapping into their pride in the community, pride in their families, pride in a legacy).
3. *Make pride a priority.* Using pride on an everyday basis to motivate is the key to obtaining long-term results.

Pride-building people are aware that instilling pride along the way is the *only way* to gain long-term success from it. Therefore, it is more important for people to be proud of what they are doing every day than it is for them to be proud of accomplishing their goals and getting the wanted results. Good leaders appeal to emotions rather than rational compliance; that is why their internal compass is always pointing to pride.

## Conclusion

The really good news is that a person does not have to work for a peak performance enterprise to experience pride and the motivation that comes with it. Institutional-building pride motivates people in almost any environment—from top performing firms to traditional organizations to financially challenged companies.

The ability to instill pride can be learned and utilized, just like any basic performance management technique. What a manager must look out for, however, is trying to motivate employees solely by using sources that are more self-serving like monetary incentives and ego building. While money is economically necessary, it does not motivate one to excel in the long run. When a manager uses institutional-building pride sources, such as recognition, accomplishments, entrepreneurship, or team support, the general population of the workforce, especially people on the front line, are more likely to produce consistent and high-quality results.

At the base of pride-instilling motivation is emotional commitment. Employees want to feel connected to the cause, like providing the best customer service or not letting the team down. It is this connectedness to an overall objective that gives institutional-building pride its powerful force. *Managers must think beyond the compensation package.*

There are many peak-performing enterprises such as KFC, General Motors, and the Marine Corps that have clearly demonstrated that motivating by pride can lead to successful results. We should continue to look at these organizations for guidance. Pride is a powerful motivating force—one that has proven to result in improved success.

# PART VII

# Teams and Teamwork

As organizations attempt to find a distinctive "edge" and achieve their goals in a rapidly changing and highly competitive environment, more and more organizations are experimenting with teamwork. In doing so, they are hoping to realize some of the synergies that flow from the creation of fully functioning teams. Many organizations, intrigued by the success of team-based structures in automotive assembly plants and elsewhere, have experimented with the use of employee involvement systems and problem-solving teams. Others have made radical changes in their technologies, and some have organized around work teams. Butler Manufacturing uses teams to assemble an entire grain dryer; Hallmark uses teams of artists, writers, accountants, marketers, and lithographic personnel to collaborate to produce Mother's Day cards, while another complete team works on cards for Father's Day.

All three readings in this section focus their attention on various facets of teams and teamwork. The first, co-authored by Frank LaFasto and Carl Larson, is titled *When Teams Work Best.* The second reading, by noted researcher/thinker J. Richard Hackman, explains the importance of managers *Leading Teams.* The third, *Beyond Teams,* was itself prepared by a team of authors—Beyerlein, Freedman, McGee, and Moran.

In *When Teams Work Best,* LaFasto and Larson draw upon a database of interviews with and observations by 6,000 team leaders/members. They identify the work knowledge (technical experience and problem-solving skills) and teamwork factors (openness, supportiveness, action orientation, and positive personal style) that comprise an effective team member. They also introduce suggestions for individuals to use to "connect" with other workmates, as well as discussing the five steps in problem-solving and various roles for team leaders to play (focusing on the goal, ensuring a collaborative climate, building confidence, setting priorities, etc.). LaFasto and Larson previously published *Teamwork: What Must Go Right/What Can Go Wrong.*

In *Leading Teams,* author J. Richard Hackman contends that many organizations place too much emphasis on the leader as the primary cause of team behavior, as opposed to team self-management. His book identifies the five conditions necessary for team effectiveness (being a real team, having a compelling goal and an enabling structure, feeling support, and receiving expert coaching). Hackman suggests that there are four levels of team self-management, and urges organizations to evaluate team success on three measures: producing a client-desired product, growth in the team's own capabilities, and having a satisfying team experience.

J. Richard Hackman is the Cahners-Rabb professor of Social and Organizational Psychology at Harvard University, and he previously taught at Yale. He has been recognized with both the Distinguished Educator Award and the Distinguished Research Award from the Academy of Management. He has written several other books, including *Groups That Work (and Those That Don't)* and (with Greg Oldham) *Work Redesign.*

*Beyond Teams* lays out a simple premise based on research and case studies—that there can be a high organizational payoff from collaborative work systems. The authors identify ten major principles that define collaborative organizations, including an emphasis on personal accountability, facilitation of dialogue, managing tradeoffs, and "exploiting the rhythm of divergence and convergence." They also demonstrate the applicability of the ten principles across manufacturing, product development, service, and virtual office settings.

Michael Beyerlein is the author or editor of a dozen books on collaboration. He is the director of the Center for the Study of Work Teams at the University of North Texas. Craig McGee is a principal with Solutions; Linda Moran works for Achieve Global; and Sue Freedman is president of Knowledge Work Associates.

READING 1

# When Teams Work Best: 6,000 Team Members and Leaders Tell What It Takes to Succeed

***FRANK LAFASTO AND CARL LARSON***

***Summary prepared by Shannon Studden***

***Shannon Studden,*** *a Milwaukee native, has an M.S. in Industrial/Organizational Psychology from the University of Tennessee-Chattanooga. She has been an instructor of Organizational Behavior at the University of Minnesota Duluth for several years. She also works as a Product Development Specialist with Emprove, a company that creates Web-based performance appraisal systems for the health care industry.*

## ◆ THE NATURE OF TEAMS

Teams differ from individual employees in that team members must not only work toward personal and team objectives, but must collaborate with other team members. The most effective teams are made up of people who have both technical skills and the ability to work with others to reach the team's goals.

A comprehensive study was conducted, and data were collected from over 6,000 individuals who work in teams. Each person assessed his/her team members, team leader, and organization. Five different functional levels emerged from the study: team members, team relationships, team problem-solving, team leadership, and the organizational environment.

---

Frank LaFasto and Carl Larson, *When Teams Work Best: 6,000 Team Members and Leaders Tell What It Takes to Succeed.* Thousand Oaks. CA: Sage Publications, 2002.

## TEAM MEMBER CHARACTERISTICS

In order to achieve the team's goal, members need a combination of working knowledge and teamwork ability. In the area of working knowledge, members must have sufficient technical *experience* to provide practical knowledge related to the team's purpose. Members also need the ability to *problem solve;* this involves clarifying problems, helping others understand, developing ideas, providing suggestions, and making proactive decisions.

Key teamwork factors include openness, supportiveness, action orientation, and a positive personal style. *Openness* is the single most important factor in effective collaboration. It encompasses an individual's and the team's willingness to address issues and encourage exchange of ideas. Openness includes ensuring that team members have role clarity (specificity of individual roles as well as the role of the team as a whole), acknowledging and addressing performance issues (e.g., social loafing and a lack of accountability), communicating the quality of team results, and clearly identifying goals.

*Supportiveness* exists when team members have an interest in helping each other succeed. It includes behaviors such as encouraging, overlooking, helping, defending, being warm and caring, and giving team goals priority over individual goals. Defensiveness, the opposite of supportiveness, works against team effectiveness by taking energy away from the team goal. In the most effective environments, openness and supportiveness go together. In an open environment, it is possible to discuss controversial work issues. In a supportive environment, the *method* of discussion matters most.

Groups with a strong *action orientation* have a desire to do something (produce results). This requires encouraging others, suggesting strategies, and being willing to try. Action-oriented individuals and teams are more likely to emerge as leaders, perhaps proving the accuracy of the fundamental law of team success: *Action is more likely to succeed than inaction.*

A *positive personal style* reflects an underlying positive attitude. A team member with this type of attitude is typically energetic, optimistic, engaging, confident, and fun. A negative attitude, on the other hand, is exhibited by pessimism, defensiveness, and being difficult to work with. Just the presence of a few group members with negative attitudes can drain the energy from a team.

## TEAM RELATIONSHIPS

Positive relationships help produce effective teams. These relationships develop when people come together, identify opportunities, share information, solve problems collectively, and develop inventive ways to collaborate. Key prerequisites for positive work relationships include:

- Being constructive.
- Acting respectful, trusting, nonthreatening, safe, and productive.
- Being focused on important issues, staying connected, and bringing out the best traits in others.
- Developing mutual understanding.

- Seeing another's point of view, feeling understood, and acting in a self-corrective manner.
- Being willing to make changes to improve the relationship; and trusting that each person is committed to the team.

Negative relationships, on the other hand, result in high costs to organizations by diverting progress away from goals and forcing managers to spend a great deal of time solving employee conflicts. Negative relationships often emerge when one or both parties are:

- Destructive.
- Disrespectful, cynical, suspicious, or threatening.
- Focused on superfluous issues.
- Engaging in power struggles.
- Uncertain about the other's points of view.
- Feeling as though their perspectives haven't been heard.
- Not making a committed effort toward concrete changes.
- Exhibiting only a limited commitment from either or both parties.

They are similarly negative when conditions around the parties are ambiguous or not self-correcting.

Team members can gauge these attributes in a relationship by answering these four questions:

1. Did we have a constructive conversation?
2. Was the conversation productive enough to make a difference?
3. Did we understand and appreciate each other's perspective?
4. Did we both commit to making improvements?

Handling conflict well is essential to positive relationships, but this skill is consistently identified as the greatest challenge in team interactions. Any conflict resolution between team members must include openness and supportiveness in order to be successful.

Feedback is frequently mishandled during the conflict resolution process. It requires caring and courage to deliver feedback; it requires courage and maturity to accept and appreciate it. Feedback rarely works because people tend to become defensive, which then eliminates the possibility of openness. When given and received well, feedback results in increased feelings of accountability, increased job satisfaction, and improved performance.

## THE CONNECT MODEL

Leaders and team members need to create and maintain positive interpersonal relationships. Both individuals in any relationship must participate actively in the process to ensure success. Participants are encouraged to:

- Make a strong commitment to the relationship.
- Tell why the relationship is important to you.
- Indicate to the other person that you're willing to work at the relationship.
- Optimize the other's safety (assert that you will not belittle the other person and will listen to them).

- Narrow the discussion to one issue and discuss it in a non-threatening way.
- Neutralize defensiveness by asking the other person to tell you if he/she feels defensive.
- Explain and echo each perspective, by telling what you have experienced and how it makes you feel, and summarizing what the other person tells you.
- Change one behavior (what improvement each person could make).
- Track mutual results, picking a time to check in with each other at specified intervals.

## ◆ TEAM PROBLEM-SOLVING

Team members need to integrate different perspectives and funnel them into good decisions during the problem-solving process. There are three common denominators to effective problem-solving teams:

1. *Focus.* Members must have clarity of purpose and an understanding of the task at hand. It is important to have a concentrated joint effort to optimize energy. Ineffective teams have more scattered efforts and unclear objectives.
2. *Climate.* The best team climates are relaxed, informal, and fun. Members in these climates feel accepted, valued, and competent. Unhealthy climates, by contrast, are tense, critical, cynical, and formal. Bad climates develop because of personal agendas taking priority over group goals, political issues, dysfunctional behavior of group members, and inappropriate leadership styles.
3. *Communication.* Open and honest communication is essential for collaborative teamwork. Ineffective teams avoid problems and hope they go away. This can lead to bad decisions or the lack of a decision at all. None of these factors is related in any way to intelligence or rank in an organization. In fact, top management teams are consistently among the least collaborative problem solvers.

### THE DYNAMICS OF PROBLEM-SOLVING

Problem-solving involves the direction of expended energy. Mental, physical, and spiritual energy gets directed toward the goal, while drains take energy away from the goal. Successful teams are able to stay focused on the goal despite potential energy drains, while unsuccessful teams allow the drains to sap their energy. When drains take precedence, energies end up being expended on self-protection and counterproductive behaviors. Power struggles, political issues, and personality conflict diffuse group members' focus on their goals and tasks. In order to move energy toward the desired objective, the goal must be clear, elevating, compelling, and unifying. A common identity and values provide the team with immunity from energy drains.

#### Five Steps to Effective Problem-Solving

Teams need to have a willingness to address problems systematically. The method of doing so is not as important as agreeing upon a method and sticking with it. In general, any successful problem-solving system should include first a thorough analysis of problems, then examination of issues, and finally a weighing of options.

The Single Question Format is one systematic method of solving problems. The main advantages of this format are: (1) team members' attentions are concentrated on one problem, and (2) solutions are chosen only after thorough analysis. Five steps need to be addressed:

**Step 1:** *Identify the problem.* What one question do we need to answer?
**Step 2:** *Create a collaborative setting.* Determine the guiding principles for the problem-solving process, and identify the assumptions and biases possessed by group members.
**Step 3:** *Identify and analyze the issues and sub-questions.* What must be determined before the process can be completed?
**Step 4:** *Identify possible solutions.* Come up with the two or three best options.
**Step 5:** *Resolve the single question.* Which is the best solution?

### CROSS-FUNCTIONAL TEAMS

Cross-functional teams combine members from different areas of an organization, or from different organizations altogether. The combination brings together many different backgrounds, areas of expertise, and perspectives. However, loyalties to different departments and organizations, as well as deeply divided time commitments and conflicting demands, can detract from progress on cross-functional teams. This increases the likelihood that energy will be directed away from the goal. Because of these factors, it is even more crucial to agree upon and commit to a common goal early in the team's formation.

## ◆ THE TEAM LEADER

Leaders have a great deal of responsibility to ensure effective team functioning. There are six dimensions over which leaders have a great deal of control: focusing on the goal, ensuring a collaborative climate, building confidence, demonstrating sufficient technical know-how, setting priorities, and managing performance. Specific leader behaviors can ensure success on all six dimensions.

- When team leaders *focus on the goal,* they define goals in a clear and elevating way, set relatively difficult goals, help team members see their role in the goal achievement process, continually reinforce and renew the goal, and make adjustments to the goal only with clear justification.
- When leaders work to *ensure a collaborative climate,* they minimize barriers to open communication, bring up tough issues, show no tolerance for competitive or inappropriate behavior, reward collaborative behavior, publicly acknowledge the desired behaviors and outcomes, guide team problem-solving efforts, and manage their own ego and personal control needs.
- When leaders seek to *build confidence* in their team, they try to be fair and impartial, provide the team with positive experiences, keep team members informed about key issues & facts, demonstrate trust of team members, assign areas of responsibility based on members' skills and abilities, show a positive attitude, and acknowledge team members' efforts, contributions, and accomplishments.

- To *demonstrate sufficient technical know-how,* team leaders acquire and use the knowledge necessary for goal achievement, and recognize and acknowledge their own limitations.

- When it comes to *setting priorities,* team leaders stay focused on the question "What needs to happen for the team to move toward its goal?" They take on additional priorities only without careful consideration, reassess priorities when necessary, and thoroughly explain any reasons for changes in priorities to team members.

In the all-important domain of managing performance, team leaders discuss results in term of objectives, level of collaboration, management of people and resources, and personal development; give clear, constructive feedback on these four dimensions by addressing behavior, not people; and recognize superior performance.

## ◆ IMPACT OF THE ORGANIZATIONAL ENVIRONMENT

The organizational environment encompasses the psychological atmosphere resulting from organizational processes. It affects how team members communicate and make decisions, whether they feel comfortable taking risks, how open they are, and whether they are ready to share and accept diverse ideas.

A good environment produces clarity, confidence, and commitment. Clarity drives confidence, and confidence drives commitment. Clarity of goals and priorities makes decisions easier, gives clearer understanding of roles, and produces clearer courses of action. Confidence helps team members commit to a decision, state their opinion, and take action. Commitment helps team members weather the difficult times that inevitably develop during any long-term process, and keep members' action orientation engaged in order to move toward the finish line.

There are three environmental dimensions that can support or hinder teamwork:

1. *Management practices.* Leadership is a primary factor in the shaping of the organizational environment. Managers must establish goals and priorities that are readily recognized at all levels of the organization. These priorities must be emphasized often and enthusiastically. It is also important to establish clear operating principles to guide team members' daily functioning. These principles should send clear messages to team members that leaders will avoid politics, and instead dedicate their energy toward the goal and being accountable for results.
2. *Structure and processes.* Changing objectives or methods of operation without creating structure and processes to support the change is a setup for failure. Structure affects decision-making, information flow, intra- and inter-organizational boundaries, and role clarity. Processes integrate skills, abilities, and information in order to produce an outcome. Effective structure and processes result in quality decisions, strong interpersonal connections, and the alignment of information, understanding, and effort. Repeating objectives and processes in a variety of ways fosters strong communication processes by reaching all employees. A good communication process assures team members that they will be kept informed.

3. *Systems.* Information systems and reward systems consistently present problems in the environment. Teams need reliable information to make effective decisions. Unreliable information systems lead to cynicism and caution in decision-making. Reward systems are needed to encourage the team toward desired results. The traditional system of rewarding and recognizing individuals is incompatible with a team philosophy, as members attain results collectively. Just as they work as one body, teams must also be rewarded as one body.

READING 2

# Leading Teams: Setting the Stage for Great Performances

*J. RICHARD HACKMAN*

***Summary prepared by Katherine A. Karl***

***Katherine A. Karl*** *is an associate professor in the Graduate School of Management at Marshall University in South Charleston, West Virginia. She received her M.B.A. and Ph.D. in Business Administration from Michigan State University with a major in Organizational Behavior and Human Resource Management. She has taught courses in human resource management, organizational behavior, labor relations, teams and teamwork, and leadership skills. Her research publications have focused on the topics of employment termination, job values, performance feedback, and the use of videotaped feedback in management education and development. Her consulting work has included team-building seminars, assessment centers, and employee satisfaction surveys.*

## ◆ INTRODUCTION

Common knowledge suggests that teams outperform individuals, and self-managing teams perform best of all. But, do they really? Not always, and not even usually. Work teams can outperform traditional work units, but they often perform much worse. Developing, supporting, and maintaining a highly successful team is a very beneficial but rare accomplishment. There is no magical recipe for team success. The best a leader can do is to help create conditions that increase the *probability* that a team will be effective.

J. Richard Hackman, *Leading Teams: Setting the Stage for Great Performances.* Boston: Harvard Business School Press, 2002.

## WHAT CONDITIONS WILL FOSTER TEAM EFFECTIVENESS?

Teams have a greater chance of being successful when leaders: (1) create a real team rather than a team in name only, (2) set a compelling direction for the team's work, (3) design an enabling team structure, (4) ensure the team operates within a supportive organizational context, and (5) provide expert coaching.

### CREATING A REAL TEAM

First, leaders must make sure that the task is appropriate for a team. Some tasks are performed better when individuals work independently (e.g., creative writing). Second, the team should have clear boundaries. To work well together, team members need to have a clear and consistent sense of who they are. Third, it is important for leaders to clearly specify the team's level of authority. Here, there are four options: (1) teams who merely carry out the instructions of their manager (manager-led teams), (2) teams who perform the task as well as monitor and manage work process and progress (self-managing teams), (3) teams who perform, self-manage, and also design the team and its organizational context (self-designing teams), and (4) teams who do all the above as well as establish the overall direction of the team (self-governing teams). While it is possible for both self-managing and self-designing teams to make significant and valuable contributions to their organizations, the other two options are rarely successful. Manager-led teams, the first option, tend to be dysfunctional for both the people involved and the organization and invariably result in wasted human resources. The latter option, self-governing teams, are often bogged down in endless discussions about their values, purposes, and collective directions.

Finally, it is commonly held that teams should periodically introduce new members and remove existing members to prevent the team from becoming inattentive, careless, and too forgiving of one another's mistakes. In truth, teams with stable membership over a long period of time perform better than those that have constantly changing membership. Teams with stable membership are more familiar with one another, the team's work, the team's norms, team members' roles, and the work setting. As a result, team members are able to focus on getting work done rather than getting oriented.

### SETTING A COMPELLING DIRECTION

Teams with no clear sense of where they are going have endless discussions and debates about the team's purpose. As a result they are unable to manage themselves efficiently or effectively. Teams are much more effective when someone in authority sets the direction for the team's work. A compelling direction—one that is challenging, clear, and consequential—energizes team members, orients their attention and action, and engages their talents.

In setting the team's direction, leaders have four choices. They can specify neither the ends nor the means, but that may result in disorder and undesirable behaviors and outcomes. They can specify both the ends and the means, but that is a waste of human resources. They can specify the means but not the ends, which is the worst case scenario. When this happens, the team's products or services rarely satisfy those who receive them, neither growth nor learning is experienced by team members, and the team's capabilities decline over time. However, *when leaders specify the ends but not the means, team members are able to take full advantage of the team's knowledge, skill, and experience to devise creative and effective ways of accomplishing the team's purposes.*

## ENABLING TEAM STRUCTURE

Three structural features are important for effective teamwork: task design, norms, and composition.

### Team Task Design

When the team's work is designed to incorporate skill variety, task identity, task significance, autonomy, and feedback, the team is more likely to experience a state of collective internal motivation. Indeed, one of the benefits of creating teams to accomplish work is that the tasks assigned can be much larger and therefore more significant and meaningful. Autonomy can give teams the opportunity to excel by allowing team members to create new and improved work processes. However, there is always the risk that teams will use their autonomy in ways undesired by organizational leaders. Finally, feedback makes team learning and performance improvements possible.

### Team Norms

Team norms are critical because they serve to coordinate and regulate member behavior. Two key norms that foster team effectiveness are: (1) being active rather than reactive, and (2) clearly specifying a handful of critical things team members must do and things they must not do. Unfortunately, both of these require forethought, effort, and diligence because they contradict natural human tendencies. Groups and individuals tend to keep on mindlessly doing whatever they've done in the past and reacting to whatever demands their attention and response at the moment rather than actively scanning the environment for problems or opportunities. Groups and individuals also have a tendency to seek harmony and may do things that shouldn't be done in an effort to please others.

### Team Composition

Leaders need to ensure each team member has strong task skills and at least adequate interpersonal skills. Additionally, the size of the group should be small (e.g., no more than six members). Finally, the composition of the team should strike a balance between homogeneity (for compatibility) and heterogeneity (for diversity of ideas).

## A SUPPORTIVE ORGANIZATIONAL CONTEXT

A well-supported work team has (1) a reward system that provides positive consequences for good team performance (as opposed to individual performance), (2) an information system that provides accurate and reliable data and projections, (3) an educational system that provides critical training and technical assistance, and (4) the material resources necessary to carry out the team's work.

Unfortunately, providing these contextual supports is difficult, for it almost always involves changing the answers to the following questions: (1) Who decides? (2) Who is responsible? (3) Who gains? and, (4) Who learns? In other words, providing teams with a supportive organization context often results in changes in the authority or privileges of currently advantaged organizational members.

One of the biggest challenges faced by those implementing teams involves changing reward systems so that recognition and reinforcement are contingent on excellent team performance. Team-based reward systems are critical in sustaining collective motivation and getting team members to think of "us" rather than "me." However, in most organizations performance appraisal and compensation systems are set up to measure and reward individual contributions, not team accomplishments.

Another critical challenge involves making changes in the accessibility of existing information and control systems. Providing teams with up-to-date and reliable information is not an easy feat for many reasons:

1. *The really good stuff is a secret.* To prevent key information from getting in the hands of competitors, some organizations keep information secret. Unfortunately, this "secret" information could often have been used by the team to improve its performance.
2. *Providers and users speak different languages.* The information is provided in a format that may make sense to the provider, but is either nonsensical or burdensome to the user.
3. *Information.* A flood is as bad as a drought. Due to improvements in information system technologies, teams may have more information available than they can adequately process. Too much information can be as much a handicap for a team as too little information.
4. *Information is power.* In many organizations, access to information is controlled by senior executives, and some of those executives are very reluctant to share information because doing so diminishes their sense of personal power.

## EXPERT COACHING

The previously mentioned conditions—compelling direction, enabling team structure, and supportive organizational context—provide the foundation for exceptional team performance. No amount of coaching can make a team successful without a sound team foundation. However, when these conditions are favorable, coaching can be crucial to minimizing process losses and increasing process gains. *Process loss* occurs when a group accomplishes less than it theoretically should, given its resources and member talents. *Process gain* occurs when the collective efforts of the team exceed what the individual members could have achieved working independently.

### What should be the *content* of team coaching interventions?

It is a common misconception that team coaching interventions should focus on improving interpersonal relationships. In truth, interpersonal conflicts are more often a consequence of, rather than a cause of, poor team performance. Thus, coaching interventions are more effective when the focus is on the team's task-performance processes. More specifically, team coaching interventions should focus on: (1) the amount of effort team members apply to their collective work, (2) the appropriateness of the performance strategies they utilize to accomplish their work, and (3) the level of knowledge and skill the team applies to its work.

Coaching that addresses effort is motivational in nature and seeks to build shared commitment to the team and its work and to minimize *social loafing,* or the tendency for team members to slack off. Strategy-focused coaching is consultative in nature and seeks to minimize thoughtless reliance on habitual routines and helps team members find or invent new performance strategies that are more appropriate to changing situational requirements and opportunities. Coaching that addresses knowledge and skill is educational in character and seeks not only to develop team members' knowledge and skills, but to prevent team members from failing to fully utilize the knowledge and skills of all its members.

### *When* should coaching be provided?

The beginning of a team's life is a good time for motivational coaching. At this point the coach needs to get all team members to understand and accept that the team is collectively responsible for accomplishing the team's work. The beginning is the wrong time for strategy-focused coaching. A team needs to experience the task before it can benefit from strategy interventions. Thus, the midpoint of a team's work cycle is the best time for a strategy-focused coaching intervention. People don't learn well when they are in a hurry, preoccupied, or anxious. Thus, educational coaching is most effective at the end of work cycle when team members have some protected time.

### *Who* should be the coach?

It is not important that a team leader or advisor always serve as coach. Peer-to-peer coaching can also be effective. What is most important is that effective coaching be available to a team. Ideally coaching should be shared. It should be provided by a number of individuals at different times and for different purposes.

## WHAT DO EFFECTIVE LEADERS DO?

Rather than focusing on traits (who the leader should be) or behavioral style (how the leader should behave), effective leaders know what to do. They make sure they have created a real work team with some stability over time. They know about providing a compelling direction, enabling team structure, supportive organizational context, and expert coaching.

Effective leaders also know when to do it. They pay close attention to timing. They move swiftly and assuredly when opportunities present themselves, but never try to force an intervention when the timing is not right. Astute leaders are aware that change initiatives are rarely successful during periods of equilibrium and that major interventions have a greater chance of success during turbulent times.

Effective leaders have both *emotional maturity and courage.* Leaders who are emotionally mature are more capable of dealing with their own anxieties and those of others. Courage is essential because creating the conditions necessary for successful team performance is usually a revolutionary endeavor and people, especially leaders, often get hurt in revolutions.

Finally, effective leaders neither micro-manage nor totally abdicate their role as leader. To build teamwork, the leader needs to let the team work. Thus, the team's potential is rarely realized when leaders attempt to personally manage every aspect of the team's work. Equally wrong is the leader who merely stays out of the way, assuming that the magic of teamwork comes automatically. The bottom line is that a leader cannot *make* a team great. However, once the favorable conditions are in place—compelling direction, enabling team structure, supportive organizational context—a leader can help members take full advantage of those favorable conditions and thereby increase the chance that greatness will occur.

# Beyond Teams: Building the Collaborative Organization

*MICHAEL M. BEYERLEIN, SUE FREEDMAN, CRAIG MCGEE, and LINDA MORAN*

*Summary prepared by David L. Beal*

*David Beal is a retired Operations Manager and Vice President of Manufacturing for Lake Superior Paper Industries and Consolidated Papers Inc. in Duluth, Minnesota. Under his leadership, the all-salaried workforce was organized into a totally self-reliant team system using the principles of socio-technical design to create a high performance system. Dave teaches in the Labovitz School of Business and Economics at the University of Minnesota Duluth, where his areas of interest include designing and leading self-directed team-based organizations, teamwork, and production and operations management. He received his B.S. in Chemical Engineering from the University of Maine in Orono, Maine with a fifth year in Pulp and Paper Sciences.*

## ◆ INTRODUCTION

The challenges organizations face today continue to grow as a result of a rapidly changing environment, not the least of which includes the proliferation of new technology, a dynamic global market place, and (more recently) the threat of terrorism. Contemporary organizations must be structurally flexible, capable of adapting to changing markets, and able to compete and win on a national and frequently international scale. *Collaborative Work Systems* (CWS) provide the fundamental principles and means to meet these challenges. Collaboration and CWS are not new; they are simply the principles and practices that make organizations and teamwork succeed. There are ten major principles for successful collaboration and a set of characteristics that collaborative organizations have that effectively apply these principles.

---

Michael M. Beyerlein, Sue Freedman, Craig McGee, and Linda Moran, *Beyond Teams: Building the Collaborative Organization.* San Francisco: Jossey-Bass/Pfeiffer, 2003.

Organizations that fail to embrace the collaborative work systems approach exhibit a contrasting set of defining characteristics.

Managers and employees at all levels working together can outperform individuals acting alone, especially when the outcome requires a variety of creative abilities, multiple skills, careful judgments, and the knowledge and experience that different employees possess in achieving organizational goals. CWS are the means to achieve these goals and not an end in and of themselves.

## RATIONALE FOR COLLABORATIVE WORK SYSTEMS

Collaborative work systems put into practice a disciplined principle-based system of collaboration necessary to be successful in a rapidly changing environment. All organizations collaborate to some extent in order to achieve their goals, including how the organization serves its customers and meets its financial objectives. CWS carry collaboration to a much higher level and therefore outperform organizations that do not consistently apply the principles of collaboration as a disciplined practice, or do not make collaboration the means to achieve business objectives and the goals of the organization.

Organizations that not only value collaborative practices, but consciously apply and nurture these practices with passion and conviction at all levels create a definite competitive advantage over organizations that simply assume collaborative practices will occur. Strategic direction and leadership at the top of the organization is paramount to achieving a CWS. While team-based organizations and self-directed work systems depend on collaborative practices, these organizations may not go far enough in the degree or variety of collaboration to reach the full potential that a CWS has.

Collaborative work systems are a key strategy for achieving superior business results. While employees create value through collaborative practices, their ability to perform and to be highly productive is often limited by the barriers the organization creates. These barriers stifle the collaborative practices employees are expected to have. Key employees at all levels solve problems, make and act on important decisions, invent new practices and improved methods of doing business, build relationships, and strategically plan for the future. The effectiveness of their processes and practices and the work system the employees are in determines the degree to which they reach their full potential. A high level of collaborative capacity will stimulate both formal and informal learning and enhance the effectiveness of work done at all levels.

When collaboration becomes both a strategy and competency for achieving business goals and a major part of the organizational culture, then:

- Organizational barriers to a collaborative work system are broken down.
- Employees at all levels know when and how to collaborate to achieve business results without wasting valuable time and resources.
- Managers and leaders in the organization create systems that are highly flexible, functionally adaptable, and fast to react to a changing environment.
- The waste that occurs within a functional silo and between functional silos diminishes and is replaced with a high level of cross-functional cooperation.
- Teams become accountable for their results and hold themselves to a high standard.

- The organization becomes a highly interdependent, interacting, and interconnected system of processes and functions that continuously performs at a high level.

Collaborative work systems do not require formal teams or a team-based system (i.e., an organizational arrangement where teams are the basic unit of organizational structure), but their collaborative capacity and competency are enhanced by the use of these structures. Since teams are frequently the most common form of business collaboration, the design, management, and work processes that make collaboration within and between teams successful are important features to discuss.

## THE PRINCIPLES OF COLLABORATIVE ORGANIZATIONS

The ten principles of collaborative work systems are:

**1.** *"Focus collaboration on achieving business results."* Collaboration is necessary to achieve the goals and strategies necessary for long-term success. It is not an end in itself, but a means to an end. This principle focuses the organization on a common goal where everyone understands their role in the broader context of achieving intermediate and overall corporate objectives. When collaboration is focused on achieving business results, everyone is focused on common goals and objectives and is in the business of getting results with very few self-serving obstacles. Employees know what needs to be done and can go about doing it in an efficient and effective manner. When collaborative efforts are not focused on business results, conflicts and disagreements will occur and employees may sub-optimize their own functional areas, sometimes at the expense of achieving overall organizational goals.

**2.** *"Align organizational support systems to promote ownership."* This principle stems from an understanding that all systems of support must be congruent with the goals and principles of the organization. If a collaborative work system is a defined strategy to achieve the goals of the organization, then all systems must support the who, when, where, and why of collaborative practices. These systems include management systems, organizational design, performance management systems, and information and communication systems. Support systems that create a sense of ownership have a much greater chance of success in creating a competitive advantage. When these systems are aligned, employees are rewarded for acting in a predictable and consistent manner toward achieving individual, intermediate, and overall corporate goals and objectives. When it is not working, employees are sent mixed messages that collectively produce organizational chaos and poor performance.

**3.** *"Articulate and enforce a few strict rules."* This principle applies to the policies, practices and methods that drive decision-making within organizations. Everyone needs to understand what needs to be done within a framework of a few highly understood rules. These rules must be consistently applied and individuals held accountable for their application. The application of this principle gives individuals and teams of individuals a common understanding of what needs to be done without limiting their ability to accomplish it. It also allows them to break down barriers and make and act on important decisions toward the accomplishment of the goals and objectives.

Organizations with too many rules suffer from inaction and an unwillingness to take risks, while an organization with too few rules struggles from a lack of direction and consistency.

**4.** *"Exploit the rhythm of divergence and convergence."* This principle provides a balance between creating new and exciting ways of getting the job done, and the discipline necessary to get the job done. Both of these are processes by which participants are allowed to diverge with their ideas and generate different ways of getting the job done, and also converge to a level of agreement necessary to move forward to get the job done. Managing the process of divergence and convergence is important to goal accomplishment. The process also has a rhythm that is recognizable. As collaboration within and between teams and individuals at different levels and across functional boundaries occurs, complex activities take place toward the accomplishment of the stated goals and objectives. Each cycle accomplishes an intermediate objective that allows the next step or iterative cycle to occur. When the rhythm of divergence and convergence is effectively managed, new ideas and ways of getting the job done naturally occur, while the disciplined commitment to accomplish the objective in the expected time frame is achieved.

**5.** *"Manage complex tradeoffs on a timely basis."* Making timely and effective decisions requires the skills, knowledge, and a process for effective decision-making. When the collaborative unit is faced with complex, interrelated, or interdependent decisions, tradeoffs frequently have to be made between contradictory criteria or information. Managing these tradeoffs for effective decision-making sometimes requires specialized skills, knowledge, and information that the collaborative unit must recognize and acquire on a timely basis. When complex decisions are made on a timely basis, the collaborative unit can move forward with increased confidence.

**6.** *"Create higher standards for discussion, dialogue, and information sharing."* Collaborative processes can be very complex and highly important to goal attainment. These processes must be well managed by leaders that recognize the need for good organization, coaching, and facilitation skills. Higher standards mean that participants have direct access to relevant information, expert opinions, and advice, new and improved capabilities for effective decision-making, and a sense of excitement and commitment to be involved in a CWS. When the collaborative capacity of an organization is not increased through coaching or training of the participants, decision-making suffers, deadlines and expectations are more difficult to meet, and participants seek a safe haven by sticking to their own opinions and perspectives. Getting "out of the box" and taking a risk will become a rare event.

**7.** *"Foster personal accountability."* When organization members are personally accountable for their own role and responsibilities in the collaborative process, the capability of the collaborative unit will improve. Accountability means that participants will build capability to achieve goals by breaking down the barriers to goal attainment, putting the goal ahead of self-serving considerations, and tackling the tasks of getting the job done with confidence, risk taking, and timeliness. Participants simply do what needs to be done and act in support of the collaborative process. When there is a lack of accountability, participants fail to acknowledge their responsibility or mistakes, and they will usually act in support of their own self-serving interests.

**8.** *"Align authority, information and decision-making."* This principle means that teams and participants have all the tools, including the authority to make important decisions, the skills, knowledge and information for effective decision-making, and the resources and support to act and carry out the decisions they make for effective goal attainment. When these are present decisions are timely, well executed, and participants are committed with a high degree of responsibility for their participation on the collaborative unit. When authority, information, and decision-making are not aligned, participants experience a loss of both support and direction, a lack of ownership in the process, and chaos or confusion when decisions and plans have to be revisited.

**9.** *"Treat collaboration as a disciplined process."* This principle means that CWS organizations must recognize and support the principles as a strategy for goal accomplishment. Making collaboration a disciplined process requires the skills, knowledge and training of a critical mass of participants that can pass on their expertise in successfully conducting collaborative processes. When organizations are competent at collaboration, they are able to manage multiple interdependent and interacting processes at the same time. These organizations will have good organization skills, the ability to quickly hurdle obstacles and break down barriers, easy access to relevant information, excellent communication skills, and the ability to make good decisions and act on those decisions in a timely manner. When collaboration is not treated as a disciplined process, meetings are not very productive or goal oriented, participants are frustrated by the lack of goal accomplishment, and managers with authority may try to micro-manage the activities of the collaborative unit.

**10.** *"Design and promote flexible organizations."* The successful organization today must be quick to respond to all sorts of changing business conditions and structurally flexible in its ability to get the work done and compete in a dynamic business environment. Flexible organizations respond with different structures, both formal and informal to maximize the speed and effectiveness of what needs to be done to be successful. The increasing complexity and dynamic nature of competing in a global marketplace requires that organizations react with different structures based on the situation. These organizations break down the barriers that traditional organizations have in a way that improves their ability to compete and respond to changing business conditions. Information and decision-making are moved to those who have to take action, rather than those who control the action of others. Flexible organizations have leaders that decentralize decision-making for maximum effectiveness and manage the organization with a high level of cross-functional capability. When organizations are structurally inflexible, their collaborative activities are less effective, they waste valuable resources, and decisions take a lot longer to make and implement.

## APPLICATIONS OF THE PRINCIPLES

Manufacturing facilities produce tangible products from physical materials with the support of functionally based staff organizations. They have become flatter in organizational structure, more flexible in their ability to get the work done in many different ways, and faster to react to the market place and remain competitive. As manufacturing organizations integrate vertically and horizontally to achieve a competitive advantage, they have also integrated new work systems such as "team based organizations," high performance systems," "self-reliant teams," and "socio-technical systems." When properly applied, these principle-based systems can produce superior performance. All of these systems represent changes in how work is organized and how the empowerment of employees has moved leadership down to the productive process or shop floor. As organizations become flatter and more flexible, the opportunities to collaborate become more numerous. The leadership in organizations must make clear expectations of the "how" and "when" to formally and informally collaborate. The "when" occurs when more than one person is required to make a decision and when effective implementation requires the acceptance or the decision is executed by a group of employees.

Collaboration in service settings needs to occur when the skills, knowledge and expertise needed resides in more than one employee, when the decisions or tasks are interdependent with other employees or parts of the organization, when decisions require the acceptance of a group of employees for effective implementation, and when multiple teams or areas need to share resources or have a common understanding for goal accomplishment. On the other hand, collaboration can be wasteful when there is not good direction or leadership for collaborative processes, when the practice of "command and control" of employees makes the empowerment of employees an abstract thought, and when management fails to share important information with employees or give employees direct access to information necessary to accomplish their tasks.

New product development creates unique and creative opportunities. Expertise in functional organizations is organized into silos as opposed to product or customer-based organizing structures. Another design is the team-based model, in which integration teams oversee the coordinated efforts and assignments of new product development teams. Global pressures, the threat of declining profit margins if new products are not developed, and the time to produce new products to pre-empt the competition are challenges these organizations face. The question is when, where and who should collaborate to maximize the use of the valuable resources. It is also important to establish the training, expectations and the time frame for effective collaboration.

The ten principles can also be applied in "virtual work settings." *Virtual organizations* are "groups of individuals working on shared tasks while distributed across space, time and/or organizational boundaries." They are unique in that they traverse organizational and functional boundaries that exist at multiple national and sometimes international locations. The participants in virtual settings are not located at the same site, but it is still possible to apply the principles of CWS to virtual work settings.

## Conclusion

Collaborative Work Systems are principle-based systems that are consciously designed and nurtured for high performance. A CWS allows the creative capacities and talents of their employees to continuously increase through knowledge sharing and mutual support.

Individuals collaborating effectively in pursuit of common goals and objectives will consistently outperform individuals acting alone or in functional silos, especially when the task requires multiple skills, knowledge, different experiences, and creative abilities. As the work and the accomplishment of tasks become more complex, flexible organizational structures and collaborative practices must be carefully thought out and executed to meet the varied challenges the organization faces. When organizations apply the ten principles of collaboration, employee ownership and involvement increases, decision-making is more consistent and execution is more effective, positional power is replaced with knowledge and leadership, and employees learn and grow at a much faster rate. The organization is also quicker to respond to the business environment, more flexible in its ability to accomplish objectives in different ways, and flatter in an organizational structure that values cross-functional competencies.

# Leadership

PART VIII

The 1990s was the "decade of the leader", a trend that continues today. Nationally we seem to be looking for the hero who can turn us around, establish a new direction, and pull us through. Organizations are searching for visionary leaders—people who by the strength of their personalities can bring about a major organizational transformation. We hear calls for charismatic, transformational, and transactional leadership. Innumerable individuals charge that the problems with the American economy, declining organizational productivity, and lost ground in worldwide competitive markets are largely a function of poor management and the lack of good organizational leadership.

Several years ago the concept of emotional intelligence (EI) emerged in the popular press. It was suggested that EI is an important leader characteristic, contributing to the leader's ability to manage more effectively not only his/her own behavior but also relationships with followers. In *Primal Leadership: Realizing the Power of Emotional Intelligence,* Daniel Goleman (author of *Emotional Intelligence* and *Working with Emotional Intelligence),* Richard Boyatzis, and Annie McKee draw upon their examination of EI and its role in the leadership process. A central question driving their work asks how emotional intelligence drives organizational performance, that is, How does the EI of the leader travel through the organization such that it affects the bottom line? In answering this question, they highlight the contagiousness of emotions. Leaders whose personalities exude emotion—energy and enthusiasm—spread the same to their followers. Leaders, on the other hand, whose personalities emit negativity transfer the same to their followers. Goleman and his colleagues argue that positive emotions are associated with organizational success, while negativity contributes to organizational hardships.

Daniel Goleman is the co-director of a consortium conducting research on emotional intelligence at Rutgers University; Richard Boyatzis is on the faculty at Case Western Reserve University; and Annie McKee serves on the faculty in the School of Education at the University of Pennsylvania. In recent years all three authors have conducted research on EI within the context of many organizations.

Jim Collins, in *Good to Great,* studied the 11 companies (out of 1,435) that had made a major transition from many years of mediocrity to many subsequent years of outstanding achievements. He discovered a series of contributors to success, including a culture of discipline, technology accelerators, a focus on doing things well, the importance of breakthrough momentum, the willingness to confront brutal reality while maintaining hope, and managing people well. In addition, he discovered that the great firms were typically led by "level 5" executives—those who combined modesty/humility with a fearless will.

Jim Collins operates a management research laboratory in Boulder, Colorado. He previously held positions at McKinsey & Company and Hewlett-Packard, and was on the faculty at Stanford University's Graduate School of Business. He is the co-author of *Built to Last* and *Beyond Entrepreneurship.*

The third reading in this section focuses on the narcissistic personality. Instead of casting the leader/manager with the narcissistic personality as out-of-place in corporate America, Michael Maccoby, in *The Productive Narcissist: The Promise and Peril of Visionary Leadership,* argues that these are the very individuals organizations need in highly competitive and turbulent times. "Nice-guy" leaders full of Daniel Goleman's highly touted emotional intelligence may well serve a useful purpose in big companies in stable and mature industries. A new paradigm of leadership—the "productive narcissist"—is needed for those organizations where industrial and competitive demands call for large-scale innovation. These are individuals like Jack Welch, Steve Jobs, Oprah Winfrey, and Bill Gates who are characterized by having a precise vision for how things *should be,* and the tendency to never listen to voices of reason and authority.

Michael Maccoby has over thirty years of consulting experience and is the president of the Maccoby Group. Dr. Maccoby is the author (or co-author) of several books, including *The Gamesman* and *Why Work? Motivating the New Workforce.*

# Primal Leadership: Realizing the Power of Emotional Intelligence

***DANIEL GOLEMAN, RICHARD E. BOYATZIS, and ANNIE MCKEE***

***Summary prepared by John Kratz***

***John Kratz*** *is an instructor in the Labovitz School of Business and Economics at the University of Minnesota Duluth. He teaches business-to-business marketing, advertising and marketing communications, international marketing, and fundamentals of selling. He has over twenty years of experience working in consumer packaged goods sales and marketing, having served in a variety of business development and marketing management positions with Gage Marketing, MCI, Actmedia, The Pillsbury Company, and Land O'Lakes, Inc. His interest in emotional intelligence research lies in its potential application for improving sales force performance. He holds an M.B.A. from the University of Minnesota's Carlson School of Management.*

## INTRODUCTION

The ever-accelerating rate of change brought on by a globalizing world economy, a diversifying workforce, and technological innovation makes enormous demands on organizational leaders desiring to instill widespread change and encourage new

---

Daniel Goleman, Richard Boyatzis, and Annie McKee, *Primal Leadership: Realizing the Power of Emotional Intelligence.* Boston: Harvard Business School Press, 2002.

organizational learning. Extensive field research indicates that most executive education and leadership development efforts fail to produce the anticipated results. The reason is not only because of *how* they are implemented, but also because of what they do *not* do. *For the most part, leadership-training processes do not take into account the power that emotion plays in influencing individual and organizational behavior.*

Leadership effectiveness is rooted in the ability to perceive, identify, and successfully manage the emotional states of ourselves as well as those of others. This is the essence of *primal leadership.*

## WHAT IS EMOTIONAL INTELLIGENCE?

*Emotional intelligence* (EI) is a set of competencies that distinguish how people manage feelings and interactions with others. It is the ability to identify one's own emotions, as well as those of one's co-workers or employees. EI is separate from, but complementary to, academic intelligence (i.e., cognitive capacities measured by IQ). Emotional intelligence skills such as empathy and self-awareness are synergistic with such cognitive skills as analytical and technical proficiencies. Effective leaders have competency in both sets of skills. EI competencies are learned abilities rather than innate characteristics, with each one uniquely contributing to leader effectiveness.

## EMOTIONAL INTELLIGENCE AND ASSOCIATED COMPETENCIES

EI consists of two sets of competencies, and four different domain areas. *Personal* competencies are those that determine how effectively people manage themselves, and *social* competencies are those that determine how effectively they manage their interpersonal relationships. The four domains of EI include self-awareness, self-management, social awareness, and relationship management. Each element influences individual, group and organization performance. *Self-awareness and self-management are personal competence components, while social awareness and relationship management are social competence components.*

### Self-Awareness

- **Emotional self-awareness:** Reading one's own emotions and recognizing their impact; using "gut sense" to guide decisions.
- **Accurate self-assessment:** Knowing one's strengths and limits.
- **Self-confidence:** Having a sense of one's self-worth and capabilities.

### Self-Management

- **Emotional self-control:** Keeping disruptive emotions and impulses under control.
- **Transparency:** Displaying honesty and integrity; trustworthiness.
- **Adaptability:** Showing flexibility in adapting to new situations or overcoming obstacles.
- **Achievement:** Demonstrating the drive to improve performance to meet inner standards of excellence.
- **Initiative:** Being ready and willing to act and seize opportunities.
- **Optimism:** Looking for, and seeing, the up side in events.

### Social Awareness

- **Empathy:** Sensing others' emotions, understanding their perspective, and taking an active interest in their concerns.
- **Organizational awareness:** Reading the currents, decision networks, and politics at the organizational level.
- **Service:** Recognizing and meeting follower, client, or customer needs.

### Relationship Management

- **Inspirational leadership:** Guiding and motivating with a compelling vision.
- **Influence:** Possessing a range of tactics for persuasion.
- **Developing others:** Bolstering others' abilities through feedback and guidance.
- **Change catalyst:** Initiating, managing, and leading in a new direction.
- **Conflict management:** Resolving disagreements.
- **Building bonds:** Cultivating and maintaining a web of relationships.
- **Teamwork and collaboration:** Cooperating with others and building effective teams.

## ◆ EMOTIONS: THE PRIMAL DIMENSION OF LEADERSHIP

Some managers may view emotions and moods as trivial, but few would discount that they influence people's behaviors as they work with others. At its most basic level, the primal task of leadership is emotional—to generate good feelings in those they lead. Leaders who cannot distinguish and guide emotions in the right direction may fail in achieving intended outcomes when working with other people.

*Resonant leaders* are attuned to people's feelings and move them in a positive emotional direction. For example, a resonant leader may consciously choose to use self-deprecating humor to skillfully defuse tense situations or use warmth and empathy to communicate bad news. Resonance comes naturally to emotionally intelligent leaders. An EI leader makes work more meaningful for others by effectively connecting with others at an emotional level, thereby creating a more supportive and nurturing work environment.

The opposite of resonant leadership is *dissonant leadership:* being out of touch with people's feelings. Dissonant leaders alienate their colleagues because they lack well-developed personal and social competency skills.

## ◆ THE NEUROANATOMY OF LEADERSHIP

Research reveals physical bases in the brain for people's interpersonal behaviors. The two types of intelligence, EI and IQ, are controlled in different parts of the brain. Cognitive and analytical intellect is controlled by the neocortex, the most recently evolved layers at the top of the brain, while the center of control for emotions is the limbic brain, the more primitive subcortex region of the brain. Although these neural regions managing rational thought and emotion are found in different areas of the brain, they have closely intertwined connections. *Understanding this interwoven relationship provides the foundation for understanding the concept of primal leadership.*

The limbic brain commandeers the rational region of the brain during emergencies to ensure safety or survival. (i.e., alert drivers instantaneously brake sharply to avoid hitting a deer that jumps out in front of their car.) The area of the brain responsible for this "fight or flight" response is the amygdala. The amygdala serves as an emotional radar, always on the alert for emotional emergencies. This subconscious survival mechanism, developed over 100 million years of human evolution, can be so overriding that it often "hijacks" our emotional response to present-day threats (i.e., when someone cuts us off while driving we tend to experience rage and may temporarily act out of character).

Extensive circuitry between the amygdala and the prefrontal area of the brain monitors emotional responses (feelings) to sensory perceptions, serving as a regulator that safeguards against potentially self-defeating behavior (i.e., recognizing that you need to take a couple of deep breaths before saying something you might regret). *Emotionally intelligent leaders monitor and regulate their feelings, and make effective decisions about how best to respond in any given social situation.*

## ◆ INADEQUECIES OF TRADITIONAL LEADERSHIP TRAINING

The problem with the content of most leadership training programs is that they are directed primarily at the rational-thinking part of the brain. That is, most leadership training, by its very design, limits potential learning because it ignores the emotional centers of the brain. Leadership training should address both the rational and emotional facets.

Some of the cited shortfalls of traditional leadership training include:

- Attempting to change only the person and ignoring the surrounding emotional culture.
- Driving the change process from the wrong organization level. Transformative leadership development must start at the top and must be viewed as a strategic priority.
- Ignoring many of the EI competencies.

The most successful leadership development initiatives are based on the idea that meaningful change occurs through a comprehensive process involving individuals in the organization, the teams in which they work, and the organization's culture.

Effective leadership development processes should be focused on intellectual and emotional learning. This can, in part, be achieved through the use of active participatory work, experiential learning and coaching, team-based simulations, and a mix of learning techniques.

## ◆ SIX LEADERSHIP APPROACHES

Research drawn from EI assessments of nearly 4000 executives identifies six distinct leadership styles requisite for creating resonance within organizations. The most effective leaders use one or more of these approaches, skillfully switching between the various styles depending on their analysis of the situation. The six distinct leadership styles, how they create resonance, and when they are best deployed, are outlined below.

**Visionary Leadership**

- Builds resonance by moving people toward the firm's mission.
- Most effective when a firm needs a new vision or direction.

**Coaching Leadership**

- Connects what a person wants with the organization's goals.
- Best used to increase employee performance by building long-term capabilities.

**Affiliative Leadership**

- Creates harmony by connecting people to each other.
- Most appropriate for motivating employees during stressful times.

**Democratic Leadership**

- Gets commitment by valuing people's input and participation.
- Invaluable for building consensus and obtaining valuable input from employees.

**Pacesetting Leadership**

- Builds resonance by setting challenging goals.
- Most effective to achieve superior results from a motivated and competent team.

**Commanding Leadership**

- Reduces fears by providing clear direction during an emergency.
- Most appropriately used during a crisis or to jump-start a turnaround.

## Conclusion

Primal leadership is a fundamental determinant of organizational effectiveness and superior business performance. Managers leading solely using their expertise and intellect miss a vital component of leadership. Neurological research indicates that the four core EI competencies are not innate talents; they are learned and teachable abilities, each of which can contribute to making leaders more effective. The most effective leaders skillfully switch between one of more of the six distinct approaches of EI leadership. Primal leadership operates best through leaders who create resonance by creating an emotional climate nurturing innovation, performance, and lasting customer relationships.

READING 2

# Good to Great: Why Some Companies Make the Leap . . . and Others Don't

*JAMES C. COLLINS*

What catapults a company from merely good to truly great? A five-year research project searched for the answer to that question, and its discoveries ought to change the way we think about leadership. The most powerfully transformative executives possess a paradoxical mixture of personal humility and professional will. They are timid and ferocious. Shy and fearless. They are rare—and unstoppable.

In 1971, a seemingly ordinary man names Darwin E. Smith was named chief executive of Kimberly-Clark, a stodgy old paper company whose stock had fallen 36% behind the general market during the previous 20 years. Smith, the company's mild-mannered in-house lawyer, wasn't so sure the board had made the right choice—a feeling that was reinforced when a Kimberly-Clark director pulled him aside and reminded him that he lacked some of the qualifications for the position. But CEO he was, and CEO he remained for 20 years.

What a 20 years it was. In that period, Smith created a stunning transformation at Kimberly-Clark, turning it into the leading consumer paper products company in the world. Under his stewardship, the company beat its rivals Scott Paper and Procter & Gamble. And in doing so, Kimberly-Clark generated cumulative stock returns that were 4.1 times greater than those of the general market, outperforming venerable companies such as Hewlett-Packard, 3M, Coca-Cola, and General Electric.

Smith's turnaround of Kimberly-Clark is one of the best examples in the twentieth century of a leader taking a company from merely good to truly great. And yet few

---

From *Harvard Business Review.* "Level 5 Leadership: The Triumph of Humility and Fierce Resolve," by Jim Collins (January 2001). 

people—even ardent students of business history—have heard of Darwin Smith. He probably would have liked it that way. Smith is a classic example of a *Level 5 leader*—an individual who blends extreme personal humility and intense professional will. According to our five-year research study, executives who possess this paradoxical combination of traits are catalysts for the statistically rare event of transforming a good company into a great one. (The research is described in Exhibit 1, "One Question, Five Years, Eleven Companies.")

"Level 5" refers to the highest level in a hierarchy of executive capabilities that we identified during our research. Leaders at the other four levels in the hierarchy can

◆ EXHIBIT 1 ◆

## One Question, Five Years, Eleven Companies

The Level 5 discovery derives from a research project that began in 1996, when my research teams and I set out to answer one question: can a good company become a great company and, if so, how? Most great companies grew up with superb parents—people like George Merck, David Packard, and Walt Disney—who instilled greatness early on. But what about the vast majority of companies that wake up partway through life and realize that they're good but not great?

To answer that question, we looked for companies that had shifted from good performance to great performance—and sustained it. We identified comparison companies that had failed to make that sustained shift. We then studied the contrast between the two groups to discover common variables that distinguish those who make and sustain a shift from those who could have but didn't.

(*continued*)

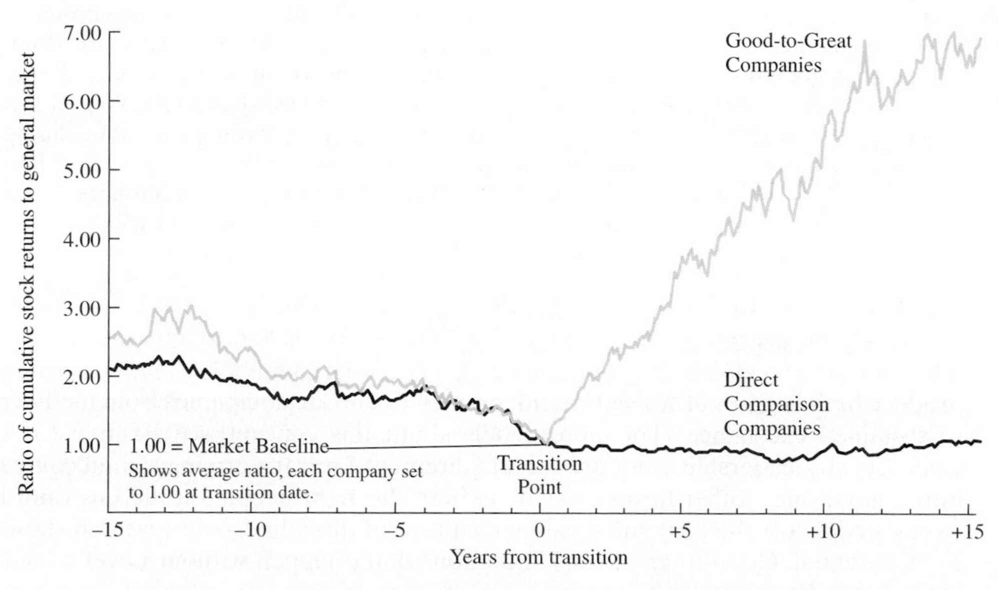

*(continued)*

More precisely, we searched for a specific pattern: cumulative stock returns at or below the general stock market for 15 years, punctuated by a transition point, then cumulative returns at least three times the market over the next 15 years. (See the graph.) We used data from the University of Chicago Center for Research in Security Prices, adjusted for stock splits, and all dividends re-invested. The shift had to be distinct from the industry; if the whole industry showed the same shift, we'd drop the company. We began with 1,435 companies that appeared on the *Fortune* 500 from 1965 to 1995; we found 11 good-to-great examples. That's not a sample; that's the total number that jumped all our hurdles and passed into the study.

Those that made the cut averaged cumulative stock returns 6.9 times the general stock market for the 15 years after the point of transition. To put that in perspective, General Electric under Jack Welch outperformed the general stock market by 2.8:1 during his tenure from 1986 to 2000. A dollar invested in a mutual fund of the good-to-great companies in 1965 grew to $420 by 2000—compared to $56 in the general stock market. These are remarkable numbers, made all the more so by the fact that they came from previously unremarkable companies.

For each good-to-great example, we selected the best direct comparison, based on similarity of business, size, age, customers, and performance leading up to the transition. We also constructed a set of six "unsustained" comparisons (companies that showed a short-lived shift but then fell off) to address the question of sustainability. To be conservative, we consistently picked comparison companies that if anything, were in better shape than the good-to-great companies were in the years just before the transition.

With 22 research associates working in groups of four to six at a time from 1996 to 2000, our study involved a wide range of both qualitative and quantitative analyses. On the qualitative front, we collected nearly 6,000 articles, conducted 87 interviews with key executives, analyzed companies' internal strategy documents, and culled through analysts' reports. On the quantitative front, we ran financial metrics, examined executive compensation, compared patterns of management turnover, quantified company layoffs and restructurings, and calculated the effect of acquisitions and divestitures on companies' stocks. We then synthesized the results to identify the drivers of good-to-great transformations. One was Level 5 leadership.

Since only 11 companies qualified as good-to-great, a research finding had to meet a stiff standard before we would deem it significant. Every component in the final framework showed up in all 11 good-to-great companies during the transition era, regardless of industry (from steel to banking), transition decade (from the 1950s to the 1990s), circumstances (from plodding along to dire crisis), or size (from tens of millions to tens of billions). Additionally, every component had to show up in less than 30% of the comparison companies during the relevant years. Level 5 easily made it into the framework as one of the strongest, most consistent contrasts between the good-to-great and the comparison companies.

produce high degrees of success but not enough to elevate companies from mediocrity to sustained excellence. (For more details about this concept, see Exhibit 2.) And while Level 5 leadership is not the only requirement for transforming a good company into a great one—other factors include getting the right people on the bus (and the wrong people off the bus) and creating a culture of discipline—our research shows it to be essential. Good-to-great transformations don't happen without Level 5 leaders at the helm. They just don't.

◆ EXHIBIT 2 ◆

## The Level 5 Hierarchy

The Level 5 leader sits on top of a hierarchy of capabilities and is, according to our research, a necessary requirement for transforming an organization from good to great. But what lies beneath? Four other layers, each one appropriate in its own right but none with the power of Level 5. Individuals do not need to proceed sequentially through each level of the hierarchy to reach the top, but to be a full-fledged Level 5 requires the capabilities of all the lower levels, plus the special characteristics of Level 5.

**LEVEL 5** LEVEL 5 EXECUTIVE
Builds enduring greatness through a paradoxical combination of personal humility plus professional will.

**LEVEL 4** EFFECTIVE LEADER
Catalyzes commitment to and vigorous pursuit of a clear and compelling vision; stimulates the group to high performance standards.

**LEVEL 3** COMPETENT MANAGER
Organizes people and resources toward the effective and efficient pursuit of predetermined objectives.

**LEVEL 2** CONTRIBUTING TEAM MEMBER
Contributes to the achievement of group objectives; works effectively with others in a group setting.

**LEVEL 1** HIGHLY CAPABLE INDIVIDUAL
Makes productive contributions through talent, knowledge, skills, and good work habits.

## ◆ NOT WHAT YOU WOULD EXPECT

Our discovery of Level 5 leadership is counterintuitive. Indeed, it is countercultural. People generally assume that transforming companies from good to great requires larger-than-life leaders—big personalities like Iacocca, Dunlap, Welch, and Gault, who make headlines and become celebrities.

Compared with those CEOs, Darwin Smith seems to have come from Mars. Shy, unpretentious, even awkward, Smith shunned attention. When a journalist asked him to describe his management style, Smith just stared back at the scribe from the other side of his thick black-rimmed glasses. He was dressed unfashionably, like a farm boy wearing his first J. C. Penney suit. Finally, after a long and uncomfortable silence, he said "Eccentric." Needless to say, the *Wall Street Journal* did not publish a splashy feature on Darwin Smith.

But if you were to consider Smith soft or meek, you would be terribly mistaken. His lack of pretense was coupled with a fierce, even stoic, resolve toward life. Smith grew up on an Indiana farm and put himself through night school at Indiana University by working the day shift at International Harvester. One day, he lost a finger on the job. The story goes that he went to class that evening and returned to work that very next day. Eventually, this poor but determined Indiana farm boy earned admission to Harvard Law School.

He showed the same iron will when he was at the helm of Kimberly-Clark. Indeed, two months after Smith became CEO, doctors diagnosed him with nose and throat cancer and told him he had less than a year to live. He duly informed the board of his illness but said he had no plans to die anytime soon. Smith held to his demanding work schedule while commuting weekly from Wisconsin to Houston for radiation therapy. He lived 25 more years, 20 of them as CEO.

Smith's ferocious resolve was crucial to the rebuilding of Kimberly-Clark, especially when he made the most dramatic decision in the company's history: sell the mills.

To explain: shortly after he took over, Smith and his team had concluded that the company's traditional core business—coated paper—was doomed to mediocrity. Its economics were bad and the competition weak. But, they reasoned, if Kimberly-Clark was thrust into the fire of the *consumer* paper products business, better economics and world-class competition like Procter & Gamble would force it to achieve greatness or perish.

And so, like the general who burned the boats upon landing on enemy soil, leaving his troops to succeed or die, Smith announced that Kimberly-Clark would sell its mills—even the namesake mill in Kimberly, Wisconsin. All proceeds would be thrown into the consumer business, with investments in brands like Huggies diapers and Kleenex tissues. The business media called the move stupid, and Wall Street analysts downgraded the stock. But Smith never wavered. Twenty-five years later, Kimberly-Clark owned Scott Paper and beat Procter & Gamble in six of eight product categories. In retirement, Smith reflected on his exceptional performance, saying simply, "I never stopped trying to become qualified for the job."

## NOT WHAT WE EXPECTED EITHER

We'll look in depth at Level 5 leadership, but first let's set an important context for our findings: we were not looking for Level 5 or anything like it. Our original question was can a good company become a great one, and, if so, how? In fact, I gave the research teams explicit instructions to downplay the role of top executives in their analyses of this question so we wouldn't slip into the simplistic "credit the leader" or "blame the leader" thinking that is so common today.

But Level 5 found us. Over the course of the study, research teams kept saying, "We can't ignore the top executives even if we want to. There is something consistently unusual about them." I would push back, arguing, "The comparison companies also had leaders. So what's different here?" Back and forth the debate raged. Finally, as should always be the case, the data won. The executives at companies that went from good to great and sustained that performance for 15 years or more were all cut from the same cloth—one remarkably different from that which produced executives at the comparison companies in our study. It didn't matter whether the company was in crisis or steady state, consumer or industrial, offering services or products. It didn't matter when the transition took place or how big the company. The successful organizations all had a Level 5 leader at the time of transition.

Furthermore, the absence of Level 5 leadership showed up consistently across the comparison companies. The point: Level 5 is an empirical finding, not an ideological one. And that's important to note, given how much the Level 5 finding contradicts not only conventional wisdom but much of management theory to date. (For more about our findings on good-to-great transformations, see Exhibit 3).

◆ EXHIBIT 3 ◆

## Not by Level 5 Alone

Level 5 leadership is an essential factor for taking a company from good to great, but it's not the only one. Our research uncovered multiple factors that deliver companies to greatness. And it is the combined package—Level 5 plus these other drivers—that takes companies beyond unremarkable. There is a symbiotic relationship between Level 5 and the rest of our findings: Level 5 enables implementation of the other findings, and practicing the other findings may help you get to Level 5. We've already talked about who Level 5 leaders are; the rest of our findings describe what they do. Here is a brief look at some of the other key findings.

*First Who:* We expected that good-to-great leaders would start with the vision and strategy. Instead, they attended to people first, strategy second. They got the right people on the bus, moved the wrong people off, ushered the right people to the right seats—and then they figured out where to drive it.

*Stockdale Paradox:* This finding is named after Admiral James Stockdale, winner of the Medal of Honor, who survived seven years in a Vietcong POW camp by hanging on to two contradictory beliefs: his life couldn't be worse at the moment, and his life would someday be better than ever. Like Stockdale, people at the good-to-great companies in our research confronted the most brutal facts of their current reality—yet simultaneously maintained absolute faith that they would prevail in the end. And they held both disciplines—faith and facts—at the same time, all the time.

*Buildup-Breakthrough Flywheel:* good-to-great transformations do not happen overnight or in one big leap. Rather, the process resembles relentlessly pushing a giant, heavy flywheel in one direction. At first, pushing it gets the flywheel to turn once. With consistent effort, it goes two turns,

(*continued*)

*(continued)*

then five, then ten, building increasing momentum until—bang!—the wheel hits the breakthrough point, and the momentum really kicks in. Our comparison companies never sustained the kind of breakthrough momentum that the good-to-great companies did; instead, they lurched back and forth with radical change programs, reactionary moves, and restructurings.

*The Hedgehog Concept:* In a famous essay, philosopher and scholar Isaiah Berlin described two approaches to thought and life using a simple parable: the fox knows a little about many things, but the hedgehog knows only one big thing very well. The fox is complex; the hedgehog simple. And the hedgehog wins. Our research shows that breakthroughs require a simple, hedgehog-like understanding of three intersecting circles: what a company can be the best in the world at, how its economics work best, and what best ignites the passions of its people. Breakthroughs happen when you get the hedgehog concept and become systematic and consistent with it, eliminating virtually anything that does not fit in the three circles.

*Technology Accelerators:* The good-to-great companies had a paradoxical relationship with technology. On the one hand, they assiduously avoided jumping on new technology bandwagons. On the other, they were pioneers in the application of carefully selected technologies, making bold, far-sighted investments in those that directly linked to their hedgehog concept. Like turbo-charges, these technology accelerators create an explosion in flywheel momentum.

*A Culture of Discipline:* When you look across the good-to-great transformations, they consistently display three forms of discipline; disciplined people, disciplined thought, and disciplined action. When you have disciplined people, you don't need hierarchy. When you have disciplined thought, you don't need bureaucracy. When you have disciplined action, you don't need excessive controls. When you combine a culture of discipline with an ethic of entrepreneurship, you get the magical alchemy of great performance.

## ◆ HUMILITY + WILL = LEVEL 5

Level 5 leaders are a study in a duality: modest and willful, shy and fearless. To grasp this concept, consider Abraham Lincoln, who never let his ego get in the way of his ambition to create an enduring great nation. Author Henry Adams called him "a quiet, peaceful, shy figure." But those who thought Lincoln's understated manner signaled weakness in the man found themselves terribly mistaken—to the scale of 250,000 Confederate and 360,000 Union lives, including Lincoln's own.

It might be a stretch to compare the 11 Level 5 CEOs in our research to Lincoln, but they did display the same kind of duality. Take Colman M. Mockler, CEO of Gillette from 1975 to 1991. Mockler, who faced down three takeover attempts, was a reserved, gracious man with a gentle, almost patrician manner. Despite epic battles with raiders—he took on Ronald Perelman twice and the former Coniston Partners once—he never lost his shy, courteous style. At the height of the crisis, he maintained a calm business-as-usual demeanor, dispensing first with ongoing business before turning to the takeover.

And yet, those who mistook Mockler's outward modesty as a sign of inner weakness were beaten in the end. In one proxy battle, Mockler and other senior executives called thousands of investors, one by one, to win their votes. Mockler simply would not give in. He chose to fight for the future greatness of Gillette even though he could have pocketed millions by flipping his stock.

Consider the consequences had Mockler capitulated. If a share-flipper had accepted the full 44% price premium offered by Perelman and then invested those shares in the general maket for ten years, he still would have come out 64% behind a shareholder who stayed with Mockler and Gillette. If Mockler had given up the fight, it's likely that none of us would be shaving with Sensor, Lady Sensor, or the Mach III—and hundreds of millions of people would have a more painful battle with daily stubble.

Sadly, Mockler never had the chance to enjoy the full fruits of his efforts. In January 1991, Gillette received an advance copy of *Forbes.* The cover featured an artist's rendition of the publicity-shy Mockler standing on a mountaintop, holding a giant razor above his head in a triumphant pose. Walking back to his office, just minutes after seeing his public acknowledgment of his 16 years of struggle, Mockler crumpled to the floor and died from a massive heart attack.

Even if Mockler had known he would die in office, he could not have changed his approach. His placid persona hid an inner intensity, a dedication to making anything he touched the best—not just because of what he would get but because he couldn't imagine doing it any other way. Mockler could not give up the company to those who would destoy it, any more than Lincoln would risk losing the chance to build an enduring great nation.

## ◆ A COMPELLING MODESTY

The Mockler story illustrates the modesty typical of Level 5 leaders. (For a summary of Level 5 traits, see Exhibit 4.) Indeed, throughout our interviews with such executives, we were struck by the way they talked about themselves—or rather, didn't talk about themselves. They'd go on and on about the company and the contributions of other executives, but they would instinctively deflect discussion about their own role. When pressed to talk about themselves, they'd say things like, "I hope I'm not sounding like a big shot," or "I don't think I can take much credit for what happened. We were blessed with marvelous people." One Level 5 leader even asserted, "There are lot of people in this company who could do my job better than I do."

◆ EXHIBIT 4 ◆

## The Yin and Yang of Level 5

| Personal Humility | Professional Will |
|---|---|
| Demonstrates a compelling modesty, shunning public adulation; never boastful. | Creates superb results, a clear catalyst in the transition from good to great. |
| Acts with quiet, calm determination; relies principally on inspired standards, not inspiring charisma, to motivate. | Demonstrates an unwavering resolve to do whatever must be done to produce the best long-term results, no matter how difficult. |
| Channels ambition into the company, not the self; sets up successors for even more greatness in the next generation. | Sets the standard of building an enduring great company; will settle for nothing less. |
| Looks in the mirror, not out the window, to apportion responsibility for poor results, never blaming other people, external factors, or bad luck. | Looks out the windows, not in the mirror, to apportion credit for the success of the company—to other people, external factors, and good luck. |

By contrast, consider the courtship of personal celebrity by the comparison CEOs. Scott Paper, the comparison company to Kimberly-Clark, hired Al Dunlap as CEO—a man who would tell anyone who would listen (and many who would have preferred not to) about his accomplishments. After 19 months atop Scott Paper, Dunlap said in *Business Week:* "The Scott story will go down in the annals of American business history as one of the most successful, quickest turnarounds ever. It makes other turnarounds pale by comparison." He personally accrued $100 million for 603 days of work at Scott Paper—about $165,000 per day—largely by slashing the workforce, halving the R&D budget, and putting the company on growth steroids in preparation for sale. After selling off the company and pocketing his quick millions, Dunlap wrote an autobiography in which he boastfully dubbed himself "Rambo in pinstripes." It's hard to imagine Darwin Smith thinking, "Hey, that Rambo character reminds me of me," let alone stating it publicly.

Granted, the Scott Paper story is one of the more dramatic in our study, but it's not an isolated case. In more than two-thirds of the comparison companies, we noted the presence of a gargantuan ego that contributed to the demise or continued mediocrity of the company. We found this pattern particularly strong in the unsustained comparison companies—the companies that would show a shift in performance under a talented yet egocentric Level 4 leader, only to decline in later years.

Lee Iacocca, for example, saved Chrysler from the brink of catastrophe, performing one of the most celebrated (and deservedly so) turnarounds in U.S. business history. The automaker's stock rose 2.9 times higher than the general market about halfway through his tenure. But then Iacocca diverted his attention to transforming himself. He appeared regularly on talk shows like the *Today Show* and *Larry King Live,* starred in more than 80 commercials, entertained the idea of running for president of the United States, and promoted his autobiography, which sold 7 million copies worldwide. Iacocca's personal stock soared, but Chrysler's stock fell 31% below the market in the second half of his tenure.

And once Iacocca had accumulated all the fame and perks, he found it difficult to leave center stage. He postponed his retirement so many times that Chrysler's insiders began to joke that Iacocca stood for "I Am Chairman of Chrysler Corporation Always." When he finally retired, he demanded that the board continue to provide private jet and stock options. Later, he joined forces with noted takeover artist Kirk Kerkorian to launch a hostile bid for Chrysler. (It failed.) Iacocca did make one final brilliant decision: he picked a modest yet determined man—perhaps even a Level 5—as his successor. Bob Eaton rescued Chrysler from its second near-death crisis in a decade and set the foundation for a more enduring corporate transition.

## ◆ AN UNWAVERING RESOLVE

Besides extreme humility, Level 5 leaders also display tremendous professional will. When George Cain became CEO of Abbott Laboratories, it was a drowsy family-controlled business, sitting at the bottom quartile of the pharmaceutical industry, living off its cash cow, erythromycin. Cain was a typical Level 5 leader in his lack of pretense; he didn't have the kind of inspiring personality that would galvanize the company. But he had something much more powerful: inspired standards. He could not stand mediocrity in any form and was utterly intolerant of anyone who would accept that idea that good is good enough. For the next 14 years, he relentlessly imposed his will for greatness on Abbott Labs.

Among Cain's first tasks was to destroy one of the root causes of Abbott's middling performance: nepotism. By systematically rebuilding both the board and the executive team with the best people he could find, Cain made his statement. Family ties no longer mattered. If you couldn't become the best executive in the industry, within your span of responsibility, you would lose your paycheck.

Such near-ruthless rebuilding might be expected from an outsider brought in to turn the company around, but Cain was an 18-year insider—and a part of the family, the son of a previous president. Holiday gatherings were probably tense for a few years in the Cain clan—"Sorry I had to fire you. Want another slice of turkey?"—but in the end, family members were pleased with the performance of their stock. Cain had set in motion a profitable growth machine. From its transition in 1974 to 2000, Abbott created shareholder returns that beat the market 4.5:1, outperforming industry superstars Merck and Pfizer by a factor of two.

Another good example of iron-willed Level 5 leadership comes from Charles R. "Cork" Walgreen III, who transformed dowdy Walgreens into a company that outperformed the stock market 16:1 from its transition in 1975 to 2000. After years of dialogue and debate within his executive team about what to do with Walgreens' food-service operations, this CEO sensed the team had finally reached a watershed: the company's brightest future lay in convenient drugstores, not in food service. Dan Jorndt, who succeeded Walgreen in 1988, describes what happened next:

> Cork said at one of our planning committee meetings, "Okay, now I am going to draw the line in the sand. We are going to be out of the restaurant business completely in five years." At the time we had more than 500 restaurants. You could have heard a pin drop. He said, "I want to let everybody know the clock is ticking." Six months later we were at our next planning committee meeting and someone mentioned just in passing that we had only five years to be out of the restaurant business. Cork was not a real vociferous fellow. He sort of tapped on the table and said, "Listen, you now have four and a half years. I said you had five years six months ago. Now you've got four and a half years." Well, that next day things really clicked into gear for winding down our restaurant business. Cork never wavered. He never doubted. He never second guessed.

Like Darwin Smith selling the mills at Kimberly-Clark, Cork Walgreen required stoic resolve to make his decisions. Food service was not the largest part of the business, although it did add substantial profits to the bottom line. The real problem was more emotional than financial. Walgreens had, after all, invented the malted milk shake, and food service had been a long-standing family tradition dating back to Cork's grandfather. Not only that, some food-service outlets were even named after the CEO—for example, a restaurant chain named Cork's. But no matter, if Walgreen had to fly in the face of family tradition in order to refocus on the one arena in which Walgreens could be the best in the world—convenient drugstores—and terminate everything else that would not produce great results, then Cork would do it. Quietly, doggedly, simply.

One final, yet compelling, note on our findings about Level 5: because Level 5 leaders have ambition not for themselves but for their companies, they routinely select superb successors. Level 5 leaders want to see their companies become even more successful in the next generation, comfortable with the idea that most people won't even know that the roots of that success trace back to them. As one Level 5 CEO said, "I want to look from my porch, see the company as one of the great companies in the world someday, and be able to say, 'I used to work there.' " By contrast, Level 4 leaders often fail to set up the company for enduring success—after all, what better testament to your own personal greatness than that the place falls apart after you leave?

In more than three-quarters of the comparison companies, we found executives who set up their successors for failure, chose weak successors, or both. Consider the case of Rubbermaid, which grew from obscurity to become one of *Fortune's* most admired companies—and then, just as quickly, disintegrated into such sorry shape that it had to be acquired by Newell.

The architect of this remarkable story was a charismatic and brilliant leader named Stanley C. Gault, whose name became synonymous in the late 1980s with the company's success. Across the 312 articles collected by our research team about Rubbermaid, Gault comes through as a hard-driving, egocentric executive. In one article, he responds to the accusation of being a tyrant with the statement, "Yes, but I'm a sincere tyrant." In another, drawn directly from his own comments on leading change, the word "I" appears 44 times, while the word "we" appears 16 times. Of course, Gault had every reason to be proud of his executive success: Rubbermaid generated 40 consecutive quarters of earnings growth under his leadership—an impressive performance, to be sure, and one that deserves respect.

But Gault did not leave behind a company that would be great without him. His chosen successor lasted a year on the job and the next in line faced a management team so shallow that he had to temporarily shoulder four jobs while scrambling to identify a new number-two executive. Gault's successors struggled not only with a management void but also with strategic voids that would eventually bring the company to its knees.

Of course, you might say—as one *Fortune* article did—that the fact that Rubbermaid fell apart after Gault left proves his greatness as a leader. Gault was a tremendous Level 4 leader, perhaps one of the best in the last 50 years. But he was not at Level 5, and that is one crucial reason why Rubbermaid went from good to great for a brief, shining moment and then just as quickly went from great to irrelevant.

## THE WINDOW AND THE MIRROR

As part of our research, we interviewed Alan L. Wurtzel, the Level 5 leader responsible for turning Circuit City from a ramshackle company on the edge of bankruptcy into one of America's most successful electronics retailers. In the 15 years after its transition date in 1982, Circuit City outperformed the market 18.5:1.

We asked Wurtzel to list the top five factors in his company's transformation, ranked by importance. His number one factor? Luck. "We were in a great industry, with the wind at our backs." But wait a minute, we retorted, Silo—your comparison company—was in the same industry, with the same wind, and bigger sails. The conversation went back and forth, with Wurtzel refusing to take much credit for the transition, preferring to attribute it largely to just being in the right place at the right time. Later, when we asked him to discuss the factors that would sustain a good-to-great transformation, he said, "The first thing that comes to mind is luck. I was lucky to find the right successor."

Luck. What an odd factor to talk about. Yet the Level 5 leaders we identified invoked it frequently. We asked an executive at steel company Nucor why it had such a remarkable track record of making good decisions. His response? "I guess we were just lucky." Joseph F. Cullman III, the Level 5 CEO of Philip Morris, flat out refused to take credit for his company's success, citing his good fortune to have great colleagues, successors, and predecessors. Even the book he wrote about his career—which he penned at the urging of his colleagues and which he never intended to distribute widely outside the company—had the unusual title *I'm a Lucky Guy.*

At first, we were puzzled by the Level 5 leaders' emphasis on good luck. After all, there is no evidence that the companies that had progressed from good to great were blessed with more good luck (or more bad luck, for that matter) than the comparison companies. But then we began to notice an interesting pattern in the executives at the comparison companies: they often blamed their situations on bad luck, bemoaning the difficulties of the environment they faced.

Compare Bethlehem Steel and Nucor, for example. Both steel companies operated with products that are hard to differentiate, and both faced a competitive challenge from cheap imported steel. Both companies paid significantly higher wages than most of their foreign competitors. And yet executives at the two companies held completely different views of the same environment.

Bethlehem Steel's CEO summed up the company's problems in 1983 by blaming the imports: "Our first, second, and third problems are imports." Meanwhile, Ken Iverson and his crew at Nucor saw the imports as a blessing: "Aren't we lucky; steel is heavy, and they have to ship it all the way across the ocean, giving us a huge advantage." Indeed, Iverson saw the first, second, and third problems facing the U.S. steel industry not in imports but in management. He even went so far as to speak out publicly against government protection against imports, telling a gathering of stunned steel executives in 1977 that the real problems facing the steel industry lay in the fact that management had failed to keep pace with technology.

The emphasis on luck turns out to be part of a broader pattern that we came to call *the window and the mirror.* Level 5 leaders, inherently humble, look out the window to apportion credit—even undue credit—to factors outside themselves. If they can't find a specific person or event to give credit to, they credit good luck. At the same time, they look in the mirror to assign responsibility, never citing bad luck or external factors when things go poorly. Conversely, the comparison executives frequently looked out the window for factors to blame but preened in the mirror to credit themselves when things went well.

The funny thing about the window-and-mirror concept is that it does not reflect reality. According to our research, the Level 5 leaders *were* responsible for their companies' transformations. But they would never admit that. We can't climb inside their heads and assess whether they deeply believed what they saw in the window and the mirror. But it doesn't really matter, because they acted as if they believe it, and they acted with such consistency that it produced exceptional results.

## BORN OR BRED?

Not long ago, I shared the Level 5 finding with a gathering of senior executives. A woman who had recently become chief executive of her company raised her hand. "I believe what you've told us about Level 5 leadership," she said, "but I'm disturbed because I know I'm not there yet, and maybe I never will be. Part of the reason I got this job is because of my strong ego. Are you telling me that I can't make my company great if I'm not Level 5?"

"Let me return to the data," I responded. "Of 1,435 companies that appeared on the *Fortune* 500 since 1965, only 11 made it into our study. In those 11, all of them had Level 5 leaders in key positions, including the CEO role, at the pivotal time of transition. Now, to reiterate, we're not saying that Level 5 is the only element required for the move from good to great, but it appears to be essential."

She sat there, quiet for a moment, and you could guess many people in the room were thinking. Finally, she raised her hand again. "Can you learn to become Level 5?" I still do not know the answer to that question. Our research, frankly, did not delve into how Level 5 leaders come to be, nor did we attempt to explain or codify the nature of their emotional lives. We speculated on the unique psychology of Level 5 leaders. Were they "guilty" of displacement—shifting their own raw ambition onto something other than themselves? Were they sublimating their egos for dark and complex reasons rooted in childhood trauma? Who knows? And perhaps more important, do the psychological roots of Level 5 leadership matter any more than do the roots of charisma or intelligence? The question remains: can Level 5 be developed?

My preliminary hypothesis is that there are two categories of people: those who don't have the Level 5 seed within them and those who do. The first category consists of people who could never in a million years bring themselves to subjugate their own needs to the greater ambition of something larger and more lasting than themselves. For those people, work will always be first and foremost about what they get—the fame, fortune, power, adulation, and so on. Work will never be about what they build, create, and contribute. The great irony is that the animus and personal ambition that often drives people to become a Level 4 leader stands at odds with the humility required to rise to Level 5.

When you combine that irony with the fact that boards of directors frequently operate under the false belief that a larger-than-life, egocentric leader is required to make a company great, you can quickly see why Level 5 leaders rarely appear at the top of our institutions. We keep putting people in positions of power who lack the seed to become a Level 5 leader, and that is one major reason why there are so few companies that make a sustained and verifiable shift from good to great.

The second category consists of people who could evolve to Level 5; the capability resides within them, perhaps buried or ignored or simply nascent. Under the right circumstances—with self-reflection, a mentor, loving parents, a significant life experience, or other factors—the seed can begin to develop. Some of the Level 5 leaders in our study had significant life experiences that might have sparked development of the seed. Darwin Smith fully blossomed as a Level 5 after his near-death experience with cancer. Joe Cullman was profoundly affected by his World War II experiences, particularly the last-minute change of orders that took him off a doomed ship on which he surely would have died; he considered the next 60-odd years a great gift. A strong religious belief or conversion might also nurture the seed. Colman Mockler, for example, converted to evangelical Christianity while getting his M.B.A. at Harvard, and later, according to the book *Cutting Edge,* he became a prime mover in a group of Boston business executives that met frequently over breakfast to discuss the carryover of religious values to corporate life.

We would love to be able to give you a list of steps for getting to Level 5—other than contracting cancer, going through a religious conversion, or getting different parents—but we have no solid research data that would support a credible list. Our research exposed Level 5 as a key component inside the black box of what it takes to shift a company from good to great. Yet inside that black box is another—the inner development of a person to Level 5 leadership. We could speculate on what that inner box might hold, but it would mostly be just that, speculation.

In short, Level 5 is a very satisfying idea, a truthful idea, a powerful idea, and, to make the move from good to great, very likely an essential idea. But to provide "ten steps to Level 5 leadership" would trivialize the concept.

My best advice, based on the research, is to practice the other good-to-great disciplines that we discovered. Since we found a tight symbiotic relationship between each of the other findings and Level 5, we suspect that conscientiously trying to lead using the other disciplines can help you move in the right direction. There is no guarantee that doing so will turn executives into full-fledged Level 5 leaders, but it gives them a tangible place to begin, especially if they have the seed within.

We cannot say for sure what percentage of people have the seed within, nor how many of those can nurture it enough to become Level 5. Even those of us on the research team who identified Level 5 do not know whether we will succeed in evolving to its heights. And yet all of us who worked on the finding have been inspired by the idea of trying to move toward Level 5. Darwin Smith, Colman Mockler, Alan Wurtzel, and all the other Level 5 leaders we learned about have become role models for us. Whether or not we make it to Level 5, it is worth trying. For like all basic truths about what is best in human beings, when we catch a glimpse of that truth, we know that our own lives and all that we touch will be the better for making the effort to get there.

# The Productive Narcissist: The Promise and Peril of Visionary Leadership


***MICHAEL MACCOBY***

***Summary prepared by Kjell R. Knudsen***



***Kjell R. Knudsen*** *is Dean of the Labovitz School of Business and Economics, University of Minnesota Duluth. A native of Norway, he first came to the United States on a Fulbright Scholarship to attend Gonzaga University. He received his M.B.A. and Ph.D. in Management from the University of Minnesota's Carlson School of Business. Dr. Knudsen worked for Minnesota Systems Research Inc., the Royal Norwegian Council for Industrial and Scientific Research (NTNF), and the Norwegian Center for Organizational Learning (NORCOL). He founded the UMD Center for Economic Development, and served as the UMD Project Manager and also as Co-Chair of the Board of Directors of Soft Center Duluth, a software development program. Dr. Knudsen has published on management and organizational development, economic development, and business education. Dr. Knudsen lives in Duluth with his wife Rosemary. They have one daughter, Christa.*


---


Michael Maccoby, *The Productive Narcissist: The Promise and Peril of Visionary Leadership.* New York: Broadway Books, 2003.

## A LOOK AT PRODUCTIVE NARCISSISTS

During times of profound change, leaders emerge who have the personality type that Freud classified as narcissistic. Narcissistic leaders can be both productive and unproductive. Productive narcissists are not necessarily successful, but unproductive narcissists have little or no chance of being successful. Productive narcissists are above all visionary and risk takers; they also possess strategic intelligence and can lead their organizations to be highly successful and sustain that success. Unfortunately, productive narcissists are incredibly difficult to work for.

## PERSONALITY TYPES

To understand narcissistic leaders it is important to understand the concept of personality type and to recognize different types. Personality typing is a common activity as people interact with others in everyday life; it helps people find explanations for other people's behavior in their personality. Based on observed patterns of behavior, people ascribe to others certain personality traits.

In everyday language, narcissism usually conjures up a negative image of someone as egotistic, self-centered, and self-absorbed. However, *narcissism defines a personality type that can be both positive and negative.* Personality type is the core self to which is added attitudes and values that individuals learn as they mature, and this combination determines the way in which people respond to their surroundings. Psychiatrist Sigmund Freud identified the three personality types of erotic, obsessive, and narcissistic; Eric Fromm added the marketing type to constitute a four-part typology.

The *erotic* personality is centered on loving and being loved. In its most productive form, people with this type of personality are thoughtful caretakers wanting to do the right thing for others. As leaders, productive erotics create a "family" context that provides substantial emotional support for others. At its most productive, the erotic personality is a developer of other people, nurturing them and giving support to their development. The downside of the erotic personality type is dependency and fear of drawing negative reactions from others. As leaders, unproductive erotics are afraid to make decisions that may be unpopular. They tend to fret over such decisions and try to avoid taking a stand on anything that may be controversial.

The *obsessive* personality attempts to live up to an internalized standard of high ideals and high expectations. As opposed to the erotic personality type that is driven by what others may think or how others may react to a person, obsessives live by an internal standard. As leaders, they make great "number twos." The productive obsessive is a manager as opposed to a leader. Obsessives are driven by a need for highly structured systems and policies as opposed to vision and dreams. The unproductive obsessives become pedantic and inflexible, eventually driving people around them away as they are more concerned with following procedure than getting things accomplished.

*Marketing* personality types are centered on meeting the needs of their surroundings in terms of what is needed to impress and succeed. These are people who love to network and interact in social and business settings. As productive leaders, marketing types rely on their radar to tell them what is needed to meet situational needs. As leaders, they adapt well in order to get things accomplished. Also, the marketing types are eager to pursue self-improvement and keep themselves looking good in terms of personal grooming and fitness. Marketing types who are leaders know how to look the part. The unproductive marketing types are the ones that are all fluff with little substance, they are all "smoke and mirrors." They say and do whatever they deem is necessary to "make a sale." As leaders, this unproductive marketing type leaves a pattern of confusion and followers who don't know what comes next.

The *narcissistic* personality type in contrast to the others is self-directed. These leaders are not concerned with what others might think, but attempt to satisfy an internal ideal or an outside market. Narcissists seek to enlist others in their own vision and to make it a reality. In this sense, the narcissist is free of social control and therefore able to pursue his or her vision without regard to what others might think or do. Narcissistic leaders reject the status quo and focus on how they think things ought to be. They create the world in their own image. Unfortunately, they do not listen much.

Narcissists have usually grown up in one of three different family situations. One context is characterized by the presence of a strong supporting mother with an absent or failed father. The second includes a strong mother whose own ambitions have been frustrated and who pushes her son (or daughter) to achieve her dreams. The third situation includes a strong mentor from outside the family.

## ◆ PRODUCTIVENESS

People who fully live up to their own potential are productive. Six important elements are included in living up to one's potential; they are:

1. Being free as opposed to dependent;
2. Being rational as opposed to irrational;
3. Being active in the sense of being the driving force with passion and enthusiasm as opposed to being reactive;
4. Having understanding in terms of knowing what powers one possesses as opposed to not knowing;
5. Having purpose as opposed to drifting aimlessly; and
6. Having perseverance as opposed to quitting easily.

People can be more or less productive, so *productiveness is a matter of degree.* Also, the degree of productiveness can vary over time. All of the four personality types described above can be productive or unproductive at a certain place and time.

## ◆ PRODUCTIVE NARCISSISTS

Productive narcissists want to change the world. Their independence and freedom allow them to act even though they may fear failure. The difference between the narcissist and the other personality types in this regard is not that the narcissist isn't afraid, it is that the narcissist goes ahead and does what he or she wants to do anyway. Given their vision of how things ought to be, and their commitment and passion to making their vision a reality, they use every means available to them to achieve it. Narcissistic leaders live in the real world. Even though they have strong visions and dreams, they have the ability to focus on what is realistic and can be done. They have the ability to act to have their vision become reality, and the ability to enlist others in their visions. Productive narcissists are very charismatic. They also know how to judge their surroundings in terms of who is with them or against them, and they tend to be black and white in their view of others. Narcissistic leaders do not give up easily. Finally, they have a sense of humor even to the point of being self-deprecating.

*The key to understanding narcissistic leaders is the role of vision.* Once they have their vision in place, they mobilize every resource available to achieve it. Productive narcissists have no life to speak of other than working to achieve their vision with whatever means are available to them. Everything and everybody become instruments at their disposal to achieve their goals and their vision. Narcissists are not workaholics in the usual sense; they are simply driven to achieve their goals and vision and have little room for anything else in their lives.

These very positive aspects of narcissistic leaders include their:

1. Ability to create visions and meaning for organizations and followers
2. Ability to act independently and take risks
3. Passion and commitment
4. Ability to inspire followers to achieve the vision
5. Sensitivity to surroundings
6. Sense of humor

On the less positive side, productive narcissists tend not listen to others very well. They are so committed to their own vision and convinced of being right that they do not believe they need anyone else. Also, narcissists do not readily trust anyone but themselves. Another trait of the productive narcissist is being overly sensitive to criticism. In fact, narcissists can easily interpret even positive comments as criticism. The productive narcissists can be so alert and sensitive to their surroundings that it turns into paranoia where they feel discriminated against or persecuted. Other times it results in an almost unnatural need for secrecy to protect against any intrusion. Narcissistic leaders frequently have temper tantrums and put people down, often in public. They have little or no interest in the consequences of their behavior on others.

Productive narcissists can be overly competitive. They strongly feel that they have to be the best. They love to beat their competition and they turn situations into a competition even though it may be totally unnecessary. On a Sunday sail with the family, a narcissist is likely to locate another sailboat in the vicinity and have a race, even though no one else knows that there is one. Narcissists can be overly concerned with control and become micromanagers. Things have to be done their way and they need to know everything. They want no surprises. Delegation is not something a narcissistic leader does easily. Given the drive toward their own visions and the view of others as instruments to their achievement, narcissists are often lonely and isolated. In their quest to use others for their own purposes, they don't form many close relationships.

An interesting characteristic of productive narcissists is their tendency to see a vision more or less as achieved once it is clear and articulated. This leads to a tendency to exaggerate reality. The facts in many ways are what they say they are. An example of this would be the manipulation of financial data to affect the stock price of a company. Productive narcissists rarely engage in self-reflection. They have little or no interest in learning about themselves. They are occupied with making decisions that

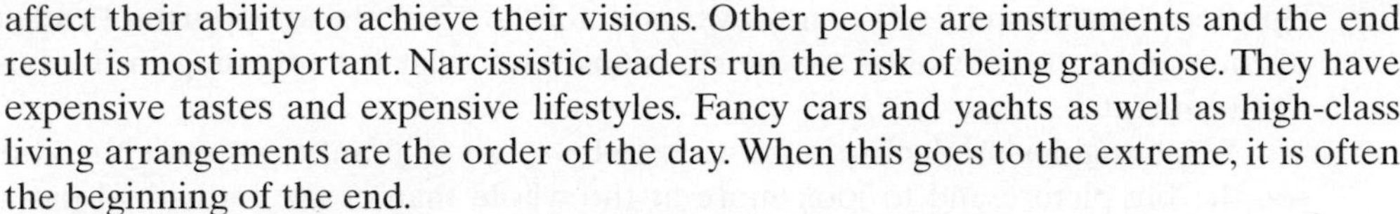

affect their ability to achieve their visions. Other people are instruments and the end result is most important. Narcissistic leaders run the risk of being grandiose. They have expensive tastes and expensive lifestyles. Fancy cars and yachts as well as high-class living arrangements are the order of the day. When this goes to the extreme, it is often the beginning of the end.

The less positive traits of the productive narcissist include:

1. Lack of ability (willingness) to listen
2. Overly sensitive to criticism and resultant feelings of paranoia
3. Put others down and exhibit anger
4. Controlling and overly competitive
5. Lonely and isolated
6. Exaggerate situations and make things up
7. Little self-knowledge
8. Given to grandiosity

## ◆ STRATEGIC INTELLIGENCE

To be a successful leader, especially in times of significant change, intense competition, and volatility, strategic intelligence is far more important than emotional intelligence. Leaders primarily characterized by emotional intelligence (i.e., ability to listen, sensitivity to feelings, empathy, and consensus decision making) fall short in a context where things are changing rapidly and there is upheaval. Vision and ability to act to create a "new world" are needed in times of profound change. In this situation, the productive narcissist with strategic intelligence excels. Emotional intelligence, which is primarily concerned with interpersonal relations, falls short in the face of a situation that demands vision and action to create a "new order." Any of the personality types described can have strategic intelligence and all leaders need some level of emotional intelligence. However, productive narcissists who want to stay on top of their organizations and achieve lasting success need strategic intelligence. In fact, many productive narcissists can rise to the top of an organization, but only a productive narcissist with strategic intelligence can stay on top and sustain success. There are five elements of strategic intelligence:

1. Ability to anticipate the future
2. Ability to think of the system as a whole
3. Visioning
4. Ability to get people to work for a common purpose and implement a vision
5. Ability to form successful partnerships

Successful CEOs are able to craft and put in place strategies to take advantage of opportunities in the marketplace. Successful strategies are based on correctly anticipating the future in the form of opportunities that become reality. This ability to anticipate the future is more than simply forecasting or carrying a present trend forward. Accurately anticipating the future is not based on linear thinking, but on the ability to deal with complex relationships and developments. It is like putting together a puzzle and then acting on it. Foresight involves investing resources in opportunities that cannot be seen because they are in the future. Foresight is often based on intuition and "gut feel." Successful leaders, however, are able to "see" these opportunities because of their intimate knowledge of their business and what is happening in the business environment.

What enables productive narcissists to be so good at anticipation is the ability to see the big picture and to look more at the whole than at the individual parts. This ability to foresee or anticipate the future coupled with the ability to see and deal with the big picture in a systemic way is what ultimately enables the successful leader to create a vision and enlist others in working to achieve it, both as employees and external partners. Foresight and ability to see the "big picture" involve intellectual and critical thinking skills; the ability to create a practical vision and enlist others in achieving it involves the ability to motivate and partner to achieve the vision. Visioning, motivating, and partnering are the practical skills needed to move a social system to focus on a common purpose and to achieve it. Strategic intelligence does not consist of five parts that are independent of each other; if any one of the parts is missing, it may be a fatal flaw in the leader's ability to achieve success.

## WORKING WITH A PRODUCTIVE NARCISSIST

Productive narcissists are very difficult to collaborate with, work for, or even be around. In fact, the question is almost more *why* a person would choose to work for one than how. For those people that do work with a productive narcissist (either by choice or by chance) these are some helpful guidelines:

1. Find out what your own personality type is.
2. Become an expert in your field.
3. Become an effective partner.
4. Don't get your own ego involved.
5. Accept the importance of protecting the image of the narcissist.

It helps a great deal if you know and understand what personality type you yourself are in working with a productive narcissist (even if you yourself are one). Self-knowledge (understanding your own behavior and reactions) is a great help in working with others; it will help you understand which of your needs can be met at work and which ones you have to get fulfilled outside of work.

One of the important aspects of working with productive narcissists is to be an expert in an area where they have a weakness that is crucial to their success. Since narcissists use people to achieve *their* ends, it is critical to be an expert at something they need. The reward for the person being "used" in this way is to be able to share in the success of the narcissist.

To partner effectively with a productive narcissist, it is important to understand what your personality type is. An erotic needs to understand that he or she is not going to get much in the way of warm praise. Erotic personality types have to get their needs satisfied outside of work. Obsessive personalities have a real opportunity to become "number two's." Narcissists are usually not very good at details and are able to see the value of someone who can take care of details for them. However, chances are that there will be little in the way of approval or acknowledgement of contributions made. Marketing types need to try to dip underneath superficiality and develop some deep knowledge to be useful to the narcissist. Also, narcissists are very good at seeing through people and grow tired of empty flattery quickly. Narcissists cannot stand people who go "where the wind blows." Narcissists working for narcissists simply need to let their boss call the shots and be in charge and do all they can to make him or her successful.

In working with a productive narcissist, it is important to recognize that there is only room for one ego—his or hers. There is little if any praise to be had and in addition there is often blame to be received, justified or not. In fact, the narcissist is likely to take credit for all ideas that are successful and blame someone else for all of their own ideas that go sour. The highest praise a narcissist can give is probably the absence of being fired! Because these situations often introduce a high level of stress, especially for an erotic personality, it is advisable to seek situations outside work that meet the needs that cannot be satisfied in the work situation. The only problem is that the productive narcissist expects everyone to work around the clock.

In working for productive narcissists, it is very important to protect their image. This is because narcissists are very sensitive to criticism. Therefore, it is important to let them take credit, whether they deserve it or not. It is also important to accept blame, whether deserved or not. Public criticism of a narcissistic boss is not a good idea if you want to keep your job.

It is important to recognize and learn how to deal with the narcissists' weaknesses. Since they don't listen well, it is important to present things by making it clear how it will benefit them. Productive narcissists are strategic and they are looking for people that can help them achieve their goals, or people who can prevent them from making mistakes that will affect their image negatively. The way to deal with the overly sensitive nature of productive narcissists is to simply take whatever they dish out. They will not know if they have hurt you and in fact they may not care, so arguing or taking them to task is likely to accomplish little but disaster. It is very important to take a narcissist's mild paranoia seriously; often it can be dealt with by humor. However, if the person becomes irrational or you think the person is out of control, it may be best to quit, especially if you are asked to do something you consider to be unethical.

In terms of the narcissists' need to be over-controlling and over-competitive, it is important again to show how it hurts their ability to achieve their goals. Sometimes it is also possible to ignore some of the requests made by narcissists, as they often forget what it was they wanted to control. This will work best when the requests are not that important to the narcissist. However, it is important to be strategic about this. The best way to deal with a narcissist's angry outburst is to take it, since it usually blows over. Also, don't expect an apology. None will be offered and there will be no explanation. The lack of knowledge that characterizes productive narcissists often makes others who don't understand them want to confront them. This is not a good idea and it will not lead to anything positive. Again, the way to deal with the lack of self-knowledge is to focus on consequences that may hurt the narcissist's ability to reach his or her goal.

Productive narcissists isolate themselves. To deal with this you need to have some value to offer as a partner. If you are already a partner or the narcissist trusts you, you may be able to suggest others that could be valued partners. Finally, it is important to be on the lookout for signs of excessive grandiosity. Given clear excess, it is time to get out. Recent corporate examples (e.g., Enron) are good illustrations of corporate excess and their consequences.

## ◆ THE FUTURE OF PRODUCTIVE NARCISSISTS

Only productive narcissists with a high level of strategic intelligence can bring the world forward in a time of upheaval and rapid change. Recent scandals brought on by narcissistic corporate leaders will seriously threaten our ability as a society to deal with future economic and social upheaval and change if it leads us to reject the productive narcissists as leaders. Despite recent scandals brought on by narcissistic leaders, when change is needed and a "new order" needs to be established, the narcissistic personality is the one best suited to take on the task. Classic positive examples are Napoleon (during the time after the French Revolution), Martin Luther (the Reformation) and Martin Luther King Jr. (the civil rights movement), among others. Each of these leaders created a new order with lasting impact on the world. Other positive examples are Bill Gates at Microsoft and Jack Welch while he was at General Electric. To be able to move forward when there is profound change and upheaval, we need leaders who are willing to take large risks and who can give meaning and direction to our society and businesses. In these situations we need productive narcissists with highly developed strategic intelligence.

# Managing Diversity

## PART IX

A wide range of biases (such as racism, ageism and sexism) are unfortunately still entrenched in pockets in some segments of society and—sadly—exhibited in its organizations. Despite powerful federal and state laws, potent corporate policy statements, widespread efforts at enlightenment, and extensive training programs, many public and private organizations still have, for example, a limited number of female upper level managers. A number of different groups within society find themselves singled out and subjected to discriminatory treatment. (See, for example, the class-action allegations of lower pay and limited promotional opportunities for women at Wal-Mart as discussed in "People problems on every aisle," *Workforce Management* February 2004, pp. 26–34.)

Many interesting books and articles have been written on the rapidly changing demographics in the United States, and the implications that those trends have for businesses and organizations. The popular press reminds us almost daily that diversity in the workplace is not only increasingly common, but also a critical factor for success in the twenty-first century marketplace. As a consequence of these dramatic demographic trends and the need for constructive response, Part IX highlights the issues of gender diversity and its management in the workplace.

*The Inclusion Breakthrough* argues that every employee should be valued as a vital component of the organization's success. Authors Miller and Katz suggest a unique view of diversity, one in which fair treatment gets redefined to mean that every employee gets treated according to their needs so that they can do their best work. Diversity exists within every individual, and should therefore be leveraged through a culture of inclusion so as to best create a competitive advantage. This can be achieved, the authors contend, through a four-stage process of laying a foundation for change, mobilizing the effort, institutionalizing it, and sustaining the change.

The authors are top executives of the Kaleel Jamison Consulting Group. Frederick Miller (President and CEO) served on the Board of Directors for the American Society for Training and Development, and was the editor of *The Promise of Diversity.* Judith Katz (Executive Vice President) has written extensively on change management, oppression and diversity, and inclusive organizations. Her previous book was *White Awareness: Handbook for Anti-Racism Training.*

# The Inclusion Breakthrough: Unleashing the Real Power of Diversity

***FREDERICK A. MILLER and JUDITH H. KATZ***

***Summary prepared by Kristina A. Bourne***

***Kristina A. Bourne*** *is a doctoral candidate in organization studies at the University of Massachusetts in Amherst, where she also obtained an M.B.A. and a Women's Studies Graduate Certificate. She received a Bachelor of Business Administration with a concentration in marketing and a Bachelor of Arts with a concentration in French and economics from the University of Minnesota Duluth. Her academic interests include gender and organization. She is currently working on her dissertation in the area of women business owners, and on a collaborative research project focusing on alternative work arrangements.*

An *inclusion breakthrough* is a powerful transformation of an organization's culture to one in which *every* individual is valued as a vital component of the organization's success and competitive advantage. In the past, diversity has been seen as something that must be managed, tolerated, or molded to fit the dominant culture. Even those organizations that embrace diversity usually see it as an end in itself, rather than connected to the main mission of the organization. Such views create a *diversity in a box* strategy for most organizations, limiting the potential and power of diversity. With an inclusion breakthrough, differences are understood as mission-critical, not something extra linked only to human resource policies and practices.

Underpinning an inclusion breakthrough is the assumption that *diversity can be found in all individuals.* Everyone has his or her own unique backgrounds, experiences, and perspectives. Hiring people from different backgrounds, however, is not

Frederick A. Miller and Judith H. Katz, *The Inclusion Breakthrough: Unleashing the Real Power of Diversity.* San Francisco: Berrett-Koehler, 2002.

enough if the organization values sameness in ways of thinking, style, and behavior. Organizations can break out of the diversity in a box model by transforming their culture to one that values and supports the various dimensions of diversity, and unleashing its power.

Barriers to inclusion, ranging from blatant disregard for differences (such as the lack of accommodations for people with disabilities) to more subtle forms (such as exclusion from the afternoon golf game) are still widespread. Change efforts, however, should not stop at leveling the playing field by breaking down these barriers. Creating an environment where all people can be more productive means raising the playing field by continually examining processes to ensure that everyone feels valued for their contribution to the organization's success. *Leveraging diversity requires a culture of inclusion to support it.*

## THE FUNDAMENTALS OF AN INCLUSION BREAKTHROUGH

An inclusion breakthrough is a cycle—each element builds on the previous to raise the entire bar of expectations for organizations. This cycle positively impacts organizations by continuously increasing job satisfaction, attracting and retaining talented individuals, developing thriving communities, and tapping into market potential. Creating a culture of inclusion requires organizations to examine the following five key processes:

- Defining a new set of competencies
- Aligning policies and practices
- Leveraging a diverse labor force
- Connecting with local community
- Increasing value to marketplace

### DEFINING A NEW SET OF COMPETENCIES

Organizations today are plagued with incompetence such as inadequate communication skills, underutilized assets, internal rivalry, turnover of talented workers, and lack of cooperation across units. To unleash creativity and enable people to perform at their highest level, organizations must require new competencies and develop infrastructures that support them.

Working collaboratively and partnering across a diverse pool of people requires an environment in which individuals feel their unique perspective contributes to the overall success of the organization. People's experience of an organization is often based on the behavior of their immediate supervisor and members of their work group. A culture of inclusion, therefore, requires *all* people, no matter what position or level in the organization, to demonstrate the following new *inclusive competencies:*

- Greet others genuinely
- Understand difference as a force for new ideas and resolve disagreements
- Listen to each team member's ideas and perspectives
- Share information clearly and honestly
- Ensure that everyone understands the overall vision and how each task relates to it
- Realize that every member has a contribution to make

- Understand that others' experiences and perspectives can add innovative ideas
- Encourage quiet members to share their thoughts
- Respect other team members' time and personal/family responsibilities
- See mistakes as learning opportunities for improvement

These key competencies create a workplace that encourages communicating across differences, resolving conflict, and valuing every individual as a contributor to the overall mission. These new competencies, however, are not static and must be continuously re-evaluated in light of changes in the external and internal environment.

## ALIGNING POLICIES AND PRACTICES

Developing a new set of inclusive competencies will only be effective if they are integrated into the formal rules and policies of the organization, requiring both the written and unwritten practices to change. Even the so-called "soft policies," those that help people feel connected to and supported by the organization, must be re-evaluated to enable individuals to feel respected for their unique contribution while working in diverse situations. Old assumptions must be abandoned. For example, no longer is the office Christmas party "everyone's holiday."

In order to achieve an inclusion breakthrough, organizations must go beyond what they are already doing, raising the bar of the old baseline of actions to new levels. Table 1 lists current and updated policies and practice that allow people from a variety of social identity groups to perform at their highest level. The goal is not to treat everyone the same. *Fairness gets redefined as treating everyone according to their needs so that they can do their best work.*

## LEVERAGING A DIVERSE LABOR FORCE

*Just having people who represent diverse social identity groups in the organization is not enough; an environment must be created that unleashes that diversity.* Diversity in a box creates a situation where everyone is expected to fit within its walls. Dismantling these limits creates an environment where people feel safe to bring forward new ideas and perspectives when their difference is valued and respected as integral to the organization's strategic mission.

### The Biases among Us

Unleashing the potential of a diverse workforce requires organizations to address the barriers preventing everyone from succeeding. Organizational practices reflect societal and individual belief systems. Racism, sexism, heterosexism, ageism, and other prevalent "isms" are like a boulder of oppression that builds momentum as it rolls down the hill. Condescending and patronizing comments maintain the dominance of the one-up group. Sexism is prevalent when men are admired for leaving early to go to their child's school activity, while women are judged negatively for leaving early to pick their child up from daycare. Systematic racism exists when white women express concern about their organization's glass ceiling, while ignoring the fact that more women of color are concentrated at the lower levels. Doing nothing allows the boulder of bias to roll on. The only way to have a true inclusion breakthrough is to stop this boulder of oppressive beliefs with sustained, positive action.

**TABLE 1** The Old and the New Baseline for Inclusive Policies and Practices

| *Addressing Issues Relating to . . .* | *The Old Baseline* | *The New Baseline* |
|---|---|---|
| Age | • Recruits young people<br>• Values the experience of people who are 50 and older | • Recognizes that young people are investments in the future<br>• Develops young people quickly<br>• Extends the retirement age<br>• Includes 50+ people in high-potential groups |
| Lesbians, Gays, and Bisexuals | • Creates an environment that is safe for people to come out<br>• Offers domestic partner benefits | • Invites people's partners to company events<br>• Encourages people to talk about their personal lives<br>• Offers benefits that take into account the unique needs of lesbians and gays<br>• Recognizes that not all customers are heterosexual |
| Nationality | • Offers additional pay for language skills<br>• Recruits people from different countries | • Recognizes a variety of holidays and customs<br>• Includes representatives from all the organization's geographic locations on board of directors and senior management team<br>• Develops local talent |
| Organizational Hierarchy | • Values and respects people at the lower levels<br>• Provides career development opportunities for all people | • Recognizes that all people contribute to the organization<br>• Listens to all voices at all levels<br>• Creates participatory decision-making processes |
| People of Color | • Actively recruits and retains people of color<br>• Has minimal representation at all levels<br>• Acknowledges differentiation between groups (e.g., African American, Latinos) | • Demonstrates a critical mass throughout organization<br>• Acknowledges multiracial identity<br>• Develops two-way mentoring across racial lines (versus one-way mentoring to fit into old culture) |
| People with Disabilities | • Complies with the Americans with Disabilities Act<br>• Provides medical benefits that address disabled people's particular needs<br>• Recognizes the contributions of people with disabilities | • Creates an environment where people feel safe to express their unique needs<br>• Proactively recruits and retains people with disabilities<br>• Represents people with disabilities in marketing campaigns<br>• Provides more funding for accommodations |
| White Men | • Ensures that the white men are included in inclusion efforts<br>• Recognizes that there is more than one type of white man | • Develops two-way mentoring so white men can learn about their own diversity and expand their perspective<br>• Acknowledges work/family issues |

(*continued*)

TABLE 1 (Continued)

| *Addressing Issues Relating to . . .* | *The Old Baseline* | *The New Baseline* |
|---|---|---|
| Women | • Shows representation at all levels<br>• Addresses sexual harassment<br>• Acknowledges the structural barriers to women's advancement<br>• Values the work women do at all levels | • Eliminates subtle forms of harassment<br>• Addresses the sticky floor (i.e., barriers that keep women of color at the bottom)<br>• Develops two-way mentoring across women and men<br>• Applies flexible scheduling to all levels of the organization<br>• Includes men in parental polices |

### Attracting and Retaining a Talented Workforce

Hanging on to new talent is difficult in today's high-turnover environment. Most people change jobs and/or organizations every few years, making recruitment and retention of talented individuals a strategic priority. When people walk out the door in a year or two, they take with them their talent and training, often heading to the competitor's door. The traditional strategy of "bringing them along slowly" doesn't work when employee turnover is high. Further, "outsider status" must be eliminated. People of color, people with an accent, and people from other social identity groups must not be ignored or made to prove that they can fit in. All members must be nurtured and developed, because all members create value for the organization.

### An Employer of Choice

Becoming an employer of choice means asking why, given complete freedom, people would work for your organization. The following are key characteristics that talented individuals from diverse backgrounds report as significant in selecting an employer.

- The leaders are highly knowledgeable and inspirational.
- The organization is positioned for growth.
- Policies support work, life, and family integration.
- Ample growth and development opportunities exist (e.g., educational support).
- People feel respected by their colleagues.
- The environment is physically and emotionally safe.
- People are recognized as business partners (e.g., profit-sharing programs).
- People have access to all job-relevant information.
- Roles, responsibilities, performance expectations, and reward systems are openly stated.

If organizations want their employees to invest their time and energy into the organization, then organizations need to invest their time and energy into those people; this is the new two-way employment agreement.

## CONNECTING WITH THE LOCAL COMMUNITY

To be competitive, an inclusion strategy should not only focus on the inside of the organization, but the outside. Attracting talented people requires attractive communities in which they will live. The quality of the water supply, school systems, transportation, and other community resources must be high. Organizations should go beyond a one-way relationship with local communities based on tax breaks and other incentives to investing in educational, recreational, and health facilities. Organizations are, after all, dependent on local communities for people, suppliers, distributors, customers, and investors.

### INCREASING VALUE TO THE MARKETPLACE

Diversity in a box places customers outside of its walls. An inclusion breakthrough sees customers as central players in the organization's success. Traditionally, diverse customers are segmented into niches, which treats social identity groups as monolithic categories. Leveraging diversity in the marketplace requires organizations to expand their view of customers and link them to their core business strategy. The range of tastes and preferences within each social identity category must be recognized. Tapping into this market potential requires more than the token representative of each social group. *All* people in the organization must have the competencies to understand the unique features of each social group.

## BUILDING AN INCLUSION BREAKTHOUGH

Creating an environment in which all members of the organization feel supported to perform at their highest level requires a methodology for an inclusion breakthrough. Most organizations will go through four phases: laying the foundation for change, mobilizing change efforts, making change an everyday activity, and sustaining and challenging the new change.

### PHASE I: LAYING THE FOUNDATION FOR CHANGE

The most important piece of the foundation is the support from the top. Senior executives must lead and model the new competencies and provide resources to help people change to new, and initially uncomfortable, ways of behaving and interacting. Senior leaders need to link the change to the core business mission by creating an organizational imperative that clearly describes how a culture change will positively impact the organization as a whole, thereby creating value for each individual.

Laying the platform for change also requires a comprehensive organizational assessment that examines and documents a baseline of the current culture, resources, practices, and opportunities. Assessment is itself a tool for change; asking people about their experiences and concerns opens a space for change to occur. Data can be collected from surveys or by focus groups that assemble people by different social identities—part-time workers, individuals over 55, Asian-American managers—providing a forum for a diversity of views. Senior leaders must be receptive to honest and frank feedback about the organization's culture.

Senior leaders cannot create the change alone; learning partners should be selected to share their experiences and perspectives with senior leaders on a continuous basis. These individuals should not be seen as token representatives for differences, but as vital partners in the change effort, who offer insights to voices in the organization that otherwise go unheard. Further, a change leadership team, including individuals from various social identity groups and the dominant group, should be created to broaden the scope of the efforts.

## PHASE II: MOBILIZING CHANGE EFFORTS

This phase begins with developing an initial 12-to-18-month plan to implement the widespread culture change. At this stage, senior leaders should provide frequent and clear communication so that everyone in the organization is aware of the forthcoming changes. For example, the CEO can send a personal letter to each employee that describes the inclusion breakthrough as mission-critical. A core group should be selected to model the changes by integrating the new competencies into their everyday work lives. Intense education sessions will also allow groups of people in the organization to learn the new competencies. For example, human resource staff will need to learn how to integrate the new inclusive policies. Further, managers at all levels will need to integrate the new skills for leveraging diversity into their behaviors. Managers can often resist the culture change because in order for them to have climbed to their current position, they had to follow the rules of the old culture, to which they became comfortable.

Breaking down both overt and subtle forms of discrimination is also an integral component of this phase. For example, organizations need to take a close look at the gender wage gap, lagging advancement opportunities for people of color, and disregard for the family needs of lesbian and gay members. Processes must be created to address these forms of discrimination.

Finally, networking groups and buddy systems should be formalized. In one organization, a networking system was established in which each group linked its existence with the overall mission, was supported by a senior executive (usually not from the group's primary identity group), and belonged to an overall group of networks, which regularly meet to align each group's activities with business objectives. After two years, the benefits of such a networking system included new talented recruits, new relationships with business partners from various social identity groups, and new products that met the needs of different customers. In buddy systems, the success of new hires is both the responsibility of the new employee and the established team member, who are matched in the recruiting process.

## PHASE III: MAKING CHANGE AN EVERYDAY ACTIVITY

For the culture change to become a core part of the organizational mission, a longer term strategic plan must be developed to integrate the new diversity concepts into every aspect of the organization, especially training and education. Managers, with their vital role in training and mentoring, must practice the new behaviors and hold their direct reports accountable for them. As new competencies get cultivated, effective performance-measuring systems must be established and formalized in order to verify that people's, including managers', behaviors align with the new inclusion policies and practices.

In one organization, a comprehensive plan to make the inclusion breakthrough an everyday reality included mandatory education sessions on the organizational imperative for every employee, a multi-day training on leveraging diversity for managers, a reorganization of managers according to the new competencies, and the identification of change agents to model the new skills in their teams. Just two years after the changes were made, people felt more than twice as favorable toward their managers and were more committed to the organization.

### PHASE IV: SUSTAINING AND CHALLENGING THE NEW CHANGE

An inclusion breakthrough is not static; rather, it is a dynamic process that must be continually recreated. Periodic reviews allow organizations to assess the change progress. Revisiting the organizational imperative will show where advancements have been made and where gaps are still present.

Leadership groups will evolve, bringing in new ideas and perspectives. Communication of the new culture should remain open both internally and externally. *To be successful, an inclusion breakthrough must be ever changing, and continuously improving as people, strategies, customers, and environments change.*

## BREAKING DIVERSITY OUT OF THE BOX

Diversity in a box may feel more comfortable in the short run, but breaking out of the box will set free the organization's underutilized human potential. Stepping out of the box opens a space for individuals to feel respected, valued, and supported so they can perform to their highest level. Changing one organization at a time just might change the world by unleashing the real power of diversity.

PART

X

# Organizational Change in Dynamic Environments

A philosopher once noted that a person never steps into the same river twice, for the flowing current is always changing. Contemporary organizations have their own "river"—a turbulent environment around them. Consequently, managers of today's organizations are being called on to integrate their operations with a rapidly changing external environment. To bring about this integration, they must often adapt their organization's internal structure, processes, and strategies to meet these environmental challenges. The ability to manage change is far different from the ability to manage and cope with the ongoing and routine side of the organization.

Experts frequently advise American managers to invest in research and development (R&D) to keep their product mix current. Some companies (e.g., 3M Corporation) derive as much as 25 percent of their revenues from products introduced in the past five years. Nevertheless, many critics charge that one of the reasons for the decline in the competitiveness of U.S. industry revolves around its failure to innovate at sufficiently high levels. Clearly, organizations need to manage change, stimulate renewal, and develop organizational cultures in which "tempered radicals" can thrive.

*Whole-Scale Change* explains how 15 authors from Dannemiller Tyson Associates have blended systems theory and process consultation with practical methodologies to create powerful processes for change. The authors suggest that by tapping the wisdom and creativity of organizational employees, solutions will be both systems-based and characterized by a strong sense of ownership on the part of its stakeholders. The authors challenge readers to examine whether they have the right pattern of success, strategic direction, functions, form, resources, and information. They draw heavily upon sociotechnical systems theory, Beckhard's resistance to change model, and Kurt Lewin's action research model to create a dozen guiding principles for whole-scale change. Finally, they suggest that successful change can be sustained through the use of four key principles.

Clayton M. Christensen, professor of business administration at the Harvard Business School, and Michael E. Raynor, a director at Deloitte Research (the research arm of Deloitte Consulting) teamed up to write *The Innovator's Solution: Creating and Sustaining Successful Growth. The Innovator's Solution* is a sequel to *The Innovator's Dilemma,* authored by Dr. Christensen. In this later book, Christensen and Raynor explore how managers become blinded by "disruptive innovations" because of their preoccupation with their existing businesses and most profitable customers. In *The Innovator's Solution,* the authors reveal how organizations that are capable of sustaining growth get beyond this crippling dilemma. These organizations have managed to create a "disruptive growth engine." By drawing upon organizational examples, Christensen and Raynor identify and discuss the forces that cause managers to make bad decisions and they offer insight as to how to make disruptions succeed.

The third reading in this chapter focuses on the work of Debra E. Meyerson in her book *Tempered Radicals: How Everyday Leaders Inspire Change at Work.* Debra E. Meyerson holds a joint appointment on the School of Business and Education faculties at Stanford University. In this book Meyerson describes the perilious life and tightropes walked by people who attempt to bring about change within organizations. Based upon hundreds of interviews with people who have struggled to do good work and bring about organizational improvements through change, this book details the day-to-day problems, challenges, dangers, realities, and rewards that are associated with change efforts. Tempered radicals represent that group of people that balance organizational conformity with individual rebellion. They often find themselves at odds with the organization's core culture, yet they are often those individuals who are a source of new ideas and approaches, and as a result promote organizational learning and change.

# Whole-Scale Change: Unleashing the Magic in Organizations

***DANNEMILLER TYSON ASSOCIATES***
***Summary prepared by Warren L. Candy***

***Warren L. Candy*** *is vice president for generation for Minnesota Power, an electric services company located in Duluth, Minnesota, where he is responsible for the operations of their generating resources in both Minnesota and North Dakota. His interests include high-performance organizational design, sustainable leadership development, and sociotechnical systems implementation. He received his diploma in production engineering from Swinburne Institute of Technology in Melbourne, Australia.*

## ◆ WHAT IS WHOLE-SCALE CHANGE?

In today's world, with its ever-changing environment and new technologies, we are faced with unparalleled demands and expectations both at work and at home. These demands are requiring both employees and the people who lead them to discover new approaches to organizational change which enables us to adapt, change, and then to change all over again! The "whole-scale change" methodology provides a common-sense way to tap into and unleash the wisdom present in every workforce.

The roots of whole-scale change are deep and varied. From past experiences it was found that to get "large-scale change" in organizations, large groups of people need to be quickly connected around the development of common, deep, accurate, and focused strategies. These microcosms of the organization are able to see and work

Dannemiller Tyson Associates. *Whole-Scale Change: Unleashing the Magic in Organizations.* San Francisco: Berrett-Koehler Publishers, 2001.

the whole system. From a common database organizations can see what needs to be different in their work and their work structures and processes. Change can begin at the very moment of understanding and acceptance, which should lead to success both now and into the future.

To shift the whole system at one time you must be able to think in the same way that the whole system thinks. Microcosms, real subsets of the larger group that represent all the voices and wisdom of the organization, are the best windows through which to view the entire system quickly and effectively in real time. By having a critical mass of microcosms experience a paradigm shift, the entire organization is better able to move and accept the change.

The essence of the whole-scale change is to cause profound, timely, and far-reaching change in *human* systems through the involvement of large numbers of people in small-group activities, and the synthesis of their combined knowledge within large-group events.

## ◆ IS WHOLE-SCALE CHANGE A JOURNEY OR A PROCESS?

Whole-scale change combines a number of different processes to help an organization adapt to meet the challenges of its environment. It takes the organization on an action-learning journey, unleashing the power of the microcosm, uniting multiple realities, and creating paradigm shifts and changes in the way the organization sees its future actions. Whole-scale change is thus both a change journey and a change process.

Whole-scale change uses three models as guides through the process: converge/diverge model, action learning model, and the DVF formula of creating paradigm shifts.

### CONVERGE/DIVERGE MODEL

This model (from the work of Lawrence and Lorsch in *Organization and Environment*) represents a connected flow that integrates the individual (in small groups) with the whole system (in large groups) to expand their database of information (diverge), to combine their multiple realities (converge), to explore possibilities (diverge), and to ultimately make systemwide decisions (converge).

In the ebb and flow of convergence/divergence, large-group events accelerate the change journey; they bring together the critical mass that combines everything people have been learning from their individual and small-group efforts into the whole picture. In the larger group they make the decisions that will move them ahead deeper and faster.

### THE ACTION LEARNING MODEL

Based on Kurt Lewin's Action Research Model, the whole-scale change model is an application of both systems thinking and action learning, aimed at keeping the system whole at every step of the way.

The steps of the action learning model are

1. Creating a common database of our multiple realities, and a shared understanding and strategic focus.

2. Identifying implications of how does this impact us, where are we currently, and what are the possibilities for us?
3. Creating the future we see by picturing and creating a shared vision of what we need to be.
4. Agreeing on a change strategy that is based on closing the gap between where we are and where we want to be, and identifying possibilities for action.
5. Connecting around specific actions of what is significant, and who will be responsible and when it will get done.
6. Action learning and planning the next steps of Plan, Do, Check, Act.
7. Go back to Step 1.

Shared information is the common thread that connects each of these steps in the learning cycle, because the focus is on creating wholeness at each step of the way by asking the following linking questions:

- What's next?
- Who needs to be involved?
- What conversations need to take place?
- What will be different because these conversations take place?

### THE DVF FORMULA: CREATING PARADIGM SHIFTS

Developed from the work of Richard Beckhard (*Organizational Transitions: Managing Complex Change,* 1987), this version of the model explains what it takes to bring about real change in an organization, or in an individual, and is represented here by the following formula:

$$D \times V \times F > R$$

where $D$ is the level of dissatisfaction with the current situation, and describes "why we must change, and the reason for us to do anything differently."

$V$ is the vision of a positive possibility, and the common end point that the organization is seeking to achieve.

$F$ is the first concrete steps taken in moving in the direction of the vision.

Thus, $D \times V \times F$ reflects its strength of the "drive for change."

$R$ is the level of resistance to change that exists within all individuals and organizations.

If $D$, $V$, or $F$ is zero, the drive for change cannot overcome the resistance to change.

## ◆ WHOLE-SCALE ORGANIZATIONAL DESIGN

Whole-scale organizational design builds on the sociotechnical systems (STS) model. The essence of STS is the integration of three organizational elements: the social (or people element), the technical (or process element), and the infrastructure (or support) element.

- The social system incorporates all of the needs and wishes of people, the structuring of jobs and work, and the understanding of what really motivates people in organizations.

- The technical system refers to the processes and procedures that the organization needs to accomplish its work, which defines the tasks that make up the work of people.
- The infrastructure system refers to the support systems that need to be in place to enable the people to accomplish the work that needs to be done. They include such areas as recognition and rewards, training, compensation, and performance feedback.

The principles that underlie the STS Model follow:

- All three elements—social, technical, and infrastructure—in any organization are interdependent and therefore cannot be analyzed independently.
- Powerful solutions and designs come from looking at all three elements together.
- The right design for any organization comes from looking at and integrating all three elements.
- The answers are everywhere, and are in everyone.

## ◆ THE GUIDING PRINCIPLES OF WHOLE-SCALE CHANGE

From many years of hands-on experience with large-scale organizational change, the following principles have been found to be the most compelling and enduring.

- Tap into the power of the microcosm.
- Uncover the collective wisdom of the people within the organization.
- Look at the whole system because piecework solutions cannot resolve complex systemwide problems.
- Believe passionately that people actively support what they help create.
- Continuously reexamine and adapt to results at different points throughout the change process.
- Create self-sufficiency for "smarter" organizations.
- Plant the seeds of generative relationships (where groups of people with diverse objectives work together on a common project for the benefit of all the participants).
- Use reality as a key driver by continually focusing on the simultaneous and often conflicting realities that exist in organizations.
- Build and maintain a common database of shared information and perceptions.
- Think about the future before you plan.
- Have your purpose drive all of your choices and decisions.
- Honor both the past and the present as you create the future by acknowledging where you have been and where you currently are.
- Keep the flame of change burning.

## THE STAR OF SUCCESS: SIX KEYS TO A SUCCESSFUL JOURNEY

A model found to be helpful and descriptive in whole-scale change is known as the "Star of Success." The Star of Success is a five-pointed star with "pattern of success" in the middle and "strategic direction," "processes and systems," "form," "resources," and "shared information" at each of the points, forming an integrated and continuous model for organizational change.

Because whole-scale change is an applied systems theory, the Star of Success provides an excellent organizational model. The Star of Success focuses an organization on six vital questions.

1. Do we have the right pattern of success?
2. Do we have the right strategic direction?
3. Do we have the right functions?
4. Do we have the right form?
5. Do we have the right resources?
6. Do we have the right information?

The Star of Success model provides an objective way for the members of an organization to focus their time, money, and energy by asking the critical questions in ways that make sense for the entire organization.

*Do we have the right pattern of success?*

- What is our purpose? What is our fundamental reason for being?
- What are our values? What do we live by when the "going gets tough"?
- What do we do?
- Why do we do it?
- For whom do we exist?
- Why, or why not, are we achieving results?
- Are we likely to continue to succeed into the future?

*Do we have the right strategic direction?*

- What is our preferred future?
- What is going on in our external environment?
- What is our mission? What business are we in?
- Who are our stakeholders?
- What value do we choose to create for our stakeholders?
- How do we intend to create and deliver that value?
- What does success look like? When will we get there?
- How will we measure our performance?

*Do we have the right functions, processes, systems, ways, and means?*

- What work needs to be done?
- What are the core and support processes?
- How will we do the work?
- What systems are needed to enable the work to be done?

*Do we have the right form, relationships, and connectivity between people?*

- What are the reporting relationships?
- Where are the organizational boundaries?
- What are the needed functional roles and relationships?
- How are decisions going to be made and kept?
- What is the power distribution?
- What are the needed external relationships?
- What are the needed internal relationships?

*Do we have the right resources, capabilities, and abilities?*

- Are people committed to the strategic direction?
- Are people committed to each other?
- Do we have the right skills and knowledge?
- Do we have the right facilities, equipment, and software?
- Do we have the needed financial resources?

*Do we have the right shared information?*

- What is the common context?
- What common data and information do we need?
- How are we going to create this data and knowledge?

## SUSTAINING THE MOMENTUM

The momentum of a major change effort is sustained when the organization anchors the required changes in the fiber of the organization while at the same time maintaining its ability to respond to the next set of challenges. Experience has shown that to sustain momentum for change, the most important point of the Star of Success is the fifth and final point of "shared information." When an organization has been able to share and understand a set of information across all of its parts in a way that creates and maintains a common worldview, it has achieved the ability to sustain change.

Four principles help sustain and drive the implementation of change.

1. Keep the system whole.
   - Have a purpose and meaning for the organization/department.
   - Stay connected as a community.
   - Receive feedback on how I/we are doing.
   - Give people a voice.
2. Engage as many microcosms as possible.
3. Build critical mass.
   - Continually expand the circle of involvement.
   - Hold large-group meetings.
4. Keep the flame of change burning with energy.

$$Energy = Meaning \times Hope \times Power$$

Where

- *Meaning* comes from embracing the Purpose, Vision, Values, and plans for the organization.
- *Hope* comes from knowing that the organization is being successful in its change efforts, because people see demonstrable results.
- *Power* comes from having a critical mass of the organization actively engaged in the change effort, exercising their ability to influence.

## ◆ WHOLE-SCALE CHANGE IN CLOSING

As a result of the integration of large-group processes with work design and change for a whole-scale approach, organizations have been able to reduce the cycle time on creating solutions and implementation strategies by one-half to two-thirds. This improved performance has occurred because of the immediate implementation of new ways of working by the small-group microcosms that are involved and are fully participating in data collection, synthesis, and decision-making.

Whole-scale change has become a process that allows the simultaneous creating and implementation of new organizations with whole system involvement. Our ever-changing environment, combined with the warp speed of technology development, requires leaders to uncover new approaches that harness the tumult, speed, and complexities of this new world, and to use them to the organization's advantage. Whole-scale change provides just such a new approach for large organizational change and improvement.

# The Innovator's Solution

CLAYTON M. CHRISTENSEN, MICHAEL E. RAYNOR, and SCOTT D. ANTHONY

Summary prepared by Warren L. Candy

***Warren L. Candy*** *is a Senior Vice President at Allete Minnesota Power, a diversified electric utility located in Duluth, Minnesota, where he is responsible for generation, transmission, distribution, mining, and customer operations in Minnesota, Wisconsin, and North Dakota. His interests include sustainable organizational design, leadership excellence, and socio-technical systems. He received his Bachelor of Science degree in Production Engineering from Swinburne Institute of Technology in Melbourne, Australia.*

## ◆ SUSTAINING CORPORATE GROWTH

Research and observation of hundreds of both successful and unsuccessful growth-orientated businesses have resulted in the identification of a number of key theories and practical responses for creating and sustaining new growth in business. Growth is important to all management teams because companies create shareholder value through profitable growth. However, approximately one company in ten is able to sustain the kind of growth that translates into above average increases in shareholder returns for more than a few years at a time. It's hard to know how to grow, but pursuing growth the wrong way can be worse than no growth at all.

As the core business approaches maturity, investors demand new growth, and executives develop seemingly sensible strategies to generate it. Although they often invest aggressively, many times their plans still fail to create the needed growth fast enough. Probably the most daunting challenge in delivering growth is that once you fail to deliver it, the odds of ever regaining past levels of success are very low. It has been shown that of all the companies whose growth has stalled, only 4 percent are able to successfully reignite their growth, even to a rate of 1 percent above GNP!

---

Clayton M. Christensen, Michael E. Raynor, and Scott D. Anthony, *The Innovator's Solution: Creating and Sustaining Successful Growth.* Boston: Harvard Business School Press, 2003.

What *can* make the process of innovation more predictable comes from an understanding of the forces that act upon those individuals and the management teams building the business. When comprehended and properly applied, these forces can powerfully influence what managers can choose to do, and what they cannot choose to do.

A dearth of good ideas is rarely the core problem in a company that struggles to launch exciting new-growth businesses. The problem is in the shaping process itself. The major obstacle for growth-seeking managers is that the exciting growth markets of tomorrow are most likely small and off the radar screen today. Managers who understand these forces, and learn to harness them in making key decisions, will develop successful new-growth businesses much more consistently than historically seemed possible.

## ◆ FUNDAMENTAL ISSUES AND PRINCIPLES

The following set of issues highlight some of the most important decisions that need to be addressed by managers. The answers to the underlying questions, and the essential principles supporting them, can guide managers as they successfully grow new and profitable businesses.

### OUTPERFORMING YOUR COMPETITION

A key management question is always "What could our competition do to outperform us?" A natural follow-up question becomes "What courses of action could actually give *us* the upper hand?" A new market entrant is more likely to beat the incumbent with disruptive innovations, rather than with sustaining innovations. *Disruptive innovations* occur where the challenge is to commercialize a simpler, more convenient product that sells for less money, a product that appeals to a new or unattractive customer set. This compares to *sustaining innovations,* where the goal is to deliver a better product that is sold for more money to an already attractive set of customers.

Disruptive innovations don't attempt to bring better products to established customers in established markets. Rather, they disruptively redefine the market by introducing products and services that are not as good as the currently available products, but instead offer other benefits such as being simpler, more convenient, less expensive, and more appealing to a new, or less demanding, customer group.

This distinction is important for innovators seeking to create new-growth businesses. Whereas the current leaders of the industry will almost always triumph in battles of sustaining innovation, successful disruptions are most likely to be launched by the new entrant companies.

### IDENTIFYING DESIRED PRODUCTS

Managers appropriately ask the questions, "What products should we be developing?" "Which improvements will our customers want?" and "Which new products will be rejected out of hand?" Managers need to rethink their perceptions and opinions of why customers actually use or don't use their products and services. In reality, customers "hire" products to do specific jobs that regularly arise in their lives and that need to get done under specific circumstances. Companies that target their products at the circumstances in which customers find themselves, rather than the customers themselves, can launch predictably successful products.

## IDENTIFYING BEST CUSTOMERS

As managers create new business ventures, they must ask themselves "Which initial customers will constitute the most viable foundation upon which to build a successful business?" The first step is to find the ideal customers for low-end disruptions. They are the current users of the mainstream products who seem disinterested in offers to sell them improved performance products. They may be willing to accept improved products, but they are often unwilling to pay for them.

A *new-market disruption* is an innovation that enables a large population of people who previously lacked the money or skill to now begin buying and using a product, and doing the job for themselves. However, a product that purports to help non-consumers do something that they weren't already prioritizing in their lives is unlikely to succeed.

## INTERNAL VS. EXTERNAL ACTIVITY

A key decision for the long-term sustainability of any organization revolves around the activities required to design, produce, sell, and distribute products and services—Which ones should be done internally? Which ones should be done externally by partners and suppliers?

Traditionally this decision has been made around the organization's core competency model, which suggests that if something fits your core competency then you should do it inside the organization. If it is not a core competency and another firm can do it better, then you should rely on them to do it. The problem with this approach is that what might seem to be a non-core activity today might become an absolutely critical competence to have mastered in a proprietary way in the future, and vice versa. The real question to be asked, and the decision to be made, is "What do we need to master today, and what will we need to master in the future, in order to excel on the path of improvement that customers will define as important to them?"

Core competence is a dangerously inwardly looking notion. Competitiveness is far more about doing what *customers* value than it is about doing what you think you are good at. Staying competitive as the competition shifts requires a willingness and an ability to learn new things rather than to hold onto what has been successful in the past.

## AVOIDING THE COMMODITIZATION OF PRODUCTS

As organizations grow, they need to maintain strong competitive advantage and attractive profits within a marketplace that, over time, is trending toward commoditization. *Commoditization* is a natural and inescapable process that occurs as new markets coalesce around proprietary products that become increasingly difficult to differentiate from the competition. Attractive future profits can often be found elsewhere in the value chain, in different stages or layers of value added, usually in the places where previously profit was hard to attain.

## CONSIDERING DISRUPTIVE GROWTH

One ongoing responsibility for all management teams is to ensure that the optimal organizational design and structure is in place to facilitate ongoing business growth. Many potentially successful innovations fail not because of market forces, but because the management of the organization is not up to the task. Those capabilities that were assets in sustaining circumstances become liabilities when disruption is needed. To be confident that managers can handle the new challenges placed before them, executives need to examine in detail the types of actual problems that they have had to deal with in the past, and diminish their emphasis on broad leadership attributes that are believed to be inherently important (e.g., good communicator; results oriented). By focusing on a person's ability to learn and adapt, managers can avoid the trap of assuming that those skills that are important today are those that will still be required in the future. In many ways this results in a paradox: *the managers that corporate executives have come to trust most today because they have consistently delivered the needed results in the core business cannot be trusted to shepherd the creation of new business ventures tomorrow.*

## ESTABLISHING A STRATEGY THAT WORKS

Most questions that are raised about strategy focus on its substance. However, the crucial question really relates to the *process* of strategy formulation, i.e., using the right process in the right circumstances. Although senior management can become obsessed with finding the right strategy, they can actually wield greater leverage by managing the processes used to develop the strategy, and by making sure that the right process is used under the right circumstances.

Within organizations there are essentially two types of strategies—deliberate and emergent. *Deliberate strategies* are the product of a conscious and analytical plan based on rigorous analysis of data. *Emergent strategies* are responses to unanticipated opportunities, problems, and successes that were unforeseen in the deliberate strategy-making process. The emergent process should dominate in circumstances where the future is hard to read and in which it is not clear what the right strategy should be. Alternatively, the deliberate process should dominate once a winning strategy has become clear and effective implementation is crucial.

# ◆ PREFERRED SOURCES OF CAPITAL

As companies seek to grow and expand, three key issues emerge for senior management to consider. These focus on: (1) identifying whose investment capital will help the firm succeed, (2) determining whose capital might be the "kiss of death," and (3) exploring what sources of money will help the firm most at different stages of its development. The best resource for facilitating success in a growth-oriented business is money that is "patient for growth but impatient for profit." By contrast, money should be impatient for growth in later stage, deliberate-strategy circumstances after a winning strategy has emerged.

## THE ROLE OF SENIOR EXECUTIVES

One reason that many soaring hot-product companies flame out is that the key initial resource, the founding team, fails to institute the processes or the values that will help the company continue to develop and initiate disruptive products and services. The CEOs of all companies play a critical role in sustaining the growth of the business.

Senior executives have three roles to play in ensuring repeated disruptive growth in their organizations. First, they must stand astride and manage the interface between the disruptive growth businesses and the mainstream businesses. Second, these executives must shepherd the internal processes which repeatedly create new organizational growth. Third, they must sense when circumstances are changing and respond appropriately.

*The larger and more complex a company becomes, the more important it is for senior managers to train employees at every level to act autonomously.* Doing so will help them make prioritized decisions that are consistent with the strategic direction and business model of the organization. Senior management's role is to decide when to keep their hands off the new business, and when to get involved.

## Conclusion

Managers need to know how to use a key number of theories and principles to create and sustain continuous organizational growth. An integrated body of theory derived from the successes and failures of hundreds of different companies has been developed, and each of these address a different aspect of the "innovator's dilemma."

READING 3

# Tempered Radicals: How People Use Differences to Inspire Change at Work

DEBRA E. MEYERSON

At one point or another, many managers experience a pang of conscience—a yearning to confront the basic or hidden assumptions, interests, practices, or values within an organization that they feel are stodgy, unfair, even downright wrong. A vice president wishes that more people of color would be promoted. A partner at a consulting firm thinks new M.B.A.s are being so overworked that their families are hurting. A senior manager suspects his company, with some extra cost, could be kinder to the environment. Yet many people who want to drive changes like these face an uncomfortable dilemma. If they speak out too loudly, resentment builds toward them; if they play by the rules and remain silent, resentment builds inside them. Is there any way, then, to rock the boat without falling out of it?

Over the past 15 years, I have studied hundreds of professionals who spend the better part of their work lives trying to answer this question. Each one of the people I've studied differs from the organizational status quo in some way—in values, race, gender, or sexual preference, perhaps (see the side bar "How the Research Was Done"). They all see things a bit differently from the "norm." But despite feeling at odds with aspects of the prevailing culture, they genuinely like their jobs and want to continue to succeed in them, to effectively use their differences as the impetus for constructive change. They believe that direct, angry confrontation will get them nowhere, but they don't sit by and allow frustration to fester. Rather, they work quietly to challenge prevailing wisdom and gently provoke their organizational cultures to adapt.

---

From the October 2001 *Harvard Business Review* article by Debra E. Meyerson, "Radical Change, the Quiet Way," pp. 92–100. 

I call such change agents *tempered radicals* because they work to effect significant changes in moderate ways.

In so doing, they exercise a form of leadership within organizations that is more localized, more diffuse, more modest, and less visible than traditional forms—yet no less significant. In fact, top executives seeking to institute cultural or organizational change—who are, perhaps, moving tradition-bound organizations down new roads or who are concerned about reaping the full potential of marginalized employees—might do well to seek out these tempered radicals, who may be hidden deep within their own organizations. Because such individuals are both dedicated to their companies and masters at changing organizations at the grassroots level, they can prove extremely valuable in helping top managers to identify fundamental causes of discord, recognize alternative perspectives, and adapt to changing needs and circumstances. In addition, tempered radicals, given support from above and a modicum of room to experiment, can prove to be excellent leaders. (For more on management's role in fostering tempered radicals, see the sidebar "Tempered Radicals as Everyday Leaders.")

Since the actions of tempered radicals are not, by design, dramatic, their leadership may be difficult to recognize. How, then, do people who run organizations, who want to nurture this diffuse source of cultural adaptation, find and develop these latent leaders? One way is to appreciate the variety of modes in which tempered radicals operate, learn from them, and support their efforts.

To navigate between their personal beliefs and the surrounding cultures, tempered radicals draw principally on a spectrum of incremental approaches, including four I describe here. I call these *disruptive self-expression, verbal jujitsu, variable-term opportunism,* and *strategic alliance building.* Disruptive self-expression, in which an individual simply acts in a way that feels personally right but that others notice, is the most inconspicuous way to initiate change. Verbal jujitsu turns an insensitive statement, action, or behavior back on itself. Variable-term opportunists spot, create, and capitalize on short- and long-term opportunities for change. And with the help of strategic alliances, an individual can push through change with more force.

Each of these approaches can be used in many ways, with plenty of room for creativity and wit. Self-expression can be done with a whisper; an employee who seeks more racial diversity in the ranks might wear her dashiki to company parties. Or it can be done with a roar; that same employee might wear her dashiki to the office every day. Similarly, a person seeking stricter environmental policies might build an alliance by enlisting the help of one person, the more powerful the better. Or he might post his stance on the company intranet and actively seek a host of supporters. Taken together, the approaches form a continuum of choices from which tempered radicals draw at different times and in various circumstances.

But before looking at the approaches in detail, it's worth reconsidering, for a moment, the ways in which cultural change happens in the workplace.

## ◆ HOW ORGANIZATIONS CHANGE

Research has shown that organizations change primarily in two ways: through drastic action and through evolutionary adaptation. In the former case, change is discontinuous and often forced on the organization or mandated by top management in the wake of major technological innovations, by a scarcity or abundance of critical resources, or by sudden changes in the regulatory, legal, competitive, or political landscape. Under such circumstances, change may happen quickly and often involves significant pain. Evolutionary change, by contrast, is gentle, incremental, decentralized, and over time produces a broad and lasting shift with less upheaval.

The power of evolutionary approaches to promote cultural change is the subject of frequent discussion. For instance, in "We Don't Need Another Hero" (HBR, September 2001), Joseph L. Badaracco, Jr., asserts that the most effective moral leaders often operate beneath the radar, achieving their reforms without widespread notice. Likewise, tempered radicals gently and continually push against prevailing norms, making a difference in small but steady ways and setting examples from which others can learn. The changes they inspire are so incremental that they barely merit notice—which is exactly why they work so well. Like drops of water, these approaches are innocuous enough in themselves. But over time and in accumulation, they can erode granite.

Consider, for example, how a single individual slowly—but radically—altered the face of his organization. Peter Grant* was a black senior executive who held some 18

◆ EXHIBIT 1 ◆

## A Spectrum of Tempered Change Strategies

The tempered radical's spectrum of strategies is anchored on the left by *disruptive self-expression:* subtle acts of private, individual style. A slightly more public form of expression, *verbal jujitsu,* turns the opposition's negative expression or behavior into opportunities for change. Further along the spectrum, the tempered radical uses *variable-term opportunism* to recognize and act on short- and long-term chances to motivate others. And through *strategic alliance building,* the individual works directly with others to bring about more extensive change. The more conversations an individual's action inspires and the more people it engages, the stronger the impetus toward change becomes.

In reality, people don't apply the strategies in the spectrum sequentially or even necessarily separately. Rather, these tools blur and overlap. Tempered radicals remain flexible in their approach, "heating up" or "cooling off" each as conditions warrant.

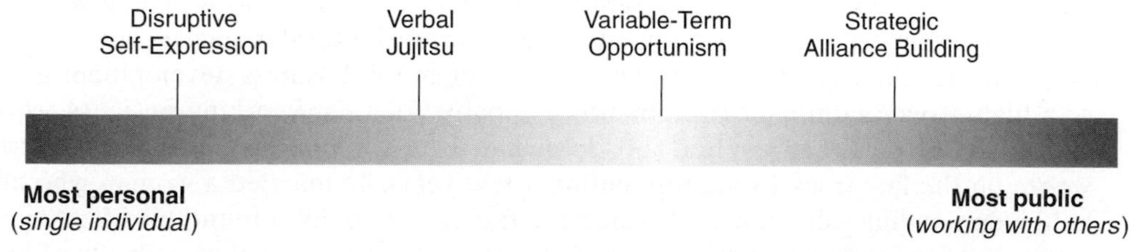


*With the exception of those in the VA hospital and Allied Domecq cases, all the names used through this article are fictitious.

positions as he moved up the ladder at a large West Coast bank. When he first joined the company as a manager, he was one of only a handful of people of color on the professional staff. Peter had a private, long-term goal: to bring more women and racial minorities into the fold and help them succeed. Throughout his 30-year career running the company's local banks, regional offices, and corporate operations, one of his chief responsibilities was to hire new talent. Each time he had the opportunity, Peter attempted to hire a highly qualified member of a minority. But he did more than that—every time he hired someone, he asked that person to do the same. He explained to the new recruits the importance of hiring women and people of color and why it was their obligation to do likewise.

Whenever minority employees felt frustrated by bias, Peter would act as a supportive mentor. If they threatened to quit, he would talk them out of it. "I know how you feel, but think about the bigger picture here," he'd say. "If you leave, nothing here will change." His example inspired viral behavior in others. Many stayed and hired other minorities; those who didn't carried a commitment to hire minorities into their new companies. By the time Peter retired, more than 3,500 talented minority and female employees had joined the bank.

Peter was the most tempered, yet the most effective, of radicals. For many years, he endured racial slurs and demeaning remarks from colleagues. He waited longer than his peers for promotions; each time he did move up he was told the job was too big for him and he was lucky to have gotten it. "I worked my rear end off to make them comfortable with me," he said, late in his career. "It wasn't *luck.*" He was often angry, but lashing out would have been the path of least emotional resistance. So without attacking the system, advancing a bold vision, or wielding great power, Peter chipped away at the organization's demographic base using the full menu of change strategies described below.

## DISRUPTIVE SELF-EXPRESSION

At the most tempered end of the change continuum is the kind of self-expression that quietly disrupts others' expectations. Whether waged as a deliberate act of protest or merely as a personal demonstration of one's values, disruptive self-expression in language, dress, office decor, or behavior can slowly change the atmosphere at work. Once people take notice of the expression, they begin to talk about it. Eventually, they may feel brave enough to try the same thing themselves. The more people who talk about the transgressive act or repeat it, the greater the cultural impact.

Consider the case of John Ziwak, a manager in the business development group of a high-growth computer components company. As a hardworking business school graduate who'd landed a plum job, John had every intention of working 80-hour weeks on the fast track to the top. Within a few years, he married a woman who also held a demanding job; soon, he became the father of two. John found his life torn between the competing responsibilities of home and work. To balance the two, John shifted his work hours—coming into the office earlier in the morning so that he could leave by 6 P.M. He rarely scheduled late-afternoon meetings and generally refused to take calls at home in the evening between 6:30 and 9. As a result, his family life improved, and he felt much less stress, which in turn improved his performance at work.

At first, John's schedule raised eyebrows; availability was, after all, an unspoken key indicator of commitment to the company. "If John is unwilling to stay past 6," his boss wondered, "is he really committed to his job? Why should I promote him when others are willing and able to work all the time?" But John always met his performance expectations, and his boss didn't want to lose him. Over time, John's colleagues adjusted to his schedule. No one set up conference calls or meetings involving him after 5. One by one, other employees began adopting John's "6 o'clock rule"; calls at home, particularly during dinner hour, took place only when absolutely necessary. Although the 6 o'clock rule was never formalized, it nonetheless became par for the course in John's department. Some of John's colleagues continued to work late, but they all appreciated these changes in work practice and easily accommodated them. Most people in the department felt more, not less, productive during the day as they adapted their work habits to get things done more efficiently for example, running meetings on schedule and monitoring interruptions in their day. According to John's boss, the employees appreciated the newfound balance in their lives, and productivity in the department did not suffer in the least.

Tempered radicals know that even the smallest forms of disruptive self-expression can be exquisitely powerful. The story of Dr. Frances Conley offers a case in point. By 1987, Dr. Conley had already established herself as a leading researcher and neurosurgeon at Stanford Medical School and the Palo Alto Veteran's Administration hospital. But as one of very few women in the profession, she struggled daily to maintain her feminine identity in a macho profession and her integrity amid gender discrimination. She had to keep her cool when, for example, in the middle of directing a team of residents through complicated brain surgery, a male colleague would stride into the operating room to say, "Move over, honey." "Not only did that undermine my authority and expertise with the team," Dr. Conley recalled later, "but it was unwarranted and even dangerous. That kind of thing would happen all the time."

Despite the frustration and anger she felt, Dr. Conley at that time had no intention of making a huge issue of her gender. She didn't want the fact that she was a woman to compromise her position, or vice versa. So she expressed herself in all sorts of subtle ways, including in what she wore. Along with her green surgical scrubs, she donned white lace ankle socks—an unequivocal expression of her femininity. In itself, wearing lace ankle socks could hardly be considered a Gandhian act of civil disobedience. The socks merely said, "I can be a neurosurgeon and be feminine." But they spoke loudly enough in the stolid masculinity of the surgical environment, and, along with other small actions on her part, they sparked conversation in the hospital. Nurses and female residents frequently commented on Dr. Conley's style. "She is as demanding as any man and is not afraid to take them on," they would say, in admiration. "But she is also a woman and not ashamed of it."

Ellen Thomas made a comparable statement with her hair. As a young African-American consultant in a technical services business, she navigated constantly between organizational pressures to fit in and her personal desire to challenge norms that made it difficult for her to be herself. So from the beginning of her employment, Ellen expressed herself by wearing her hair in neat cornrow braids. For Ellen, the way she wore her hair was not just about style; it was a symbol of her racial identity.

Once, before making an important client presentation, a senior colleague advised Ellen to unbraid her hair "to appear more professional." Ellen was miffed, but she didn't respond. Instead, she simply did not comply. Once the presentation was over and the client had been signed, she pulled her colleague aside. "I want you to know why I wear my hair this way," she said calmly. "I'm a black woman, and I happen to like the style. And as you just saw," she smiled, "my hairstyle has nothing to do with my ability to do my job."

Does leaving work at 6 PM or wearing lacy socks or cornrows force immediate change in the culture? Of course not; such acts are too modest. But disruptive self-expression does do two important things. First, it reinforces the tempered radical's sense of the importance of his or her convictions. These acts are self-affirming. Second, it pushes the status quo door slightly ajar by introducing an alternative modus operandi. Whether they are subtle, unspoken, and recognizable by only a few or vocal, visible, and noteworthy to many, such acts, in aggregation, can provoke real reform.

## VERBAL JUJITSU

Like most martial arts, jujitsu involves taking a force coming at you and redirecting it to change the situation. Employees who practice verbal jujitsu react to undesirable, demeaning statements or actions by turning them into opportunities for change that others will notice.

One form of verbal jujitsu involves calling attention to the opposition's own rhetoric. I recall a story told by a man named Tom Novak, an openly gay executive who worked in the San Francisco offices of a large financial services institution. As Tom and his colleagues began seating themselves around a table for a meeting in a senior executive's large office, the conversation briefly turned to the topic of the upcoming Gay Freedom Day parade and to so-called gay lifestyles in general. Joe, a colleague, said loudly, "I can appreciate that some people choose a gay lifestyle. I just don't understand why they have to flaunt it in people's faces."

Stung, Tom was tempted to keep his mouth shut and absorb the injury, but that would have left him resentful and angry. He could have openly condemned Joe's bias, but that would have made him look defensive and self-righteous. Instead, he countered Joe with an altered version of Joe's own argument, saying calmly, "I know what you mean, Joe. I'm just wondering about that big picture of your wife on your desk. There's nothing wrong with being straight, but it seems that you are the one announcing your sexuality." Suddenly embarrassed, Joe responded with a simple, "Touché."

Managers can use verbal jujitsu to prevent talented employees, and their valuable contributions, from becoming inadvertently marginalized. That's what happened in the following story. Brad Williams was a sales manager at a high-technology company. During a meeting one day, Brad noticed that Sue, the new marketing director, had tried to interject a few comments, but everything she said was routinely ignored. Brad waited for the right moment to correct the situation. Later on in the meeting, Sue's colleague George raised similar concerns about distributing the new business's products outside the country. The intelligent remark stopped all conversation. During the pause, Brad jumped in: "That's an important idea," he said. "I'm glad George picked up on Sue's concerns. Sue, did George correctly capture what you were thinking?"

With this simple move, Brad accomplished a number of things. First, by indirectly showing how Sue had been silenced and her idea co-opted, he voiced an unspoken fact. Second, by raising Sue's visibility, he changed the power dynamic in the room. Third, his action taught his colleagues a lesson about the way they listened and didn't. Sue said that after that incident she was no longer passed over in staff meetings.

In practicing verbal jujitsu, both Tom and Brad displayed played considerable self-control and emotional intelligence. They listened to and studied the situation at hand, carefully calibrating their responses to disarm without harming. In addition, they identified the underlying issues (sexual bias, the silencing of newcomers) without sounding accusatory and relieved unconscious tensions by voicing them. In so doing, they initiated small but meaningful changes in their colleagues' assumptions and behavior.

## VARIABLE-TERM OPPORTUNISM

Like jazz musicians, who build completely new musical experiences from old standards as they go along, tempered radicals must be creatively open to opportunity. In the short-term, that means being prepared to capitalize on serendipitous circumstances; in the long term, it often means something more proactive. The first story that follows illustrates the former case; the second is an example of the latter.

Tempered radicals like Chris Morgan know that rich opportunities for reform can often appear suddenly, like a $20 bill found on a sidewalk. An investment manager in the audit department of a New York conglomerate, Chris made a habit of doing whatever he could to reduce waste. To save paper, for example, he would single-space his documents and put them in a smaller font before pressing the "Print" button, and he would use both sides of the paper. One day, Chris noticed that the company cafeteria packaged its sandwiches in Styrofoam boxes that people opened and immediately tossed. He pulled the cafeteria manager aside. "Mary," he said with a big smile, "those turkey-on-focaccia sandwiches look delicious today! I was wondering, though . . . would it be possible to wrap sandwiches only when people asked you to?" By making this very small change, Chris pointed out, the cafeteria would save substantially on packaging costs.

Chris gently rocked the boat by taking the following steps. First, he picked low-hanging fruit, focusing on something that could be done easily and without causing a lot of stir. Next, he attacked the problem not by criticizing Mary's judgment but by enrolling her in his agenda (praising her tempting sandwiches, then making a gentle suggestion). Third, he illuminated the advantages of the proposed change by pointing out the benefits to the cafeteria. And he started a conversation that, through Mary, spread to the rest of the cafeteria staff. Finally, he inspired others to action: eventually, the cafeteria staff identified and eliminated 12 other wasteful practices.

Add up enough conversations and inspire enough people and, sooner or later, you get real change. A senior executive named Jane Adams offers a case in point. Jane was hired in 1995 to run a 100-person, mostly male software-development division in an extremely fast-growing, pre-IPO technology company. The CEO of the company was an autocrat who expected his employees to emulate his dog-eat-dog management style. Although Jane was new to the job and wanted very much to fit in and succeed, turf wars and command-and-control tactics were anathema to her. Her style was more collaborative; she believed in sharing power. Jane knew that she could not attack the

◆ EXHIBIT 2 ◆

## How the Research Was Done

This article is based on a multipart research effort that I began in 1986 with Maureen Scully, a professor of management at the Center for Gender in Organizations at Simmons Graduate School of Management in Boston. We had observed a number of people in our own occupation academia who, for various reasons, felt at odds with the prevailing culture of their institutions. Initially, we set out to understand how these individuals sustained their sense of self amid pressure to conform and how they managed to uphold their values without jeopardizing their careers. Eventually, this research broadened to include interviews with individuals in a variety of organizations and occupations: business people, doctors, nurses, lawyers, architects, administrators, and engineers at various levels of seniority in their organizations.

Since 1986, I have observed and interviewed dozens of tempered radicals in many occupations and conducted focused research with 236 men and women, ranging from midlevel professionals to CEOs. The sample was diverse, including people of different races, nationalities, ages, religions, and sexual orientations, and people who hold a wide range of values and change agendas. Most of these people worked in one of three publicly traded corporations—a financial services organization, a high-growth computer components corporation, and a company that makes and sells consumer products. In this portion of the research, I set out to learn more about the challenges tempered radicals face and discover their strategies for surviving, thriving, and fomenting change. The sum of this research resulted in the spectrum of strategies described in this article.

company's culture by arguing with the CEO; rather, she took charge of her own division and ran it her own way. To that end, she took every opportunity to share power with subordinates. She instructed each of her direct reports to delegate responsibility as much as possible. Each time she heard about someone taking initiative in making a decision, she would praise that person openly before his or her manager. She encouraged people to take calculated risks and to challenge her.

When asked to give high-visibility presentations to the company's executive staff, she passed the opportunities to those who had worked directly on the project. At first, senior executives raised their eyebrows, but Jane assured them that the presenter would deliver. Thus, her subordinates gained experience and won credit that, had they worked for someone else, they would likely never have received.

Occasionally, people would tell Jane that they noticed a refreshing contrast between her approach and the company's prevailing one. "Thanks, I'm glad you noticed," she would say with a quiet smile. Within a year, she saw that several of her own direct reports began themselves to lead in a more collaborative manner. Soon, employees from other divisions, hearing that Jane's was one of the best to work for, began requesting transfers. More important, Jane's group became known as one of the best training grounds and Jane as one of the best teachers and mentors of new talent. Nowhere else did people get the experience, responsibility, and confidence that she cultivated in her employees.

◆ EXHIBIT 3 ◆

## Tempered Radicals as Everyday Leaders

In the course of their daily actions and interactions, tempered radicals teach important lessons and inspire change. In so doing, they exercise a form of leadership within organizations that is less visible than traditional forms but just as important.

The trick for organizations is to locate and nurture this subtle form of leadership. Consider how Barry Coswell, a conservative, yet open-minded lawyer who headed up the securities division of a large, distinguished financial services firm, identified, protected, and promoted a tempered radical within his organization. Dana, a left-of-center, first-year attorney, came to his office on her first day of work after having been fingerprinted—a standard practice in the securities industry. The procedure had made Dana nervous: What would happen when her new employer discovered that she had done jail time for participating in a 1960s-era civil rights protest? Dana quickly understood that her only hope of survival was to be honest about her background and principles. Despite the difference in their political proclivities, she decided to give Barry the benefit of the doubt. She marched into his office and confessed to having gone to jail for sitting in front of a bus.

"I appreciate your honesty," Barry laughed, "but unless you've broken a securities law, you're probably okay." In return for her small confidence, Barry shared stories of his own about growing up in a poor county and about his life in the military. The story swapping allowed them to put aside ideological disagreements and to develop a deep respect for each other. Barry sensed a budding leader in Dana. Here was a woman who operated on the strength of her convictions and was honest about it but was capable of discussing her beliefs without self-righteousness. She didn't pound tables. She was a good conversationalist. She listened attentively. And she was able to elicit surprising confessions from him.

Barry began to accord Dana a level of protection, and he encouraged her to speak her mind, take risks, and most important, challenge his assumptions. In one instance, Dana spoke up to defend a female junior lawyer who was being evaluated harshly and, Dana believed, inequitably. Dana observed that different standards were being applied to male and female lawyers, but her colleagues dismissed her "liberal" concerns. Barry cast a glance at Dana, then said to the staff, "Let's look at this and see if we are being too quick to judge." After the meeting, Barry and Dana held a conversation about double standards and the pervasiveness of bias. In time, Barry initiated a policy to seek out minority legal counsel, both in-house and at outside legal firms. And Dana became a senior vice president.

In Barry's ability to recognize, mentor, and promote Dana there is a key lesson for executives who are anxious to foster leadership in their organizations. It suggests that leadership development may not rest with expensive external programs or even with the best intentions of the human resources department. Rather it may rest with the open-minded recognition that those who appear to rock the boat may turn out to be the most effective of captains.

For Chris Morgan, opportunity was short-term and serendipitous. For Jane Adams, opportunity was more longterm, something to be mined methodically. In both cases, though, remaining alert to such variable-term opportunities and being ready to capitalize on them were essential.

## ◆ STRATEGIC ALLIANCE BUILDING

So far, we have seen how tempered radicals, more or less working alone, can effect change. What happens when these individuals work with allies? Clearly, they gain a sense of legitimacy, access to resources and contacts, technical and task assistance, emotional support, and advice. But they gain much more—the power to move issues to the forefront more quickly and directly than they might by working alone.

When one enlists the help of like-minded, similarly tempered coworkers, the strategic alliance gains clout. That's what happened when a group of senior women at a large professional services firm worked with a group of men sympathetic to their cause. The firm's executive management asked the four-woman group to find out why it was so hard for the company to keep female consultants on staff. In the course of their investigation, the women discussed the demanding culture of the firm: a 70-hour work-week was the norm, and most consultants spent most of their time on the road, visiting clients. The only people who escaped this demanding schedule were part-time consultants, nearly all of whom happened to be women with families. These part-timers were evaluated according to the same performance criteria including the expectation of long hours as full-time workers. Though many of the part-timers were talented contributors, they consistently failed to meet the time criterion and so left the company. To correct the problem, the senior women first gained the ear of several executive men who, they knew, regretted missing time with their own families. The men agreed that this was a problem and that the company could not continue to bleed valuable talent. They signed on to help address the issue and, in a matter of months, the evaluation system was adjusted to make success possible for all workers, regardless of their hours.

Tempered radicals don't allow preconceived notions about "the opposition" to get in their way. Indeed, they understand that those who represent the majority perspective are vitally important to gaining support for their cause. Paul Wielgus quietly started a revolution at his company by effectively persuading the opposition to join him. In 1991, Allied Domecq, the global spirits company whose brands include Courvoisier and Beefeater, hired Paul as a marketing director in its brewing and wholesaling division. Originally founded in 1961 as the result of a merger of three British brewing and pub-owning companies, the company had inherited a bureaucratic culture. Tony Hales, the CEO, recognized the need for dramatic change inside the organization and appreciated Paul's talent and fresh perspective. He therefore allowed Paul to quit his marketing job, report directly to the CEO, and found a nine-person learning and training department that ran programs to help participants shake off stodgy thinking and boost their creativity. Yet despite the department's blessing from on high and a two-year record of success, some managers thought of it as fluff. In fact, when David, a senior executive from the internal audit department, was asked to review cases of unnecessary expense, he called Paul on the carpet.

Paul's strategy was to treat David not as a threat but as an equal, even a friend. Instead of being defensive during the meeting, Paul used the opportunity to sell his program. He explained that the trainers worked first with individuals to help unearth their personal values, then worked with them in teams to develop new sets of group values that they all believed in. Next, the trainers aligned these personal and departmental values with those of the company as a whole. "You wouldn't believe the changes, David," he said, enthusiastically. "People come out of these workshops feeling so much more excited about their work. They find more meaning and purpose in it, and as a consequence are happier and much more productive. They call in sick less often, they come to work earlier in the morning, and the ideas they produce are much stronger." Once David understood the value of Paul's program, the two began to talk about holding the training program in the internal audit department itself.

Paul's refusal to be frightened by the system, his belief in the importance of his work, his search for creative and collaborative solutions, his lack of defensiveness with an adversary, and his ability to connect with the auditor paved the way for further change at Allied Domecq. Eventually, the working relationship the two men had formed allowed the internal audit department to transform its image as a policing unit into something more positive. The new Audit Services department came to be known as a partner, rather than an enforcer, in the organization as a whole. And as head of the newly renamed department, David became a strong supporter of Paul's work.

Tempered radicals understand that people who represent the majority perspective can be important allies in more subtle ways as well. In navigating the course between their desire to undo the status quo and the organizational requirements to uphold it, tempered radicals benefit from the advice of insiders who know just how hard to push. When a feminist who wants to change the way her company treats women befriends a conservative Republican man, she knows he can warn her of political minefields. When a Latino manager wants his company to put a Spanish-language version of a manual up on the company's intranet, he knows that the white, monolingual executive who runs operations may turn out to be an excellent advocate.

Of course, tempered radicals know that not everyone is an ally, but they also know it's pointless to see those who represent the status quo as enemies. The senior women found fault with an inequitable evaluation system, not with their male colleagues. Paul won David's help by giving him the benefit of the doubt from the very beginning of their relationship. Indeed, tempered radicals constantly consider all possible courses of action: "Under what conditions, for what issues, and in what circumstances does it make sense to join forces with others?"; "How can I best use this alliance to support my efforts?"

Clearly, there is no one right way to effect change. What works for one individual under one set of circumstances may not work for others under different conditions. The examples above illustrate how tempered radicals use a spectrum of quiet approaches to change their organizations. Some actions are small, private, and muted; some are larger and more public. Their influence spreads as they recruit others and spawn conversations. Top managers can learn a lot from these people about the mechanics of evolutionary change.

Tempered radicals bear no banners; they sound no trumpets. Their ends are sweeping, but their means are mundane. They are firm in their commitments, yet flexible in the ways they fulfill them. Their actions may be small but can spread like a virus. They yearn for rapid change but trust in patience. They often work individually yet pull people together. Instead of stridently pressing their agendas, they start conversations. Rather than battling powerful foes, they seek powerful friends. And in the face of setbacks, they keep going. To do all this, tempered radicals understand revolutionary change for what it is—a phenomenon that can occur suddenly but more often than not requires time, commitment, and the patience to endure.

PART

# XI

# Managerial Decision-Making

Managers at all levels of organizations make decisions. Some of these are relatively trivial and some are powerfully significant. Some managers make decisions frequently and others engage in the process more infrequently. Some managers make decisions intuitively and others follow a more systematic process. Nevertheless, in a systems framework, *all* decisions eventually affect the success of the enterprise. It is critical to discover useful frameworks for how managers should approach the decision process so as to avoid common errors and increase the probability of success. This becomes increasingly true for "high-stakes" decisions with large potential payoffs, or when managers are faced with crisis situations.

Paul C. Nutt, in *Why Decisions Fail,* asserts that up to two-thirds of all decisions are either failure-prone or based on questionable tactics. He examined 400 top-level strategic decisions and fifteen monumental fiascoes to identify the three most common blunders that managers make—rushing to judgment, misusing resources, and failure-prone tactics. Under these conditions, managers often make the bad decision undiscussable such that no one can learn from it. He concludes by suggesting alternative tactics that decision-makers could use to avoid these traps, including owning up to past mistakes.

Nutt is a professor of management sciences and public policy and management at The Ohio State University's Fisher College of Business. He received his Ph.D. from the University of Wisconsin–Madison, and was named a Fellow in the Decision Sciences Institute. Nutt serves on the editorial board for several publications, including the *Strategic Management Journal.* He is the author of six other books, including *Managing Planned Change* and *Making Tough Decisions.*

Authors Murnighan and Mowen, in *High-Stakes Decision-Making,* point out that managers often need to make key decisions under tight time pressures and incomplete information, but still must use a systematic process for doing so. They start by asking managers to analyze their situation based on (1) whether or not a problem really exists, and (2) whether or not action needs to be taken. Next, they describe a variety of classic traps that decision-makers fall into, including time snares, decision myopia, illusions of causality, and hindsight bias. Finally, they prescribe a seven-step (SCRIPTS) process for approaching and analyzing complex, high-risk decisions that focuses on Search, Causes, Risks, Intuition, Perspectives, Time Frame, and Solving the Problem.

J. Keith Murnighan is the Harold H. Hines Jr. Distinguished Professor of Risk Management in the Kellogg School of Management at Northwestern University, and a specialist in negotiations and decision-making. He has a Ph.D. in Social Psychology from Purdue University, and is a Fellow in the Academy of Management. His co-author, John C. Mowen, is Regents Professor and Noble Chair of Marketing Strategy at Oklahoma State University. His Ph.D. is from Arizona State University, and he is a past president of the Society for Consumer Psychology. Professor Mowen specializes in managerial and consumer decision-making.

Ian Mitroff and Gus Anagnos examine a series of internally and externally caused corporate crises (e.g., Egypt Air, Nike, the Intel chip, Exxon Valdez, the Challenger explosion). On the basis of these examples, the authors suggest that any organization could be susceptible to similar catastrophes caused by human error, accident, or criminal acts. All organizations are vulnerable unless they set proactive mechanisms in place that will detect early warning signals and prepare a crisis portfolio that details their advance preparations and likely responses. The authors also discuss the creation of a corporate culture that helps to control and contain the damage once it occurs.

Mitroff is the Harold Quinton Distinguished Professor of Business Policy in the Marshall School of Business at the University of Southern California, and is the Director of USC's Center for Strategic Public Relations. He is the author or co-author of twenty-two books, including *Crisis Leadership: Planning for the Unthinkable.* Mitroff is president and Gus Anagnos is vice president of the consulting firm Comprehensive Crisis Management.

# Why Decisions Fail: Avoiding the Blunders and Traps that Lead to Debacles

**_PAUL C. NUTT_**

**_Summary prepared by Paul C. Nutt_**

***Paul C. Nutt** is a professor of management sciences in the Fisher College of Business at The Ohio State University. He received his Ph.D. degree from the University of Wisconsin-Madison and a B.S.E and M.S.E from the University of Michigan. His research interests include organizational decision-making, leadership, and radical change. He has written over 100 articles and seven books on these topics that have received numerous awards from the Decision Sciences Institute, The Academy of Management, INFORMS, The Center for Creative Leadership, AAMC, FACHE, and others. He is a Fellow in the Decision Sciences Institute. Trade discussions of his work have appeared in the* Wall Street Journal, Fast Company, *and PRI's* Marketplace. *He serves on several editorial review boards and regularly consults for public, private, and nonprofit organizations on strategic management, decision-making, and international business.*

## ◆ INTRODUCTION

With the rash of recent corporate scandals, the public rightfully wonders if corporate managers are able to make sound decisions. The answer is unnerving. Based on a multi-decade study of real-life organizational decisions, about *half of all business decisions end in failure.* Vast sums of money are spent to make decisions that result in no ultimate value for the organization. Worse yet, some managers make the same

---

Paul C. Nutt, *Why Decisions Fail: Avoiding the Blunders and Traps that Lead to Debacles.* San Francisco: Berrett-Koehler, 2002.

mistakes over and over again. Research shows that failed decisions share three common blunders: managers rush to judgment, misuse their resources, and repeatedly use failure-prone tactics to make their decisions.

## A STUDY OF DECISION-MAKING

A 25-year research effort developed a unique database of more than 400 decisions made by top managers in private, public and nonprofit organizations across the United States. A wide variety of decisions have been studied, from purchasing equipment to renovating space to deciding which products or services to sell. About half of the decisions were not fully used after just two years—one of the key indicators of failure. One-third of the decisions were *never* used. These failure figures would be even higher if it were possible to study a random selection of decisions. The "story behind the story" of EuroDisney, the Firestone tire recall, the Denver International Airport (DIA), Quaker's acquisition of Snapple, Shell's disposal of the Brent Spar oil platform, and other equally devastating decision debacles were studied and documented, providing insights into why decisions fail. Lesser known failures were found to have the same features as the debacles, except they didn't attain the notoriety. Failure could not be blamed on events that can't be controlled, such as fickle customers and down markets. Instead, *failure typically stems from blunders that point unsuspecting decision-makers toward traps that ensnare them.* In this sense, most of these decision-making failures are actually preventable.

## THE BLUNDERS

Three deadly blunders led to failed decisions and debacles. The *rush to judgment* blunder crops up when managers identify a concern and latch onto the first remedy that they come across. Managers seem to believe that concerns and solutions come in pairs. They fear the threat of an unresolved concern—and they do so with good reason, as higher executives are quick to question them and pressure them for an answer. As the pressure mounts, managers find it nearly impossible not to grab the first solution that they find. However, *failure is four times more likely when decision-makers embrace the first idea they come across without taking the time to investigate what is motivating their action and then seeking out possible remedies.*

The second blunder—*misuse of resources*—occurs when managers spend their time and money during decision-making on the wrong things. For example, decision-makers collectively spend millions of dollars to defend hastily selected ideas with a defensive evaluation and devote little or nothing to other aspects of decision-making, such as gathering intelligence about the concerns prompting action, finding who may block action, setting expectations, and uncovering actions that can meet expectations.

The third blunder is *failure-prone tactics.* Two-thirds of the decisions studied applied failure-prone tactics. Success can increase by as much as 50 percent when better tactics are used. Following good decision-making practices costs very little, especially when compared to the costs of a debacle.

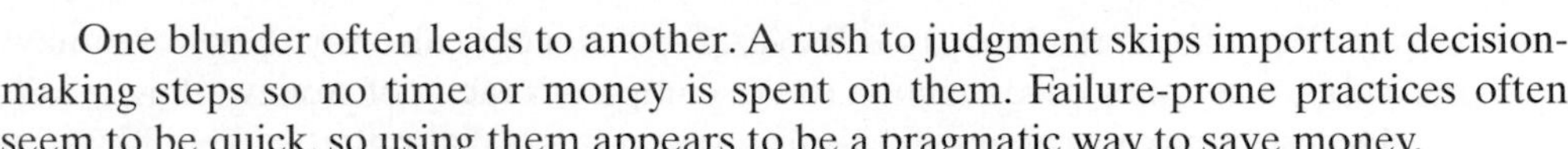

One blunder often leads to another. A rush to judgment skips important decision-making steps so no time or money is spent on them. Failure-prone practices often seem to be quick, so using them appears to be a pragmatic way to save money.

## FAILURE TRAPS AND WAYS TO AVOID THEM

Managers that blunder find themselves caught in one or more traps. When trapped, managers are apt to make a bad call that makes failure likely. The blunders create traps and these traps bring about failure that crops up in all failed decisions. Seven common traps were uncovered:

- Not taking charge by reconciling claims
- Failing to deal with the barriers to taking action
- Providing or receiving ambiguous directions
- Engaging in a limited search and no innovation
- Misusing evaluation
- Overlooking ethical questions
- Failing to learn

### NOT TAKING CHARGE BY RECONCILING CLAIMS

To start a decision-making effort, powerful and influential stakeholders make a claim and attempt to get it endorsed. Other claims are overlooked. If decision-makers buy into a claim without looking further, they are apt to get trapped. The initial claim often omits what aroused the claimant, it may be disconnected from the concerns of people, it may fail to identify their perceived needs or their considerations, and it may neglect to suggest perceived opportunities. The relationship of a concern or a consideration with a claim's arena of action may be suspect, as in Smithburg's beliefs about the connection of an acquisition with the need for defensive restructuring for Quaker. Adopting the implied arena of action (e.g., an acquisition) is ill-advised when such a motivating concern or consideration is used to defend it. The concerns and considerations motivating a claim are seldom spelled out, leading people to speculate about what they may be. In the debacles studied there were no attempts to analyze the claim or to uncover competing claims, although gathering this kind of intelligence is highly and widely recommended.

Instead, decision-makers select among the claims being offered by a select group of powerful insiders and forge ahead with the selected claim, and its implied arena of action. When decision-makers are silent about their concerns and considerations, people make their own judgments about what a decision is really about, and its importance. These judgments often elude the decision-maker. Skeptics and people who have something to lose each are handed a platform to raise objections. To discredit the decision and the decision-maker, opponents call attention to what seems to be an error, faulty logic, or a misrepresentation to question the legitimacy of a claim, and its arena of action. The decision-making effort must then scale this slippery slope to be successful. Many of the debacles studied had hidden concerns, suggesting very different claims than the ones pushed by decision-makers. At Ford, officials expressed surprise when told that many insiders were troubled by the company's failure to recall the

Explorer and fix its tendency to roll over. Ford's leaders also say they were unaware of the public's very negative reaction to the company's tactic of stonewalling recalls.

Decision-makers can avoid this trap by finding a claim that stakeholders can support. Insight into people's concerns and considerations broadens one's views of what needs fixing, and suggests an arena of action that stakeholders can support. Demonstrating awareness of people's views gives any decision-making effort legitimacy. Stakeholders who understand the arguments presented and see how they point to an arena of action that accounts for important things are more apt to support the proposal. When people see a claim as valid, momentum is created as word spreads to others.

## FAILING TO MANAGE FORCES STIRRED UP BY A DECISION

Decision-makers in the debacles studied implemented a preferred course of action with either an edict or with persuasion. When using an edict, the best one can hope for is indifference—that people either do not care enough to resist or will believe that resistance is futile. If the edict fails, decision-makers may resort to persuasion, now trying to explain why the decision has value. This is fouled by the previous power play, even if power is applied incrementally. Using persuasion from the outset is somewhat more effective. Selling an idea with persuasion can work if stakeholders are indifferent to what decision-makers want to do. Persuasion has little effect, however, on people who believe they have something to lose. There are better ways to get a decision adopted.

Edicts and persuasion fail because neither manages the social and political forces stirred up by a decision. The decision-makers in the debacles had no idea what enflamed their opponents and assumed it stemmed from self-serving interests. People's worries fester and grow when their interests and commitments are ignored. Being more forthcoming about reasons and motives can neutralize opposition. Involving potential critics in the decision-making process at least clarifies their views for you. And involvement may shift the critic from a position of opposition to one of support.

Successful decision-makers push implementation to the front of their decision-making efforts to uncover and manage people's interests and commitments. If power must be shared, teams can be created and involved in making the decision. People are more apt to disclose their interests when they are in such an arrangement. Even when disclosure is limited, the act of negotiating a solution promotes ownership in the agreed-upon plan that increases its prospect of success. Even when not forced to do so, savvy decision-makers use participation because it improves the chance of a successful implementation. Another effective approach, called networking, helps demonstrate the necessity of acting. Current performance is documented, and credible performance norms are identified. Using this information, key stakeholders are shown the importance of a decision by decision-makers, collecting and managing interests with each encounter. People are more likely to be supportive when networking makes them aware of performance shortfalls and the level of performance that is possible. *Networking makes the need to act credible.*

## AMBIGUOUS DIRECTIONS

Direction identifies the expected results of a decision. In failed decisions, directions are either misleading, assumed but never agreed to, or unknown. Using economic benefits to justify the arena is both misleading and dangerous. Critics were given a platform to question the arena. Opponents of the Denver International Airport (DIA) asked if there was a better way to spend $500 million to produce economic gains for the greater Denver area. Misrepresenting the expected benefits provides an opportunity to attack the decision. Being clear about what is to be gained by having an arena puts a "best face" on such projects. Many major infrastructure projects, such as mass transit systems, are put in jeopardy when champions trumpet "economic benefits" as the expected outcome. Debacles often had bloated or unrealistic expectations that made them failure-prone.

Directions that were not understood by key players pose difficulties. Thwarting a takeover seemed to be Smithburg's aim in masterminding Quaker's acquisition of Snapple. It became the implicit direction behind the key decision, but this was never codified or explained. Smithburg's failure to be clear about his aims prompted insiders to make their own assumptions. It is easy to see how people could assume a different direction. What about profit? Insiders who assumed that a profit direction guided the Snapple purchase would find the decision wrong-headed. Thwarting a takeover would make the rationale behind Smithburg's decision clearer but would prompt other questions, but at least would steer people away from looking for profit-enhancing ideas.

Being clear about expected results was often set aside in the debacles by a rush to find a remedy. Fearing criticism, decision-makers act as if they must have a way to deal with a claim as soon as one is acknowledged. The need to disarm the real or the potential critic makes it hard to admit doubt. Doubt can be a powerful positive force pushing one to think deeply about what is needed. The leaders substitute an answer (the acquisition of Snapple) for thinking about the aim of profit possibilities. The idea (the Snapple acquisition) eliminated discussion about what might create profits at Quaker and what would be the best way to realize this aim. The idea and its assumed benefits displaced the need to think about the results the company hoped to produce. People will see these benefits differently and form different impressions about what is wanted. Without clarity about the reasons for taking action, disputes arise as people push courses of action that deal with their idiosyncratic notions of expected results. Such disputes are a prime cause of conflict in decision-making. The recommended action is discussed but not the hoped-for results that prompted it. People pushing a preferred course of action often fail to tell others what results they are trying to realize. Setting an objective clears away this ambiguity and conflict. Being clear about what is wanted also mobilizes support and guides the search for answers.

## LIMITED SEARCH AND NO INNOVATION

*Decision-makers often embrace a quick fix.* Having an "answer" eliminates ambiguity about what to do, but keeps the decision-maker from looking for other ideas that could be better. Smithburg was wedded to buying and turning around companies. Shell was drawn to deep-sea disposal of waste materials because it was legal.

Decision-makers that avoid a quick fix are confronted with a new challenge: the allure of current business practices. It is difficult to move away from the tangible to the unknown. In the debacles, many of the proposed actions copied the business practices of others to reduce time and cost. These costs are almost always underestimated, as is the time to do the required tailoring.

Decision-makers drawn to a quick fix or to "how others do it" are also pulled away from innovation and search. The search for ideas, and for an innovative one that provides "first mover" advantage, is often waylaid by the desire for a quick fix and the lure of current business practices. When a clear direction is set, however, conducting a search and seeking an innovative response reduces the risk of failure.

## MISUSING EVALUATIONS

Once a quick fix is uncovered, many decision-makers strike a defensive posture and collect information to argue for its adoption. More time and money was spent doing this type of evaluation than all the other decision-making activities combined. Smithburg knew Snapple's price, but little else. Shell officials spent huge sums on "evaluations." It was hardly a surprise that each commissioned evaluation spoke glowingly of the idea. The money spent on defensive evaluations that justify such actions would be better spent to find a more beneficial action.

Evaluation is valuable when used to compare the benefits of a preferred course of action to performance norms and to determine the risk in realizing the benefits. Expected results must be clear before such an evaluation can provide pertinent information. If one adopts a profit direction for the Snapple decision, best and worst case assumptions about sales and product synergies can be analyzed to determine risk. This would have exposed the Quaker board to factors that limit synergies (the incompatibility of distribution and manufacturing for Snapple and Gatorade) and sales (public dislike of Snapple Products), lowering revenue projections and the likelihood of turning a profit. Such an evaluation can be used to uncover the level of risk in the purchase decision and strip away ambiguity and conflict. Factors that drive revenues and profits upward and downward were ignored in the debacles, so risk was hidden. Substituting benefit and risk assessments for defensive evaluations improves the prospect of success.

## IGNORING ETHICAL QUESTIONS

Tough decisions pose ethical dilemmas. The DIA supporters ignored questions about who pays, who benefits, and who decides. Many large-scale infrastructure projects such as sports arenas, rapid transit systems, and arts centers share this failing.

Values that lurk behind an ethical position were never understood in the debacles. Shell executives saw their disposal plan as pragmatic. Others saw it as unethical. When the actions of decision-makers appear unethical it can prompt whistleblowing by insiders or boycotts by outsiders, as in the Shell case. Even when these extreme reactions are avoided, decision-makers plant the seeds of distrust when their behavior appears to be unethical to insiders or to outsiders.

To avoid distrust, whistle blowing, and boycotts, these ethical issues must be confronted. To do this, people should be encouraged to speak out and pose ethical questions during decision-making deliberations. Create forums for ethical concerns to be voiced, explore options uncovered in the decision-making effort, and offer mediation to those who disagree. The forum allows a decision-maker to look for values behind the positions of people who oppose them. The decision-maker can often affirm these values and make a minor modification in a claim or a preferred course of action to carry on much as before. Had Shell officials affirmed the values of the groups that opposed them by addressing disposal questions they would have cut the ground from under the arguments of Greenpeace, and blunted any attempted boycott. If this fails, offer mediation. Shell officials could have held hearings and conferences to find out what their critics were saying, looking for unwarranted criticisms and misunderstandings to be diffused. At best, new insights can develop. If not, the leaders can take steps that show they considered the views of their critics—a position that boosts the legitimacy of a proposed action. Companies using mediation win lawsuits involving whistle-blowing. Companies without it usually lose them.

### FAILING TO LEARN

Guiding decision-makers away from failure-prone tactics requires learning. But learning is thwarted when managers have no tolerance for mistakes and errors, or a failed decision. In such an environment, people conceal bad outcomes. To make things worse, chance events make outcomes muddy. Good decision-making practices cannot guarantee good outcomes, because of chance events. Bad luck, such as when product demand falls below expectations because of unexpectedly bad weather, can be mistaken for bad decision-making practices. Good luck, such as windfall profits due to favorable increases in interest rates or consumer interest in a product, can cover up failure-prone decision-making practices.

A failed decision puts people in a no-win situation when there is no tolerance for failure. Individuals in such a bind have but two options: own up or cover up. An own up approach makes the day of atonement today; a cover up makes it tomorrow or perhaps never. Put in this bind, people will seldom own up to a failure and likely will delay the day of atonement as long as they can. Several acts of deception are necessary to pull this off. Offsetting bad news with good news sidetracks potentially threatening questions. The cover-up is two tiered: the distorted good news and the blatant act of creating misleading information. These games of deception become undiscussable in the minds of the presenters because to reveal them would also reveal the "lose-lose" position created for the organization. There must be a cover up of the cover up to cover one's tracks. Put in this situation, people engage in a paradoxical behavior; *they make undiscussable the key aspects of a decision from which others need to learn.*

The real culprit in this process is the perverse incentive that keeps decision-makers from owning up. A perverse incentive always has this effect, making it difficult for people to come forward with their insights about what happened and why. Subordinates are often aware when things are going badly, but they are not inclined to share what they know in a punishment-driven environment. Many higher ups make it clear they tolerate no opposition to their pet projects. In each case, perverse incentives create barriers to learn why a decision went wrong and how to avoid a similar failure in the future. It is essential to create an environment in which decisions can be openly discussed so as to avoid this blame-finding mentality.

## ◆ IMPLICATIONS FOR MANAGERS

*The prospect of decision-making success dramatically improves when managers avoid the traps discussed above.* To do so, managers should probe to uncover hidden concerns, take steps to manage the social and political forces that can block an idea, identify the results wanted, search widely and encourage innovation, and estimate benefits linked to expected results along with the risk in realizing them. Ethical dilemmas often go undetected as decisions are made and crop up later, causing responsible people considerable embarrassment. This can be avoided if decision makers encourage ethical questions to be voiced as the decision-making effort unfolds. Perverse incentives get people to adopt a defensive posture that blocks learning how to improve decision-making. Perverse incentives must be rooted out and a win-win environment created before learning can occur.

READING 2

# The Art of High-Stakes Decision-Making: Tough Calls in a Speed-Driven World

*J. KEITH MURNIGHAN*
*and JOHN C. MOWEN*

*Summary prepared by Linda Rochford*

**Linda Rochford** *is Associate Professor of Marketing at the University of Minnesota Duluth. Her interests include formulating and implementing marketing strategy and the development and marketing of new products. Her work has been published in such outlets as the* Journal of Product Innovation Management *and the* Journal of the Academy of Marketing Science. *She has held various technical, marketing, and management positions for 3M and Cargill. She earned her Ph.D. in Marketing, M.B.A. and B.S. in Chemistry from the University of Minnesota.*

## ◆ INTRODUCTION

Managers can benefit from a systematic method for making *high stakes decisions—those nonroutine, high-risk decisions, often made under time pressure with ambiguous or incomplete information, that have serious consequences.* Equally important, managers need to recognize barriers to effective decision-making. Awareness of these barriers is the first step in making sound decisions.

SCRIPTS is an acronym for a seven-step process for making sound, high stakes decisions. It includes these phases:

1. *Search* for signals of threats and opportunities.
2. Find the *causes.*

J. Keith Murnighan and John C. Mowen, *The Art of High-Stakes Decision Making: Tough Calls in a Speed-Driven World.* New York: John Wiley & Sons, 2002.

3. Evaluate the *risks.*
4. Apply *intuition* and emotion.
5. Take different *perspectives.*
6. Consider the *time* frame.
7. *Solve* the problem.

To truly appreciate this structured method, it's important to understand the conditions that impede good decision-making and how the seven-step process is designed to minimize or eliminate these impediments.

## EXAMINING THE STEPS

### IS THERE A PROBLEM?

The first step is searching for signals of threats and opportunities. The process of accurately identifying the problem is critical for good decision-making. The most basic issue here is whether there in fact even *is* a problem. Is the decision-maker actually facing a threat or opportunity? Decision-makers face four possible scenarios. They may:

- Correctly diagnose that a problem exists and take action to solve the problem.
- Correctly determine that no problem exists and take no action.
- Mistakenly decide a problem exists and take action when there really is no problem, resulting in a "needless blunder."
- Mistakenly ignore a problem that exists and fail to take action, producing a "missed opportunity."

The challenge is to avoid "needless blunders" and "missed opportunities." Even if a decision-maker is fortunate enough to avoid these pitfalls, there is still the danger of getting behind the *power curve.* The power curve refers to the compounding effects of delaying action. A familiar example is the huge long-term difference between investing a fixed amount for retirement at age 25 versus 45. The total amount of interest earned favors early investors and penalizes those that wait until later. Because reaching a decision, acting on that decision, and seeing results from the action all take time, there is a time lag before the intended effect is realized. The size of the lag increases to a point beyond which it is simply not possible to catch up. This produces a *zone of false hope,* the point at which action has been taken too late to have an impact on the problem. For example, failing to respond in a timely fashion to a new product introduction from a competitor can put a company in the zone of false hope where there is no chance of recapturing the ground lost in the market, and the odds of success for the firm have dropped significantly.

### THRESHOLD FOR ACTION

The power curve and the need for timely problem identification and action raise the issue of how to set the threshold for action, or "set the trigger" for decision-making. The trigger metaphor illustrates how decision-makers have to weigh the amount of evidence or information necessary before taking action. A "sticky trigger" requires a preponderance of evidence before acting—for example, the decision to go to war should require a sticky trigger because of the tremendous political, economic, and human risks and consequences from taking such action. A "hair trigger" might be set for a decision where the failure to act has great consequences. A "hair trigger" might be set for product recall where the public's safety is at risk. Johnson and Johnson's handling of the Tylenol product tampering is a situation where it was better for them to overreact to protect the public (and they did just that). Johnson and Johnson's handling of the Tylenol situation—a combination of rapid product recall and production of a tamper resistant package—may have seemed costly and extreme at the time, but because of the rapid and extensive action taken on the problem, public trust in the Tylenol brand was quickly re-established and even strengthened. Finally, a "neutral trigger" is set for problems where it is not necessary to be neither particularly conservative, nor particularly aggressive in response.

## BARRIERS TO SOUND DECISION-MAKING

One of the biggest challenges faced by decision-makers is the tendency to overestimate the probability of success. The *overconfidence bias* blinds managers to signals of threats, increasing the risk of making an error in one of two ways: (1) failing to collect necessary information, and (2) influencing how the trigger is set. In other words, since overconfident people assume that things will turn out well, they are lax in their search for opportunities and threats in the situation analysis. They tend to underestimate the risk of the threats and overestimate the odds of success in exploiting opportunities or overcoming threats.

Decision-makers fall into this trap when they base decisions on incomplete information—the *illusion of correlation* (e.g., focusing on the number of correct forecasts by Wall Street pundits rather than asking how many of the forecasts were incorrect). A dramatic example of failing to look at all of the information is demonstrated by the Challenger spacecraft disaster. NASA decision makers looked at O-ring failure caused by burn-through from the rocket fuel at different launch temperatures. However, they didn't consider the other half of the picture—how often was there no burn-through at different launch temperatures. When the complete picture is examined, what looked like almost equal odds of having failure above and below 65 degrees launch temperature produced a radically different outcome—100 percent failures at lower temperatures and about a 20 percent chance of failure above the temperature threshold.

Once threats and opportunities have been identified, the SCRIPTS model calls for determining the underlying cause. Treating a symptom of a problem rather than taking action on the underlying cause will only delay solution and risk getting behind the power curve. A single cause can generate many symptoms, may share symptoms with other causes, and there may be more than one root cause, particularly for high-stakes decisions. In other words, determining causality can be very difficult. Most high stakes problems are caused by a number of complex factors. What otherwise might be a fairly benign event can act as a tripwire on this set of complex factors to create a serious and dramatic event. The *tipping point* is the threshold event—often a seemingly trivial or minor factor—that pushes the system into failure.

Decision-makers must guard against *illusions of causality,* inaccurately attributing causes to problems. An example of the illusion of causality is the *illusion of perfor-*

*mance*—giving oneself credit for good outcomes and attributing poor outcomes to anyone else in greater proportion than is merited by the facts. Another example is *hindsight bias* that leads decision-makers to retrospectively overestimate how well a problem or outcomes from a problem could have been anticipated.

One technique for identifying problem causes is *root-cause analysis.* A fundamental part of root-cause analysis is dissecting the sequence of events leading up to the problem including both human decision-making and physical systems and processes.

After identifying the problem and its cause, the consequences of taking action—risk assessment—should be considered. Risks can include social or monetary risk for the decision-maker, risk to life and health, information risk, as well as catastrophic "sink the boat" risk. Risk analysis helps to determine where the threshold for action—the decision trigger—is set.

Risk assessment can be plagued by distortions of probability estimates and outcome evaluations. Distortions can occur for a number of reasons. More recent, more familiar, or more vivid, information is more easily accessible and remembered—the *availability bias*—making this the information that is inappropriately used in determining potential outcomes. The law of decreasing margin effect suggests that the first loss or gain has more impact than subsequent losses or gains. Consequently, decision-makers are apt to take more risks to try to break a losing streak—often taking reckless chances—and are very conservative about making decisions that could risk interrupting a winning streak. Decision-makers can also be blinded to very real risks by "summit fever"—the temptation to achieve their goals so tantalizingly close that very unreasonable risks are undertaken.

## USING INTUITION AND MULTIPLE PERSPECTIVES

Relying on intuition for high stakes decisions seems risky. However, intuition can be valuable if used carefully. Intuition can be used to validate decisions made using rational decision-making or when the rational decision-making process does not lead to a clear decision. Intuition may be the only option in crisis situations where there is no time for a more time consuming, rational process. The systematic decision model calls for the use of guided intuition to make fast, experienced based decisions under very short time deadlines.

It makes sense to look at problems and potential decisions through various frames of reference to counteract the normal tendency to confirm one's own frame or perspective. Multiple professional perspectives should be used to help place the decision-maker in the role of other organizational stakeholders—such as engineering, production, legal, accounting, marketing, and even competitors—and to ensure that the ethical dimensions of the decision are fully explored.

## IT'S ABOUT TIME

One of the most interesting challenges in decision-making is how managers use and view time. High stakes decisions are often characterized by time pressure. Different cultures may view time as a linear concept—one event following the next in a sequential fashion. Most western cultures consider time linear. Other organizational cultures—agricultural societies, academic institutions—view time as circular because the same sequence of events takes place year after year. Procedural time is perhaps the most unpredictable because the ending point is dependent on completing a particular process where unforeseen circumstances can compress or extend the time needed to finish a process. An example of procedural time is a surgery. Even if the average length of time for a procedure is two hours, the surgery isn't finished until all of the necessary procedures have been completed which could vary considerably around the average. Consider the frustration of a linear time–oriented individual working in a circular time–oriented organization. The linear oriented individual may be frustrated that more speed and effort is not put into solving problems that the organization may consider as temporary and cyclical.

Even without different perspectives on time, decision-makers face time traps. Time traps are the present versus future time trade offs made in confronting problems. Decision myopia, time snares, and time fences are all examples of time traps.

*Decision myopia* is associated with over-valuing present outcomes over future outcomes. These managers want immediate gratification. This can lead to short-term thinking at the expense of the long-term health of the individual or organization. *Time snares* are related to decision myopia. Time-snared decision-makers let short-term positive outcomes cause an action that leads to long-term negative outcomes. For example, General Mills was criticized for boosting quarterly sales by shipping much larger orders to customers than the customer had asked for. At some point, customers will rebel against carrying extra inventory, and this can affect the buyer-seller relationship. Sales may drop significantly as customers simply don't need to or want to buy any more goods.

*Time fences,* on the other hand, occur when an action that would lead to long-term gains is stopped because it also causes short-term negative outcomes. For example, the political will to balance the federal budget almost always runs up against a time fence. Most politicians do not want to face the short-term sacrifices needed in order to achieve the longer range benefit.

High stakes decisions often must be made under time pressure. Time pressure creates a number of effects on decision-makers that can make for poorer decisions. For example, decision-makers under time pressure will increase the speed with which they process information for a decision, but they will compensate by reducing the amount of information considered. Decision-makers under fire will also tend to let emotions carry them away, which interferes with more rational analysis or guided intuition. To minimize the negative effects of time pressure on crisis decision-making, organizations should pre-plan responses to potential problems and utilize dress rehearsals of crisis situations to practice responses.

## SOLVING THE PROBLEM

The entire SCRIPTS process culminates with solving the problem. The first step in solving the problem is setting the threshold for action. The *risk ratio* is used to quantitatively set the trigger and is defined as follows:

$$\text{Risk ratio} = \frac{\text{the value of a needless blunder}}{(\text{the value of a needless blunder}) + (\text{the value of a missed opportunity})}$$

The risk ratio is then adjusted qualitatively based on each of the risk factors identified previously. This is an important step, as not all risks can be assigned financial values.

The second step in solving the problem is to determine the probability of successfully responding to the problem. This is accomplished by identifying the specific actions and milestones that need to take place, as well as the probability of achieving each of these. The conditional probability is calculated to compute the overall probability of achieving the expected outcome across multiple milestones. The results of such an estimate are often sobering due to the tendency to overlook the conditional nature of the outcome.

The last step in solving the problem is to compare the likelihood of success to the risk ratio. This is called the *confidence margin.* The decision-maker should not proceed if the likelihood of success is less than the risk ratio (i.e., if the confidence margin is negative). If multiple alternatives have positive confidence margins, the alternative with the greatest confidence margin should be the best choice.

## Conclusion

Novice and veteran decision-makers can learn and gain from examining their past decision-making experiences as a vehicle for developing new ways of thinking. Master decision-makers practice their decision-making on lower stakes decisions in order to learn from the process. Then, when a real crisis arises, they can have a higher expectation of responding coolly and creatively. This is perhaps one of the most valuable lessons and benefits of practicing a systematic problem-solving and decision-making process.

# Managing Crises Before They Happen

**_IAN I. MITROFF, with GUS ANAGNOS_**

**_Summary prepared by Allen Harmon_**

***Allen Harmon*** *is president and general manager of WDSE-TV, the community licensed PBS member station serving Northeastern Minnesota and Northwestern Wisconsin. Before joining WDSE, Mr. Harmon held a series of senior management positions in a regional investor-owned electric utility. He earned an MBA from Indiana University and has completed the University of Minnesota Carlson School of Management Executive Development Program. He has served as an adjunct instructor in the School of Business and Economics at the University of Minnesota Duluth (an experience that heightened his respect for academia).*

Since 1900, there have been 28 major industrial accidents in which 50 or more people have lost their lives. Nearly half of those accidents have occurred in the last 15 years. Crises, from Bhopal and Columbine to the Exxon Valdez and ValuJet, no longer seem as much aberrations as they do an integral feature of our modern information systems society. They have become a part of our language, recalling an entire chain of events with a single word.

In 1982, five people died as a result of taking poisoned Tylenol capsules. The perpetrators were never caught. The event marked the opening of a new discipline, crisis management (CM); Tylenol maker Johnson & Johnson's reaction to the situation became the field's first benchmark. It is impossible to know for sure what forces kept others from pursuing the skills needed in a world where crisis is commonplace. Johnson & Johnson appears still to believe that no amount of prior planning could have better prepared them for such a crisis. With the benefit now of nearly 20 years of experience, crisis managers disagree. Although the qualities demonstrated under fire by Johnson & Johnson's management—commitment to values, managerial skill, and candor—are necessary to successful crisis management, they alone are not sufficient to assure success.

Ian I. Mitroff, with Gus Anagnos, *Managing Crises Before They Happen: What Every Manager Needs to Know about Crisis Management.* New York: American Management Association, 2001.

## WHAT IS CRISIS MANAGEMENT?

Distinct from the disciplines of emergency and risk management, which deal with natural disasters, CM focuses primarily on man-made crises: environmental contamination, fraud, product tampering, and other products of human failings. Unlike natural disasters, these events are not inevitable. Neither are they fully preventable. Crisis management is a system of planning, preparing, and acting to substantially limit both the duration and damage caused by these crises, with the objective of allowing the company to recover from crisis more quickly and with less lasting damage. The practice of CM goes far beyond the popular perception that it is simply a matter of controlling media relations. Like environmentalism or TQM, CM done well is done by the organization systemically. Like these other systemwide initiatives, the linkages formed in implementing CM systemically can produce additional benefits for the organization, and require senior management's embrace to be effected.

## A BEST PRACTICES METHOD

Five elements comprise a best practices model of crisis management; each element must be managed before, during, and after the crisis event. Organizations should view the model as a benchmark for their own CM effort.

### IDENTIFYING CRISIS TYPES AND THEIR RISKS

Every organization needs to plan for at least one crisis in each of seven types or families of crises, because each type can happen to any organization:

- **Economic:** Strike or labor unrest, labor shortage, stock price or earnings decline, market crash
- **Informational:** Loss of confidential or proprietary information, false information, tampering with computer records
- **Physical:** Loss of key physical plant or equipment
- **Human resource:** Loss of key personnel, acts of workplace violence or vandalism, rise in accidents or absenteeism
- **Reputational:** Damage to corporate image, rumors, gossip, slander
- **Psychopathic acts:** Product tampering, hostage taking or kidnapping, terrorist acts
- **Natural disasters:** Fire, flood, earthquake, explosions

Although the exact situation the organization will encounter will rarely be the one for which a plan has been developed (and will often be a combination of several problems occurring simultaneously as a crisis in one family often sets in motion one in another), the critical benefit to the organization comes from thinking about the unthinkable before it happens. Having done so by itself improves the organization's ability to avoid paralysis when the unthinkable occurs.

Preparing for at least one crisis of each type enhances traditional risk management techniques, which tend to focus on preparing for reoccurrence of events the organization has already experienced.

## DEVELOPING MECHANISMS FOR MANAGING CRISES

Having a crisis management plan is not as important as the capability to deal with crises, which is usually developed through the creation of the plan. The planning process provides a mechanism for anticipating crises; other mechanisms are needed to sense and react to crisis, contain the damage, then learn from and redesign effective organizational procedures for dealing with future crises.

It is in learning and redesign, the most important of these mechanisms, that organizations' crisis management performance most often comes up short. Except in cases of criminal acts or negligence, the goal of the crisis postmortem should be no fault learning that will better prepare the organization for the next event.

## UNDERSTANDING THE SYSTEMS THAT GOVERN ORGANIZATIONAL BEHAVIOR

Understanding any complex organization requires developing an appreciation for its technology, structure, human factors, culture, and ultimately the psychology of its top management. Each impacts the organization's ability to deal with crisis before, during, and after the event.

Technology, the most visible part of many organizations, does not exist in a vacuum. No matter how reliable the technology, it is operated by humans who, over time, are likely to make intentional or unintentional errors. Human factors engineering can reduce, but not eliminate, the potential for those errors to create crisis. The structure of a complex organization creates additional "errors" that affect the organization's crisis management performance. By creating opportunities (or even incentives) to distort information, the organization's structure can help or hinder the delivery of the right information to the right people in the organization so that the right decisions can be made. When these factors do not work appropriately, critical time can be lost in dealing with the crisis.

Deeper within the organization lie its culture and the psychology of its top management. Like individuals, organizations are prone to resorting to defense mechanisms to deny vulnerability; the defense mechanisms employed by organizations mirror the classic Freudian mechanisms used by individuals. The extent to which these defensive mechanisms are at work in the organization will determine the organization's receptiveness to crisis management.

## DEVELOPING RELATIONS WITH STAKEHOLDERS

Effective response to crisis requires coordination and cooperation among a wide range of internal and external parties, from the organization's employees to local, state, and national authorities. The development of relationships and sharing of plans among these stakeholders must be attended to years in advance if the organization is to develop the capabilities required for smooth operation in the face of a major crisis.

## ASSESSING CM CAPABILITIES THROUGH THE USE OF SCENARIOS

A good crisis scenario—a plan for how the unthinkable will occur—is the final element of the model. It tests the organization's CM capability, how the other four elements perform. A "good" scenario involves the occurrence of a chain reaction of events that the organization has not previously considered at the worst possible of times, and contemplates the failure of the most predictable of systems.

## BEFORE THE CRISIS: DETECTING ITS SIGNALS

Effective crisis management is more than reaction to the crisis once it occurs; it requires anticipating the crisis while there is still time to avert it. Fortunately, all crises send out a repeated train of early warning signals. If those signals can be detected, separated from the organizational noise, amplified and acted upon, many crises could be averted. Thus, effective crisis management requires that the organization develop appropriate detectors for the variety of signals that may presage crisis and have in place a means to react.

Different types of potential crises will emit different sorts of signals, and the organization must be prepared to detect them all. For example, we would expect the signals that foreshadow a product tampering incident to be different from those preceding a major equipment failure. Early warning signals can be differentiated along two dimensions: their source (internal or external) and their type (technical or people). In general the four resulting types apply to organizations of all types. Organizations need to develop receptors for each signal type from internal technical signals, such as the output of a process control system, to external people signals, such as a complaint from neighbors that something at the plant doesn't smell right. Any such signal could be the key to averting a crisis!

Once the signal is detected, the organization must have in place a mechanism for acting on it. A signal that does not relate to the normal operating repertoire may be seen by many, but not acted upon if no one knows what to do about it. In the aftermath of most crises, it usually turns out that at least one person in the organization knew about an impending crisis. Too often, that person lacked the power to bring the issue to the attention of the organization. Open lines of communication and clear reporting sequences for problem signs (and for parts of problem signs, as it may take information from several sources to put together the whole picture), an emphasis on safety, and a culture that rewards signal detection are all elements of effective crisis management.

If an organization takes but one step toward implementing crisis management, the development of signal detection capabilities throughout the organization is the one it should take. In many cases sensors and supporting databases are already in place, and need only be reconceptualized to play a role in CM.

## TELLING THE TRUTH

Telling the truth plays a central role in dealing with all crises. Because the human-caused crises with which CM is concerned are in principle preventable, the public is often rightly outraged when they occur. Revealing anything less than the truth to avoid acknowledging responsibility only feeds the public's rage, extending the crisis and increasing the damage done.

It is folly to assume that there is today such a thing as a secret. The voracious appetite of the modern 24 hours a day, 365 days a year news media eliminates any assurance that what is said behind closed doors will remain there. New technologies allow for intrusion into even the most private nooks and crannies of our lives. To believe that one's secrets can be kept is self-delusional. The question is no longer *whether* our worst and darkest secrets will be revealed for public scrutiny, but *when,* under what *circumstances,* and by *whom.* The issue for the crisis manager is not whether to tell the truth, but how much of the truth to tell, and when.

When faced with the classic reporter's three-part question "When did you first know about the problem, what did you do about it, and if you didn't know about it, why not?" how should the crisis manager respond? The answer: With nothing but the truth, and with as much of the truth as is required to put an end to the crisis (which is probably far more than one is comfortable revealing). Better yet, of course, is for the crisis manager to preempt the reporter's question altogether by choosing to reveal the same information on one's own terms.

Does the crisis manager "tell all"? No, there *is* a limit. The revelations stop after what is needed to put an end to the crisis is said, before the world hears what it wants to gloat over.

## ◆ VICTIMS AND VILLAINS

In the aftermath of almost all human-caused crises there are but two possible outcomes. The organization involved will either be perceived as a *victim,* or it will be perceived as the *villain.* The line between the two is drawn by the creativity and character the organization displays in dealing with the crisis. Over time, most individuals and organizations embroiled in crises tend to be perceived as villains; maintaining the role of victim requires continual, ongoing effort.

Victims are those organizations or persons to whom harm is done, whether intentional or not. One who unintentionally or unknowingly causes harm to another, or does harm despite doing everything possible to avert it, is also potentially a victim. Villains are responsible for knowingly allowing or causing harm to another. Repentant villains acknowledge the wrong they have done and take measures to correct it. Other villains deny what they did to avoid responsibility; the most loathsome of villains pose as victims themselves, and therefore by their denial of responsibility they set off more crises.

In seeking the most positive outcome for the organization, the crisis manager clearly wants to avoid being associated with the vilest of villains. That requires first, recognizing and acknowledging the true victim of the situation and avoiding the temptation to cast oneself in the role. Second, the organization must assume responsibility for its action or inaction in the situation.

How the organization communicates the acceptance of its responsibility bears on the outcome of the crisis situation. Technical explanations may be true, but will be seen to most outsiders as an effective dodge of responsibility. The logic that works within the organization may seem completely illogical to outsiders; in responding to the crisis, the organization must see the crisis from the perspective of the true victim. The organization must be aware of and responsive to the emotional reactions of the true victims. In the course of dealing with the crisis, the organization must be sensitive to the potential for alienating victims, customers, or shareholders by actions that solve the problem for the organization, but not for other stakeholders.

## CREATIVITY IN CRISIS MANAGEMENT

Crisis management is most effective when viewed not as implementation of a set of process steps, but instead as an exercise in creative problem solving. Organizations that nurture and encourage creativity—thinking "outside the box"—are those most likely to succeed in managing crisis situations. Similarly, those organizations that can successfully integrate critical quantitative thinking and emotional intelligence, not just "walking in their stakeholders' shoes" but "getting inside their heads" to know what they consider important, are most likely to find solutions to crisis situations that satisfy all stakeholders.

Along the way, organizations need to ask whether they truly understand the crisis from the stakeholders' perspective. Too often crisis management efforts have been directed to solving the wrong problem—the problem as seen from the organization's perspective.

## THINKING SYSTEMICALLY

The disproportionate number of the twentieth century's major industrial accidents, occurring in the last 15 years, yields a clue that the world has indeed changed. Our society has become more complex, and our interactions are more tangled. Today's problems require systems thinking if we are to formulate them for effective solution. In today's society, it is difficult to identify simple cause-effect relationships, because one thing rarely causes another. Instead, any particular effect is the result of a number of contributing factors. So, too, it is with crises. Managing crisis requires identification of the full range of factors that contribute to one's situation in order to formulate an effective response.

Given the complexity of the systems with which the crisis manager must deal, it is important to assess the effect of proposed corrective actions to ensure that they won't in fact make matters worse.

# Ethics and Values

PART

# XII

Almost daily, newspaper and television reports appear that document unethical activities engaged in by organizations, their executives, and their employees. The corporate world has been rocked by reports of scandal and corruption. Simultaneously, the past several years have seen an increase in the number of schools of business that have introduced ethics courses into their curricula. A large number of organizations are actively discussing ethical behavior, developing codes of conduct or codes of ethics, and making statements about the core values of their organizations.

A number of books have explored the ethical dilemmas that managers face, the core principles that guide ethical decision-making, and the need for linking corporate strategy and ethical reasoning. However, questions still surround which values ethical leaders should hold, and how those values could be conveyed to their employees. The four books represented in this part address the need for managers to be ethical and credible.

James M. Kouzes and Barry Z. Posner surveyed 15,000 managers, analyzed 400 case studies, and interviewed 40 managers prior to writing *Credibility,* their second major book on leadership. (Their earlier work was *The Leadership Challenge.*) They discovered that employees want their leaders to be honest, forward-looking, inspiring, competent, and supportive. Most-admired leaders were highly principled, held clear and strong values, were optimistic and hopeful, and demonstrated their belief in the worth of others. Kouzes and Posner urge readers to strengthen their credibility through a continuous internal dialogue, staying in touch with their constituents, developing others' capacities, affirming shared values, and sustaining employee hopes. Kouzes is president of TPG/Learning Systems, and Barry Posner is professor of organizational behavior at Santa Clara University. Another book by Kouzes and Posner is *Encouraging the Heart.*

Greed and corporate corruption is the backdrop for the second reading in this section on ethics and values. *Saving the Corporate Soul & (Who Knows?) Maybe Your Own* was written by David Batstone. Mr. Batstone was a founding editor of the magazine *Business 2.0* and a contributor to several newspapers (*The New York Times, Chicago Tribune, San Francisco Chronicle*). His writings have focused on ethics, business, spirituality, and culture. In this book, Mr. Batstone discusses eight principles for the creation and preservation of integrity and profitability. A central theme of the book, as captured in its title, suggests that corporate and personal success can be achieved without the "sacrifice of one's soul." Confronting the current furor over corporate irresponsibility, Batstone talks about what is necessary for the revitalization of today's corporations and the people who manage them.

Warren G. Bennis joins Robert J. Thomas in the authorship of *Geeks and Geezers: How Era, Values, and Defining Moments Shape Leaders.* Warren Bennis is professor and founding chairman of The Leadership Institute at the University of Southern California. He has made the study of leadership a major vocation, having authored twenty-seven books on leadership and change. His co-author, Robert J. Thomas, is an associate partner and senior fellow with the Accenture Institute for Strategic Change. He is also the author of *What Machines Can't Do.* Bennis and Thomas have also collaborated on the book *Crucibles for Leadership.*

*Geeks and Geezers* presents a detailed description and differentiation between the leadership philosophy and style of our youngest and oldest leaders. The Geeks (the youngest leaders) are under the age of thirty-five; they matured in front of the computer screen during the dot.com era. The Geezers (our oldest leaders) are over the age of seventy and matured during the Great Depression and World War II. The authors discuss the processes through which each of these leader groups emerged, and the role which that era played in shaping their vales and leadership styles. It appears as though regardless of one's generation, virtually every leader has experienced at least one transformational experience—what is called a "crucible"—a make-or-break experience and a significant leadership defining event.

*Authentic Leadership: Rediscovering the Secrets to Creating Lasting Value* is the last reading in this section on ethics and values. Drawing upon his twenty-year leadership position at Medtronics, a world-leading medical technology company, Mr. George offers lessons on leading with heart and compassion—a guide for character-based leadership. He identifies what he believes to be five essential dimensions of authentic leadership—purpose, values, heart, relationships, and self-discipline—and discusses how they can be developed.

Bill George, the author of *Authentic Leadership,* is the former chairman and CEO of Medtronics. The Academy of Management recognized Mr. George as Executive of the Year, and the National Association of Corporate Directors and *Business Week* recognized him as Director of the Year. Currently, he serves as executive-in-residence at Yale University and sits on the boards of Goldman Sachs, Novartis, and Target.

# Credibility

*JAMES M. KOUZES and BARRY Z. POSNER*

*Summary prepared by Gregory R. Fox*

***Gregory R. Fox*** *is the Vice Chancellor for Finance and Operations at the University of Minnesota Duluth. He earned his master's degree at the University of Washington, and received a Bush Mid-Career Leadership Fellowship. He has developed instructional support materials for the Newstrom and Bittel book* Supervision: Managing for Results.

Leadership is many things—a series of actions, an encounter between people, an intangible, a performing art. Leadership does not, and cannot, exist independently, for it is a *reciprocal relationship* between those who choose to lead and those who decide to follow. There have been dramatic changes in the nature of the relationship between leader and subordinate (employer-employee) during the past decade. Most significant has been an increased awareness of the leader's need to serve others, to build seamless partnerships with others, and to build a community of individuals and teams at work. Wise leaders have become servers, supporters, partners, and providers, building their relationships on mutual obligations, commitments, and collaboration. This changing leader-follower relationship increasingly creates *servant leaders* who value the role of serving, and giving to, those with whom they work.

## ◆ KEY LEADERSHIP CHARACTERISTICS

In a survey, 15,000 managers were asked to identify their seven most admired leadership characteristics from a set of twenty qualities. The results of the survey, subsequent case studies, and in-depth interviews were remarkably consistent. The most desirable characteristics (those selected by more than half of the respondents) identified for leaders were honest, forward-looking, inspiring, and competent. *Honesty appears to be essential to leadership,* with 87 percent of the respondents selecting that characteristic.

Results also suggest that *competence* (being capable, effective, challenging, and encouraging), while still widely cherished as a leader characteristic, *is valued somewhat less today than in the past.* This could be seen as a cause for concern if companies start being led by visionary and inspirational individuals who do not have the complex skills needed to implement their visions. In contrast to the decline in valuing competence, the leader quality that has increased most in value during the last ten years is

---

James M. Kouzes & Barry Z. Posner, *Credibility: How Leaders Gain It and Lose It, Why People Demand It.* San Francisco: Jossey-Bass, 1993.

*supportiveness.* This characteristic originally ranked eleventh and now ranks sixth overall as an admired leadership attribute. This change reflects a strong societal trend toward empowerment, and indicates that people are searching for more understanding and encouragement from their leaders.

The qualities of honesty (trustworthiness), inspiration (dynamism), and competence (expertise) in combination are often referred to as source credibility. *Credibility is believed to be the primary foundation of future global leadership,* although it has often been overlooked in the past.

Studies done by Lou Harris, The Opinion Research Corporation, and others suggest that there is a significant gap between the value that constituents place on credibility and the likeliness it will occur in their place of work. The recent savings and loan and Wall Street scandals and religious fraud have led to a sense of betrayal and public disillusionment. Fueling this disillusionment have been recent reports of chief executive officer compensation at up to 150 times the level of the average worker in manufacturing and service industries. When employees believe that management does not "walk their talk," a *credibility gap*—a strong sense of cynicism—occurs, which weakens the bond that is required for effective leadership.

Earning credibility is done one-to-one, a little at a time, through personal contact with constituents. Managers are encouraged to "Do what you say you will do"—and then substitute "we" for "you" in that motto to build a bond with those they are serving. Three critical elements for strengthening leader credibility are clarity, unity, and intensity. *Clarification* of values, visions, and aims helps others understand the guiding principles. *Unity* is the degree to which people understand, agree on, and support the clarified values and directions. *Intensity* is the strength of commitment to deeply held aims and aspirations.

When leaders demonstrate credibility through clarity, unity, and intensity, workers tend to feel enthusiastically motivated, challenged and inspired, capable and powerful, as well as respected, valued, and proud. The predictable employee outcomes of these feelings include pride in belonging, strong team spirit, congruence of personal and organizational values, organizational commitment, and sense of ownership. Credible leadership stimulates employees to contribute their time and talents to a common purpose.

## THE SIX DISCIPLINES

Leaders earn credibility, respect, and loyalty when they demonstrate that they believe in the self-worth of others. Leaders must appreciate others, affirm others, and develop others. They must demonstrate these behaviors persistently and tenaciously. Through the study of leaders and leadership, six disciplines that underlie credibility emerge. They are as follows (see additional details in Table 1):

- Discovering yourself (clarifying your values)
- Appreciating constituents (talking and listening to them)
- Affirming shared values (striving for consensus and community)
- Developing constituents' capacity (constantly educating)
- Serving a purpose (becoming servant leaders)
- Sustaining hope (maintaining energy and optimism)

**TABLE 1** The Six Leadership Disciplines

| ***Discovering Yourself*** ***Leaders Should*** | ***Developing Capacity*** ***Leaders Should*** |
|---|---|
| Keep a journal | Stop making decisions |
| Discover their life themes | Stop talking at staff meetings |
| Assess their values | Set up coaching opportunities |
| Audit their ability to succeed | Invite people to assume responsibility |
| Seek mastery experiences | Give everyone a customer |
| Ask for support or help | Have an open house |
| Evaluate the five "Ps" of personal mission: | Share the big picture |
| • Proficiency | Enrich people's jobs |
| • Product | Let constituents be the teachers |
| • People | Use modeling to develop competencies |
| • Place | |
| • Purpose | |
| ***Appreciating Constituents and Their Diversity*** ***Leaders Should*** | ***Serving a Purpose*** ***Leaders Should*** |
| Be accessible, even at home | Manage by storytelling |
| Listen everywhere and listen well | Create heroes |
| Learn your constituents' stories | Speak with confidence |
| Step outside your cultural experience | Reduce fear |
| Keep in touch with your constituents | Ask questions |
| Become an employee for a day | Hold yourself accountable |
| Be the first to take a risk | Keep score |
| Know what bugs your constituents | Conduct a personal audit |
| Practice small wins | Conduct an organization audit |
| | Get everyone to champion values |
| ***Affirming Shared Values*** ***Leaders Should*** | ***Sustaining Hope*** ***Leaders Should*** |
| Get together to start drafting your group's credo | Exercise |
| Make sure there is an agreement around values | Write your vision for the future |
| Conduct a values survey | Set goals and make a plan |
| Connect values with reasons | Choose flexible optimism |
| Structure cooperative goals | Suffer first |
| Make sure everyone knows the business | Nurture optimism and passion |
| Be an enthusiastic spokesperson for shared values | Go visiting |
| Say "yes" frequently | Dispute your negative beliefs |
| Go slow to go fast | Reclarify your values |
| Establish a sunset statute for your credo | |

## SELF-DISCOVERY

A review of those individuals who are identified as the most admired leaders reveals that they are people who are highly principled, with strong beliefs. Their individual values clarify what they will or will not do, directly contributing to their credibility as leaders. In addition, strong personal values assist in resolving conflicts and serve to motivate others.

Those interested in leadership are encouraged to write their own personal leadership philosophy and then evaluate what has been written. This assessment is aimed at identifying the values that are expressed in this credo. Exercises like this make it possible for those interested in the study of leadership to assess what values are most evident in effective leaders.

Another important characteristic associated with self-discovery is developing confidence and self-efficacy. This requires identifying the skills, knowledge, and abilities that are necessary to represent the values you claim with moral force. Effective leaders identify the skills necessary for their job. They acquire competence (mastery) in each of these areas and then expand the skills they have to be more effective in a wide variety of circumstances. They observe successful role models, seek social support from others, and manage the stresses in their lives. Then they seek to exhibit optimal performance, or *flow,* through goal setting, becoming immersed in their roles, avoiding distraction through intense attention to the present, and learning to enjoy their current activities.

## APPRECIATING CONSTITUENTS

Effective leaders recognize that organizations (and individuals) are enriched through diversity. They seek to create cultures where each person values and affirms others, relationships are collaborative, co-workers develop a sense of shared history, and the whole person (work and family elements) is recognized. These leaders keep their minds open, appreciate the uniqueness in others, solicit and use feedback from others, trust others, and stimulate constructive controversy.

## AFFIRMING SHARED VALUES

Leaders seek a common core of understanding—an identification of shared values and consensus around paradigms. They struggle to identify common ground, they advocate cooperative community of purpose, and they foster consensus around key issues. They create drafts of underlying creeds, and demonstrate flexibility as revisions are sought and made.

## DEVELOPING CAPACITY

Credible leaders believe in the abilities of others to grow and develop. They empower others through distributed leadership; they provide educational opportunities for building others' knowledge and skill; they encourage a sense of ownership in employees; and they inspire confidence in employee abilities to act responsibly and capably. They invite employees to accept mutual responsibility for results, and share information and feedback that allows others to grow.

## SERVING A PURPOSE

Leaders must have a strong sense of faith in what they are doing, and why. They recognize their servant leader role and set examples that others can follow. They are visibly "out front" demonstrating their priorities, staying in touch with their constituents, and making an impression on others through storytelling, "utilizing the teachable moment" when others are particularly susceptible to learning, and standing up for their beliefs. Perhaps most importantly, they create enduring organizational systems and structures that reinforce and support their values long after the leader has departed.

### SUSTAINING HOPE

People struggle. People get discouraged. People lose hope. These are moments when credible leaders need to be proactive, demonstrating that it is possible to regain internal control over external events. Leaders can inspire others to take initiative courageously, to balance hope and work for reasonable results, and to enjoy themselves along the path. And leaders are encouraged to demonstrate the acceptability of being caring, loving, and compassionate in the workplace so as to inspire others to do so, too.

## Conclusion

Currently, the work world is experiencing a fundamental restructuring. There are no guarantees that a perfectly executed leadership plan will result in a satisfying, successful worklife. Credible leaders, those most in touch with their constituents, feel the pain most strongly. Leaders seeking to establish their credibility are urged to develop understanding and learn to love the struggle. But a caveat is in order: *Excessive emphasis on any one of the six disciplines can damage a leader's credibility.*

Leaders can strengthen their credibility by engaging in a dialogue about the fundamental tension between freedom and constraint. In nearly every workplace, more freedom is becoming commonplace; at the same time, institutions will continue to have some sharp constraints. The dialogue will focus on questions of how many, how much, and what type.

The success of leaders should be measured by whether they left their organization a better place than they found it. To respond to the organizational struggle, credible leaders need to be optimistic, hopeful, and inspiring. They need to discover their own selves, appreciate the diversity of others, and recognize that renewing credibility is a continuous struggle. They need to take risks, accept the associated pain and excitement, and revel in the exhilaration of becoming continual learners about what it means to be leaders. In short, they need to be credible—to themselves and to others.

READING 2

# Saving the Corporate Soul & (Who Knows?) Maybe Your Own

***DAVID BATSTONE***

***Summary prepared by Gary P. Olson***

***Gary P. Olson*** *is Executive Director of the Center for Alcohol and Drug Treatment, Duluth, Minnesota. He is responsible for the overall direction of this regional nonprofit corporation. His areas of interest include corporate strategy, employee participation, and effectiveness. He received his M.B.A. from the University of Minnesota Duluth.*

## ◆ INTRODUCTION

Public concern over corporate irresponsibility is deep and widespread. Corporate scandals have filled the headlines, ruined careers, and bankrupted retirement accounts. Yet millions of workers, from clerks to executives, rely on corporations for their livelihood and investors count on them to grow and prosper. At the same time, public markets have had unrealistic expectations for growth, leading to a short-term vision by executives and compromising long-term sustainability.

Ultimately, the confidence and trust of employees and the public are as important to the success of the corporation as quarterly performance. This can only be achieved and maintained when the corporation acts in a principled way. Substantial evidence supports the notion that principled corporations outperform the market over the long term. A principled company will strengthen its reputation, avoid costly legal battles, and more effectively manage its business network. In a principled corporation, profits do not overshadow its other priorities, particularly its reputation. A corporation that

David Batstone, *Saving the Corporate Soul & (Who Knows?) Maybe Your Own.* San Francisco: Jossey-Bass, 2003.

embraces the following principles will be a better place to work, to do business with, and to invest in:

- The interests of corporate leaders are closely aligned with those of their customers, employees, shareholders, and communities.
- The company's operations are open and visible to all stakeholders.
- The corporation is a positive force in the communities in which it operates.
- Products are accurately represented, and there is a commitment to customers before and after a sale.
- Workers are treated as valued team members.
- The corporation fully accepts responsibility for its environmental impact.
- The corporation is committed to diversity in its workforce and markets.
- The transnational corporation will apply the same principles overseas that inform its activities at home.

## PRINCIPLED LEADERSHIP

Corporate workers make decisions every day that affect employees, customers, and the community at large. Without leadership and support from the executive and board level to act in a principled way, their decisions may undermine the integrity of the corporation and lead to unexpected or even disastrous consequences. In other words, *principled leadership starts at the top.*

The personal interests of corporate leaders should be aligned with those of employees, customers, shareholders, and the communities in which they do business. Their actions should support the viability of the corporation in a responsible way. If trust and confidence among employees is lacking, investor confidence can also suffer. When corporate leaders display integrity, don't cut corners, and act responsibly, that trust can be earned.

One indication of principled leadership is whether or not the business model is built for both present and future earnings. Is it sustainable? An example of an unsustainable business plan is when growth targets are based on shareholder expectations rather than actual consumer demand. Unrealistic growth targets can lead to ill-advised marketing, capital investments, and other expenditures. Customer surveys and actual orders can be used to develop sales projections, giving a more realistic estimate.

In many corporations, executives reap the rewards while employees bear most of the risk. Both shareholder value and jobs have suffered while executives cashed in their stock options and companies went bankrupt. Bonuses have been paid to executives following wage concessions from workers. A principled corporation links executive compensation with company performance. The way directors and executives report their compensation is also important, particularly in the areas of share ownership and stock options. Holding periods for stock options, for example, can ensure that executives place the interests of the corporation above personal gain. Finally, excessive wage gaps between executive and non-executive employees can indicate something other than a long-term strategy on the part of leadership.

Since the ultimate control over the character of a corporation takes place at the board level, the integrity and independence of the board is crucial. It is the board's responsibility to protect the interests of all the stakeholders: employees, customers, shareholders, and the public. Although management representation is important, the CEO alone should not recruit board members, and board members should be expected to disclose any conflicts of interest and business relationships with the corporation on whose board they might serve. Employees can and should have a representative on the board, since they have the most to lose. Finally, shareholders should have a democratic process to influence company policy when corporate boards get off track.

## ◆ TRANSPARENCY

The most important relationships a corporation can have are based on trust. Shareholders must have confidence that the results reported by the company are genuine. Employees who are expected to stake their careers and personal security on a company need to trust its commitment to value. Customers expect to get what they pay for and trust the company to stand behind their products.

One of the biggest problems corporate integrity has faced has been in the area of financial reporting. Clear, accurate, verifiable company reports, access to information by employees and shareholders, and rational accounting practices are critically important. A transparent corporate culture is enhanced when reports to employees and investors disclose details on operations, finances, and other important affairs. Shareholders count on independent auditors to report accurately a company's performance and avoid conflicts of interest. A company committed to transparency will ensure that accounting assumptions are clear, real earnings are reported, cash flows are detailed clearly, and write-offs are fairly stated. Transparency means operating with honesty, integrity, and openness so that a company's operations can be judged realistically by anyone who cares to look.

Participation by employees in key decisions is another aspect of transparency. Not all decisions are open for debate, but the rationale behind those decisions can be shared. When ideas are in the earliest stages of consideration, wide input is encouraged as part of the decision-making process.

Finally, when a company makes promises, it needs to stand behind them. Trust is built when the promises made by an individual employed by the company are honored even if it hurts the company in the short term.

## ◆ COMMUNITY

Corporations rely on the resources, labor, and infrastructure of the communities in which they operate. A single-minded focus on profitability can lead to a disregard of the source of their success. Insensitivity to the interests of community can lead to a backlash by employees and customers that can damage the company's reputation and limit its opportunities.

The ways in which a corporation builds a relationship with the community are wide-ranging. Structured programs that encourage employees to become involved in community projects have been very successful. These programs can improve employee satisfaction as well as improve the company's image. Direct investment in community development is another way corporations can build support. The goal is to build social capital: community support that can come to the aid of the corporation at critical moments.

It is as important to assess the return on investment for community engagement, as is any other enterprise activity. Sometimes the development of its own workforce is a primary consideration. In other situations, it is the correlation between the resources invested and the goals of the program.

## ◆ CUSTOMER SERVICE

A company that presents its products honestly and serves its customers beyond the initial transaction builds loyalty and support. Marketing campaigns that focus on obfuscation more than clarification are a sign of corporate dishonesty.

There are a few simple questions that can determine the level of customer care.

- Can the promises a company makes about a product be delivered?
- When a company fails to deliver on its promises, can it make it right?
- Does a company respond in a meaningful way to customer feedback?

Customer loyalty and retention are at the top of the list of management challenges, but customers need a good reason to believe in a company. Trust and fairness at each point of contact with a company will determine whether that loyalty is earned. Each component of customer service should be broken down and evaluated and all employees of the company should interact with customers periodically. Decision-making should be pushed to those employees closest to the customer and employees should be rewarded for acquiring new customers and retaining them.

## ◆ THE VALUE OF WORKERS

The extent to which workers are treated as partners in the business enterprise can be critical to long-term success. Historically, workers have been viewed as a capital expense, but when employees align their personal interests with those of the company this relationship can result in a significant competitive advantage. This is particularly true when superior quality is important in a product or service.

There are many ways to achieve this objective: profit-sharing, participation in governance, involvement in decision-making, creation of career advancement opportunities, employee stock ownership programs (ESOPs), and others. Perhaps the ultimate form of employee participation is worker ownership of the company. Since the U.S. government declared employer contributions to ESOPs tax deductible, the trend toward employee ownership has accelerated. Although most employee-owned companies are small, some large corporations like United Airlines are majority-owned by workers.

Although no company can guarantee job security or compensation, employee involvement can minimize the human cost of the business cycle. When workers become true partners and that partnership is fully supported by the company's structure, then everyone is more likely to pull in the same direction. Enhancing the role of employees as stakeholders in the company can alter the labor-management paradigm, build trust and confidence, and improve company performance in important ways.

## ◆ RESPECT FOR THE ENVIRONMENT

Ignoring the impact of the corporation's activities on the environment can lead not only to unplanned expense, but can also undermine the company's reputation and the public trust. There have been a number of high-profile cases of environmental damage caused by corporations that led to serious consequences, both financially and to the company's reputation.

Until recently it was seen as government's role to protect the environment through regulation, and the firm's job to operate within those guidelines. The consumer-led environmental movement has given the environment a new and important position as a virtual corporate stakeholder. Important public interest groups now work together with government, but often go considerably further in their concern for the environment. Consumers are also making decisions about products and companies based on their environmental record. *These changing social values present the corporation with a powerful challenge.*

Though it can be difficult to meet both consumers' expectations and the demands of militant environmentalists, a number of large corporations have begun to look beyond the regulations to address these social concerns. These companies have moved beyond a compliance mentality toward an outcome-informed process of environmental management.

One of the terms used to describe a merger between business and environmental concern is *sustainable development.* Corporate goals and strategies for achieving sustainability start with pollution control and compliance with existing regulations. The participation of external stakeholders and the creation of environmental management systems within the firm are important additional steps. In order to be effective, sustainability needs to be a key factor in planning and integrating management systems that consider the environmental impact of product development and production each step of the way.

## ◆ DIVERSITY

Diversity is not just about skin color, gender, sexual orientation, or religion. Diversity is not a euphemism for affirmative action. *Diversity is about reflecting the values and cultures of the customer and the community in which you operate.* Sometimes companies must make a special effort to avoid a narrow-minded view of who is a desirable employee or customer. This is simply a sound business practice.

To achieve a balanced workforce, managers should be evaluated on their track record for hiring, retaining, and promoting minorities and women. Any process that excludes individuals, customers, or employees in an arbitrary way needs to be examined and corrected. This is certainly true when trying to diversify the customer base. Some of the essential steps in a diversity effort are to:

- Establish a physical presence in an under-represented community
- Build strong connections with local interest groups
- Work to strengthen the neighborhood
- Recruit and employ representatives from the community
- Design products and services that meet local needs

## THE GLOBAL PERSPECTIVE

A principled corporation that operates globally should apply the same principles overseas that inform its activities at home. The rights of workers, respect for the community, protection of the environment, and fair trading practices are equally important for the transnational corporation. Developing nations can provide valuable assets to the corporation, yet they should not have to sacrifice genuine economic development in the process. There is no question that transnational corporations can contribute to the improvement of standards of living in impoverished economies. If those corporations operate transparently and engage the population of the country in which they operate, they may be able to avoid some of the pitfalls that await the insensitive or unaware.

# Geeks and Geezers: How Eras, Values, and Defining Moments Shape Leaders

*WARREN G. BENNIS and ROBERT J. THOMAS*

*Summary prepared by Stephen B. Castleberry*

***Stephen B. Castleberry (Ph.D.)** is a professor of marketing at the University of Minnesota Duluth where he teaches courses in research, selling, and ethics. He was the previous holder of the UARCO Professor of Sales and Marketing Chair at Northern Illinois University and has served as department chairperson at two universities. He has published over thirty refereed journal articles in national publications on topics such as sales teams, sales training, listening, and ethics, and is co-author of the text* Selling: Building Partnerships. *He serves on the editorial boards of several journals, has done consulting work for international as well as regional businesses, and owns a publishing company. He also appeared in eight segments of a PBS special on personal selling called* The Sales Connection.

Individual factors such as class, intelligence, wealth, beauty, and genetics have long been studied for their influence upon leadership traits. What has not been studied as much is the influence of another demographic factor, the era in which the leader matured as an adult. An interesting distinction, for example, can be seen when one compares environmental influences from the era of the early 1950s with that of the 1990s.

---

Warren G. Bennis and Robert J. Thomas, *Geeks and Geezers: How Era, Values, and Defining Moments Shape Leaders.* Boston: Harvard Business School Press, 2002.

## ◆ GEEZERS AND THE ERA OF LIMITS

*Geezers,* highly successful leaders who are now over seventy years old, were in their maturing years (mid to late twenties) during 1945–1954. Interviews with twenty-five geezers revealed the following environmental influences and characteristics:

- Although there was great hope and promise after World War II, this was tempered by fears of nuclear war and a stock market crash.
- To be successful in business it was important to be a team player and follow the company's rules and norms. Firms were highly respected by employees.
- Level of experience was highly correlated with respect. Those who worked hard, were patient, and learned the ropes were rewarded. Advancement took time.
- Americans trusted institutions. For example, organized religions had substantial influence in communities.
- It was assumed that most men would choose one career and have a traditional family. Work-life balance was missing, with families being treated as secondary in importance when compared to the firm's wishes.
- Raised during the Depression, geezers sought financial security in order to offer their families a better life than they had growing up.
- Many were war veterans who exhibited service-based maturity and had practical, goal-oriented attitudes and philosophies.
- Heroes were numerous and widely available (e.g., FDR, Ghandi, Winston Churchill) and their presence had profound impacts on the ideas and behaviors of citizens.
- Leaders were more comfortable leading alone and stressing a "command and control" mentality.

## ◆ GEEKS AND THE ERA OF OPTIONS

Contrast that portrait of geezers with what life was like for *geeks,* those successful leaders under thirty-five years old, who experienced their maturing years (mid to late twenties) during 1991–2000, and you'll find a world of difference. Based on interviews with eighteen geeks, the following highlights the types of environmental influences and characteristics of leaders that matured during that era:

- An expectation of lifetime employment for the "loyal company man" of the 50s was replaced with contract workers, part-timers, and a lack of corporate loyalty toward workers, as companies downsized and outsourced in a never-ending cycle of cost reductions.
- Opportunities seemed endless, and included ones like becoming an entrepreneur and getting rich overnight in the dot.com craze. Newly emerging leaders were impatient to realize their ambitions.
- Women flocked into the workforce.
- It was a period of great economic prosperity.

- Institutions went through drastic changes. Organized religion lost much of its importance, the definition of what constituted a "family" changed, and public education was in crisis as evidenced by falling test scores.
- They feel a responsibility to the communities that surround them and fully expect to change the world into a better place.
- They don't expect to stay with one company all their lives. They saw what happened to their parents, who were jettisoned out of companies to which they had been very loyal.
- They don't expect to remain in one career all their lives. In fact, they expect to have something closer to nine different careers.
- Success is defined as being challenged, having power, and charting history.
- Lessons are learned primarily from life, not from formal instruction or from reading "the classics."
- Balance between work and personal life is of paramount importance.
- Heroes, of which there are very few contemporary ones, tend to be people with whom they have had personal contact (a coach or parent). It's just too easy for "traditional" heroes (e.g., politicians) to be discredited in the ever-present world dominated by the media and Internet.

## ◆ CRUCIBLES OF LEADERSHIP

Emerging leaders enter life's trials and opportunities with leadership skills based upon individual factors and the influences of the era in which they lived while maturing as a young adult. But how do these people become truly gifted leaders? By a crucible. The *crucible* is a metaphor that calls to mind the melting pots and caldrons that alchemists employed in their attempts to change worthless metals into gold. In leadership terms, *crucibles are those transforming events or situations that radically change a person's leadership abilities and skills.* Crucibles are where leaders start asking themselves elemental questions, like "Who do I want to be? Why I am here on earth?" "How should I relate to people?" Every one of the forty-three leaders studied had experienced at least one such crucible.

Crucibles are not necessarily painful, and therefore emerging leaders may even seek them out. For example, working with a chosen mentor can be a crucible. Arthur Levitt, Jr. created crucibles for himself by constantly seeking out new challenges in the form of new careers that would stretch and grow his leadership skills. For Geoff Keighley his unpainful crucible was discovering his own power and uniqueness, while pretending to be a magician at a birthday party in the second grade. For Liz Altman, it was spending a year in Japan, whose culture shocked and challenged her.

In other situations, crucibles represent difficult circumstances that test and mold. For example, Sidney Rittenberg was put in a Chinese prison on charges of spying. For Mike Wallace it was the sudden death of his oldest son. Vernon Jordan credits the many racial slurs he encountered from a Georgia governor as his crucible. Not surprisingly, World War II was a crucible for many of the geezers in the study.

## THE OUTCOMES OF CRUCIBLES: LEADERSHIP COMPETENCIES

### 1. ADAPTIVE CAPACITY

Truly successful leaders come through their crucibles, not with a sense of bitterness or frustration, but with a vision about who they are or who they might become. It is this *adaptive capacity* that sets them apart from non-leaders who experience the same types of crucibles. Even when failure occurred during a crucible, it was seen as a friend, not a foe. Why? Because the leader finds new abilities, new appreciation, and new resolve for future encounters. The leader often creates a story around the experience that instills resolve, and reminds the leader of the lessons learned. This story is almost always shared with others, and can become a legend.

### 2. ENGAGING OTHERS BY CREATING SHARED MEANING

What good is it to have a vision unless others know about it and agree with it? That's why one of the very first jobs of successful leaders is to communicate their vision to followers and have them buy into it, even to the point of accepting the vision as their own. Leaders convert an inspiring personal vision into a shared meaning for their followers.

### 3. A DISTINCTIVE VOICE LOUD ENOUGH TO PROVIDE LEADERSHIP

Leaders have self-confidence and are aware of their abilities. They know who they are and have the emotional intelligence to know how to relate to their followers effectively. Their "voice" stands out in a distinctive way for others to hear.

### 4. INTEGRITY AND A STRONG SENSE OF VALUES

All leaders studied had a strong set of values, which includes components such as a desire for justice, an appreciation for the value and rights of all people, a compelling desire to do the right things, and integrity. Their integrity—a critical component of success—is composed of three components:

- **Ambition.** The drive for gain and growth. The focus can be on rewards for the individual, the good of the community, or both.
- **Competence.** The skills component of integrity, it includes expertise in critical leadership skills.
- **Moral compass.** The ability to differentiate good and evil and the recognition that we do not live our lives alone.

All three components must be present and in balance for true integrity to be present. *While it is easy to understand the dangers of unbridled ambition and lack of competence, less recognized is the danger of having a moral compass, but having no ambition or competence.* An example would be Huey Long or Father Charles Coughlin, who had a great moral compass, but lacked competence or ambition to achieve goals, leading people into false dreams and follies.

## ANOTHER TRAIT OF SUCCESSFUL LEADERS: BEING PUPPIES

When examining the geezers in this study, an additional trait was identified: neoteny. *Neoteny* is the youthful, almost puppy-like quality that attracts others to oneself. It is to have energy, to stimulate and enjoy being stimulated, to be curious, to have a contagious laugh and to feel alive. Charisma may in fact be an outcome of neoteny. It is probably the neoteny of successful older leaders that attracts younger people to seek mentoring relationships with them. It can also be a reason that many older leaders actually enjoy mentoring younger people, because many young people exhibit neoteny too.

## THE LEADERSHIP MODEL—A SUMMARY

Based on results of interviews with the forty-three geeks and geezers, a model of leadership emerged. Leaders are the product of individual factors in the context of the era during which they reached maturity. They go through a life-transforming event or experience called a crucible, which gives meaning and direction to life and leadership. This results in improved competencies in adaptability, engaging others in shared visions, finding their own distinctive powerful and effective voice, and integrity.

One can find many examples, beyond the forty-three persons interviewed for the study, who display the leadership model in action. For example, September 11, 2001 provided a crucible by evoking life-changing leadership skills for leaders like New York Mayor Rudolph Giuliani and President George W. Bush.

## HOW CAN WE INCREASE THE POOL OF LEADERS?

*There are many people who have the capacity to be great leaders, but they have never had the opportunity to test their skills or utilize them.* Here are some suggested ways to increase our pool of available leaders:

- **National level**—Increase the opportunities for service (Peace Corps, Teach for America, AmeriCorps, City Year programs).
- **Firm level**—Invest in leadership training, encourage employees to spend time reflecting on lessons learned in day-to-day activities, systematically rotate employees through various departments, provide life-work balance for geeks who seek it, and offer sabbaticals.
- **Individual level**—Learn how to learn, build networks across generations and cultures, stay active through exercise, be optimistic, spend time thinking and reflecting, find ways to practice leadership, and strive to develop one's own level of neoteny.

READING 4

# Authentic Leadership

**_BILL GEORGE_**

**_Summary prepared by Randy Skalberg_**

***Randy Skalberg*** *is an assistant professor of taxation and business law at the University of Minnesota Duluth where he has taught courses in Corporate and Individual Tax, Business Law and Corporate Ethics. He holds a B.S.B. in Accounting from the Carlson School of Management at the University of Minnesota, a J.D. from the University of Minnesota Law School, and an L.L.M. in Taxation from Case Western Reserve University in Cleveland, Ohio. He has served as an in-house Tax Counsel to* Fortune 500 *corporations including Metris Companies and The Sherwin-Williams Company, and also served in the tax department at Ernst & Young's Minneapolis office. He is admitted to practice law in Minnesota, as well as before the U.S. Tax Court.*

## ◆ AUTHENTIC LEADERSHIP

*Authentic leadership* involves those actions taken by people of high integrity who are committed to building enduring organizations relying on morality and character. It means being your own person as a leader. A leader's authenticity is based not only on differentiating right and wrong (the classic "moral compass") but also on a leadership style that follows qualities of your heart and mind (passion and compassion) as well as by your intellectual capacity. All too often, society has glorified leaders based on high-style and high-ego personalities instead of personal qualities that provide for true, quality leadership.

## ◆ DIMENSIONS OF A LEADER

An authentic leader practices the five dimensions of leadership: Purpose, Values, Heart, Relationships, and Self-Discipline. *Purpose* focuses on the real reasons people choose to become leaders—not the trappings of power, the glamour, or the financial

Bill George, *Authentic Leadership: Rediscovering the Secrets to Creating Lasting Value.* San Francisco: Jossey-Bass, 2003.

rewards that go with leadership. *Values* provide the "true north" of a leader's moral compass. Failure of leadership values lies behind the failure of Enron, but more importantly, leadership values have been critical in the growth of virtually all of America's long-term corporate success stories. An example of *Heart* in leadership is provided by Marilyn Nelson, CEO of Carlson Companies. She took over an organization bordering on crisis from previous years of "hard-nosed" management and created a program called "Carlson Cares," which has resulted in both corporate growth and an improved bottom line. The *Relationship* dimension debunks the myth that a great leader needs to be distant and aloof to prevent the relationship from interfering with "hard" decisions. An authentic leader creates close relationships as part of leadership. The existence and fostering of such relationships is actually a sign of strength in leadership, not an indicator of weakness. Consistency is the hallmark of *Self-discipline* in a leader. Consistency enables employees who work with the leader to know where he or she stands on important issues and to rely on even the most difficult decisions the leader has made.

## LEADING A BALANCED LIFE

One of the key characteristics of authentic leadership is the focus on the journey rather than the destination. The leader must recognize that a career is rarely a straight-line path to success (and most likely should not be), but rather it is a journey wherein all of the leader's experiences contribute to overall success.

This concept of success implies not merely financial or professional success, but the overall success that comes from leading a *balanced life*—one that recognizes the importance of work, family, friends, faith and community service, with none of them excluding any of the others. Leaders who subordinate everything else in life to their work do not develop organizations as well as those who live a more balanced life. Living such a life and allowing their employees to do so as well creates higher levels of commitment to the organization and in turn, improves the organization's bottom line. *Balancing work, family, social, and spiritual aspects of your life and providing a meaningful amount of time to each provides the leader with richness in life* that is unavailable to someone who chooses an eighty-hour week and is simply a "company person." The balance between work and family life is a substantial challenge, especially in today's two-career families. One of the challenges every leader will face is the impact of increased time demands from the organization on his or her family. The "delicate balance" between work and family life continues to be very difficult to achieve.

In addition to work/family balance, friendships are important. True friendships offer a place to share your emotions outside your family and without workplace involvement. This sharing process is an important part of the process of personal development. Equally important is the mentoring process. Contrary to the traditional view of mentoring, where an older person provides one-way advice to a younger person, true mentoring is a two-way process where both parties learn from each other. This two-way process acknowledges that mentoring is not merely the older generation telling "war stories," but a process where younger employees and students can provide insight into the questions that young leaders have about the business world. Finally, community service is an essential part of authentic leadership. Through community service, leaders have an opportunity to work with people of lesser economic means. *Getting in touch with people helps develop both the heart of a leader and sensitivity for the difficulties of the lives of others.*

## ◆ ORGANIZATIONAL MISSION AS MOTIVATION

A common phrase in today's business world (some would say almost a mantra) is "maximizing shareholder value." While that might be an appropriate goal for a company seeking a white knight in a takeover battle, it is fundamentally flawed as a long-term business model. The best way to create real long-term value for a company's shareholders is to be a *mission-driven organization*—one that utilizes its mission statement as an integral part of managing the organization, not merely a plaque that hangs on the CEO's wall. The best organizations have a corporate mission that inspires creative employees to develop innovative products and provide superior service to the customer. This strategy creates a self-sustaining business cycle. In Medtronic's case, this mission is to "alleviate pain, restore health and extend life" of the patient consumer which creates demand from physicians who are the immediate customers.

## ◆ CUSTOMER FOCUS

Every company's purpose boils down to serving its customers well. If it does this better than any of its competitors, and does it over the long term, it will ultimately create more shareholder value than its competitors. *Customer-focused quality* relies for its success on measurements that focus externally on customers, and uses customer feedback as the ultimate measurement of quality. The role model for customer focus must be senior management. If senior management is focused on internal operations instead of on customer service, the company will eventually fail to an environment that empowers and rewards employees who provide high quality sales and service to the customer.

## ◆ TEAM FOCUSED MANAGEMENT

CEOs are given credit when companies succeed, but it is largely a myth that the CEO is primarily responsible for the success of a company. Many of the great corporate success stories of the past twenty-five years—Intel, Nokia, Hewlett-Packard, Microsoft, Coca-Cola, and Pepsi—have all been managed by a team at the top, not merely by a single high-powered CEO. Upon being named CEO of Medtronic, Bill George immediately proposed a partnership (as opposed to a traditional boss-subordinate relationship) with Vice Chair Glen Nelson. This was critical to Medtronic's success. Nelson, an M.D., brought a critical perspective on the relationship of the practice of medicine and technology to the management team, while George brought experience in high technology management from his previous employer, Honeywell.

## PITFALLS TO GROWTH

*There are seven key pitfalls to sustainable corporate growth: lack of mission, underestimation of core business, single-product dependence, failure to spot change, changing strategy with changing culture, ignoring core competencies, and over-reliance on growth through acquisition.* Avoiding each of these pitfalls requires disciplined leadership to recognize the problem and aggressively solve it without immediately retreating into a dangerous cost-cutting mode. This type of leadership in the face of inevitable criticism from securities analysts and the media will provide inspiration to the organization and rejuvenate its growth.

## OVERCOMING OBSTACLES

A key obstacle for Medtronic involved litigation in the implantable defibrillator market. A former Medtronic employee held patent rights to the first implantable defibrillator and went to work for Eli Lilly, a Medtronic competitor. Lilly used the patents to prevent Medtronic from developing its own defibrillator, a product that was critical to its core pacemaker business. Medtronic and Lilly litigated this patent claim to the U.S. Supreme court, where Medtronic won the right to develop its implantable defibrillator. Even after this victory though, Medtronic still had to negotiate a cross-licensing agreement with Lilly, clear FDA approval, and face the challenge of another competitor (Guidant) that reached the market with a dual chamber defibrillator prior to Medtronic. This 15-year struggle proved worthwhile, however, since Medtronic now enjoys greater than 50 percent market share in the implantable defibrillator market.

## ETHICAL DILEMMAS

Socially responsible organizations need to confront directly the issue of ethical standards in international business. Medtronic discovered shortly after acquiring the Italian distributor of Medtronic's Dutch pacemakers that the distributor was depositing large sums in a Swiss bank account, presumably to pay off Italian physicians who were Medtronic customers. George confronted the recently hired president of Medtronic Europe about the account and terminated him for violating Medtronic's corporate values. The termination caused uproar within Medtronic Europe, but in the twelve years since this incident, the Dutch pacemaker subsidiary has responded with outstanding performance.

A second crisis arose in Japan, where two Medtronic-Japan managers were arrested and put in jail for giving airline tickets to a physician so that he could give speeches at two international transplant conferences. The arrests were part of a series of arrests of executives of foreign pacemaker manufacturers apparently based on the Ministry of Health's frustration at its inability to force the manufacturers to reduce prices in the Japanese market. The two managers were eventually released from jail following a guilty plea and returned to work. But, George took the critical step in visiting Japan to reestablish confidence in Medtronic-Japan's employees and meet with officials from the Ministry of Health. This visit led to the creation of an industry-wide code of conduct approved by the Ministry of Health. Medtronic continues to be a leader in the medical device industry in Japan and has not agreed to mandated price concessions.

## ◆ GROWTH BY ACQUISITION

In the fall of 1998 Medtronic engaged in a series of acquisitions costing a total of $9 billion. Medtronic's growth had been in sharp decline, so George decided to make a series of bold moves. These included the acquisition of Physio-Control, a manufacturer of manual defibrillators used in hospitals. George had to overcome internal resistance to the Physio-Control deal, as well as others based on a poor history of acquisition integration at Medtronic. After overcoming that resistance in the Physio-Control deal, the groundwork was set for two more acquisitions in 1998 and 1999—Sofamor Danek, the world's leading spinal surgery company, and AVE, the leader in the U.S. stent business.

By late January 1999 Medtronic had completed five acquisitions at a total cost of $9 billion. Next Medtronic faced the more difficult task of integration. Most acquisitions that fail do so not from financial issues or lack of strategic vision, but rather from cultural clashes within the newly merged entities. Medtronic took a proactive approach to integration focusing on four key issues: leadership of the business, financial leadership, business integration, and cultural integration. George formed integration teams for each company led by a Medtronic executive and including Medtronic employees and employees from the acquired company.

## ◆ SHAREHOLDERS COME THIRD

George's executive philosophy was described in an article in *Worth Magazine,* quoting him as saying, "Shareholders come third." George expected some backlash from the article, but surprisingly received none. The theory is simple. Customers are first, employees are second, and shareholders come third. Only by truly meeting the needs of the first two stakeholder groups does the successful company have any chance of satisfying the shareholders. *The key to meeting shareholder expectations is transparency.* Medtronic is completely transparent about every corporate event inside the company with respect to shareholders, a policy that can be contrasted with the Kozlowski-led Tyco which hid major corporate expenditures from its own board of directors, much less the shareholders.

## ◆ CORPORATE GOVERNANCE

The key to improved corporate governance is to restore power to boards of directors to govern corporations. The board should play an important role as a check on the company's executives and a means of ensuring long-term as opposed to short-term focus. One key to creating this type of board is to have a majority (perhaps two-thirds) of truly independent board members that have no business relationship to either the corporation or the executives. This will ensure that the directors can truly act independently of the CEO, not merely as "inside" directors who serve at the pleasure of the CEO.

## PUBLIC POLICY AND RISK TAKING

Medtronic found itself cast in a leadership role in reform of the U.S. Food and Drug Administration. The key issue in the reform movement was the steadily increasing approval time for new drugs. Drugs that were already in use in foreign countries were taking months, and in many cases years, to be approved in the U.S., and American patients were dying without access to life-saving medications. George presented his ideas about the need for reform at the Food & Drug Law Institute in Washington, D.C. and went on to work with the late Senator Paul Wellstone to generate bipartisan support for the Food and Drug Modernization Act of 1996. Today, new drugs are approved in less than six months, as opposed to twenty-nine months at the height of the FDA's delay problems.

## SUCCESSION PLANNING FOR THE CEO

One of the most critical and often overlooked steps in a CEO's career is succession. Almost as many CEO succession processes fail as succeed. If the board working with the incumbent CEO fails to identify a qualified and appropriate internal candidate, they are often forced to look outside the organization for a "star" CEO, a process that more often than not fails, as happened at Xerox and Maytag. One of the key factors is a lack of clarity on the CEO's part about how and when he or she will step aside. The CEO should identify a retirement date well in advance (Bill George announced his retirement date one year in advance), develop a succession plan, and make the transition as seamless as possible. This transition method is critical not only to employees and shareholders who desire consistent leadership, but also to the new CEO who knows when he or she will take over. This prevents the new CEO from being forced to choose between waiting around and moving on to other opportunities.

PART

# XIII

# Managing Emotions at Work

Topics of interest to managers encompass a wide array of themes, and these are constantly changing and evolving. This section includes a sampling of topics that have received substantial attention in recent years, all revolving around the focus of employee emotions and feelings. The topics in this section include employee enthusiasm, mindsets regarding change, toxic experiences at work, and the positive psychology underlying authentic happiness. These readings are designed to raise issues, provide an opportunity for reflection on oneself, and stimulate conversations regarding the balance between emphasis on corporate profits and employee (and personal) needs.

The first book summarized in this edition of *The Manager's Bookshelf* has a simple and surprisingly nonbusiness-sounding title: *Fish!* Like several other books (e.g., *The One Minute Manager, Zapp!, Heroz,* and *Who Moved My Cheese?*), which have also sold in large numbers, *Fish!* is short (about 100 pages), easy and quick to read, engaging, and written in the form of a parable. The authors (Lundin, Paul, and Christensen) provide a creative way to convey a central message—that work can (and should be) a joyful experience for all involved. Like any of the books summarized in this edition, we urge you to read the original source in its entirety and then reflect about what you have read. What are the roles of "fun" and "play" at work? Can such an environment be created? Is the conceptual foundation of the authors' message a solid one? Do negative implications as well as positive ones arise from creating a joyful experience at work?

Authors Lundin, Christensen, and Paul and Chart House Learning have also collaborated in the preparation of other products extending the *Fish!* philosophy and practice. Their follow-up books include *Fish! Tales, Fish! Sticks,* and *Fish! For Life,* and they also have a wide array of videos, calendars, training programs, apparel, and other related products available at their Web site, www.charthouse.com/home.asp. We think you will discover that despite the brevity, simplicity, and creative format of *Fish!,* useful ideas for action and debate can be found in this and almost any type of managerial literature. Like all ideas, of course, they need to be tested for their soundness, validity, and applicability.

Spencer Johnson (co-author of *The One Minute Manager* and *The Present*) has produced another book selling millions of copies titled *Who Moved My Cheese?* The book catapulted to the top of best-seller lists for *USA Today, Publisher's Weekly, The Wall Street Journal,* and *Business Week,* with some companies (e.g., Southwest Airlines and Mercedes-Benz) ordering thousands of copies to distribute to their employees. Written in the form of a fable about two mice and two small people living in a maze, Johnson suggests that change is rampant around us, and thus employees must anticipate, monitor, and adapt to change quickly in order to survive. Unfortunately, fear—and the tendency to cling to the familiar and comfortable past—prevents some people from letting go of old beliefs, attitudes, and paradigms. Readers interested in a critical view of the book should examine Jill Rosenfeld's article, "This Consultant's Whey is Cheese-y" (*Fast Company,* November 2000, pp. 68–72).

Toxic bosses and organizational cultures exist in many workplaces even in this enlightened era, and their impact is often compounded by the presence of combative customers, impossible deadlines, and unexpected tragedies. The results of this insidious organizational toxicity include lower productivity, job stress, workplace sabotage, and labor-management disputes. *Toxic Emotions at Work* provides a description of the positive roles that toxin handlers can engage in to reduce and even minimize the adverse impacts of toxic pain. They can listen with compassion, facilitate the discussion of emotions, intercede on behalf of colleagues, and reframe painful situations. Frost concludes his book with a three-stage model for managing toxicity that identifies strategies for prevention, intervention, and restoration.

Peter J. Frost received his Ph.D. from the University of Minnesota, and currently is the Edgar F. Kaiser Professor of Organizational Behaviour on the Faculty of Commerce of the University of British Columbia. In addition to *Toxic Emotions at Work,* he is the co-author of many other books, such as *HRM Reality, Doing Exemplary Research, Organizational Reality,* and *Reframing Organizational Culture.* In 2003, Peter Frost received the George R. Terry Book Award from the Academy of Management for *Toxic Emotions at Work.*

The last book included in this section is *Authentic Happiness,* by Martin Seligman. The book draws upon psychological research on "positive psychology" to suggest that happiness can be cultivated by individuals if they choose to identify and draw upon their existing "signature strengths," such as humor, optimism, kindness, creativity, and generosity. The resulting positivism can serve as a buffer against negative life events and misfortunes, help individuals attain their personal growth goals while improving the world around them, and move them toward achieving authentic contentment. Putting it more simply, Seligman argues that good character coupled with optimism leads to lasting happiness.

Martin Seligman is the Fox Leadership Professor of Psychology at the University of Pennsylvania, where he has initiated work on learned helplessness, depression, optimism and pessimism, motivation, personality, and positive psychology. He is the former president of the American Psychological Association. Included in his bibliography of 20 books and 170 articles are *Helplessness, What You Can Change and What You Can't, Abnormal Psychology,* and *Learned Optimism.*

# Fish!

*Stephen C. Lundin, Harry Paul, and John Christensen*

Mary Jane Ramirez is a manager who must create an effective team out of a set of employees who have historically been less than helpful to each other and generally unenthusiastic about teamwork. While taking a walk at lunchtime one day, she encounters a strange but compelling sight—the fishmongers of Seattle's Pike Street Fish Market. These employees have created a bustling, fun-filled, joyful work atmosphere both for themselves and for their customers. Through a series of conversations with Lonnie and some deep self-reflectiveness, she gradually uncovers some ideas that will guide her future behavior.

Using the fish market as a metaphor for other organizations, several key premises about employees are identified, and these lead logically to a short series of recommendations for personal effectiveness. The premises (underlying assumptions) include:

- Life is short, and our moments of life are precious. Therefore, it would be tragic for employees to just "pass through" on their way to retirement. Managers and employees both need to *make each moment count.*
- Most people prefer to work in a job environment that is *filled with fun.* When they find this fun or create it, they are much more likely to be energized and release their potential.
- People also like a work environment where they feel they can *make a difference* in the organization's outcomes. They need some capacity to assess their contribution toward those outcomes.
- Almost any job—no matter how simple or automated—has the potential to be performed with *energy and enthusiasm.*
- Employees may not always have the opportunity to choose whether to work, or the work to be done itself. However, they will always have some degree of choice about the *way* in which they do their work. At the extreme, each employee can choose to be ordinary, or to be world famous. One path is dull; the other is exciting.
- Employees can legitimately act like a bunch of *adult kids* having a good time as long as they do so in a respectful manner (not offending co-workers or customers). When they do act as kids (along with choosing to love to the work they do), they can find happiness, meaning, and fulfillment every day.

---

Stephen C. Lundin, Harry Paul, and John Christensen, *Fish! A Remarkable Way to Boost Morale and Improve Results.* New York: Hyperion, 2000.

Based on these premises, four recommendations are offered to employees for their personal effectiveness:

1. Every morning, before you go to work, *choose your attitude* for the day (and make it a positive one).
2. Make an effort to introduce an element of *play* into your work environment; it will benefit you and all those around you.
3. Make a commitment to make someone else's day *special* for them. Do something that will create a memory, engage them in a meaningful interaction, or welcome them to your organization.
4. While you are at work, seek to be *present* with them. Focus your energy on them; listen attentively and caringly; pay attention to the needs of your customers and co-workers.

Following these simple prescriptions will make the work experience joyful for all involved, just as it has for the employees and customers of Seattle's Pike Street Fish Market.

# Who Moved My Cheese?

*SPENCER JOHNSON, M.D.*

*Summary prepared by Gary Stark*

***Gary Stark*** *is an assistant professor of management at Washburn University. He earned his Ph.D. in Management from the University of Nebraska in 1999. Gary's research interests include recruiting, work-life balance, and the study of how and why people seek feedback on their work performance. He was previously on the faculty of the University of Minnesota Duluth. Prior to his academic life Gary earned his B.S. and M.B.A. degrees at Kansas State University and worked in Chicago as a tax accountant.*

## ◆ A REUNION

Several former classmates met in Chicago one Sunday, the day after their class reunion. After discussing the difficulties they had been having with the many changes in their lives since high school, one of the classmates, Michael, volunteered a story that had helped him deal with the changes in his life. The name of the story was "Who Moved My Cheese?"

## ◆ THE STORY

The story revolved around four characters who spent their lives in a maze. The maze was a giant labyrinth with many deadends and wrong turns. But those who persisted in the maze were rewarded, for many rooms in the maze contained delicious Cheese. Two of the characters in the maze were littlepeople named Hem and Haw. Two were mice named Sniff and Scurry. The characters spent every day at Cheese Station C, a huge storehouse of Cheese. However, the mice and the littlepeople differed in their attitudes about Cheese Station C. These attitudes affected their behaviors. The mice, Sniff and Scurry, woke up early each day and raced to Cheese Station C. When they got there they took off their running shoes, tied them together, and hung them around

---

Spencer Johnson, M.D. *Who Moved My Cheese? An Amazing Way to Deal with Change in Your Work and in Your Life.* New York: Putman Books, 1998.

their necks so that they would be immediately available should they need to move on from Cheese Station C. And Sniff and Scurry did something else to make sure that they were ready to move on if the need arose. Every day upon arrival at Cheese Station C Sniff and Scurry carefully inspected the Station and noted changes from the previous day.

Indeed, one day Sniff and Scurry arrived at Cheese Station C and found that the Cheese was gone. Sniff and Scurry were not surprised because they had been inspecting the Station every day and had noticed the Cheese supply dwindling. In response to the Cheeselessness, Sniff and Scurry simply did as their instincts told them. *The situation had changed so they changed with it.* Rather than analyze the situation, they put on their running shoes (taken from around their necks) and ran off through the maze in search of new Cheese.

The littlepeople, Hem and Haw, were different. Long ago, when they first found Cheese Station C they had raced to get there every morning. But, as time went on, Hem and Haw got to the Station a little later each day. They became very comfortable in Cheese Station C and, unlike Sniff and Scurry, never bothered to search for changes in the Station. They assumed the Cheese would always be there and even came to regard the Cheese as their own. Unfortunately, unlike Sniff and Scurry, they did not notice that the Cheese was disappearing.

When they arrived on the fateful day and discovered the Cheese had run out in Cheese Station C, Hem and Haw reacted differently than Sniff and Scurry. Instead of immediately searching for new Cheese they complained that it wasn't fair. Finding Cheese was a lot of work in their maze and they did not want to let go of the life they had built around this Cheese. They wanted to know who moved their Cheese.

Hem and Haw returned the next day still hoping to find Cheese. They found none and repeated the behaviors of the day before. Eventually Haw noticed that Sniff and Scurry were gone. Haw suggested to Hem that they do as Sniff and Scurry had and go out into the maze in search of new cheese. Hem rebuffed him.

A similar scenario played out day after day in Cheese Station C. Hem and Haw returned every day hoping to find the Cheese they believed they were entitled to. They became frustrated and angry and began to blame each other for their predicament.

In the meantime, Sniff and Scurry had found new Cheese. It had taken a lot of work and they dealt with much uncertainty, but finally, in a totally unfamiliar part of the maze they found Cheese in Cheese Station N.

Still, day after day, Hem and Haw returned to Cheese Station C in hopes of finding their Cheese. And the same frustrations and claims of entitlement continued. Eventually, however, Haw's mindset began to change. He imagined Sniff and Scurry in pursuit of new Cheese and imagined himself taking part in such an adventure. He imagined finding fresh new Cheese. The more he thought about it the more determined he became to leave. Nevertheless, his friend Hem continued to insist that things would be fine in Cheese Station C. Hem figured that if they simply *worked harder* they would find their Cheese in Cheese Station C. He feared he was too old to look for Cheese and that he would look foolish doing so. Hem's concerns even made Haw doubt himself until finally one day Haw realized that he was doing the same things over and over again and wondering why things didn't improve. Although Haw did not like the idea of going into the maze and the possibility of getting lost, he laughed at how his fear was preventing him from doing those things. His realization inspired him to write a message to himself (and perhaps to Hem) on the wall in front of him. "*What Would You Do If You Weren't Afraid?*" (p. 48), it said. Answering his own question, Haw took a deep breath and headed into the unknown.

Unfortunately, a long interlude without food from Cheese Station C had left Haw somewhat weak. He struggled while searching for new Cheese and he decided that if he ever got another chance he would respond to a change in his environment sooner than he had to the situation in Cheese Station C.

Haw wandered for days and found very little new Cheese. He found the maze confusing, as it had changed a great deal since the last time he had looked for Cheese. Still, he had to admit that it wasn't as dreadful as he had feared. And whenever he got discouraged he reminded himself that however painful the search for new Cheese was, it was better than remaining Cheeseless. The difference was that *he was now in control.* Haw even began to realize, in hindsight, that the Cheese in Cheese Station C had not suddenly disappeared. If he had wanted to notice he would have seen the amount of Cheese decreasing every day, and that what was left at the end was old and not as tasty. Haw realized that maybe Sniff and Scurry had known what they were doing. Haw stopped to rest and wrote another message on the wall. The message read: "*Smell the Cheese Often So You Know When It Is Getting Old*" (p. 52).

Haw was often scared in the maze for he did not know if he would survive. He wondered if Hem had moved on yet or was still frozen by his fears. However, Haw's confidence and enjoyment grew with every day as he realized that the times he had felt best in this journey was when he was moving. He inscribed this discovery on the wall of the maze: "*When You Move Beyond Your Fear, You Feel Free*" (p. 56).

Soon Haw began painting a picture in his mind of himself enjoying all his favorite Cheeses. This image became so vivid that he gained a very strong sense that he would find new Cheese. He stopped to write on the wall: "*Imagining Myself Enjoying New Cheese Even Before I Find It, Leads Me to It*" (p. 58). Outside a new station Haw noticed small bits of Cheese near the entrance. He tried some, found them delicious, and excitedly entered the station. But Haw's heart sank when he found that only a small amount of Cheese remained in what was once a well-stocked station. He realized that if he had set about looking for new Cheese sooner he might have found more Cheese here. He wrote these thoughts on the wall: "*The Quicker You Let Go of Old Cheese, the Sooner You Find New Cheese*" (p. 60).

As Haw left this station he made another important self-discovery. He realized what made him happy wasn't just having Cheese. What made him happy was not being controlled by fear. He did not feel as weak and helpless as when he remained in Cheese Station C. Haw realized that moving beyond his fear was giving him strength and wrote that: "*It Is Safer to Search in the Maze Than Remain in a Cheeseless Situation*" (p. 62). Haw also realized that the fear he had allowed to build up in his mind was worse than the reality. He had been so afraid of the maze that he had dreaded looking for new Cheese. Now he found himself excited about looking for more. Later in his journey he wrote: "*Old Beliefs Do Not Lead You to New Cheese*" (p. 64). Haw knew that his new beliefs had encouraged new behaviors.

Finally it happened. What Haw had started his journey looking for was now in front of his eyes. Cheese Station N was flush with some of the greatest Cheeses Haw had ever seen. Sure enough, his mouse friends Sniff and Scurry were sitting in the Cheese, their bellies stuffed. Haw quickly said hello and dug in.

Haw was a bit envious of his mouse friends. They had kept their lives simple. When the Cheese moved, rather than overanalyze things, Sniff and Scurry moved with it. As Haw reflected on his journey he learned from his mistakes. He realized that what he had written on the walls during his journey was true and was glad he had changed. Haw realized three important things: (1) the biggest thing blocking change is yourself; (2) things don't improve until you change yourself; and (3) there is always new Cheese out there, whether you believe it or not. Indeed he realized running out of Cheese in Cheese Station C had been a blessing in disguise. It had led him to better Cheese and it had led him to discover important and positive things about himself.

Although Haw knew that he had learned a great deal he also realized that it would be easy to fall into a comfort zone with the new store of Cheese. So, every day he inspected the Cheese in Cheese Station N to avoid the same surprise that had occurred in Cheese Station C. And, even though he had a great supply of Cheese in Cheese Station N, every day he went out into the maze to make sure that he was always aware of his choices, that he did not have to remain in Cheese Station N. It was on one of these excursions that he heard the sound of someone moving toward him in the maze. He hoped and prayed that it was his friend Hem, and that Hem had finally learned to . . . "*Move with the Cheese and Enjoy It!*" (p. 76).

## BACK AT THE REUNION

After the story the former classmates recounted situations in which they had to face changes in their work and their personal lives and they discussed which maze character they had acted most like. Most resolved to act more like Haw when dealing with changes they would face in the future. All agreed the story was very useful and that they would use the wisdom contained within to guide them.

# Toxic Emotions at Work

**PETER J. FROST**

**Summary prepared by Gary J. Colpaert**

***Gary J. Colpaert** received a B.A. in Business Administration from the University of Minnesota Duluth and a Masters degree in Health Care Administration from the University of Wisconsin in Madison. He worked for the U.S.S. Great Lakes Fleet, with his responsibilities there including marketing, sales, and running the day-to-day operations of the commercial fleet. After leaving Duluth, Gary held the position of Vice President-Clinical and Support Systems at Children's Hospital of Wisconsin and then became the Executive Vice President of the Blood Center of Southeast Wisconsin. Gary is currently the Administrative Director of the Eye Institute in Milwaukee. He has developed and implemented internal coaching programs, a Winning at Work program, and a Leadership Intensive Program. He leads a men's group whose members are interested in leading an authentic life of leadership and service, and he also has a meditation practice that includes a yearly ten-day period of silence.*

## ◆ OVERVIEW

Work organizations and their leaders sometimes take actions—intentional and unintentional—that produce emotional pain in their employees. That pain can become toxic and thus have a negative effect on the organization. Alternatively, there is a meaningful role for compassion in an organization, and managers face the task of handling toxic emotions and their consequences for those people who experience pain in the workplace. In short, *compassionate companies can improve their toxin-handling practices.*

Organizations by their very nature create a regular supply of emotional pain. New bosses, mergers, layoffs, stifling or confusing policies, salary decisions and even the way that changes are communicated can all be sources of emotional pain felt by all organizational members. If the pain cannot be dissipated it will, at a minimum, become a

---

Peter J. Frost, *Toxic Emotions at Work: How Compassionate Managers Handle Pain and Conflict.* Boston: Harvard Business School Press, 2003.

source of decreased productivity and a toxic condition that renders significant negative consequences for the organization and its staff.

Most organizational leaders lack the awareness to encounter and neutralize toxins and therefore an informal structure of toxin handlers emerges which takes on the difficult (often unsupported) work of maintaining emotional homeostasis. The large amount of emotional pain caused by organizations, the unrecognized value of engaging this pain, and the already heavy workload of toxin handlers puts the organization at risk for not having the capacity to deal with the emotional pain it creates.

## SPECIFIC SKILLS NEEDED BY AN EFFICIENT TOXIN HANDLER

A Gallup poll of two million employees revealed the value of compassionate managers, finding that most people value having a caring boss higher than money or the fringe benefits they receive. It takes some basic skills to be an effective toxin handler.

- Reading emotional cues of others and themselves.
- Keeping people connected and in communication.
- Acting to alleviate the suffering of others.
- Mobilizing people to deal with their pain and get back to a stable state.
- Building a team environment that rewards compassionate action.

The impact of using these skills to diminish the emotional pain of even one person in the organization can have a significant positive impact on the whole organization.

## USEFUL PRACTICES

Compassionate organizations promote a healthy, productive culture through a set of policies, procedures, and belief systems that produce generative responses from people at all levels of the organization. Useful compassionate practices include:

- Identifying a link between the emotional health of the organization and the bottom line;
- Recognizing and rewarding managers who are good at handling emotional pain;
- Using hiring practices that emphasize attitude as well as technical skill;
- Maintaining fair-minded practices consistent with loyalty, responsibility, and the fostering of community in the workplace;
- Implementing intervention strategies during times of distress and initiating rehab strategies to ensure long-term vitality; and
- Building a culture that values compassion.

Studies reveal a direct correlation between harmony in the workplace (as a result of these compassionate practices) and company profits. For example, there is a 20 percent increase in survival probability for firms that are one standard deviation above the mean as compared to organizations one standard deviation below the mean on the dimension of valuing human resources.

## ◆ TOXIN HANDLERS

The work of the toxin handler is to respond compassionately to pain in the organization, to reduce its impact, and to enable people to return to constructive behaviors. Toxin handlers have complex profiles. They are caregivers, leaders, social architects, and builders of productive systems of relationships. Their work reflects five major themes:

- **Listening**—providing moments of human compassion by giving attention and consideration to the pain of others;
- **Holding space for healing**—providing support and time needed for healing;
- **Buffering pain**—reframing communications, using political capital, building relationships, displaying personal courage;
- **Extricating others from painful situations**—making the decision to get people out of the situation causing the pain; and
- **Transforming pain**—framing pain in constructive ways by changing the view of painful experiences and coaching.

## ◆ BURNOUT CAN OCCUR

The potential toll on toxin handlers is, not surprisingly, burnout. Without support and the ability to "decompress," the toxin handler can suffer psychological, physical, and professional setbacks. Often anger and guilt are the first symptoms of problems developing within the toxin handler. It is imperative for a toxin handler to manage negative emotions because the effects of stress last a significant period of time. Stress impairs the immune system and has been shown to influence the brain's neurological pathways.

Paying attention to others more than themselves has its costs, and the potential for becoming addicted to helping others is real. A trap that toxin handlers may frequently fall into is having an agenda for the person being helped. Another particular problem that handlers often face is that they may not know how to handle their own pain. If they over-identify with the role, they may have the incorrect perception that there is no one else they can count on for help. It may be difficult to maintain their perspective or to manage their time when results of this type of work are ambiguous. Adding to the potential for burnout is that all of this work is in addition to the stress and strain of their life experience outside of work.

## ◆ PROVIDING ASSISTANCE

Healing the handlers is possible when there is a clear personal vision of why they are helping someone, when they are provided with the tools and skills to protect themselves, and when conversations are held that recognize and bring into consciousness the intention to not get overly involved emotionally with the people in pain.

A game plan for self-protection that includes options for action is critical for long-term success. World-class athletes, for example, overcome stress through methods including hydration, physical movement, mental change of channels, balanced eating programs, and emotionally changing channels. It is also necessary to build up one's reserves in advance, and this can be fostered by:

- **Increasing one's physical strength**—keeping fit; getting a massage.
- **Boosting one's emotional capacity**—staying positive; not taking things personally; accepting what you can't change.
- **Regenerating mental capacity**—refocusing the mind; creating personal space; developing mental sanctuaries; learning to say no.
- **Building spiritual capacity**—being clear on values; revering one's life balance.

## ◆ AIDING AND SUPPORTING TOXIN HANDLERS

What handlers and their organizations can do at the interface between the handler, the organization, and the person in pain is to generate an increased level of organizational understanding, respect, and language for the role and work of toxin handling. This results in the toxin handler's feeling connected and less isolated. There is power in naming this work as a positive, contributing factor in the organization's success. The way in which this work is spoken about is a critical factor in building a compassionate organization. For example, the question "What did you do at work today?" is typically difficult for a toxin handler to answer. A positive way for the toxin handler to answer this question is to acknowledge that there is a lot of pain in the office and to express feeling that progress is being made towards shifting the situation. Other positive actions for the handlers to systematically manage and diffuse the emotional pain in organizational life include:

- Acknowledging the dynamic by naming the work, giving it legitimacy, and creating a forum to talk about it.
- Offering support, by encouraging toxin handlers to meet with professionals/ experts for assistance.
- Assigning handlers to safe zones, by sending toxin handlers to an outside conference.
- Modeling healthy behavior, by having top leaders demonstrate and reinforce the behaviors.
- Creating a supportive culture, by allowing them to learn from each other.

## ◆ WHAT DO COMPASSIONATE LEADERS DO?

Leaders sometimes create painful messes by themselves. When this happens, they need a repertoire of personal pain-handling skills. Compassionate leaders:

- Pay attention, because there is always pain in the room.
- Put people first, so as to keep the feelings and the well-being of staff in mind when decisions are made.
- Practice professional intimacy by empathizing without clouded judgment or over-identification.

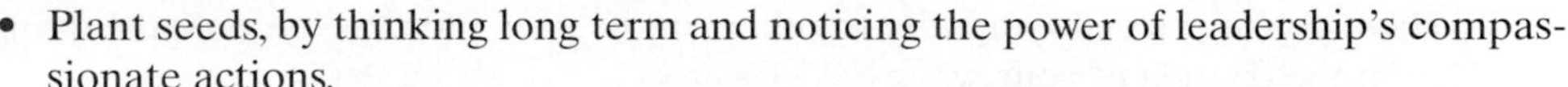

- Plant seeds, by thinking long term and noticing the power of leadership's compassionate actions.
- Push back, by addressing the toxic sources whether they be people or systems.

Leaders must be willing to place responsibility where it belongs (with whomever is accountable for the toxicity) and then sharpen the practices listed above so that the organization is responsive to pain.

## ◆ THREE MAJOR STRATEGIES

The compassionate company is more than just the leaders and gifted people who excel at handling toxic situations. The institutional venues and structures necessary to create healthy and productive workplaces can be compared to a biological system. Toxins are natural by-products in a biological system. Using the metaphor, three sets of strategies become apparent for use before, during, and after the toxic situation.

1. *Prevention* can be accomplishing by choosing new people wisely, developing existing staff, being fair minded, and setting a healthful tone.
2. *Intervention* can be implemented by dealing with downturns, dealing with acute trauma, being visible, creating meaning for the pain, and providing a context to talk about the pain.
3. *Restoration and recovery* occurs when managers demonstrate patience and trust, provide guidance, acknowledge pain, and then focus on constructive actions for resolving it.

## ◆ ORGANIZATIONAL AND INDIVIDUAL CAPACITY FOR HANDLING TOXIC SITUATIONS

The following list of questions can help the organization make an assessment of its organizational capacity and individual capacity for compassionate response(s).

For *organizational* capacity, consider:

What is the breadth of resources that can be provided to the people in need—money, work flexibility, or physical aid as well as others' time and attention?
What is the volume of resources (time and attention) required by the people who are suffering?
How quickly can a response to the suffering be delivered?
How specialized is the need in the organization?

For *individual* capacity, consider:

Can you listen and be aware of grief and maintain awareness of your own and others' response to it?
Do you know how to support initiatives that come from subordinates that may be outside of organizational norms?

Have you expressed sympathy to others in the past and can you imagine doing that in the context of your work life?

Can you deal with fast moving changes in circumstances that have an emotional focus?

## Conclusion

Paying attention to these kinds of questions and pondering how the person or the organization would answer them is an effective initial response. This can lead to a greater acknowledgement of the emotional toxicity and pain, broader self-awareness in the organization, and (hopefully) utilization of the strategies for increasing the capacity for compassionate responses within the organization.

# Authentic Happiness: Using the New Positive Psychology to Realize Your Potential for Lasting Fulfillment

***MARTIN E. P. SELIGMAN***

***Summary prepared by Cathy A. Hanson***

***Cathy A. Hanson** is the Director of Human Resources for the City of Azusa, California. She is responsible for all aspects of human resources within a dynamic city environment. A majority of her career has been spent in the human resources departments of* Fortune 100 *companies (Mars, Disney, and Kraft). Her areas of interest include high performance work teams (both private and public sector), change management, and team building. She received an M.B.A. from the University of Southern California and a B.A. in Business Administration at the University of Minnesota Duluth.*

---

Martin E. P. Seligman, *Authentic Happiness: Using the New Positive Psychology to Realize Your Potential for Lasting Fulfillment.* New York: Free Press, 2002.

## INTRODUCTION TO POSITIVE EMOTIONS

Most people would like to experience more positive emotion than negative emotion in their (work) lives. However, the focus of modern psychology has been on helping people deal with negative emotions. Little time has been spent on answering questions such as Who experiences a plentiful amount of positive emotions? Who does not? What factors enhance these emotions? and What can individuals (and managers) do to build on and experience more positive emotions?

To begin to address these issues, positive psychology has identified personal strengths that (when used) lead to feelings of happiness, pleasure, and gratification. Three criteria were identified to help define these strengths:

- The strength is valued in almost every culture.
- The strength is not a means to another end.
- The strengths are flexible, adaptable, and moldable.

These criteria were applied to a vast array of research, and six core virtues (and their underlying signature strengths) were identified: wisdom and knowledge, courage, love and humanity, justice, temperance, and spirituality and transcendence. When people identify their own key signature strengths and practice them on a daily basis, this results in greater feelings of happiness, pleasure, and gratification, and therefore they experience more positive emotions.

## EFFECTS OF POSITIVE EMOTIONS

When it comes to important life decisions, research suggests that people who utilize their signature strengths on a daily basis are smarter (make wiser choices) than people who do not. Other implications of positive emotions include:

- Happy people tend to rely on their positive past experiences when faced with daily challenges, whereas less happy people tend to be more skeptical/doubtful. Based upon their past experiences, happy people tend to assume that their current outcomes will also be positive.
- A positive, optimistic state of mind helps people think in a way that is creative, open minded, and unguarded. A negative, more pessimistic state of mind, however, contributes to a fight-or-flight way of thinking. People in this state of mind tend to focus on what is wrong and how to eliminate it.
- A positive state of mind contributes to a totally different way of thinking and perceiving than a negative state of mind.
- According to direct evidence, positive emotion predicts health and longevity, and consequently helps cushion the downfalls of aging.
- People who experience more positive emotion tend to enjoy higher job satisfaction, earn a higher income, and be more productive in their jobs than their less happy counterparts.
- People characterized by positive emotions tend to endure pain better, and they tend to take additional safety and health precautions.
- When faced with a personal or business challenge, a positive mindset will likely lead to more creative and open-minded solutions.

## INCREASING THE LEVEL OF HAPPINESS

Research suggests that happiness and a person's self-set barriers to happiness depend on three factors:

1. *Set range.* This is the general fixed range of happiness and sadness experienced by an individual; it is largely based on heredity and can be wide or narrow. The set range can be influenced by the *Hedonic treadmill,* which is the tendency to adapt to good things that happen by taking them for granted. This necessitates more and more good things in order to experience the same level of happiness again and again. Other than understanding one's inclination to be affected by the treadmill, there is little that can be done to greatly influence a person's set range.
2. *Circumstances.* Some conditions that can raise the level of happiness include:
   - **Money.** Studies have revealed that as purchasing power increases so does average life satisfaction. However, once the Gross National Product reaches $8,000 per person, the correlation disappears. The significance a person places on money influences happiness more than the actual amount of money itself.
   - **Marriage.** Studies have shown that marriage is powerfully related to happiness. However, it is not clear whether happier people get married or whether marriage makes people happier.
   - **Social life.** Studies show that happy people lead more fulfilling social lives. Again, it is not clear whether happy people are more social or whether a social life makes people happier.
   - **Negative/positive emotion.** Evidence suggests only a moderate correlation between positive and negative emotion and overall happiness. Therefore, experiencing a lot of positive emotion only moderately protects a person from experiencing negative emotions.
   - **Age.** Research shows that life satisfaction increases with age, but the experience of intense emotions, both positive and negative, decreases with age and experience.
   - **Health.** When it comes to health, *the biggest impact on happiness is a person's subjective perception of health.* Research has shown that objective measures of good health are only slightly related to happiness.
   - **Religion.** The presence of religious beliefs and practices has been shown to increase happiness by instilling hope about the future.

   In simple terms, the level of happiness can presumably be improved by changing one's circumstances. People should get married, develop a fulfilling social life, strive to experience more positive than negative emotions, value their health, and find a religion that provides them with a sense of hope. By contrast, education, climate, race, or gender hasn't been shown to have much of an effect on happiness.
3. *Voluntary variables.* These are intellectual and emotional choices that are made by people. These discretionary changes can be divided into three time frames: past, present, and future.
   - **Past.** According to research, there are three ways to increase happiness about the past: People can let go of the belief that the past (*their* past) predicts the future; they can increase their gratitude about the good things that have happened in the past; and they can learn to forgive (and forget) negative things that have happened in their past.

- **Present.** Two things have been shown to increase happiness in the present—pleasures and gratifications. *Pleasures* are enjoyable feelings that are fleeting and involve little thinking, but can be nurtured and enhanced. Pleasures can be enhanced in three distinct ways. These include:
  - **a.** *Finding new pleasant experiences to enjoy.* Habituation involves experiencing something that is initially pleasurable, but over time and exposure it loses its ability to elicit the same level of happiness. By contrast, positive people consciously inject as many pleasing events as possible into their work and personal lives and spread these factors out over time, thereby enhancing their feelings of pleasure and avoiding habituation.
  - **b.** *Savoring the positive.* Positive people become aware of the pleasure and then consciously and deliberately focus on the feelings of pleasure. In order to savor the pleasure, people are encouraged to share it with others, or store and revisit pleasurable memories.
  - **c.** *Practicing mindfulness.* Positive people live in the here and now. Meditation is one useful way to increase mindfulness of the present.
- **Future.** There are two important dimensions that illustrate one's style when contemplating the future—permanence and pervasiveness. *Permanence* is the belief that bad events are unchangeable; this mindset determines how soon a person will give up when faced with adversity. *Pervasiveness* at one extreme, is the belief that bad events influence all aspects of one's life; at the other extreme it is the belief that events are confined to the one area that experienced failure. An optimist will more likely believe that good events are pervasive, while a pessimist is more inclined to believe that good events are caused by specific and temporary factors. A pessimist will believe that bad events are pervasive and permanent. In order to increase happiness about the future and experience hope, negative pessimistic thoughts must be recognized, understood, and logically argued against.

  Unlike pleasures, *gratifications* cannot be nurtured and enhanced; they are simply experienced by demonstrating one's personal strengths and virtues. This typically occurs only after much effort, but the result is worthwhile; a positive person will experience a more meaningful life.

## ◆ USING STRENGTHS TO ACHIEVE VIRTUES

There are six virtues that are endorsed across every major religious and cultural tradition—wisdom and knowledge, courage, love and humanity, justice, temperance, and spirituality and transcendence. However, they are difficult if not impossible to measure. When these six virtues are considered together they capture the notion of good character. The paths to the six virtues and to the resultant good character come through the utilization of a person's *signature strengths*—unique characteristics that are measurable, acquirable, demonstrated across situations, lead a person to feel gratified, are valued by most cultures, and are not a means to another end. In order to achieve the virtues a person must identify and build on their signature strengths in each of the six virtue areas. In order to identify the overall top five signature strengths, twenty-four components of the six virtues must be explored.

- **Wisdom and knowledge.** There are six routes to display wisdom. These include curiosity and interest in the world, love of learning, judgment/critical thinking/openmindedness, ingenuity/originality/practical intelligence/street smarts, social intelligence/personal intelligence/emotional intelligence, and perspective.
- **Courage.** There are three ways to display courage. These include valor/ bravery, perseverance/industry/diligence, and integrity/genuineness/honesty.
- **Love and humanity.** There are two paths to humanity and love. These include kindness/generosity, plus loving/allowing oneself to be loved.
- **Justice.** There are three routes to display justice. These include citizenship/duty/teamwork/loyalty, fairness/equity, and leadership.
- **Temperance.** There are three routes to display temperance. These include self-control, prudence/discretion/caution, and humility/modesty.
- **Spirituality and transcendence.** There are seven routes to display transcendence. These include appreciation of beauty and excellence, gratitude, hope/optimism/ future-mindedness, spirituality/sense of purpose/faith/religiousness, forgiveness/mercy, playfulness/humor, and zest/passion/enthusiasm.

Once a person has identified which of the twenty-four components *most* describe who they are, they will have identified their strengths. (Additionally, identifying the twenty-four components that are *least* like themselves identifies their weaknesses.) From the former list the individual's strengths can be identified. *These signature strengths are the ones that most accurately describe a person's true self.* In order to identify the top five signature strengths, individuals should ask themselves which of these descriptors apply to each of the twenty-four components:

- a sense of ownership and authenticity
- a feeling of excitement while displaying it
- a rapid learning curve as the strength is first practiced
- continuous learning of new ways to enact the strength
- a sense of yearning to find ways to use it
- a feeling of inevitability in using the strength rather than exhaustion while using it in
- the creation and pursuit of personal projects that revolve around it
- joy, zest, enthusiasm (even ecstasy) while using it.

## Summary

Organizations and their managers should seek to provide opportunities for employees to experience an increased level of positive emotions at work. In order to enhance positive emotions and thereby create a more meaningful and purposeful life, employees—and their managers—need to recognize their set range, change happiness-influencing circumstances, change voluntary variables in the past, present, and future, and identify and utilize their signature strengths each and every day in all aspects of their lives.

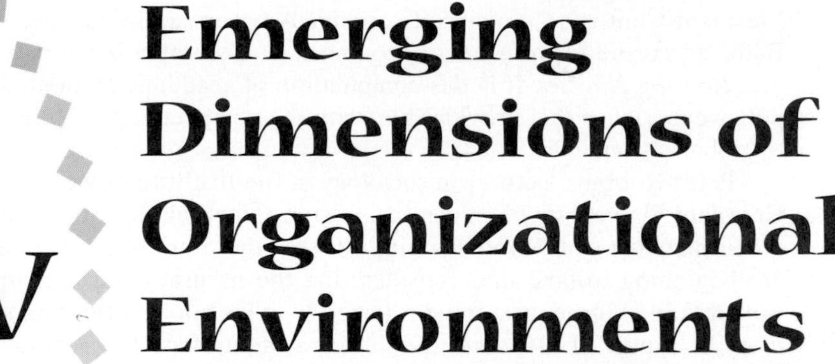

# PART XIV Emerging Dimensions of Organizational Environments

The external environment in which organizations operate has become increasingly complex, adding new challenges and responsibilities for those who manage. The world has moved from international trade to multinationalism to globalization. The global arena is a new domain for many organizations, and it holds key lessons to be learned. The dynamics generated by organizations doing business in the global arena are leading toward the creation of a borderless world. The emergence of the World Trade Organization finds corporations, not nation-states, coming together and playing a significant role in defining the conduct of commerce in this new world.

In addition to an increasingly borderless world, new technologies are having a profound impact upon organizations and the way business is conducted and how work is performed. While the exportation of blue-collar manufacturing jobs has been occurring for some time, with increasing frequency we are now hearing about the exportation of call services, computer information technology/software engineering, architecture, financial services, and accounting jobs. The digital culture is here!

With increasing concerns about global warming, the emergence of the Green party, and the continued lobbying and strength of a variety of environmental groups, an increasing number of organizations are starting to consider ways of integrating environmental concerns into the conduct of their business.

In this, the final section of *The Manager's Bookshelf: A Mosaic of Contemporary Views,* we have chosen to include three readings focused on emerging dimensions of organizations—globalization, the greening of the corporation, and the digital culture.

The first reading focuses on globalization. Joseph Stiglitz, in *Globalization and its Discontents* challenges conventional wisdom which suggests that globalization (i.e., free trade and open markets) is inevitable, beneficial, and without viable alternatives. The central theme of Stiglitz's work is captured by the words of Michael J. Mandel, chief economist for *Business Week* magazine—"Globalization is not helping many poor countries. Incomes are not rising in much of the world, and adoption of market-based policies such as open capital markets, free trade, and privatization are making developing economics less stable, not more."[1]

Joseph Stiglitz won the Nobel Prize in Economics in 2001, served as chairman of President Clinton's Council of Economic Advisors, and was chief economist at World Bank. Today, he is professor of economics at Columbia University and the author of *The Roaring Nineties.* It is this combination of academic credentials and "real world" policy experience that provides him with the perspective to challenge the current rush to globalization.

Peter Robbins, lecturer in sociology in the Institute of Water and Environment at Cranfield University, examines social-environmental corporate cultures and styles of green management. Robbins point out that there are a number of corporations that are beginning to take into consideration the natural environment as a part of their way of doing business—a trend referred to in his book's title as *Greening the Corporation.* As a part of his work, the author examines ARCO Chemical, Ben & Jerry's, Shell, and The Body Shop. Based upon his analysis of these four companies' environmental philosophies and practices, he develops a framework intended to help other organizations deal with the dilemmas of combining traditional business objectives (i.e., earning a profit) with healthy environmental objectives.

The last reading in this section is written by Rosabeth Moss Kanter. She is professor of business administration at the Harvard Business School, a consultant, business and government advisor, and author. She has written several best-selling books, among them: *Frontiers of Management, World Class: Thriving Locally in the Global Economy, Innovation: Breakthrough Thinking at 3M, Dupont, GE, Pfizer and Rubbermaid, Men and Women of the Corporation, When Giants Learn to Dance, The Challenge of Orgnizational Change: How Companies Experience It and Leaders Guide It,* and *The Change Masters: Innovation and Entrepreneurship in the American Corporation. The Times* named Kanter one of the 100 most important women in America and one of the 50 most powerful women in the world.

In *Evolve: Succeeding in the Digital Culture of Tomorrow*, Rosabeth Moss Kanter explores what she calls e-culture with an eye toward helping us understand how cyberspace is going to transform organizations and the way we live and work. Kanter reveals insider stories and lessons learned from such companies as Barnes and Noble, IBM, eBay, IBM, Sun Microsystems, and Williams-Sonoma, providing the reader with insight into pitfalls and best practices from organizations on the Internet highway.

[1]Michael J. Mandel. Where global markets are going wrong. *Business Week,* June 17, 2002, p. 17.

# Globalization and Its Discontents

*JOSEPH E. STIGLITZ*

*Summary prepared by Sanjay Goel*

***Sanjay Goel*** *(Ph.D., Arizona State University) is an assistant professor of management at the University of Minnesota Duluth. His research and teaching interests are primarily in the areas of strategic and international management, corporate governance, and the management of innovation and technology. His prior work experience includes management consulting in the agribusiness sector, where he was involved in new project appraisals and project monitoring. Currently he assists start-ups in high-tech industries with building strategic and governance expertise.*

## ◆ THE ISSUE OF GLOBALIZATION

*Globalization* involves the closer economic integration of the countries and peoples of the world. It has been brought about by the enormous reduction of costs of transportation and communication, and the breakdown of the artificial barriers to the flows of goods, services, capital, knowledge, and people across the borders. In recent years the issue of globalization and its impact on countries, their public and private institutions, and their citizens, has attracted a lot of attention. The interest is not merely academic; the pace of globalization has increased dramatically in recent years, even as its benefits are heatedly debated. The debate is complicated because even people who argue for globalization cannot quite ignore the pain it causes (sometimes even to themselves). At the same time, even the most strident opponents of globalization can see visible signs of how it has benefited themselves in very tangible ways.

Joseph E. Stiglitz, *Globalization and Its Discontents.* New York: W. W. Norton & Company, 2002.

## THE BENEFITS OF GLOBALIZATION

What have been the positive effects of globalization? Opening up to international trade has helped many countries grow far more quickly than they would otherwise have done. Export-led growth was the centerpiece of the industrial policy that made people in much of Asia far better off. Globalization has also reduced the sense of isolation felt in much of the developing world, and has given many people in the developing countries access to knowledge well beyond the reach of even the wealthiest in any country a century ago. Foreign aid, another aspect of the globalized world, for all its faults still has brought benefits to millions, often in ways that have almost gone unnoticed. For instance, guerrillas in the Philippines were provided jobs by a World Bank-financed project as they laid down their arms; irrigation projects have more than doubled the incomes of beneficiary farmers; education projects have brought literacy to the rural areas.

## GLOBALIZATION: DOES EVERYONE BENEFIT?

*Proponents of globalization, however, confuse the means with the ends.* To them, globalization itself is progress. Many of the promises of globalization, however, are just that—mere promises—with an uncertain time horizon of payoff to parties who are affected negatively. In the transition, globalization causes pain and suffering to people who are not part of decisions about globalization. In fact, *there is a growing divide between the haves and the have-nots,* which has left increasing numbers in the Third World in dire poverty, living on less than a dollar a day. The actual number of people living in poverty has actually *increased* by almost 100 million at a time when the total world income actually increased by an average of 2.5 percent annually. Neither has globalization succeeded in ensuring political and economic stability. Crises in Asia and in Latin America have threatened the economies and the stability of all developing countries. Globalization and the introduction of a market economy did not produce the promised results in Russia and most of the other economies making the transition from communism to the market. The West made the promises of unprecedented prosperity. Instead, globalization brought unprecedented poverty. In contrast, China, which designed a transition on its own, was wildly successful. Whereas in 1990 China's GDP was 60 percent that of Russia, by the end of the decade the numbers had been reversed.

The West pushed many countries willy-nilly into globalization. Critics of globalization in these countries, as well as in the West, accuse Western countries of hypocrisy. The Western countries have pushed poor countries to eliminate trade barriers, but kept up their own barriers. This prevented developing countries from exporting their agricultural products and deprived them of desperately needed export income. This hurt farmers in developing countries and consumers in Western countries. Protests by people in the know, or those who were close to the decision-making, were brushed aside, and special commercial and financial interests prevailed. Even when not directly guilty of hypocrisy, the West has controlled the globalization agenda, ensuring that it garners a disproportionate share of the benefits, at the expense of the developing

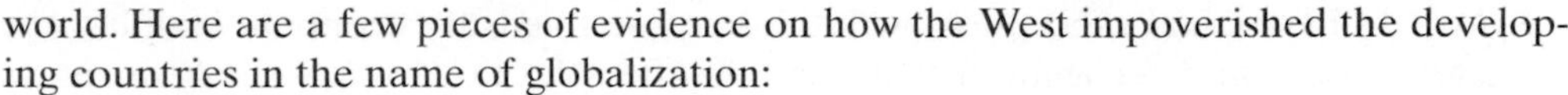

world. Here are a few pieces of evidence on how the West impoverished the developing countries in the name of globalization:

- The advanced industrial countries declined to open up their markets to the goods of the developing countries, while insisting that those countries open up their markets to the goods of the wealthier countries. The advanced industrial countries continued to subsidize agriculture, making it difficult for the developing countries to compete, while insisting that the developing countries eliminate subsidies on industrial products.
- A study of *terms of trade* (the prices which countries get for the products they produce and export) indicates that after the last trade agreement in 1995, the net effect was to lower the prices some of the poorest countries in the world received relative to what they paid for their imports, making the latter worse off.
- Western banks benefited from the loosening of capital market controls in Latin America and Asia, but those regions suffered when inflows of speculative hot money that had poured into countries suddenly reversed. Trade talks were used to strengthen intellectual property protections throughout the world. However, marginal increase in incentives to innovate also meant that thousands of people in countries such as Brazil and India were condemned to death by their own governments. The Western drug companies couldn't sell much to these citizens anyway at the prices they set.
- When projects initiated by the West but funded by private capital fail, the poor people in the developing countries still must repay the loans. Therein lies the rub—*when people suffer the consequences of decisions that they do not understand and had no voice in, it creates discontent.* Gradually, as the awareness spreads that this discontentment is not just an individual feeling, but is shared by others, it leads to full-blown revolt via sporadic voices and widespread, organized protests as witnessed in Seattle (1999) at the World Trade Organization conference, and Genoa (2001), among other places. While the general benefits of globalization have been more widely welcomed, the more narrowly defined economic aspects of globalization have been the subject of controversy, as well as the international institutions that have written the rules.

## THE ROLE OF INSTITUTIONS THAT GOVERN GLOBALIZATION

There are three main institutions that govern globalization: the International Monetary Fund (IMF), the World Bank, and the World Trade Organization (WTO). There are, in addition, other institutions that play a role in the international economic system. These include a number of regional banks and a large number of United Nations organizations (the United Nations Development Program [UNDP] and the UN Conference on Trade and Development [UNCTAD], for example). The IMF and the World Bank came into existence shortly after World War II, as part of a concerted effort to finance the rebuilding of Europe and to save the world from future economic depressions. The World Bank was given the former role—that of reconstruction and rebuilding. The task of ensuring global economic stability was assigned to IMF.

In its original conception, with the purpose to ensure economic stability, the IMF was based on a recognition that markets often did not work well. As a result, IMF could then ensure stability by proving to be the lender of last resort, introducing liquidity in the form of loans to those countries facing an economic downturn, and pressuring countries to do their fair share to maintain global aggregate demand. Thus, the IMF was founded on the belief that there was a need for collective action at the global level for economic stability. The UN serves the same purpose in ensuring political stability. The IMF is a public institution, established with money provided by taxpayers around the world, even though it does not report directly to either the citizens who finance it, or those whose lives it affects. Ministries of finance and central banks of the world's governments control it, with effective voting power determined by a country's economic power. Only one country, the United States, has an effective veto.

The IMF has changed subtly, but markedly, since it was constituted. While it was founded due to the recognition that markets are fallible, the *IMF now champions market supremacy with ideological fervor.* While it was at one time also concerned about increasing aggregate demand (via lowering taxes, increasing government spending, lowering interest rates, etc.), today the IMF champions just the opposite by controlling the purse strings. Countries are provided funds only if they engage in policies such as cutting deficits, raising taxes, or raising interest rates. The IMF's market fundamentalists believe in the power of the markets (as opposed to their fallibility) with a religious fervor. They believe that all markets are perfect, and all governments corrupt. Their solutions are to promote fiscal austerity, privatization, and *market liberalization* (the elimination of rules and regulations in many developing countries that are purportedly designed to stabilize the flows of volatile money into and out of the country) in every country with an economic crisis. As a result, the prescriptions of the current IMF are not tailored to specific political, cultural, historic, and even economic conditions of the countries to which they are applied at financial gunpoint.

Here are some specific examples of how IMF's one-size-fits-all market-based prescriptions were wrong, and even perverse, in their effects on the people they were purportedly supposed to help:

- In the East Asian crisis of 1997–1998, countries such as Thailand and Indonesia followed IMF policies almost to the letter, partially because they were also desperate to raise money. In pushing for bank restructuring, in pushing capital market liberalization prematurely, and in underestimating the importance of the interregional impacts, by which the downfall of one country contributed to that of its neighbors, the IMF caused grievous harm to these countries and its citizens and entrepreneurs, and actually delayed their recovery. The primary institutions that benefited were financial institutions in the West that were able to pull out their money from these troubled countries. Countries that listened to, but did not follow, the IMF's advice (such as South Korea and Malaysia) recovered faster, even as they were paying the price for interregional impacts due to the IMF's intervention in Indonesia and Thailand.
- In Russia, the IMF ignored the role of institutions of domestic capitalism (such as the United States' Federal Reserve Bank, the Stock Exchange Commission, the Federal Trade Commission, etc.) that have developed in industrialized countries

over decades, providing order, and checks and balances. Rather, the IMF, again relying on ideology of markets, placed its faith on prices, private property, and profits. This led to rapid inflation, erasing the savings of most Russians, and actually transferred economic power to the Russian Mafia in the name of neo-entrepreneurs. Eventually, the bailout by the IMF was used by Wall Street to pull out their money, and by the Mafia to transfer the money out to safe havens such as Switzerland.

## ◆ MANAGERIAL LESSONS

Given the way in which these institutions operate within the context of globalization, several managerial implications are offered:

1. Managers may have an ethical responsibility toward stakeholders who are affected by managerial decisions, yet these stakeholders have no voice in those decisions.
2. The dominant goals of an organization may change subtly over time. The cumulative effect of these subtle changes may lead to the antithesis of an organization's original mission.
3. *Organizational ideology may be a powerful straitjacket,* coloring all problems with the same hue, and limiting the number of solutions considered. Once this happens, the organization may hire extremely smart newcomers, with intellect and wisdom and questioning spirit, who are either quickly steeped in organizational ideology, or leave the stifling organizational culture. There is no room for dissenters or doubters.
4. Once the organizational ideology becomes a straitjacket, there is no room for any new information to lead to a change. All outcomes, even the most discordant ones, are rationalized either as positive outcomes, or explained away as random shocks or faults of other actors.
5. Managers can avoid the pathology of ideological straitjacket by encouraging debate, opening up dialogue with other institutions, and involving affected stakeholders in the decision process. The resultant climate restores the credibility of the organization (thereby ensuring its survival and legitimacy), as well as increases the welfare of other stakeholders by providing solutions that are tailored to the cultural, historic, and social context of the problem.

# Greening the Corporation: Management Strategy and the Environmental Challenge

*PETER THAYER ROBBINS*

*Summary prepared by Robert Stine*

***Robert Stine** is Associate Dean of the College of Natural Resources, University of Minnesota and Leader of the Natural Resources and Environment Capacity Area for the University of Minnesota Extension Service. His interests include leadership, organizational management, and natural resource management and utilization. He received his Ph.D. in Forest Policy from the University of Minnesota, M.S. from Oregon State University, and bachelors degree from Indiana University.*

## ◆ INTRODUCTION

During the twentieth century, approximately ten million chemicals were created in laboratories around the world. Most of these chemicals are "building blocks" that are used to manufacture millions of end-products, many of which are toxic in nature. Either in the manufacturing process or as part of an end-product, these chemicals create

Peter Thayer Robbins, *Greening the Corporation: Management Strategy and the Environmental Challenge.* London: Earthscan Publications, 2001.

environmental challenges for corporations, primarily in the areas of air pollution, toxics, and water pollution. Large agricultural and pharmaceutical corporations must also deal with the issues of biotechnology and biodiversity.

For many years, corporations paid little attention to the environmental impacts of their operations. However, beginning in the 1980s some businesses began to view the environment as a business opportunity. Others began to consider environmental and social issues in their business practices. Collectively, these practices became known as *greening the corporation.*

## ◆ ECOLOGICAL MODERNIZATION

Corporations tend to navigate their way through environmental issues at two levels. The first is at the macro level, where corporations interact with the societies in which they operate. One view on this macro level is the theory of *ecological modernization,* which holds that society (including corporations) can modernize itself out of ecological crises. It does this by integrating economics, natural sciences, corporate management, politics, regulators, and other factors to develop solutions. The ultimate goal is to continue development of modern, industrialized societies that include both economic growth and environmental responsibility.

Ecological modernization has three components, all of which impact a corporation's response to environmental issues. The first component involves institutional learning, or how well corporations respond to critical events and public opinion. Those companies that respond to environmental crises or issues by improving practices and including environmental considerations in their decisions tend over time to become more "green" (i.e., less damaging to the environment).

The second component of ecological modernization deals with how corporations view environmental issues. If they are viewed as "technocratic projects," simply something that needs a technological response to be fixed, then corporations take environmental actions only when they think it benefits their economic interest. In this case, environmental concerns are often considered only after economic objectives have been met. The result is that the environment sometimes wins and—at least in the short term—the corporate bottom line always wins.

The final component of ecological modernizations deals with cultural politics. Democratic, informed debate within a corporation can often lead to changes in how the environment is viewed. So rather than a problem that needs a technological fix, environmental challenges can be viewed as opportunities. Such a mindset is perhaps most often found in small corporations that have a "social-environmental" perspective.

## ◆ CORPORATE CULTURE AND MANAGEMENT STYLE

Ecological modernization only partially explains the process of corporate responses to environmental issues, because it deals primarily with the macro or social environment in which corporations operate. A fuller explanation, at a more micro level of corporate management, is supplied by looking at corporate culture and management style.

## CORPORATE CULTURE

Corporate culture refers to the set of norms found in organizations. Two typical corporate cultures are role and power. In a *role culture,* the role or job description is often more important than the individual who currently fills it. Role cultures are characteristic of organizations that operate in stable or non-competitive markets. A *power culture* is usually found in small, founder led, entrepreneurial organizations. Power cultures tend to have few rules and procedures, little bureaucracy, and control mechanisms that are exercised by the founder(s) mostly through the selection of key people.

Relative to environmental issues, there are subsets of these corporate cultures. For example, a corporation can have a role culture where safety is the highest priority. Such a culture is focused primarily on preventing accidents, and the role everyone in the corporation plays in preventing accidents is highly structured.

Similarly, another corporation could have a role culture where the highest priority is placed on environmental action that builds shareholder value. These corporations might concentrate on pollution prevention, energy conservation, and renewable energy sources—all fairly conservative approaches—as a way of building shareholder value while at some level addressing environmental issues.

Corporations with a power culture, typically led by the founder, have an opportunity to be more proactive relative to environmental issues because the founder can decree it so. For example, Ben & Jerry's, a manufacturer of ice cream and frozen yogurt, has a philosophy of "linked prosperity," which integrates economic, social, and environmental goals. It is a philosophy that comes directly from the founders.

The Body Shop, another founder-led organization, manufactures cosmetics, and has a power culture with a stated philosophy of "profits and principles." While wealth creation is important, the company also actively addresses environmental issues such as energy conservation, waste management, and product life-cycle assessment. The founder has been actively engaged in environmental issues, including fighting the use of animals for product testing, worldwide.

## MANAGEMENT STYLES

*Corporate environmental management* styles can be divided into four categories, each more "green" in terms of its environmental progressiveness. The four styles are compliance-oriented management, preventative management, strategic environmental management, and sustainable development management.

*Environmental compliance management* is the least progressive of the four styles, and reflects a traditional approach to environmental issues. Corporations exhibiting this style respond to environmental issues primarily to comply with legislation or litigation. Any innovative practices are generally directed toward better compliance with environmental laws.

*Preventative environmental management* goes beyond simply complying with regulations and moves toward pollution prevention and reduced consumption of resources. The majority of companies responding to a United Nations survey fell in this category. They respond to environmental issues in ways that will maintain and protect markets, or in ways that will save them money. Within companies that employ a preventative management style, managers are kept informed of environmental issues with the goal of preventing accidents and liabilities. Audits and assessment of risks and hazards are often used to ensure a preventative approach to operations.

*Strategic environmental management* incorporates environmental goals into the overall economic strategy of the corporation, often anticipating and pursuing potential green markets. Corporations using this strategy may conduct cradle to grave analyses or environmental research, and they generally respond to environmental issues in a more proactive fashion. This type of environmental management strategy is usually coordinated by the highest level managers within a corporation, and these companies also actively engage in public relations campaigns to reinforce their public image.

*Sustainable development management* is the most progressive and proactive of the four styles. Relatively few corporations worldwide are practicing this style. One defining characteristic of such organizations is that they strive to take a leadership role in their industries in response to environmental challenges. They typically institute their environmental programs worldwide, including developing countries. Typical of a sustainable development style would be statements such as:

- "We will develop and market products with superior environmental properties that will meet highest efficiency requirements."
- "We will opt for manufacturing processes that have the least possible impact on the environment."
- "We will participate actively in, and conduct research in, the environment field."
- "We will conduct a total review regarding the adverse impact of our products on the environment."
- "We will strive to attain a uniform, worldwide environmental standard for processes and products."

There is some question about whether any corporation can be truly sustainable in the very long term. However, as social expectations change and corporate operations expand into developing countries, *corporations that manage environmental challenges well can reap financial rewards.* If the challenges are mismanaged or ignored, corporations can incur high costs and liabilities.

## Conclusion

The interaction between corporations, society, and the environment is still evolving. Corporations are generally reacting to society's concerns about protecting the environment, but in different ways. Some still view environmental issues as simply a problem to be resolved or avoided. Many have a more proactive view, and look for ways to incorporate environmental issues into their business practices in a way that helps them create wealth. Finally, there are some corporations that are actively integrating economic, environmental, and social goals in an effort to become fully "green."

# Evolve! Succeeding in the Digital Culture of Tomorrow


***ROSABETH MOSS KANTER***

***Summary prepared by Rajiv Vaidyanathan***



***Rajiv Vaidyanathan** is associate professor of marketing at the University of Minnesota Duluth. He received his Ph.D. from Washington State University. He also has several years of business and consulting experience. His research interests include the examination of how consumers perceive prices and evaluate advertised deals, as well as the marketing implications of e-commerce. His research has been published in several journals, including the* Journal of the Academy of Marketing Science, Journal of Business Research, Journal of Marketing Education *and* Journal of Product & Brand Management, *as well as in the proceedings of several national and international marketing conferences.*


## ◆ INTRODUCTION

Many managers found themselves blindsided by the rapid growth and development of e-businesses. Even after the dot-com crash, smart leaders have realized that the e-business model has altered the way business is and can be conducted in this Internet-enabled world. An analysis of the new Internet model reveals that while the technology, network economics, and speed are quite different, they still face the age-old problems of leadership, organization, and change.

The Internet and its associated technologies affect businesses by playing the roles of both a stimulus and a facilitator of a new organizational culture. This new phenomenon, termed *e-culture,* is a collaborative, community-based culture that forms the

Rosabeth Moss Kanter, *Evolve! Succeeding in the Digital Culture of Tomorrow.* Boston: Harvard Business School Press, 2001.

core of e-business. Evolving to embrace this e-culture is key to taking full advantage of the Internet age. In this new age, it is important for managers to understand why they need to change, what to change, and how best to effect this change in leading, organizing, working, and thinking about their organizations.

## THE IMPORTANCE OF COMMUNITY

A key element of e-culture is the idea of *community,* which is a group of individuals with shared experiences, values and goals who voluntarily feel a sense of group identity and work together for the good of all. Ironically, while Web sites tout the "I" and "my" as core elements of their personalized experience, it is the power of the collective network of individuals that is essential to the success of on-line businesses. Within organizations, a true sense of community needs to involve more than shared dress styles or parties. There are seven elements of an ideal community:

1. *Membership:* Customers, users, employees, partners, and other affected parties all feel a shared responsibility to each other and understand their rights and their obligation to speak up.
2. *Fluid boundaries:* Ties between members extend in all directions and in many ways. Members may vary in their involvement in parts of the community over time, but still identify with the core of the organization.
3. *Voluntary action:* Members participate in their community because they want to. They do more than just their jobs because they know that they can effect change in their community.
4. *Identity:* A community exists in the minds of its members. Irrespective of physical location, the collective thoughts of members who believe that it exists make it so.
5. *Common culture:* The boundaries of a community are defined by the shared language and understandings among its members. Such commonalities assure the interchangeability and seamless information passage necessary to harness the power of the community.
6. *Collective strength:* The bonds among members of a community result in a collective strength that gives the shared ideals of the community its power to effect change.
7. *Collective responsibility:* Most successful communities have members who understand the importance of serving the needs of the community. Being an insider in a variety of real and virtual communities is necessary to grow quickly and effectively.

Understanding community dynamics is important in both online and offline environments. The idea of building community cannot simply be given lip service, but must be used to effectively meet the needs of the community. Otherwise the community may rise up against the business. In an e-culture, the same empowerment that allows members of a community to marshal their resources towards the good of the business also allows them to employ those same resources against the business. Many dot-coms have all the style and flash of e-businesses, but none of the substance. While the dot-com busts focused more on raising venture capital, the successful companies put an emphasis on the experience of their users or customers. Instead of arrogance, the firm needs confidence with the humility to learn and change based on the rapidly changing environment, maintaining a balance between technology, marketing, and content.

## KEY ELEMENTS OF e-CULTURE

Developing a Web site does not constitute Internet success. Too many companies have invested millions of dollars in a haphazard collection of Web sites across the organization with no clear evaluation of cost savings or incremental revenues. They ask various units to develop Web sites and Web capabilities based on interest or expertise within the unit, without any idea of how these efforts contribute to the overall business strategy. Success requires that businesses rethink the role of technology and networks in altering relationships with employees, customers, suppliers, intermediaries, and other stakeholders. What is essential is not cosmetic change, but systemic change; substantive change is always difficult. Building an e-culture involves overcoming all the barriers to change that exist in almost every business—lack of senior executive support, lack of technological or Web-specific expertise, resistance from key markets, suppliers or employees, lack of capital for new innovations, internal rivalries, and more. Success is defined not by having an online presence, but developing and implementing a sustainable e-business model. This requires an understanding of the four key elements of operating in the e-culture mode.

1. *Treating strategy as improvisational theater.* Just as improvisational theater involves skilled players interacting with the environment in many alternate ways to find a path to follow, managers need to rethink their approach to strategy. They must move from planning every last detail before making one big bet to exploring several avenues with small experiments in order to figure out what will work best in the uncertain environment. In contrast to the classical model, here strategy emerges from action. This rapid-fire improvisational approach to discovery-based strategy is at the heart of e-culture.

   The inherent assumption of the improvisational approach is that it is difficult to predict the reaction of people to something that is completely new to them, that has not been invented, or that has not yet happened. Skilled improvisers modify their approach based on the reaction of the audience to initial "feelers." Improvisation does not mean arbitrarily shooting from the hip. Rather it requires an overriding *theme* that provides the focus for the action. Amazon's initial focus on delivering a massive assortment of books in a quick, easy manner online allowed for some flexibility in approaches, while maintaining a focus. Improvisation also requires a *theater* that is fairly independent of the established organizational structure. For example, some e-businesses let the improvisational show evolve in "skunk works" or other theater structures that lend themselves to the development of e-culture. A third requirement of the improvisational approach is a skilled set of *actors* who are comfortable in this uncertain environment. The approach requires people who can act quickly in rapidly changing conditions without full information and also think on their feet while multi-tasking (paying attention to a multitude of things at once).

   Next, all good improvisational theater requires actively involving the audience in the production. While paying attention to the needs of customers has always been essential for success in business, e-business requires a high sensitivity to multiple audiences. These audiences may include present and potential customers, employees, peers, and others. Finally, improvisation requires recognizing constant change and striving for continuously improved interactions with the audience. Similarly, e-business involves ensuring the development of successively improved products and business models over time.

2. *Opening up to a network of partners.* The rush to get "big everywhere fast" requires maximizing every possible connection available to the business to scale-up rapidly. Good alliance managers or *collabronauts* are able to identify the best synergistic relationships that benefit all the partners in the relationship. They work at building and maintaining alliances that use personal relationships to harness the power of several parties toward a common goal. Such alliances are often complicated and sometimes tenuous. Successful collabronauts are able to effectively manage these relationships and integrate the forces for the good of the organization. Good network relationships should be built not to establish short-term deals, but to take advantage of future potential discoveries of value to the partners. This involves nurturing partnerships. While deals are done when the paperwork is signed, networks are built on the foundation of a deal. Network partners get embedded in each other's business and use carefully cultivated human relationships to manage tensions among partners. The keys to success are choosing the best partners, dealing with them based on their strategic importance, investing in them, building some interdependence so the success of each partner contributes to the success of all, open sharing of information through integrated networks, formal contracts, and absolute integrity in dealings.
3. *Moving from cell-like entities to integrated communities.* Successful e-businesses are significantly more likely than unsuccessful businesses to have departments that collaborate with each other, have conflict seen as a creative instead of disruptive force, have the freedom to do anything in support of the business that is not explicitly prohibited, and have decisions made by the people with the most knowledge instead of the highest rank. Building an e-culture involves reconstructing the organization to allow for interactions that don't degenerate into turf wars. While some collaborative environments can be built through cross-functional teams that bridge the marketing and technical worlds, true collaborative *communities* have a bottom-up approach that lets all participants in the organization feel like stakeholders.
4. *Creating a culture to attract and hold world-class talent.* The heart of any e-culture and collaborative community is people. Most employees expect equitable compensation and thus money is rarely the differentiating factor in picking among jobs. Instead, the keys to keeping quality employees lie in the three elements of community—the "three M's" of mastery, membership, and meaning. *Mastery* refers to the perceived future potential of the job. Organizational commitment in the form of training, clear paths to success, challenging work, and some ability to share in the future of the organization all add up to the "stickiness" of a job. The best people strive for achievement and greater responsibility, while shying away from the status quo. E-businesses must allow employees to stretch and feel empowered to effect change, while still having clear boundaries and priorities. *Membership* involves ensuring that employees build strong and warm personal

ties with other employees so they have a feeling of community. This can be achieved through welcome parties, mentoring, support of personal interests, adequate recognition, and mutual trust and respect. Successful e-businesses also provide their employees with a sense that their efforts contribute to more than the company's bottom line. Most dot-coms are characterized by strong social values through community service activities that are often performed jointly to build a shared set of values and identity. This gives the employees a sense of *meaning* to their work.

## ◆ THE HEART OF e-CULTURE: CHANGE

Whether a traditional organization is seeking to transform itself into an Internet-enabled organization, or a dot-com is looking to build and grow in an online world, there are no quick ways to riches on the Web. At the heart of e-culture is the need for change. Organizations need to change their internal structures in order to adapt to a constantly changing external environment. *Change needs to be a way of life and must be seen as a creative force within the organizations.* Building such a nimble organization requires a commitment to go beyond cosmetic alterations and a willingness to embrace major strategic change.

## ◆ GETTING CHANGE ROLLING

One big massive overhaul is not enough. The entire organization needs to operate in a way that allows for rapid and continuous change. In order to get this change rolling, leaders must work on a set of elements that all build toward systemic change. These are:

1. *Common theme, shared vision:* It is important to get everyone in the organization on the same page by clearly articulating and communicating the vision for the "e-volved" organization.
2. *Symbols and signals:* Small acts can symbolize the seriousness of the leadership to truly change the way things are going to operate. Even something simple like redefining the use of office space may symbolize how the new organizational structure will alter communication flows and relationships in the organization.
3. *Guidance structure and process:* Assigning accountability for steering the change at the macro-organizational level is important in ensuring that all the change efforts are aimed in the right direction.
4. *Education, training, action tools:* Change does not happen at all levels of the organization with grand announcements and symbolic gestures. Leaders must inform employees of the impact on their day-to-day activities and provide the tools necessary to effect change at their level.
5. *Champions and sponsors:* Every effort at change requires someone who is actively campaigning for the change and ensuring the support of "sponsors" who will execute the change.
6. *Quick wins and local innovations:* Once the vision is established, it is important to implement some innovations at the local level to demonstrate that change is

achievable and beneficial. Approaching this as improvisational theater will ensure demonstrable action that is consistent with the overarching vision of the "directors."

7. *Communications and best practice exchange:* To avoid chaotic change, multidirectional flow of information is critical. Leaders need to know what the local units are doing and the local units need to know what the leaders are expecting. Sharing information among peers also allows for the emergence of "best practices" that make the implementation of change more efficient.
8. *Policy, procedures, system alignment:* All the organizational policies and procedures need to be reexamined in light of the new vision to ensure that they are aligned. Change in vision without supportive changes in policies and procedures will either lead to frustration or inaction.
9. *Measures, milestones, and feedback:* As the organization evolves, it is important for everyone to know if the change is proceeding along the right track. Feedback on successes can improve morale and build consistency in efforts toward the change.
10. *Rewards and recognition:* No change is possible without people at the grassroots overcoming the inevitable obstacles to change. Appropriately rewarding supporters of change will highlight the heroes who can then serve as role models for the rest.

These elements of getting change rolling can be seen as a wheel, with each of the ten elements forming the spokes of the wheel. True change requires not going through the process once, but constantly cycling through the elements as the change efforts gather momentum and making adjustments based on the reactions of the various audiences to the change. Operating in an e-culture necessitates operating in an environment of constant, evolving change.

## ◆ LEADING CHANGE: SKILLS FOR CHANGEMASTERS

While the importance of change has been rehashed in business books over many years, the Internet-enabled world has dramatically altered the rate and the scope of this change. The demand to "get big everywhere fast" requires altered views on how to overcome resistance to change. Effecting this broad-based change involves seven essential skills that reflect a style that is basic to e-culture. The best leaders of change in an organization, the *changemasters,* are those individuals who effectively sponsor, lead, and manage the process of systemic change within an organization. Ideally, they should possess or develop these seven key skills.

**Skill 1:** *Continuous environmental monitoring.* The best changemasters are so tuned into the environment that they instinctively identify needs in the marketplace and even the need to change within the organization. They also are able to anticipate and deal with problems before they become disasters. They constantly have their antennae up and monitor multiple information sources for ways to make things better. Just as great improvisational actors are tuned in to their environment so that they can sense changes and react to them, changemasters don't assume they know their customers or are better than their competitors. They don't surround themselves with people who agree with them. They do not bask in their success or revel in the failures of their competitors. They verge on the paranoid as they look for signs that someone else could innovate them into oblivion.

**Skill 2:** *Breakthrough thinking.* While the best e-business leaders are finely attuned to changes in the environment, they also have the ability to use this information to generate exciting new ideas. These leaders are able to put the pieces of information together a little differently and analyze the buffet of strategic options in unique ways. They see distinctive patterns and are not bound by convention in their approaches to problems. This is what makes them innovators as opposed to imitators. Breakthrough thinking can be developed within the organization by encouraging managers to dissect both their successes and failures and look for special juxtapositions that provided unexpected results, by going "off the beaten path" on trips to see how things are done in other environments quite differently, by conducting large brainstorming sessions, and even holding talent shows that poke fun at tradition.

**Skill 3:** *Inspiring a vision.* In order to get stakeholders to rally around an idea, it needs to be condensed into a meaningful and inspiring vision. The vision needs to be communicated in a manner that gets everyone excited about the prospects. Visions must combine aspirational goals with pragmatic values that tell the employees what's in it for them. The vision must be clear as to the organization's destination, its role in changing the world, the positive outcomes and benefits to each person, evaluation metrics that benchmark success, an image or slogan that succinctly summarizes the goal, and a tangible first step that highlights the attainability of the vision. The vision can best be communicated not in a written placard or laminated wallet card. Rather, the passion and enthusiasm of the leaders and their aggressive pursuit of the vision is what gives it legs.

**Skill 4:** *Building a coalition.* Ensuring successful change also requires leaders to go beyond a mandate for change. It involves building a coalition of forces that work for the change. Leaders need to understand the politics of the organization and the barriers to change, while serving as community organizers who use their personal networks to build a consensus aligned with the vision. Successful changemasters start by sounding people out about the idea to find out where people stand and make adjustments based on their feedback. They then creatively try to make the necessary deals to get the resources to implement the idea. Finally, they monitor the results and make adjustments based on the reactions of all the parties involved as the coalition of people backing the idea gets larger.

**Skill 5:** *Nurturing the team.* In a sense, the team working on the idea is a micro-community. Just like any group of individuals is not a community, it takes a shared sense of identity, a shared vision, clear goals, and mutually-agreed-upon deadlines to make a group a team. The role of the change agent is to ensure that the bonds necessary to turn a task force into a team develop. Leaders must provide the team with time and space to get their creative energies flowing. The leader must provide the tools for communication among members and be an advocate for the efforts of the team through the rest of the organization. It is the leader's responsibility to obtain the resources necessary to let the team operate effectively and efficiently.

**Skill 6:** *Having persistence and perseverance.* Managing change is an active process. Good changemasters don't step aside as the change gets rolling. Rather, they actively monitor progress and resolve the problems that emerge. In that fast-paced and unknown Internet-enabled world, it is not unusual for unexpected obstacles to arise, forecasts to fall short, momentum to start slowing, and critics of the plan to start growing louder. The successful leader understands the need to improvise and be flexible enough to adapt to the challenges. Constantly boosting the enthusiasm of a hardworking group and persevering on the vision in the face of doubters and critics is an essential skill of a successful changemaster. Leading change involves a great deal of determination to make sure the enthusiasm and motivation don't fade in the face of obstacles.

**Skill 7:** *Providing appropriate recognition.* Celebration for a job well done is a core part of e-culture. Given the frenetic pace of change and heightened expectations of the people working in e-business environments, it becomes important to recognize achievement not only for its motivational value, but also to build support for the efforts from others in the organization and from partners. People recognized and rewarded for engaging in change are more likely to keep the change rolling—an important goal of e-businesses.

## Conclusion

The technological revolution has changed the face of business. However, it does not provide a simple and solitary answer to the question of how businesses should change. Rather it opens up myriad possibilities on how businesses can successfully respond. The solution to operating in this new environment is to be flexible enough to change in ways that allow for continuous change. Building new value propositions in new environments requires not just change, but *sustainable change.* Sustainable change requires a fundamental change in the people and processes at the heart of the organization. These people cannot simply be told to change. They must internalize the need to change and voluntarily alter their behaviors to make the organization competitive in the new world.

Leaders in this e-culture need to inspire, motivate, and guide the change, while staying focused on the vision. They must ensure that the stage is set, the players are trained and prepared, and the audiences are ready before trusting them to improvise and adapt to the changing world. The actual pace of change will vary across organizations, but ultimately the goal is fundamental change and the building of a close-knit community with shared goals and identities. Community involves an enmeshed network of human relationships. Building an e-culture does not mean isolated, faceless individuals depending exclusively on electronic communications. Rather, successful e-cultures depend on closer human relationships where the *people* communicate effectively to voluntarily achieve mutually beneficial goals. This is the essence of "evolving" to succeed in the new digital culture.

# Glossary of Terms

**Acting mindfully** Operating in a manner that allows a manager to better notice the unexpected in the making and halt its development. (Weick and Sutcliffe)

**Action orientation** Having a tendency to act, to do something regardless of consequences. (LaFasto and Larson)

**Adaptive capacity** The ability to find new skills, new appreciation, a new vision, and new resolve for future encounters based on an experience of change. (Bennis and Thomas)

**Ambiguity** Inability to characterize important aspects of a decision such as arena of action, objectives, or remedies. (Nutt)

**Ambition** The drive for gain and growth. (Bennis and Thomas)

**Amygdala** The part of the brain that triggers emotional reactions before the thinking brain has a chance to pick up the signal. (Frost)

**Arena of action** The remedy implied by the concerns and considerations that initiates action. (Nutt)

**Authentic leadership** Actions by people of high integrity who are committed to building enduring organizations relying on morality and character. (George)

**Availability bias** The fallacy of allowing the recency and amount of publicity given to information to be remembered and given more weight than it merits. (Murnighan and Mowen)

**Balanced life** Leading a life that recognizes the importance of work, family, friends, faith and community service, with none of them excluding any of the others. (George)

**Balanced path** The approach that harmonizes worker fulfillment with enterprise performance. (Katzenbach)

**Balanced scorecard** A means of measuring an organization's strategy map along four key dimensions—financial, customer, internal business process, and learning/growth (Kaplan and Norton); a method of reporting on corporate performance that emphasizes the entire value chain (internal and external processes rather than historical lagging indicators), not just financial indicators. (Conger, Lawler, and Feingold)

**Boulder of oppression** Overt and subtle forms of discrimination based on individual, organizational, and societal belief systems that value one social identity group over another (e.g., racism, sexism, ageism, heterosexism). (Miller and Katz)

**Burnout** The effects of a mismatch between the needs of an employee and the demands of a job, which can be manifested by an erosion of emotions, frustration, and health symptoms. (Cascio)

**Business unit** A unit within an organization that has control over both revenues and costs, and therefore can calculate its own profit or loss over any period of time. (Kaplan and Norton)

**Changemasters** Those individuals in an organization who sponsor, lead, and manage the process of systemic change within an organization. (Kanter)

**Cheese** A metaphor for anything that employees are seeking (as rewards for their efforts) or elements of their environment with which they are familiar (that cause confusion if changed). (Johnson)

**Choice-structuring process** A process whose goal is to produce sound strategic choices that lead to successful action. (Argyris)

**Circumstance-based categorization** Segmentation of products and services. (Christensen)

**Climbers** Companies that lagged their peers in the first period, but achieved performance better than their peers in the second. (Joyce, Nohria, and Roberson)

**Collaboration** A coordinated effort among team members to attain an outcome. (LaFasto and Larson); One possible result of conflict resolution in which both sides work together to get what each needs. (Thomas)

**Collaborative work system** A form of organization that practices a disciplined system of collaboration and a set of ten principles to achieve superior results so as to be successful in a rapidly changing environment. (Beyerlein, Freedman, McGee, and Moran)

**Collabronauts** Managers who are good at building and maintaining alliances that use personal relationships to harness the power of several parties toward a common goal. (Kanter)

**Commoditization** The process that transforms profitable, differentiated, proprietary products into undifferentiable commodities. (Christensen)

**Community** A group of individuals with shared experiences, values, and goals who feel a sense of group identity and work together for the good of all. (Kanter)

**Compassionate organization** Organizations that promote a culture of and a set of practices and respectful policies that produce generative responses from their people and link the emotional health of the organization with the bottom line. (Frost)

**Compassionate responding** The capacity to listen to grief and to provide sympathy and support in a relatively short time. (Frost)

**Competence** The component of integrity that includes expertise in critical leadership skills. (Bennis and Thomas)

**Competitive advantage** Structure, human resources, processes, knowledge, culture, and other aspects of the organization that provide a sustainable edge in the marketplace. (Lawler); The edge a firm can gain over its competitors by providing equivalent benefits at a lower price, or greater benefits that compensate for a higher price than competitors charge. (Porter)

**Consequence management** A management philosophy that rewards and punishes on the basis of the consequences or results of individual action. (Katzenbach)

**Containment** The ability of an organization (derived from resilience and deference to expertise) to recover from unexpected negative events. (Weick and Sutcliffe)

**Context** The situational background surrounding a decision. (Nutt)

**Converge/diverge** The process of moving back and forth from small group to large group to integrate the combined wisdom of the entire system. (Dannemiller Tyson)

**Core competencies** Technical areas of organizational expertise that can support the pursuit of strategic objectives and provide the basis for sustained competitive advantage. (Lawler)

**Credibility** A combination of honesty, inspiration, and competence in leaders that inspires workers to be motivated, feel valued, and act ethically. (Kouzes and Posner)

**Credibility gap** The difference between what leaders say and what they do. (Kouzes and Posner)

**Crisis management** The discipline of planning, preparing, and acting to substantially limit both the duration and damage caused by human-made crises with the objective of allowing the organization to recover from a crisis more quickly and with less lasting damage. (Mitroff)

**Crisis scenario** A plan for how the unthinkable will occur, which is used to test the organization's crisis management capability. (Mitroff)

**Crisis type** One of the seven families of crises: economic, informational, physical, human resource, reputational, psychopathic acts, and natural disasters. (Mitroff)

**Critical mass** The set of key decision-makers and decision-influencers necessary for success. (Dannemiller Tyson)

**Cross-selling** Selling several products to the same customers as a way to realize revenue synergies. (Kaplan and Norton)

**Crucibles** Those transforming events or situations that radically change a person's leadership abilities and skills. (Bennis and Thomas)

**Culture** The way in which the organization brings together large numbers of people and imbues them for a sufficient time with a sufficient similarity of approach, outlook, and priorities to enable it to achieve collective, sustained responses that would be impossible if a group of unorganized individuals were to face the same problem. How things really get done in an organization. (Weick and Sutcliffe)

**Customer-focused quality** A quality measurement that focuses externally on cus-

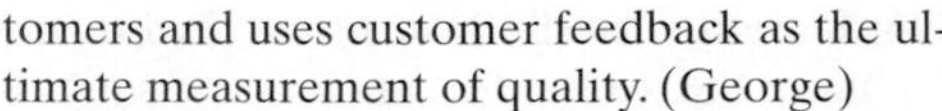

tomers and uses customer feedback as the ultimate measurement of quality. (George)

**Cycle time** The amount of time spent from beginning to completion of a task or project (Thomas)

**Death spiral** The opposite of a virtuous spiral, this deteriorating condition flourishes in organizations that mishandle their human capital, in turn causing both individual and organizational performance decline. (Lawler)

**Decision myopia** Events in the present are valued more than those that will occur in the future, resulting in a tendency for decision-makers to overweight present outcomes and underweight future outcomes. (Murnighan and Mowen)

**Deliberate strategy** Improved understanding of what works and what doesn't based on deliberate, conscious, and analytical decision-making. (Christensen)

**Differentiation** Providing something unique that is valuable to buyers and for which they are willing to pay a price premium. (Porter)

**Differentiation** Realizing that we are all unique individuals, responsible for our own survival and well-being, while enjoying the expression of our being in action. (Csikszentmihalyi)

**Disruptive innovations** A strategy that targets new less demanding customers with products and services that, although not as good as the currently available products, appeal due to simplicity, cost, or convenience. (Christensen)

**Disruptive self-expression** The art of using modest changes in one's language, dress, office decor, or behavior to slowly initiate change in the work atmosphere. (Meyerson)

**Dissonant leadership** The ability to generate discord by being unresponsive to other people's feelings. (Goleman, Boyatzis, and McKee)

**Diversity** Commitment to the principle that a company's employees and customers reflect the values and the cultures of the community in which it operates. (Batstone)

**Diversity in a box model** An organizational belief that differences should be managed, tolerated, or molded to fit the dominant organizational culture. (Miller and Katz)

**Downsizing** An intentional, proactive management strategy, which can include reductions in the firm's financial, physical, and human assets. (Cascio)

**Drive to acquire** The innate human need to obtain objects and increase our relative status. (Lawrence and Nohria)

**Drive to bond** The innate human need to form reciprocal bonds with others. (Lawrence and Nohria)

**Drive to defend** The innate human need to protect our selves and what we hold dear. (Lawrence and Nohria)

**Drive to learn** The innate human need to make sense of ourselves and of our world. (Lawrence and Nohria)

**Ecological modernization** A theory that society can modernize itself out of ecological crises by integrating economics, natural sciences, corporate management, politics, regulators, and other factors to develop solutions that allow both economic growth and environmental responsibility. (Robbins)

**e-Culture** A collaborative, community-based culture that forms the core of e-business. (Kanter)

**Effective managers** Managers who manage themselves and others so that both employees and the organization benefit. (Blanchard and Johnson)

**Emergent strategy** The cumulative effect of day-to-day prioritizations identifying unanticipated opportunities, problems, and successes. (Christensen)

**Emotional fortitude** The ability to be honest with oneself and deal honestly with business realities, based upon the four qualities of authenticity, self-awareness, self-mastery, and humility. (Bossidy)

**Emotional intelligence** A set of competencies distinguishing how people manage feelings and interactions with others. (Goleman)

**Empathy** The ability to sense what people are feeling through receiving and interpreting verbal and nonverbal messages. (Goleman)

**Enlightened management systems** Organizations where employees are assumed to be at the highest levels of the need hierarchy, are capable of self-actualization, and are receptive to management practices that keep people informed, provide clarity of direction, and challenge them to stretch and grow. (Maslow)

**Enriched jobs** Jobs that create three psychological conditions: experience of meaningfulness, experience of responsibility, and feedback or knowledge of results. (Lawler)

**Environmental compliance management** The organization meets minimal expectations by focusing primarily on complying with environmental laws or litigation. (Robbins)

**Erotic personality** A person who is centered on loving and being loved. (Maccoby)

**Espoused theories** The beliefs and values people hold about how to manage their lives. (Argyris)

**Ethics** Value-based positions taken by a decision's stakeholders. (Nutt)

**Evolutionary change** Cultural changes induced through gentle, incremental, decentralized approaches that have lasting effects but less upheaval. (Meyerson)

**Execution** The disciplined and systematic process of exposing reality (key information) through robust dialogue and acting on it with intensity and rigor. (Bossidy)

**Executive discipline** The implied rules executives follow to enforce individual accountability and consequence management. (Katzenbach)

**External commitment** Commitment that is triggered by management policies and practices that enable employees to accomplish their tasks. (Argyris)

**Extrinsic motivation** Anything that can be bestowed upon employees from others to stimulate their motivation and provide satisfaction to them. (Ventrice)

**Extrinsic rewards** Rewards that come from external sources, such as money, prestige, and acceptance. (Thomas)

**False spiral** A spiral that occurs when an organization or individual believes it has started a virtuous spiral, when in fact it is simply an illusion. (Lawler)

**Feedback** Information regarding results of one's efforts (how well one is performing). (Blanchard and Johnson)

**Flow** Full involvement with life. (Csikszentmihalyi)

**Frame** A conceptual window, mindset, or paradigm that illuminates some aspects of a decision and obscures others. (Nutt)

**Fraudulent spiral** A spiral that can be easily mistaken for a virtuous one, but it is caused by deceitful activities. (Lawler)

**Fundamental attribution error** Propensity to place the cause for another person's outcomes on themselves (blame the victim) rather than bad luck or external factors. (Murnighan and Mowen)

**Geeks** Successful leaders under 35 years old who came into maturity during the 1991–2000 decade. (Bennis and Thomas)

**Geezers** Highly successful leaders who are now over 70 years old who came into maturity during the period of 1945–1954. (Bennis and Thomas)

**Globalization** The closer integration of the countries and peoples of the world which has been brought about by the enormous reduction of costs of transportation and communication, and breaking down the artificial barriers to the flows of goods, services, capital, knowledge, and people across the borders. (Stiglitz)

**Good character** A moral state that is demonstrated when a person utilizes signature strengths and demonstrates a combination of the six virtues. (Seligman)

**Hedonic treadmill** Ability to adapt to positive experiences that requires more and more of the experience in order to feel the same level of happiness that was experienced initially. (Seligman)

**High performance work practices** Management policies and practices (e.g., open communications, information sharing, performance-based pay systems, empowered teams, and extensive training opportunities) that focus on developing and making the most effective use of an organization's human assets. (Cascio)

**Highly reliable organizations (HRO)** Organizations that operate under very trying conditions all the time, yet manage to have fewer than their fair share of accidents. Examples include power grid dispatching centers, air traffic control systems, nuclear aircraft carriers, nuclear power plants, hospital emergency departments, and hostage negotiation teams. (Weick and Sutcliffe)

**Hindsight bias** Inability to look objectively at a decision's outcome and to have anticipated the consequences of a decision, resulting in decision-makers overestimating how well a problem or outcomes from a problem could

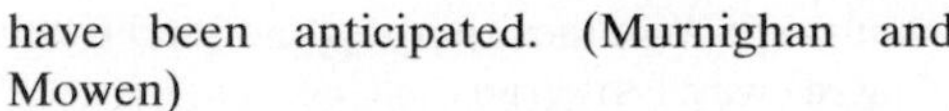

have been anticipated. (Murnighan and Mowen)

**Hundred-year manager** Manager who leads the business and makes decisions based upon the belief that the company will still be operating one hundred years from now. (Csikszentmihalyi)

**Illusion of control** Decision-maker acts as though s/he can influence purely chance events. (Murnighan and Mowen)

**Illusion of correlation** Condition occurring when decision makers focus exclusively on the cell in the matrix that corresponds with a "hit," while ignoring how many times they were wrong. (Murnighan and Mowen)

**Illusion of performance** Attributing internal factors (oneself) as the explanation for good outcomes and attributing external factors as the explanation for bad outcomes in greater proportion than merited by the facts. (Murnighan and Mowen)

**Illusion of the run** The concept of regression to the mean as the probable outcome, due to the fact that chance is one of the factors in affecting success and failure. (Murnighan and Mowen)

**Illusions of causality** Various flawed mental processes that lead the decision-maker to inaccurately conclude that causality exists when it does not or that there is no causality when it does exist. (Murnighan and Mowen)

**Improvisational theater** An approach where skilled actors work on developing an interactive and dramatic product without a script and based on the reaction of other players and the audience. (Kanter)

**Inclusion breakthrough** When an organization creates a culture in which every individual is valued as a unique and vital component of the organization's success. (Miller and Katz)

**Inclusive competencies** Workplace behaviors that encourage communicating across differences, resolving conflict, and valuing every individual as a unique contributor to the organization's mission. (Miller and Katz)

**Inside-out management** Commitment derived from energies internal to human beings that are activated because getting a job done is intrinsically rewarding. (Argyris)

**Institutional-building pride** Intrinsic pride that is based on emotional commitment that tends to further collective rather than strictly individual sets of interest. (Katzenbach)

**Integration** Creating conditions at work such that individuals can best achieve their own goals by directing their efforts toward the success of the enterprise. (McGregor)

**Integration** Realizing that however unique and independent people are, they are also completely enmeshed in networks of relationships with other human beings. (Csikszentmihalyi)

**Integrity** An unwavering adherence to principles on which mutual trust can be based. (Csikszentmihalyi)

**Integrity** The ability to do the right thing, which is comprised of three components: ambition, competence, and a moral compass. (Bennis and Thomas)

**Intrinsic motivation** Factors such as job design, meaningful tasks, and feeling trusted that provide an internal source of satisfaction for employees because the reward comes from within. (Ventrice)

**Intrinsic rewards** Rewards that come from internal sources, generating positive emotions such as initiative and commitment. (Thomas)

**J. M. Keynes** Influential economist who provided prescriptions (e.g., deficit spending) for governments to help the economy climb out of recessions. (Stiglitz)

**Leadership capacity** The amount of leadership time and talent available to a group or organization at a specific point in time. (Katzenbach)

**Leadership characteristics** A desired combination of heart, purpose, values, relationships, and self-discipline. (George)

**Learning** A means to find pitfalls that made a decision fail to meet expectations. (Nutt)

**Learning disability** A way of thinking in organizations that keeps managers and others from making necessary changes and adapting to environmental needs. (Senge)

**Level 5 leader** A person who builds enduring greatness through a paradoxical combination of personal humility plus professional will and fearlessness. (Collins)

**Leveraging diversity** A strategy based on the belief that diversity can be found in all individuals because of each person's unique background, experiences, and perspectives and when acknowledged unleashes the power of human creativity. (Miller and Katz)

**Liberalization of capital markets** The elimination of rules and regulations in many developing countries that are purportedly designed to stabilize the flows of volatile money into and out of the country. (Stiglitz)

**Limbic center** The "emotional center" of the brain that sorts incoming messages based on their relevance to human needs. (Lawrence and Nohria)

**Listening to pain** The core competence of the toxin handler that involves listening with compassion and providing a moment of human connection. (Frost)

**Losers** Companies that lagged peers in both periods. (Joyce, Nohria, and Roberson)

**Low-end disruptions** The process of attacking the least profitable and most over-served customers at the low end of the original value network. (Christensen)

**Manager-led teams** Teams who merely perform the task by carrying out the instructions of their manager or leader. (Hackman)

**Managing By Wandering Around (MBWA)** The process of having managers spend a substantial portion of their time meeting with customers, vendors, and employees to learn their needs. (Peters and Waterman)

**Marketing personality** Persons who are centered on meeting the needs of their surroundings in terms of what is needed to impress and succeed. (Maccoby)

**Mindful anticipation** The useful mindset resulting from a preoccupation with potential failure, reluctance to simplify interpretations, and sensitivity to operations that enables HROs to respond effectively to unexpected events. (Weick and Sutcliffe)

**Mission-driven organization** An organization that utilizes its mission statement as an integral part of managing the organization, not merely a plaque that hangs on the CEO's wall. (George)

**Mobilization** The process of shaking up, or unfreezing, an organization to make it clear that change is needed. (Kaplan and Norton)

**Model I** The management theory that individuals use to protect themselves, while unilaterally treating others in the same (undifferentiated) way. (Argyris)

**Model II** The management theory that relies upon valid information, free and informed choice, and internal commitment. (Argyris)

**Moral compass** The ability to differentiate good and evil, along with the recognition that leaders do not live their lives alone. (Bennis and Thomas)

**Narcissistic leaders** Leaders who reject the status quo, focus on how they think things ought to be, and create the world in their own image. (Maccoby)

**Narcissistic personality** A person who is self-directed, not concerned with what others might think, free of social control, and attempts to satisfy a vision of an internal ideal or an outside market. (Maccoby)

**Neoteny** The youthful, almost puppy-like quality that attracts others to an individual. It is to have energy, to stimulate and enjoy being stimulated, to be curious, to have a contagious laugh, and to feel alive. (Bennis and Thomas)

**New logic organization** A firm with a set of strategies for the pursuit of an organization's objectives that stress product- and customer-focused designs, the effective use of human resources, participatory business involvement, and performance-based compensation systems. (Lawler)

**New-design plants** Organization-wide approaches to participative management in which group members participate in selection decisions, the layout facilitates workgroup tasks, job design revolves around teams, and pay systems are egalitarian. (Lawler)

**New-market disruptions** The process of creating new value networks and products that are more affordable to own. (Christensen)

**Obsessive personality** A person who attempts to live up to an internalized standard of high ideals and high expectations. (Maccoby)

**Open system** An arrangement of interrelated parts interacting with its external environment. (Dannemiller and Tyson)

**Openness** Willingness to address issues, speak one's mind, and listen to others' ideas. (LaFasto and Larson)

**Organizational design** The set of activities necessary to determine the strategic direction

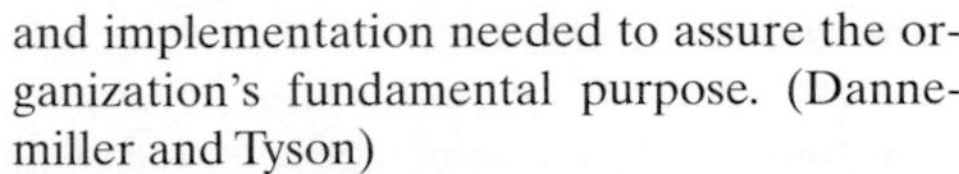

and implementation needed to assure the organization's fundamental purpose. (Dannemiller and Tyson)

**Organizational restructuring** Planned changes in a firm's organizational structure that affect its use of people, including the possibility of workforce reductions. (Cascio)

**Organizations** Those systems in which people come together in communities to accomplish something meaningful. (Dannemiller and Tyson)

**Outside directors** Board members who are not employees of the firm or consultants paid by the firm, and are not related to or social acquaintances of members of senior management. (Conger, Lawler, and Finegold)

**Owning up** Admitting to errors or flaws in a decision-making process. (Nutt)

**Paradigm shift** A change to a new paradigm or model having new rules, boundaries, and behaviors. (Dannemiller and Tyson)

**Peak performers** Any group of employees whose emotional commitment enables them to deliver products or services that constitute a sustainable competitive advantage for their employers. (Katzenbach)

**Peer recognition** Formal or informal efforts by co-workers to praise employees for their positive contributions at work. (Ventrice)

**Performance-based pay** Compensation systems that reward individuals based on the extent to which their behaviors and outcomes contribute to the achievement of organizational goals. (Lawler)

**Personality type** The core self, to which is added the attitudes and values learned, that determines the way in which someone responds to their surroundings. (Maccoby)

**Play** The introduction of joy, fun, and enthusiasm into a work environment. (Lundin, Paul, and Christensen)

**Positive personal style** An attitude and disposition portraying energy, optimism, confidence, and fun. (LaFasto and Larson)

**Power culture** An organizational culture that depends on a central source of power, typically the organization's founder, that spreads throughout the organization. (Robbins)

**Power curve** Relationship between time and the effects of taking action. (Murnighan and Mowen)

**Preventative environmental management** An approach that emphasizes pollution prevention and reduced consumption of resources. (Robbins)

**Primal leadership** The theory that leadership effectiveness is rooted in the primordial regions of our brain governing our ability to perceive and identify our emotional states. (Goleman, Boyatzis, and McKee)

**Principled leadership** Corporate leadership ensures that all of the firm's operations meet or exceed standards developed in accordance with publicly stated principles and values. (Batstone)

**Problem** The difference between what is actually happening and what you want to happen. (Blanchard and Johnson)

**Process gain** The increment that occurs when the collective efforts of the team exceed what the individual members could have achieved working independently. (Hackman)

**Process loss** The deficiency that occurs when a group accomplishes less than it theoretically should, given its resources and member talents. (Hackman)

**Processess** The patterns of interaction, coordination, communication, and decision-making through which inputs are transformed into outputs. (Christensen)

**Productive narcissists** People (often leaders) who want to change the world. (Maccoby)

**Productiveness** The process of fully living up to one's potential by being free, rational, passionately active, knowing their powers, having purpose, and persevering. (Maccoby)

**Productivity** Employee output in terms of the quantity and quality of work completed. (Blanchard and Johnson)

**Professional intimacy** Working in a way that honors the integrity of the position, the person, and the organization at a level of connection deeper than normal. (Frost)

**Property conception** A view of the corporation as the private property of the shareholders. The board members are held to be agents of the shareholder/owners and concerned primarily with the financial return on their investment. (Conger, Lawler, and Finegold)

**Rationality** A way of thinking about a decision that stresses analysis and logic. (Nutt)

**Recognition** A personalized acknowledgement of an employee's accomplishments toward organizational goals. (Ventrice)

**Reframing** Informally or formally translating communications in the organization in such a way that emotional pain will be reduced or deflected from reaching the intended audience. (Frost)

**Reprimand** Negative verbal feedback provided when undesirable employee behavior and performance occur. (Blanchard and Johnson)

**Resonant leadership** The ability to move others in a positive direction by being responsive to their feelings. (Goleman, Boyatzis, and McKee)

**Responsible restructuring** An alternative to "slash and burn" workforce reductions, wherein employee' ideas and efforts form the basis of sustained competitive advantage by addressing underlying competitive problems. (Cascio)

**Risk ratio** A formula used to quantitatively determine where the trigger for decision-making should be set, determined by dividing the value of a needless blunder by the sum of the value of a needless blunder + the value of a missed opportunity. (Murnighan and Mowen)

**Robust dialogue** The candid exchange of information and feelings, requiring open minds, a desire to hear new information, extensive questioning, critical thinking, and a drive toward closure. (Bossidy)

**Role clarity** Clear understanding of one's responsibilities as a team member, both within oneself and by others. (LaFasto and Larson)

**Role culture** An organizational culture where the role or job description is more important than the individual who fills it (a typical bureaucracy). (Robbins)

**Role of malice** The actions of managers that are designed to degrade others or to undermine the confidence or self esteem of others. Creating pain may be a source of control to assure there are no challenges to authority. (Frost)

**Root cause analysis** Process used to help accurately determine the underlying cause(s) for a problem while minimizing biases such as the illusion of causality. (Murnighan and Mowen)

**Safe zones** Created spaces where toxin handlers are moved out of the stressful situations within the organization for a period of time in order to let them re-energize and rest. (Frost)

**Selective adaptation** Choice of a method or action that accommodates identified conditions rather than ignoring or going against those facts. (McGregor)

**Self-actualizing employees** Those persons who institute their own ideas, make autonomous decisions, learn from their mistakes, and grow in their capabilities. (Maslow)

**Self-awareness** Being aware of your moods and feelings in the present moment. (Goleman)

**Self-designing teams** Teams who perform, self-manage, and also design the team and its organizational context. (Hackman)

**Self-governing teams** Teams who perform a task, self-manage, and design themselves as well as establish the overall direction of the team. (Hackman)

**Self-managing teams** Teams who perform a task as well as monitor and manage work process and progress. (Hackman)

**Self-serving pride** Individualistic pride that comes from drives for power, ego, and materialism. (Katzenbach)

**Set range** Fixed range of happiness a person experiences that is determined primarily by heredity. (Seligman)

**Shared vision** The capacity to create and hold a shared picture of the future across a set of individuals. (Senge)

**Signature strength** A strength that is measurable, acquirable, demonstrated across situations, leads a person to feel gratified, is valued by most cultures, and is not a means to another end. (Seligman)

**Social entity conception** A broad view of the corporation as a public entity with responsibility and accountability to many *stakeholders* including employees, customers and the community. (Conger, Lawler, and Finegold)

**Social loafer** A passive group member who fails to carry one's weight and relies on others for progress and results. (LaFasto and Larson)

**Social operating mechanisms** Formal or informal interactions where integrative dialogue occurs such that barriers are broken

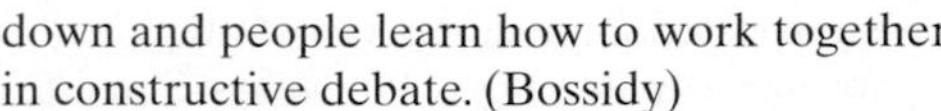
down and people learn how to work together in constructive debate. (Bossidy)

**Social skills** Handling emotions in relationships with other co-workers and accurately reading social situations. (Goleman)

**Soul** The energy a person or organization devotes to purposes beyond itself. (Csikszentmihalyi)

**Span of control** The number of subordinates reporting directly to a supervisor. (Thomas)

**Speculative "hot" money** Money that comes into and out of a country, often overnight, frequently betting on whether a currency is going to appreciate or depreciate. (Stiglitz)

**Stakeholder** Any party (e.g., a community, the firm's employees, suppliers, a governmental entity, or environmental activist organization) which has an enduring interest or investment in the performance and ethos of the firm. A stakeholder is distinguished from but inclusive of equity investors called shareholders. (Conger, Lawler, and Finegold)

**Stickiness factor** The packaging of information to make it irresistible. (Gladwell)

**Stockdale paradox** The capacity by some executives to simultaneously confront the most brutal facts of their current reality while maintaining faith that they will prevail in the end. (Collins)

**Strategic alliance building** The process of enlisting allies—like-minded, similarly tempered co-workers—to increase one's clout and gain a sense of legitimacy. (Meyerson)

**Strategic environmental management** An approach that incorporates environmental goals into the overall economic strategy of the corporation, often anticipating and pursuing potential green markets. (Robbins)

**Strategic intelligence** The combination of abilities to anticipate the future, think in terms of the system as a whole, engage in visioning, get people to work for a common purpose, and form successful partnerships. (Maccoby)

**Strategy map** A logical relationship diagram that specifies the relationship among shareholders, customers, business processes, and an organization's competencies. (Kaplan and Norton)

**Summum bonum (chief good)** The belief that whereas people desire other goods (such as money or power) because they believe those things will make them happy, they really want happiness for its own sake. (Csikszentmihalyi)

**Supportiveness** A desire and demonstrated willingness to help others succeed. (LaFasto and Larson)

**Sustainable development management** An approach that blends economic, social, and environmental goals. An organization subscribing to this philosophy often takes environmental leadership roles in the industry, and typically incorporates environmental programs across the entire organization. (Robbins)

**Sustaining innovations** A strategy that offers demanding high-end customers better performance than that which was previously available. (Christensen)

**Synergy** Working together, cooperating, combining in a cooperative action to yield an outcome that is greater than the sum of its parts (Covey); revenue enhancement or cost reductions achieved by increasing markets or sharing services across product lines or business units. (Kaplan and Norton)

**Systemic change** Deep organizational change that goes beyond cosmetic alterations to major strategic reconstruction of policies, procedures, and hierarchical structures within an organization. (Kanter)

**Team basics** The five elements necessary to achieve real team performance: size, purpose and goals, skills, working approach, and mutual accountability. (Katzenbach)

**Tempered radicals** Change agents who work to effect significant changes in moderate ways. (Meyerson)

**Terms of trade** The prices which countries get for the products they produce and export. (Stiglitz)

**Theories in use** The actual rules or master programs that individuals use to achieve control. (Argyris)

**Theory X** A set of assumptions that explains some human behavior and has influenced conventional principles of management. It assumes that workers want to avoid work and must be controlled and coerced to accept responsibility and exert effort toward organizational objectives. (McGregor)

**Theory Y** A set of assumptions offered as an alternative to Theory X. Theory Y assumes that work is a natural activity, and given the right conditions, people will seek responsibility and apply their capacities to organizational objectives without coercion. (McGregor)

**Time fence** Action that would lead to long-term gains is stopped because it also causes short-term negative outcomes (the opposite of a time snare). (Murnighan and Mowen)

**Time snare** Problem occurring when decision-makers let the prospect of short-term positive outcomes cause an action that leads to long-term negative outcomes. (Murnighan and Mowen)

**Tipping point** A dramatic moment in an epidemic or trend, positive or negative in nature, when everything can suddenly change. (Gladwell)

**Tipping point** A seemingly innocuous event that could be the tripwire that pushes the system over the edge and creates a serious problem; a small change that can result in a large, sudden and dramatic effect that can multiply geometrically. (Murnighan and Mowen)

**Tough decisions** A class of decisions that have ambiguity, uncertainty, and conflict. (Nutt)

**Toxic tandem** A toxic boss who has a toxic handler regularly by his/her side. (Frost)

**Toxin handlers** Those leaders, managers, and staff that tend to the emotional pain of the people in the organization and work to bring harmony and balance and remove stress and tension. (Frost)

**Transparency** All of the firm's products are honestly presented and its operations are visible to any and all stakeholders. (Batstone)

**Tumblers** Companies who exhibited better-than-peer performance in the first period, followed by under-performance in the second. (Joyce, Nohria, and Roberson)

**Uncertainty** Doubt about the magnitude of future conditions, such as interest rates. (Nutt)

**Undiscussables** Topics or processes in decision-making that managers believe should be withheld from debate. (Nutt)

**Unexpected event** The negative surprise that occurs when either expected strategy or performance outcomes fail to materialize or when unexpected impediments to strategy and performance materialize. (Weick and Sutcliffe)

**Value chain** The discrete value-producing activities within a firm that are potential sources of competitive advantage. (Porter)

**Value network** The context within which a firm establishes a cost structure and operating processes with suppliers and partners. (Christensen)

**Values** The standards by which employees make prioritized decisions. (Christensen)

**Variable-term opportunism** A flexible approach to initiating change, ranging from capitalizing on serendipitous opportunities to making proactive changes. (Meyerson)

**Verbal jujitsu** The art of taking undesirable, demeaning statements or actions from others, deflecting their force, and turning them into opportunities for change. (Meyerson)

**Virtual organizations** Companies that have groups of individuals working on shared tasks while distributed across space, time, and/or organizational boundaries. (Beyerlein, Freedman, McGee, and Moran)

**Virtues** The six components (wisdom and knowledge, courage, love and humanity, justice, temperance, spirituality and transcendence) that when taken together describe a person of good character. (Seligman)

**Virtuous spiral** The ultimate competitive advantage, it is a win-win relationship that is a source of positive momentum that creates higher and higher levels of individual and organizational performance. (Lawler)

**Warrior spirit** A deep emotional commitment that causes important segments of a workforce to emerge as the enterprise's primary competitive advantage; engendering that spirit demands resurgent sources of emotional energy and clear channels, or management approaches, for aligning that energy. (Katzenbach)

**What-if questioning** Examining key assumptions about payoffs to determine the risk in adopting an alternative. (Nutt)

**Wholescale change** The process of uncovering and achieving the organization's aspirations, yearnings, and longings by involving and engaging a critical mass, if not the entire organization. (Dannemiller Tyson)

**Winners** Companies outperforming their peers in both periods of examination (Joyce, Nohria, and Roberson)

**Workforce** All of the employees across the baseline of the organization who either make the products, design the services, or deliver the value to the customer. (Katzenbach)

**Working group** Any small group collaborating to accomplish a common purpose or goal. (Katzenbach)

**Zero-defects** The idea, arising from Total Quality Management principles, that the ultimate goal of continuous improvement is to have absolutely no errors made. (Thomas)

# Bibliography of Inclusions


Argyris, Chris (2000). *Flawed Advice and the Management Trap.* New York: Oxford University Press, Inc.

Batstone, David (2003). *Saving the Corporate Soul & (Who Knows?) Maybe Your Own.* San Francisco: Jossey-Bass.

Bennis, Warren G. and Thomas, Robert J. (2002). *Geeks and Geezers: How Era, Values, and Defining Moments Shape Leaders.* Boston: Harvard Business School Press.

Beyerlein, Michael M., Freedman, Sue, McGee, Craig, and Moran, Linda (2003). *Beyond Teams: Building the Collaborative Organization.* San Francisco: Jossey-Bass/Pfeiffer.

Blanchard, Kenneth and Johnson, Spencer (1981). *The One Minute Manager.* LaJolla, CA: Blanchard-Johnson.

Bossidy, Larry and Charan, Ram, with Charles Burck (2002). *Execution: The Discipline of Getting Things Done.* New York: Crown Business.

Cascio, Wayne F. (2003). *Responsible Restructuring: Creative and Profitable Alternatives to Layoffs.* San Francisco: Berrett-Koehler.

Christensen, Clayton M. and Raynor, Michael E., and Scott D. Anthony (2003). *The Innovator's Solution: Creating and Sustaining Successful Growth.* Boston: Harvard Business School Press.

Collins, James, C. (2001). *Good to Great: Why Some Companies Make the Leap . . . and Others Don't.* Cambridge, MA: Harvard Business School Press.

Conger, Jay A., Lawler III, Edward E., and David L. Finegold (2001). *Corporate Boards: Strategies for Adding Value at the Top.* San Francisco: Jossey-Bass.

Covey, Stephen R. (1989). *The Seven Habits of Highly Effective People: Restoring the Character Ethic.* New York: Simon and Schuster.

Csikszentmihalyi, Mihaly (2003). *Good Business: Leadership, Flow, and the Making of Meaning.* New York: Penguin Putnam.

Dannemiller Tyson Associates (2001). *Whole-Scale Change: Unleashing the Magic in Organizations.* San Francisco: Berrett-Koehler.

Deming, W. Edwards (1986). *Out of the Crisis.* Cambridge, MA: MIT Press.

Frost, Peter J. (2003). *Toxic Emotions at Work: How Compassionate Managers Handle Pain and Conflict.* Boston: Harvard Business School Press.

George, Bill (2003). *Authentic Leadership: Rediscovering the Secrets to Creating Lasting Value.* San Francisco: Jossey-Bass.

Gladwell, Malcolm (2000). *The Tipping Point.* Boston, MA: Little, Brown, & Co.

Goleman, Daniel, Boyatzis, Richard, and McKee, Annie (2002). *Primal Leadership: Realizing the Power of Emotional Intelligence.* Boston: Harvard Business School Press.

Hackman, J. Richard (2002). *Leading Teams: Setting the Stage for Great Performances.* Boston: Harvard Business School Press.

Johnson, Spencer, M. D. (1998). *Who Moved My Cheese?* New York: Putnam Books.

Joyce, William, Nitin Nohria, and Bruce Roberson (2003). *What (Really) Works: The 4 + 2 Formula for Sustained Business Success.* New York: Harper Collins.

Kanter, Rosabeth Moss (2001). *Evolve! Succeeding in the Digital Culture of Tomorrow.* Boston: Harvard Business School Press.

Kaplan, Robert S. and Norton, David P. (2001). *The Strategy-Focused Organization.* Cambridge, MA: Harvard Business School Press.

Katzenbach, Jon R. (2003). *Why Pride Matters More than Money.* New York: Crown Business.

Katzenbach, Jon R. (2000). *Peak Performance: Aligning the Hearts and Minds of Your Employees.* Cambridge, MA: Harvard Business School Press.

Kouzes, James M. and Posner, Barry Z. (1993). *Credibility.* San Francisco: Jossey-Bass.

LaFasto, Frank and Larson, Carl (2002). *When Teams Work Best: 6,000 Team Members and Leaders Tell What It Takes to Succeed.* Thousand Oaks, CA: Sage Publications.

Lawler III, Edward E. (2000). *Rewarding Excellence.* San Francisco: Jossey-Bass.

Lawler III, Edward E. (2003) *Treat People Right! How Organizations and Individuals Can Propel Each Other into a Virtuous Spiral of Success.* San Francisco: Jossey-Bass.

Lawrence, Paul R. and Nohria, Nitin. (2002). *Driven: How Human Nature Shapes Our Choices.* San Francisco: Jossey-Bass.

Lundin, Stephen C., Paul, Harry, and Christensen, John (2000). *Fish!* New York: Hyperion.

Maccoby, Michael (2003). *The Productive Narcissist: The Promise and Peril of Visionary Leadership.* New York: Broadway Books.

Maslow, Abraham H. (1998). *Maslow on Management.* New York: John Wiley & Sons.

McGregor, Douglas (1960). *The Human Side of Enterprise.* New York: McGraw-Hill.

Meyerson, Debra E. (2003). *Tempered Radicals: How Everyday Leaders Inspire Change at Work.* Boston: Harvard Business School Press.

Miller, Frederick A. and Katz, Judith H. (2002). *The Inclusion Breakthrough: Unleashing the Real Power of Diversity.* San Francisco: Berrett-Koehler.

Mitroff, Ian I. with Anagnos, Gus (2001). *Managing Crises Before They Happen.* New York: American Management Association.

Murnighan, J. Keith and Mowen, John C. (2002). *The Art of High-Stakes Decision-Making: Tough Calls in a Speed-Driven World.* New York: John Wiley & Sons.

Nutt, Paul C. (2002). *Why Decisions Fail: Avoiding the Blunders and Traps that Lead to Debacles.* San Francisco: Berrett-Koehler.

Peters, Thomas J. and Waterman, Robert H. Jr. (1982). *In Search of Excellence.* New York: Harper and Row.

Porter, Michael E. (1985). *Competitive Advantage: Creating and Sustaining Superior Performance.* New York: Free Press.

Robbins, Peter Thayer (2001). *Greening the Corporation: Management Strategy and the Environmental Challenge.* London: Earthscan Publications.

Seligman, Martin E. P. (2002). *Authentic Happiness: Using the New Positive Psychology to Realize Your Potential for Lasting Fulfillment.* New York: Free Press.

Senge, Peter M. (1990). *The Fifth Discipline.* New York: Doubleday.

Stiglitz, Joseph E. (2002). *Globalization and Its Discontents.* New York: W.W. Norton & Company.

Thomas, Kenneth W. (2000). *Intrinsic Motivation at Work.* San Francisco: Berrett-Koehler.

Ventrice, Cindy (2003). *Make Their Day: Employee Recognition That Works.* San Francisco: Berrett-Koehler.

Weick, Karl E. and Kathleen M. Sutcliffe (2001). *Managing the Unexpected: Assuring High Performance in an Age of Complexity.* San Francisco: Jossey-Bass.

# Index

## M

# TOPICS AND SKILLS IN ENGLISH

# TOPICS AND SKILLS IN ENGLISH

## Student's Book

Vivien Barr and Clare Fletcher

Edward Arnold
A division of Hodder & Stoughton
LONDON BALTIMORE MELBOURNE AUCKLAND

# Acknowledgements

The publisher would like to thank the following for permission to reproduce or adapt copyright material:
The Controller of Her Majesty's Stationery Office
The London Borough of Barnet
British Telecom
Harrow Observer



First published in Great Britain 1983
Third impression 1988

*British Library Cataloguing Publication Data*

Barr, Vivien
Topics and skills in English.
Student's book
1. English language — Text books for foreigners
I. Title II. Fletcher, Clare
428.2'4 PE1128
ISBN 0 340 28708 X



Typeset in Century Schoolbook by Macmillian India Ltd.
Printed and bound in Hong Kong for Edward Arnold, the educational academic and medical publishing division of Hodder and Stoughton Limited, 41 Bedford Square, London WC1B 3DQ by Colorcraft Ltd.

# Contents

# Introduction

**Topics and Skills in English** comprises a book, a cassette and a study guide. It is intended for adults and young people who need to improve their practical English. They may be studying in part-time or full-time classes or on their own. For some, their aim may be to express themselves more effectively as individuals dealing with outside people and organisations; others may be preparing for employment.

The **book** can be used as a course book or relevant units can be selected. The Topic Table and Skills Index will help you to see at a glance the work covered in a unit, and also to find related material in other units. The Topic Units in the book are designed to give useful information as well as to teach and practise different language activities. This information is printed on a grey background and can be read through and referred to as with any handbook. The Skills Units each introduce and practise the skill intensively in carefully controlled stages. Reading, listening and diagrammatic material is provided in the book and this can be supplemented with material related to a particular interest, area of work or locality. The particular difficulties of those learning English as a second language are recognised in the structures listed in the Topic Table, and in the listening material on the **cassette**.

The **Study Guide** is for teachers and independent students. Information printed on a grey background is useful for both; other material is directed primarily at teachers. The Study Guide includes notes, keys to the exercises and full tapescripts.

# Unit 1 Health

## Section 1: Introduction

### A

Everyone living in Britain can get free medical treatment under the National Health Service. People can do one or more of these things when they need medical help:

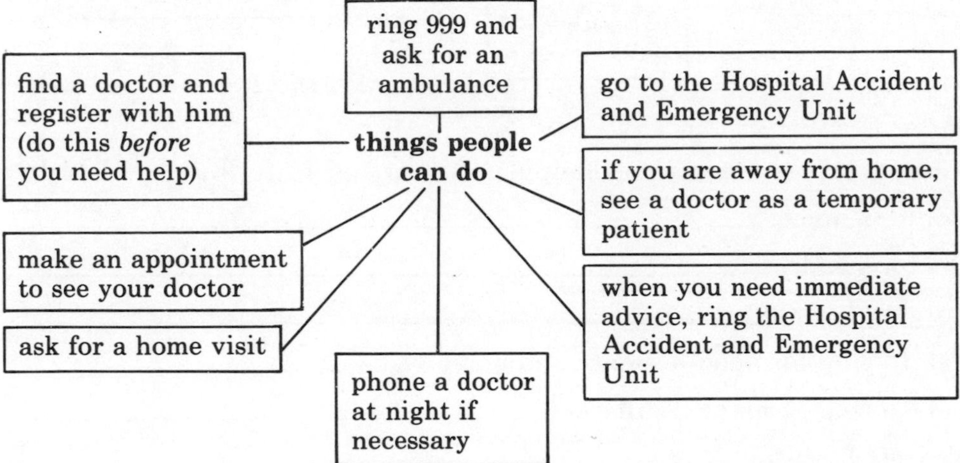

things people can do
ring 999 and ask for an ambulance
find a doctor and register with him (do this *before* you need help)
go to the Hospital Accident and Emergency Unit
if you are away from home, see a doctor as a temporary patient
make an appointment to see your doctor
ask for a home visit
when you need immediate advice, ring the Hospital Accident and Emergency Unit
phone a doctor at night if necessary

### B

Use the diagram above to advise each of these people. Suggest what each one should do.

1 Ann Howe's mother, who is 82, has got a bad attack of flu.
2 Jean Whitmore whose father has just had a heart attack.
3 John Martin who is away from home and has suddenly got a painful rash all over his hands.
4 Janet Miller who thinks she might be pregnant.
5 Bill Johnson who has sprained his ankle.
6 Jack Rogerson who has a very bad sore throat and cough.
7 Anita Bristow who has moved to a new area. Her old doctor cannot treat her any more.
8 Ray Gosling who has severe backache and needs time off work.
9 George Macey who is lying awake in the middle of the night with very severe stomach pains.
10 Mary Gordon whose daughter has fallen off the swing and has hurt her arm badly. It looks as if it might be broken.

# Section 2: Patient and doctor

## A

When the doctor sees the patient he will do one or more of these things:

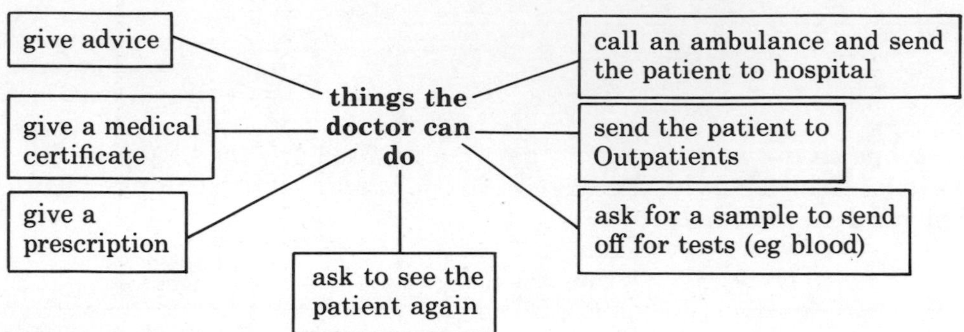
things the doctor can do
give advice
give a medical certificate
give a prescription
ask to see the patient again
call an ambulance and send the patient to hospital
send the patient to Outpatients
ask for a sample to send off for tests (eg blood)

## B

Find out some information about your doctor and write down the details:

Doctor's name: ______________________

Doctor's address: ______________________

Surgery hours: ______________________

Tel. to ring for appointments and home visits: ______________________

Tel. to ring at night if different: ______________________

Nearest hospital: ______________________

## C

Match each of the words on the left with the correct definition on the right.

1 surgery
2 prescription charge
3 Outpatients Department
4 prescription
5 Casualty Department
6 medical certificate
7 General Practitioner

a) Accident and Emergency Department in a hospital.
b) A note from the doctor to show that you are ill and cannot work.
c) Money you pay the chemist for medicine on prescription.
d) An instruction from the doctor. The patient takes this to the chemist.
e) Family doctor.
f) A hospital department. Patients go there by appointment but do not stay there.
g) The doctor's room where he treats patients.

# Section 3: In the doctor's surgery

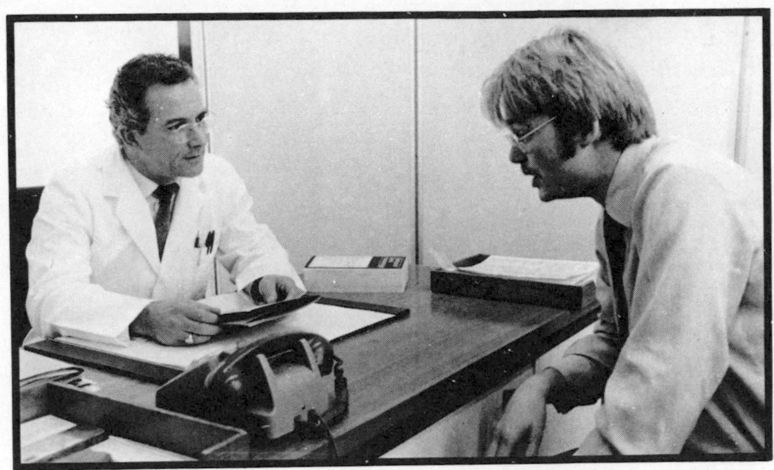

## A

Listen to a doctor talking to a patient. He is trying to find out what is wrong. Here are some of the questions he asks. Write down the patient's replies:

What can I do for you?
Where exactly is this pain?
When do you get it?
How long have you had this pain?
When you get the pain, how long does it last?
Do you have any other symptoms?

Practise this conversation in pairs.

## B

<u>Here are some more symptoms</u>

I feel : hot
: cold
: sick
: dizzy
: tired
: weak
: depressed

It hurts : under my arm
: in my chest
: in my groin

I've got : stomach ache
: backache
: toothache
: diarrhoea
: constipation

I've got a : high temperature
: fast pulse
: sore throat
: headache
: rash
: cough

I keep : being sick
: sweating
: shivering
: dropping things
: bursting into tears

The pain is : mild
: quite bad
: severe

## C

Work in pairs

A) Someone in your family is very ill. Ring the doctor for advice. Describe the patient's symptoms.
B) You are the doctor. Ask questions to find out what is wrong.

## D

Illnesses

Match each illness with the right part of the body. Use a dictionary to help you.

| Parts of the body | Illness |
|---|---|
| eyes | gastric 'flu |
| head | 'flu |
| throat | bronchitis |
| chest | measles |
| stomach | tonsillitis |
| all over | conjunctivitis |
| | appendicitis |
| | migraine |

## E

Listen to the doctor talking to another patient. Answer these questions:

a) What is wrong with her?
b) What treatment does the doctor prescribe?

Listen again.
The patient asks the doctor some questions. She wants him to explain things to her. Write down the questions she asks.

## F

Making things work for you

1 Practise asking a doctor to explain. What can you say? Reply to these things a doctor might tell you:

You've got gingivitis.
Here's a prescription for Doxtol.
I'm afraid you've got pleurisy.
Take two tablets night and morning until it clears up.

2 You may also need to persuade him that something is more serious than he thinks. What can you say?

a) You want him to come to see your child as soon as possible. She is too ill to take to the surgery. The doctor says: "Bring her into the surgery tomorrow". What can you say?
b) You have a bad pain. He says: "This is nothing to worry about. The pain will go away". What can you say?
c) You have a bad rash. He says: "Take this. It'll clear it up." You don't know what it is or how to take it. What can you say?

# Section 4: Medicine

## A

Prescriptions

1 Your doctor may give you a prescription to take to the Chemist. Some patients have to pay a prescription charge for each item. Others do not have to pay: they are *exempt*.

2 Look at the back of the prescription form and find out who is exempt. Make sure you know what to do if you are exempt or getting medicine for somebody who is exempt.

ONLY IF THE PATIENT IS EXEMPT FROM PRESCRIPTION CHARGES COMPLETE THIS DECLARATION
(BEFORE going to the pharmacy)

I DECLARE that the patient named overleaf

please tick one box only

☐ is under 16 years of age

☐ is a woman aged 60 or over

☐ is a man aged 65 or over

☐ holds a current Family Practitioner Committee exemption certificate

☐ holds a current prepayment certificate (FP96)

☐ is covered by a Department of Health and Social Security exemption certificate

☐ is a War/Service pensioner with an exemption certificate Ref. No. (if available) . . . . . . . . . . . . . . . . . . . .

AND THAT I AM

please tick one circle

○ the patient

○ the patient's parent or guardian

○ the patient's representative

I understand that enquiries may be made to check this Declaration and that a deliberately false statement may lead to prosecution.

Signed . . . . . . . . . . . . . . . . . . . . . . . . . . . . . . . . Date . . . . . . . . . .

NAME AND ADDRESS-If your FULL address appears overleaf write "As overleaf"
(Block letters)

. . . . . . . . . . . . . . . . . . . . . . . . . . . . . . . . . . . . . . . . . . . . . . . . . . .

. . . . . . . . . . . . . . . . . . . . . . . . . . . . . . . . . . . . . . . . . . . . . . . . . . .

3 Are these people exempt or not? Tick the right box.

| | *exempt* (pays nothing) | *not exempt* (must pay) |
|---|---|---|
| Mrs. Peel, aged 62 | ☐ | ☐ |
| Mr. West, aged 62 | ☐ | ☐ |
| Anita Jones, aged 15 | ☐ | ☐ |
| Sheila Weston, aged 22 | ☐ | ☐ |
| John Barclay, aged 5 | ☐ | ☐ |

4 Imagine you are Mrs. Peel's neighbour and you are collecting medicine for her. Fill in the form correctly.

5 It is not quite clear on the form exactly who is exempt. The DHSS booklet *NHS Prescriptions: How to get them free* will give much more information. Some patients who can get free medicine may have to fill in another form first. Always ask if you are not sure.
*Example*: My son is 17 and still at school. Does he have to pay for his tablets?

Use the example to help you ask about your sister and brother.
a) Your sister has just had a baby. Ask if there is any charge for her medicine.
b) Your brother is unemployed. Ask if you have to pay for his tablets.

## B

You can get some medicine without a prescription. There will be directions on how to take it. Before you take any medicine or use any cream, inhalant or special shampoo, make sure you know what it is and exactly how to use it. You can ask the chemist about medicine on or off prescription.

## C

The next exercises give you practice in reading directions. Always ask, though, if you are in any doubt. Here are some useful questions:

What is this?
How do I take it?
How often should I take it?
How much should I take?
Can I stop taking it as soon as I feel better?

## D

Collect tablets, medicines and creams that you have at home and read what is written on them. Here are some of the words you may find. Add to these lists. Check on the meaning of words if you are not sure.

| What is it? | How do you take it? | Warnings | |
|---|---|---|---|
| tablet | swallow | *Complete the following*: | *Other important words*: |
| ointment | rub in gently | Keep out of . . . | Paediatric |
| lozenge | hold under tongue & allow to dissolve | Do not exceed . . . | Junior |
| inhalant | sniff | Not to be taken . . . | Infants |
| antiseptic | gargle | For external . . . | |
| bandage | dilute | | |
| | bathe | | |
| | dissolve in water | | |

## E

Use the directions from medicines to fill in this chart.
One has been done for you.

| NAME | On prescription? | What is it? | What is it for? | DIRECTIONS How much? (DOSE) | | | How? | How Often? | | | When? |
|---|---|---|---|---|---|---|---|---|---|---|---|
| | | | | ADULTS | CHILDREN | BABIES | | ADULTS | CHILDREN | BABIES | |
| Boots cold relief | No | powder | colds | 1 sachet | Do not give without medical advice | — | Mix with hot water and drink | Max 4 in 24 hrs | — | — | At bedtime and every 4 hours during the day |
| | | | | | | | | | | | |

# Section 5: Hospital

## A

There are three main places in a hospital where patients may be treated. These are the Outpatients Department, the Accident and Emergency Unit (A & E) and the Wards. The diagram shows which patients are treated in these three places. Put the names of each place in the diagram.

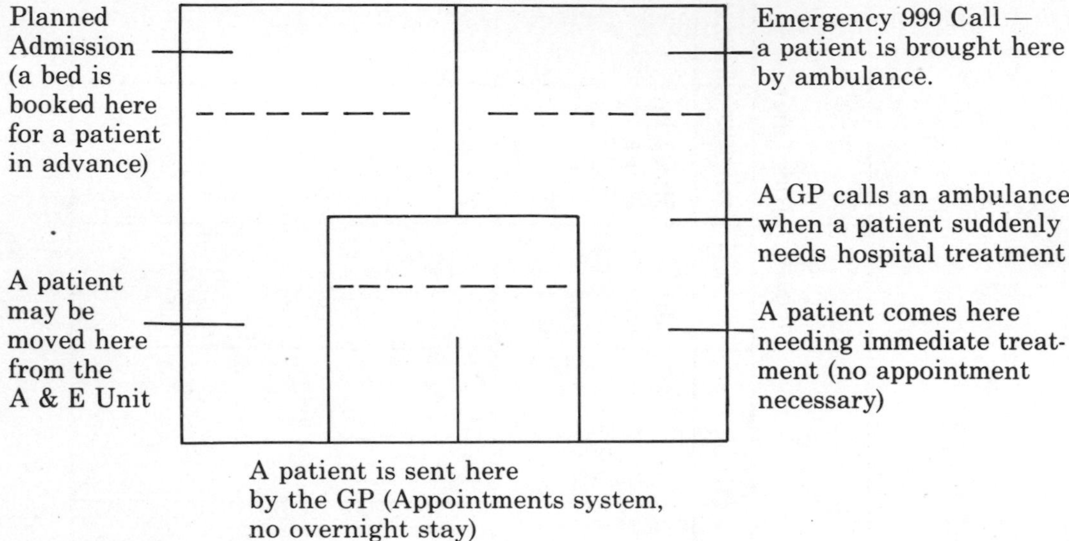

Planned Admission (a bed is booked here for a patient in advance)
A patient may be moved here from the A & E Unit
Emergency 999 Call — a patient is brought here by ambulance.
A GP calls an ambulance when a patient suddenly needs hospital treatment
A patient comes here needing immediate treatment (no appointment necessary)
A patient is sent here by the GP (Appointments system, no overnight stay)

## B

Calling an ambulance

Ambulances
Nurses Home
Education centre
Nursing Management
Gynaecology ward
Radiotherapy unit
X-ray
Wards
Childrens unit
Pathology
Out-patients
Car park
Physics & Nuclear
Ultrasound

1 Listen to two 999 calls to the ambulance service.

2 Put the items below into the right order:

Say what is wrong.
Give your phone number.
Dial 999.
Say which service you need.
Say where the ambulance must come to.

3 Now practise calling an ambulance.

a) Someone has fallen downstairs in your house and cannot move.
b) There has been an accident at the end of your road. Both drivers are hurt.
c) You are out shopping. And old man has collapsed in the street.

## C

In the Accident and Emergency Unit

1 If a patient is well enough, he has to answer questions in the Accident and Emergency Unit. A nurse asks these questions and fills in a REGISTRATION FORM.

2 Listen to a nurse asking a patient questions.
Fill in as much as possible on the registration form from the patient's replies.

**Paxton Hospital**
**Accident and Emergency Department**

| Surname: | Sex: | Title: | Date and time: |
|---|---|---|---|
| First Forename: | Second Forename: | | |
| Address: | | | |
| Tel No: | Postal Code: | | |

Date of Birth: Place of Birth: Religion:

Occupation of patient: * Next of Kin:
Relationship:
Address:

Tel.

GP's Name and Address:

## D Planned admission to a hospital ward

1 A patient who knows beforehand that he/she will be going into hospital may receive a letter like this:

**PRESTON PARK HOSPITAL**

Whitton Road, Giggeston GA3 5BG Tel 54982

Dear Mrs. Green.

This letter gives you information about your planned stay in this hospital.

You will be in Victoria ward. Please arrive at the ward between 4·30 pm and 6·30pm on Tuesday 17 February.

What to bring: You should bring nightclothes, toilet articles, a handtowel and a bathtowel, slippers and a dressing-gown. There is no space to store your clothes. We suggest that a member of your family or a friend comes with you, and when they leave they can take your clothes. You will have a locker in which you can keep small items such as books and soft drinks. You will be able to buy small items when the Hospital Shop trolley visits the ward; you may like to have some money for this, but you are advised not to bring large sums of money or other valuables.

Visiting hours are 12 noon - 8 pm every day.

What to expect: When you arrive, a member of the nursing staff will take down some details of your personal and medical history. During your time in hospital, you will receive treatment in the ward, and you may also go to another department of the hospital, such as Physiotherapy. Nurses check each patient's pulse, temperature etc, and keep a record.
Medical staff make a regular ward round to examine patients and discuss their treatment. There may be several doctors and other staff, the ward sister, and medical students on a ward round.

When the doctor thinks a patient is well enough to go home, the patient is discharged. Your expected date of discharge is

Saturday 21 February

Yours sincerely

J.G. Prior

J G Prior
Hospital Secretary

2 Imagine you are going into hospital. Use the information in the letter from the hospital to do these things:
   a) Make a list of things to take with you.
   b) Write a note to leave at home for your family, telling them your ward and visiting hours.
   c) You will be away from work. Fill in the form below for your employer:

**REQUEST TO BE ABSENT FROM WORK FOR HOSPITAL TREATMENT**

NAME:. . . . . . . . . . . . . . . . . . . . . . . . . . . . . . . . . . . . . . . . . .

FIRST DAY OF ABSENCE: . . . . . . . . . . . . . . . . . . . . . . . . . . . . . . .

DATE OF RETURN TO WORK (if known): . . . . . . . . . . . . . . . . . .

ADDRESS WHILE IN HOSPITAL:. . . . . . . . . . . . . . . . . . . . . . . . .

. . . . . . . . . . . . . . . . . . . . . . . . . . . . . . . . . . . . . . . . . . . . . .

. . . . . . . . . . . . . . . . . . . . . . . . . . . . . . . . . . . . . . . . . . . . . .

. . . . . . . . . . . . . . . . . . . . . . . . . . . . . . . . . . . . . . . . . . . . . .

SIGNATURE:. . . . . . . . . . . . . . . . . . . . . . . . . . . . . . . . . . . . . . . .

APPROVED BY:. . . . . . . . . . . . . . . . . . . . . . . . . DATE . . . . . . . . . .
Head of Department

# E

## Hospital Vocabulary

1 Here are some definitions of words we use in connection with hospitals. Fill in the missing letters if you can.
   a) nearest relative: n______ of k______
   b) coming into hospital: ad____ss____n
   c) coming out of hospital: d__sch__rge
   d) finding out what is wrong with a patient: d__ag__os__s

2 A GP (General Practitioner) is a general doctor. Many doctors in hospitals are specialist doctors. There are also special wards which are used for patients who are in hospital for similar reasons.

| Specialist Ward | Specialist Doctor | Definition |
|---|---|---|
| 1) psychiatric ward | psychiatrist | |
| 2) obstetric or maternity ward | obstetrician | |
| 3) geriatric ward | geriatrician | |
| 4) gynaecological ward | gynaecologist | |
| 5) surgical ward | surgeon | |
| 6) orthopaedic ward | orthopaedic surgeon | |
| 7) paediatric ward | paediatrician | |

Fill in the right definition for each doctor from the list below. Use a dictionary to help you.

treats old people; treats children; treats women having babies; treats injuries to bones; treats mental illness; performs general operations; treats women's illnesses.

# Unit 2 Using the telephone

## Section 1: Introduction

This unit deals with business calls *between a person and an organisation*.

A

Listen to some telephone calls and make notes. There are six calls on the tape. The notes for the first call are done for you:

Caller: Lesley Turner

Call to: Derwent Television

Purpose: To arrange for somebody to come and repair a television

B

Listen to four telephone calls. Decide: was the call good, or are there difficulties? Think carefully about what the caller said and how. Then tick the right comment or comments below:

| | CALL | | | |
|---|---|---|---|---|
| | 1 | 2 | 3 | 4 |
| What the caller said was just right. | | | | |
| The caller said too much. | | | | |
| The caller said too little. | | | | |
| The caller was not well prepared. | | | | |
| The caller was difficult to understand. | | | | |
| The caller's manner was not very good. | | | | |

# Section 2: Making telephone calls

## A

Making an appointment

1 Listen to someone making an appointment. Follow the words below, and see how the prompts help you.

| Receptionist | Caller | Prompt |
|---|---|---|
| Dr Green's surgery | Hello. I'd like to make an appointment to see Dr Green | Greeting + say why you are ringing |
| Can I have your name, please? | Yes, it's Joe Carson. The surname is Carson, C..A..R..S..O..N | Give information |
| 4.30 tomorrow? | That's fine. 4.30 tomorrow. Thank you very much. | Accept the appointment + repeat details to check + thank |
| Thank you. Goodbye | Goodbye. | Goodbye. |

1 Now practise the call in pairs. First read the words. Then see if the caller can manage with just the prompts.

2 Mrs Smith is ringing to make an appointment to see the Headmaster. Her son, Billy Smith, is in Class 3A. Listen to the call.

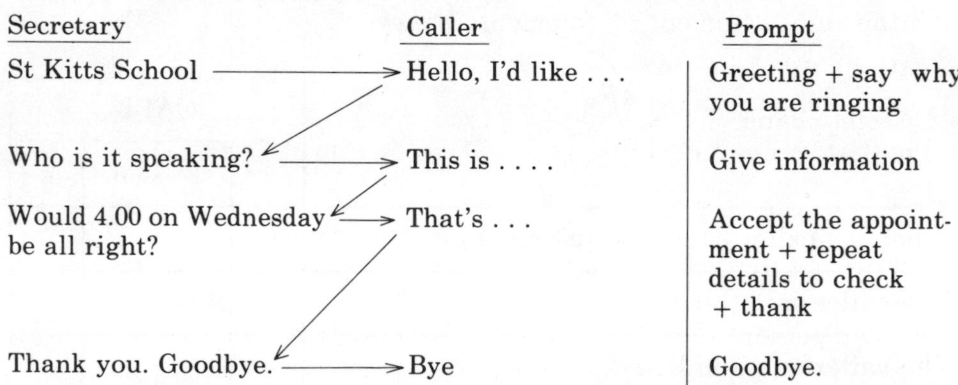

| Secretary | Caller | Prompt |
|---|---|---|
| St Kitts School | Hello, I'd like . . . | Greeting + say why you are ringing |
| Who is it speaking? | This is . . . . | Give information |
| Would 4.00 on Wednesday be all right? | That's . . . | Accept the appointment + repeat details to check + thank |
| Thank you. Goodbye. | Bye | Goodbye. |

Now practise the call in pairs, using the prompts to help you.

3 Listen to Jane Woods making an appointment to see a solicitor at Rexham Law Centre. Take down the time and the solicitor's name and then practise the call in pairs.

NB Make sure you and your partner change roles.

## B Changing or cancelling appointments

Listen to Joe Carson and Mrs. Smith ringing back to change their appointments. Then practise each call. The caller can try to use just the prompts.

| 1 Receptionist | Caller | Prompt |
|---|---|---|
| Dr. Green's surgery → | Hello, this is Joe Carson speaking. I have an appointment with Dr. Green, and I'm afraid I can't come. | Greeting + give name + why you are ringing |
| When was it for? → | 4.30 tomorrow. I'm sorry I can't come then because I have to collect my neighbour's child from school. Could I please have a later appointment? | Give information + apologise + give a reason + ask for what you want. |
| Can you come at half-past five? → | That's fine. 5.30 tomorrow. Thank you very much. | Accept the appointment. repeat the details to check. thank |
| Thank you. Goodbye. → | Goodbye | Goodbye |

| 2 Secretary | Caller | Prompt |
|---|---|---|
| St. Kitts School | | Greeting + give name + say why you are ringing |
| When was it for? | | Give information Apologise + give a reason. Ask for what you want |
| What about the same time the following Wednesday? | | Accept, + repeat details. |
| I hope Billy is better soon. Goodbye. | | Thank. Goodbye. |

3 Listen to Jane Woods cancelling her appointment at the Law Centre.
4 Practise cancelling an appointment. Imagine you are Joe Carson, cancel your doctor's appointment.

## C
## Further practice: Appointments

a) One person in each group is the receptionist. He or she needs to work on p 16 and study it first on his or her own.
b) The others in the group are patients. They will ring up the receptionist in turn. They will work from p 18. Decide first in a group who is going to make each call.
c) Patients and receptionist come together. Patients phone in turn. The receptionist should write names in the appointments diary. Patients should make a note of the doctor, and the day and time of the appointment.

Receptionist

You work as a medical receptionist in a practice with three doctors.
Keep a clear record of all appointments.
(Write in pencil so that you can change appointments.)
Here is your appointments diary for tomorrow and the day after.

Day ................ Date ................

| | Dr. GREEN | Dr. HENRY | Dr. PRINCE |
|---|---|---|---|
| 8·45 | | | Ms. Karen Mace |
| 9·00 | Mrs. Joan Keeble | | William Banks |
| 9·15 | Mr. Harold Brind | Mrs. Champa Shah | |
| 9·30 | | Mr. Kwok Ukwe | |
| 9·45 | | | |
| | | | |
| | | | |
| 4·30 | | NO APPOINTMENTS | |
| 4·45 | | Dr. Henry works | |
| 5·00 | | morning surgery | |
| 5·15 | Jeanette South | only | no appointments after 5·00pm |
| 5·30 | Pauline Dart | | Dr. Prince goes |
| 5·45 | | | out on visits |

Day . . . . . . . . . . . . . . . Date . . . . . . . . . . . . .

| | Dr GREEN | Dr HENRY | Dr PRINCE |
|---|---|---|---|
| 8·45 | Lisa Misty | NO APPOINTMENTS | |
| 9·00 | | DR. HENRY WORKS | |
| 9·15 | Mrs. Eliza Pringle | AFTERNOON SURGERY | |
| 9 30 | | ONLY | |
| 9·45 | | | |
| 10·00 | | | |
| | | | |
| | | | |
| 5·00 | | | |
| 5·15 | | Harold Martin | |
| 5·30 | | | |
| 5·45 | | James Ironstone | |
| 6·00 | | | Janet Williamson. |
| 6·15 | | | |
| 6·30 | | | |

Practice

Morning surgery on . . . . . . is from . . . . to . . . . . .

I'm afraid the last appointment is at . . . . . . . .

Dr. . . . . . . . only does morning surgery on . . . . . . . . .

I'm afraid the only appointment left is . . . . . . . . . .

Patients

1 Decide in the group which patient(s) you are going to be. Choose a doctor and a time when you want an appointment.

| Name of patient | Doctor | Time |
|---|---|---|
| Mrs Kay Brown<br>Mr Paul Fielding<br>Janet White<br>Carl Driberg<br>Jenny Lipton<br>Freda Somer<br>Gemma James<br>John Buxton–you want an appointment for your wife, Anthea Buxton.<br>Nila Patel–you want an appointment for your mother, Mrs Surekha Patel.<br>Mrs Farley–you want an appointment for your son, James Farley | Dr Prince<br>Dr Henry<br>Dr Green | Today or tomorrow.<br>Tomorrow morning, early.<br>Tomorrow morning, any time.<br>Tomorrow afternoon.<br>The day after tomorrow, early in the morning.<br>The day after tomorrow, in the morning.<br>The day after tomorrow, in the afternoon. |

Remember to make a note of the doctor, and the day and time of the appointment you are given.

2 Patients phone again to change or cancel their appointments. Remember to give your name, and the day and time of your old appointment.

Reasons for changing or cancelling

a) You do not need to see the doctor any more.
b) You cannot come tomorrow afternoon because there is a special meeting at work. Ask for another appointment.
c) You forgot that you have your driving test then. It isn't urgent. You will ring next week for another appointment.
d) Try to get an appointment sooner. You feel worse and you would like to see the doctor as soon as possible.
e) Your son is not well, so you cannot come to see the doctor. Cancel your appointment and say you will ring again.
f) Change your appointment. Your central heating has broken down and they are coming to fix it at the time of your appointment.
g) Give your own reasons.

## D Finding out

1 Listen to somebody telephoning to find out information. Decide which of these places the caller is phoning, and fill in the information on the form below:—

British Rail Passenger Enquiries
Brooks Travel Agency
Royal Theatre Box Office

| Place phoned: ................................................ |
| --- |
| Purpose of call: ................................................ |
| Information received:................................................ |

2 With a partner, practise telephoning the other two places listed, and asking for information. Plan your call first.
3 When you have had enough practice, try making some real phone calls.

Suggestions

Look up the telephone numbers in the directory and use the Yellow Pages. If you have problems, see Unit 10, Alphabetical Order, p. 96.

a) Find out the times of trains from Charing Cross to Canterbury on weekdays between 0900 and 1100 hours.
b) Ring two or three companies and find out how much it costs to rent a colour TV.
c) Find out what time the main film starts in your local cinema.
d) Find out how much it costs to send a bunch of red roses to your favourite person by Interflora.

# Section 3: Dealing with organisations

## A

Large organisations usually have a telephone switchboard, and several extensions. The person at the switchboard answers the telephone, and then puts the call through to the right extension.

## B

1 Getting through to the right person, when you know who to ask for

If you know the name of the person, the department, or an extension number, ask for this. You may have to speak to one or two other people before you get through to the right person. Only explain what you want when you are speaking to the right person.

2 Listen to this telephone call. You might like to write down what people say. You will hear three people:
   the caller, Mr. Thomas
   the switchboard operator at Coles & Fowler
   the Personnel Officer, Mrs Grant

3 Listen to another call. This time you will hear 4 people. Work out who they are.

4 Now work in groups of three: a caller, a switchboard operator, and the person in the organisation. Practise getting through to the right person. Change parts, so you practise everything.

Caller: Remember

| | |
|---|---|
| Asking for someone: | Could I speak to the Personnel Officer, please?<br>I'd like to speak to Mr Atkins, please. |
| Asking for an extension department or section: | Could I have Extension 22?<br>Could I have Accounts?<br>Could I have the Accounts Department? |

| Organisation | Ask for: |
|---|---|
| a) Coles & Fowler | Mrs Grant, in Personnel |
| b) Truppins | Mr Clark, Radio & TV Department |
| c) Green and Sherwood | Miss Harris in Accounts |
| d) Butt & Walker | Extension 23 (Mr J Butt) |
| e) Paxton Hospital | The Ward Sister, Jones Ward |
| f) Owners Building Society | Mortgage Records Department |

5 Listen to another call. What is different about this call?

6 In your group of three, practise dealing with a wrong connection. The person in the organisation can choose which department answers the phone.

## C Getting through to the right person when you do not know who to ask for.

1 When you ring an organisation for the first time, you may not know what department or extension to ask for. The call will go to the switchboard first. The person at the switchboard needs to know just enough about the purpose of your call to put you through to the right department. Do not go into details until you are sure you are speaking to the right person or department.

2 Listen to somebody phoning Lesleys department store.

| | |
|---|---|
| Switchboard: | Lesleys. Can I help you? |
| Caller: | Hello. I'd like to find out some information about garden chairs. |
| Switchboard: | Just a moment, I'll put you through to the Garden Furniture section. |
| Assistant: | Garden Furniture. |
| Caller: | Hello, I'd like to find out some information about garden chairs. |
| Assistant: | Yes, what would you like to know? |
| Caller: | Have you any folding chairs in stock? |

3 You are going to make some calls like this. First do some practice: Imagine you are the switchboard operator at Lesleys. You receive enquiries and have to decide where to put them through to.
Below is a list of the different departments, sections and extensions at Lesleys, and a list of enquiries. For each enquiry, decide where you would put it through to.

| Department or Section | |
|---|---|
| Accounts Section | Ext. 22 |
| Personnel Dept. | Ext. 23 & 24 |
| Electrical goods | Ext. 25 |
| Radio & TV | Ext. 26 |
| Garden furniture | Ext. 27 |
| DIY Dept: | |
| electrical tools | Ext. 28 |
| hand tools | Ext. 29 |
| Soft furnishing Dept | |
| bedlinen | Ext. 30 |
| curtains | Ext. 31 |
| upholstery | Ext. 32 |

**Enquiries**

1 Hello, I'd like to find out about cassette recorders.
2 Good morning, I'd like to find out if you have any job vacancies.
3 Good afternoon, I'd like to enquire about electric drills.
4 Hello, could I speak to somebody about electric clocks?
5 Good morning, I'd like to find out what fridges you have in stock.
6 Good afternoon, could I please talk to someone about the curtains I ordered?
7 Hello, I have a query about the bill I have received for some garden chairs.

4 Imagine you are going to telephone Lesleys. For each of the situations below, decide what you should say to the switchboard operator. (If you want some help you can look again at the enquiries in exercise 3.)

a) You have always wanted to work in a shop. You have a lot of experience of DIY. You would like a job at Lesleys.

b) You are thinking of buying a new fridge. Your old fridge was satisfactory until it got very old: it is made by Tricity. Your sister says that her Phillips fridge is very good.

c) You ordered some curtains six weeks ago. You were told that they would take three weeks, but when you rang up after three weeks you were told that the material hadn't come in, and they would take several weeks more. You want to know if they are ready.

d) As a birthday present for your brother, you are thinking of buying a Western XJ60 cassette recorder. You want to know how much it costs at Lesleys.

e) You bought a cheap electric clock at the market last year. It went wrong. You have decided to buy a good quality electric clock this time, and want some advice about good makes.

f) You bought some garden chairs recently. You paid for the chairs when they were delivered. Now you have received another bill for them.

g) You have been given a Lesleys Gift Token for £15. You would like to buy an electric drill, but you aren't sure if you can get one for £15.

5 Now practise making calls. Look again at the call in C2. Work in groups of three. Take it in turns to be the caller, the switchboard operator, and somebody in the department. The caller is telephoning about the situations in C4: the switchboard operator has the list of departments in C3.

## D Dealing with organisations: SUMMARY

1 If you know who you want to speak to, do not explain what you want until you are speaking to that person.

2 If you do not know who to ask for, explain briefly why you are ringing. (You may need to do this more than once.)

# Section 4: Telephone Talk: a summary of useful phrases

| DEALING WITH ORGANISATIONS: GETTING THROUGH TO THE RIGHT PERSON | |
|---|---|
| | Could I have { extension thirty-four? / extension two one six? / the Personnel Department? } |
| | Could I speak to / I'd like to speak to { Mr Smith. / the Personnel Manager } |
| | I'd like to { enquire / find out } about . . . |

| UNDERSTANDING THE SWITCHBOARD OPERATOR | RESPONDING |
|---|---|
| It's ringing for you.<br>Trying to connect you.<br>Putting you through. | Thank you. |
| I'm sorry, the line is engaged at the moment. Will you hold? | a) Yes please.<br>b) I'll hold on for a minute.<br>c) No thank you. I'll ring again later. |

| UNDERSTANDING THE PERSON WHO ANSWERS | RESPONDING |
|---|---|
| Accounts (Department). | Could I speak to Mr Smith, please? |
| Mr Smith speaking./Speaking. | Good morning, Mr Smith . . . |
| Who's calling?/Who's speaking? | My name is . . .<br>This is . . . |
| I'm afraid Mr Smith is not available at the moment. | d) Could I leave a message?<br>e) I'm ringing to . . . Could somebody else help me? |
| Mr Smith isn't here. Can I take a message? | f) Yes please. This is . . . .<br>g) No thank you. I'll try again later. |
| Could you hold on a moment please?<br>Hold on a minute. | Yes, certainly. |
| I'll get him for you. | Thank you. |
| I'll see he gets the message | Thank you. |
| Can I help you? | I'd like to { find out about . . . . / book tickets for . . . . / make an appointment . . . . / etc. } |

Exercise: Here are some phrases that you might hear in a personal telephone call. For each one, decide what you should say in a business call.

Hang on a sec.
Hi!
No, he's out.
Yeah, sure.
Cheerio.

## Section 5: Making a sequence of calls

### A

First, listen to Tony Simpson ringing up about his television. As he talks, the receptionist fills in a request form. Fill it in as you listen.

**DERWENT RENTAL CO**

Request for TV Repair DATE: ____________________

Customer's name: ____________________

address: ____________________

____________________

tel. no: ____________________

Appointment date: ____________________

time: ____________ SIGNED: ____________

### B

Now listen to two more calls from Tony Simpson to the Derwent Rental Co. What is his problem? What does he say when he insists that things are put right?

### C

Practise the sequence of calls with a partner. Make sure you change roles.

# Section 6: Telephone directories and operator services

## A Telephone directories

If you know the name and address of a person or organisation, but not their telephone number, you can look in a telephone directory. If you want to find a business or service, eg a locksmith, look in the Yellow Pages. This may be a section in the ordinary telephone directory, or it may be a separate directory.
The Unit *Alphabetical Order* on pages 96–105 gives practice in finding things quickly in directories.

## B Telephone Dialling Codes

Sometimes you want to ring a telephone number like Oxford 722771. If you live outside Oxford, you will need the booklet *Telephone Dialling Codes*. This gives an alphabetical list of places and their dialling codes. It tells you that the code for Oxford is 0865, so you dial 0865 722771.

Use your *Telephone Dialling Codes* booklet. Find the dialling codes for these places:

| | | | |
|---|---|---|---|
| Birmingham | ____________ | Newcastle | ____________ |
| Manchester | ____________ | Slough | ____________ |
| Edinburgh | ____________ | Cambridge | ____________ |
| Coventry | ____________ | Windsor | ____________ |
| London | ____________ | Hertford | ____________ |

## C Operator Services

In a telephone directory or dialling code booklet, there is a list of operator services. Find the list, and decide which number these people should ring:

a) Mr Singh has dialled a number several times, and keeps getting the same wrong number.
b) Ms Parker's phone is silent – there is no dialling tone.
c) Mr O'Connell wants to telephone a friend who lives in Birmingham. He knows the friend's address, but not his telephone number.
d) Mrs Ball's little girl has swallowed a piece of plastic and cannot breathe properly.

## D Charges

The dialling code booklet may contain the list of telephone charges or there may be a separate leaflet of up-to-date charges. Use the list to find this information:

a) Mrs McCall lives in your area and wants to phone someone in Edinburgh, someone else in London, and a third person who lives in Brighton. How much will each call cost?
b) Mr Cheung lives in your area and wants to phone his sister in Hong Kong. How much will it cost?
c) What are the different rates and times for inland calls?

# Extension work

## Practice calls

Practise these calls with a partner. If you can, put your calls on tape. Listen, and decide how good your call is.

1 **North Thames Gas**
46 Station Road, Pinkham. Tel: 466378

Dear Customer

We are replacing old gas mains in your street. We need to put new gas pipes in your house. Would you be kind enough to telephone Miss O'Callan, Extension 234, to arrange a time for us to do this work.

Yours sincerely

John Boyant.

Area Manager

2 Telephone a hospital to find out visiting hours. Find out if a friend or relation in hospital is well enough for you to visit.
3 Your child has got to go into hospital to have an operation, and will be away from school for four weeks. Tell the school, and arrange to get some work for him/her to do.
4 You have lost your bag, with your wallet and keys in it. Report it to the local police.
5 You have just got off the bus and realise that you have left your bag on the bus. Ring the bus garage, and ask them to look for your bag when the bus arrives at the garage. You will collect it from the garage.

## Real calls

Use the telephone directory and telephone to find out things you want to know.

Suggestions:

a) the opening hours of a local shop or library.
b) the time of the last bus or train on your route.

# Unit 3 A place to live I

## Section 1: Introduction

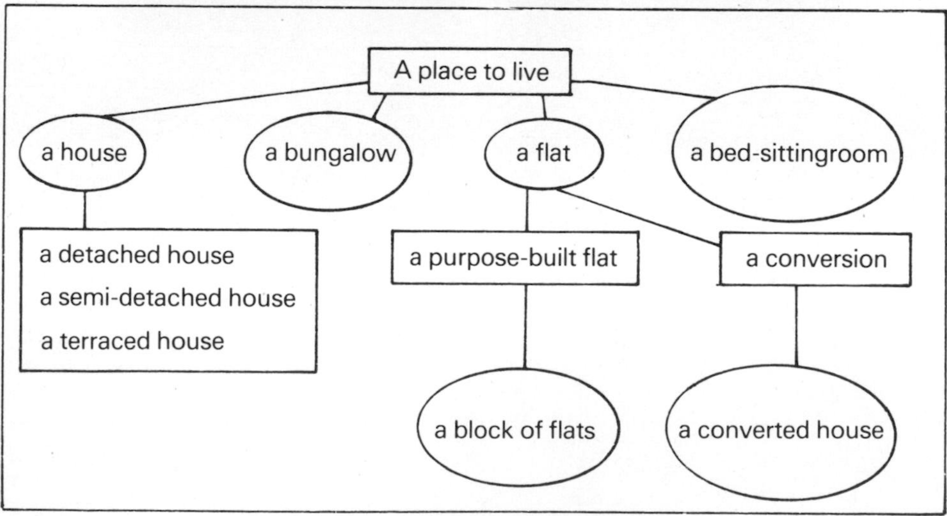


Use words from the diagram to label the five pictures above.

## Section 2: Asking for facts

Ask questions, and fill in this questionnaire for other people in the class.

| Name | | | | |
|---|---|---|---|---|
| Type of accommodation | | | | |
| Town | | | | |
| No. of rooms | | | | |
| Kitchen at front or back | | | | |
| No. of years at that address | | | | |

## Section 3: Descriptions

A

Listen to this description of a flat, and label the rooms.

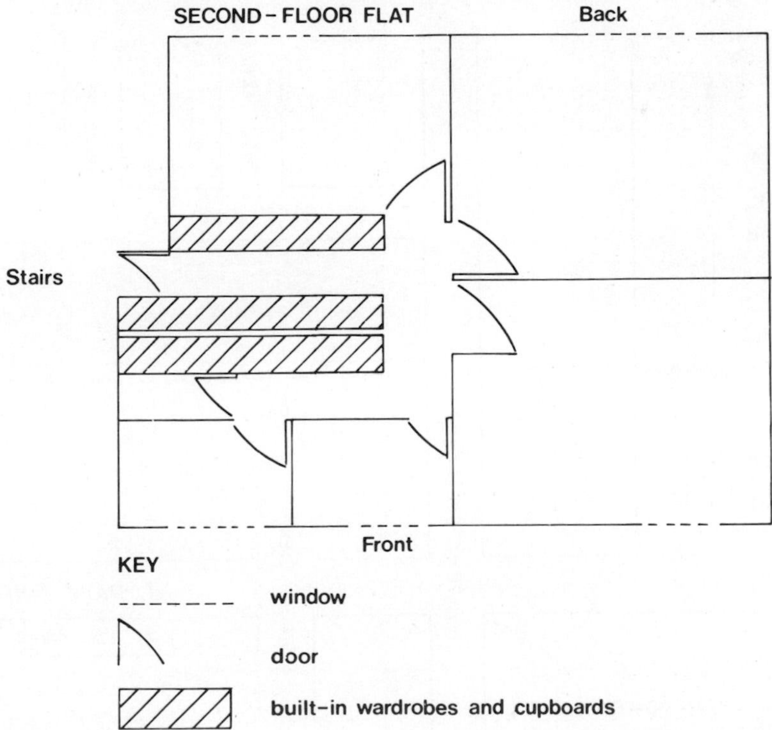

B

Describe the flat you have labelled on page 29. Mention the floor it is on, the number of rooms, and the position of the rooms. Remember to use the correct prepositions:

eg on the {ground / first / second} floor — in the {sitting room / kitchen / bathroom}

at the {back / front} — in front of / next to / opposite / between

C

Describe the place where you live. Add more information. Draw a plan of it if you can.

## Section 4: Giving directions

You can help people to find where you live by giving them directions, and also by drawing a sketch map.

Listen to somebody giving directions to his house from the station. On the sketch map below, draw arrows to show where to go, and mark the right house.

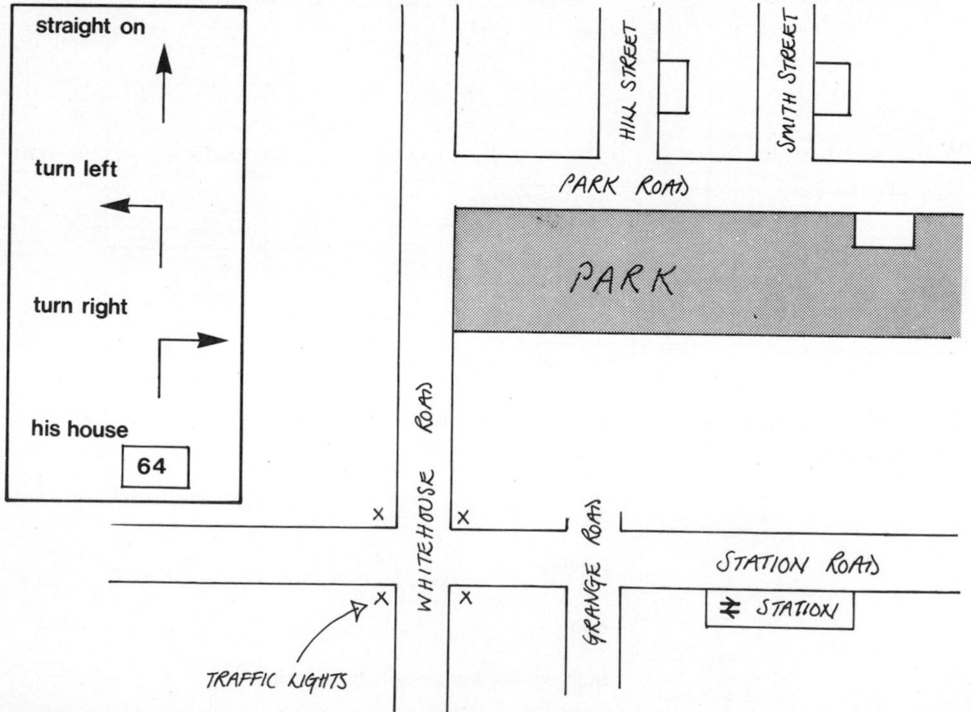

## Further practice

1 Give directions to your home from the nearest station or bus stop. Draw a sketch map with arrows, if you can. A street map of the area may help you.

2 Give directions, with a sketch map if possible, to the place where your class is held.

## Section 5: Comparisons

A

Listen to somebody talking about the house she grew up in and the flat she lives in now. What are the main differences?

B

Listen again. Write down the words she uses to compare the two places: notice some words end in *—er*, some have *more* in front:
eg small*er* *more* convenient

C

Write sentences comparing the two places, using the words in your list:
eg The house was *more difficult* to clean than the flat.
The flat is *smaller* than the house.

D

Write sentences comparing the place you grew up in and the place you live in now.

## Extension work

Imagine you can choose where to live and the type of building. Write a description.

# Unit 4 Filling in forms

## Section 1: Understanding the purpose of forms

A

1 Here are the titles of some forms:

Harrow Further Education College
ENROLMENT FORM

Sunburst Holidays
BOOKING FORM

FAMILY ALBUM ORDER FORM

Park Hospital
Patient's Record Card

Harry & Parsons: Application
for the post of .............

**WHAT IS EACH FORM FOR?**

booking

enrolling

applying

ordering or buying

Giving information

2 Look again at the forms. Say which *type* of form you need to fill in:

a) You have been accepted for a course. You need an__________ form.
b) You want to apply for a job. You need an__________form.
c) You want to buy goods by post from a catalogue. You need an__________form.
d) You want to fix up a holiday. You need a__________form.

B

Understanding the purpose of parts of forms.
Forms have different parts, which each have a purpose. Look at this order form and a) notice the different parts, b) fill it in.

Saying what you want

Giving information about yourself

Signature – showing that you really mean what you say on the form.

ORDER FORM

Please send me ___ shirts at £11.95 each (plus 50p postage and packing each).

Please indicate size, colour and quantity required:

| | Small | Medium | Large |
|---|---|---|---|
| Blue | | | |
| Pink | | | |

I enclose a cheque/P.O. for £___ payable to Super Shirts Ltd.

---

Name & Address ..............................

..............................

Signature ..................Date ..........

## Section 2: Seeing how forms ask for information

A

Here are some things that forms often ask for.
Read the examples. If there are any headings that you do not understand, look them up in the GLOSSARY p. 131.

Surname: .....Peterson
First name(s): James Michael
Address: 92 Earls Road
London SW6

Tel: 01-874 7412
D.O.B: 9/7/49
Age in years: 33
Marital Status: Single
Sex: Male
Place of Birth: Sydney
Nationality: Australian

Surname: ..................
First Name (s): ..............
Address: ..................
..................
..................
Tel:..................
D.O.B: ..................
Age in years: ..............
Marital Status:..............
Sex: ..................
Place of Birth: ..............
Nationality: ..............

Now fill in the information for yourself.
Remember: English forms fit English names. If your naming system is different, it is important to work out which name to put as your surname, because forms are filed by *surname*.

## B

Here are some headings from forms. Some of them mean the same. Group together the headings which mean the same. There are five groups.

| | |
|---|---|
| Forenames | Postal address |
| Vacancy applied for | Surname |
| Applicant's surname | Place of birth |
| Address | Employment now sought |
| Title of job applied for | Permanent address |
| Private address | Application for the post of . . . . . . |
| First names | Country of birth |
| Country of origin | Christian names |

## C

Giving the same information in different ways

Study these sections from three different forms:

NAME.....Jane Maria SMITH........ ...Miss.
(title)

ADDRESS...97 Eastcote Avenue...............
.....Pinner, Middx...Postcode HA7 7AK.

SIGNATURE...Jane M. Smith...............

---

Surname: (PRINT) SMITH Initials: J.M. ~~Mr~~/~~Mrs~~/Miss

Home Address: (PRINT) 97. EASTCOTE AVENUE, PINNER, MIDDX.
HA7 7AK

I declare that the information given in this form is, to the best of my knowledge, complete and correct. Signed Jane M. Smith

---

| | | | | | | | | | | | | | | | | | | | | |
|---|---|---|---|---|---|---|---|---|---|---|---|---|---|---|---|---|---|---|---|---|
| Surname | S | M | I | T | H | | | | | | | | | | | | | | | |
| Forename(s) | J | A | N | E | | M | A | R | I | A | | | | | | | | | | |
| Permanent address | 9 | 7 | | E | A | S | T | C | O | T | E | | A | V | E | N | U | E | | |
| | P | I | N | N | E | R | | M | I | D | D | X | | H | A | 7 | | 7 | A | K |

I agree to send payment or return the goods within two weeks of receipt

SIGNATURE: Jane M. Smith

Now fill in these sections from forms for yourself:

NAME.............................................. ..........
(title)

ADDRESS...................................................................

.................................Postcode..................

Signature ...................................................

Surname:(PRINT) Initials: Mr/Mrs/Miss

Home Address:(PRINT)

I declare that the information given in this form is, to the best of my knowledge, complete and correct. Signed

| | | | | | | | | | | | | | | | | | | | | | | | | |
|---|---|---|---|---|---|---|---|---|---|---|---|---|---|---|---|---|---|---|---|---|---|---|---|---|
| Surname | | | | | | | | | | | | | | | | | | | | | | | | |
| Forename(s) | | | | | | | | | | | | | | | | | | | | | | | | |
| Permanent address | | | | | | | | | | | | | | | | | | | | | | | | |
| | | | | | | | | | | | | | | | | | | | | | | | | |

I agree to send payment or return the goods within two weeks of receipt

SIGNATURE:

D

Showing your answer

Sometimes you are given several possible answers, and asked to choose. Here are some of the ways you are asked to show your answer.

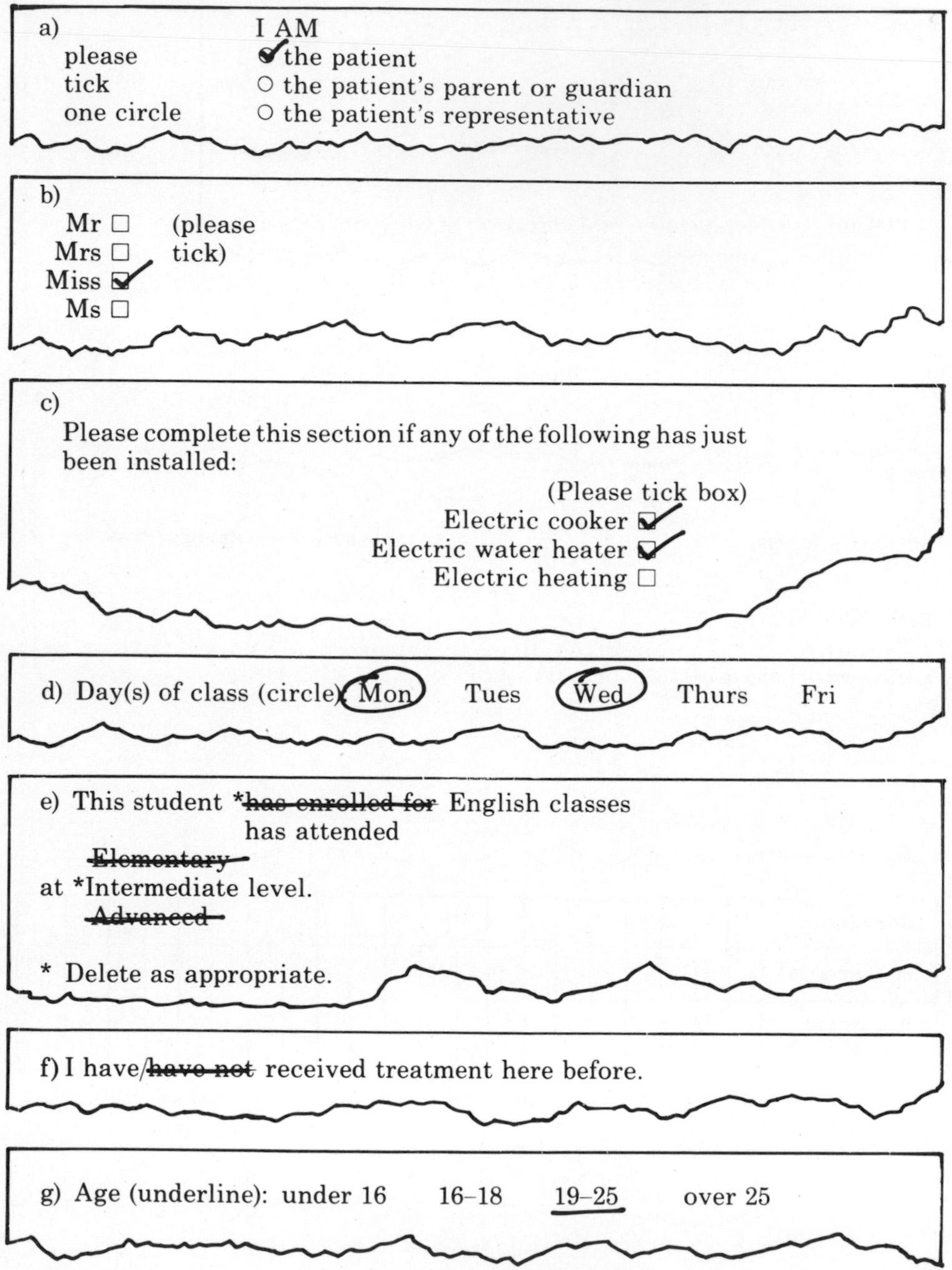
a) please tick one circle

I AM
✔ the patient
○ the patient's parent or guardian
○ the patient's representative

b) (please tick)
Mr ☐
Mrs ☐
Miss ☑
Ms ☐

c) Please complete this section if any of the following has just been installed:
(Please tick box)
Electric cooker ☑
Electric water heater ☑
Electric heating ☐

d) Day(s) of class (circle): Mon Tues Wed Thurs Fri

e) This student *~~has enrolled for~~ / has attended English classes at *~~Elementary~~ / Intermediate / ~~Advanced~~ level.
* Delete as appropriate.

f) I have/~~have not~~ received treatment here before.

g) Age (underline): under 16 16–18 19–25 over 25

It is important to follow the instructions, and show your answers in the right way. If you do not, you may leave out some information, or make more work for the person dealing with your form.

E

Showing your answer — practice

Give the information asked for. Follow the instructions carefully.

NAME: (Block capitals) . . . . . . . . . . . . . . . . . . . . . . . . . . . . . . . . . . . . . . . . . . .

1 I am doing this exercise * in class
at home
somewhere else

2 Time of day: (underline) morning afternoon evening

3 Today is: (circle) Monday Tuesday Wednesday Thursday Friday

4 I find this work very difficult ☐ (please tick one box)
quite difficult ☐
not very difficult ☐

5 I find this work very useful ○ (please tick one circle)
quite useful ○
not very useful ○

6 I *have/have not filled in a job application form in the last three months.

7 Are you looking for a job at the moment? *YES/NO

8 Which activities in English are you most interested in improving? Tick one or more activity:
speaking ☐
understanding spoken English ☐
reading ☐
writing ☐
spelling ☐

*delete as appropriate

SIGNATURE: . . . . . . . . . . . . .

## F

Study the form below. Find all the places where the person filling in the form has left out information. Mark these . Find all the places where the person has given the information, but has not shown the answer in the right way. Mark these . The first line is done for you.

PARK INSTITUTE ENROLMENT FORM

Please use block capitals

Full name . . J P Callaghan . . . . . . . . . . . . . . . . . . . . . . . .

Address. . . 96 Hambledon Place, . . . . . . . . . . . . . . . . . . . . . .

Wembley, Middx . . . . . . . . . . . . . . . . . . . Postcode: . . . . . . . . . . . . . .

Place and date of birth . Wembley . . . . . . . . . . . . . . . . . . . . . . . .

Marital status (circle) Single ✓ Married Widowed Divorced

COURSE ENROLLED FOR

| Course no. | | | | | Course Title |
|---|---|---|---|---|---|
| 2 | 4 | 6 | 9 | 1 | woodwork |
| | | | | | |
| | | | | | |

I ~~have~~/have not attended a course at this institute before.
Day(s) of classes: *Mon Tues Wed Thurs Fri
No. of hours per week (circle): under 1 2-(4) 5–8 over 8
Are you attending on Day Release?* ~~YES~~/NO
If YES, give you employer's name and address and the name of your supervisor: . Brendel Hark Ltd, . . . . . . . . . . . . . . . . . . . . .

. Mill Lane, . . . . . . . . . . . . . . . . . . . . . . . . .

. Edgware . . . . . . . . . . . . . . . . . . . . . . . . . .

Supervisor: . . . . . . . . . . . . . . . . . . . . . . . . . . . . . . . . . . . . .

* delete as appropriate

Signature: . . . J. P. CALLAGHAN. . . . . . Date: . . . . . . . . . . . . . . .

FOR OFFICE USE ONLY
Course (s) – Woodwork
Fee assessed by (initials) –
checked by –
Fee payable : £ . . . . . .

Fee paid by student ☐ (tick)
Fee paid by employer ☐

# Section 3: Finding your way round a form

## A

Forms use 'signposts' to help you find your way round the form:
**heavy**
**bold** } type
*italics*
LARGE LETTERS

and also: — sections and sub-sections
— numbers
— letters

Here are some questions to help you use the 'signposts' on the form on the next page.
Do NOT read the whole form first. Read a question and then look at the form to answer it.

1 What is the purpose of this form? ______
2 The form is divided into three columns, left, middle and right. The middle column is for you to write in.
The column on the left is ______
The column on the right is ______
3 Look at the middle column. How many sections are there to fill in? ______
4 In which section do you give personal details?
______
5 In which section do you say what sort of licence you want?
______
6 In Section 2 there are five sub-sections. Are they marked with numbers or letters? ______
7 Look at Section 3. How many sub-sections are there? ______
8 Under "Notes to help you" there are two headings. Write down the two headings. ______
9 The note headed ADDRESS refers to one part of the form. Which part? Give the Section and Sub-section. ______
10 Is this the whole form or not? Find the words that tell you. ______
______

## B

Now fill in all three sections for yourself, first in pencil and then in ink. If you have a current full licence, imagine you have lost it.

Department of Transport

1

Please do not write above this line

# Application for a Driving Licence

D1
JULY/82

## Notes to help you

If you need more information before you fill in this form please ask at your post office for leaflet D100.
**To drive a heavy goods vehicle or a public service vehicle you need an additional licence. Consult a Traffic Area Office.**

## Address

A business, club or hotel address cannot be accepted unless you live there permanently.
If you have no permanent address in England, Scotland or Wales, give the name and address of a person in England, Scotland or Wales through whom you may be contacted at any time.

## Types of Licence

**Full licence**
You may apply for this if during the last 10 years you have
- (i) held a British full licence
- or (ii) passed the British driving test
- or (iii) held a full licence issued in Northern Ireland, the Channel Islands or the Isle of Man.

Otherwise you may only apply for a provisional licence.

Please read Notes then complete in **BLACK INK** and **BLOCK LETTERS**

## 1 Applicant

a. Surname 4
Christian or forenames 5

Please tick box or state other title such as Dr, Rev.

b. Mr 1 Mrs 2 Miss 3
Other title 6

Your full permanent address in Great Britain (see note on left)

c. Address
7
Post Town 8
Postcode (Your licence may be delayed if the postcode is not quoted) 9

d. Please tick box Male 1 Female 2 10

e. **Please enter your date of birth** Day Month Year 11

f. If you hold a licence from the Driver and Vehicle Licensing Centre please enter your Driver Number in the box below.

12

### Official Use Only

Provisional - 1
Full - 2
Rec. type 2

Cont. No. 3

**Provisional Licence**
To enable you to drive motor vehicles with a view to passing a driving test.
If you are a motorcyclist you may have to take a test in two parts. You will not need a provisional licence if you hold a full licence which states that it has the effect of a provisional licence to drive other groups of vehicles.
If you are applying for your first provisional licence do not drive until you receive it.

**IMPORTANT:** From 1.10.82 you must apply for motorcycle entitlement if you require it by ticking the box at 2(c). The term motorcycle includes scooter, but not moped. If you are under 17 your motorcycle entitlement will start from your 17th birthday.

**Duplicate Licence**
To replace a lost, stolen, destroyed or defaced licence.

**Exchange Licence**
For a driver
(i) who has passed a driving test
or (ii) whose existing licence contains endorsements no longer current (see leaflet D100)
or (iii) who requires provisional motorcycle entitlement to be added to his licence (see leaflet D100)

## 2 Licence required

a. Please tick box if you have **never** held a British licence (full or provisional) ☐

b. Please tick the type of licence you require (see note 'Types of licence' on left)

Full ☐ Provisional ☐ Duplicate ☐ Exchange ☐

c. Please tick box if you also require provisional motorcycle entitlement (see IMPORTANT note on left). ☐

d. When do you want your new licence to begin?
**A licence cannot be backdated.**
**Application may be made during the 2 months before commencement date.**

Day ___ Month ___ Year ___ 14

e. If you have passed a driving test since the issue of your last licence write the new Group passed here
**and enclose the pass certificate.** ____________

## 3 Last Licence

Please give details of your last licence **and enclose it with this form**

a. If your last licence was surrendered on disqualification write S/D
**or** if you have not previously held a licence, write NONE ____________

b. **Type of licence i.e. Provisional or Full** ____________

c. Expiry date ____________

d. If your last licence has been lost, stolen, destroyed or defaced please tick the appropriate box below. If a lost licence is later found and is still current you must return it to DVLC but keep any licence issued to you in the meantime.

Lost or stolen ☐ Destroyed ☐ Defaced and I enclose it ☐

e. Name and/or address on licence **if different from that at 1 above**

Surname ____________ 20
Christian or forenames ____________ 21
Address ____________
____________
Post Town
Postcode (please quote) ____________ 27

**Please continue overleaf**

MC ☐ 13
DRE ☐ 15 End ☐ 16
Iss. No. ☐ 17
TPC ☐ 18
Ent. ☐ 19
MP ☐ 22 RE ☐ 23 VDOB ☐ 24
MIM ☐ 25 Amount ☐ 26
DAM ☐ 28

# Unit 5 A place to live II

## Section 1: Information about types of housing

### A

Read the text below, and then fill in the information asked for in the chart opposite:

1 Council houses and flats These are owned by the Council. You can ask the Council to put you on the list of people waiting for a Council house or flat; if you live in bad conditions or have other problems, you may get a place more quickly, but most people have to wait a long time. Single people usually can't get Council places. The Council looks after the house, and does repairs, but they are sometimes slow. There are usually a few rules for council tenants. For example, they may not be able to keep pets, or paint the front door a different colour.

2 Privately rented houses and flats These are usually more expensive, and in some areas there are not many. The law gives tenants in privately rented places some rights. Sometimes you can get the rent reduced, and sometimes the maximum rent is fixed by law—the owner cannot charge more. There may be rules about the things people can and cannot do, especially if the owner lives in the same house. Places to rent are advertised in newspapers and in newsagents' windows. Accommodation agencies and some estate agents have details too.

3 Owner-occupied houses and flats The people who live in these houses and flats own them. Usually they have borrowed the money to buy the house or flat from a Building Society. This money is called a mortgage. (Councils and banks also lend money for mortgages.) You need a large sum of money for a deposit and expenses. You can get information about houses or flats for sale from newspaper advertisements or estate agents.

4 Housing Associations They charge low rents, to help people who find it difficult to get a house or flat in another way (eg old people, one-parent families). Local Councils usually have a list of Housing Associations in their area, or they may be listed in the Yellow Pages telephone directory.

| Type of housing | Money | Who is this type of housing meant for? | Disadvantages | Where to get information |
|---|---|---|---|---|
| Council | | | | |
| Privately rented | | | | |
| Owner-occupied | | | | |
| Housing Association | | | | |

## B

Match each of the words on the left with the correct definition on the right.

1 rent
2 rates
3 tenant
4 solicitor
5 local authority
6 occupier
7 owner-occupier
8 mortgage
9 landlord/landlady

A the person who lives in a house or flat
B a lawyer who deals with buying and selling houses or flats
C money lent by a building society or bank to pay for a house or flat
D money paid by tenants to landlords
E somebody who owns a room, flat or house which they let to somebody else to live in.
F somebody who owns the house he/she lives in
G somebody who rents accommodation
H the Council
I money paid to the Council

## Section 2: Applying to the Council

### A

If you want to apply for a council house or flat, you have to fill in a housing application form. Fill in the form on the next page.

### B

Imagine you have received the following letter from the Council. With a partner, practise telephoning to arrange to see the flat.

Dear Sir/Madam

I have pleasure in offering you the tenancy of 4 Long Walk, a house on the Bellcrest Estate. Please telephone my Allocations Section so that arrangements can be made for you to view the house.

If you decide to refuse this offer, please indicate your reasons for doing so and return this letter, together with the Conditions of Tenancy, without delay.

This offer will be withdrawn if you have not contacted this office within two weeks.

Yours faithfully

R Cooper

R J Cooper
Housing Manager

## COUNCIL HOUSING APPLICATION

All questions must be answered fully in block capitals and the declaration signed overleaf.

1) Details of persons (yourself first) for whom accommodation is required

| SURNAME | OTHER NAMES | RELATIONSHIP TO YOURSELF | DATE OF BIRTH | MALE/ FEMALE |
|---|---|---|---|---|
| | | | | |
| | | | | |
| | | | | |
| | | | | |

**2 YOUR PRESENT ACCOMMODATION**

a) ADDRESS ______________________________

b) TELEPHONE NO. HOME______________ WORK __________

| | BED-ROOMS | LIVING ROOMS | KITCHEN | BATH-ROOM | W.C. |
|---|---|---|---|---|---|
| c) NO. OF ROOMS USED BY YOU AND YOUR FAMILY ONLY | | | | | |
| d) NO. OF ROOMS SHARED WITH OTHER RESIDENTS | | | | | |

e) DO YOU HAVE TO CLIMB STAIRS TO REACH YOUR PRESENT HOME YES/NO IF YES, HOW MANY______________________

f) HOW LONG HAVE YOU LIVED AT YOUR PRESENT ADDRESS __

**3 FACILITIES** Please indicate (by ticking the appropriate column) if you have sole use of or share the following facilities:

| | OWN USE | SHARED USE | NONE |
|---|---|---|---|
| a) A FIXED BATH OR SHOWER | | | |
| b) A WASH BASIN | | | |
| c) A KITCHEN SINK | | | |
| d) A COOKER | | | |
| e) AN INSIDE W.C. | | | |
| f) AN OUTSIDE W.C. | | | |

g) DO YOU HAVE HOT & COLD WATER SUPPLY FOR YOUR BATH YES/NO WASH BASIN YES/NO KITCHEN SINK YES/NO

**4 TENANCY DETAILS** (*Please tick appropriate box*)

| ARE YOU | TENANT | OWNER OCCUPIER | SHARING WITH RELATIVES | SHARING WITH PERSONS NOT RELATED TO YOU | A HOUSING ASSOCIATION TENANT |
|---|---|---|---|---|---|
| | | | | | |

PLEASE GIVE NAME & ADDRESS OF LANDLORD ______________________

______________________________________________________________

**5 MEDICAL FACTORS**

DO YOU, OR ANY PERSON INCLUDED IN THIS APPLICATION, USE A WHEELCHAIR YES/NO

ARE YOU, OR ANY PERSON INCLUDED IN THIS APPLICATION, REGISTERED BLIND OR DISABLED WITH THIS COUNCIL. YES/NO IF YES, PLEASE GIVE REGISTRATION NO ______________________
ARE THERE ANY OTHER SERIOUS MEDICAL PROBLEMS, IN RELATION TO YOUR PRESENT HOUSING, WHICH YOU WISH THE COUNCIL TO TAKE INTO CONSIDERATION ______________________

**6 OTHER FACTORS**

a) IF YOU ARE MARRIED WITHOUT CHILDREN, WOULD YOU BE PREPARED TO ACCEPT HOUSING IN A TOWER BLOCK YES/NO

b) IF YOU ARE SINGLE, ARE YOU INTERESTED IN SHARING ACCOMMODATION YES/NO

c) IF YOU ARE ELDERLY, WOULD YOU LIKE TO BE CONSIDERED FOR A FLAT WHERE A WARDEN IS AVAILABLE YES/NO

d) PLEASE STATE THE ADRESSES AT WHICH YOU HAVE LIVED DURING THE LAST FOUR YEARS:

| | FROM | | TO | |
|---|---|---|---|---|
| | MONTH | YEAR | MONTH | YEAR |
| | | | | |
| | | | | |
| | | | | |
| | | | | |

e) ARE THERE ANY OTHER FACTORS WHICH YOU WISH TO BE TAKEN INTO ACCOUNT, SUCH AS NOTICE TO QUIT, HARASSMENT BY YOUR LANDLORD, DAMPNESS, DISREPAIR ETC. IF SO, PLEASE GIVE DETAILS

______________________________________________________________

______________________________________________________________

______________________________________________________________

**DECLARATION**

I DECLARE THAT ALL INFORMATION GIVEN IN THIS APPLICATION IS CORRECT, AND I UNDERTAKE TO NOTIFY THE HOUSING DEPARTMENT IF THERE IS ANY CHANGE IN MY CIRCUMSTANCES AFFECTING THIS APPLICATION.

SIGNED: MR/MRS/MISS DATE

## Section 3: Finding a place to rent—newspaper advertisements

### A

Advertisements use abbreviations so that information can be fitted into a small space. Here are some advertisements from a local newspaper.

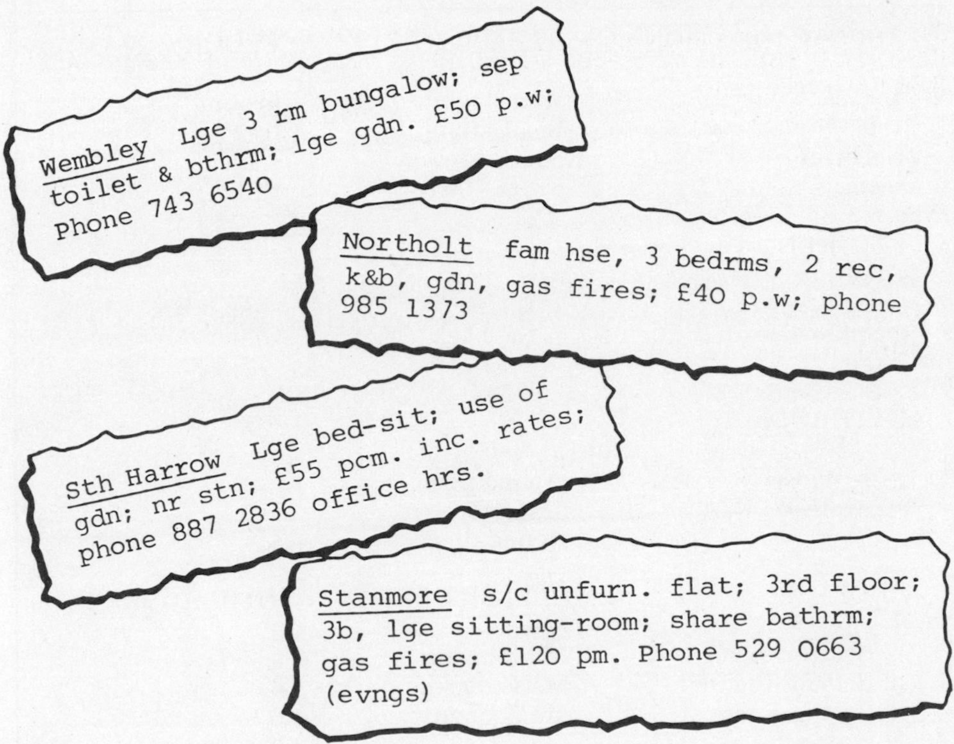

Wembley Lge 3 rm bungalow; sep toilet & bthrm; lge gdn. £50 p.w; Phone 743 6540
Northolt fam hse, 3 bedrms, 2 rec, k&b, gdn, gas fires; £40 p.w; phone 985 1373
Sth Harrow Lge bed-sit; use of gdn; nr stn; £55 pcm. inc. rates; phone 887 2836 office hrs.
Stanmore s/c unfurn. flat; 3rd floor; 3b, lge sitting-room; share bathrm; gas fires; £120 pm. Phone 529 0663 (evngs)


Work out what the abbreviations mean. Write out the advertisements in full.

### B

Here is information about four families. Decide which of the four places in A you would recommend for each family. Give reasons.

a) Mr & Mrs Brown. 2 children. They want a garden and central heating, and good public transport. Can pay up to £45 pw.
b) Mr & Mrs White. 2 children. They want large rooms. Can pay up to £35 pw.
c) Miss Johnson. Wants a place on her own. Must be near public transport.
d) Miss Williamson. Single parent, has 4 children. Wants central heating. Can pay up to £38 pw.

## Further practice

Find some advertisements for places to rent in your local paper. Write them out in full.

## C

You are going to hear a telephone call from somebody who wants to rent a place to live. While you listen, tick the correct information below:

| ACCOMMODATION | AREA | FLOOR |
|---|---|---|
| house | Wembley | ground |
| flat | Wealdstone | first |
| bedsitter | South Harrow | second |
| room | North Harrow | third |
| **KITCHEN** | | |
| small | at the front | shared use |
| medium sized | at the back | sole use |
| large | | |
| **BATHROOM** | | |
| with W. C. | ground floor | |
| separate W. C. | first floor | |
| | second floor | |
| **ADDRESS** | **CALLER'S NAME** | **TIME AGREED** |
| 42 Brerton Road | Mr Johnson | 5.45 pm |
| 42 Betton Road | Mr Thomson | 6.00 pm |
| 42 Breton Road | Mr Ronson | 6.15 pm |
| 42 Briton Road | | 6.30 pm |

## D

Listen to another telephone call. Write down the information.

## E

Work in pairs. Choose one of the places advertised in A. Practise ringing up and asking questions about it. Arrange a time to go and see it.

## F

You are going to hear two people talking about a place they have been to see. Look at the advertisements in A again (or look at the information from these advertisements which you wrote in full), and decide which place they are discussing.

# Section 4: Linking words

## A

1 Make a list of advantages of having a ground-floor flat, instead of a top-floor flat.
eg There are no stairs for old people to climb.

2 Make a list of disadvantages.

3

Remember how to link the advantages and disadvantages:

1 Linking two points which are the *same*: ALSO

Example:

| ADVANTAGE | | ADVANTAGE |
|---|---|---|
| You don't have to carry shopping upstairs. | ALSO | There are no stairs for old people to climb. |

'You don't have to carry shopping upstairs. Also, there are no stairs for old people to climb.'

2 Linking two points which are *different*: ON THE OTHER HAND

Example:

| ADVANTAGE | | DISADVANTAGE |
|---|---|---|
| Your visitors can get to your flat quickly. | ON THE OTHER HAND | Other people's visitors may knock at your door with enquiries. |

'Your visitors can get to the flat quickly. On the other hand, other people's visitors may knock at your door with enquiries.'

4 Say and write some advantages and disadvantages. Link them with 'Also', or 'On the other hand'.

B

Write about the advantages and disadvantages of
- your present home
- having central heating
- being an only child
- driving a car/riding a bicycle/using public transport/walking

# Section 5: Finding a place to buy

A Newspaper advertisements:

People who want to buy somewhere to live can look at advertisements in newspapers. Find some advertisements for properties for sale in your area, and work out what they mean.

B

Estate agents:

1 People who want to buy somewhere can also go to estate agents. Estate agents have lists of properties for sale. They can also give you more details of a particular house or flat.

Remember: Estate agents work for the owner of a house who wants to sell it. They give information to the person wanting to buy. Some of the things they say and write are facts, some are opinions.

2 FACTS AND OPINIONS

"The sitting room has three windows" is a FACT.
We could count the windows, and everybody would agree that there are three.
"The sitting room is beautiful" is an OPINION.
Different people have different opinions. Some people may think the sitting room is beautiful; others may not agree.

3 Study the two information sheets from an estate agent, on pages 51–2. Underline the facts. Put a (ring) round the opinions. The first part is done for you.

# Chislum & Floggit

Estate Agents

This is an outstanding property, built of brick, with a tiled roof. The attractive view from the house will delight you.

Three reception rooms: front – 18′ × 12′ and 14′ × 12′, – with bay windows and attractive open fireplaces; rear – 20′ × 14′ – an exceptional room of great character. Luxurious carpeting in all reception rooms. Kitchen with fitted units and stainless steel sink and draining board. 3 electric sockets in every room.

Two beautifully decorated large front bedrooms with fitted wardrobes and open fireplaces; back bedroom with view over garden. Large bathroom with bath and shower. Separate lavatory. Fitted carpets throughout.

Huge natural back garden, a delight for a keen gardener.

£45,000

# Chislum & Floggit
Estate Agents

Modern semi-detached house in desirable residential area, within easy reach of shops and station. Five minutes' walk from Stainham primary school. Excellent condition throughout.

2 reception rooms: front 12′ × 12′, rear 14′ × 12′. Convenient kitchen, well-equipped, with back door opening onto paved area.

Open staircase. 3 bedrooms, one with fitted wardrobe. Well-arranged bathroom with attractive matching bath, basin and WC.

Gas-fired central heating.

Well-kept gardens at front and back.

£35,000

4 You are going to hear two people talking about one of the houses on p. 51 and p. 52, after they have seen it.
   (a) Find out which house they have seen.
   (b) Find out what they now know about the house, which they didn't know from the information sheet.

5 The Shaftesbury family are looking for a house. Mrs Shaftesbury has just been appointed head of Stainham primary school. Mr Shaftesbury will continue working in town. They have three children and a large dog. John is taking A level examinations next summer. Wendy likes having friends round to listen to records and Sandra sings with a group. The family have a car, but Mrs Shaftesbury can't drive. They hope to sell their present house for about £40,000.

Which of the two houses sounds more suitable for the Shaftesbury family? Give reasons.

Remember Link your points with 'Also', 'On the other hand'.

Consider Position: convenient or inconvenient, close to or a long way from station etc.
Accommodation: number of rooms, size of rooms
Price:
Other points: easy to look after, heating, garden, etc.

## Extension work

1. Facts can be looked at in different ways. Read these two descriptions of the same flat, one by an estate agent, one by a friend of yours.

Estate agent

An attractive ground-floor flat in a converted cottage. Conveniently close to the station, it stands in a natural garden. The flat is not occupied and so is ready for immediate occupation.

The interior is freshly decorated. There is a large front room which is light and airy. The rooms at the back are pleasantly shaded, and are ideal for bedrooms. In the large bedroom, the new occupant can choose the position of the light. The small bedroom is next to the bathroom.

Friend

You can't see the front door from the road because the grass in the front garden is so long and the bushes are so big. When you get inside, the noise from the trains is so loud that you can't have a conversation. Someone has recently painted over the rust on the window frames and the damp marks on the walls but the house obviously hasn't been lived in for months.

At the back, there are tall bushes right outside the windows, so the back rooms are dark. In the front room, the windows don't fit properly, so the wind blows in. There are supposed to be two bedrooms, but one is so small that if you put a bed in it, you couldn't get anything else in. And the bigger one has no electric light.

Notice the different way the two accounts talk about the same thing. In two columns, write out the phrases that talk about the same thing. The first one has been done for you.

| Estate agent | Friend |
|---|---|
| conveniently close to the station | the noise from the trains is so loud that you can't have a conversation. |

2. Give a description of the place where you live, pointing out its good and bad points for somebody who wants to rent or buy it.
3. Write a short essay entitled *Where I live now*. You can plan your essay like this, using work you have done already.

Introduction Describe the house/flat/room you live in.
(Look back at what you wrote in *Unit* 3 *A Place to Live I*, section 3 C, p. 30.)

Advantages and disadvantages
(Look back at what you wrote in *Unit* 3 *A Place to Live II*, Section 4 B, p. 50.)

Compare it with one or more places where you have lived in the past
(Look back at what you wrote in *Unit* 3 *A Place to Live I*, Section 5 D, p. 31.)

# Unit 6 Writing formal letters

## Section 1: What is a formal letter?

A

A formal letter is a letter to someone who is not known as a friend. There are some rules for writing formal letters: rules for punctuation, for beginning and ending a letter and for arranging the letter (LAYOUT)
In the first part of this unit, you will see some differences between formal letters and other things which are sent by post.

B

Here is one morning's post delivered to the Blue Ark restaurant. The owner lives above the restaurant. This morning he received: 1) a letter from a firm, 2) a letter from a friend, 3) a postcard and 4) a letter from someone he does not know.
Read them and 1) decide which is which
2) write the owner's name and address

22 Grove End
Byfleet
Lincs
17/3/8-

Dear Ronald
Many thanks for your letter. It really cheered us up. Lucy is well on the way to recovery now; the worst is over.
It would be great to see you all. When Lucy is a bit stronger we've promised ourselves Sunday lunch at the Ark. If you were free, we could do something in the afternoon. I'll ring nearer the time, Best wishes Tom

43 Honey Lane
Daxford
DA3 6HC

17th March 198-

The Owner
The Blue Ark
23 Fortune Avenue
Daxford
DA4 8HD

Dear Sir,

I am looking for a position as a waitress. I have had some experience and would very much like to work at The Blue Ark

I enclose a Personal Record, giving details of my background. I hope to hear from you if there is a vacancy now or likely to be one in the near future.

Yours faithfully,

Emma Jones

Emma Jones

---

Phillip & Sons, Ltd.
90-96 High Street, Daxford, DA4 2HC
Tel: 40551/2/3
Telex: 728537

17th March 198-

Mr. R.S. Honiton,
The Blue Ark,
23, Fortune Avenue,
Daxford,
DA4 8HD

Dear Mr. Honiton,

Mr. John Campbell

Mr. Campbell has applied for a job with this firm as a canteen manager. He has given your name as a referee.

I would be grateful if you could let us have a confidential reference. A stamped addressed envelope is enclosed.

Yours sincerely

G. Johnson.

G. Johnson
Personnel Officer

---

Good to see the family again after such a long time. Having a lazy time sun bathing and eating good food. Hope all well, see you back in Daxford. Love.
Jamie

Mr. R.S. Honiton
23. Fortune Avenue
Daxford.
DA4 8HD

## C

1 Read the letter from a friend again. Fill in this information from the letter:

Name of the person who wrote it: ______________________
Address of the person who wrote it: ______________________
______________________________________________

Date: ______________________________________
How does the letter begin? Dear ______________________
How does the letter end? B ______________________
Does the letter include Mr Honiton's address? YES/NO

2 Read the letter from Emma Jones again. Fill in this information:

Emma Jones' address: ______________________
Postcode:
______________________________________________

Date of the letter: ______________________
Dear______________
Yours______________
Does Emma Jones know Mr Honiton's name? YES/NO
Does the letter include Mr Honiton's address? YES/NO

3 Read the letter from a firm again. Fill in this information:

Name of firm: ______________________
Address of firm: ______________________
Postcode:______________ Tel No: ______________
Date of the letter: ______________________
Name of the person who wrote it: ______________________
Position of the person who wrote it; ______________________
Does the writer know Mr Honiton's name? YES/NO
Does the letter include Mr Honiton's address? YES/NO

Remember: Dear + name goes with Yours sincerely
Dear Sir } goes with Yours faithfully
Dear Madam }

## D

Discuss the differences between the letter from a friend, and the two formal letters.

## E

There are different styles for formal letters in English. You have to keep to the rules, but you can choose the style. Compare the letter from the firm and the letter from Emma Jones. Look at the differences in punctuation.
It is best to learn one style and use it for all formal letters. This unit will teach a blocked style with open punctuation; this is the style Emma Jones uses.

# Section 2: Layout

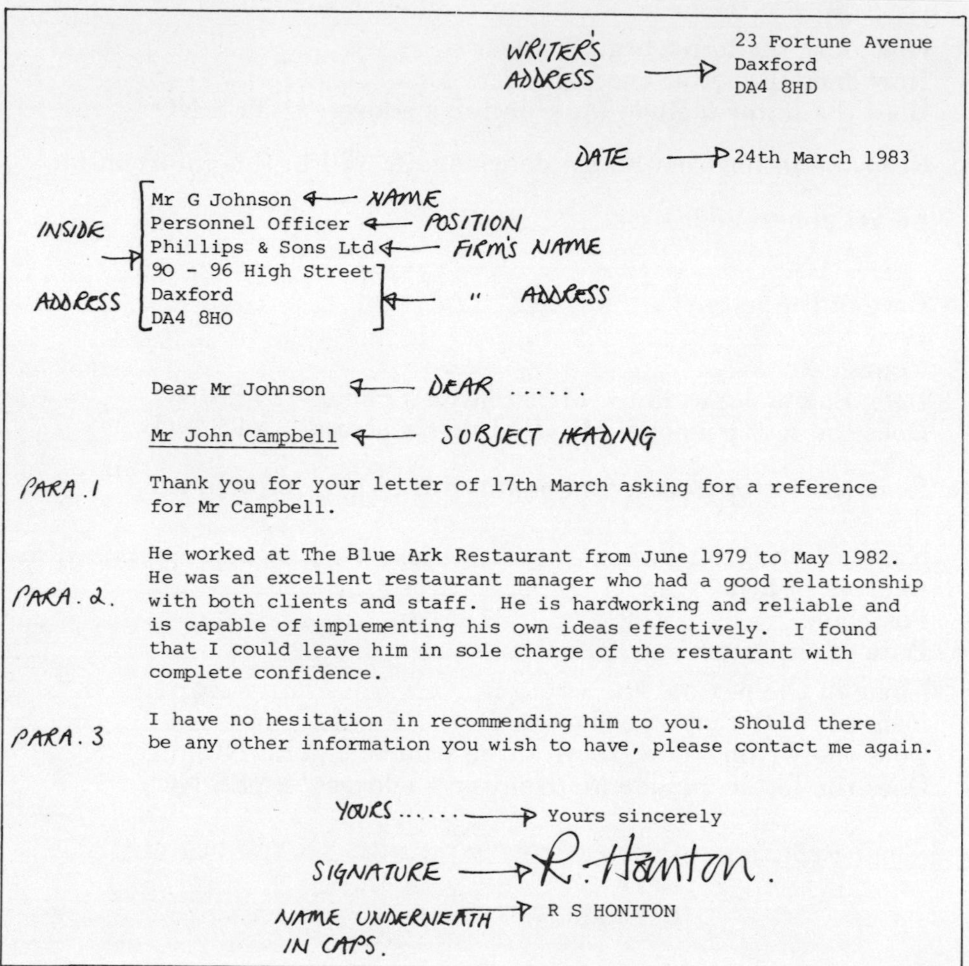

23 Fortune Avenue
Daxford
DA4 8HD

24th March 1983

Mr G Johnson
Personnel Officer
Phillips & Sons Ltd
90 - 96 High Street
Daxford
DA4 8HO

Dear Mr Johnson

Mr John Campbell

Thank you for your letter of 17th March asking for a reference for Mr Campbell.

He worked at The Blue Ark Restaurant from June 1979 to May 1982. He was an excellent restaurant manager who had a good relationship with both clients and staff. He is hardworking and reliable and is capable of implementing his own ideas effectively. I found that I could leave him in sole charge of the restaurant with complete confidence.

I have no hesitation in recommending him to you. Should there be any other information you wish to have, please contact me again.

Yours sincerely

R. Hanton.

R S HONITON



A

This letter has all the different parts labelled. Study it carefully.
Look at the LAYOUT — This is where the parts of the letter go on the page.
Look at the use of CAPITAL LETTERS.
This letter has a subject heading, but many formal letters do not have one.
Remember: the writer's name never goes at the top of a letter.

## B

Practise the LAYOUT of a formal letter

Use the information in the table below, and write it with the correct layout for a formal letter. The first one is done for you.

| Date | Letter from: | Letter to: |
|---|---|---|
| 22/3/83 | J B Sutton<br>24 Abingdon Road<br>London NW5 8JH | The Manager<br>Scottish National Bank<br>19 King Street<br>Edinburgh ED6 8NG |
| 5/11/83 | Joan Parker (Mrs)<br>Flat 4 78 Hillside<br>Crescent<br>Birmingham BJ7 4TG | Ms E T Smith<br>Claims Department<br>Commercial Union Assurance Co<br>17 Darling Street<br>Birmingham BH8 3FT |
| 8/1/82 | N S Lee<br>287 Carmelite Road<br>Horsham<br>W Sussex, HO2 3 BN | Mr G McDonald<br>Sales Manager<br>Norris & Sons Ltd Francis Way<br>Sheffield SH4 8HN |
| 9/2/84 | B Joshi 47 High Road<br>North Salford M3 9ED | The Environmental Health<br>Officer<br>Civic Centre Salford M4 5SA |
| 30 Dec 83 | YOU | Mrs G O'Flanagan<br>Brookland Books<br>1 Brookland Avenue<br>Norwich NO2 3BC |

Example

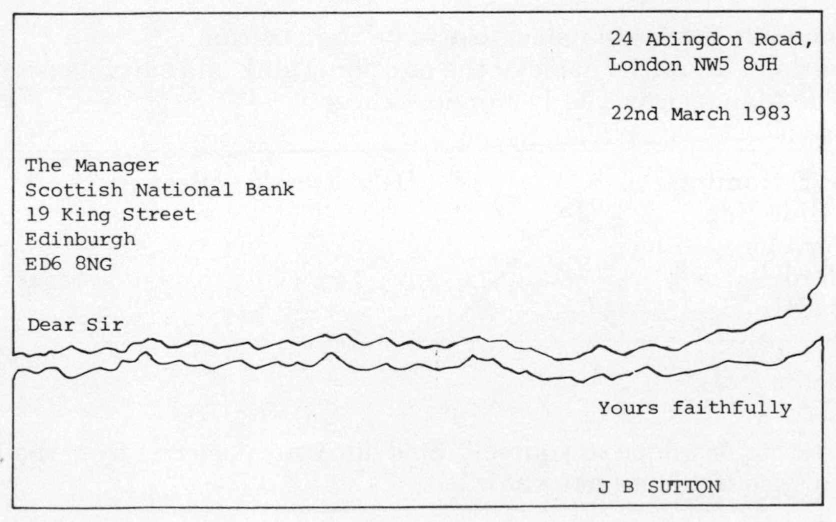
24 Abingdon Road,
London NW5 8JH

22nd March 1983

The Manager
Scottish National Bank
19 King Street
Edinburgh
ED6 8NG

Dear Sir

Yours faithfully

J B SUTTON

## C Notice how things go together

| ENVELOPE | INSIDE ADDRESS | DEAR . . . . . | YOURS. . . . . . |
|---|---|---|---|
| Mr *R S Honiton<br>The Blue Ark<br>23 Fortune Avenue<br>Daxford<br>DA4 8HD | Mr R S Honiton<br>The Blue Ark<br>23 Fortune Avenue<br>Daxford<br>DA4 8HD | Dear Mr * Honiton | Yours sincerely |
| *Remember: you need initials with the surname on an envelope and in the inside address; you never use initials after Dear. . . . . You begin the name and address on an envelope about halfway down. Use the same style and punctuation as for the inside address | | | |
| Mr G Johnson<br>Personnel Officer<br>Phillips & Sons plc<br>90–96 High Street<br>Daxford<br>DA4 8HO | Mr G Johnson<br>Personnel Officer<br>Phillips & Sons plc<br>90–96 High Street<br>Daxford<br>DA4 8HO | Dear Mr Johnson | Yours sincerely |
| If you know the name and the position, write them both | | | |
| The Owner<br>The Blue Ark<br>23 Fortune Avenue<br>Daxford<br>DA4 8HD | The Owner<br>The Blue Ark<br>23 Fortune Avenue<br>Daxford<br>DA4 8HD | Dear Sir | Yours faithfully |
| If you don't know the name, just write the position.<br>If you don't know the name or the position, think of a suitable position: eg. The Manager or The Personnel Officer | | | |
| Mr R S Honiton<br>The Blue Ark<br>23 Fortune Avenue<br>Daxford<br>DA4 8HD | X | Dear Ronald | Best wishes |

## D

Address an envelope to yourself. Find out your postcode from the local Post Office if you do not know it.

# Section 3: Writing Letters

## A

A Letter of Enquiry

145 Winton Road
POTTERTON
Lincs
PS3 2GJ

8 January 198-

The Manager
Key Insurance Co
46 Granthan Ave
KINGSLEY
Lincs
KL5 7FD

Dear Sir

I am interested in car insurance and house contents insurance. I would be grateful if you would send me some information. I look forward to hearing from you.

Yours faithfully,

Janet Sanders

JANET SANDERS (Mrs)

Study this letter carefully. Use it to help you write the two letters of enquiry below.

Write to:

| a) The Manager | b) The Manager |
|---|---|
| National Building Society | Lutton Tool Hire plc |
| 48–50 Pentforth Street | 2 Phillips Street |
| Trendley | Trendley |
| Brenton | Brenton |
| TB2 4TS | TB3 5FS |

Enquire about:

| opening a savings account | hiring a floor polisher |
|---|---|

## B

### How to plan a formal letter

Purpose: before you write a formal letter decide carefully about the purpose of it. Why are you writing? The answer could be one or more of these things:

to ask for something, eg information, a form, an appointment, a refund

to apply for something

to give information

to ask somebody to do something

to apologise

to confirm details or arrangements

to query something

to send something

to complain

### Starting points + openings

Starting point:

| | |
|---|---|
| interest: | I am interested in . . . |
| something you sent: | |
| a) a letter you wrote: | I wrote to you on . . . asking for . . . |
| b) payment: | I sent a cheque for . . . on . . . |
| c) order: | I ordered a . . . on . . . |
| a conversation: | Following our conversation yesterday, I would like to . . . |
| a letter you received: | Thank you for your letter of 22nd April*. (*This is always the date on the letter, not when it arrived.) |
| an arrangement or an appointment: | I have an appointment to collect the keys from your office on . . . at . . . |
| advertisement: | I am writing in reply to your advertisement. |
| a subject heading is often a good opening: | Savings Account no. RB 65432<br>This account . . . |

Look back at all the formal letters in this unit.
For each one:

1. Decide why the person is writing
2. Decide the starting point
3. Write out the opening

## C

### How to plan a formal letter

Here are some sentences from letters.

1. I am sorry I have not replied to your letter before.
2. I enclose a postal order for £15.07.
3. I would be grateful if you would send someone to repair the leaking pipe outside the kitchen window.
4. I would like to apply for the job of fitter advertised in The Daily Herald yesterday.
5. Please send me an application form for the job of porter advertised in last week's Daily News.
6. I feel that this delay is quite unsatisfactory.
7. I wish to query my latest tax assessment.
8. I would like to confirm that I will be able to attend the interview on . . . . . . at . . . . . . .
9. I last received Unemployment Benefit for the week ending . . . . . . .
10. Thank you for your letter asking me to come for an interview on . . . at . . . .

For each one, answer these questions:
How much can you say about why the person is writing?
Could this be the opening? If not, write a suitable opening.

### Ending a formal letter

Here are some useful endings to choose from. Sometimes there is no need for a closing sentence.

1. I look forward to hearing from you.
2. I apologise for the inconvenience caused.
3. I enclose a stamped addressed envelope for your reply.
4. I hope you will not let me down again.
5. I look forward to meeting you.
6. I look forward to hearing from you as soon as possible.

### Planning a formal letter

Think of the purpose and the starting point.
Choose the right kind of opening and ending from the suggestions in this section.
Remember: paragraphs in formal letters are usually short.

## D

### Replying to formal letters

1 Read the letter below carefully. It asks Ms Marley to do two things. Make sure you know what they are.

**EASTLEIGH GAS BOARD**
High Road, Winterton, W16 7HR
Tel.: 85221/223

26th September 198-

Ms S J Marley
16 Wellington House
Alexander Road
Winterton
W14 6PE

Dear Madam

The New World VI Cooker which you ordered is now available. We look forward to receiving from you the outstanding £210 so that we can proceed to deliver the cooker.

Please let us know when you would like the cooker delivered. We need at least three working days' notice.

Yours faithfully

F. Jones

F. Jones
Area Manager

Plan your reply (Imagine you are Ms Marley)

Starting point: the letter
Opening:
Why you are writing: to send a cheque and give a date and time

Write the letter

You received this card.
Fill in the date
and time you asked
for in your letter.

> **EASTLEIGH GAS BOARD**
>
> Appointment to deliver cooker
> confirmed for.......am/pm
>
> signed: R Matthews

You stayed at home all day but no one turned up. You tried to phone but there was no reply.

Write a second letter — plan it carefully.

Starting point:
Opening:
Why you are writing: give information
complain
ask for another appointment
Ending:

2 Read the letter below. Write a reply confirming the arrangement. Remember to plan it first. Use the same subject heading.

> **Winterton College**
>
> Bounds Green Winterton W19 9NY Tel 34 77890
>
> 6 May 198-
>
> Mr J Kingsley
> 135 Farley Close
> Winterton
> W14 6PL
>
> Dear Mr Kingsley
>
> General Clerical Course 65/06
>
> Thank you for your application for this course.
>
> We would like you to attend an introductory meeting, followed by a personal interview on Thursday, 17th May, from 9.30 am to 1.30 pm.
>
> Please confirm that you will be able to attend. I look forward to hearing from you.
>
> Yours sincerely
>
> J B Marsh
>
> J B Marsh (Mrs)
> Admissions Officer

After the interview, another letter arrived. Reply to it.

**Winterton College**

Bounds Green Winterton W19 9NY Tel 34 77890

24th May 198-

Mr J Kingsley
135 Farley Close
Winterton
W14 6PL

Dear Mr Kingsley

General Clerical Course 65/06

Following your interview on May 17, I am happy to be able to offer you a place on this course.

Please confirm in writing that you wish to accept this place. For our students' records we need a black and white or colour passport photograph of you. We also need to know the name and address of your General Practitioner.

Yours sincerely

J B Marsh

J B Marsh (Mrs)
Admissions Officer

## Extension work

1. You ordered a size 14 white cotton shirt on March 17th from Langhans Mail Order Company. You sent a cheque for £10. On June 14th you received a blue and pink coat.
   Write to:
   The Sales Director, Langhans, 16 Frooley High Street, Bamsworth, BA6 4LR.
2. Write to the Head of your local school. Choose one of the following reasons:
   You would like to ask him or her to write a reference for you.
   You wish to ask if your child could miss the last week of term because you are all going on holiday.
   You wish to arrange an appointment to discuss your child's progress.

3. Reply to this advertisement in your local paper.
(Make up an address for Mrs O'Sullivan)

> Baby sitter wanted 3 nights a week:
> Regular, reliable, must live nearby.
>
> Write to Mrs Jane O'Sullivan
>
> ....................
>
> ....................

4. Confirm a telephone booking for yourself for one night at the Falcon Hotel, Brook Street, Braxford, BR6 2LW
5. An old car has been left outside your house. It has been there for weeks, and is in a dangerous condition. Write to the Highways Department of the local Council.
6. You have telephoned the box office at the Pavilion Theatre, Daxford, to book tickets for the musical 'Happy Days'; 2 tickets at £5.50 each for the Saturday after next. Confirm the booking and send a cheque or postal order.
7. Write to the BBC Ticket Unit, Broadcasting House, London, W1A 4WW, asking for tickets for a radio or TV show.

# Unit 7 Looking for work

## Section 1: Looking at Jobs

### A

YOU AND JOBS Think carefully about the kind of job you would like. Think about what you can do. Study the chart below, and tick the box or boxes which show how you feel.

| What would you feel about jobs in which these things happen? | I'd like that | I wouldn't mind that | I wouldn't like that | I'm sure I could do it | I'm not sure I could do it | I couldn't do it |
|---|---|---|---|---|---|---|
| You work largely on your own | | | | | | |
| You work with people of different ages and backgrounds | | | | | | |
| You have to answer the phone and take messages | | | | | | |
| You deal with members of the public | | | | | | |
| You have to take responsibility for money, equipment or other staff | | | | | | |
| You have to work some Saturdays | | | | | | |
| You get dirty | | | | | | |
| You have to be good at Maths | | | | | | |
| You have to be able to drive | | | | | | |
| You have to be able to type | | | | | | |
| You mainly work out of doors | | | | | | |
| You work shifts | | | | | | |
| You have to do overtime | | | | | | |
| There is no overtime | | | | | | |
| You have to carry things | | | | | | |
| You have to wear protective goggles, overalls, gloves or head-covering | | | | | | |
| You have to wear a uniform | | | | | | |
| You start on a low wage but get training | | | | | | |
| You work some evenings | | | | | | |

## B

### What does the job involve

1 Match the job in the left-hand column with the correct description in the right-hand column.

1) A receptionist
2) A secretary
3) A cashier
4) A sales assistant
5) An accounts clerk
6) A ward orderly
7) An office junior
8) A personnel officer
9) A catering assistant

A) works in the kitchen preparing food, serving it and washing up.
B) helps customers find what they want, arranges goods on display and may take money.
C) take dictation, types, and assists the boss.
D) greets people when they first come in, makes appointments and answers the phone.
E) takes money, works at a till and gives change.
F) helps with filing, does general clerical work, runs errands and often receives training.
G) works in a hospital doing general domestic work such as cleaning or serving meals.
H) deals with orders, invoices, petty cash, etc.
I) deals with staff, especially hiring them.

2 Listen to the tape. You will hear four people talking about the work they do. Find out which job each one has.

3 Write a brief description of a job or jobs you are interested in (like the descriptions in ex 1).

## C

### Classification of Jobs

1 To save time, job vacancies are classified, or listed under headings. Decide what heading each of these jobs would come under in the newspaper or Job Centre:
SALES ASSISTANT, COOK, CLERICAL ASSISTANT.

2 Study the headings below and put them into alphabetical order. Then underline the headings you would want to look at.

HOSPITAL, PART-TIME, PRINTING TRADES, TEMPORARY, ACCOUNTANCY, CATERING, SECRETARIAL, SHOP & STORE STAFF, SCHOOL LEAVERS & JUNIORS, FASHION & TAILORING, GENERAL VACANCIES, CLERICAL, ELECTRONICS, MANAGERIAL, COMPUTER PERSONNEL, CLEANING, FACTORY WORK, BUILDING & CONSTRUCTION, SKILLED, UNSKILLED, LATEST VACANCIES.

3 Here are five more headings; each is similar to one of the headings in the last section. Write the correct heading in the space.

Retail: Shop + Store Staff ____ Industrial ____
Office work: ____ Miscellaneous: ____
Domestic: ____

4 Here are three jobs. Which heading in ex. 2 would you put them under?
Manager ____
Clerk ____ Secretary ____

## Section 2: Finding a vacancy

### A

Newspapers

1 Job advertisements appear in national daily and Sunday papers, evening papers and local papers. Public libraries have copies of most papers.

2 Look quickly at the job advertisements and answer the questions below as briefly as you can. Do not read the advertisements fully. Look at the headings, the job (in heavy type) and the end of each advertisement.

a) How many columns are there? ____

b) How many headings are there? ____

c) How many jobs are there under Hairdressing? ____

d) How many jobs are there under Office? ____

e) How many jobs mention part-time? ____

f) Look at the advertisements under General.
How many ask you to phone? ____
How many ask you to write? ____
How many ask you to go there? ____

g) Look at the advertisements under Office.
How many ask you to phone? ____
How many ask you to write? ____
How many ask you to go there? ____
Which advertisement asks you to phone or write for an application form and further details? ____

h) Write down all the abbreviations you can find.
Next to each, write the word or words in full.

# EMPLOYMENT

66 General

**HOMEWORKERS**

ADDRESSING FORMS

Please call at:

9, INVERNESS PLACE, W2

Between 10 a.m. and 12 noon and 2 p.m. to 4 p.m.

**TRAINEE PRODUCTION ASSISTANT**, girl or boy to train as production assistant to designer, small group, W11. Organising ability an advantage, small offset printing production control / studio work / camera work. Potentially managerial position. Please write to – Box No. T513, 17 Grove Road, London W6.

**T.V. FIELD ENGINEER.** Estate car, salary approximately £6,600. Immediate vacancy. — Tel. 01-793 4036

67 Hairdressing

**HAIR STYLIST**

Part-time experienced.

Perhaps your family has grown up and you would like to resume hairdressing.

**JOHN OF MAYFAIR**

26, CONNAUGHT STREET
LONDON W2
Tel: 970 4278

**LADIES HAIRDRESSER**

FULL OR PART TIME

Good wage and condition
Ring for further information

**Tel. 796 1670**

68 **Hospital & Nursing staff**

**SRNS/SENs** required for day duties, weekend work and short visits. — Tel. 865 5621, Bleep No. 2524.

69 Hotel Staff

**CHAMBERMAID / DAILY HELP,** M/F, for small friendly hotel, Paddington area, 8 a.m. to 12.30, 6 days, good pay and condition. — Tel. 955 3375.

**FULL AND PART TIME BARMAIDS**

Also Snack bar Assistant. Small friendly house in W1 area near Middlesex Hospital. Excellent salary. References most essential.

PLEASE PHONE
PROPRIETOR ON

**220 2452**

72 Office

**ARABIC SPEAKING RECEPTIONIST**

Required for luxury flats, NW8. Must be numerate, with typing and telex experience. Good salary.

Please phone Manager on:

**984 4498**
(No Agencies)

**ASSISTANT AUDIO SECRETARY**

To senior partner in legal firm.

Knowledge of conveyancing and litigation matters essential, ability to work on own initiative. Fast, accurate typing, friendly young office adjacent to Parsons Green Tube, SW6. Excellent salary for right person.

**Telephone:**
**494 0901**

**AUDIO SECRETARY**

To collect from and deliver to solicitors in W1

Telephone:
**798 2226**

Ask for Mr. N. F. Allan

**ACCOUNTANT:** Small rapidly expanding central London firm, require semi senior. Excellent prospects and experience given to successful candidate. Salary negotiable. — Tel. 01-955 7151

**COPY TYPIST**

Age 30 plus, salary £4,000 plus LV's, four weeks holiday, staff pension scheme.

Apply: Mr. Peebles

48, PALL MALL
LONDON SW1

**Tel. 201 0125**

**EXPERIENCED ACCOUNTS CLERK**

With computer experience to run small companies books in friendly office.

Salary negotiable.

Apply in writing to:

The Accountant

**BOAT SHOWROOMS OF LONDON**

286, KENSINGTON
HIGH STREET, W14

**General Assistant** required by the Horticultural Association. Varied work including office duties. Send for application form and particulars to the Staff Officer, Horticultural Association, Malden Avenue, London W6 32R.

**Clerical Assistant** wanted by the London Tourist Agency. For further details and an application form, ring 863 0043 (24 hours). Quote reference no. 42/003.

INNER LONDON
EDUCATION AUTHORITY

**North Westminster School, Penfold Street, London NW1 6RX**

A vacancy exists for a

**PERSONAL SECRETARY**

TO THE HEADMASTER

Responsible for arranging engagements, correspondence and general assistance. This challenging post demands a flexible approach.

Applicants should possess English language 'O' level and RSA Stage II in Shorthand and Typing or equivalent.

Salary dependent on age and experience but not less than £4,767 (inclusive) at age 21.

Further details and application forms available from Mr. E. Goss, School Secretary, Tel: 442 2281.

3 There are many things you want to know about a job. Think of some things.
When you are seriously interested in an advertisement, read it very carefully. Note what information it gives and what is missing, so that you can make sure you find out everything you need to know. Here are some notes on the last advertisement:—

Job : Personal Secretary to the Headmaster.

Organization : North Westminster School.

Kind of Work : Secretarial

Number of vacancies : 1

Area : London NW1

Training and prospects : ? none, probably

Hours : ?

Money : ? but not less than £4,767 at age 21

Canteen or L.V's : School dinners?

Permanent or Temporary : Permanent?

How to apply : Phone for application form and further details

Name of person to contact : Mr. E. Goss.

PERSON WANTED

Age : ?

Experience : ?

Qualifications : English Language O level
RSA stage II in Shorthand and Typing
or equivalent.

4 Now use the same method to make notes on the vacancy for the Accounts Clerk. Where the advertisement does not tell you something, put ? and think how you could ask about it.

5 Make notes in the same way on a newspaper advertisement which interests you.

B

Job Centres

1 These are run by the government and are free for employers and for people looking for jobs. They are usually in prominent positions in the High Street. Anyone can walk in and read the job vacancies on the display boards. People register for employment in Job Centres. Also, if people might be able to get money from the government, they go from the Job Centre to the unemployment benefit office. There the staff tell them if they can get any benefit.

## Inside the Job Centre

2 Inside the Job Centre vacancies are displayed on boards which people look at on their own. Each vacancy is on a separate card and cards are classified under headings. These headings show the kind of work or the kind of person wanted for jobs in that group. When people find suitable vacancies on the board they go to the desk and give in the details. The exact procedure varies from one Job Centre to another: in some you take the card to the desk; in others you just give in the number of the card on the board. The person behind the desk asks some relevant questions and may then contact the employer to arrange an interview. Once an interview is arranged, people are given an introduction card to take to the interview.

3 Here are some instructions about what to do in the Job Centre. Put them in the right order. Use the paragraph above to check.

a) Answer questions about yourself.
b) Take the details to the desk (*either* take the card *or* write down the number).
c) Read the display boards.
d) Find the right headings on the display boards.
e) Take the introduction card to the interview.
f) Find a suitable vacancy or vacancies.
g) Write down any details about your interview which are not on the introduction card.

4 Find your local Job Centre. Go there. Find out the opening hours. Find out the exact procedure. (Do people take the cards to the desk, or just write down the numbers?)
Write down any headings for vacancies which are different from the list you have seen in Section 1 C, page 69. Write down some vacancies which interest you.

5 What happens at the desk in the Job Centre

Listen to the conversation on tape. Notice the questions you have to answer. Make a note of the main ones.

# C

## Careers Offices

There is a Careers Office in each district. Careers Officers give help and advice to younger people (usually 24 or younger) and will give information on courses of all kinds and job opportunities. Anyone can walk in, but it may be necessary to make an appointment to talk to a Careers Officer.

## D

Employment Agencies

These are privately run, and charge the employer money for finding an employee. These agencies have information about vacancies. An interviewer discusses them with you, and tries to put you in touch with an employer. Unlike the Job Centres, employment agencies often deal only with one kind of work, for example temporary office work or industrial jobs. Even if there is no suitable vacancy displayed in the window, people can go into an agency and give details about themselves. The agency may telephone them later with information about a suitable vacancy.

## E

Signs outside factories or shops

Some firms do not use Job Centres or Employment Agencies to find employees. Instead, signs are displayed outside the workplace.

## F

Walking in and asking if there are any vacancies

1 You can try to find work by going into some of the larger shops and asking if there are any vacancies. Ask to speak to the manager. (You might find it helpful to look at Unit 9 *Interviews*, sections 4–6, pages 92–5.)

2 Listen to two people trying this. Notice the words they use. Use these as a model, and try it yourself.

## G

Here are words used by people looking for work in different situations.

'May I see the manager for a moment, please?'
"I see you have got a vacancy for a fitter. I'd like to apply for the job."
"I was made redundant last Friday and I'd like to register for employment, and claim unemployment benefit."
"I'm looking for an office job.'

Which is the right situation for each one?
— in a Job Centre.
— in an Employment Agency.
— in a workplace which has a vacancy displayed outside.
— in a workplace with no vacancy displayed outside.

# Section 3: Applying

## A

### Applying by phone

1 Many advertisements ask you to telephone the organisation.

Some give a name to ask for.
Some give a position to ask for.
Some give a first name only.
Some just give a number.

2 Look back at the advertisements on page 71, and try to find an example of each; for one kind there is no example.

3 What to say at the beginning:
"Good morning. May I please speak to Mr Phillips?"
"Good morning. May I please speak to the Proprietor?"
"Hello. I'm ringing about the . . . . . . . . job you advertised. The advert says I should speak to Rosie."
"Hello. Could I have the . . . . . Department please?"
"Could I have extension 12, please?"
"Hello. I'm ringing about the chambermaid job you advertised."

### Practice

4 First, make notes on this advertisement. What information is given and what is missing?

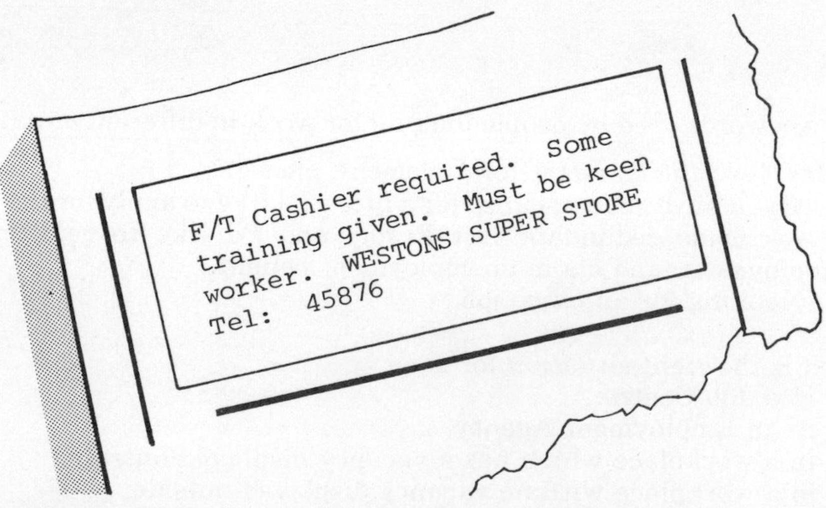

F/T Cashier required. Some
training given. Must be keen
worker. WESTONS SUPER STORE
Tel: 45876

5 Listen to three people phoning up about this job. For each call, tick the comments below which apply:

| | Call 1 | Call 2 | Call 3 |
|---|---|---|---|
| sounded confident | | | |
| sounded nervous | | | |
| sounded polite | | | |
| was well prepared | | | |
| said too much | | | |
| said too little | | | |
| asked sensible questions | | | |

6 Listen again to the best call. Notice that the caller says these things:
her name.
the job.
her work experience.
questions about hours and money.
the name of a referee.

You are going to practise applying for this job. Prepare your answers and questions.

7 Practise the call with a partner. The words of the telephonist and the manager are given on page 78. Make sure you change roles.

8 Choose another advertisement from page 71 which asks you to telephone. With a partner, practise ringing up about that job. Remember: Study the advertisement carefully first.

## B

### Phoning for an application form

1 Many large organisations, such as government departments, hospitals and schools, ask you to fill in a special application form when you apply for a job. Check advertisements carefully to see if they tell you to phone to apply, or tell you to phone or write for an application form and further details.

Practise the call in A6 in pairs. Make sure you change roles.

Telephonist: Weston's. Good morning.
Caller:
Telephonist: Oh yes. I'll put you through to Mr Fortis. He's the manager.
Manager: Mr Fortis speaking.
Caller:
Manager: Ah, yes. Have you been a cashier before?
Caller:
Manager: Could you give me a number I could ring for a reference?
Caller:
Manager: Right. Thank you. I'll get in touch with him later.
Caller:
Manager: Well, we work a basic 38-hour week. There's a rota for staff.
Caller:
Manager: £69.50. Now, could you come in and see me? What about tomorrow at 9.30?
Caller:
Manager: What is your full name?
Caller:
Manager: Do you know where the shop is? It's 442 High Road, on the corner of Brent Street.
Caller:
Manager: OK. I'll see you tomorrow morning then.
Caller:

2 Look back to the newspaper advertisements on page 71. How many mention an application form?

3 Listen to someone phoning to ask for a form. In the list below tick the things the caller says:

- his name
- his age
- the job
- his work experience
- his address
- questions about hours and money
- his present occupation
- where he saw the job advertised
- the name of a referee

4 Listen now to someone leaving her name and address on an answering machine, in reply to the next to last advertisement on page 71.

5 Now prepare what *you* would say in reply to the advertisement. Remember that your name and address must be clear. Spell any street name or surname unless it is very well known and your pronunciation is very clear. If a tape recorder is available, record yourself. Then put away the advertisement while you listen to yourself, and see how clear you are.

Remember When you phone for an application form:

- Your call will be brief.
- There is usually no need to talk to anyone who will deal directly with your application.
- Do not tell the person taking your name and address about yourself or about your experience.
- You probably cannot ask any questions about the job. Wait until you read the further details.
- Make it clear exactly what job you are interested in. If the job has a reference number, give that as well as the name of the job.

## C

### Writing a letter asking for an application form

Check how to set out a formal letter correctly. Now write in reply to the advertisement for the Horticultural Association on page 71. Here are some suggestions to help you:

*I should like to apply for the . . . . . vacancy advertised in . . . . . on . . . . . . I would be grateful if you would send me . . . . . .*

# Unit 8 Job application forms

## Section 1: Filling in forms

Filling in an application form is important! If your application form is good, you may get an interview, and may get the job. If your application form is not good, you won't get an interview.

Different organisations have different forms, but all of them ask for:
- PERSONAL DETAILS
- INFORMATION ABOUT EDUCATION/TRAINING/QUALIFICATIONS
- PRESENT OCCUPATION
- PREVIOUS EMPLOYMENT
- NAMES AND ADDRESSES OF REFEREES

Some ask about HEALTH and LEISURE INTERESTS.

See page 33 in *Filling in Forms* for help with PERSONAL DETAILS.

## Section 2: Education/Training/Qualifications

Look carefully at this part of a form filled in by Keith Reilly.

| Education and training since age 11 | | | |
|---|---|---|---|
| From | To | School/college/training course | Qualifications |
| 1971 | 1976 | Charlton High School Birmingham. | C.S.E.<br>English : Grade 3<br>Gen Science : " 1<br>History : " 2 |

Now fill in this part for yourself. Make sure you a) give the right information b) spell correctly c) write neatly.

| Education and training since age 11 | | | |
|---|---|---|---|
| From | To | School/college/training course | Qualifications |
| | | | |

## Section 3: Present occupation and previous employment

A Look carefully at this part of a form.

Present employment

| Employer | Position | Date commenced |
|---|---|---|
| I am unemployed | — | — |

Previous employment in chronological order*

| Employer | Position | From | To | Reason for Leaving |
|---|---|---|---|---|
| Gordon Davis Garages Small Heath | Mechanic | 1976 | '79 | To get experience with different cars |
| Renault Services Birmingham 4 | " | 1979 | '81 | My family moved to London |

* in chronological order = in the order in which they happened, with the earliest first.

B Reasons for Leaving

Here are some reasons why people left their jobs:

- — had an argument with the boss
- — was made redundant
- — was bored in the job
- — was dismissed for bad attendance
- — was injured at work
- — moved to a new area
- — had a baby
- — to get more experience
- — to get more responsibility
- — to improve my skills

Discuss these. Which reasons could you put on a form? If you do not want to explain exactly why you left, you can put *Domestic reasons* or *Personal reasons*. (Remember that you may have to say more at an interview.)

C

Now fill in this part for yourself.

Present employment

| Employer | Position | Date commenced |
|---|---|---|
| | | |

Previous employment in chronological order

| Employer | Position | From | To | Reason for Leaving |
|---|---|---|---|---|
| | | | | |

## Section 4: References

A

Nearly all employers ask for references before they give somebody a job.

In a *reference*, somebody who knows you writes about you to the employer. On an application form, you are asked to give the name and address of people who will write *references* for you. The people are sometimes called *referees*.
Always *ask* people if they will write a reference for you before you give their name on an application form.
Choose — your employer or previous employer
— a teacher at school, college, a training course
— somebody who knows you well or has known you a long time.
Don't choose a member of your family.

B

Signature

There may be a Declaration that what you have written is true. You sign the form to show that you mean what you have written.

C

Look carefully at this part of the form:

REFERENCES Give the name and address of two referees.
If you are employed, one should be your present employer.
(previous employer)

NAME: J.P. Tindall NAME: Dr. G. Perkins

POSITION: Service Manager POSITION: Family Doctor

ADDRESS: Renault Services ADDRESS: 26 Love Lane

Daneton Road Birmingham 4PT. 8LM.

Birmingham 4BJ 7HA

Signed: K. Reilly

D

Now fill in this part of a form for yourself.

REFERENCES Give the name and address of two referees.
If you are employed, one should be your present employer.

NAME: .................... NAME: ....................

POSITION: .................... POSITION: ....................

ADDRESS: .................... ADDRESS: ....................

.................... ....................

.................... ....................

Signed: ....................

## Section 5: Making the form fit you

Remember that forms have to fit many people, so sometimes they may not fit you exactly. You can change things on a form to fit you.
Look at some examples where people have successfully changed a form to fit them.

REFERENCES ~~Present~~ Most recent Employer .... J.P. Salmon ..........
...J.P. Salmon Ltd. 42 High St. NW4 6HP......

WORK EXPERIENCE
Position
Employer I had my own retail business in Vietnam

EXAMINATIONS: S.S.C. in India (similar to G.C.E. O level) English, Science, Hindi, Gujarati, Mathematics...

## Section 6: Covering letter

When you send your completed application form you need to send a brief covering letter.
Here is an example of what to say.

```
Dear Sir

I should like to apply for the clerk-typist vacancy
advertised in the New Standard on 24 May.

I enclose a completed application form, and look forward
to hearing from you.

Yours faithfully
```

Check how to set out a formal letter correctly with addresses, date etc. Look back at Unit 6, *Writing Formal Letters*, pages 58–61, if necessary.

Choose a job which you have seen advertised, fill in this application form and write a covering letter.

| Job Applied For: | | | |
|---|---|---|---|
| Surname MR/MRS/MISS (Block letters) | | First names | |
| Maiden name (if any) | | | |
| Private address | | Tel. No. | |
| Married or single | | Date of Birth | |
| Place of Birth | Nationality | | |
| Are you a registered disabled person? | | YES/NO | |
| Present employment (give details) | | | |

Previous employment (in chronological order)

| From (date) | To (date) | Post and Employer |
|---|---|---|
| | | |

Education since age 11 years, and examinations taken

| From (year) | To (year) | School or College (state if part-time) | Examination and result |
|---|---|---|---|
| | | | |

REFEREES

Present employer (if not employed, give your employer when you were last employed. If at school or college, give Principal.)

Name. . . . . . . . . . . . . . . . . . . . . . . . . . . . . . . . . . . . . . . . . . . . . . . . . . . . . .

Address . . . . . . . . . . . . . . . . . . . . . . . . . . . . . . . . . . . . . . . . . . . . . . . . . . . . . .

REFEREES

1 Name
Status
Address

2 Name
Status
Address

DECLARATION I declare that the information given in this application is, to the best of my knowledge, complete and correct.

Signed Date

# Section 7: Personal record

A Sometimes you need to write to apply for a job.
You can send a personal record sheet, with a covering letter.

You know the things application forms ask for:

PERSONAL DETAILS
INFORMATION ABOUT EDUCATION/
TRAINING/QUALIFICATIONS
PRESENT OCCUPATION
PREVIOUS EMPLOYMENT
REFERENCES

Put the same things in your personal record. But if, for example, you have not passed any exams, you can leave Examinations out of your personal record.

B Study this Personal Record Sheet. Compare it with the parts of an application form filled in by Keith Reilly in sections 2, 3, & 4, pages 80–3.

Name: Rajendra Patel
Address: 94 Hellman Drive, Wealdstone, Harrow HA3 8JK
Tel: 01–863 4562
Date of Birth: 3/4/62

Education and training

1973–78 Government School, Baroda, India. I passed SSC (equivalent to GCE O level) in English, Maths, Geography, General Science, Hindi and Gujarati.
1979–80 Evening classes in Leicester, in English and Book-keeping.

Employment

1978–80 I worked in my uncle's supermarket in Leicester. I helped in the running of the shop, and learnt to do the accounts.
1980–81 In London, I was a packer at Drona Ltd, manufacturers of electrical components. I was made redundant in July 1981.

At present I am unemployed. I am attending Workseekers' English classes at Harrow College of Further Education, to improve my English. I would like a job where I can use my book-keeping.

References Mr E P Tomlinson, Staff Manager, Drona Ltd 731 High Road, NW9 7NM

Mrs C S Freeman, Lecturer, Harrow College of F. E. Whitefriars Centre, Tudor Road, Wealdstone, Harrow HA3 8NB

C Write a personal record sheet for yourself.

# Unit 9 Interviews

## Section 1: Getting an interview

When organisations ask people to write a letter or fill in a form to apply for a job, they then choose a number of suitable people to interview. Those people receive letters asking them to come for an interview.

Deacon & Co. advertised for a laboratory assistant. The Personnel Officer received 28 completed application forms. She drew up a list of seven people she wanted to interview, and sent them each a similar letter. Here is one of the letters:

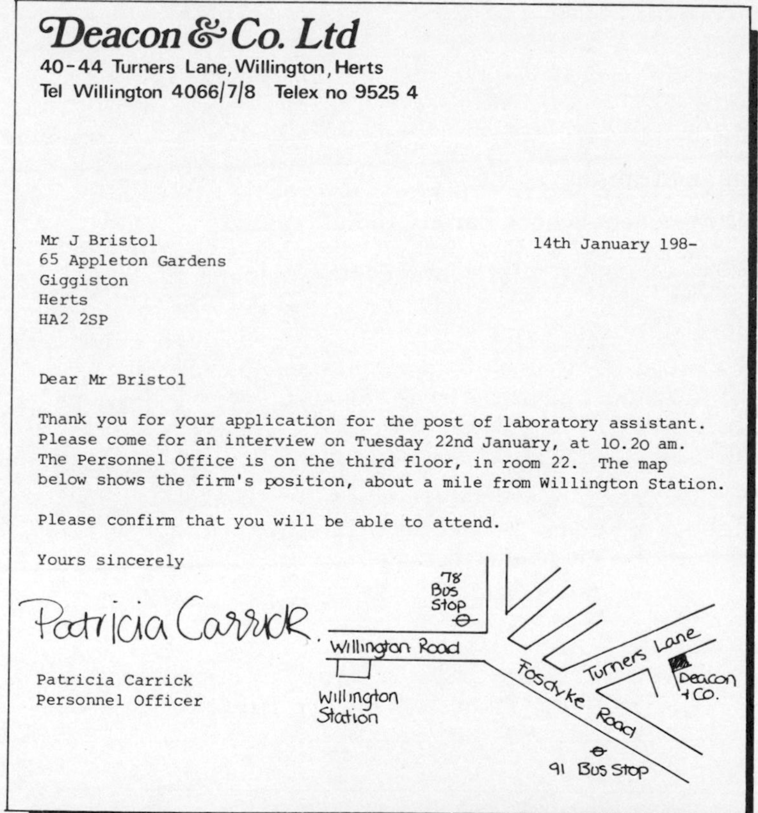

**Deacon & Co. Ltd**
40-44 Turners Lane, Willington, Herts
Tel Willington 4066/7/8 Telex no 9525 4

Mr J Bristol
65 Appleton Gardens
Giggiston
Herts
HA2 2SP

14th January 198-

Dear Mr Bristol

Thank you for your application for the post of laboratory assistant. Please come for an interview on Tuesday 22nd January, at 10.20 am. The Personnel Office is on the third floor, in room 22. The map below shows the firm's position, about a mile from Willington Station.

Please confirm that you will be able to attend.

Yours sincerely

Patricia Carrick

Patricia Carrick
Personnel Officer



Notice the last sentence. It is important that the Personnel Officer knows who is coming. That is why a letter like this asks for confirmation.

# Section 2: Replying to the letter

## A

Below are letters from three of the people who were asked to come for an interview. On the cassette there are telephone calls from two more people. Read the letters and listen to the calls. Then fill in the form on page 90.

65 Appleton Gardens
Giggiston
Herts HA2 2SP

January 15th 198-

Ms P Carrick
Personnel Officer
Deacon & Co Ltd
40 - 44 Turners Lane
Willington
Herts

Dear Ms Carrick

Thank you for your letter of 14th January asking me to come for an interview.

I would like to confirm that I will be able to attend on Tuesday, January 22nd, at 10.20 am.

Yours sincerely

J. Bristol.

John Bristol

Dear Miss Carrick

Thank you for your letter of January 14th, asking me to come for an interview.

I am afraid I will not be able to attend as I have accepted another job.

Yours sincerely

K. Somer

K Somer

Dear Miss Carrick,

Thank you for your letter of 14th January, asking me to come for an interview on January 22nd. at 9.45 am.

I am very interested in the laboratory assistant job. Unfortunately, however, this is a difficult time for me, since I work three mornings a week at the moment, one of which is Tuesday morning. I feel I cannot let my employer down as the firm is shortstaffed. I also work on Monday and Thursday mornings. I am free any time on Wednesdays and Fridays, and after 2.00 pm. on the other three days.

I would be very grateful if you could give me another time. I am sorry for any inconvenience caused.

Yours sincerely

Jean Kent

Jean Kent (Mrs)

Fill in the response column on this form, choosing the right words from these:

confirmed
asked for another time
asked for another day
not coming.

| POST: Laboratory Asst. | | INTERVIEW: TUES. JAN. 22ND |
|---|---|---|
| TIME | NAME | RESPONSE |
| 0930 | Mr Keith Somer | |
| 0945 | Mrs Jean Kent | |
| 1005 | Mr Harvey Grant | |
| 1020 | Mr John Bristol | |
| 1035 | Miss Mary Garvey | |
| 1055 | Mr Martin Coomer | |
| 1115 | Miss Jane Arnold | |

Section A shows you how people reply to the letter asking them to come for an interview. Now you are going to practise replying.

## B

Imagine you are either Mary Garvey or Martin Coomer. You have received a letter asking you to come for an interview at Deacon & Co. Miss Garvey's interview is at 1035. Mr Coomer's is at 1055. Write the reply. Use this address: 58 Firtree Ave, Dorley, Herts. Decide whether to confirm, ask for another day or time (make sure there is a good reason) or say you are no longer available.

## C

Imagine *you* have been asked to come for an interview for this job, at 1130. Decide whether to confirm, ask for another day or time (make sure there is a good reason) or say you are no longer available. Practise telephoning the company.

## Section 3: Planning the journey

If you are asked to go for an interview, you need to plan your journey. You may need to use a street map and a bus or train timetable. You will need plenty of time to find the building and to find your way inside it.

Plan the journey for Mr J Bristol. It takes him at least ten minutes to walk from home to Giggiston station. Look at the letter inviting him to come for an interview. Check the time of his interview. Work out how much time he should allow to get from the station to the company. Using the train timetable below, work out exactly when John Bristol needs to leave home in order to be in good time for his interview.

**TIMETABLE**

| | | | | | | | | | | |
|---|---|---|---|---|---|---|---|---|---|---|
| Kinney | 0905 | 0925 | 0945 | 1005 | 1025 | 1045 | 1105 | 1125 | 1145 | 1205 |
| Giggiston | 0909 | 0929 | 0949 | 1009 | 1029 | 1049 | 1109 | 1129 | 1149 | 1209 |
| Dorley | 0913 | 0933 | 0953 | 1013 | 1033 | 1053 | 1113 | 1133 | 1153 | 1213 |
| Fillingborough | 0918 | 0938 | 0958 | 1018 | 1038 | 1058 | 1118 | 1138 | 1158 | 1218 |
| Holler | 0921 | 0941 | 1001 | 1021 | 1041 | 1101 | 1121 | 1141 | 1201 | 1221 |
| Praxton | 0924 | 0944 | 1004 | 1024 | 1044 | 1104 | 1124 | 1144 | 1204 | 1224 |
| Willington | 0928 | 0948 | 1008 | 1028 | 1048 | 1108 | 1128 | 1148 | 1208 | 1228 |
| Barnup | 0932 | 0952 | 1012 | 1032 | 1052 | 1112 | 1132 | 1152 | 1212 | 1232 |
| Hillingside | 0936 | 0956 | 1016 | 1036 | 1056 | 1116 | 1136 | 1156 | 1216 | 1236 |
| Dorley | 0940 | 1000 | 1020 | 1040 | 1100 | 1120 | 1140 | 1200 | 1220 | 1240 |

Notes for John Bristol (Fill in the spaces)

Job:
Interview DAY/DATE/TIME:
Firm + address:
Leave home at:
Train leaves from ________________ at ________________
arrives at ________________ at ________________

NB Remember to take letter with map.

# Section 4: Preparing for an interview

Before an interview, think what an employer wants, and what you can offer.

## A What an employer wants

An employer knows what the job requires. He wants to know if you are the best person for the job.

1 Look again at the list on page 68 of things that can happen in a job, and think what things are required for each of these jobs:
warehouseman, traffic warden, cashier, accounts clerk.

2 Think about what is required for the job you hope to get.

## B What you can offer

Be prepared to talk about yourself, your abilities and personal qualities.

1 Abilities Write true sentences about yourself beginning: *I can* . . . Use the list given here to choose from and add any ideas of your own.

drive / type / do mental arithmetic / operate a cash register / answer the phone / take messages / do filing / write out bills / follow a map efficiently / operate a lathe / use a sewing-machine etc.

2 Personal qualities Write true sentences about yourself beginning: *I am* . . . Use the list given here to choose from and add any ideas of your own.

punctual / reliable / hardworking / thorough / keen to learn / able to learn quickly / able to get on with people / well-organized / good with machines / a quick worker / able to work without supervision / ambitious

3 Expanding Try to say a little more

For example: In my last job I enjoyed the contact with customers. I am able to get on with people.

or I am able to get on with people. I enjoyed mixing with people of different ages and backgrounds on the College course.

## C

Listen to people with little or no experience answering questions.

## D Advice

— Sound positive, polite and confident.
— Ask, if you do not understand.
— Ask, if you do not hear clearly.
— Try not to say just YES or NO – say a little more.

## E

What kind of questions are you likely to be asked?

Here are some answers to typical interview questions.
Try to work out the questions.

a) Yes, I'm a good timekeeper.
b) I'm hardly ever ill. In my last job I missed about 3 days in $2\frac{1}{2}$ years.
c) I came to this country in 1972.
d) I've always been interested in accounts work. Figure-work is what I enjoy most.
e) Yes, I would like to ask a few questions.

# Section 5: Pattern of an interview

## A

It is difficult to guess in advance what questions you are going to be asked at an interview. However, you can prepare some answers since most interviews follow a kind of pattern. There are often five stages:

1. Opening Questions. The interviewer wants to start the interview. He or she may just go over personal details from your form.
2. Questions about you and your experience. The interviewer wants to find out more about what you have done in the past and what you are like as a person. He or she will ask what you are doing at the moment and probably about your future plans.
3. Explanation of the job & questions. The interviewer explains what the job involves. He or she will often ask you questions about why you want the job and whether you could do it.
4. A chance for you to ask questions
5. The end of the interview. The interviewer will show by words and tone of voice that he or she wants the interview to finish.

## B

Job interview on tape

1 Listen to the interview and notice the five stages in the pattern.
2 Listen a second time and write down the questions the interviewer asks.
3 Listen a third time and concentrate on the answers.
How long is the answer?
How soon does he reply to the question?
What information does he have to have ready?
How does he sound? Choose the words which fit:
shy, difficult to understand, confident, sleepy, polite

## C

1 Prepare your answers to the interviewer's questions which you wrote down.
2 With a partner, practise a job interview. Make sure you change roles.

## D

Advice

— Listen carefully to the questions.
— Think what the questions really mean.
— Think about the length of your answer. Some questions need longer answers than others.
— Have details of your education, experience and referees ready.
— Be clear about when you can start.

# Section 6: Further practice

## A

Sometimes interview questions are not straightforward. It is important to know what the interviewer is trying to find out from you.
Look at the two groups of questions. The first group shows what the interviewer *says*. The second group shows what the interviewer *means*. Match each question in the first group with a question in the second group.

1. Why did you leave your last job?
2. How well do you get on with people?
3. What are you doing at the moment?
4. Tell me about any relevant work experience you have had.
5. Why do you want this job?
6. Can you take responsibility?

(a) Are you easy to work with or do you cause trouble?
(b) Can you be trusted to work without supervision?
(c) Can you show me that you have thought seriously about the work you would be doing here?
(d) I'm worried that your reason for leaving your last job may show something bad about you.
(e) What have you done in previous jobs which will help with this one?
(f) I'd like to hear about your present job to see how much responsibility you have and to find out if it connects with this job in the type of work you have to do.

## B

Questions for you to ask

Prepare questions of your own. Try to show interest in the organisation and the work, not just in the money and in the holidays.
Remember you haven't got the job, so use *would* not *will*. Try to limit your questions to a maximum of four. You can ask the interviewer to say more about something he mentioned before but make sure you do not ask a question which has already been covered in the interview.
Here are some examples of questions:

Would I work in this room?
Would I be able to move to another section?
Would I get any training?
Is there a chance of promotion?

Write down a question on each of these:

size of company;   hours;   holidays;   money

## C

Imagine that you have gone to an interview. What would you say in answer to these questions?

1. You got here all right then?
2. How long have you lived in . . . . . . . . . . . ?
3. Tell me what you are doing at the moment.
4. What about previous work experience?
5. Are you punctual and reliable?
6. What about your health record?
7. Why do you want this job?
8. Do you mix easily? Get on with people?
9. We could only take you on for six months, initially.
10. The work can be fairly tiring.
11. Are you interested in promotion?
12. Are there any questions you'd like to ask me?
13. Would you be prepared to work one Saturday in three?
14. Is there someone I could write to for a reference?

## D

Listen to another interview. Discuss the things that go wrong.

# Section 7: Summary

Read through the whole section on interviews again and then make a list of all the advice.

# Unit 10 Alphabetical Order

## Section 1: Check your skill

### A

Check how good you are at finding names in alphabetical order in a telephone directory. Time yourself, and see how long it takes you to find the phone numbers for these people, from the telephone directory extract opposite.

| Time started: | Name | Telephone number |
|---|---|---|
| | Adair William | |
| | Absolom N G | |
| | Acton Hospital | |
| | Ackerley P W | |
| | Abrey N | |
| | Adam G J | |
| | Ace Fish Bar | |

Time finished:
Time taken:

If you did it in less than five minutes, go on to section 4 page 102. If it took you more than five minutes, you need more practice. Sections 2 and 3 will help you. When you have worked through sections 2 and 3, come back and do exercise B — see if you have improved.

### B

Time yourself, and see how long it takes you to find the phone numbers for these people.

| Time started: | Name | Telephone number |
|---|---|---|
| | Acacia Garden Centre | |
| | Acton J W | |
| | Ackerman A E | |
| | Abse Dr D | |
| | Adamou Andreas | |
| | Ace R | |
| | Adam J G | |

Time finished:
Time taken:

Abrey F, 123 Claremont Rd NW2 ........ 01–**494** 5086
Abrey M.F, 103 Coppett's Rd N10 ........ 01–**970** 7385
Abrey N, 4 Netherlands Rd,Barnet ........ 01–**442** 3792
Abrey Rnld, 20 Prayle Gro NW2 ........ 01–**483** 3991
Abrey R, 6 Nighthawk,The Concourse NW9 ........ 01–**220** 5845
Abrey R.C, 24 Layfield Rd NW4 ........ 01–**201** 6679
Abrey R.C, 8 Woodfield Dv,E Barnet ........ 01–**792** 5809
Abrines A, 22 Crown Rd,Borehamwood ........ 01–**765** 9527
Abrol R, 26 Ashcombe Pk NW2 ........ 01–**970** 4289
Abry C.A, 46 Seymour Ct,Crest Rd NW2 ........ 01–**984** 3906
Absalom F.O, 8b Mapesbury Rd NW2 ........ 01–**955** 4736
Absalom H.D, 6 Gayton Cres NW3 ........ 01–**220** 9366
Absalom N.G, 39 Oakroyd Av ........ **Potters Bar** 43999
Absalom P, 8b Mapesbury Rd NW2 ........ 01–**225** 5530
Abse Dr D, 85 Hodford Rd NW11 ........ 01–**442** 1961
Absolon Edw.J.M, 44 Somerset Rd,New Barnet ........ 01–**494** 7496
Absolon E.M, 23 Netherlands Rd,New Barnet ........ 01–**793** 7047
Abson J, 9 Woodleigh Av N12 ........ 01–**970** 3890
Abstracta Construction Ltd,Display Shopftg Exhibitions,
Unit C,Staples Cnr Tdg Est,Edgware Rd NW2... 01–**971** 2511
Abubakar N, 6 Elaine Ct,Haverstock Hl NW3 ........ 01–**955** 8910
Abu-Samra N, 34 Meadway NW11 ........ 01–**201** 8706
Abushadi K.M, 84 Ashbourne Clo N12 ........ 01–**225** 0701
Abuzaid A.I, 20 Court Ho Gdns N3 ........ 01–**483** 3749
Abuzeid A.M, 86 Brook Rd NW2 ........ 01–**793** 9589
Abuzeinah R, 138 Dollis Hl La NW2 ........ 01–**970** 5280
**AC BEARINGS, Ball Brngs,**
**Turpins Wks,Oaklands Rd NW2**... 01–**483** 6218
Acacia garden Centre,
826 Hertford Rd,Enfield... **Lea Valley** 719144
Academy Car Service,Car Hire—
1 Watford Wy NW4 ........ 01–**793** 6446
Do. ........ 01–**970** 6699
Do. ........ 01–**201** 4155
Do. ........ 01–**234** 1982
Academy Cinemas—
Academy One, 165 Oxford St W1 ........ 01–**792** 2981
Academy Two, 165 Oxford St W1 ........ 01–**984** 5129
Academy Three, 167 Oxford St W1 ........ 01–**955** 8819
Acato Yeko, 17 Church Va N2 ........ 01–**220** 5240
Acceleration,Mtr Acces, 4 The Broadway NW7 ........ 01–**225** 8677
Accent Graphics Ltd,Typstrs, 683 High Rd N12 ........ 01–**442** 5330
Do. ........ 01–**494** 0039
Do. ........ 01–**793** 5995
Accessories & Spares (Whetstone),
1378 High Rd N20... 01–**955** 9523
Accountability, Mngmt Information Advisers,
176 Finchley Rd NW3... 01–**971** 6816
**ACCOUNTING ASSOCIATES,Emplymt Consits,**
**168 Finchley Rd NW3**... 01–**225** 0202
Acctim Services Ltd,Wtch Rprs,
45 Woodhouse Rd N12... 01–**234** 2355
Acculith 76,Photolithographers—
Brakeshear Ho, High St,Barnet ........ 01–**442** 9818
Do. ........ 01–**483** 1927
Accurate Builders Ltd,Bldg,Civ Engineering Contr,
7 Crescent Rd N3... 01–**494** 7921
AccuRay (U.K.) Ltd,Consit Engs—
Stockingswater La,Enfield ........ 01–**955** 5255
Accurso J, 6 Stanford Rd N11 ........ 01–**970** 1597
Accurso S, 27 Hollyfield Av N11 ........ 01–**971** 9184
**AC-DELCO DIVISION OF GENERAL MOTORS Ltd,**
**(Replacement Parts Operation), Stag La NW9**... 01–**984** 6541
Ace Cine Trucking, 14b Downshire Hl NW3 ........ 01–**765** 3002
Ace Fish Bar, 238 Archway Rd N6 ........ 01–**793** 8880
Ace R, 2 Windermere Rd N10 ........ 01–**792** 7002
Achampong Phillip, 62 Westbere Rd NW2 ........ 01–**494** 9083
Achara E.U, 101 Hamilton Rd NW11 ........ 01–**483** 9528
Acharya B.N, 4 Windsor Rd N3 ........ 01–**442** 3566
Acharya C.N, 6 Dawpool Rd NW2 ........ 01–**234** 7161
Acharya G, 31a Alma Rd,Enfield ........ 01–**225** 0058
Acharya I, 80 Review Rd NW2 ........ 01–**224** 5937
Acharya M.B, 29 Queen's Av N3 ........ 01–**220** 5149
Acharya N.N, 42 The Circle NW2 ........ 01–**201** 6573
Acharya P.H, 39 Highworth Rd N11 ........ 01–**955** 0183
Acharya P.J, 20 Ashurst Rd N12 ........ 01–**224** 2396
Acheampong E, 9 Heber Rd NW2 ........ 01–**225** 3053
Acheapong J, 29 Sandhurst Rd NW9 ........ 01–**442** 0827
Achilleas N, 30 Clitterhouse Rd NW2 ........ 01–**494** 5813
Achilleos C, 57 Kynaston Rd,Enfield ........ 01–**793** 9947
Achilleos C, 54 Scotland Gn Rd,Enfield ........ 01–**955** 0569
Achilleos P.G, 168 Broadlands Av,Enfield ........ 01–**971** 1727
Achilleos S, 148 Review Rd NW2 ........ 01–**984** 0349
Aching B, 101 Sandhurst Rd NW9 ........ 01–**970** 0394
Achjadi A.S, 129 Finchley La NW4 ........ 01–**765** 5808
Achler L, 19 Summerlee Av N2 ........ 01–**792** 7830
Achurch L.J, 18 Parsonage Gdns,Enfield ........ 01–**483** 5999
Achuthan K, 224 Chapter Rd NW2 ........ 01–**234** 7751
Acker W, 19 Keats Gro NW3 ........ 01–**224** 5138
Ackerley P.W, 9 Birchwood Ct,Edgware ........ 01–**201** 7956
Ackerman A.E, 8 Covert Wy,Hadley Wd ........ 01–**220** 5118
Ackerman Bernd, 100 Dollis Hl La NW2 ........ 01–**225** 2932
Ackerman B, 17 Gilda Av,Enfield ........ 01–**955** 6276
Ackerman Dorothea, 7 Holmfield Av NW4 ........ 01–**442** 2288
Acme Electric Co.(Finsbury) Ltd—
Hyde Ho, Edgware Rd NW9 ........ 01–**494** 6151
The Hyde NW9 ........ 01–**793** 1040
**ACME SIGNS & DISPLAYS Ltd,Point of Sales Aids,**
**Green St,Enfield**... 01–**970** 8251
Acock H, 18 Manesty Ct,Ivy Rd N14 ........ 01–**984** 0325
Acorn, 1 Whitchurch La,Edgware ........ 01–**971** 0220
Do. ........ 01–**955** 0229
Acorn Fashions, Ladies Wear—
Hampstead, 84 Heath St NW3 ........ 01–**765** 6171
Highgate, 13 Highgate High St N6 ........ 01–**792** 6781
Acott D, 120 Ivy Rd NW2 ........ 01–**483** 7374
Acott F, 17 Radnor Gdns Enfield ........ 01–**234** 7911
A'Court H.A,
2 Vicarage Fm Cotts,Hadley Rd,Enfield... 01–**245** 5077
Acquah-Asare G, 4 Avenue Ct,Farm Av NW2 ........ 01–**201** 6741
Acquarone de Jimenez S, 27 Frognal NW3 ........ 01–**220** 2521
Acquaviva A, 13 Richmond Rd,Barnet ........ 01–**234** 5074
Acropolis, Arts & Designs,
12 Dalmeny Rd,New Barnet... 01–**494** 8949
Acropolis Steak House, 93 Colney Hatch La N10 ........ 01–**764** 4613
Acteson C.G, 3/1 Glengall Rd,Edgware ........ 01–**971** 2160
Action Associates (Agencies) Ltd,Ins Broks,
46 Cricklewood Bdwy NW2... 01–**984** 4648
Action Sports Ltd,Sporting Gds,
162 High St,Barnet... 01–**955** 6783
Actionplan Ltd,(Sales & Mngmt Selection), 01–**792** 0739
125 High St,Edgware ........ 01–**442** 0786
Acton G.D, 15 Elmstead Clo N20 ........ 01–**224** 1543
**ACTON HOSPITAL, 46 Gunnersbury La W3** ........ 01–**220** 2277
Acton J.W, 90 Longford Ct,Belle Vue Est NW4 ........ 01–**224** 3853
Acton M.B, 49 Lavender Av NW9 ........ 01–**225** 7434
Acton T, 68 Woodgrange Gdns,Enfield ........ 01–**234** 3952
Acton W.T, 96 Broadoak Av,Enfield ........ **Lea Valley** 74428
Actor's Charitable Trust The—
(Housekeeper), 83 Lawn Rd NW3 ........ 01–**483** 1001
Actual Workshop The,
Muswell Hl Centre,Hillfield Pk N10... 01–**494** 1353
Acuna B, 48a Minster Rd NW2 ........ 01–**792** 9984
**A-CUT-ABOVE, Hrdsg Salon—**
9a Church St,Enfield ........ 01–**793** 5490
Acutt J.C, 474 Baker St,Enfield ........ 01–**765** 5490
Acworth Miss W.B, 65 Frognal NW3 ........ 01–**955** 2880
ACYC Youth Club, Thirleby Rd,Edgware ........ 01–**970** 0911
Adadia P, 56 Marsh Dv NW9 ........ 01–**971** 6162
Adair William J, 14 Stanhope Av N3 ........ 01–**984** 6508
Adalian Yvonne,
5 Litchfield Ct,Litchfield Wy NW11... 01–**970** 8921
Adam, Unisex Hairstyles, 12 Muswell Hl Bdwy N10 01–**765** 9300
Adam A, 15 Rudall Cres NW3 ........ 01–**792** 8574
Adam Adair, Hair Stylist,
50 Shenley Rd Borehamwood... 01–**971** 3465
Adam D.P, 78 Blake Rd N11 ........ 01–**442** 8611
Adam & Eve,Snack Bar, 763 High Rd N12 ........ 01–**984** 0753
Adam Mrs Grace J, 2 Crescent Rd,Enfield ........ 01–**234** 2097
Adam G.J, 13 Victoria Clo,New Barnet ........ 01–**224** 1971
Adam J, 15a Bracknell Gdns NW3 ........ 01–**201** 6968
Adam J, 24 Grand Av N10 ........ 01–**220** 7602
Adam J.G, 9 Tretawn Pk NW7 ........ 01–**225** 5865
Adam J.L, 46 Alexandra Gdns N10 ........ 01–**442** 0439
Adam J.R, 21 Sutherland Wy ........ **Cuffly** 3280
Adam, Kennedy & Co,Est Agts—
127 Hertford Rd,Enfield ........ 01–**955** 5061
18 Southbury Rd,Enfield ........ 01–**483** 5555
Do. ........ 01–**792** 8282
Adam Leonhard, 20 Edgeworth Cres NW4 ........ 01–**765** 7961
Adam M, 5/12 Lindfield Gdns NW3 ........ 01–**970** 2598
Adam Paul,Tlr, 16 Ballard's La N3 ........ 01–**984** 3785
Adam P, 17 Fletton Rd N11 ........ 01–**971** 2969
Adam S, 9 Austell Hts,Austell Gdns NW7 ........ 01–**970** 4013
Adam S.H, 15 Alderney Ho,Eastfield Rd, Enfield ........ 01–**955** 5709
Adam W.V.M, 8 Ronald Ct,Hadley Rd,New Barnet ... 01–**765** 1540
Adamantos A, 36 Exeter Rd NW2 ........ 01–**793** 1714
Adamastor Press & Literary Agency Ltd,
6 Somerton Rd NW2... 01–**792** 8101
Adames P, 88 Eton Rse,Eton Coll Rd NW3 ........ 01–**494** 5485
Adam-Harkness V, 56b Hale La NW7 ........ 01–**483** 3343
Adami B, 39 Cheviot Gdns NW2 ........ 01–**442** 8389
Adami L.F, 67 Avenue Rd N14 ........ 01–**234** 4718
Adamiak D.J, 36 Queen's Av N20 ........ 01–**225** 8501
Adamis R, 23 Cresham Rd,Edgware ........ 01–**224** 9638
Adamley Textiles Ltd,Prntrs,
37 Oakleigh Pk Sth N20... 01–**225** 2776
Adamopoulos C, 5a St. Andrews Rd NW9 ........ 01–**234** 5257
Adamou Andreas, 7 Audley Rd NW4 ........ 01–**442** 5784
Adamou D.A, 3 Highwood Ct,High Rd N12 ........ 01–**483** 0376
Adamou N.B,
12a Seymour Ct Colney Hatch La N10... 01–**494** 9534
Adams A, 59 Brookfield Cres NW7 ........ 01–**792** 3375
Adams A, 32a Coppetts Rd N10 ........ 01–**793** 6665
Adams A, 75 Burnham,Fellows Rd NW3 ........ 01–**765** 9258
Adams Alfred, 19 Hadley Ridge,Barnet ........ 01–**955** 8177
Adams A, 50 Horsham Av N12 ........ 01–**970** 0528

## Section 2: Putting things in alphabetical order

### A

Arrange the things in each group below in alphabetical order.
Remember:

If the first letter is the same, look at the second letter.
If the first and second letters are the same, look at the third letter.
If the first word is the same, look at the second word.

a) Greece
India
Nigeria
China
Argentina
Pakistan
Spain
Jamaica

b) Painters
Plumbers
Publishers
Printers
Photographers
Porters

c) mad
majority
magazine
mallet
machine
magistrate
maid

d) Jackman Street
Johns Street
Jillian Close
Jubilee Gardens
Jebb Road
Johns Lane

e) Staplers
Typewriters
Stationery trays
Photocopiers
Desks
Filing cabinets

### B

The lists a) – e) come from *reference books*. Libraries keep reference books in a reference section so that they are always there for people to look things up in.
Look at each list, and decide which reference book it comes from. Fill in the chart:

Atlas
A–Z Street Atlas
Dictionary
Office Supplies Catalogue
Yellow Pages Telephone Directory

| | | You might find them in |
|---|---|---|
| a) | countries | |
| b) | services | |
| c) | words | |
| d) | street names | |
| e) | office equipment | |

## C

### People's names

Remember: In official lists of names, it is *surnames* that are most important.

1 Look at the surnames, and put these names into alphabetical order:

| Surname | First name |
|---|---|
| Jones, | Mary |
| Pepper, | John |
| Shipman, | Peter |
| Johnson, | Anne |
| Adams, | Henry |
| Shah, | Dilip |
| Lee, | Yukwah |
| Barker, | Susan |

2 The names below must be written in the register in alphabetical order of surname. If two people have the same surname, look at their first names. Write out the names in the register in the correct order (the first one is done for you).

Mary Brown
John Bell
Suzanna Liu
Peter James
Barbara Chambers
Kumud Kanji
Anne Adamson
Martin McKay
Isabel Smith
Sangita Patel
Brian O'Donovan
Raju Patel
Alison Smith
Andrew Zachary

| CLASS REGISTER | |
|---|---|
| Surname | First name |
| BELL | JOHN |

## Further practice

Make a list, in alphabetical order, of the people in your family or the people in your class.

## Section 3: Finding things in alphabetical order

A Find the advertisement for each of these things in the newspaper extract opposite, and write down the price:

| (*column* 2) | *price* | | *price* |
|---|---|---|---|
| Carry cot | | Lady's winter coat | |
| Coffee Table | | Ferguson record player | |
| Chest of drawers | | Hoover | |
| Cupboard | | (*all columns*) | |
| Desk | | Camera | |
| (*column* 3) | | Cupboard | |
| Football boots | | Kitchen sink | |
| Kitchen wall unit | | Electric fan heater | |
| Gent's shoes | | | |

B The first word of an advertisement can be the make, a number or something else. The things below are also in the classified ads, but not in this order. Find each advertisement and then underline the first word in the book.

Phillips hood-style hair-dryer
set of four dinner chairs
Fridge freezer, Hotpoint, Iced Diamond.
M & S coat, wool, for three-year-old child

## Further practice

1 With a partner, practise telephoning about something you want to buy.
2 Find the classified advertisement in your local paper. Which of the things on this page are also advertised in your paper?
3 Make a list of ten names from the telephone directory extract on page 97—mix up the names so they are NOT in alphabetical order. Exchange lists with another student, and find the numbers.
4 Arrange the names from ex 1 in alphabetical order.
5 The people listed in exercise A page 96 are being invited to a meeting. Choose four people and for each one, look up their address, and write an envelope to them — you can use pieces of paper the same size and shape as an envelope, or draw the shape on paper. Check how to address an envelope in the Unit *Writing Formal Letters* on page 60.

**8 FT. x 4 FT.** board with rounded ends, suitable for train layout, as new; £19.99. — 442 081

**ACTION MAN** Bionic Eye tank and trolleys, Action Man equipment, video game. £7. — 483 6324.

**ALADDINIQUE** paraffin heater, £6. — 984 2277.

**AURORA** motor racing set, complete with 12 volt transformer, bridges, instructions, etc.: boxed, as new, £18. — 201 9044

**BABY** cradle including mattress, good condition, £15.00. — 494 8825.

**BABY'S** cot and mattress. £9.50. — 765 8017 evenings.

**BED** and mattress, 3 ft x 6ft, £15. — 970 3275.

**BEDSPREAD** 4'6" green and beige Italian material, plain beige valance, £18.50. — 970 3784.

**BELLING** 2-bar electric fire, coal effect, in teak frame. £10. — 234 7467.

**BELLING** dark wood electric fire, coal effect, 28in high, 22in long, excellent condition, £13 ono. — Northwood 26617.

**BERRY** Magicoal 3 bar electric fire, coal effect, teak surround, perfect working order, £18. — 11 Alfriston Ave., N. Harrow.

**BUNK BEDS,** 3ft wide without mattresses, reasonable condition, £15. — 494 2501.

**CAMEL** coat, full length, size 14, brand new. £19.95. — 984 1573.

**CAMERA** 35mm Konicas f1.8, 48mm lens 1 500 sec, real leather case, excellent condition, £17. — 955 4703 after 6pm.

**CAMPING** Gaz, international de luxe Superbluet new cylinder gas C2, with whistling kettle; £7.50 complete; as new. — 955 0521.

**CARAVAN**, old but useable for hot dog bar, free. — 40 Sitwell Grove, Stanmore. — 971 5785.

**CAR** centre console, full length, cassette compartment armrest, fits Escort, Capri, Viva, Avenger, Cortina II, III, IV, V, vgc, £10.00. — 494 2692.

**CARMEN** conditioning curl, complete set of 20 heated rollers, in excellent condition, hardly used, £6.50. — 984 3762.

**CARPET**, Axminster, green, 12ft x 9ft, £15. — 971 3784.

**CARPET** Axminster, all wool, gold brown autumn design, 9 x 12, good condition,

**CARPET**, good quality, patterned gold, £12.50, approx 12ft x 12ft. — 494 1014.

**CARRYCOT,** blue flowers, navy inside, £8. — 793 7250.

**CHEST** of 5 drawers, modern; £15; good condition. — 955 6790.

**CHEST** of drawers, 3ft light oak veneer, good condition, perfect for small bedroom and bedside table, £9. — 483 3367.

**CHILD'S** coat, all wool, M. & S., age 3, blue tweed, £3.50. — 483 4498.

**CHILD'S** pedal tractor and Fisher-Price television, bus, excellent condition, will separate. £15 ono. — 971 4256.

**CLOTHES** airer, for use over bath or free-standing, £3. — 984 5544.

**COFFEE** table, 2½ft square top, 1ft 9in circular glass inserted. 1ft 9in under shelf, in light oak, excellent condition, £19.99. — 955 8928

**COMPUTER** battle ship game. £16. — 792 4651

**COPPER** immersion tank, 25 gallons capacity, good condition, £15. — 483 8387.

**CORTINA** Mk III gearbox, v.g.c. £19.99, guaranteed. — 971 6176.

**COT** and mattress, perfect condition, £19.50. — 984 5850.

**COT** and mattress and transfers, aiso bottle warmer, will separate, both very good condition. £19. — 984 2769.

**COT** blankets, three, lemon, satin bound, good condition, £5. — 442 0250.

**COT,** excellent condition, £19.50. — 984 9707.

**CUPBOARD**, white formica topped, very sturdy, ideal for kitchen or toy cupboard, £5 o.n.o. — 793 7252.

**CYCLE,** adult (small), 26" wheels, 5 gears, new tyres, chain, £19.99. — 234 6224 after 4pm.

**DESK,** teak finish, suitable for child, £10.00. — 955 2116.

**DIMPLEX** 3 bar electric fire, coal effect, bronze surround, conceals standard fireplace recess, £5. — 483 6912.

**DUVET,** double bed size, feather and down, 10.5 tog rating, 100% cotton, cambric case, £15. — Evenings after 6pm 494 2668.

**ELECTRIC** coal-effect fire, Belling, 3 bars; £8. — 483 8669.

**ELECTRIC** fan heater, two speeds, v.g.c. £14. — 792 1396.

**ELECTRIC** fire, Morphy Richards, 2kw, good condition, with new 15in spare element. — 442 0835.

**ELECTRIC** fire, 2 bars, good condition; £10. — 703 2614.

**ELECTRIC** log effect fire, 3 bars and Mothercare baby walker, £15. — 955 8146.

**ELECTRIC** organ, Hitorgan, Bontempi 22 keys; £15. — 3 Crossway, Pinner.

**EMBROSSE** lamb coat, size 12 14, recently cleaned and remodelled, would make excellent winter coat, £18. — 225 0610.

**EMMANUELLE** video tape, hardly used. £19.90. — 204 2034 after 6pm.

**ENGLISH ELECTRIC** washing machine, needs repair, £5. — 971 1776.

**EVENING** dress, elasticated multi-coloured fully sequinned top with 2½ in. straps, long mauve skirt, size 14, £15. — 970 4782.

**EVENING** short jacket, black velvet and lurex, colourful, ideal for occasions, size 14, new £12.95, offers. — 955 6917.

**FERGUSON** record player, good condition, non-stereo, £17.25, connections for stereo, tape, radio. — 984 7996 after 3.30pm.

**FERGUSON** stereogram attractive teak finish, good condition, £19.99. — 220 9500.

**FIAT** 500 front and rear bumpers, good

**FOOTBALL** boots, size six, as new, £5. — 793 2508.

**FOUR** thick foam dinner chairs, practically new, £19.99 the set, may separate. — 984 3717.

**FRIDGE,** Electra, works ok, £19.99 ono. — 970 4516.

**FUR** box jacket, beautiful coney, beige, size 14, £19.99. — 955 2154.

**FUR** coat, size 44-46, as new (Debenhams last year); £19.99 — 483 8263.

**GAS** convector fire, neat and good looking model, £15 ono. — 984 4287.

**GAS FIRE,** Flavel Debonair with thermostat, good condition, £19.95. — 793 4514.

**GAS** fire, modern, excellent condition, £18. — 792 2523.

**GAS** fire, Sahara imitation log, £19.99. — 984 7669.

**GENTLEMAN'S** dark grey suit, unworn, large size, for tall man; £19.99. — 971 3904.

**GENT'S** shoes, high quality, one pair brown, one pair black. Oxford type, size 9½ 10, £14 separable. — 955 8318.

**HEADBOARD,** white, 4ft 6in, with two small oak shelves, bed or wall fitting, £12. — 442 5911 after 7pm.

**HOOD** hairdryer, Philips, complete with foldaway stand, perfect condition; £10. — 984 1357.

**HOOVER** Junior upright, vacuum cleaner, good working condition, some tools, spare bags and driving rings. £12. — 483 4088.

**HOTPOINT** Iced Diamond fridge freezer, needs compressor but otherwise immac. £10. — 220 6101.

**IMPORTED** from USA, electronic baseball and two games age eight-adult, also two board games vgc, £18. — 483 8574 10am-6pm.

**IRONING** board, in good condition, £5. — 955 7293.

**JEAN** Varon long brown chiffon evening dress, beautiful details, size 10, worn twice, £19. — 984 2980.

**KITCHEN** sink, double bowl, stainless steel top, £5. — 971 2545.

**KITCHEN** utensils, bric-a-brac, good condition; £5.50 ono. — 201 1606.

**KITCHEN** wall clock, square, battery operated, brand new, still boxed, £4.50. — 970 8059 evenings.

**KITCHEN** wall unit, Hygena, blue white, size 36" x 39", excel. condition, £19.99 ono. — 792 5032.

**KNOCKOUT** boxing game, Perfection and Connect Four. £10, will separate. — 483 1213.

**LADIES** late Victorian gold plated bracelet, £15. — 792 8162.

**LADIES** leather ¾ jacket, size 16, also mid-brown winter coat, both vgc, £15, will separate. — 494 0307.

**LADIES** winter coat, Air Force blue, with hood, sized 34 bust. £10. — 984 3328.

**LADY'S** black patent court shoes, never worn, size 5½, "Pedro Garcia" make, £8. — 955 0708 after 7pm.

**LADY'S** full-length single breasted brown leather coat, with belt, size 10, as new, £19.99. — 984 3358.

**LADY'S** off-white raincoat, size 10, bundle dresses, blouses, top, skirts, trousers, sizes 10 14, £16 ono, separable. — 984 3872.

**LADY'S** size 14 dresses, one lamb's wool and mohair, other attractive polyester jersey, both blue, £10, separable, perfect. — 792 9534.

**LADY'S** washable velvet sweaters, several different colours, long sleeves; in perfect condition; size 12; 6 for £12.50. — 483 7520.

**LARGE** teak-finish wall unit; £18. — 234 4162.

6 Copy ten names from the telephone directory on to small cards — one name on each card. Mix up the cards, then put them into alphabetical order. Then you can exchange cards with another student, or combine twenty cards and put them into alphabetical order.

How can you help in class, at work etc, by putting things in alphabetical order?

- — student record cards
- — lists of stationery and equipment
- — catalogue cards in a library.

Now you have done some practice, go back to page 96 and do exercise B — see if you have improved.

# Section 4: Finding the right page in reference books

## A

1 To help you find the right page, the first and last things on each page are put at the top as GUIDEWORDS:

Examples

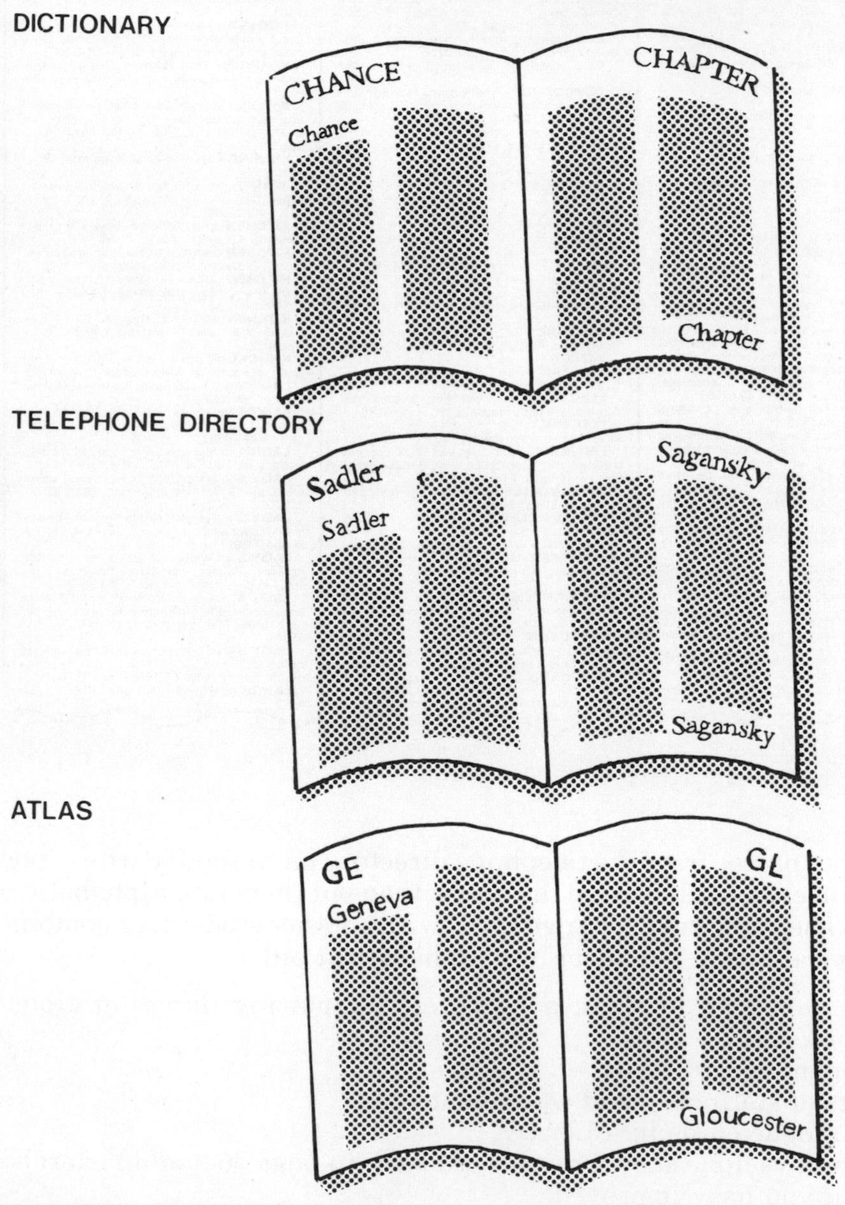

When you are looking for something, you can see from the guidewords on a page if the thing you want is on that page or not.

eg in a Street Atlas:
Guidewords: **HER-HILL**

Are these roads listed on that page or before or after?

| Roads | Answers | |
|---|---|---|
| Harris Avenue | before | (Ha . . . is before He . . .) |
| Hidcote Lane | on the page | (Hid . . . is between Her and Hill) |
| Hipley Road | after | (Hip . . . is after Hill) |

2 Look at the guidewords and decide if each thing is on that page or before or after.

| Street Atlas | Answers | Telephone Directory | Answers |
|---|---|---|---|
| **Her-Hill** | | **Sadler-Sagansky** | |
| Heywood Street | | Saffet | |
| Hendon Lane | | Sabington | |
| Hilldown | | Sanger | |
| Hetherington Road | | Saenger | |
| Halifax Road | | Sadoo | |
| Hindes Way | | Sidhu | |
| Hilary Close | | Sagger | |

| Atlas | Answers | Dictionary | Answers |
|---|---|---|---|
| **GE-GL** | | **Chance-chapter** | |
| Ghandi Dam | | chaos | |
| Gillingham | | change | |
| Galapagos | | challenge | |
| Ghana | | chat | |
| Gdansk | | chapel | |
| Gothenbury | | chime | |
| Georgetown | | channel | |
| Glasgow | | chaplain | |

## B

The Yellow Pages Telephone Directory lists businesses which provide a service. If you have a problem, you may be able to find the service you need by looking in the Yellow Pages. For each problem below, choose the service required, and find the guidewords for the page you need.

| Problem | Service required | Guidewords in Yellow Pages |
|---|---|---|
| a) Your water pipes have burst | 1) Optician | o) Garden Centres — Gas Installers |
| b) Your eyes need testing | 2) Removal firm | p) Gift shops—Grocers |
| c) You have to get to the airport very late at night | 3) Radio and TV repair | q) Microfilming — Midwives |
| d) You have to move house | 4) Plumber | r) Millers — Model Shops |
| e) Your television isn't working properly | 5) Glazier | s) Model Shops—Motor Cycles |
| f) You have a broken window | 6) Minicabs | t) Newsagents — Office cleaning |
| | 7) Garden Centre | u) Oil companies — Painters |
| | 8) Printer | v) Painters — Photographers |
| | | w) Piano tuners—Printers |
| | | x) Publishers — Railway equipment |
| | | y) Raincoats — Refrigeration |
| | | z) Refrigerator Repairs — Rent Officer |

## C

Using guidewords to find things quickly

Here are some exercises to practise finding things in a book. You may have these books at home or in the classroom, or you may go and look at them in a library.

1 ATLAS

Here is a list of places. Look up each place in the index of an atlas, and find out the page where the place appears on a map.

| PLACE | PAGE | PLACE | PAGE |
|---|---|---|---|
| Washington DC, USA | | Torremolinos, Spain | |
| Delhi, India | | Santiago, Chile | |
| Malta | | Manchester, England | |
| Ontario, Canada | | Hong Kong | |
| Berne, Switzerland | | Nairobi, Kenya | |

2 Look up the place where you were born in the index of an atlas. Find the map. Use the other information in the index to find the place on the map.

3 DICTIONARY
Look up each of the words below in a dictionary, and write down the word which comes before and the word which comes after it.

| | Word before it | WORD | Word after it |
|---|---|---|---|
| Example: | grove | grow | growl |
| | | peanut | |
| | | sister | |
| | | switch | |
| | | halt | |
| | | moan | |
| | | serious | |
| | | idea | |
| | | place | |
| | | count | |

4 TELEPHONE DIRECTORY
There is a list of names in Section 2 exercise C1, page 99. Look up those surnames in your local telephone directory, and write down the guidewords on the page(s) where each surname appears.

| | Surname | Guidewords |
|---|---|---|
| Examples: | Jones | Johnston — Jones<br>Jones — Jones<br>Jones — Joshi |

## Extension work

1 In this Unit, you have looked at various reference books which list things in alphabetical order. Look quickly through the unit, and make a list of all the reference books mentioned.

2 On page 106 are some situations where people need information. Find out the information, using newspapers and reference books (your local library will have copies of them for you to look at). Make a note of where you find the information.

| | Information | Where did you find it? |
|---|---|---|
| A wants to go to the cinema. What is on at the nearest cinema? | | |
| B has to write to a company in Boston. She knows Boston is in America, but doesn't know which state. | | |
| C knows that his friend lives in your area. He *thinks* the road is called Elm Avenue. Is there a road called Elm Avenue? | | |
| D's car has broken down during a journey in your area. He is a member of the AA, but doesn't know the telephone number of the nearest AA office. | | |
| E has also had a breakdown, but is not a member of the AA. She needs to find a garage with a breakdown service. | | |
| F is not sure how to spell these words: harass? or harrass? embarass? or embarrass? Check the correct spelling. | | |
| G wants to buy a second-hand bicycle. Is there one for sale? If so, how much? | | |
| H has had his keys stolen. He cannot get into his flat until he can get an expert to take the lock off the front door. Find the phone number of a locksmith. | | |
| I must contact the Careers Service (which is run by the local authority). What is the phone no? | | |

3 Use an encyclopaedia to find out:
What is Alexander Bell famous for?
Who flew the first aeroplane, and when?

4 Make a list, in alphabetical order, of people and places you may need to contact quickly, and their telephone numbers:
eg doctor, hospital, plumber
Keep your list by your phone.

# Unit 11 Language at work

## Section 1: Talking about a job

A

If you are in a job, you should be able to tell somebody what you do.
eg I'm a ward orderly. I clean the wards, and I help serve meals to patients.
My last job was as a clerical assistant. I dealt with enquiries, and sent out orders for stationery and equipment, and did the post.

B

You should also be able to say:—
(1) what organisation you work for
(2) where it is
(3) what it does (if the name doesn't show this).
eg I'm a packer at Anders & Macheson, in Watford. They make electrical components.
I've got a job as a clerk with Barclays Bank. I work at the Piccadilly branch.

C

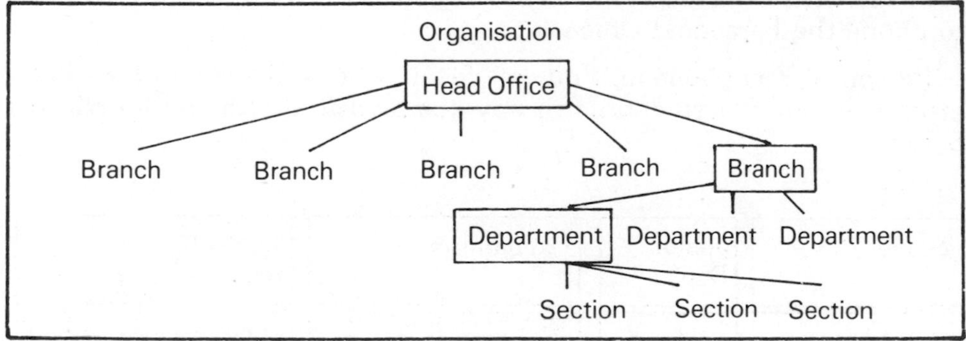


In a large organisation, you should be able to say which part of the organisation you work in.
eg I work for Hammonds, at the Wembley branch. I'm an assistant in the food department, in the produce section. My section sells fruit and vegetables.

D

Think of the job you do now, or a job you used to do, or a job you would like. Talk about the job, as in the examples A–C.

## Section 2: Phoning work when you are ill

### A

If you are ill and cannot go to work, you should telephone the organisation you work for and inform them. Remember that in a large organisation, you will have to get through to the right section.

### B

1 Listen to somebody phoning to say she is ill. What section does she work in? What is wrong with her? How long will she be away from work?
2 Listen again and notice exactly what she says.

### C

Practise phoning to say that you are ill.

Sometimes you have to phone on behalf of a relative or neighbour. When you get through to the right section, say:
"I'm phoning for my sister . . . . . . . "
"I'm phoning for my next-door neighbour, Peter Jenkins. . . . "

Practise with a partner. At Morrow Electronics, staff who are ill have to phone the Personnel Office.

Person A. You phone in. You can decide who is ill—you or somebody else. You can choose details in any combination from the four boxes below.

| Name | Job or Dept. | Explanation | Time off required |
|---|---|---|---|
| Carol Harvey<br>Jane Smith<br>Burt Ford<br>Michael Blake<br>Donald Parsons<br>Anne Mason<br>John Winsor<br>Clare Newton | Packing Dept.<br>Accounts<br>Office Manager<br>Computer operator<br>Assembly Dept. | shut fingers in car door<br>gastric flu<br>bronchitis<br>fell downstairs this morning and twisted an ankle.<br>a heavy cold<br>terrible toothache | today<br>today and tomorrow<br>today & ?<br>Doctor says at least 3 days<br>Hard to tell — you'll ring again the day after tomorrow. |

Person B. You work in the Personnel Office. When somebody phones in, you fill in the information in the Sickness Book:—

| SICKNESS BOOK | | | | | |
|---|---|---|---|---|---|
| Date | Surname | First Name | Job or Dept. | Reason for absence | Time off required |
| | | | | | |
| | | | | | |
| | | | | | |
| | | | | | |
| | | | | | |
| | | | | | |

## Section 3: Understanding an organisation

A

In any organisation, you need to know how it is organised and who is there to help you.

## B

Some organisations provide written information for their employees. Here is an information sheet which is given to all drivers and conductors when they join the Giggiston Bus Company.

INFORMATION FOR EMPLOYEES:

Giggiston Bus Company has ten garages and a Head Office. The Personnel Department and Wages Office are at Head Office in Giggiston. All staff have four weeks holiday a year. Office staff work 9am – 5 pm.

Each garage is arranged in the following way:

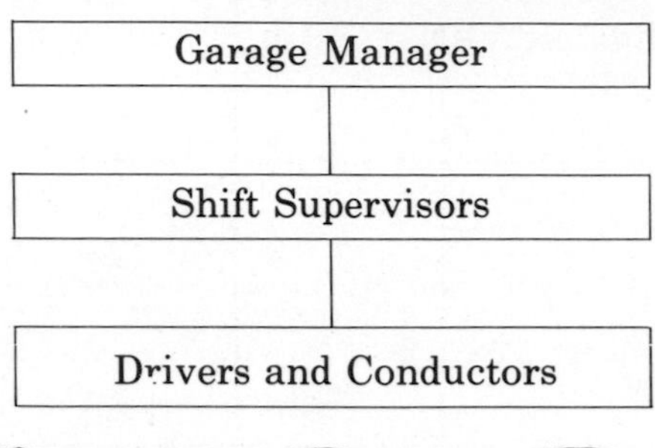


Read the rest of the information sheet below in order to complete these sentences:—

a) Office staff work office hours (9–5); bus drivers work __________

b) If bus drivers are ill and cannot go to work they should ________

c) If bus drivers want to arrange time off for holidays, they should go to see ________________

d) The number of weeks' holiday is decided by __________

Drivers and conductors belong to one of the ten garages of the Company. Each garage has seven shift supervisors and a garage manager. Drivers, conductors and shift supervisors work shifts. The garage manager decides who works which shift. The different shifts are:
5 am – 1 pm, 8 am – 4 pm, 2 pm – 10 pm, 4 pm – midnight.

The shift supervisor's job is to arrange which bus each driver and conductor take out on their shift.

If drivers or conductors are ill and cannot come to work, they should telephone their shift supervisor at the beginning of the shift. When they plan their holidays, they should arrange with the garage manager which weeks they can have off. The length of the working week, the number of weeks' holiday and the rates of pay are all agreed betweeen Giggiston Bus Company and the trade union.

## C

Say what you can about these people, using information from the sheet:

Office staff
Drivers
The garage manager
A shift supervisor

## D

If people do not understand the structure of the organisation, they may ask you to do things which you cannot do. Here are some things you could say:

I'm afraid I can't { help you. / do that. / tell you. } You'll have to see the supervisor.

I'm sorry. I don't know. I'll have to ask Head Office.

If a driver asks a shift supervisor to change his times of work, the shift supervisor could say: ______________________________

## E

Oral Practice

a) As a bus driver or conductor, phone your shift supervisor to say that you are ill and cannot come to work today.
b) Decide what dates you would like for your holiday. Ask the manager.
c) You are a bus driver. You would like to change your shift next week. The garage manager does not like making changes. Try and find another driver who is willing to change shifts with you. Then ask the garage manager if you can change.

## F

Make sure that you know, in your job:
Is there a Personnel Department?
Is there a trade union?
Who should you contact in these situations?
you are ill and cannot come to work.
your pay is wrong one week or month.
a machine which you use is faulty.
you need some more equipment.
you want to arrange your holiday.
you need to arrange time off eg to go to the dentist.
Will you be paid if you are ill?
When do you need a medical certificate if you are ill?

# Section 4: Describing a procedure

## A

There are two different ways of describing a job.

1 Sometimes we are interested in the person and what he or she does. Here is a librarian talking about her job.

"I deal with new books. I take the books to the librarian's room, where I unpack them and count them. Then I inspect them. If there are damaged books, I send them back to the publisher. Then I catalogue the satisfactory books. I give each book an index number, and I fill in a catalogue card for each one. I write the author and title of the book, and the index number, on the card. I keep the cards in a box, and I file them alphabetically, by surname of author. Then I put the books on the shelves. We arrange the books according to subject."

We are interested in the person, the librarian, and in what she does, so she uses the active form of the verb: "I *take* the books . . ."

2 Sometimes we are interested in the *procedure*, not in the person. We talk about what happens, not about the person doing it. Then we use the passive form of the verb: eg New books *are taken* . .

## B

The procedure can be shown in a diagram:

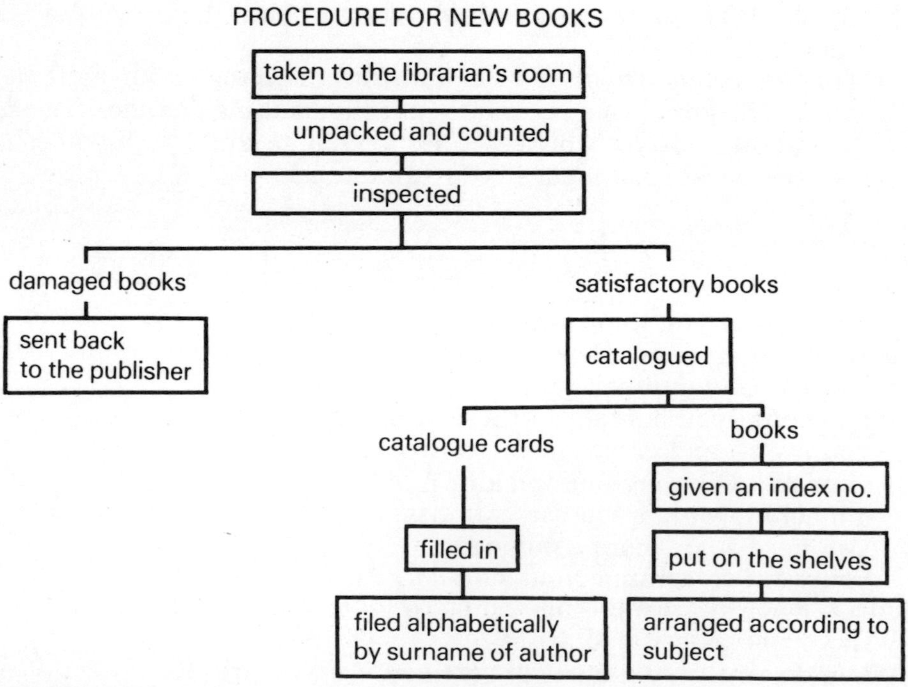

PROCEDURE FOR NEW BOOKS

taken to the librarian's room

unpacked and counted

inspected

damaged books

sent back to the publisher

satisfactory books

catalogued

catalogue cards

filled in

filed alphabetically by surname of author

books

given an index no.

put on the shelves

arranged according to subject

## C

You have looked at a diagram showing the procedure for new books. Now use the diagram to write out the same procedure in sentences. Begin:

New books are taken to the librarian's room, where they are unpacked and counted. Then they are inspected. Damaged books . . . . . . . .

## D

Here is a notice displayed in the storeroom at Wilkins & Widdowson plc.

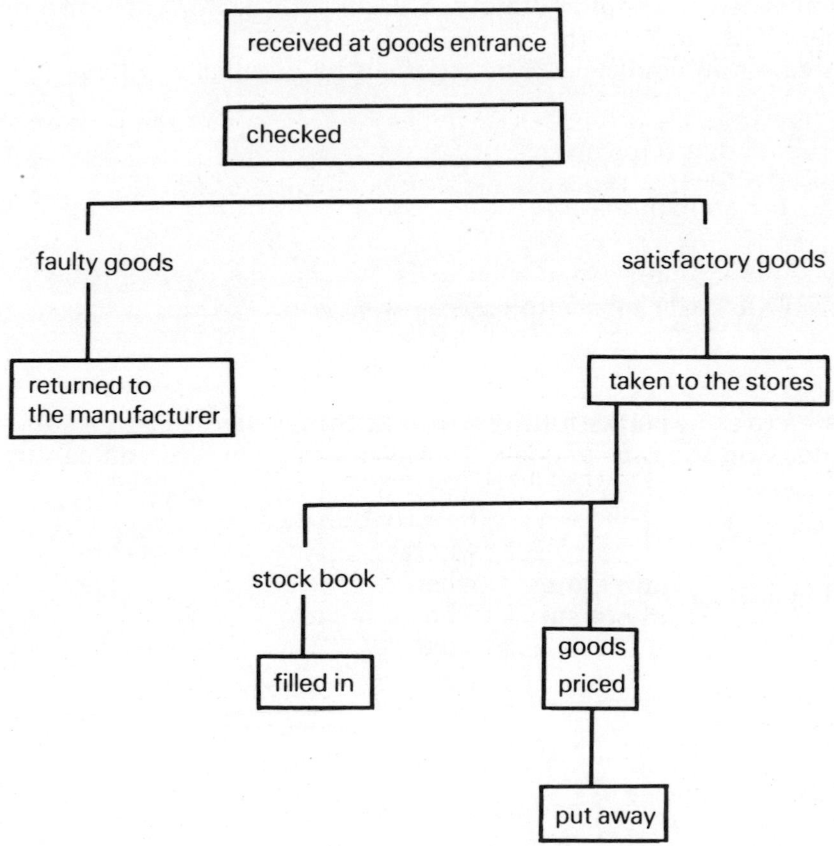


Explain to a new employee what happens when goods are delivered. You can help the new person by putting in words like:

First, then, next, after that, finally.

# Section 5: Understanding spoken instructions, asking for an explanation, taking messages

## A

Understanding spoken instructions

1 When you are asked to do something, always check that you have understood. Repeat the main points.

2 Listen to two examples of somebody checking.
3 Then listen to people telling you to do things. For each one, decide where it is, or what the person's job is.
4 Listen again, and repeat the main points of what you have to do.

## B

Asking for an explanation

1 If you do not understand what to do, you cannot check. Instead, you have to ask the person to explain it to you.

2 Listen to two examples.
3 Listen to some people telling you to do things. If you are not sure what to do, stop the tape and ask. Here are some phrases you can use:

I'm sorry. { I don't know / I'm not sure } { how to ....... / where ....... / when ........ / who ......... / what ........ / which ....... }

Can you please { explain? / tell me? / show me? / help me? }

## C Taking messages

1 When you answer the telephone, you may have to take a message for somebody. Always put the date and time of the telephone call, and your name in case there is a query about it.

2 Listen to this call. Compare the notes the receptionist made during the call and the message she wrote after it.

Tues. 9·15 for: Mr Price
Fr: Mr Parson, Folley + Co Ltd. 592 8661 Ext. 42 pl. ring asap.

**Barclay & Tyson Ltd**

Telephone Message | Date: 10/11/81
--- | ---
For: Mr Price | Time: 9·15 am.

From: Mr Parson, Fully + Co. Ltd. 01. 592 8661 EX 42

Please ring Mr. Parson as soon as possible

T. Glynn (RECEPTION)

3 Listen to this call. Use the notes to write out the message.

10/11 10·30 For: Mrs Sharma, Food Dept.
Fr: Mr Glaxo. Greyson Foods. Ring to-d or asap 448·2261 EX·12

**Barclay & Tyson Ltd**

Telephone Message | Date:
--- | ---
 | Time:

4 Listen to four more calls. For each call, make notes and write out the message.

5 You now have the details of six telephone calls. Practise each of the six calls with a partner. (Remember to change roles.)

## D Making Notes

1 If you are asked to do something long or complicated, make notes so you can remember what to do.

2 Listen to two examples. Make notes of what to do.
If it is difficult, you can ask the speaker to slow down or to repeat something

3 Go back and listen again to the two examples. Notice ways of asking somebody to slow down or repeat something.

4. Listen to people telling you what to do. Make notes of the main points.

# Section 6: Instructions, warnings and safety notices

## A

Here are some notices warning people or telling people how to do things. Notice the different language used:—

| Passive verbs | Direct instruction:— |
|---|---|
| 1 THIS BOX MUST BE HANDLED WITH CARE AND NOT LAID ON ITS SIDE | HANDLE THIS BOX WITH CARE. DO NOT LAY IT ON ITS SIDE |
| 2 TO BE STORED AT A TEMPERATURE NOT EXCEEDING 16C (61F) | |
| 3 ALL ACCIDENTS ARE TO BE REPORTED TO THE SUPERVISOR IMMEDIATELY | |

Phrases meaning 'never':—

| | |
|---|---|
| 4 Under no circumstances should you attempt to open more than one drawer at the same time. | |
| 5 Do not use an abrasive on stainless or chromium parts and on no account clean them with metal polish. | |
| 6 Liquids on this shelf are poisonous and should in no circumstances be consumed, and should so far as possible be kept away from open wounds. | |

Verbs of advice

| | |
|---|---|
| 7 You are advised to check your change carefully, as mistakes cannot be rectified afterwards. | |
| 8 It is recommended that all filing cabinets are loaded starting from the bottom drawer and working upwards. | |

Often a direct instruction is easier to understand. Look back to the first notice. Write direct instructions like this for the other notices.

## B

1 Some notices warn that something might happen.

For example:— OVERHEATING MAY OCCUR IF THE PHOTOCOPIER IS RUN FOR MORE THAN THREE MINUTES CONSECUTIVELY

The notice warns that if . . . . . . . . . . ., then something might happen. People have to work out for themselves what they should do or not do.
2 Change the notice about the photocopier into a direct instruction.
3 Look at the warning notices below. For each notice:
a) Underline what might happen.
b) Change the notice into a direct instruction.

| | |
|---|---|
| 1 Fingermarks can damage the disc | |
| 2 If screws are not properly tightened, excessive wear will result | |
| 3 These filing cabinets are liable to fall forward if more than one loaded drawer is opened | |
| 4 Many common household aerosol sprays and polishes will cause permanent damage to the television screen. | |

# Section 7: Language skills in combination

## A

In this unit, you have practised:

— listening
— phoning
— keeping a written record
— understanding instructions.

In this final section, we have a work situation where somebody has to do all these things together.

## B

The Greenhill Garage is a self-service petrol station with a repair and breakdown service.

1 Sometimes a driver puts petrol in his car and drives away without paying. Jonathan Chan is a new cashier at the Greenhill Garage. Listen to an experienced cashier telling him what to do if a driver leaves without paying.
2 Listen again, and make a note of what to do.
3 The things on the tape are not in the right order for the cashier. Put them in the right order.
4 Look at the notice on page 120, PROCEDURE IN CASE OF NON-PAYMENT, which is displayed above the cashier's desk. What is mentioned in that notice, which was not mentioned by the cashier you listened to?

5 Listen to a cashier phoning the police. As you listen, fill in the information on the Report Chart for Non-payment below.

| REPORT CHART FOR NON-PAYMENT | | | | |
|---|---|---|---|---|
| Date | Time | Reg. No. | Description of car: colour, make, etc | Description of driver |
| Reported to police by: ........................ Amount owing: | | | | |

6 Work in pairs. A is the cashier; B is a policeman or policewoman. CASHIER: A driver has left without paying. Choose details in any combination from the information below. Then phone the police to report it. Afterwards, fill in the Report Chart.

Rolls-Royce **HBT 738V** £11.25
Fiat 127 **OWK 826T** £7.64
Mini **BYO 183W** £22.15
Ford Cortina **AMT 72P** £9.26
Ford Fiesta **KKO 491K** £17.84

| REPORT CHART FOR NON-PAYMENT | | | | |
|---|---|---|---|---|
| Date | Time | Reg. No | Description of car: colour, make, etc | Description of driver |
| Reported to police by: ........................ Amount owing: | | | | |

POLICEMAN/WOMAN: As the cashier reports the incident, make notes of the relevant information. Afterwards fill in the Report Chart.

| REPORT CHART FOR NON-PAYMENT | | | | |
|---|---|---|---|---|
| Date | Time | Reg. No. | Description of car: colour, make, etc | Description of driver |
| Reported to police by: .................. Amount owing: | | | | |

| PROCEDURE IN CASE OF NON-PAYMENT |
|---|
| Record registration number of car<br>colour<br>make<br>Note driver's description<br>Record amount owing<br>Telephone police<br>Fill in report chart |

← This notice is displayed above the cashier's desk.

## C. Breakdown service

The Greenhill Garage runs a 24-hour breakdown service. At night, when drivers ring to report their problem, the cashier answers the phone. He writes down the information, and then phones the mechanic on duty and gives him the information. Then the mechanic goes out to deal with the problem.

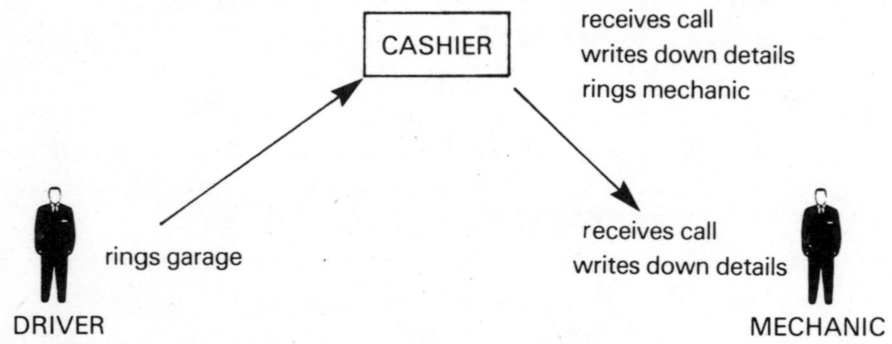


BREAKDOWN 1

You are the cashier on night duty. Listen to a call from a driver. As you listen, write down the information on the BREAKDOWN SERVICE FORM.

BREAKDOWN 2

a) Now imagine you are a driver. You are going to telephone the Greenhill Garage to report a breakdown. Decide where you have broken down. Then either make up details of the car and breakdown, or choose details in any combination from the three boxes below:

| Make | Registration | Problem |
|---|---|---|
| Austin Allegro | PGC 403T | The engine stopped, and won't start again. |
| Fiat 127 | ALN 862P | The oil warning light is on. |
| Ford Cortina | LTD 832X | The front wheel has come off. |
| Metro | MCP 792R | The engine is making a terrible noise. |
| Mini | BCG 993W | There is a leak from the petrol tank. |
| Renault 6 | | |

Prepare your telephone call.

b) Work with a partner, as a driver and a cashier.
The driver telephones to report a breakdown.
The cashier answers the phone and writes down the details on a BREAKDOWN SERVICE FORM
Make sure you change roles.

c) Now each person has a BREAKDOWN SERVICE FORM filled in. Find a new partner, and work as the cashier and the duty mechanic.
The cashier telephones the mechanic to give him the information from the BREAKDOWN SERVICE FORM.
The mechanic answers the phone and writes down the details.

BREAKDOWN SERVICE FORM

Name of caller: ______________ Nature of breakdown: ________
______________________________________________

Type of vehicle: ________ Colour: ________ Reg. No: ________

Location: ______________________________________

Call received by: ________ Date: ____________ Time: ________

BREAKDOWN SERVICE FORM

Name of caller: ____________ Nature of breakdown: __________
______________________________________________

Type of vehicle: ________ Colour: __________ Reg No: ________

Location: ______________________________________

Call received by: ________ Date: ____________ Time: ________

# SKILLS INDEX

The skills are taught systematically in SKILLS UNITS, and are also practised in other units.

Language at work
Sickness Book, section 2, p 109
Report Forms for details of non-payment, section 7, p 119
Breakdown Service Form, section 7, p 121

| | |
|---|---|
| WRITING FORMAL LETTERS | Writing formal letters, pp 55–67<br>A place to live<br>Read letter from Council, section 2, p 44<br>Looking for work<br>Write a letter asking for an application form, section 3, p 79<br>Job application forms<br>Write a covering letter, section 6, p 84<br>Interviews<br>Read a letter from a company, and read replies, section 2A, p 89<br>Write a letter in reply, section 2B, p 90<br>Alphabetical order<br>Address envelopes, section 3 (further practice), p 100 |
| ALPHA-BETICAL ORDER | Alphabetical order pp 96–105<br>Looking for work<br>Heading in Classified Ads and Job Centre, section 1C, p 69<br>Job advertisements, section 2A, p 71 |

# Health

## Language activity

| | |
|---|---|
| Listening | Conversation between doctor and patient, section 3, p 3<br>999 calls, section 5, p 9<br>Questions and answer in Accident & Emergency Department, section 5, p 9 |
| Oral work | Describe symptoms, ask for explanation, persuade doctor to come, section 3, p 4<br>Phoning (see SKILLS) |
| Transfer of information | Directions from medicine to chart, section 4, p 7<br>Label diagram of hospital from written information, section 5, p 8<br>From taped dialogue between patient and nurse, to form, section 5, p 9<br>From hospital's letter to—list of things to take, note for family, form at work, section 5, pp 10–11 |
| Reading | Information about what to do when you need medical help, section 1, p 1<br>Back of prescription form, section 4, p 5<br>Directions on medicines, section 4, p 7.<br>Letter from hospital about planned admission, section 5, p 10 |
| Writing | Written record of information about your doctor, section 2, p 2<br>Forms (see SKILLS) |

## Skills

Using the telephone, calling an ambulance, section 5, pp 8–9
Forms: Fill in the back of the prescription form, section 4, p 5
Fill in Accident & Emergency Department form, section 5, p 9

## Structures

I feel . . .
It hurts . . . section 3, p 3
I've got . . .
I keep______ing.
wh-questions, section 3, p 3

# A Place to live 1

## Language Activity

| | |
|---|---|
| Listening | Listen to a description of a flat and label plan, section 3, p 29<br>Listen to directions and follow on map, section 4, p 30<br>Listen to comparison of old house and present home, sec. 5, p 31 |
| Oral Work | Ask for facts about people's homes, section 2, p 29 |
| Diagrams | Plan of flat — understand and label, section 3, p 29<br>Sketch map — understand and label, section 4, p 30<br>Draw a plan of your own home, section 3 p 30<br>Draw a sketch map to your own home, section 4, p 31. |
| Transfer of information | Spoken description of flat to labelled plan, section 3, p 29<br>Directions to marked map, section 4, p 30 |
| Writing | Describe a room/flat/house and your own home, section 3, p 30 and extension work p 31.<br>Write directions, section 4, p 31<br>Extension work |

## Skills

Filling in forms: simple questionnaire form, section 2, p 29

## Structures

Questions, section 2, p 29
Comparisons, section 5, p 31
  – er
  more –
Prepositions, section 3, p 30

Extension work could include the Conditional
  my ideal house *would* be . . . . . .
  if I could choose where to live . . . .

# A Place to live 2

## Language activity

| | |
|---|---|
| Listening | Phone calls arranging to view, section 3C and D, p 48<br>Dialogue about a house – identify which one, section 3F and 5B4, pp 48 and 53 |
| Oral work | Phoning — Council to arrange to view, section 2B, p 44.<br>— answer to newspaper advert, section 3, p 48.<br>Discuss which of several properties best fits a family and explaining reasons, sections 3B + 5B(5), pp 47, 53<br>Use linking words to discuss various advantages and disadvantages, section 4 p 49 |
| Transfer of Information | Text about types of houses to chart, section 1, p 42<br>From letter to phone call, section 2, p 44<br>Spoken information in phone call to info. sheet, section 3C, p 48<br>From newspaper advertisement to phone call, section 3E, p 48<br>Information from 2 texts to table, extension work. |
| Reading | Text: information about types of housing, section 1, p 42<br>Letter from Council, section 2B, p 44<br>Newspaper advertisements, section 3A, p 47<br>Information sheets from Estate Agents – distinguishing fact from opinion, section 5B + extension work, pp 50–4 |
| Writing | Forms (see SKILLS)<br>Use linking words to write about advantages & disadvantages, section 4, pp 49–50<br>Describe the place you live in now, extension work, p 54<br>Essay: where I live now, extension work, p 54 |

## Skills

| | |
|---|---|
| Using the Telephone: | phone in reply to a letter from the Council, section 2, p 44<br>phone a private landlord to arrange to see accommodation, section 3E, p 48 |
| Filling in Forms: | application for Council Housing, pp 45–6 |

## Structures

Linking words: also
on the other hand pp 49–50

# Looking for work

## Language activity

| | |
|---|---|
| Listening | Listen to people talking about their jobs, identify each job, section 1, p 69<br>Listen to people asking about vacancies, section 2F, p 75<br>Listen to people phoning about a job, section 3A, p 77<br>Listen to people phoning for an application form, section 3B, p 78 |
| Oral work | Practise telephoning about a job, section 3A, p 77<br>" " for an application form, sec. 3B, p 78 |
| Diagrams | Fill in responses on chart, "You and Jobs", section 1, p 68 |
| Reading | Information about places to look for work, sec. 2, pp 70–5<br>Job advertisements: scanning and intensive reading, section 2A, p 71, section 3, p 76 |
| Writing | Describe a job, section 1, p 69<br>Make notes on advertisements, section 2A, p 70<br>Write a letter asking for an application form, section 3C, p 79 |

## Skills

| | |
|---|---|
| Using the Telephone: | Apply by phone, section 3A, p 76<br>Phone for an application form, section 3B, pp 77–9 |
| Writing Formal Letters: | Ask for an application form, section 3C, p 79 |
| Alphabetical Order: | Headings in classified ads and Job Centre, section 1, p 69<br>Job advertisements in alphabetical order, section 2A, p 71 |

## Structures

____ing: Like____ing, wouldn't mind____ing, section 1, p 68
Present simple in description of jobs, section 1, p 69

# Interviews

## Language activity

| | |
|---|---|
| Listening | Phone calls confirming/asking for a change in time of an interview, section 2, p 90<br>Interview questions, section 4C, p 92<br>Whole interviews, section 5B + 6D pp 93 + 95 |
| Oral Work | Phone call to company, section 2C p 90<br>Talking about yourself, section 4 + 5, pp 92–4<br>Practice interview, section 5, p 94<br>Asking and answering questions, section 6, pp 94–5 |
| Diagrams | Train timetable, section 3, p 91 |
| Transfer of Information | From letters and phone calls to form, section 2, pp 88–90 |
| Reading | Letter from company and replies, section 1 + 2, pp 88–9<br>Matching interview questions, section 6, p 94 |
| Writing | Letter of reply, when asked for interview, section 2, p 90 |

## Skills

Using the telephone: phone the company to confirm or ask for a change in time of an interview, section 2C, p 90
Writing formal letters:
  Read a letter from a company and replies, section 1 + 2A, pp 87–9
  Write a letter in reply, section 2B, p 90

## Structures

I can . . . . . .
I am able to . . . .
I enjoyed . . . .
} section 4, p 92

Questions, section 4, p 93

# Language at work

## Language activity

| | |
|---|---|
| Listening | Somebody phoning work when ill, section 2, p 108<br>Spoken instructions, phone messages, section 5, pp 114–5<br>Greenhill Garage calls, section 7, pp 118–120 |
| Oral work | Explain how a job fits into an organisation, section 1, p 107<br>Phone work when ill, section 2, 3, pp 108, 111<br>Arrange holiday dates, change of shifts, section 3, p 111<br>Explain a procedure, section 4, p 113<br>Check instructions, ask for explanation, section 5, p 114<br>Report incident to police, pass on information heard on phone, section 7, p 119 |
| Diagrams | Structure of an organisation, section 3, p 110<br>Flowchart showing a procedure, section 4, pp 112–3 |
| Transfer of information | From phone call to sickness book, section 2, pp 108–9<br>From procedure chart to spoken/written explanation, section 4, pp 112–3<br>From phone call to form, section 7, pp 118–21 |
| Reading | Information sheet about a company, section 3, p 110<br>Description of a procedure, section 4, p 112<br>Written instructions, warning, and safety notices, section 6, pp 116–17 section 7, pp 119–20 |
| Writing | Writing out a procedure, section 4, p 113<br>Keeping a written record, sections 2, 5, 7, pp 109, 115, 119<br>Telephone messages, take notes, write message, section 5, p 115<br>Fill in details on a form, section 7, pp 119, 121 |

## Skills

| | |
|---|---|
| Using the Telephone: | phone work when ill, section 2, p 108<br>taking messages, section 5, p 115<br>Greenhill Garage calls, section 7, pp 119–121 |
| Filling in Forms: | Sickness Book, section 2, p 109<br>Report form for details of non-payment, section 7, p 119<br>Breakdown service form, section 7, p 121 |

## Structures

Present simple: saying what people do in a job, section 1, p 107
Past simple; talking about a past job, section 1, p 107
Present simple, active and passive; describing a procedure, section 4, p 112
Sequencing words, eg first, then, section 4, p 113
Various structures used for instructions and warnings, (passive infinitive, modal, passive) contrasted with imperative, section 6, pp 116–17

# Glossary

Here is a list of words connected with HOUSING, FORMS and WORK. Words which are easy to find in a dictionary are not included here.

## Housing

(words connected with these units: A Place to Live I & II).

amenities — see facilities.

converted/conversion — a *converted* house has been changed into two or more flats. These flats are *conversions*.

estate agent — a person whose business is to let or sell property.

evict/eviction order — to *evict* a tenant is to give him official notice that he must move out.

facilities or amenities in a house — things like a bath, inside lavatory, etc.

freehold/freeholder — the person who owns the *freehold* owns the ground on which the property stands. He is the *freeholder*.

furnished — let with furniture in it provided by the landlord.

harassment — unfair pressure on a tenant by a landlord to force the tenant to move out.

ground rent — money paid to the freeholder by someone who owns a *leasehold* property.

inc. = including.

lease — a legal agreement to rent or buy a property for a certain time.

leasehold — anyone who buys a *leasehold* property will not own the ground on which it stands. Ground rent will have to be paid to the *freeholder*.

mortgage — a loan from a building society or bank to buy a property.

notice to quit — an *eviction* order.

occupant/occupier — someone living in a property.

o.n.o = or nearest offer. The owner suggests a price and will accept that or the offer nearest to it.

p/b = purpose-built. Purpose- built flats are built as flats, not converted.

p.c.m. = per calendar month. The rent covers a whole month, not 28 days.

reception rooms — downstairs rooms such as dining-room and sitting-room.

residents — people living in a property.

residential area — a place where people live rather than work; not an industrial area.

self-contained — the flat has its own front door and does not share kitchen, bathroom etc, with other flats.

semi = semi-detached — a house which is attached to another house on one side only; (semi = half).
sole use — to be used by one occupier and his family only.
tenant — somebody who rents the accommodation he lives in.
tower block — a high building which has many flats in it.
unfurnished — let without furniture in it.

## Forms

(words connected with these units: Filling in Forms & Job Application Forms).
block capitals = capital letters, eg A, B, C.
block letters = capital letters, eg A, B, C.
business telephone = telephone number at work.
covering letter — a short letter to send with a form. See Job Application Forms p. 84.
CV — curriculum vitae. This is the same as a Personal Record. (see page 86)
christian name — same as *first name*.
chronological order — in order of time, starting in the past and finishing with the most recent.
country of origin — the country you were born and grew up in.
curriculum — see CV.
date — give date, month and year, or month and year.
eg 9 November 1981 or 9/11/81 or November 1981.
date of birth — Use numbers, eg 30/2/64.
declaration — part of a form where you sign to show you have written the truth.
delete as appropriate — cross out the things which do *not* apply to you.
dependants — people who depend on you financially such as your children.
D.O.B. — date of birth.
duration — length of time eg duration of stay.
expiry date — date when something runs out or is no longer valid.
F/T = full-time.
first name(s) — your personal name or names which your friends and relatives use when talking to you.
forename(s) — same as *first name*(s).
former address — previous address, usually the last address before your present one.
former surname — see maiden name.
full name — all your names, forenames + surname.
initials — the first letter of each of your names, eg. R.S.B. (Roger Simon Black). If the surname is asked for in full, then initials means the first letters of your forenames, only.
eg Surname: BLACK Initials: R.S.

maiden name — a woman's surname before she married and started using her husband's surname. (Only a married woman can have a maiden name.)
marital status — this is asking if you are *single* or *married* (or *separated*, *widowed* or *divorced*).
N/A = not applicable — You can write this on a form if the question does not apply in your case.
no. = number.
notes — advice on sections of a form. Read the notes *before* you fill in the form.
occupant/occupier — person who occupies (lives in) a house, flat or room.
OFFICE USE ONLY — do not write on this part of the form.
overleaf — on the other side of the paper.
P/T = part-time.
PTO = please turn over the piece of paper.
Permanent address = home address. This is your home address, not where you might be living temporarily during a training course.
personal record — personal details and information about your education and work experience supplied by you on a separate sheet of paper. Send it with a covering letter.
place of birth — where you were born. Give the town + the state or county + the country if not the British Isles.
post = job.
previous address — your last address before your present one.
position = job.
private phone no. = home phone number, not work phone number.
postal address = address.
print — an instruction to write in capital letters.
purpose of visit — why do you want to come here? Your answer might be one of these: to study, to visit friends or relatives, for business reasons, to set up home.
reference — something written about a person's character and abilities, especially when he or she is being considered for a job. There is an example on page 58. See also p. 82.
referee — someone who writes a reference. Often an employer or teacher.
signature — this is your first name (or initial) + surname. It must be written by hand, by you, in your own special way. It shows that you mean what you have written.
spouse = husband or wife.
status — can mean job or official position, eg teacher.
subsection — part of a section.
surname — family name. Papers are filed under people's surnames, so the surname may be asked for first.
tel. = telephone number.
title = Mr/Ms/Miss/Mrs/Dr/Prof, etc.
vacancy = job (in an advertisement or application).

work telephone no.—usually means a telephone number at your work which people outside can use to contact you during work hours.

## Work

(words connected with these units: Looking for Work, Interviews and Language at Work).

answering machine—a machine which answers the phone and records information and messages.

employee—worker.

employer—person in charge, boss.

filing cabinet—large container for files.

to file— to arrange papers in order so that people can easily find the one they need.

interviewee—the person who is interviewed, who wants the job.

interviewer—the person from the organisation who interviews.

introduction card—a card the Job Centre gives applicants to introduce them to the employer. See page 74.

miscellaneous—miscellaneous jobs do not fit under any other heading in the Job Centre or newspaper.

perm = permanent. A job which lasts for an indefinite period. You may not be a permanent member of staff until after you have finished a probationary period.

personnel = staff.

Personnel Officer/Personnel Manager—someone in an organisation who has the job of dealing with staff. For example: hiring new staff, arranging holiday dates, etc.

probation/probationary period—a period of time during which the employer decides if a worker is satisfactory or not. Find out what the law says about this. An employer can ask someone on probation to leave much more easily than he can ask a permanent employee.

procedure—a way of doing things in stages. It is often written down for employees to follow.

referee
reference }—look up in the Forms section of the Glossary.

shift/shift supervisor— in some occupations different groups of workers work different hours. Each block of time is called a shift, eg, early shift, late shift.

occupation = job.

skilled/unskilled—a skilled job is one which needs training and/or experience. The word is usually used about jobs in factories or in the building industry. Some jobs are skilled, others are unskilled.

temporary = not permanent.

unskilled—see skilled.

vacancy (*plural* vacancies)—an unoccupied post.

warden—someone who lives in a block of flats and has responsibility for the flats and/or the people living in them.